Sixth Edition

REALITY THROUGH THE ARTS

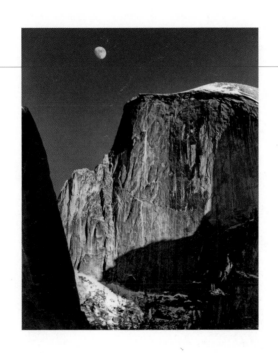

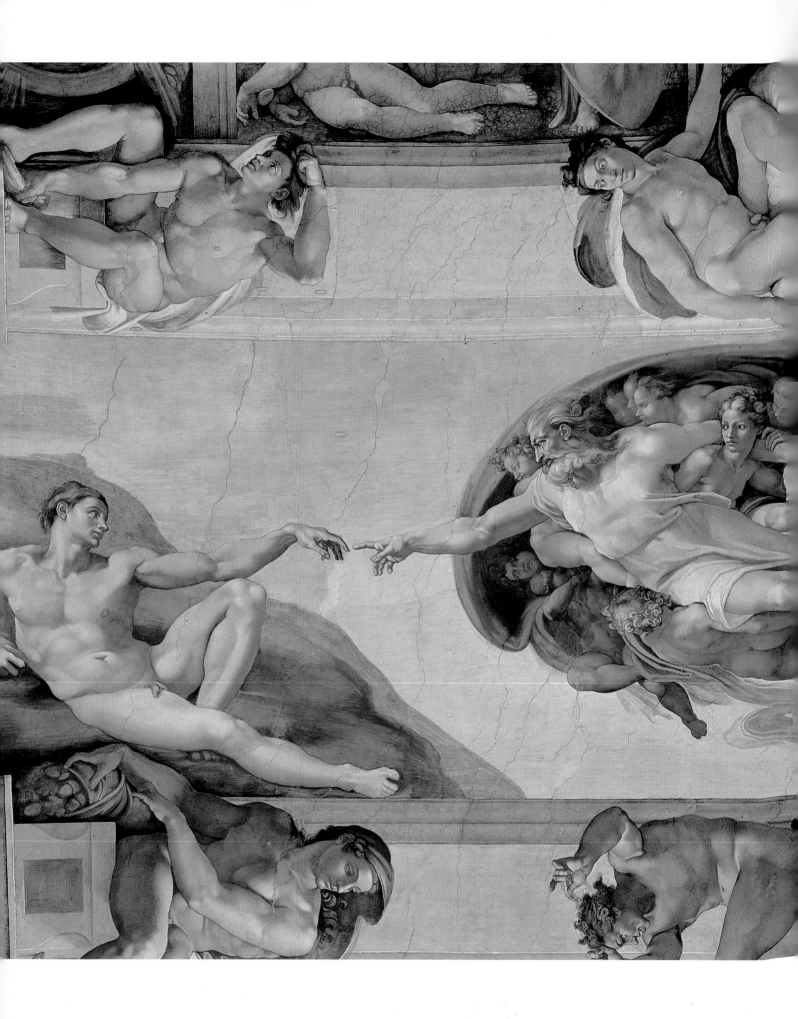

Sixth Edition

REALITY THROUGH THE ARTS

DENNIS J. SPORRE

PRENTICE HALL, UPPER SADDLE RIVER, NJ 07458

Library of Congress Cataloging-in-Publication Data

Sporre, Dennis J.
    Reality through the arts / Dennis J. Sporre.—6th ed.
        p. cm.
    Includes bibliographical references and index.
    ISBN 0–13–195858–5
      1. Arts. 2. Arts—History. I. Title.

NX440.S68 2006
700—dc22

2005053494

Editor in Chief: Sarah Touborg
Editorial Assistant: Jacqueline Zea
Acquisitions Editor: Amber Mackey
Editorial Assistant: Keri Molinari
Director of Marketing: Brandy Dawson
Manufacturing Buyer: Sherry Lewis

Credits and acknowledgments of material borrowed from other sources and reproduced, with permission, in this textbook appear on pages 430–1.

Pearson Education Ltd.
Pearson Education Australia PTY, Ltd.
Pearson Education Singapore, Pte. Ltd.
Pearson Education North Asia Ltd.

Pearson Education, Canada, Ltd.
Pearson Educación de Mexico, S.A. de C.V
Pearson Education–Japan
Pearson Education Malaysia, Pte. Ltd.

This book was designed and produced by
Laurence King Publishing Ltd, London
www.laurenceking.co.uk

Every effort has been made to contact the copyright holders, but should there be any errors or omissions, Laurence King Publishing Ltd would be pleased to insert the appropriate acknowledgment in any subsequent printing of this publication.

Senior Managing Editor: Richard Mason
Project Editor: Nicola Hodgson
Designers: Andrew Shoolbred and Greg Taylor
Picture Researcher: Emma Brown
Typesetter: Marie Doherty

Front cover: Marcel Duchamp, *Nude Descending a Staircase, No. 2*, 1912. Oil on canvas, 4 ft 10 ins x 2 ft 11 ins (1.25 x 0.6 m). Philadelphia Museum of Art (The Louise and Walter Arensberg Collection).

Back cover: Cesar Pelli, Petronas Towers, Kuala Lumpur City, Malaysia, 1997. Glass and steel, 1,483 ft (451.9 m) high. Stefano Cellai, Superstock.

Half title: Ansel Adams, *Moon and Half Dome*, Yosemite National Park, California, 1960. Ansel Adams Publishing Rights Trust.

Frontispiece: Michelangelo Buonarroti, *The Creation of Adam*, Sistine Chapel ceiling (detail), Vatican, Rome, 1508–1512.

Page 12: Diego Rivera, *Slavery in the Sugar Plantation, Tealtenago, Morelos* (detail), 1930-1. Palace of Cortez, Cuernavaca, Mexico.

10 9 8 7 6 5 4 3 2 1
ISBN 0–13–195858–5

CONTENTS

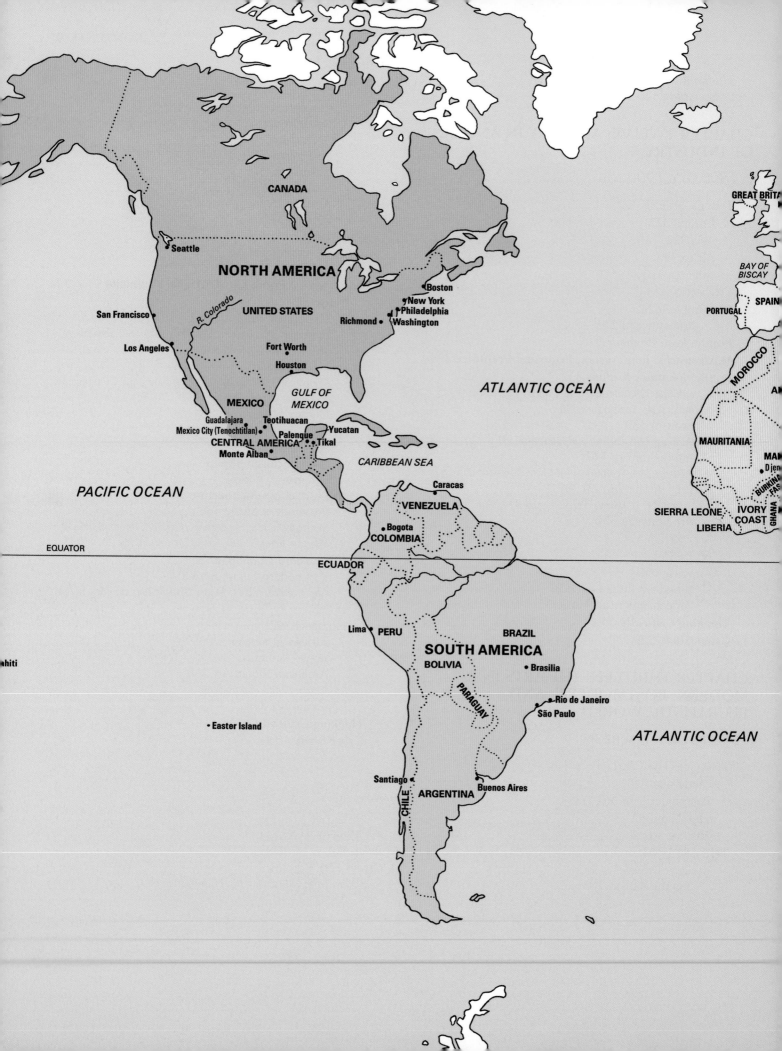

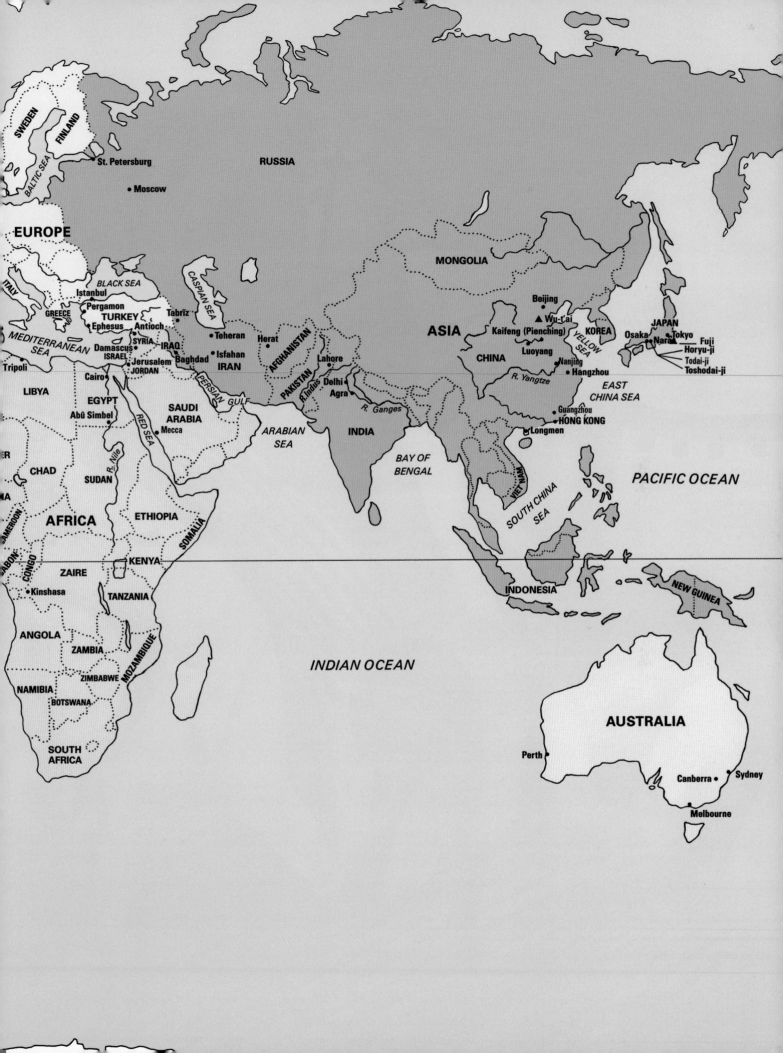

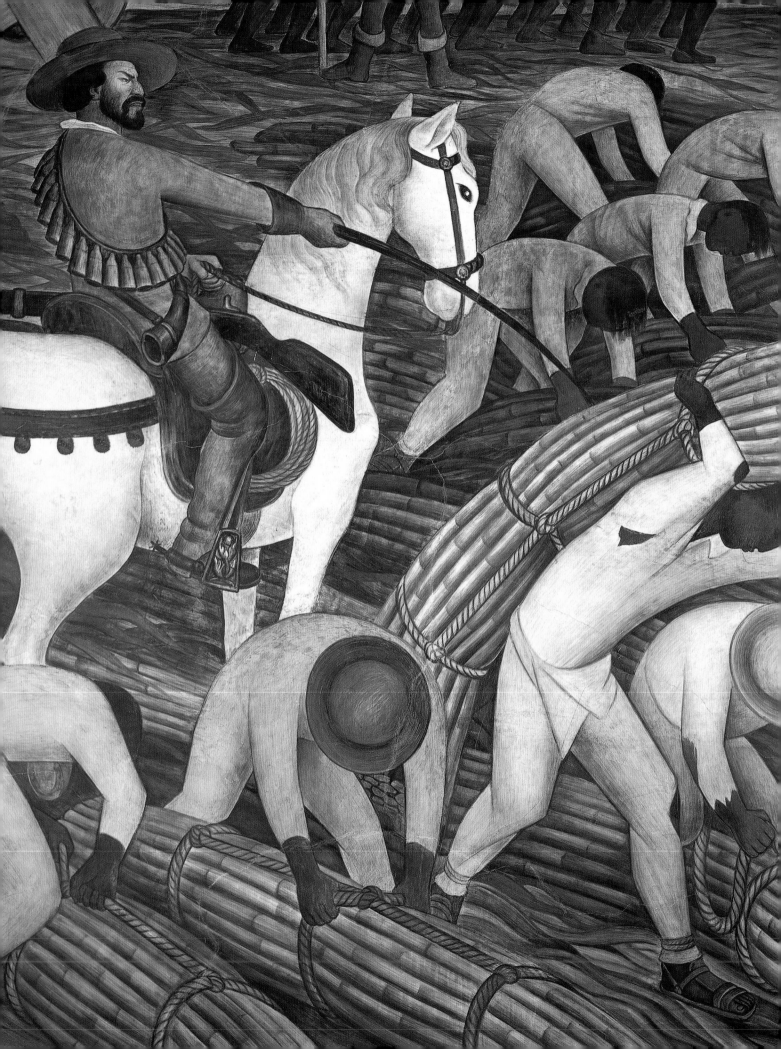

PREFACE

This book teaches basic principles and practices of the arts—drawing, painting, printmaking, sculpture, architecture, music, theatre, dance, cinema, and literature—in Western and other cultures. Designed for individuals who have limited experience of and in the arts, it provides definitions and concepts in Part I, using general terms that can help the reader approach, understand, and critically discuss the historical materials that comprise Part II.

Part I examines the media of the arts, defining and explaining important terminology, discussing how artworks are composed, and suggesting ways in which art can effect responses. The compendium approach in Part I seeks to empower readers with more polished skills of observation and greater confidence in sharing responses. Part II has a chronological arrangement, presenting a snapshot of the arts from selected world cultures while focusing on style. The text takes a "smorgasbord" rather than an in-depth approach.

This edition, the sixth, contains changes in three major areas: organization, content, and style. In terms of organization, all of the introductory materials now appear in the Introduction, as opposed to being spread among the Introduction, Part I, and Part II. I have rearranged the chapters in Part I, placing architecture immediately after sculpture. Each chapter has a new internal organization— more obviously so in Part II. Part I mainly consists of new general headings. As far as content is concerned, this edition has significant additional material in terms of illustrations, a "context" section at the beginning of each chapter in Part II, a less technical music chapter in Part I, a new accompanying music CD, new literature selections, more about photography and cinema, hyperlinks in the Profile features, and a pronunciation glossary. Stylistically, I have given the book a heavy edit to enhance the active voice. Finally, in accordance with the suggestion of the National Museum of the American Indian, I have changed references in the text from Native American to American Indian.

This book reflects many sources. It reflects the general knowledge of its author, who has spent nearly fifty years in formal and experiential relationship with the arts in the classroom and around the world. It also reflects notes taken here and there as well as formal research. In the interest of readability, however, and in recognition of its generalized purpose, the text avoids footnoting wherever possible. I hope that the method selected for presentation and documentation of others' works meets the needs of both responsibility and practicality. The bibliography gives a comprehensive list of works consulted.

In 1977, when I wrote *Perceiving the Arts* (Prentice Hall, 8th edition, 2005), I asked Ellis Grove, my colleague at The Pennsylvania State University, to prepare a chapter on film. Ten years later, that formed the basis for Chapter Six of this book. In twenty-five years of revisions of these two texts, much of Ellis's original work has been altered. Nonetheless, the basics belong to him. Any deterioration of his work results from my tinkering, and I am indebted to him and to more than two score colleagues whose insights, encouragement, and criticism at each new edition have, I hope, made each edition of *Reality Through the Arts* better than its predecessor. I also owe much to Bud Therien, who for twenty-five years was my editor and publisher at Prentice Hall and who gave me the impetus to write this book; to Amber Mackey, my editor and publisher, to Nicola Hodgson and Richard Mason, my editors at Laurence King, Ltd., in London, England; and to my wife, Hilda, whose patience, love, understanding, expertise, notetaking, and research assistance have provided me with a solid foundation from which to generate my own part of the project.

Dennis J. Sporre
Spring 2005

FACULTY AND STUDENT RESOURCES TO ACCOMPANY THE TEXT

- **Companion Website at www.prenhall.com/sporre**
  Prentice Hall's exclusive Companion Website accompanies *Reality Through the Arts*. It offers unique tools and support that make it easy for students and instructors to integrate this online study guide with the text. The site is a comprehensive resource organized in line with the chapters within the text and features a variety of learning tools. Students can test their knowledge with multiple choice, true/false, fill in the blank, and essay questions for each chapter. These quizzes offer instant scoring and feedback to help students' self-study, and they can email their quiz results directly to their instructor. Other resources include a Message Board to foster communication and collaboration, and instructors can use the Syllabus Manager to create, post, and revise a syllabus online.

- **"Music for the Humanities" CD**
  This CD features musical extracts from a broad variety of periods and styles. The CD is bound into each copy of the text and the musical selections are listed at the back of the book (see p. 432).

- **Instructor's Manual with Test Bank**
  Designed for both the novice and seasoned professor, this invaluable guide includes resources for each chapter such as: an overview, objectives, outline, lecture and discussion ideas, and further resources. The test bank consists of multiple choice, true/false, short answer, and essay questions. Contact your local Prentice Hall sales representative for more information.

- **TestGen**
  This commercial-quality computerized test management program for Windows or Macintosh allows instructors to select test bank questions in designing their own exams. Contact your local Prentice Hall sales representative for more information.

- **Fine Art Slides**
  Slides that accompany the text are available to qualified adopters. Contact your local Prentice Hall sales representative for more information.

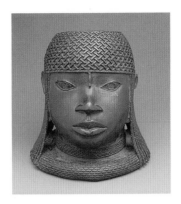

INTRODUCTION

"If we, citizens, do not support our artists, then we sacrifice our imagination on the altar of crude reality and we end up believing in nothing and having worthless dreams."

Yann Martel—*Life of Pi*

USING THIS BOOK

ORGANIZATION

The title of this book, *Reality Through the Arts*, means that art, in general and arguably, has something to do with revealing "reality" to us. Of course, we can define reality in many different ways: scientifically, spiritually, intellectually, intuitively, and so on. We might, for example, choose to define reality by using the Latin word *verisimilitude* (veh-rih-sih-MIH-lih-tood), which means "plausibility or likeness or nearness to truth." This implies further that something called "truth" exists that may or may not reflect lifelikeness as we perceive it with our senses of sight, sound, smell, taste, and touch. However, before we tie ourselves in semantic and philosophical knots so early in our study, let us suggest, simply, that the title of this book hints that by studying art, we can find a deeper understanding of the human condition and the various realities that implies: our hopes, dreams, struggles, and beliefs.

With regard to art or the arts, studying them is very much like learning to drive a car. Driving a car for the first time usually requires a preoccupation with mechanics

and an intense concentration on keeping the car moving in a straight line. As technical details become habitual, drivers can attend to more important details of driving.

When the experience of art study is new, and when we make studious attempts at doing it "right" or amass materials for a classroom assignment, often the details interfere with the larger experience. Obsession with finding specific details—what a book or teacher has indicated should be the objects of looking—frequently robs the occasion of its pleasure and meaning. Nonetheless, with practice the details do fall into place and heightened enjoyment, and a sense of personal achievement—sophistication, some might say—expands exponentially.

Getting to that point, however, requires a beginning. Perceiving anything requires an understanding of what can be perceived. The organization of this book provides a usable outline of the basics: things we can see, hear, and respond to in works of art. We focus on these basics in Part I: The Media of the Arts. In Part I we prepare to travel in the land of basic terminology. We meet the traditional art disciplines of drawing, painting, printmaking, photography, sculpture, architecture, music, theatre, cinema, dance, and literature. Each of these disciplines has its own language, to which the text introduces us. You will find many of the terms and concepts familiar, and you will think, "I know that!" At other times you will need to pause, memorize, discuss with your classmates, and refer to the music CD attached to the book (a Companion Website also is available for further study).

Each of the chapters in Part I has an identical organization comprising two basic parts. In the first part we encounter terms defining characteristics and qualities we can bring to bear when we approach a work of art. We title this part of the chapter "Formal and Technical Qualities." Formal qualities are those that have mainly to do with the larger divisions such as types and genres of the discipline. Technical qualities relate to the devices from which the artist constructs the work of art: things such as composition, melodies, and plots. In the second part of the chapter we discuss how those earlier characteristics and qualities cause works of art to affect our sense responses. We title this part of each chapter "Sense Stimuli." So, in each of Chapters 1–8 we have an aesthetic give and take: "Formal and Technical Qualities" represents our going to the work of art; "Sense Stimuli" represents the artwork coming to us.

Part II of the text (The Styles of the Arts) reveals some of the fundamentals of artistic style as it has appeared in works of art throughout history in a variety of cultures: Asian, African, European, and American. We use chronology and continents as organizing principles, but we must remember that chronology and continents represent conveniences and do not give us a true "history" of the arts. Rather, as we use them, they give us a series of snapshots only—a sampling of the art that humankind has produced over 35,000 years and the labels by which we have come to identify some of it. In our travels we will make some pretty dizzying jumps—geographically and chronologically. Think of the experience as an elaborate artistic buffet rather than an in-depth study.

Furthermore, we will confront cultures different from our own. Arguably, perhaps, we can never see a work of art from outside our own culture in the way that someone nurtured in that culture can. We cannot hope to know the historic works of our own culture in the way they were known in their own times. Nonetheless, every work of art comprises unique qualities and potential experiences for us. We can analyze, compare, and relate those qualities even if we do not know much about the context or culture that produced them. Of course, the more we know about those factors, the richer our experience becomes.

PRONOUNCING NAMES AND TERMS

Study of the arts brings us face to face with many challenging terms (many of them in a foreign language) and names. To assist acquaintanceship, each term or name not pronounced exactly as it appears is followed, in parentheses, by a pronunciation guide.

The system used in this book sometimes looks awkward. For example, the long I sound (which comprises a diphthong of ah and ee) such as in die, eye, and by, is indicated by the letter Y when the syllable stands alone or precedes a consonant. The letter Y prior to a vowel maintains its yuh sound, as in young (yuhng). The letter G, when sounded "hard" as in go or guard, is presented as GH. Again, it appears odd in some cases, such as ghoh-GHAN (Gauguin). Nonetheless, when one remembers that GH equals a hard G sound, the appearance yields to successful pronunciation.

Principle stress in a word or name is indicated by capitalization. For example, the pronunciation of "fable" would be indicated as FAY-buhl. Typically, words comprising three or more syllables also have at least one syllable of secondary stress. These are not indicated in this text. More often than not, if the primary stress is identified, the secondary stresses fall almost automatically into place.

Here is a guide to the system used in this book:

A	cat
Ah	cot
Aw	awe
Air	air, pair
Awr	core
Ay	bay
Eh	bet
Ee	see
Gh	go
Y	eye
Ih	bit
Ihng	sing
Oh	foe
Oo	food
Ow	wow
Oy	boy
Uh	bug
U	wood
Zh	pleasure
z	zip

A word of warning: pronunciation is not always universally agreed upon. Pronunciations in this text have been drawn from respected encyclopedic and dictionary sources. Even so, some may appear to flout common usage, especially of names that enjoy widespread Anglicization. Further, sounds such as French nasals and German umlauts mean little to those unfamiliar with the languages. We have made no attempt to replicate those sounds in the pronunciation prompts.

THE COMPANION WEBSITE AND ACCOMPANYING MUSIC CD

This book has a Companion Website on which a number of helpful features appear. One of these is a video containing fourteen tracks dealing with subjects such as musical forms and instruments, rhythm, perspective, subtractive and ceramic sculpture, theatre terminology, modern dance, ballet, Classical, medieval, and modern architecture, and poetry.

Attached to the book itself is a music CD containing twenty-five tracks of musical examples that are discussed in the text. These examples include pieces from Asian, African, and Middle Eastern cultures as well as examples of music ranging from the Middle Ages through to the present in Western culture. We refer to these selections (as well as many others) in the chapter on the medium of music and opera in Part I and the music sections of the chapters on style in Part II. Whenever a musical example mentioned in the text can be accessed on the accompanying CD, the note "music CD track —, (title)" appears in the text.

PUTTING THIS STUDY IN CONTEXT

For centuries, scholars, philosophers, and aestheticians have debated without general resolution a definition of "art." The challenging range of arguments encompasses, among other considerations, opposing points of view that insist on the one hand that "art" must meet a criterion of functionality—that is, be of some societal use—and, on the other hand, that "art" exists for its own sake. This text seeks to survey rather than dispute. Thus, the dilemma of art's definition remains unsolved here, despite the energizing effect that such a discussion might engender. We can, however, examine some characteristics of the arts that enhance understanding.

Art has and has had a profound effect on the quality of human life, and its study requires seriousness of purpose.

Having said that, however, we must not confuse seriousness of purpose in the study of art with a sweeping sanctification of works of art. Some art is serious, some art is profound, and some art is sacred. Yet some art is light, some is humorous, and some is downright silly, superficial, and self-serving for its artists.

The remainder of this section treats five general subjects: (1) *The Arts and Ways of Knowing* (2) *What Are Art's Main Concerns?* (3) *What Are Art's Purposes and Functions?* (4) *How Should We Perceive and Respond?* and (5) *How Do We Live with Art?*

THE ARTS AND WAYS OF KNOWING

Humans are a creative species. Whether in science, politics, business, technology, or the arts, we depend on our creativity almost as much as anything else to meet the demands of daily life. Any book about the arts tells a story about us: our perceptions of the world as we have come to see and respond to it, and the ways we have communicated our understandings to each other for thousands of years (Fig. **0.1**).

Our study in this text focuses on vocabulary and perception, as well as on history. First, however, we need an overview of where the arts fall within the general scope of human endeavor.

We live in buildings and listen to music constantly. We hang pictures on our walls and react like personal friends to characters in television, film, and live dramas. We escape to enjoy public parks, engross ourselves in novels, wonder about a statue in front of a public building, and dance through the night. All these situations involve forms called "art," in which we engage and are engaged in daily. Curiously, as close to us as these "art" activities are, in many ways they remain mysteries. How do they, in fact, fit into the larger picture of the human "reality" that we experience?

Since the human species began, we have learned a great deal about our world and how it functions, and we have changed our patterns of existence. However, the fundamental characteristics that make us human—our ability to intuit and to symbolize—have not changed. Art, the major remaining evidence we have of our earliest times, reflects these unchanged human characteristics in inescapable terms and helps us to understand the beliefs of cultures, including our own, and to express the universal qualities of humans.

As we begin this text, learning more about our humanness through art, let us start where we are. That has two implications. First, it means relying on the perceptive capabilities we already have. Applying our current abili-

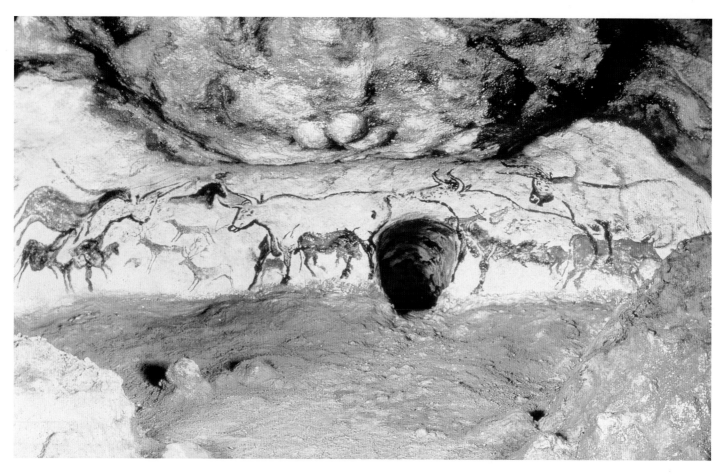

0.1 Cave chamber at Lascaux, France, early Stone Age (c. 15,000 B.C.E.).

ties to perceive will develop confidence in approaching works of art. Second, starting where we are means learning how art fits into the general scheme of the way people examine, communicate, and respond to the world around them. A course in the arts, designed to fulfill a requirement for a specified curriculum, demonstrates that the arts fit into an academic context that divides up the ways people acquire knowledge. Consequently, the first step in this exploration of the arts requires placing them in some kind of relationship with other categories of knowledge. Visual art, architecture, music, theatre, dance, literature, and film belong in a broad category of pursuit called the "humanities." The terms "arts" and "humanities" fit together as a piece to a whole. The humanities constitute a larger whole into which the arts fit as one piece. So, when we use the term "humanities" we automatically include the arts. When we use the term "arts" we restrict our focus. The arts disciplines—visual art (drawing, painting, printmaking, photography), performing art (music, theatre, dance, cinema), literature, and architecture (including landscape architecture), typically arrange sound, color, form, movement, and/or other elements in a manner that affects our sense of beauty (see p. 19) in a

graphic or plastic (capable of being shaped) medium. The humanities include the arts but also include other disciplines such as philosophy and, sometimes, history, which comprise branches of knowledge that share a concern with humans and their cultures. We begin our discussion with a look at the humanities.

The humanities, as opposed, for example, to the sciences, can very broadly be defined as those aspects of culture that look into what it means to be human. The sciences seek essentially to describe reality, whereas the humanities seek to express humankind's subjective experiences of reality, to interpret reality, to transform our interior experience into tangible forms, and to comment upon reality, to judge and evaluate. But despite our desire to categorize, few clear boundaries exist between the humanities and the sciences. The basic difference lies in the approach that separates investigation of the natural universe, technology, and social science from the search for truth about the universe undertaken by artists.

Change in the arts differs from change in the sciences in one significant way: new scientific discovery and technology usually displaces the old, but new art does not invalidate earlier human expression. The art of Picasso cannot make the art of Rembrandt a curiosity of history in the way that the theories of Einstein did the views of William Paley. Nonetheless, much about art has changed over the centuries. Part II of this text, "The Styles of the Arts," illustrates how the role of the artist can shift with the nature of the age. Using a spectrum developed by Susan Lacy in *Mapping the Terrain: New Genre Public Art* (1994), we learn that at one time an artist may be an *experiencer*; at another, a *reporter*; at another, an *analyst*; and at still another time, an *activist*. Further, the nature of how art historians see art has changed over the centuries—for example, today historians do not credit an artist's biography with all of the motivations for his or her work, and they now include in their studies works of art from previously marginalized groups such as women and minorities. These shifts in the discipline of arts history itself constitute important considerations in understanding the nature of art.

We can approach works of art with the same subtleties we normally apply to human relationships. We know that we cannot simply categorize people as "good" or "bad," as "friends," "acquaintances," or "enemies." We relate to others in complex ways. Some friendships are pleasant but superficial, some people are easy to work with, and others (but few) are lifelong companions. Similarly, when we have gone beyond textbook categories and learned how to approach art with this sort of sensitivity, we find that art, like friendship, has a major place in enriching quality of life.

WHAT ARE ART'S MAIN CONCERNS?

Among other areas, art has typically concerned creativity, aesthetic communication, symbols, and the fine arts and crafts. Let's look briefly at each of these.

Creativity

Art has always evidenced creativity—the act of bringing forth new forces and forms. How creativity functions is a subject for debate. Nonetheless, something happens in which humankind takes chaos, formlessness, vagueness, and the unknown and crystallizes them into form, design, inventions, and ideas. Creativity underlies our existence. It allows scientists to intuit a possible path to a cure for cancer, for example, or to invent a computer. The same process allows artists to find new ways to express ideas through processes in which creative action, thought, material, and technique combine in a medium to create something new. That "new thing," often without words,

triggers human experience: specifically, our response to the artwork.

In the midst of this creative process stands the art medium. Although most people can readily acknowledge the traditional media—for example, painting, sculpture, and printmaking—occasionally, when a medium of expression does not conform to expectations or experiences, many question whether the work qualifies as art. For example, Figure **0.2A** and **B** shows one gigantic installation in two parts, of blue and yellow umbrellas in the United States and Japan, respectively, created (and entirely financed) by the artists Christo and Jeanne-Claude. The umbrellas constituted the physical manifestation of a larger creative idea that the artists considered the whole work. People disagreed as to whether these inventive constructions constituted an artistic medium or a work of art.

In February 2005 these artists unveiled a similar project, called "The Gates," in New York City's Central Park. Thousands of swaths of pleated nylon billowed in the breeze from the top of 7,500 16-foot-tall gates. Like all their projects, this one comprised as much a public happening as a vast environmental sculpture and feat of engineering. It required more than 1 million square feet of vinyl and 5,300 tons of steel set along 23 miles of footpaths throughout the park. The artists themselves bore the 20-million-dollar cost.

Aesthetic Communication

Art usually involves communication. Arguably, artists need people with whom they can share their perceptions. When artworks and humans interact, many possibilities arise. Interaction may be casual and fleeting, as in the first meeting of two people, when one or both are not at all interested in the other. Similarly, an artist may not have much to say, or may not say it very well. For example, a poorly written or produced play will probably not excite an audience. Similarly, an audience member's preoccupations with other things may make perception of the play's message impossible, thus short-circuiting that part of the artistic experience. On the other hand, optimum conditions may result in a profoundly exciting and meaningful experience. The play may treat a significant subject in a unique manner, the production artists may exhibit excellent skills in manipulating the medium, and the audience may be receptive. Or the interaction may fall somewhere between these two extremes.

Throughout history, artistic communication has involved *aesthetics*. Aesthetics is the study of the nature of beauty and of art and comprises one of the five Classical fields of philosophical inquiry—along with epistemology

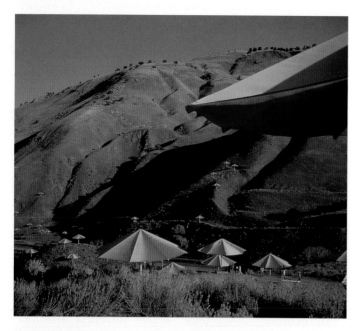

0.2A and B Christo and Jeanne-Claude, *The Umbrellas, Japan–USA*, 1984–91. (A) Valley north of Los Angeles, California, detail of 1,760 yellow umbrellas; (B) Valley in prefecture of Ibaraki, Japan, detail of 1,340 blue umbrellas. Nylon and aluminum, height of each umbrella including base 19 ft 8¼ ins (6 m); combined length 30 miles (48 km).

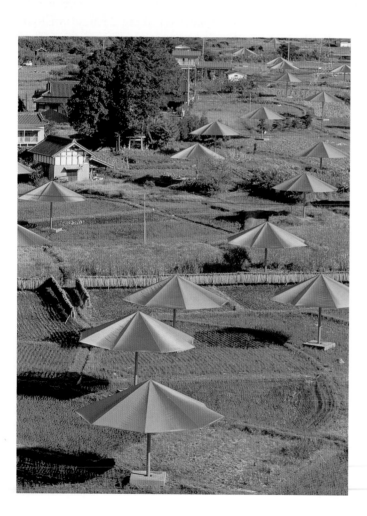

(the nature and origin of knowledge), ethics (the general nature of morals and of the specific moral choices to be made by the individual in relationship with others), logic (the principles of reasoning), and metaphysics (the nature of first principles and problems of ultimate reality). The term *aesthetics* (from the Greek for "sense perception") was coined by the German philosopher Alexander Baumgarten (1714–62) in the mid-eighteenth century, but interest in what constitutes the beautiful and in the relationship between art and nature goes back at least to the ancient Greeks. Both Plato and Aristotle saw art as *imitation* and beauty as the expression of a universal quality. For the Greeks, the concept of "art" embraced all handcrafts and the rules of symmetry, proportion, and unity applied equally to weaving, pottery, poetry, and sculpture. In the late eighteenth century, the philosopher Immanuel Kant (kahnt; 1724–1804) revolutionized aesthetics in his *Critique of Judgment* (1790) by viewing aesthetic appreciation not simply as the perception of intrinsic beauty, but as involving a judgment—subjective, but informed. Since Kant, the primary focus of aesthetics has shifted from the consideration of beauty *per se* to the nature of the artist, the role of art, and the relationship between the viewer and the work of art.

Symbols

Art also concerns symbols. Symbols are usually a tangible emblem of something abstract: a mundane object evoking a higher realm. They differ from signs, which suggest a fact or condition. Symbols carry deeper, wider, and richer meanings. Look at Figure 0.3. Some people might identify this as a plus sign in arithmetic. But it might also be a Greek Cross, in which case it becomes a symbol because it suggests many images, meanings, and implications. Artworks use a variety of symbols to convey meaning. Symbols make artworks into doorways leading to enriched understanding.

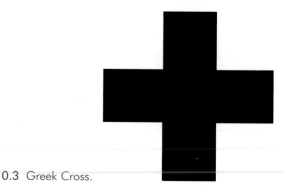

0.3 Greek Cross.

Symbols occur in literature, art, and ritual. They can be based on conventional relationships such as a rose standing for courtly love in a medieval romance. A symbol can suggest physical or other similarities between itself and its reference (the red rose representing blood) or personal associations—for example, the Irish poet William Butler Yeats's use of the rose to symbolize death, ideal perfection, Ireland, and so on. Symbols also occur in linguistics wherein words are considered arbitrary symbols and in psychoanalysis where symbols, particularly images in dreams, are regarded as repressed, subconscious desires and fears. In Judaism, the contents of the feast table and the ceremony performed at the Jewish Passover seder (the feast celebrating the exodus from slavery in Egypt) symbolize the events surrounding the Israelites' deliverance from Egypt. In Christian art, the lamb symbolizes the sacrifice of Christ.

Fine and Applied Art

One last consideration in understanding art's concerns involves the difference between *fine art* and *applied art*. The "fine arts"—generally meaning painting, sculpture, architecture, music, theatre, dance, and, in the twentieth century, cinema—are prized for their purely aesthetic qualities. During the Renaissance (see Chapter 11), these arts rose to superior status because Renaissance values lauded individual expression and unique aesthetic interpretations of ideas. The term "applied art" sometimes includes architecture and the "decorative arts" and refers to artforms that have a primarily decorative rather than expressive or emotional purpose. The decorative arts (a name first used in 1791) include handcrafts by skilled artisans, such as ornamental work in metal, stone, wood, and glass, as well as textiles, pottery, and bookbinding. They may also encompass aspects of interior design and personal objects such as jewelry, weaponry, tools, and costumes. Even mechanical appliances and other products of industrial design can be considered part of the category. Many decorative arts, such as weaving, basketry, and pottery, are also commonly considered "crafts," but the definitions of the terms remain somewhat arbitrary and without sharp distinction.

WHAT ARE ART'S PURPOSES AND FUNCTIONS?

We can also expand our understanding of art by examining some of its purposes and functions. In terms of the former—its purposes—we ask, What does art do? In terms of the latter—art's functions—we ask, How does it do it?

Purposes

Essentially, art does four things: (1) it provides a record; (2) it gives visible or other form to feelings; (3) it reveals metaphysical or spiritual truths; and (4) it helps people to see the world in new ways. Art can do any or all of these. They are not mutually exclusive.

Until the invention of the camera, one of art's principal purposes was to enact a record of the world. Although we cannot know for sure, very likely cave art of the earliest times did this. Egyptian art, ancient Greek art, Roman art, and so on until the invention of the camera all undertook, at times, to create pictorial records.

Art can give form to feelings. Perhaps the most explicit example comes in the Expressionist style of the early twentieth century (see Chapter 13). Here the emotions of the artist toward the work's content form a primary role in the work. "Feelings" can be referenced in works of art through technique—for instance, brush stroke—and through color (to isolate two visual examples), both of which have long associations with emotional content.

A third purpose of art, the revelation of metaphysical or spiritual truths, rises as an example in plainchant and the Gothic cathedrals of medieval Europe (see Chapter 10), whose light and space perfectly embodied medieval spirituality. A tribal totem, such as a Bakota ancestor (see Fig. 2.7), deals almost exclusively in spiritual and metaphysical revelation.

Finally, as a fourth purpose, most art, if well done, can assist us in seeing the world around us in new and surprising ways. Art that has abstract content may reveal a new way of understanding the interaction of life forces, as does the work of Piet Mondrian (peet MAWN-dree-ahn); see Figure **1.48** and the associated discussion.

Functions

In addition to its purposes (what it does), art also has many functions (how it does what it does), including (1) enjoyment, (2) political and social commentary, and (3) artifact. No one function has more importance than the others. Nor are they mutually exclusive; one artwork may fill many functions. Neither are the three functions just mentioned the only ones. Rather, they serve as indicators of how art has functioned in the past and can function in the present. Like the types and styles of art that have occurred through history, these three functions and others form options for artists and depend on what artists wish to do with their artworks—as well as how we perceive and respond to them.

Plays, paintings, and concerts can provide escape from everyday cares, treat us to a pleasant time, and engage us

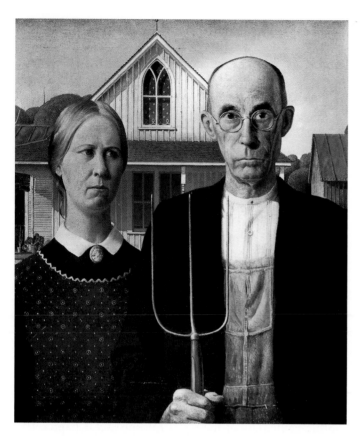

0.4 Grant Wood, *American Gothic*, 1930. Oil on beaver board, 30 × 25 ins (76 × 63 cm). Art Institute of Chicago (Friends of American Art Collection).

in social occasions. Works of art that provide enjoyment may perform other functions as well. The same artworks we enjoy may also create insights into human experience. We can glimpse the conditions of other cultures, and we can find healing therapy in enjoyment.

An artwork in which one individual finds only enjoyment may function as a profound social and personal comment to another. A Mozart symphony, for example, may relax us and allow us to escape our cares. It may also comment on the life of the composer and/or the conditions of eighteenth-century Austria. Grant Wood's *American Gothic* (Fig. 0.4) may amuse us, and/or provide a tongue-in-cheek commentary about rural America, and/or move us deeply. The result depends on the artist, the artwork, and us. We can note here, as well, that implicit in our discussion of enjoyment as a function of art rests the concept that art can exist for its own sake, alone. That is to say that many people believe that art need not have any "function" at all. "Art for art's sake" is the phrase used to describe their viewpoint, and the issue of whether art should be functional or exist purely for its own sake is worthy of discussion. Art used to bring about political change or to modify the behavior of large groups

of people has political or social functions. In ancient Rome, for example, the authorities used music and theatre to keep masses of unemployed people occupied in order to quell urban unrest. At the same time, Roman playwrights used their public platform to attack incompetent or corrupt officials. The Greek playwright Aristophanes, in such plays as *The Birds*, saw that comedy could be employed as a means of challenging the political ideas of the leaders of ancient Athenian society. In his play *Lysistrata*, he puts his message over by creating a story in which all the women of Athens go on a sex strike until Athens rids itself of war and warmongers.

In nineteenth-century Norway, the playwright Henrik Ibsen used his work *An Enemy of the People* as a platform for airing the conflict of priorities between pollution control and economic wellbeing. In the United States today, many artworks are used as vehicles to advance social and political causes, or to sensitize viewers, listeners, or readers to particular cultural situations such as racial prejudice and AIDS.

Art also functions as an artifact: a product of a particular time and place, an artwork represents the ideas and technology of that specific environment. Artworks often provide not only striking examples but occasionally the only tangible records of some peoples. Artifacts such as paintings, sculptures, poems, plays, and buildings, enhance our insights into many cultures, including our own. Consider, for example, the many revelations that we might find in a sophisticated work such as the roped pot on a stand from Igbo-Ukwu (Fig. 0.5). This ritual water pot from a village in eastern Nigeria used the *cire-perdue* or "lost-wax" process (see p. 77) and amazes us with its virtuosity. It reveals the sophisticated vision and technical accomplishment present in this ninth- and tenth-century African society.

The Igbo-Ukwu pot suggests that when we examine art in the context of cultural artifact, one of the issues we face concerns the use of artworks in religious *ritual*. We could consider ritual as a separate function of art. In fact, we may not think of religious ritual as art at all; but ritual often expresses human communication through an artistic medium.

Music, for example, when part of a religious ceremony, does this, and theatre—if seen as an occasion planned and intended for presentation—would include religious rituals as well as events that take place in theatres. Often, as a survey of art history would confirm, we cannot discern when ritual stops and secular production starts. When ritual, planned and intended for presentation, uses traditionally artistic media like music, dance, and theatre, we can legitimately study it as art, and see it also as an artifact of its particular culture.

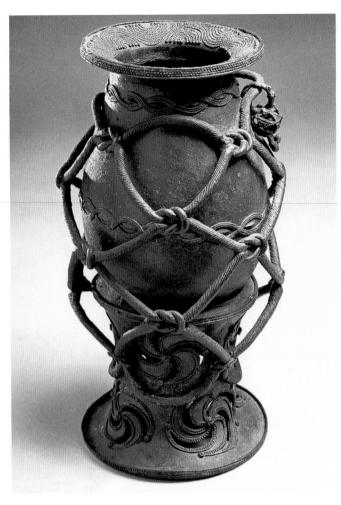

0.5 Roped pot on a stand, from Igbo-Ukwu, eastern Nigeria, 9th–10th century. Leaded bronze, height 12½ ins (32 cm). National Museum, Lagos.

HOW SHOULD WE PERCEIVE AND RESPOND?

Thus far, in putting the arts in context, we have examined *The Arts and Ways of Knowing, What Are Art's Main Concerns?* and *What Are Art's Purposes and Functions?* Now we deal with the challenge of how we approach studying them—*How Should We Perceive and Respond?* We have chosen a method of study that can act as a springboard into confident and rewarding engagement with the arts. In the first half of the book, we will examine the various media that artists use to transform their visions of human reality into works of art. In the second half of the book we will travel through history and around the world to examine the choices artists make while using their media to give artworks their particular appearance. The first half of the book is more technical than the second,

and it deals, basically, with the question, What can we see and hear in works of art? To put that question in different terms, How can we sharpen our aesthetic perception? The answer is threefold.

- First of all, we must identify those items that can be seen and heard in works of art and literature.
- Second, we must learn some of the terminology relating to those items—just as we learn any subject.
- Third, we must understand why and how what we perceive relates to our response.

It is, after all, our response to an artwork that interests us. We can *perceive* an object. We *choose* to *respond* to it in aesthetic terms.

When we have finished our examination of the two units of this text—*The Media of the Arts: What Artists Use to Express "Reality"* and *The Styles of the Arts: How Artists Portray "Reality"*—our own human reality will have broader horizons and deeper insights. We will also approach and communicate these issues with greater confidence.

HOW DO WE LIVE WITH ART?

Our final examination on the topic of putting the arts in context concerns the relationship of the arts to everyday life. Because of unfamiliarity, many individuals feel uncomfortable approaching the arts and literature. That unfamiliarity, perhaps, has been fostered by individuals, both within the disciplines and without, who try to make involvement in the arts and literature elitist, and art galleries, museums, concert halls, theatres, and opera houses open only to the knowledgeable and the sophisticated. Nothing could be further from the truth. The arts comprise elements of life with which we can and must deal and to which we must respond every day. We live with the arts because the principles of *aesthetics* permeate our existence. Specifically, the aesthetic experience is a way of knowing and communicating in and of itself, separate from other ways of knowing and communicating. It forms a significant part of our experience. Cutting ourselves off from the part of our existence that deals with aesthetic communication and knowledge forces us to cope with life with only half of our available survival tools.

The arts also play important roles in making the world around us more interesting and habitable. Artistic ideas join with *conventions* to make everyday objects attractive and pleasurable. We use the term "convention" repeatedly in this text. A convention is a set of rules or mutually accepted conditions. Conventions play important roles in everyday life.

First of all, a convention that dictates a consistent height for tables and desks controls the design. So the lower portion of the chest, from point A to point B, designs space within a height that harmonizes with other furniture in the room. If we look carefully, we can also see that the parts of the chest contain a sophisticated and interesting series of proportional and progressive relationships. The distance from A to B is twice the distance from A to D and is equal to the distance from B to C. The distances from A to F and C to E bear no recognizable relationship to the previous dimensions but are, however, equal to each other and to the distances from G to H, H to I, and I to J. In addition, the size of the drawers in the upper chest decreases at an even and proportional rate from bottom to top.

The Volkswagen shown in Figure 0.7 forms another example. Here, repetition of form reflects a concern for unity, one of the fundamental characteristics of art. The design of the early Volkswagen Beetle (or "Bug") used strong repetition of the oval. We need only look at the various parts of the Bug to see variation on this theme. Later models differ from this version and reflect the intrusion of conventions, again, into the world of design. As safety standards called for larger bumpers, the oval design of the motor-compartment hood flattened so a larger bumper could clear it. The rear window enlarged and squared to accommodate the need for increased rear vision. The intrusion of these conventions changed the design of the Beetle by breaking down the strong unity of the original composition.

Finally, as Edwin J. Delattre states when he compares the purpose for studying technical subjects to the purpose for studying the humanities or the arts, "When a person studies the mechanics of internal combustion engines the intended result is that he should be better able to understand, design, build, or repair such engines, and sometimes he should be better able to find employment because of his skills, and thus better his life. . . . When a person studies the humanities [the arts] the intended result is that he should be better able to understand, design, build, or repair a life—for living is a vocation we have in common despite our differences.

"The humanities provide us with opportunity to become more capable in thought, judgment, communication, appreciation, and action." Delattre goes on to say that these provisions enable us to think more rigorously and to imagine more abundantly. "These activities free us to possibilities that are new, at least to us, and they unbind us from portions of our ignorance about living well. . . . Without exposure to the cultural . . . traditions that are our heritage, we are excluded from a common world that crosses generations."[1] The poet Archibald

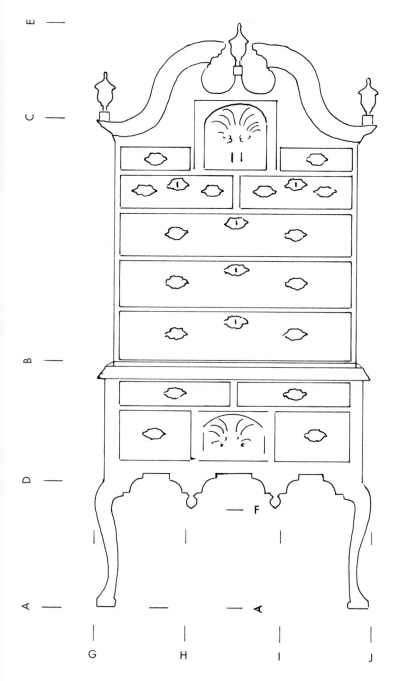

0.6 Scale drawing of an 18th-century highboy.

For example, Figure 0.6, a scale drawing of an eighteenth-century highboy, illustrates how art and convention combine in everyday items. The maker of the high chest conceived it to fill a practical purpose—to provide for storage of household objects in an easily accessible, yet hidden, place. However, while designing an object to accommodate that practical need, the cabinetmakers felt the additional need to provide an interesting and attractive object. If we perceive with discrimination and imagination, we enter an enlightening and challenging experience with this piece of furniture.

MacLeish is more succinct: "Without the Arts, how can the university teach the Truth?"

Perhaps in a broader sense, we can say we live with art because art has the potential to change our lives. Many years ago, a colleague laid on my desk a very expensive book about architecture. "From a student," he said. "Before or after grades?" I replied in my usual, insensitive, flip manner. After a pregnant pause and a bit of glaring, he told me "Sam's" story.

Sam, who was a construction worker, took our course, "Introduction to the Arts" as a night student. After the semester ended (and after the grades were posted!) Sam brought the book to my colleague, who had taught the course. At that time, such a book probably cost at least a fourth of Sam's weekly salary.

"Why?" my colleague asked Sam.

"Because you changed my life," Sam replied. "Before this course I poured concrete day in and day out. It was concrete—you know, cement, sand, stone, et cetera— just concrete. After taking this course, I can't see just bland concrete anymore. Whenever I walk onto a job site, I see patterns, colors, lines, and forms. Whenever I look at a building, I see history. I go to places I'd never dreamed of going before, and I can't believe how dull my life really was without all the things I now see and hear. I just never knew there was so much out there."

My colleague said to me, "You know, this construction worker—'Joe Sixpack' we might have called him—a man's man, had tears in his eyes; he was so taken by what he'd found out about life through art."

APPLYING CRITICAL SKILLS

We all seem to want to opine on the quality of works of art. Whatever the form or medium, judgments about the quality of an artwork vary from one extreme to another, ranging from "I like it" and "interesting" to specific reasons for its effectiveness or ineffectiveness.

Because the word *criticism* implies many different things to many people, we must first agree on what it means—or what it does not. Criticism does not necessarily mean saying negative things about a work of art. All too often we think of critics as people who pass judgments, giving their opinions on the value of a painting, sculpture, work of architecture, and so on. Personal judgment may result from criticism, but criticism implies more than passing judgment.

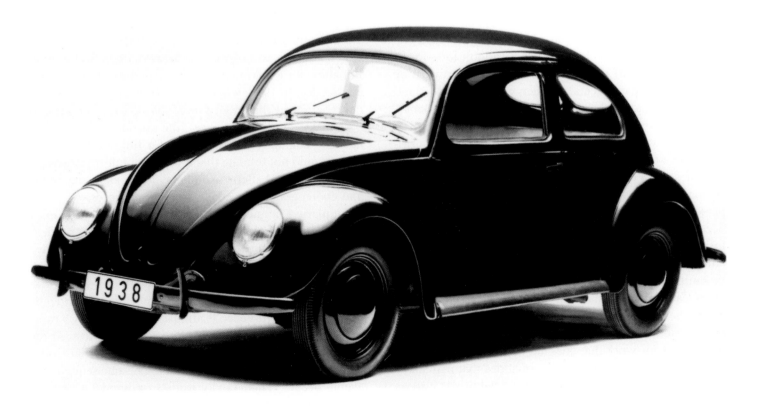

0.7 *Volkswagen Beetle, 1938.*

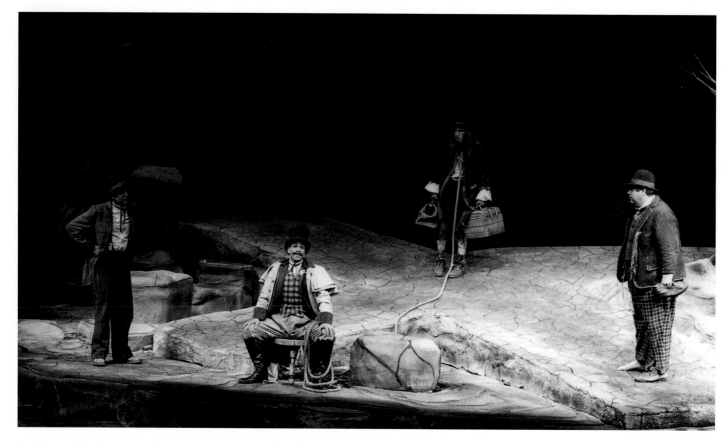

0.8 Samuel Beckett, *Waiting for Godot*, Utah Shakespearean Festival, 1990. Director: Tom Marlens.

Criticism *should* be a *detailed process of analysis to gain understanding and appreciation.* Identifying the formal elements of an artwork—learning what to look for—forms the first step of art criticism. We *describe* an artwork by examining its many facets and then we try to understand how they work together to create meaning or experience. We then try to state the nature of that meaning or experience. Only when we complete that process should criticism move to judgment.

Professional critics usually bring to the process a set of standards developed from personal experience. Whenever personal standards are applied, the process of criticism becomes complicated. First of all, knowledge of the artform may be shallow. Second, perceptual skills may be faulty; and, finally, the range of personal experience may be limited. In addition, the application of personal standards can be problematic if judgment is based on pre-established criteria: if someone believes that, say, "beauty" and/or usefulness constitute essential elements of a work of art, then any work that does not meet those criteria will be judged as faulty, despite other qualities that may make the work unique and profound. Pre-established criteria often deny critical acclaim to new or experimental approaches in art.

History resounds with examples of new artistic attempts that met with terrible receptions from so-called experts, whose idea of what an artwork ought to be could not allow for experimentation or departures from accepted practice. In 1912, when Vaslav Nijinsky (nih-JIN-skee) choreographed the ballet *Rite of Spring* to music by Igor Stravinsky (strah-VIHN-skee), the unconventional music and choreography actually caused a riot: audiences and critics could not tolerate that it did not conform to accepted musical and balletic standards. Today, both the music and choreography are considered masterpieces.

Similarly, Samuel Beckett's play, *Waiting for Godot* (1953) (Fig. **0.8**) does not have a plot, characters, or ideas expressed in a conventional manner. In this play, two tramps wait beside the road by a withered tree for the arrival of someone named Godot. The tramps tell stories to each other, argue, eat some food, and are interrupted by a character named Pozzo leading a slave, Lucky, by a rope. After a brief conversation, Lucky and Pozzo leave. At the end of the first act, a boy enters to announce that Godot will not come today. In Act 2, much the same sequence of events occurs. Then Lucky leads in a blind Pozzo. The tree has sprouted a few leaves. The play ends as the young boy returns to indicate Godot will not arrive that day either. If your standards require a successful play to have a carefully fashioned plot wrapped around fully developed characters and a clear message, then *Waiting for Godot* cannot possibly be a good play. Some people agree with such an assertion; others disagree vehemently. What, then, do we conclude? What if my criteria do not match yours? What if two experts disagree on the quality of a movie? Does that ultimately make any difference to our experience of it?

Value judgments remain intensely personal, but some opinions are more informed than others and represent more authoritative judgment. Sometimes, even knowledgeable people disagree. Disagreements about quality, however, can enhance our experience of a work of art when they lead us to think about why the differences exist. In this way, we gain a deeper understanding of the artwork. Nonetheless, *criticism* can be exercised without involving any judgment. We can thoroughly dissect any work of art—for example, we can describe and analyze line, color, melody, harmony, texture, plot, character, and/or message. We can observe how all of these factors affect people and their responses. We can spend a significant amount of time doing this and never pass a value judgment at all.

Does this discussion mean all artworks are equal in value? Not at all. It means that in order to understand what criticism involves, we must separate descriptive analysis, which can be satisfying in and of itself, from the act of passing value judgments. We may not like the work we have analyzed, but we may have understood something we did not understand before. Passing judgment may play no role whatsoever in our understanding of an artwork. But we still exercise criticism. As an exercise in understanding, criticism is necessary. We must investigate and describe. We must experience the need to know enough about the process, product, and experience of art if we are to have perceptions to share.

Now that we have examined briefly what criticism is and why we might try it, what approaches to criticisim can we employ?

TYPES OF CRITICISM

A number of ways exist to "criticize" or analyze works of art. Some are fairly straightforward, and some are relatively complex and theoretically involved. Let's begin with two basic types of criticism: formal criticism and contextual criticism. Once we have these concepts in hand, we can branch out a little to examine the theoretically involved and opposing critical theories of structuralism and deconstruction.

Formal Criticism

Formal criticism constitutes analysis that applies no external conditions or information. It attempts to explain a work's total formal aesthetic organization. When we use formal criticism, we analyze the artwork just as we find it: if it is a painting, we look only within the frame; if it is a play, we analyze only what we see and hear. Formal criticism approaches the artwork as a self-contained entity, and the work must stand on its own merits. Formal criticism is exemplified in the work of the "New Critics" such as Allen Tate (1899–1979), who insisted on the intrinsic value of a work of art and focused attention on the work alone as an independent unit of meaning. As an example of how we might go about formal criticism, consider this brief analysis of Molière's comedy of 1664, *Tartuffe* (Fig. **0.9**).

> Orgon, a rich bourgeois, has allowed a religious con man, Tartuffe, to gain complete control over him. Tartuffe has moved into Orgon's house and tries to seduce Orgon's wife while at the same time planning to marry Orgon's daughter. Tartuffe is unmasked, and Orgon orders him out. Tartuffe seeks his revenge by claiming title to Orgon's house and blackmailing him with some secret papers. At the very last instant, Tartuffe's plans are foiled by the intervention of the king, and the play ends happily.

We have just described a story. Were we to go one step further and analyze the plot, we would look, among other things, for points at which *crises* occur and cause important decisions to be made by the characters; we would also want to know how those decisions moved the play from one point to the next. In addition, we would try to locate the extreme crisis, the *climax*. Meanwhile, we would discover auxiliary parts of the plot such as *reversals*—for example, the characters' awareness of the true situation. Depending on how detailed our criticism were to become, we could work our way through each and every aspect of the plot. We might then devote some time to describing and analyzing the driving force—the *character*—of each person in the play and how the characters relate to each other. We might ask whether Molière has created fully developed characters? Are they types or do they seem to behave more or less like real individuals? In examining the *thematic* elements of the play, we would no doubt conclude that the play deals with religious hypocrisy, and that Molière had a particular point of view on that subject.

In this formal approach, information about the playwright, previous performances, historic relationships, and so on, are irrelevant. Thus the formal approach helps us to analyze how an artwork operates and to decide why the

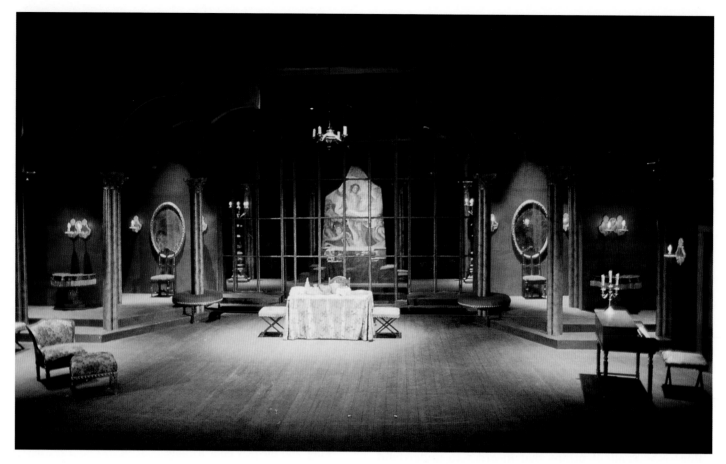

0.9 Jean-Baptiste Molière, *Tartuffe*, University of Arizona Theatre, 1990. Director: Charles O'Connor.

artwork produces the responses it does. We can apply this form of criticism to any work of art and come away with a variety of conclusions.

Of course, knowledge about how artworks are put together, what they are, and how they stimulate the senses (topics that are discussed in the first half of this text) enhances the critical process. Knowing the basic elements that comprise these formal and technical elements of the artwork gives us a ready outline on which to begin a formal analysis.

Contextual Criticism

Another general approach, contextual criticism, seeks meaning by adding to formal criticism an examination of related information outside the artwork, such as facts about the artist's life, his or her culture, social and political conditions and philosophies, and public and critical responses to the work. We can research these and apply them to the work in order to enhance perception and understanding. Contextual criticism views the artwork as an artifact generated from particular contextual needs, conditions, and/or attitudes. If we carry our criticism of

Tartuffe in this direction, we would note that certain historical events help clarify the play. For example, the object of Molière's attention was probably the Company of the Holy Sacrament, a secret, conspiratorial, and influential religious society in France at the time. Like many fanatical religious sects—including those of our own time—the society sought to enforce its own view of morality by spying on the lives of others and seeking out heresies—in this case, in the Roman Catholic Church. Its followers were religious fanatics, and they had considerable impact on the lives of the citizenry at large. If we were to follow this path of criticism, we would pursue any and all contextual matters that might illuminate or clarify what happens in the play. Contextual criticism may also employ the same kind of internal examination followed in the formal approach.

Structuralism

Structuralism is a European critical movement of the mid-twentieth century, based on the linguistic theories of Ferdinand de Saussure (soh-SUHR, 1857–1913). It applies to the artwork a broader significance, insisting that individual phenomena—in this case works of art—can be understood only within the context of the overall structures of which they are a part. These structures represent universal sets of relationships that derive meaning from their contrasts and interactions within a specific context. Structuralist criticism, associated with Roland Barthes (bahrt; 1915–80), derives by analogy from structural linguistics, which sees a "text" as a system of self-contained signs whose meaning is derived from the pattern of their interactions rather than from any external reference. This approach opposes critical positions that seek to determine an artist's intent, for example. Thus, the meaning of Molière's *Tartuffe* lies not in what Molière may have had in mind when he wrote it, but in the patterns of contextual relationships that work within the play. Finally, structuralism, which shares some common roots with formal criticism, also opposes approaches, such as deconstruction, that deny the existence of uniform patterns and definite meanings.

Deconstruction

Deconstruction, associated with the French philosopher Jacques Derrida (dare-ee-DAH; 1930–2004), was also originally associated with literary criticism, but has been applied to other disciplines. Derrida used the term *text*, for example, to include any subject to which critical analysis can be applied. Deconstructing something means "taking it apart." The process of deconstruction implies on the one hand drawing out all the threads of a work to identify its multitude of meanings and, on the other hand, undoing the "constructs" of ideology or convention that have imposed meaning on the work. All of this leads to the conclusion that there is no such thing as a single meaning in a work of art, nor can it claim any absolute truth. Inasmuch as a work can outlast its author, its meanings transcend any original intentions. In other words, the viewer or listener brings as much to the work as the artist; thus, there are no facts, only interpretations. The story of *Tartuffe*, for example, becomes only a sidebar to the interpretation that we bring to it based on our own experiences and circumstances.

Both structuralism and deconstruction are much more complex and philosophically and sociologically involved than the limited space available in this text allows us to discuss in detail. However, they illustrate the diversity of theories and approaches possible when encountering works of art. These theories—as well as the simple processes of formal and contextual criticism—merit further exploration and discussion as ways in which we can engage, analyze, come to know as best we can, and, ultimately, judge works of art.

MAKING JUDGMENTS

Now that we have made a rough definition of criticism and noted some approaches that criticism can take in pursuit of understanding and enjoyment of works of art, we can make a few brief comments about making judgments. While we may judge artworks on many levels and by many criteria, two particular characteristics stand out: artisanship and communication. Judgment of a work of art's quality probably ought to include consideration of both of these.

Artisanship

Judging a work's artisanship means judging how it has been crafted or made. Generally, such judgments require knowledge about the medium of the artwork. For example, we would have difficulty judging how a musical symphony has been crafted without having some detailed knowledge of musical composition. The same may be said of judging how well a painting, sculpture, building, or play is made. Nonetheless, some criteria exist that allow general judgment of artisanship. These criteria include *clarity* and *interest*.

Applying the standard of clarity means deciding whether the work has coherence. Even the most complex works of art need handles that allow us to approach them and begin to understand how they work. This standard of judgment has stood the test of time. Artworks have sometimes been compared to onions in that the well-made ones allow respondents to peel away translucent layers, with the removal of each layer moving us closer to the core. Some people can peel away all the layers, and some people can peel away only one or two, but a masterfully crafted work of art will have a coherence that allows virtually anyone to grasp on to some layer, if only the outer one.

Applying the standard of interest is similar to, and perhaps overlaps, applying the standard of clarity in that artists use layers of devices or qualities to capture and hold our interest. Masterfully crafted works of art employ such devices and qualities as: (1) universality (the artist's ability to touch a common experience or feeling within us), (2) carefully developed structures or focal points that lead us where the artist intends us to go, and (3) freshness of approach that makes us curious to investigate further. When we watch a tired and trite mystery, we know what is going to happen: the characters are stale clichés, and we lose interest almost immediately. A masterfully crafted work will hold us—even if we know the story, as in the case of plays such as Sophocles' *Oedipus the King* or Shakespeare's *Hamlet*.

If a work of art does not appear clear or interesting, we may wish to examine whether the fault lies in the work or in ourselves before rendering judgment.

Communication

Evaluating what an artwork tries to say offers more immediate opportunity for judgment and less need for expertise. Johann Wolfgang von Goethe (GHUHR-tuh), the nineteenth-century poet, novelist, and playwright, set out a basic, commonsense approach to evaluating communication. Because Goethe's approach provides an organized means for discovering an artwork's communication by progressing from analytical to judgmental functions, it helps us to end our discussion on criticism. Goethe suggests that we approach the critical process by asking three questions: What is the artist trying to say? Does he or she succeed? Was the artwork worth the effort? These questions focus on the artist's communication. The third question, of whether or not the project was worth the effort, raises issues such as uniqueness or profundity. A well-crafted work of art that merely restates obvious insights about the human condition lacks quality in its communicative component. One that offers profound and unique insights exhibits quality.

We should think of the arts somewhat as we think of people. Eventually we find human differences too subtle for easy classification, and the web of our relationships becomes too complex for analysis. We try to move toward more and more sensitive discrimination, so that there are those we can learn from, those we can work with, those good for an evening of light talk, those we can depend on for a little affection, and so on—with perhaps those very few with whom we can sustain a relationship for a lifetime. When we have learned this same sensitivity and adjustment to works of art—when we have gone beyond the easy categories of the textbooks and have learned to regard our art relationships as part of our own growth—then we shall have achieved a dimension in living as deep and as irreplaceable as friendship.

STYLE

The manner in which artists express themselves constitutes their style. Style is tantamount to the personality of an artwork: the body of characteristics that identifies an artwork with an individual, a historical period, a "school" of artists, or a nation. Often, styles derive from philosophical ideas, and theories of expression underlie styles such as Classicism, Romanticism, and Postmodernism, to

name a few. We will discuss these as they appear in the text. In the meantime, we can benefit from some general observations. To begin arriving at an artwork's style involves a process. It means assimilating materials, making comparisons, and drawing conclusions.

The style of any artwork can be determined by analyzing how the artist has arranged the characteristics of the medium. If the usage is similar to that of others, we might conclude that they exemplify the same style. For example, Bach and Handel typify the Baroque style in music; Haydn and Mozart, the Classical. Listening to works by these composers quickly leads to the conclusion that the ornate melodic shapes and rhythmic patterns of Bach are like those of Handel, and quite different from the flowing themes and precise concern for structure of Mozart and Haydn. The precision and symmetry of the Parthenon compared with the ornate opulence of the Palace of Versailles suggest that, in line and form, the architects of these buildings treated their medium differently. Yet the design of the Parthenon is very much a visual companion, stylistically, of Mozart and Haydn; Versailles reflects an approach to design similar to that of Bach and Handel.

HOW CAN WE ANALYZE STYLE?

Let us take our examination one step further and stylistically analyze four paintings. The first three were done by three different artists; the fourth, by one of those three. By stylistic analysis, we will determine who was the painter of the fourth.

The first painting (Fig. 0.10), *A View Near Volterra*, is by Corot (kuh-ROH). Corot has primarily used curved *line* to create the edges of the forms or shapes in the painting. Many of the forms—the rocks, trees, clouds—do not have crisp, clear edges. Color areas tend to blend with each other, giving the painting a somewhat fuzzy or out-of-focus appearance. Corot's use of palette heightens this comfortable effect. Palette encompasses the total use of color and contrast; since these illustrations are black and white, we can deal with only one aspect of palette: *value contrast*, the relationship of black, white, and gray. As with his use of line, Corot maintains subtlety in his value contrast. Movement from light to dark is gradual, and he avoids stark contrasts. He employs a full range of black, grays, and white, but does so without calling attention to their positioning. Corot's *brushstroke* is somewhat apparent: if we look carefully, we can see brush marks—individual strokes where paint has been applied—throughout the painting. We can tell that the foliage was executed by *stippling* (by dabbing the brush to the canvas as one would dot an "i" with a pencil). Thus, even though the objects portrayed are lifelike, the artist has not made any

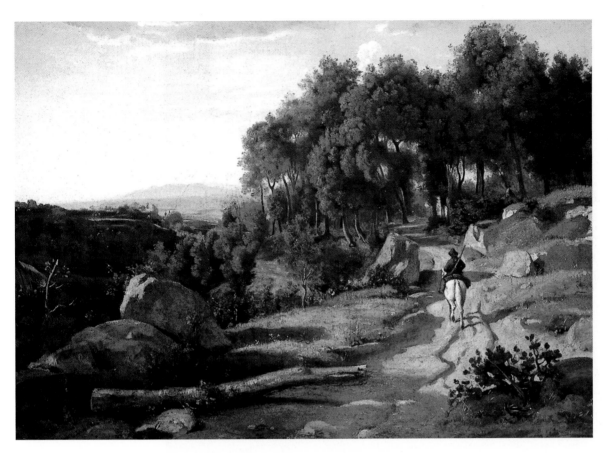

0.10 *Jean-Baptiste-Camille Corot, A View Near Volterra*, 1838. Oil on canvas, 27⅜ × 37½ ins (70 × 95 cm). National Gallery of Art, Washington, D.C. (Chester Dale Collection).

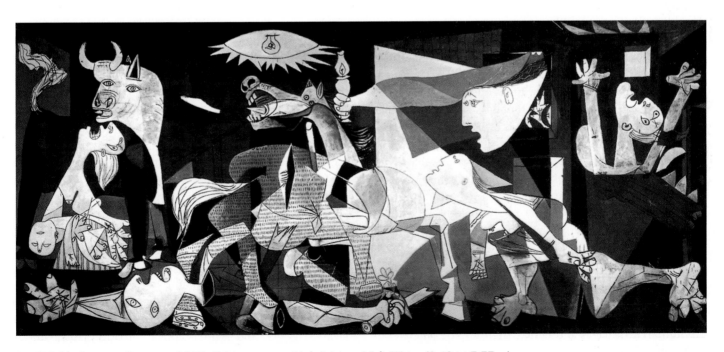

0.11 Pablo Picasso, *Guernica*, 1937. Oil on canvas, 11 ft 5 ins × 25 ft 5¾ ins (3.48 × 7.77 m). Museo Nacional Centro de Arte Reina Sofia, Madrid.

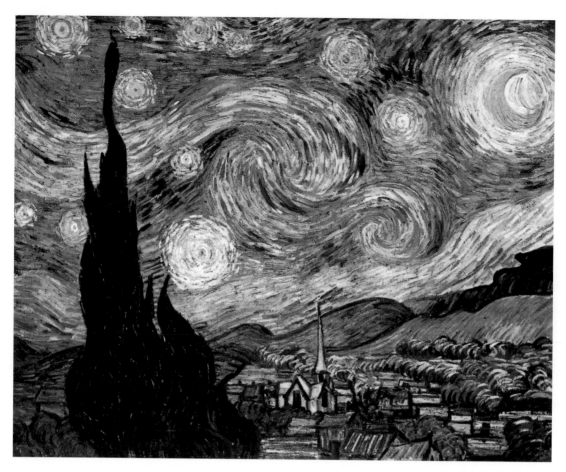

0.12 Vincent van Gogh, *The Starry Night*, 1889. Oil on canvas, 29 × 36¼ ins (73.7 × 92.1 cm). The Museum of Modern Art, New York.

attempt to hide the fact that the picture has been painted. The overall effect is lifelike, but we can see in every area the spontaneity with which Corot executed it.

The second painting (Fig. **0.11**), Picasso's *Guernica*, joins curved and straight lines, placing them in such relationships that they create movement and dissonance. The edges of color areas and forms remain sharp and distinct; there is nothing soft or fuzzy. Likewise, the value contrasts are stark and extreme. Areas of the highest value, white, force against areas of the lowest value—black. In fact, the range of tonalities is far narrower than in the previous work. Mid or medium (gray) tones appear, but they play a minor role in the effect of the palette. The tonal areas and the absence of obvious brushwork emphasize the starkness of the work.

The third painting (Fig. **0.12**), van Gogh's *Starry Night*, uses line in highly active although uniformly curved ways. Forms and color areas have both hard and soft edges, and van Gogh, like Picasso, uses outlining to strengthen his images and reduce their reality. The overall effect of line creates a sweeping and undulating movement, highly dynamic and yet far removed from the stark-

ness of the Picasso. In contrast, van Gogh's curvilinearity and softened edges yield quite different effects from the relaxed quality of the Corot. Van Gogh's value contrasts are broad, but moderate. He ranges from darks through medium grays to white, all virtually equal in importance. Even when movement from one area to another crosses a hard edge to a highly contrasting value, the result remains moderate: not soft, not stark. Brushstroke, however, gives the painting its unique personality. We can see thousands of individual brush marks where the artist applied paint to canvas. The nervous, almost frenetic use of brushstrokes makes the painting come alive.

Now that we have examined three paintings in different styles and by different artists, can you determine which of the three painted Figure 0.13? First, examine the use of line. Form and color edges are hard. Outlining appears. Curved and straight lines are juxtaposed. The effect is active and stark: unlike Corot, a bit like van Gogh, and very much like Picasso. Next, examine palette. Darks, grays, and whites appear broadly. However, the principal impression remains of strong contrast—the darkest darks against the whitest whites. This is not like

Corot, a bit like van Gogh, and most like Picasso. Finally, brushstroke is generally unobtrusive. Tonal areas are mostly flat. This is definitely not a van Gogh and probably not a Corot. Three votes out of three go to Picasso—and the style is so distinctive that you probably had no difficulty deciding, even without the written analysis. However, would you have been so certain if asked whether Picasso painted Figure **1.25**? Some differences in style are obvious; others are more subtle. It is quite a challenge to distinguish the work of one artist from another who designs in a similar fashion. However, the analytical process we just completed indicates how we can approach artworks to determine in what ways they exemplify a given style.

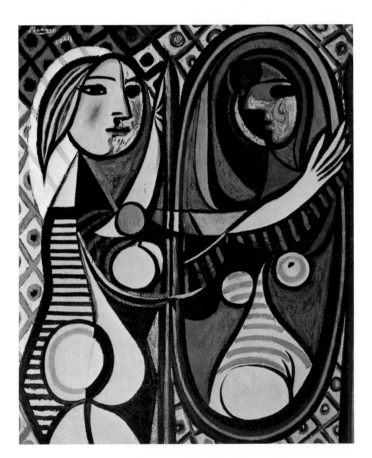

0.13 Exercise painting (see p. 56 for identification).

STYLE AND CULTURE

We sometimes recognize differences in style without thinking much about it. Our experience or formal training need not be extensive for us to recognize that the building in Figures **0.14** and **0.15** and that shown in

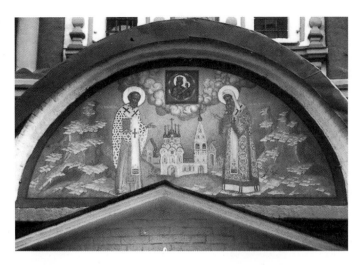

0.14 Church of Nikolai Khamovnik, Moscow, detail of front portal.

0.16 reflect different cultural circumstances. The Russian Orthodox church in Figure **0.15** is distinguishable by its characteristic domes and the icons that decorate its walls (Fig. **0.14**). The tomb in Figure **0.16** is, similarly, typically Muslim, identifiable by its arch. The decorative embellishment, in contrast to the icons of the Orthodox church, reflects the Islamic prohibition against depicting human form in an architectural decoration.

HOW DOES A STYLE GET ITS NAME?

Why is some art called Classical, some Pop, some Baroque, and some Impressionist? Some styles were named hundreds of years after they occurred—the definition resulted from extended, common usage or a historical viewpoint. For example, the Athenian Greeks, whose works we know as Classical, were centuries removed from the naming of their style. Some labels, such as Surrealist, were coined by artists themselves. Many come from individual critics who, having experienced the emerging works of several artists and noting a common or different approach, invented a term (sometimes a derogatory one) to describe it. Because of the influence of the critic or perhaps the catchiness of the term, the name came to gain general currency.

We must take care, however, when we use labels for artworks. Occasionally they imply stylistic characteristics; sometimes they identify attitudes or tendencies that are not really stylistic. Often debate exists as to which is which. For example, Romanticism has stylistic characteristics in some art disciplines, but the term also describes a broad philosophy of life. A style label can be a compos-

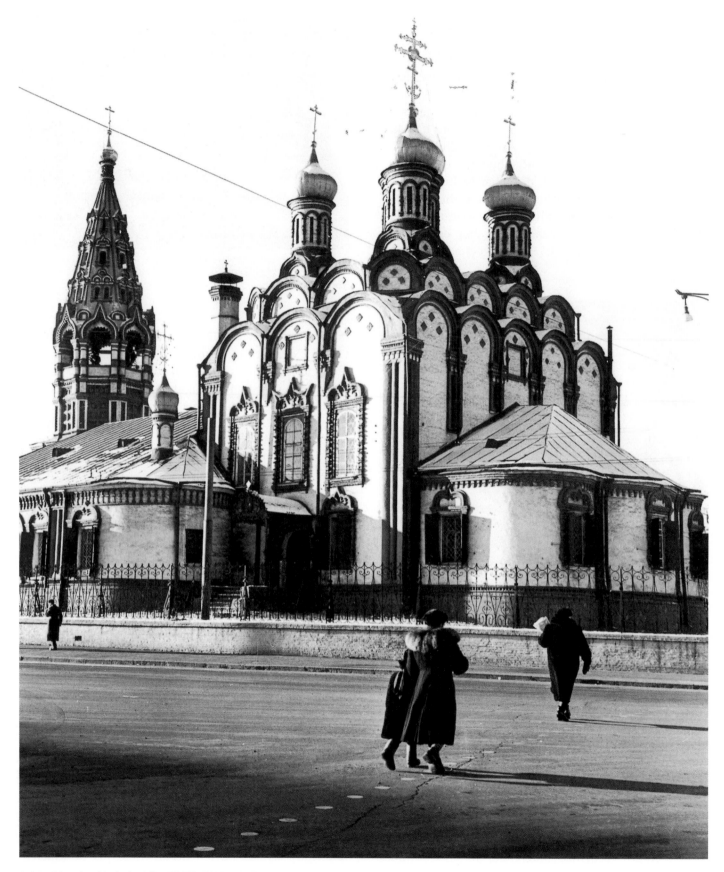

0.15 Church of Nikolai Khamovnik, Moscow, Russia, 1679–82.

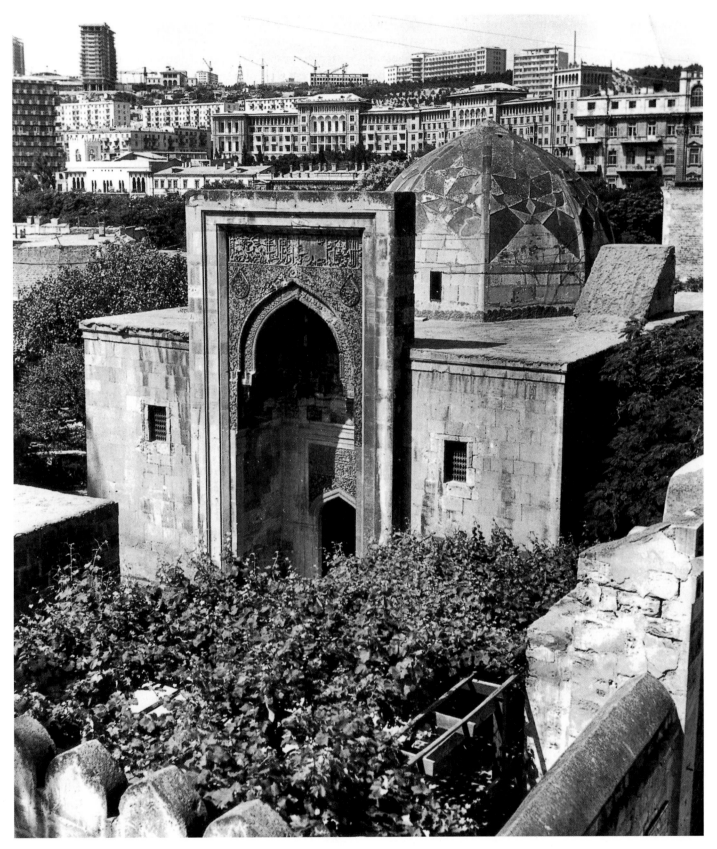

0.16 Tomb of the Shirvanshah, Baku, Azerbaijan, 15th century.

ite of several elements with dissimilar characteristics but identical objectives—for example, Post-Impressionism (see p. 347). Occasionally experts disagree as to whether certain artworks fall within the descriptive parameters of one style or another, even while agreeing on the definition of the style itself.

In addition, we can ask how the same label might identify stylistic characteristics of two or more unrelated art disciplines, such as painting and music. Is there an aural equivalent to visual characteristics, or vice versa? More often than not, similarity of objectives results in the same stylistic label being used for works that belong in quite different disciplines.

Styles do not start and stop on specific dates, nor do they recognize national boundaries. Some reflect deeply held convictions or creative insights; some are imitations of previous styles. Many styles are profound; others are superficial. Some are intensely individual.

THINKING CRITICALLY

- The artist Andy Warhol (WAHR-hall; 1928–87) reportedly said that "Art is anything you can get away with." Some people believe that art is whatever an artist says it is. Others contend that art is a vision of human reality expressed in a particular medium and shared with others. What do you agree or disagree with in these definitions? Formulate your own definition.

- The ancient Greek philosopher Aristotle (AIR-his-taht-uhl; 384–322 B.C.E.), divided the arts into "high art" and "low art." In terms of the arts of the twenty-first century, how would such a division apply? What reasons might there be, today, to separate "popular culture" from "art"?

- Some cities require new office buildings to set aside a certain percentage of their cost for artworks, such as sculptures, to be incorporated into the building. Make an argument for and against such policies.

- Public monies are often utilized to buy art, subsidize symphonies, and support individual artists. The intent is to keep art at the center of our public lives. Why would you agree or disagree with such practices? What stipulations should or should not be attached to public money used to support artistic activities?

- Do you believe that art should serve some kind of societal function, or should it exist solely for its own sake? Try setting out a case for both sides of the argument.

- Locate an object in your home that has primarily a utilitarian purpose but also exhibits some kind of artistic design. Describe how the design of the object prompts a pleasurable, aesthetic experience for you.

PART I

THE MEDIA OF THE ARTS

What Artists Use to Express "Reality"

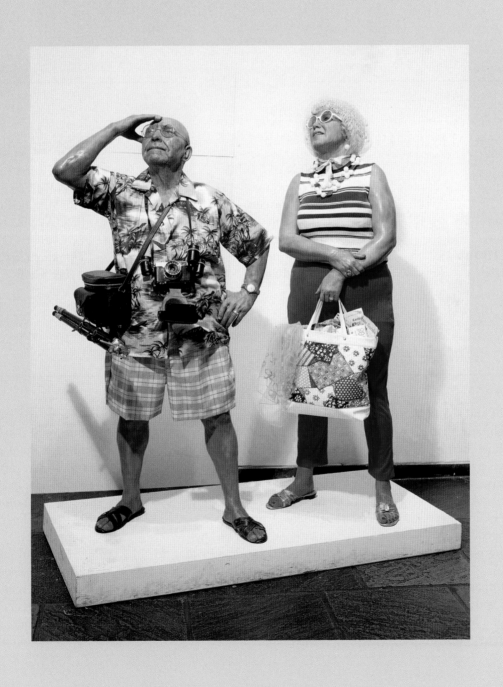

CHAPTER ONE

TWO-DIMENSIONAL ART

Drawing, Painting, Printmaking, and Photography

OUTLINE

FORMAL AND TECHNICAL QUALITIES

MEDIA
  Drawing
  Painting
  Printmaking
  Photography
Profile: Pablo Picasso
COMPOSITION
  Elements
  Principles

OTHER FACTORS
  Perspective
  Chiaroscuro
  Content
Painting and Human Reality:
  Géricault, **The Raft of the**
  "Medusa"

SENSE STIMULI

CONTRASTS
DYNAMICS
TROMPE L'OEIL
JUXTAPOSITION
FOCUS
Thinking Critically
Cyber Study

IMPORTANT TERMS

Chiaroscuro Light and shade; the balance of light and shade across the whole picture.

Composition The arrangement of line, form, mass, color, and so forth in a work of art.

Form The shape of an object within a composition.

Hue The spectrum notation of color.

Intaglio The printmaking process in which ink is transferred from the grooves of a metal plate to paper by extreme pressure.

Intensity The degree of purity of a color.

Line The basic building block of visual design; for example, a thin mark, a color edge, or an implied line.

Lithography A printmaking technique, based on the principle that oil and water do not mix, in which ink is applied to a piece of paper from a specially prepared stone.

Perspective The creation of the illusion of distance in a picture through the use of line, atmosphere, and so on.

Symmetry The balancing of like forms and colors on opposite sides of the vertical axis of a composition.

Value The relationship of lights to darks in a visual composition.

Variation The relationship of repeated items in a composition to each other.

FORMAL AND TECHNICAL QUALITIES

Two-dimensional art in the form of pictures of family, friends, music and sports stars, copies of artistic masterpieces, and original paintings and prints adorn our personal spaces. Dorm rooms, bedrooms, and living rooms seem coldly empty and depersonalized without pictures of some kind. Pictures have always been important to us. People who lived in caves 20,000 years ago drew pictures on their walls. In this chapter we shall learn about the many ways pictures can be made and how artists use two-dimensional qualities to speak to us.

Drawings, paintings, photographs, and prints differ primarily in the technique of their execution. We respond initially, however, to their content: landscapes, seascapes, portraits, still lifes, religious icons—or other subjects.

MEDIA

When we engage in two-dimensional works of art at a more technical level, we begin to notice things about the artist's choices in putting the work together. One of the choices is the work's medium. We will consider a number of media, which we break into four major categories: drawing, painting, printmaking, and photography.

Drawing

Drawing, considered the foundation of two-dimensional art, involves a wide variety of materials traditionally divided into two groups: *dry media* and *wet media*. In the discussion that follows we will note the dry media of chalk, charcoal, graphite, and pastel, and the wet media of pen and ink and wash and brush.

DRY MEDIA *Chalk* developed as a drawing medium by the middle of the sixteenth century. Artists first used it in its natural state, derived from ocher hematite, white soapstone, or black carbonaceous shale, placing it in a holder and sharpening it to a point. Chalk is a fairly flexible medium. A wide variety of tonal areas can be created, with extremely subtle transitions between them. Chalk can be applied with heavy or light pressure. It can be worked with the fingers once it is on the paper to create the exact image the artist desires, as exemplified by *Prudence* (Fig. **1.1**) by Cherubino Alberti (chair-oo-BEE-no al-BAIR-tee).

Charcoal, a burnt wood product (preferably derived from hardwood), like chalk, requires a paper with a

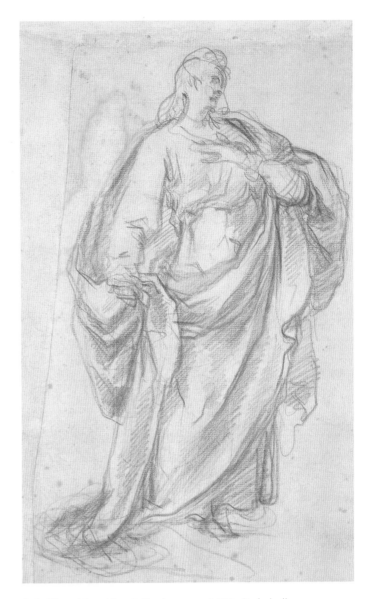

1.1 Cherubino Alberti, *Prudence*, c. 1601. Red chalk on paper, 11¼ × 7 ins (28.7 × 17.7 cm). National Gallery of Art, Washington, D.C. (Gift of William B. O'Neal, in Honor of the 50th Anniversary of the National Gallery of Art).

relatively rough surface—"tooth"—for the medium to adhere. Charcoal has a tendency to smudge easily, which dampened its early use as a drawing medium. It found wide use, however, as a means of drawing details, for example, on walls, and for murals that were eventually painted or frescoed. Today, resin fixatives sprayed over charcoal drawings can eliminate smudging, and charcoal has become a popular medium because artists find it extremely expressive. Like chalk, charcoal can achieve a variety of tonalities as seen in George Bellows's *Study for "Nude with Hexagonal Quilt"* (Fig. **1.2**).

Pastel, essentially a chalk medium, combines colored pigment and a non-greasy binder. Typically, pastels come

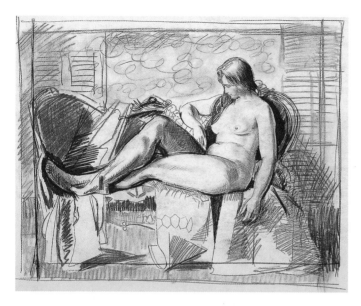

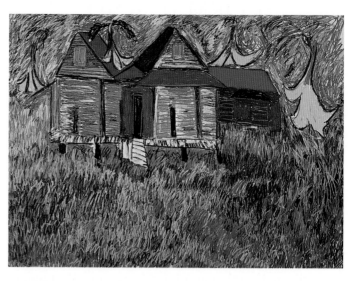

1.2 (above) George Bellows, *Study for "Nude with Hexagonal Quilt,"* 1924. Charcoal and black crayon on paper, 21⅞ × 26⅞ ins (55.5 × 68.2 cm). National Gallery of Art, Washington, D.C. (Gift of Mr. and Mrs. Raymond J. Horowitz).

1.3 (above) Beverly Buchanan, *Monroe County House with Yellow Datura*, 1994. Oil pastel on paper, 5 ft × 6 ft 7 ins (1.52 × 2 m). Bernice Steinbaum Gallery, Miami (Collection Dr. and Mrs. Harold Steinbaum).

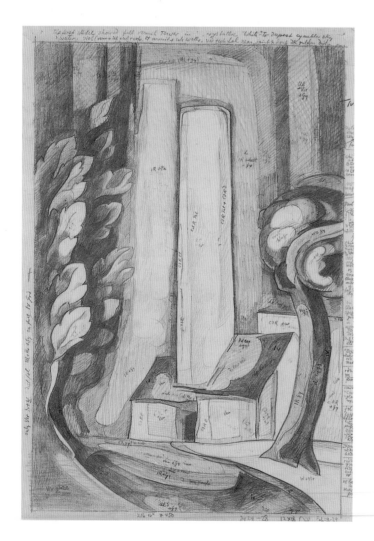

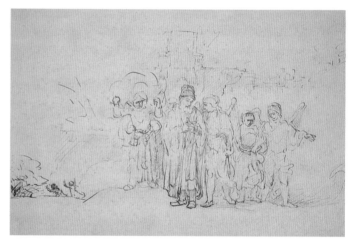

1.5 (above) Rembrandt van Rijn, *Lot and His Family Leaving Sodom*, c. 1655. Pen and light brown ink, 8⅛ × 11⅝ ins (20.5 × 29.5 cm). National Gallery of Art, Washington, D.C. (Widener Collection).

1.4 (left) Oscar F. Bluemner, *Study for a Painting*, probably 1928. Graphite on tracing paper, 19¹³⁄₁₆ × 13½ ins (50.3 × 34.2 cm). National Gallery of Art, Washington, D.C. (John Davis Hatch Collection).

in sticks about the diameter of a finger and in degrees of hardness: soft, medium, hard. The harder the stick, the less intense its color. In fact, the name "pastel" implies pale colors. Intense colors require soft pastels, but soft pastels are quite difficult to work with. A special ribbed paper helps to grab the powdery pastel, and a sprayed fixative holds the powder in place permanently on the paper. Beverly Buchanan's *Monroe County House with Yellow Datura* (Fig. 1.3) illustrates not only the breadth of color intensity possible with pastels, but also the intricacy resulting from application by a skilled hand.

Graphite, a form of carbon, like coal, finds its most common use in pencil leads. As a drawing medium it can be manufactured in various degrees of hardness. The harder the lead, the lighter and more delicate its mark, as seen in Oscar F. Bluemner's *Study for a Painting* (Fig. 1.4).

WET MEDIA *Pen and ink* is a fairly flexible medium compared to graphite, for example. Although linear, pen and ink gives the artist the possibility of variation in line and texture. Shading can be achieved by diluting the ink, and the overall qualities of the medium are fluidity and expressiveness, as we can see in Rembrandt's *Lot and His Family Leaving Sodom* (Fig. 1.5).

Wash and brush is created by diluting ink with water and applying it with a brush. Its characteristics appear similar to watercolor, which we discuss in the next section on painting media. Although difficult to control, wash and brush creates effects nearly impossible to achieve in any other medium. Because it must be worked quickly and freely, this medium has a spontaneous and appealing quality, as suggested in *Lotus* (Fig. 1.6) by Chu Ta (choo-tah).

In addition to the media just described (which may be combined in infinite variety), there exist a wide range of possibilities of an experimental and innovative nature. These include the computer, when it is used as an electronic sketchpad.

Painting

Like drawing media, painting media each have their own characteristics and, to a great extent, this dictates what the artist can or cannot achieve as an end result. In the following section we will examine five painting media: oils, watercolor, tempera, acrylics, and fresco.

Oils, perhaps the most popular of the painting media, have been so since their development around the beginning of the fifteenth century. The popularity of oils stems principally from the fact that they offer a tremendous range of color possibilities; they can be reworked; they present many options for textural manipulation; and they

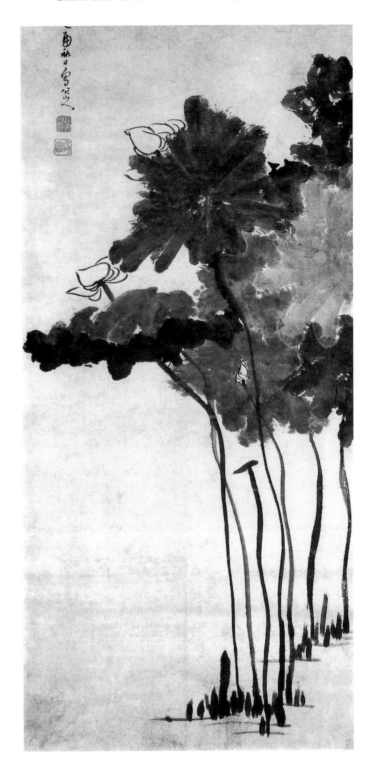

1.6 Chu Ta (Zhu Da) (Pata-shan-jen), *Lotus*, 1705. Brush and ink, 6½ × 28 ins (17 × 71 cm). Palmer Museum of Art, Pennsylvania State University.

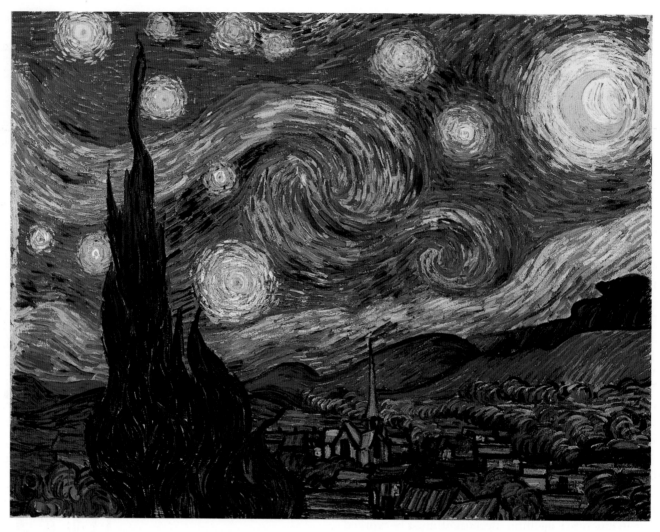

1.7 Vincent van Gogh, *The Starry Night*, 1889. Oil on canvas, 29 × 36¼ ins (73.7 × 92.1 cm). The Museum of Modern Art, New York.

are durable. If we compare two oil paintings, *The Starry Night* (Fig. **1.7**) by van Gogh (Vahn GOH) and *Holy Family with St. John* (Fig. **1.8**) by Giovanni Vanni (VAH-nee), we can see the importance of the medium in each case. Vanni creates light and shade in the Baroque tradition, and his *chiaroscuro* (key-AR-ohs-SKOO-roh) depends upon the capacity of the medium to blend smoothly among color areas. Van Gogh, on the other hand, requires a medium that will form obvious brush-strokes. Vanni demands the paint to be flesh and cloth. Van Gogh demands the paint to be paint, and to call attention to itself.

Watercolor (a broad category) includes any color medium that uses water as a thinner. The term has traditionally referred to a transparent paint usually applied to paper. Because watercolors are transparent, an artist must be very careful to control them. If one area of color overlaps another, the overlap shows as a third area combining the previous hues. Their transparency gives watercolors a delicacy that cannot be produced in any other medium, with the possible exception of wash and brush.

Tempera, an opaque watercolor medium, was employed by the ancient Egyptians, and is still used today. Tempera refers to ground pigments and their color binders—for example, gum or glue—but we know it best in egg tempera form. A fast-drying medium, it virtually eliminates brushstroke, and gives extremely sharp detail. Colors in tempera paintings appear almost gemlike in their clarity and brilliance.

Acrylics, in contrast with tempera, constitute modern, synthetic products. Most acrylics can be dissolved in water (but are water-impermeable when dry) and the binding agent for the pigment consists of an acrylic polymer. Acrylics offer artists a wide range of possibilities in both color and technique. An acrylic paint can be either opaque or transparent, depending upon dilution. It dries

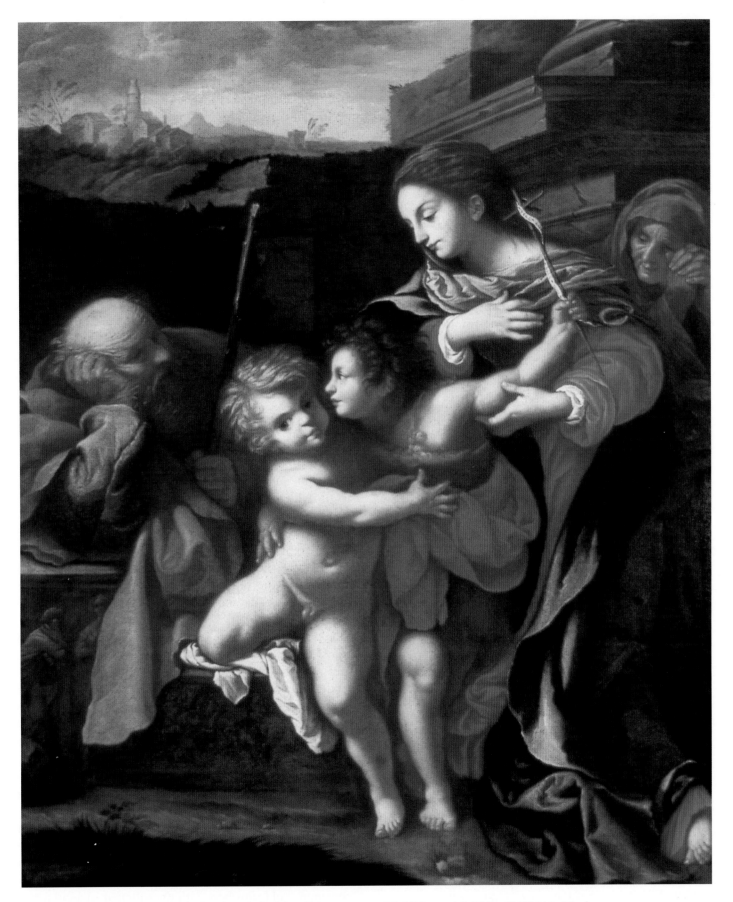

1.8 Giovanni Battista Vanni, *Holy Family with St. John*. Oil on canvas, 5 ft 10 ins × 4 ft 10 ins (1.78 × 1.47 m).
Palmer Museum of Art, Pennsylvania State University.

fast, thin, and resistant to cracking under extremes of temperature and humidity. Perhaps less permanent than some other media, it adheres to a wider variety of surfaces. It does not darken or yellow with age, as does oil.

Fresco is a wall-painting technique in which pigments suspended in water are applied to fresh wet plaster. Michelangelo's Sistine Chapel frescoes (see Figs. **11.9** and **11.10**) best represent this technique. Because the end result becomes part of the plaster wall rather than being painted on it, fresco has a long lifespan. However, it is an extremely difficult process, and once the pigments are applied, no changes can be made without replastering the entire section of the wall.

Printmaking

Printmaking falls generally into three main categories, based essentially on the nature of the printing surface. First is *relief printing*, such as woodcut (Fig. **1.9**), wood

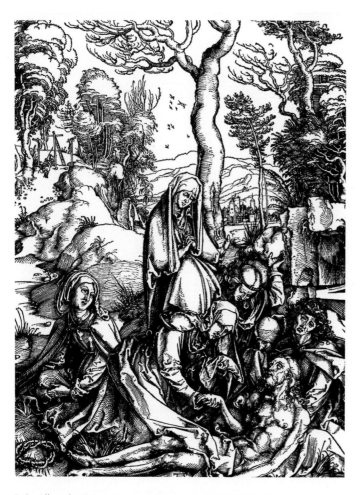

1.9 Albrecht Dürer, *Lamentation*, c. 1497–1500. Woodcut, 15½ × 11¼ ins (39 × 29 cm). Palmer Museum of Art, Pennsylvania State University (Gift of the Friends of the Museum of Art).

engraving, and linoleum cut. Second is *intaglio* (in-TAH-lyoh) including etching, aquatint, and drypoint. Third is the *planographic process*, which includes lithography, silkscreen (serigraphy), other forms of stenciling, and monoprinting. Printmakers also use other combinations and techniques, particularly photoprocesses. While interesting, the modern techniques of photoprocessing will remain outside our discussion for reasons of space.

To begin, we need to ask, What is a print? A print is a hand-produced picture transferred from a printing surface to a piece of paper. An artist prepares the printing surface and directs the printing process. The unique value of a print lies in the fact that the artist usually destroys the block or surface after making the desired number of prints. In contrast, a reproduction is not an original, but a copy of an original painting or other artwork, reproduced usually by a photographic process. As a copy, the reproduction does not bear the handiwork of an artist.

Every print has a number. On some the number may appear as a fraction—for example, $^{36}/_{100}$. The denominator indicates how many prints were produced from the plate or block. In this number, called the issue number or edition number, the numerator indicates where in the series the individual print was produced. If only a single number, such as 500, appears, also called an edition number, it simply indicates the total number of prints in the series. The numerator is an item of curiosity only; it has nothing to do with a print's value, either monetarily or qualitatively. The issue number does have some value in comparing, for example, an issue of 25 with one of 500, and usually reflects in the price of a print. However, the issue number does not solely determine the value of a print. Its quality and the reputation of the artist comprise more important considerations.

RELIEF PRINTING In relief printing (Fig. **1.10**), an artist transfers the image to paper by cutting away nonimage areas and inking the surface that remains. The image protrudes in relief from the block or plate, and produces a picture reversed from the image carved by the artist. This reversal characterizes all printmaking media. Figure **1.9** illustrates the linearity of the woodcut, and shows the precision and delicacy possible in the hands of an expert. When we first see this picture, the subtleties of the tonalities may suggest to us a painting. Until we focus more directly on individual details, the shading seems natural—not linear. On further examination, we realize that all details consist of delicate lines and that the forms have outlines. Each form's edges create a sharp break between it and the area or form next to it. Compare the linear appearance of forms here with the softened edges of forms in Giovanni Vanni's *Holy Family with St. John* (see Fig.

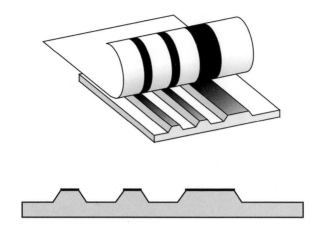

1.10 Relief printing.

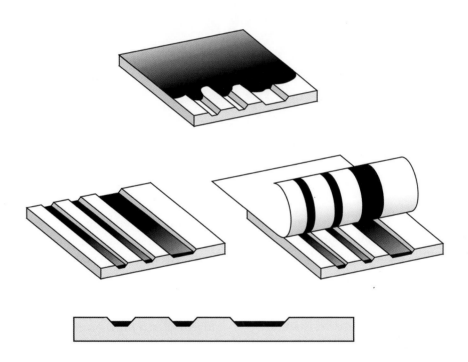

1.11 Intaglio process.

1.8). Both pictures explore strong contrasts between high and low color values (see pp. 58–59). However, the Vanni moves softly, whereas the Dürer moves relatively abruptly: Dürer has only ridges cut into a block of wood to create his images, whereas Vanni can blend with a brush areas created by oil paints. Nonetheless, the masterful skill of Dürer gives us an image of tremendous subtlety and nuanced mood.

INTAGLIO In the intaglio process (Fig. 1.11) (the opposite of relief printing), the artist transfers ink to the paper not from raised areas, but from grooves cut into a metal plate. Line engraving, etching, drypoint, and aquatint are some of the methods of intaglio.

Line engraving involves cutting grooves into the metal plate with special sharp tools. It requires great muscular control because the pressure must be continuous and

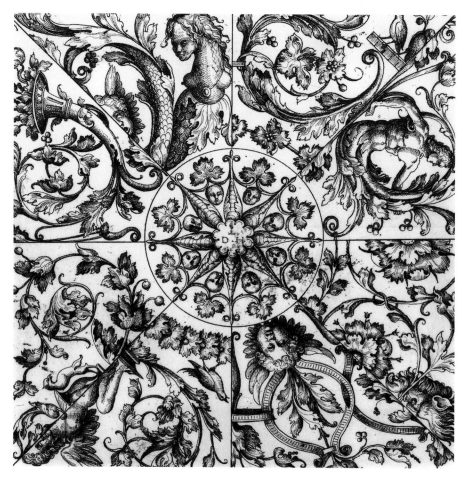

1.12 Daniel Hopfer, *Ceiling Ornament*. Etching, 10 × 8¾ ins (25 × 22 cm). Palmer Museum of Art, Pennsylvania State University.

constant if the grooves are to produce the desired image. The line-engraving process produces very precise images and represents the most difficult and demanding of the intaglio processes.

In the *etching* process, the artist removes the surface of the plate by exposing it to an acid bath. First the artist covers the plate with a thin, waxlike, acid-resistant substance called a *ground*. The artist scratches away parts of the ground to produce the desired lines then immerses the plate in acid, which burns away the exposed areas. The longer a plate stays in the acid, the deeper the resulting etches; the deeper the etch, the darker the final image. Artists wishing to produce lines or areas of differing darkness must cover the lines they do not want to be more deeply cut before further immersions in the acid. Repetition of the process yields a plate producing a print with the desired differences in light and dark lines.

Figure **1.12** consists only of individual lines, either single or in combination. The lighter lines required less time in the acid than the darker ones. Because of the precision and clarity of the lines, it is difficult to determine whether this print is an etching or an engraving. Drypoint, on the other hand, can be distinguished because it produces lines with less sharp edges.

In *drypoint* the printmaker scratches the surface of a metal plate with a needle. Unlike line engraving, which gives a clean, sharp line, the drypoint technique leaves a ridge, called a burr, on either side of the groove, resulting in a somewhat fuzzy line.

Aquatint can create a range of values from lightest gray to black and thus is useful for shading. The intaglio methods already noted consist of various means of cutting lines into a metal plate. Sometimes, though, an artist may wish to create large areas of subdued tonality. Such shadowy areas cannot be produced effectively with lines. Therefore, the artist dusts the plate with a resin substance and heats it, which affixes the resin. She then puts it into an acid bath. A rough surface, like sandpaper, results and the print has tonal areas that reflect this texture, making aquatint very recognizable.

Once prepared, whether by line engraving, etching, drypoint, aquatint, or a combination of methods, the

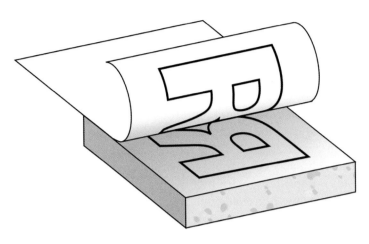

1.13 Planographic process.

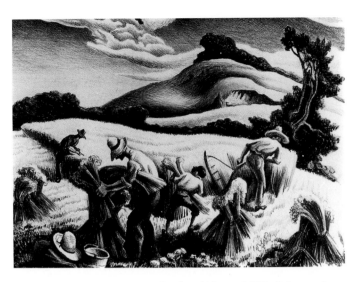

1.14 Thomas Hart Benton, *Cradling Wheat*, 1938. Lithograph, 9½ × 12 ins (24 × 30 cm). Palmer Museum of Art, Pennsylvania State University (Gift of Carolyn Wose Hull).

plate goes into a press along with a special dampened paper. Padding is placed on the paper, and then a roller forces the plate and the paper together with great pressure. The carefully applied ink, remaining only in the grooves, transfers as the paper is forced into the grooves by the roller of the press. Even if no ink had been applied to the plate, the paper would still receive an image. This *embossing* effect or *platemark* marks an intaglio process.

PLANOGRAPHIC PROCESSES In a planographic process (Fig. **1.13**), the artist prints from a plane surface—neither relief nor intaglio. *Lithography* (the term's literal meaning is "stone writing") rests on the principle that water and grease do not mix. To create a lithograph, artists begin with a porous stone—usually limestone—and grind one side until absolutely smooth. They then draw an image on the stone with a greasy substance. They can control the darkness of the final image by varying the amount of grease used: the more grease, the darker the image. After drawing the image, the artist treats the stone with gum arabic and nitric acid, and then rinses it with a petrol product that removes the image. However, the water, gum, and acid have impressed the grease on the stone, and when wetted it absorbs water only in the ungreased areas. Finally, a grease-based ink is applied to the stone. It, in turn, will not adhere to the water-soaked areas, but only where the artist has drawn. As a result, the stone can be placed in a press and the image will be transferred to the waiting paper.

In Figures **1.14** and **1.15** we see the characteristic most attributable to lithography—a crayon-drawing appearance. Because the lithographer usually draws with crayonlike material on the stone, the final print has exactly that quality. Compare these prints with Figure **1.16**, a pas-

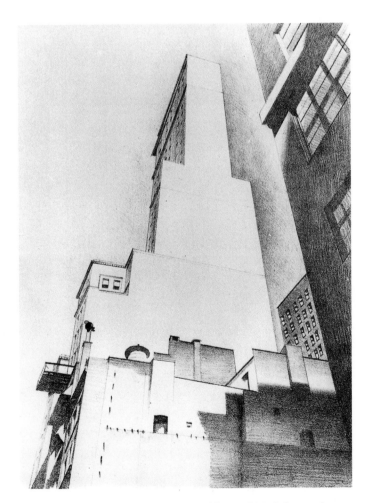

1.15 Charles Sheeler, *Delmonico Building*, 1925. Lithograph, 10 × 7⅛ ins (25 × 18 cm). Palmer Museum of Art, Pennsylvania State University.

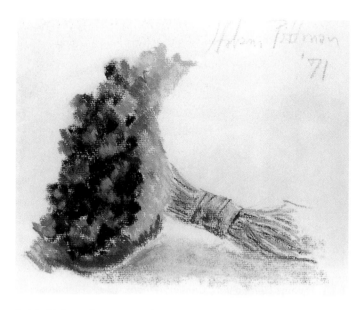

1.16 Hobson Pittman, *Violets No. 1*, 1971. Pastel, 9½ × 10¼ ins (24 × 26 cm). Palmer Museum of Art, Pennsylvania State University.

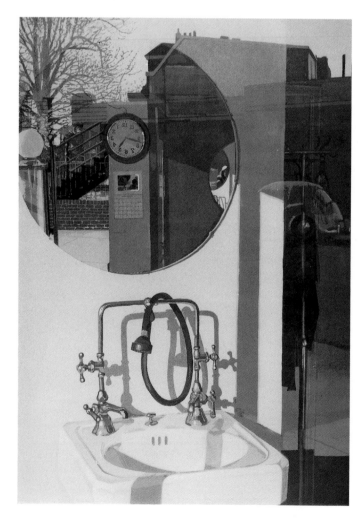

1.17 Nancy McIntyre, *Barbershop Mirror*, 1976. Silkscreen, 26½ × 19 ins (67 × 48 cm). Palmer Museum of Art, Pennsylvania State University.

tel drawing, and the point is clear. For *silkscreening*, the most common of the stenciling processes, a finely meshed silk fabric mounted on a wooden frame is used. The non-image areas are blocked out by a variety of methods, including glue or cut paper. The stencil goes into the frame and ink is applied. A rubber instrument, called a squeegee, forces ink through the openings of the stencil, through the screen, and onto the paper below. This technique allows the printmaker to achieve large, flat, uniform areas, as seen in Figure **1.17**. Here the artist has, through successive applications of ink, built up a complex composition, with highly lifelike detail.

A *monotype* or *monoprint*, as its name implies, creates a unique impression by applying printing ink to a flat surface and transferring it to paper. The method, however, excludes one of the usual main purposes of printmaking—obtaining multiple copies of a single image, because a monoprint creates a one-time image only. On the other hand, the marks and textures of the monotype differ characteristically from those drawn or painted on paper. Monoprint appeals to many artists because it requires no presses or studio equipment.

Prints reflect recognizable differences in technique. It is not always possible to discern the technique that has been used in executing a print, and some prints reflect a combination of techniques. However, in determining the method of execution, we add another layer of potential response to a work.

Photography

Photographic images (and images of its subsequent developments—motion pictures and video) provide us, primarily, with information. Cameras (Fig. **1.18**) record the world; but, in addition, through editing, a photographer can take the camera's image and change the reality of life as we see it to a reality of the imagination. In one small sense, photography constitutes a simplification of reality that substitutes two-dimensional images for the three-dimensional images of life. It also can amplify reality when a photographer takes a snapshot of one moment in time and transforms it by altering the photographic image and/or artificially emphasizing one of its parts.

PHOTOGRAPHY AND ART Photographer Ansel Adams (1902–84) viewed the photographer as an interpretive artist; he likened a photographic negative to a musical score, and the print to a performance. Thus, despite all the choices an artist may make in committing an image to film, these comprise only the beginning of the artistic process. A photographer still has the choice of size, texture, and value contrast or tonality. A photo of the grain

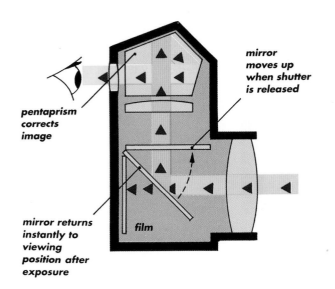

pentaprism
corrects
image

mirror
moves up
when shutter
is released

mirror returns
instantly to
viewing
position after
exposure

film

1.18 The single-lens reflex (SLR) camera.

of a piece of wood, for example, can have an enormous range of aesthetic possibilities, depending on how a photographer employs and combines these three elements.

After World War I, as photography entered its second century, significant aesthetic changes occurred. Early explorations of photography as an artform tended to employ darkroom techniques, tricks, and manipulation that created works that seemed staged and imitative of sentimental, moralistic paintings. The followers of such an aesthetic believed that for photography to be art, it must look like art.

During the early years of the twentieth century, however, a new generation of photographers arose who determined to take photography away from the previous pictorial style and its soft focus, and toward a more direct, unmanipulated, and sharply focused approach. Called *straight photography*, this approach expressed its adherents' belief in photography's unique vision. The principal American force behind the recognition of photography as a fine art, Alfred Stieglitz (STEEGH-lihts; 1864–1946), gained recognition for his clarity of image and reality shots, especially of clouds and New York City architecture, as in *The Flatiron Building* (Fig. **1.19**). In 1902, he formed the Photo-Secessionist group and opened a gallery referred to as "291" because of its address at 291 Fifth Avenue in New York City. In addition to showcasing photography, Stieglitz's efforts promoted many visual artists, including the woman who would become his wife, Georgia O'Keeffe (see Chapter 13). He also promoted photography as a fine art in the pages of his illustrated quarterly, *Camera Work*.

The adherents of straight photography found in their ranks perhaps America's most famous photographer, Ansel Adams, who became a recognized leader of modern photography through his sharp, poetic landscape photographs of the American West—for example, his photograph of *Moon and Half Dome* (Fig. **1.20**). A well-known technical innovator and pioneer in the movement to preserve the wilderness, he did much to elevate photography to the level of art. His work emphasized sharp focus and subtle variety in light and texture, with rich detail and brilliant tonal differences. In 1941, he began making photomurals for the United States Department of the Interior, a project that forced him to master techniques for photographing the light and space of immense landscapes. He developed what he called the Zone System, a means for determining the final tone of each part of the landscape.

We might think of art photography as something fairly lifelike in its presentations, and in the examples just discussed, it appears just so. Photography also, however, can present the abstract—even the nonobjective—and in the *photograms* of Man Ray (1890–1976) we see the process not of taking pictures, but of making them. In a photogram the artist places objects directly onto photographic paper and exposes them to light. Although not the first to make photograms, Man Ray has come to represent the process through his *Rayographs* (Fig. **1.21**).

DOCUMENTARY PHOTOGRAPHY Since the late nineteenth century, photographers had used photography to document social problems. During the Great Depression of the 1930s, a large-scale program in documentary photography began in the United States. Among the photographers using this approach, Dorothea Lange (1895–1965) helped develop an unsurpassed portrait of the nation. Noted for her ability to make strangers seem like familiar acquaintances, her work graphically detailed the erosion of the land and the people of rural America during the Great Depression. In *Dust Bowl Farm in Texas* (Fig. **1.22**), for example, she presents a ramshackle farmhouse with a windmill on the bleak, windswept plains of the Coldwater District north of Dalhart, Texas, during the June 1938 dust bowl. The work documents the 1930s natural disaster as environmental degradation of the landscape.

PHOTOGRAPHIC TECHNIQUES The word *camera* means "room" in Latin; in the sixteenth century, artists used a darkened room, called a *camera obscura*, to copy nature accurately. Remarkably, the camera obscura utilized the same device used by today's cameras. Specifically, a small hole on one side of the light-free room admitted a ray of light that projected the scene outside onto a semitransparent scrim cloth. The camera obscura illustrated in

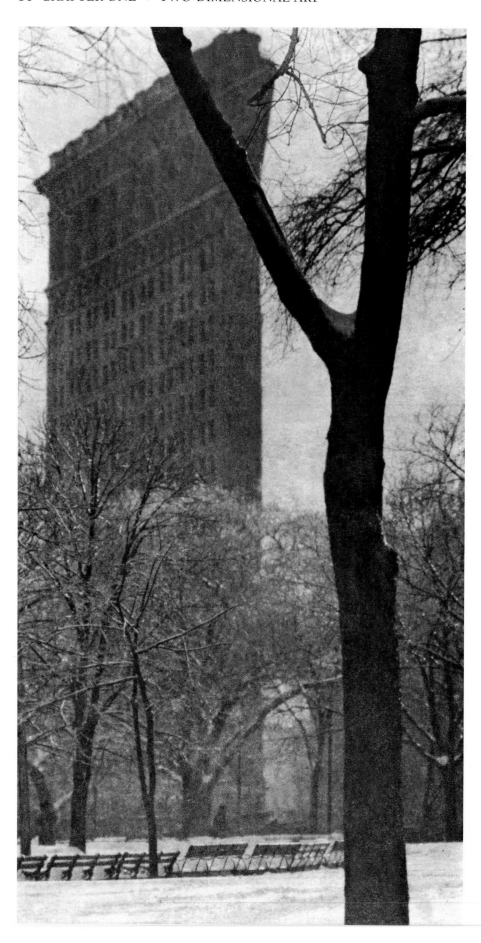

1.19 (*left*) Alfred Stieglitz, *The Flatiron Building*, from *Camera Work*, (Vol IV), 1903. 6⅝ ins × 3¼ ins. The Metropolitan Museum of Art, The Alfred Stieglitz Collection, 1933 (33.43.420-469).

1.20 (*right*) Ansel Adams, *Moon and Half Dome*, 1960. Yosemite National Park, California. Ansel Adams Publishing Rights Trust.

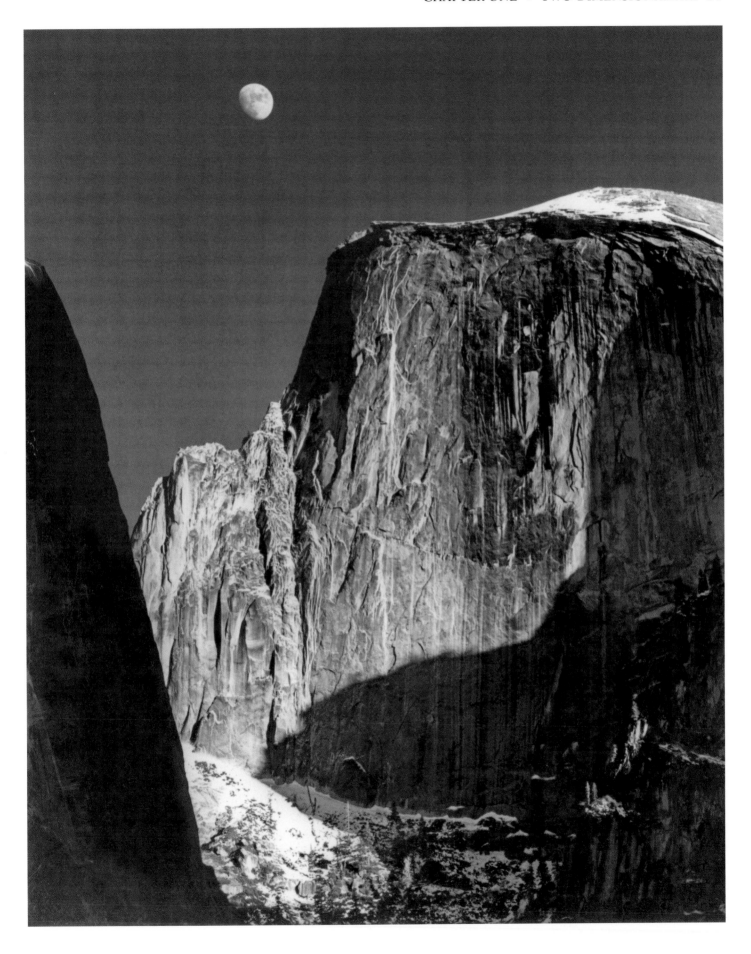

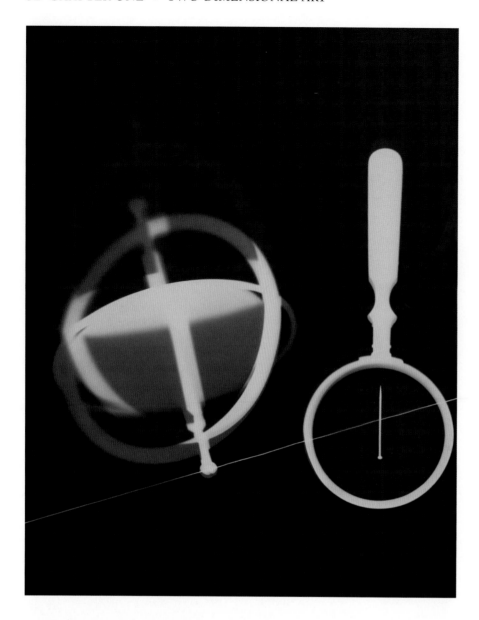

1.21 Man Ray, *Rayograph* (gyroscope, magnifying glass, pin), 1922. Gelatin silver print. Museum of Modern Art, New York.

Figure **1.23** actually has holes in two walls. The early camera obscuras were also portable, which allowed artists to set them up to project any subject matter. Of course, the camera obscura could not preserve the image it projected, and photography could not emerge until someone solved that technological problem.

The technology of photography began in England in 1839 with the invention of William Henry Fox Talbot, who achieved a process for fixing negative images on a paper coated with light-sensitive chemicals. His process, called a *photogenic drawing*, appeared at about the same time as two French inventors, Louis Jacques Mandé Daguerre (dah-GHAIR) and Joseph Nicéphore Niépce (nee-APE-suh), produced a process in which a positive image could be affixed to a metal plate. Niépce died in 1833, and Daguerre perfected the process, which now bears his name: *daguerreotype* (dah-GHAIR-oh-type).

Unfortunately, the image on the daguerreotype could not be reproduced, while the photogenic image, on paper, could. Fox Talbot realized that the negative image of the photogenic drawing could be reversed by covering it with sensitized paper and exposing the two papers to sunlight. Then the latent image on the second paper was developed by dipping the paper in gallic acid, a process that was called *calotype*.

The early technical developments of Fox Talbot were followed in 1850 by another Englishman, Frederick Archer, who, in a darkened room, poured a viscous chemical solution, liquid collodion, over a glass plate bathed in silver nitrate. Although the process required preparing, exposing, and developing the plate within a span of fifteen minutes, the results were universally accepted within the next five years, and the wet-plate *collodion* photographic process became standard.

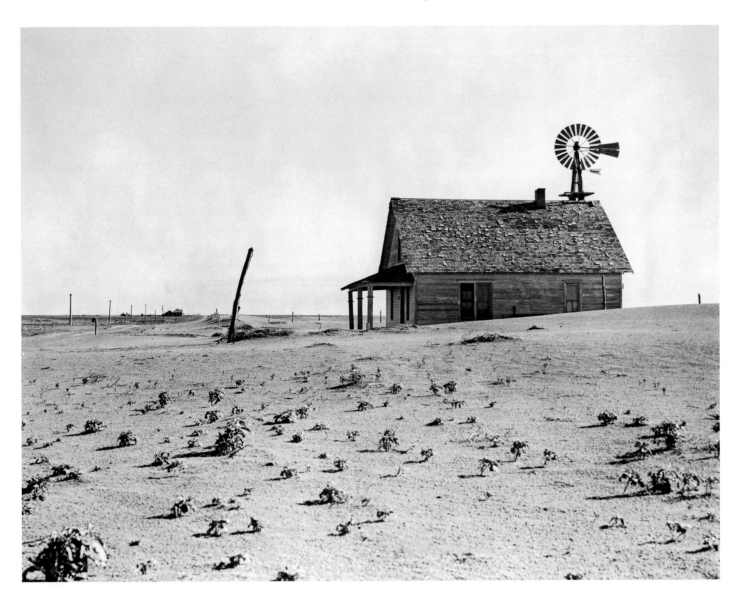

1.22 (above) Dorothea Lange, *Dust Bowl Farm in Texas*, 1938.

1.23 (right) Artist working inside camera obscura. Engraving. © Bettmann/CORBIS.

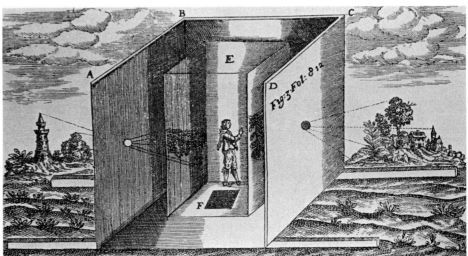

Profile

Pablo Picasso

Pablo Picasso (1881–1973), born in Málaga, on the Mediterranean coast of Spain, studied at the Academy of Fine Arts in Barcelona, but had already mastered realistic technique and had little use for school. At sixteen he had his own studio in Barcelona. In 1900 he first visited Paris, and in 1904 he settled there. His personal style began to form in the years from 1901 to 1904, a period often referred to as his Blue Period because of the pervasive blue tones he used in his paintings at that time. In 1905, as he became more successful, Picasso altered his palette, and the blue tones gave way to a terracotta color, a shade of deep pinkish red. At the same time, his subject matter grew less melancholy and included dancers, acrobats, and harlequins. The paintings he did during the years between 1905 and 1907 are said to belong to his Rose Period.

Picasso played an important part in the sequence of different artistic movements in the twentieth century. Because he and his work played significant roles in those movements, many people consider him the most important artist of the twentieth century. He said that to repeat oneself is to go against "the constant flight forward of the spirit." Primarily a painter, he also became a fine sculptor, engraver, and ceramicist. In 1917 Picasso went to Rome to design costumes and scenery for Sergei Diaghilev's Ballets Russes. This work stimulated another departure in Picasso's work, and he began to paint the works now referred to as belonging to his Classic Period, which lasted from about 1918 until 1925.

At the same time as he was working on designs for the ballet, Picasso also continued to develop the Cubist technique (see Chapter 13), making it less rigorous and austere.

His painting *Girl Before a Mirror* (see Fig. **1.26**) gives us an opportunity to study his use of color in contrast to form. For example, Picasso chose red and green perhaps because they are complementary colors and perhaps, as art historian H. W. Janson suggests, because Picasso intended the green spot in the middle of the forehead of the mirror's image as a symbol of the girl's psyche, or inner self, which she confronts with apparent anguish.

Guernica (ghair-NEE-kah; Fig. **1.24**), Picasso's moving vision of the tragedies of the Spanish Civil War, also depends on curved forms. In this painting, however, the forms are intended to be fundamental because Picasso uses no color, only white, grays, and black. *Guernica*, a huge painting, was Picasso's response to the 1937 bombing by the Fascist forces of the small Basque town of Guernica. The distortions of form that can be seen in this painting approach those of Surrealism (see Dalí's *The Persistence of Memory*, Fig. **1.41**), but Picasso never called himself a Surrealist.

Picasso continued to work in many genres with incredible speed and versatility into his nineties.

For more information on Pablo Picasso and his works, look at www.picasso.fr/anglais/index.htm; http://en.wikipedia.org/wiki/Pablo_Picasso; and at www.artcyclopedia.com.

COMPOSITION

A discussion of how any artwork is put together eventually results in a discussion of how it is composed. The elements and principles of *composition* stand basic to all the arts, and we shall return to them time and time again as we proceed.

Elements

LINE The basic building block of a visual design is line. To most of us, a line is a thin mark: ————. In two-dimensional art, "line" has three physical characteristics: (1) a linear form in which length dominates over width, (2) a color edge, and (3) an implication of continued direction.

Line as a linear form in which length dominates over width can be seen in *Composition* (Fig. 1.25) by Joan Miró (hoh-ahn mee-ROH); the figures defined by the thin outlines represent this characteristic. This can also be seen in several places in *Girl Before a Mirror* (Fig. 1.26) by Pablo Picasso (pee-KAH-soh)—for example, in defining the diamond shapes in the background, along the back of the girl's head, and down her back. The second characteristic,

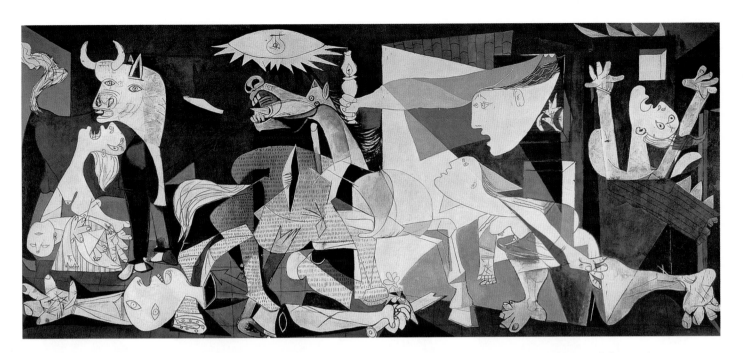

1.24 Pablo Picasso, *Guernica*, 1937. Oil on canvas, 11 ft 5 ins × 25 ft 5¾ ins (3.48 × 7.77 m). Museo Nacional Centro de Arte Reina Sofia, Madrid.

1.25 Joan Miró, *Composition*, 1933. Oil on canvas, 4 ft 3⅜ ins × 5 ft 4 ins (1.31 × 1.65 m). Wadsworth Atheneum, Hartford, Connecticut.

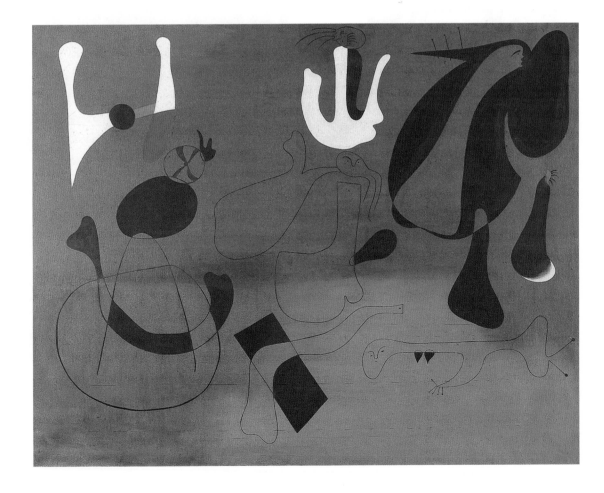

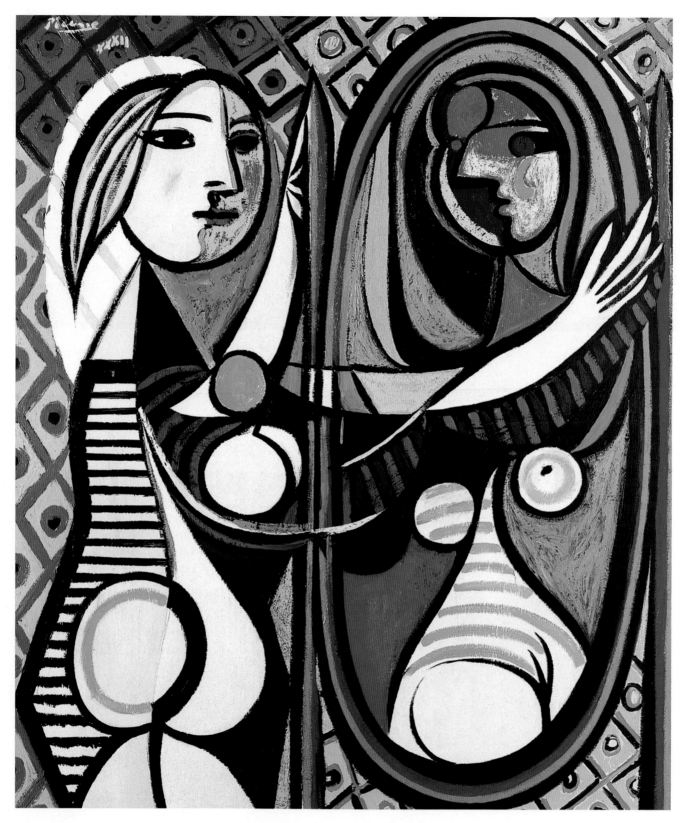

1.26 Pablo Picasso, *Girl Before a Mirror*, Boisgeloup, March 1932. Oil on canvas, 5 ft 4 ins × 4 ft 3¼ ins (1.62 × 1.3 m). The Museum of Modern Art, New York (Gift of Mrs. Simon Guggenheim).

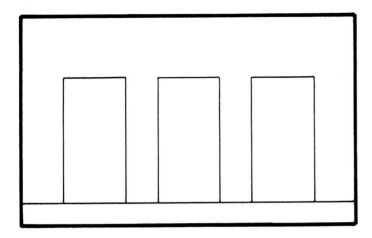

1.27 Outline and implied line.

1.28 Jackson Pollock, *Number 1, 1948*, 1948. Oil and enamel on unprimed canvas, 5 ft 8 ins × 8 ft 8 ins (1.73 × 2.64 m). The Museum of Modern Art, New York (Purchase).

line as an edge, or as the place where one object or plane stops and another begins, shows again in Figure **1.25**, as the edges where the white, black, and red color areas stop and the gray and gold backgrounds begin.

The third characteristic, implication, is illustrated by the three rectangles in Figure **1.27**. They create a horizontal "line" that extends across the design. No physical line occurs between the tops of the forms, but their spatial arrangement creates one by implication. A similar use of line occurs in Figure **1.7**, where we can see a definite linear movement from the upper left border through a series of swirls to the right border. That line is quite clear, although it constitutes not a form edge or outline but a carefully developed relationship of numerous color areas. This treatment of line appears in Figure **1.28**, although in a much more subtle and sophisticated way. By dripping paint onto canvas—a task not as easily executed as it might appear—the artist subordinated form, in the sense of recognizable and distinct areas, and thereby *focal areas*, to form a dynamic network of complex lines. The effect of this technique has a strong relationship to the actual force and speed with which the pigment was applied.

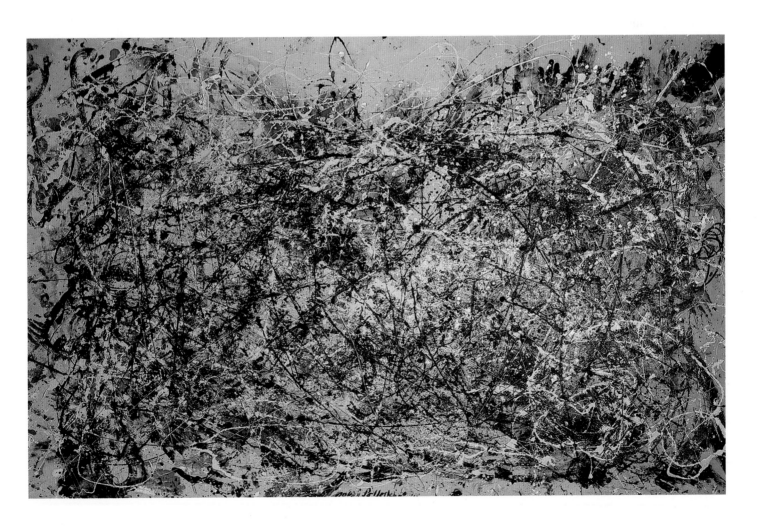

An artist uses line to control our vision, to create unity and emotional value, and ultimately to develop meaning. In pursuing those ends, and by employing the three aspects noted above, the artist finds that line has one of two simple characteristics: *curved* or *straight*. Whether expressed as an outline, as a boundary, or by implication, and whether simple or in combination, a line represents some derivative of straightness or curvedness.

FORM *Form* and line relate closely both in definition and in effect. Form is the *shape* of an object within the composition, and the word "shape" often appears as a synonym for form. Form constitutes the space described by line. In a drawing, a building is a form. So is a tree. We perceive them as buildings or trees, and we also perceive their individual details because of the line. Form cannot be separated from line in two-dimensional design.

COLOR Many ways exist by which to approach the compositional concept of color. We could begin with color as electromagnetic energy, discuss the psychology of color perception, and/or approach color in terms of how artists use it. The first two possibilities are extremely interesting, and the physics and psychology of color provide many potential crossovers between art and science and life. Nonetheless, we will limit our investigation to the last of these. The discussion that follows focuses on three color components: hue, value, and intensity.

Hue denotes the measurable wavelength of a specific color. The visible range of the color spectrum or range of colors we can actually distinguish extends from violet on one end to red on the other (Fig. **1.29**). The traditional color spectrum consists of seven basic hues (red, orange, yellow, green, blue, indigo, and violet). These are *primary hues* (red, blue, and yellow) and *secondary hues* that are direct derivatives of the primaries. In all, there exist (depending on which color theory one follows) from ten to twenty-four perceivably different hues, including these seven.

Assuming, for the sake of clarity and illustration, twelve basic hues, we can arrange them in a series (Fig. **1.30**) or turn them into a *color wheel* (Fig. **1.31**). With this visualization, artists' choices with regard to color become clearer. First, an artist can mix the primary hues of the spectrum, two at a time in varying proportions, creating the other hues of the spectrum. For example, red and yellow in equal proportions make orange, a secondary hue. Varying the proportions—adding more red or more yellow—makes yellow-orange or red-orange, which are tertiary (TUHR-shee-air-ee) hues. Yellow and blue make green, and also blue-green and yellow-green. Red and blue make violet, blue-violet, and red-violet.

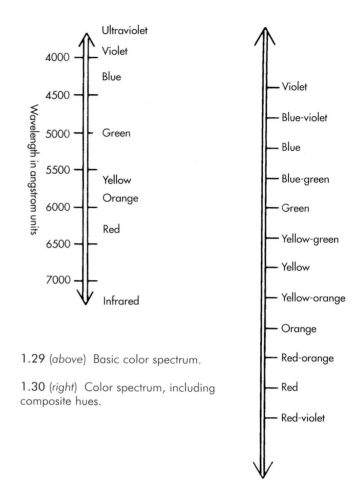

1.29 (*above*) Basic color spectrum.

1.30 (*right*) Color spectrum, including composite hues.

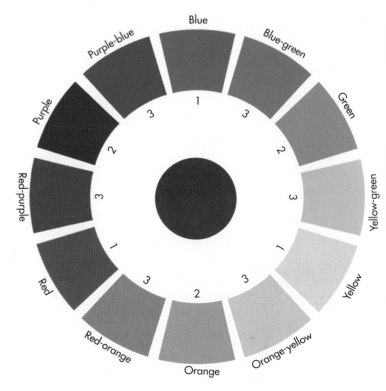

1.31 Color wheel: 1: primary hues; 2: secondary hues; 3: tertiary hues.

☐ White		☐ W	
☐ High light		☐ HL	☐ Yellow
☐ Light	Yellow-green ☐	☐ L	☐ Yellow-orange
☐ Medium light	Green ☐	☐ ML	☐ Orange
☐ Medium (gray)	Blue-green ☐	☐ M	☐ Red-orange
☐ High dark	Blue ☐	☐ MD	☐ Red
☐ Dark	Blue-violet ☐	☐ D	☐ Red-violet
☐ Low dark	Violet ☐	☐ LD	
☐ Black		☐ B	

1.32 Value scale. 1.33 Color-value equivalents.

Hues directly opposite each other on the color wheel are complementary. When mixed together in equal proportions, they produce gray.

Value, sometimes called key, is the relationship of blacks to whites and grays. The range of possibilities from black to white forms the value scale (Fig. **1.32**), which has black at one end, white at the other, and medium gray in the middle. We call the perceivable tones between black and white light or dark. The lighter, or whiter, a color, the higher its value. Likewise, the darker a color, the lower its value. For example, light pink has high value, while dark red has low value, even though they both have the same primary red as their base. Adding white to a hue (like primary red) creates a tint of that *hue*. Adding black creates a *shade*.

Some hues are intrinsically brighter than others, a factor we will discuss momentarily, but we can have a brightness difference in the same color. The brightness may involve a change in value, as just discussed—a pink versus a grayed or dull red. Brightness may also involve surface reflectance, a factor of considerable importance to all visual artists. A highly reflective surface creates a brighter color (and therefore a different response from the viewer) than does a surface of lesser reflectance, all other factors being equal. This constitutes the difference between high gloss, semi-gloss, and flat paints, for example. Probably surface reflectance concerns texture more than color. Nonetheless, the term *brilliance* often describes not only surface gloss but also characteristics synonymous with value. As just mentioned, some hues have intrinsically darker values than others. That applies to the concept we discuss next: intensity.

Intensity, sometimes also called chroma or saturation, is the degree of purity of a hue. Every hue has its own value—in its pure state each hue falls somewhere on the value scale, as shown in Figure **1.33**. The color wheel (see Fig. **1.31**) illustrates how movement around the wheel can create change in hue. Movements across the wheel alter intensity. For example, adding green to red grays the red. Therefore, because graying a hue constitutes a value change, the terms "intensity" and "value" are occasionally used interchangeably. Some sources use the terms independently but state that changing a hue's value automatically changes its intensity. Graying a hue by using its complement differs from graying a hue by adding black (or gray derived from black and white). Gray derived from complementaries, because it has hue, is far livelier than gray derived from black and white, which does not have hue.

We call the overall use of color by the artist *palette*. An artist's palette can be broad, restricted, or somewhere in between, depending upon whether the artist has utilized the full range of the color spectrum and/or whether he or she explores the full range of *tonalities*—brights and dulls, lights and darks.

MASS is the physical volume and density of an object. In two-dimensional art such as drawing, painting, printmaking, and photography, mass must be implied. The use of light and shade, texture, and perspective (see p. 62) give the figures and objects in Giovanni Vanni's *Holy Family with St. John* (see Fig. **1.8**) the appearance of fully rounded, solid mass. Vanni does all in his power to create depth of space, thus drawing attention away from the fact that the picture exists in only two dimensions.

TEXTURE, a picture's apparent roughness or smoothness, ranges from the shine of a glossy photo to the three-dimensionality of *impasto*, a painting technique wherein an artist applies pigment thickly with a palette knife. The texture of a picture falls anywhere within these two extremes. Texture may be illusory, in that the surface of a picture may be absolutely flat but the image gives the impression of three-dimensionality, so the term can be applied to the pictorial arts either literally or figuratively.

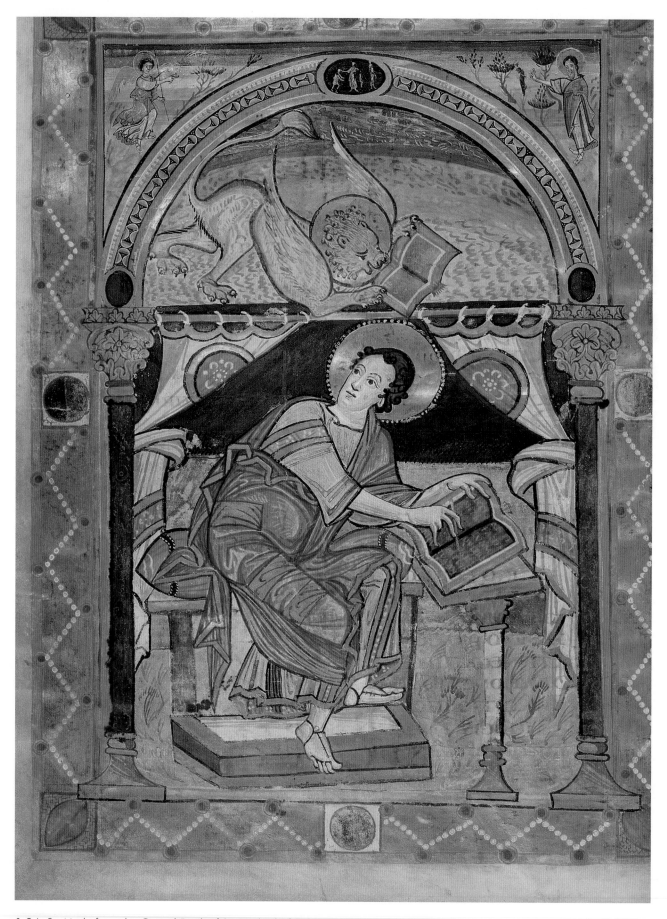

1.34 *St. Mark*, from the Gospel Book of St. Médard of Soissons, France, early 9th century. Paint on vellum, 14⅜ × 10¼ ins (37 × 26 cm). Bibliothèque Nationale, Paris.

Principles

REPETITION, or the way artists repeat or alternate items, plays an important role in composition. Repetition has three constituent parts: rhythm, harmony, and variation.

Rhythm, in technical language, is the recurrence of elements in a composition. In other words, rhythm is the repetition of lines, shapes, and objects in a picture. If the repeated elements, like the diamonds in Picasso's *Girl Before a Mirror* (see Fig. **1.26**), have the same size or importance, then we call their rhythm regular. If the repeated elements, like the circular shapes in *St. Mark* (Fig. **1.34**) have differing size and/or importance, then their rhythm we call irregular.

Harmony is the logic of the repetition. Harmonious relationships have components that appear to join naturally and comfortably. If the artist employs forms, colors, or other elements that appear incongruous or illogical, then we would use a musical term and say the picture has *dissonance.* However, we need to understand that ideas and ideals often reflect cultural conditioning or arbitrary understandings.

Variation is the relationship of repeated items to each other, like theme and variation in music (see Chapter 4). How does an artist take a basic element in the composition and use it again with slight or major changes? Picasso, the artist of Figure **1.26**, has used two geometric forms, the diamond and the oval, and created a complex painting via repetition. The diamond with a circle at its center repeats over and over to form the background. Variation occurs in the color given to these shapes. Similarly, the oval of the mirror repeats with variations in the composition of the girl. The circular motif is also repeated throughout the painting, with variations in color and size.

BALANCE is the achievement of equilibrium in a work of art. Determining whether a work is balanced or not is like dividing it into halves and evaluating whether one half or the other dominates. If the two halves seem equal, the work is balanced. As we shall see, many factors combine to affect a picture's balance, and line, form, and color all play a role. There are two general types of balance: symmetrical (formal) and asymmetrical (informal or psychological).

The most mechanical method of achieving balance, *symmetry*—specifically bilateral symmetry—involves the balancing of like forms, mass, and colors on opposite sides of the vertical axis (see Fig. **1.12**). Pictures employing absolute symmetry tend toward stability and stolidity.

Asymmetrical balance, which is sometimes referred to as psychological balance, carefully arranges unlike items

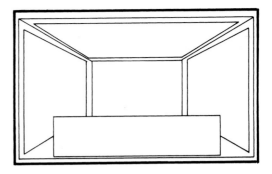

1.35 Closed composition (composition kept within the frame).

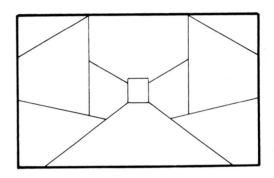

1.36 Open composition (composition allowed to escape the frame).

(see Fig. **1.25**). Every painting illustrated in this chapter is asymmetrical. Comparative discussion as to how balance has been achieved is a useful exercise, especially if we consider colors. Often color can balance line and form. Because some hues, such as yellow, have great eye attraction, they can be used to counterbalance tremendous mass and activity.

UNITY An important characteristic in a work of art is the means by which it achieves unity. A critical analysis of the elements of a painting should lead us to a judgment about whether the total statement comprises a unified one.

With regard to unity, some may speak of *closed composition,* in which use of line and form always directs the eye into the painting (Fig. **1.35**), as unified, and *open composition,* in which the eye can wander off the canvas, or escape the frame (Fig. **1.36**), as disunified. Such is not the case. Keeping the artwork within the frame is a stylistic device that has an important bearing on the artwork's meaning. For example, painting following *Classical* standards stays predominantly within the frame, illustrating a concern for the self-containment of the artwork and for precise structuring. *Anticlassical* design forces the eye to escape the frame, suggesting perhaps the world or universe outside, or the individual's place within an overwhelming cosmos. Unity does not depend on either of these conditions.

FOCAL AREAS When we look at a picture for the first time, our eye moves around it, pausing briefly at those areas that seem to be of greatest visual appeal. These comprise *focal areas*. A painting may have a single focal area from which the eye will stray only with conscious effort. Or it may have an infinite number of focal points whereby the eye bounces from one point to another on the picture—in this way, the elements vie for our attention.

Artists achieve focal areas in a number of ways—through confluence of line, by encirclement, or by color, to name just a few. To draw attention to a particular point in the picture by confluence of line, the artist may make all lines lead to that point, as in Leonardo da Vinci's *Last Supper* (see Fig. **11.8**). To create encirclement, the focal object or area may be placed in the center of a ring of objects. Focus by color means using a color that demands our attention more than the other colors in the picture. For example, bright yellows attract our eye more readily than dark blues. Wherever we look in this painting, we find some device that captures our vision and causes us to pause for a moment at an architectural element, a disciple's gesture, or even an imagined gaze of one of the disciples. A focus thus occurs. Eventually, however, any expressed or implied line in this work leads our vision to focus on the face of Christ.

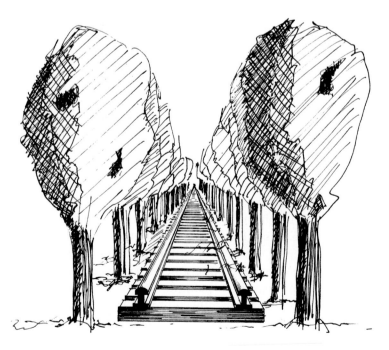

1.37 Linear perspective.

OTHER FACTORS

Perspective

Perspective indicates spatial relationships. It rests on the phenomenon that distant objects appear smaller and less distinct than objects situated in the foreground.

A number of types of perspective exist. We will discuss three: linear, atmospheric, and shifting. *Linear perspective* (Fig. **1.37**) is characterized by the phenomenon of standing on railroad tracks and watching the two rails apparently come together at the horizon (known as the *vanishing point*). Very simply, linear perspective creates the illusion of distance in a two-dimensional artwork through the convention of line and foreshortening—the illusion that parallel lines come together in the distance. Linear perspective, also called scientific, mathematical one-point, or Renaissance perspective, developed in fifteenth-century Italy (see Chapter 11). Linear perspective is the system most people in Euro-American cultures think of as perspective, because it represents the visual code they are accustomed to seeing. (See the Companion Website: Perspective.)

Atmospheric perspective indicates distance through the use of light and atmosphere. For example, mountains in the background of a picture appear distant through less detail. In the upper left of Figure **1.8**, a castle appears at a great distance. We know it is distant because it is smaller and, more important, because it is indistinct.

We find *shifting perspective* especially in Chinese landscapes and it is affected by additional factors of culture and convention. The painting *Buddhist Monastery by Stream and Mountains* by Chü-jan (Fig. **1.38**) divides the picture into two basic units—foreground and background. The foreground of the painting consists of details reaching back toward the middle ground. At that point a division occurs, so that the background and the foreground separate by an openness in what might have been a deep middle ground. The foreground represents the nearby, and its rich detail causes us to pause and ponder on numerous elements, including the artist's use of brushstroke in creating foliage, rocks, and water. Then a break appears, and the background seems to loom up or be suspended—almost as if it were a separate entity. Although the foreground gives us a sense of dimension—of space receding from the front plane of the painting—the background appears flat, a factor that serves to enhance further the sense of height of the mountains. The apparent shift in perspective, however, results from the concept that truth to natural appearance should not occur at the expense of a pictorial examination of how nature works. The artist invites the viewer to enter the painting and examine its various parts, but not to take a panoramic view from a single position. Rather, the artist reveals each part almost as though the viewer were walking through the landscape. Shifting perspective allows for a personal journey and can lead to a strong personal, spiritual impact on the viewer.

Chiaroscuro

Chiaroscuro, whose meaning in Italian is "light and shade," suggests three-dimensional forms via light and shadow without the use of outline. Artists use it to make their forms appear *plastic*—three-dimensional. Making two-dimensional objects appear to be three-dimensional depends on the artist's ability to render highlight and shadow effectively. Without them, all forms are two-dimensional in appearance.

Chiaroscuro gives a picture much of its character. For example, the dynamic and dramatic treatment of light and shade in Figure 1.39 gives this painting a quality quite different from what would have resulted had the artist chosen to give full, flat, front light to the face. The treatment of chiaroscuro in a highly lifelike fashion in Figure 1.41 helps give the painting its strangely real yet dreamlike appearance.

In contrast, works that do not employ chiaroscuro have a two-dimensional quality. This can be seen to a large extent in Figure 1.7 and also in Figures 1.24 and 1.42.

Content

Arguably, all works of art pursue verisimilitude (see p.14), and they do so with a variety of treatments of content or subject matter. We can regard treatment of content as ranging from naturalism to stylization. Included are such concepts as abstract, representational, and nonobjective (see Glossary). The word verisimilitude, again, comes from the Latin, *verisimilitudo*, and it means plausibility or likeness or nearness to truth. Aristotle, in his *Poetics*, insisted that art should reflect nature—for example, even highly idealized representations should possess recognizable qualities—and that the probable should take precedence over the merely possible. This has come to mean that the search for a portrayal of truth can sometimes mean a distortion of what we observe around us in favor of an image that, while perhaps not being lifelike, better speaks to the underlying truth of human existence than

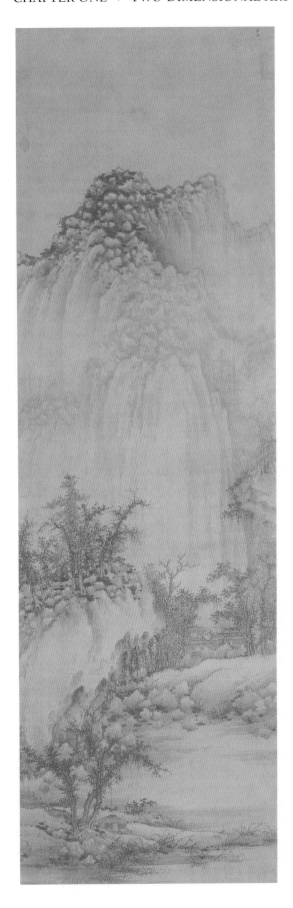

1.38 Chü-jan, *Buddhist Monastery by Stream and Mountains*, c. 960–85 C.E. Ink on silk, 33⅜ × 22⅝ ins (85.5 × 57.5 cm). Cleveland Museum of Art (Gift of Katharine Holden Thayer).

1.39 Jan Vermeer, *The Girl with the Red Hat*, c. 1665. Oil on wood, 9⅛ × 7⅛ ins (23 × 18 cm). National Gallery of Art, Washington, D.C. (Andrew W. Mellon Collection).

1.40 (*opposite*) Théodore Géricault, *The Raft of the "Medusa,"* 1819. Oil on canvas, 16 ft × 23 ft 6 ins (4.91 × 7.16 m). Louvre, Paris.

Painting and Human Reality

Géricault, The Raft of the "Medusa"

The Raft of the "Medusa" (meh-DOO-suh; Fig. **1.40**) by Théodore Géricault (zhay-ree-KOH) illustrates a criticism of social institutions in general. The painting tells a story of governmental incompetence that resulted in tragedy. In 1816, the French government allowed an unseaworthy ship, the *Medusa*, to leave port, and it was wrecked. Aboard a makeshift raft, the survivors endured tremendous suffering, and were eventually driven to cannibalism. In preparing for the work, Géricault interviewed the survivors, read newspaper accounts, and went so far as to paint corpses and the heads of guillotined criminals.

Géricault's painting captures the ordeal of the event in Romantic style, tempered by Classical and even High Renaissance influences (see Chapters 11 and 12). He creates firmly modeled flesh, lifelike figures, and a precise play of light and shade (chiaroscuro). In contrast to other paintings of the time, which expressed Classical tendencies and, hence, two-dimensionality and order, Géricault used a complex and fragmented compositional structure. He chose to base the design on two triangles rather than on one strong central triangle. In *The Raft of the "Medusa,"* the left triangle's apex is the makeshift mast, which points back toward despair and death. The other triangle moves up to the right to the figure waving the fabric, pointing toward hope and life as a rescue ship appears in the distance.

Géricault captures the moment that a potential rescue ship is sighted and sails on by. The play of light and shade heightens the dramatic effect and the composition builds upward from the bodies of the dead and dying in the foreground to the dynamic group whose final energies are summoned to support the figure waving to the ship. Thus, the painting surges with unbridled emotional response to the horror of the experience and the heroism of the survivors. It is hope followed by despair.

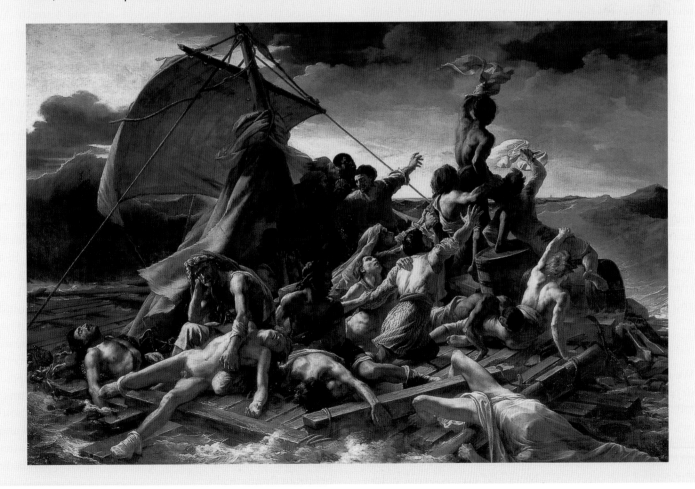

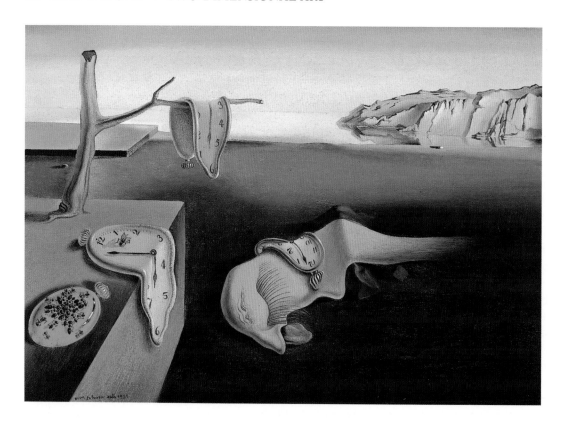

1.41 *(left)* Salvador Dalí, *The Persistence of Memory*, 1931. Oil on canvas, 9½ × 13 ins (24.1 × 33 cm). The Museum of Modern Art, New York (Given anonymously).

1.42 *(opposite)* Sir Peter Paul Rubens, *Rape of the Daughters of Leucippus*, c. 1616–17. Oil on canvas, 7 ft 3½ ins × 6 ft 10¼ ins (2.22 × 2.09 m). Alte Pinakothek, Munich.

mere lifelikeness does. So, the verisimilar, whether lifelike or not, becomes acceptable or convincing according to the respondent's own experience or knowledge. In some cases, this means enticing the respondent into suspending disbelief and accepting improbability within the framework of the work of art.

SENSE STIMULI

We do not touch pictures, and so we cannot feel their roughness or their smoothness, their coolness or their warmth. We cannot hear pictures and we cannot smell them. Concluding that a picture affects our senses in a particular way means that we respond in terms of visual stimuli that change into mental images of touch, taste, and sound.

CONTRASTS

We refer to the colors of an artist's palette as warm or cool depending upon which end of the color spectrum they fall. We think of reds, oranges, and yellows as warm colors. They are the colors of the sun and therefore call to mind our primary source of heat, so they carry strong implications of warmth. We call colors falling at the opposite end of the spectrum—blues and greens—cool colors

because they imply shade, or lack of light and warmth. As we will notice frequently, this mental stimulation has a physical basis.

Tonality and color contrast also affect our senses. The stark value contrasts of Figure **1.24** contribute significantly to the harsh and dynamic qualities of the work. The colorlessness of this monochromatic black, white, and gray comments on the tragic bombing of Guernica. In the opposite vein, the soft yet dramatic tonal contrasts of Figure **1.39** and the strong warmth and soft texture of the red hat create a completely different set of stimuli.

Many of the sense-affecting stimuli work in inseparable concert. We have already noted some of the effects of chiaroscuro, but one of the most interesting is its application to the treatment of flesh. Some flesh appears like stone; other flesh appears soft and true to life. Our response to whatever treatment has been given is tactile—we want to touch, or we believe we know what we would feel if we did touch. Chiaroscuro is essential to achieve those effects. Harsh shadow and strong contrasts create one set of responses; diffused shadows and subdued contrasts create another. *Rape of the Daughters of Leucippus* (loo-SIH-puhs; Fig. **1.42**) by Rubens (ROO-behns) presents softly modeled flesh whose warmth and softness come from color and chiaroscuro. Highlight and shadow create softness, while predominantly red hues warm the composition; our sensual response tends to heighten dramatically.

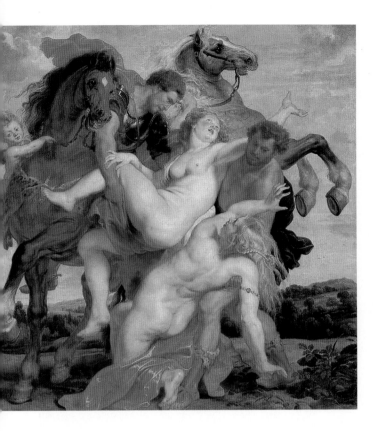

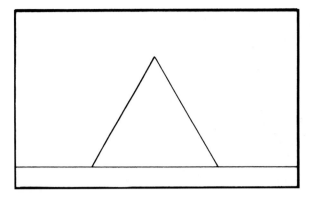

1.43 Upright-triangular composition.

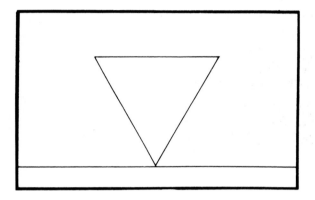

1.44 Inverted-triangular composition.

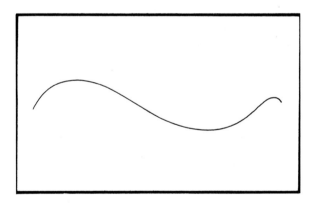

1.45 Curved line.

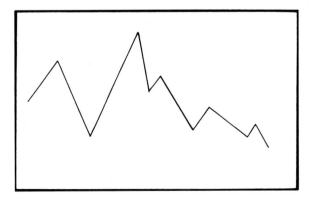

1.46 Broken line.

DYNAMICS

Although static, pictures can stimulate a sense of movement and activity and create a sense of stable solidity. The artist stimulates these sensations by using certain conventional devices. Principally vertical composition can express, for example, a sense of dignity and grandeur (see Fig. 1.50; see also Fig. 0.4). Horizontality can elicit a sense of stability and placidity. The triangle, for example, has interesting engineering possibilities because of its structural qualities. In art it has significant psychological qualities. If we place a triangle so that its base forms the bottom of a picture, we create a definite sense of solidity and immovability (Fig. 1.43). If that triangle were a pyramid sitting on a level plane, a great deal of effort would be required to tip it over. If we invert the triangle so that it balances on its apex, a sensation of instability and action results (Figs. 1.44 and 1.47). Although we can feel clearly the sensations stimulated by these simple geometric forms, we should not conclude that such devices are either explicit or limited in their communication. Nonverbal communication in the arts is not that simple. Nonetheless, basic compositional devices do influence our response and affect our perceptions.

The use of line also affects sense response. Figure 1.45 illustrates curved line and a sense of relaxation. The broken line in Figure 1.46 creates a much more dynamic and violent sensation. We can also feel that the upright

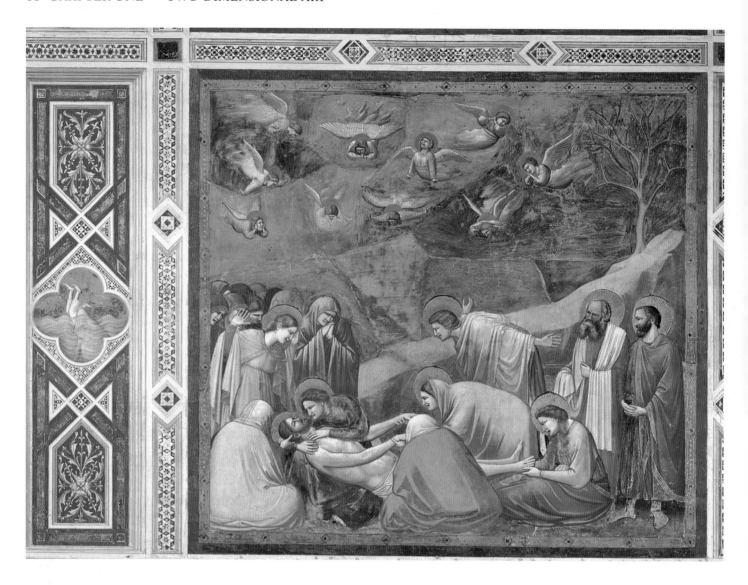

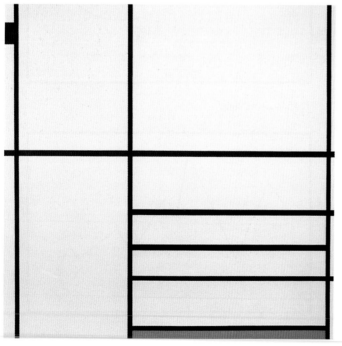

1.47 (above) Giotto, *The Lamentation*, 1305–6. Fresco, 7 ft 7 ins × 6 ft 7½ ins (2.31 × 2.02 m). Arena Chapel, Padua.

1.48 (left) Piet Mondrian, *Composition in White, Black, and Red*, 1936. Oil on canvas, 3 ft 4¼ ins × 3 ft 5 ins (1.02 × 1.04 m). The Museum of Modern Art, New York (Gift of the Advisory Committee).

triangle in Figure 1.43, although solid and stable, is more dynamic than a horizontal composition because it uses strong diagonal line, which tends to stimulate a sense of movement. Precision of linear execution can also create sharply defined forms or soft, fuzzy images. Figure 1.48 shows how straight lines and right angles can create the basic principles of life itself. Vertical lines signify vitality and life; horizontal lines signify tranquillity and death. The intersection of vertical and horizontal lines is used to represent life's tensions.

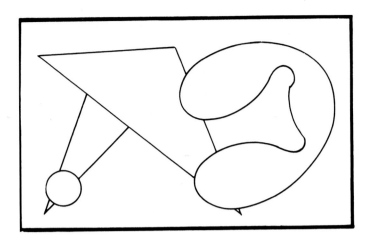

1.49 Juxtaposition of inharmonious forms.

TROMPE L'OEIL

Trompe l'oeil (tromp-LUH-yuh), or "trick the eye," gives the artist a varied set of stimuli by which to affect our sensory response. It constitutes a form of illusionistic painting that attempts to represent an object as existing in three dimensions at the surface of the painting.

JUXTAPOSITION

We can also receive stimuli from the results of juxtaposing curved and straight lines, which results in linear dissonance or consonance. Figure **1.49** illustrates the juxtaposing of inharmonious forms, which creates instability. Careful use of this device can stimulate some very interesting and specific sense responses.

The metaphysical fantasies of Giorgio de Chirico (KEE-ree-koh; 1888–1978) have Surrealist associations (see Chapter 13). Works such as *The Nostalgia of the Infinite* (Fig. **1.50**) contain no rational explanation for their juxtaposition of strange objects. They have a dreamlike quality, associating objects that are not normally grouped together. Such works lack rationality and show a world humankind does not control. In them, "there is only what I see with my eyes open, and, even better, closed."

FOCUS

Artists use focus, focal points, or emphasis to control our physical attention and, thus, sense response. Pick any work in this chapter and you will find that involuntarily your eye moves from one point on the picture to another. The areas that draw your attention constitute the work's foci. Sometimes works have a limited number of strong focal points. Sometimes works seem to have an infinite

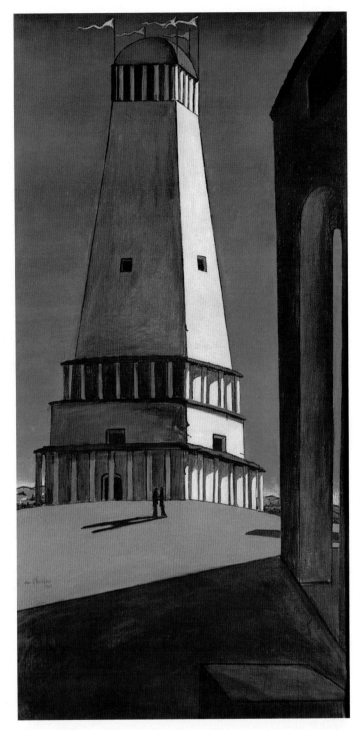

1.50 Giorgio de Chirico, *The Nostalgia of the Infinite*, 1913–14?, dated 1911 on the painting. Oil on canvas, 53¼ × 25½ ins (135.2 × 64.8 cm). The Museum of Modern Art, New York (Purchase).

number of equal focal points. For example, the work of François Boucher (boo-SHAY; 1703–70) in the Rococo tradition (see Chapter 11) gives a taste of the decorative, mundane, and somewhat erotic painting popular in the early and mid-eighteenth century. As a protégé of

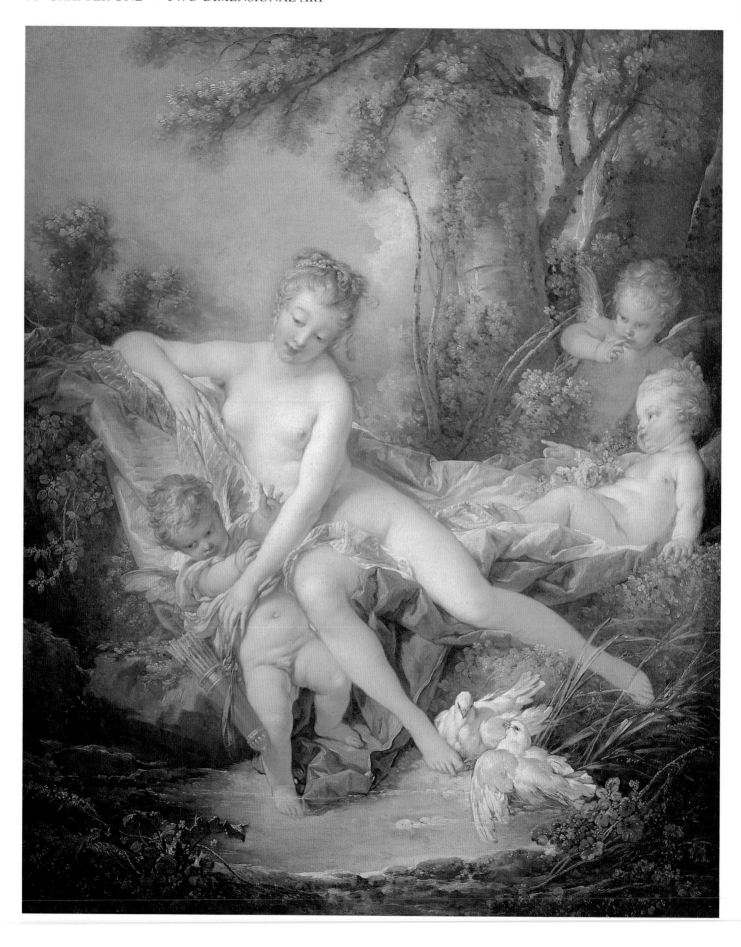

Madame de Pompadour, mistress of King Louis XV, Boucher enjoyed great popularity. His work has a highly decorative surface, and portrays pastoral and mythological settings such as shown in Figure 1.51. Boucher's figures appear amid exquisitely detailed drapery. His nearly flawless rendering technique and his displays of painterly virtuosity provide a fussily pretty work whose main subject competes with its decorative background for our attention. Each detail takes on a separate focus of its own and leads the eye first in one direction and then another.

THINKING CRITICALLY

Do a *basic analysis* of a drawing, painting, or print: pick a work of two-dimensional art and ask yourself how it reflects the qualities appropriate to the specific topics discussed in Chapter 1. Begin with the following:

* Reaction. Does the artist present clues in the work as to any response he or she might seek to achieve? In what ways does the artist stimulate emotional and intellectual response? What was your response and what means does the artist employ to evoke it?

Now build a *comparative analysis* by choosing two or more works and detailing how they reflect specific qualities described in the chapter. For example:

* Medium. What medium does van Gogh use in *The Starry Night* (Fig 1.7)? What medium does McIntyre use in *Barbershop Mirror* (Fig. 1.17)? Compare how the particular qualities of the media influence the final composition and appearance of the works.

* Line. Compare how Dürer (*Lamentation*, Fig. 1.9) and Vermeer (*The Girl with the Red Hat*, Fig. 1.39) employ the various qualities of line. How does their use of implied line, edge, and rectilinear line affect the dynamic workings of the pieces?

* Color. Compare the use of color in Vanni's *Holy Family with St. John* (Fig. 1.8) and Géricault's *The Raft of the "Medusa"* (Fig. 1.40). How do hue, value, intensity, and contrast contribute to the overall palette of each work, and how do the palettes compare?

CYBER STUDY

DRAWING (charcoal):
—Georgia O'Keeffe, *The Shell*
http://www.nga.gov/cgi-bin/pinfo?Object=56395+0+none

LINE ENGRAVING:
—Albrecht Dürer, *Angel with the Key to the Bottomless Pit*
http://sunsite.auc.dk/cgfa/durer/p-durer5.htm

LITHOGRAPHY:
—Robert Indiana, *South Bend*
http://www.nga.gov/cgi-bin/pinfo?Object=56441+0+none

PRINTMAKING (general):
http://www.artcyclopedia.com/media/Printmaker.html

ENGRAVING (general):
http://www.artcyclopedia.com/media/Engraver.html

PHOTOGRAPHY (general):
http://www.artcyclopedia.com/media/Photographer.html

1.51 François Boucher, *Venus Consoling Love*, 1751. Oil on canvas, 42⅛ × 33⅜ ins (107 × 85 cm). National Gallery of Art, Washington, D.C. (Chester Dale Collection).

CHAPTER TWO

SCULPTURE

OUTLINE

FORMAL AND TECHNICAL QUALITIES

DIMENSIONALITY
  Full-Round
  Relief
  Linear
METHODS OF EXECUTION
  Subtraction
  Construction
  Substitution
  Manipulation
COMPOSITION
  Elements

Sculpture and Human Reality:
  Michelangelo, David
  Principles
Profile: Michelangelo
OTHER FACTORS
  Articulation
  Focal Area (Emphasis)
  Ephemeral
  Found

SENSE STIMULI

TOUCH
TEMPERATURE AND AGE
DYNAMICS
SIZE
LIGHTING AND
  ENVIRONMENT
Thinking Critically
Cyber Study

IMPORTANT TERMS

Articulation The manner of movement from one element in an artwork to another.

Construction A method of execution in sculpture in which works are constructed, or built, by one element being added to another.

Full-round Sculptural works that explore full three-dimensionality.

Manipulation A method of execution in sculpture in which works are shaped by skilled use of the hands.

Proportion The relationship of shapes in a work of visual art.

Relief Sculptural works attached to a background and seen from one side only.

Substitution A method of execution in sculpture in which works are transformed from a molten to a solid state.

Subtraction A method of execution in sculpture in which works are carved.

FORMAL AND TECHNICAL QUALITIES

Sculpture is a three-dimensional art. It may take the form of whatever it seeks to represent, from pure, or nonobjective, form to lifelike depiction of people or any other entity. Sometimes sculpture, because of its three-dimensional nature, comes very close to reality in its depiction. Duane Hanson, for example (Fig. 2.1), uses plastics to render the human form so naturalistically that the viewer must approach the artwork and examine it closely to determine that it is not in fact a real person. In the remainder of this section we discuss four topics relating to how sculptors realize their works: (1) dimensionality; (2) methods of execution; (3) composition; and (4) other factors.

DIMENSIONALITY

Sculpture may be *full-round, relief,* or *linear.* Full-round works are freestanding and fully three-dimensional (Figs. 2.2 and 2.3). Relief works can be viewed from only one side—that is, projecting from a background. A sculpture utilizing materials two-dimensionally we call linear. A sculptor's choice of full-round, relief, or linearity as a mode of expression dictates to a large extent what he or she can and cannot execute, both in aesthetic and in practical terms.

Full-Round

Full-round sculptural works explore full three-dimensionality and are intended to be viewed from any angle (Fig. 2.2). Some subjects and styles pose certain constraints in this regard, however. Painters, printmakers, and photographers have virtually unlimited choice of subject matter and compositional arrangements. Full-round sculptures dealing with such subjects as clouds, oceans, and panoramic landscapes present problems for the sculptor, though. Freestanding and three-dimensional sculpture forces sculptors to concern themselves with the practicalities of engineering and gravity. They cannot, for example, create a work with great mass at the top unless they can find a way (within the bounds of acceptable composition) to keep the statue from falling over. After we have viewed numerous full-round works, we begin to note the small animals, branches, tree stumps, rocks, and other devices that have been employed to give practical stability to a work.

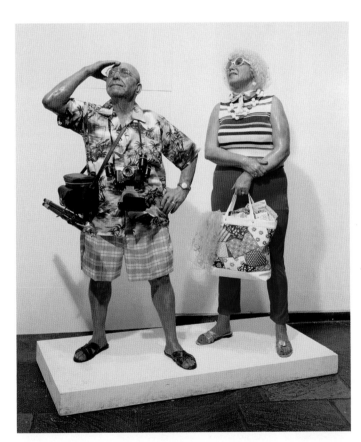

2.1 Duane Hanson, *Tourists,* 1970. Polyester-chromed fiberglass, 5 ft 6 ins × 4ft 8 ins × 3 ft 11 ins (1.7 m × 1.5 m × 0.94 m). Museum of Modern Art, Edinburgh, Scotland, UK.

2.2 (*right*) Auguste Rodin, *The Burghers of Calais,* 1866. Bronze, height 6 ft 10½ ins (2.09 m). Hirshhorn Museum and Sculpture Garden, Smithsonian Institution, Washington, D.C. (Gift of Joseph J. Hirshhorn).

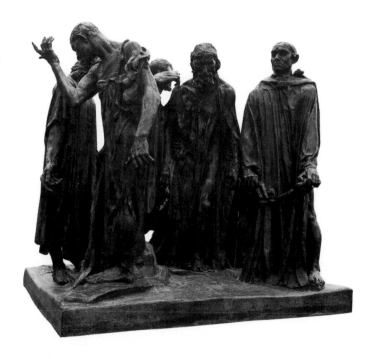

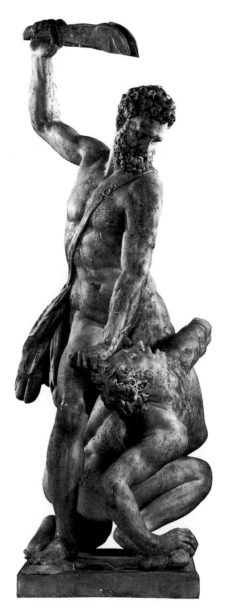

2.3 (left) Giovanni Bologna, *Samson Slaying a Philistine*, c. 1562. Victoria & Albert Museum, London.

Relief

The sculptor who creates a work in relief does not have quite so many restrictions. Since the work attaches to a background, he or she has freer choice of subjects and need not worry about their positions or supports. Clouds, seas, and perspective landscapes remain within the relief sculptor's reach, since the work requires viewing from only one side. Relief sculpture, then, is three-dimensional. However, because it protrudes from a background, it maintains a two-dimensional quality, as compared to full-round sculpture. Sometimes relief sculpture can almost reach the point of full-roundness, as the jamb statues of saints from the west portal of Chartres (shartr) Cathedral in France illustrate (Fig. 2.4). Later jamb statues from another portal of the same cathedral (see Figs. **10.27 and 10.28**) exhibit an even greater sense of emergence from their background. We call relief sculptures that project

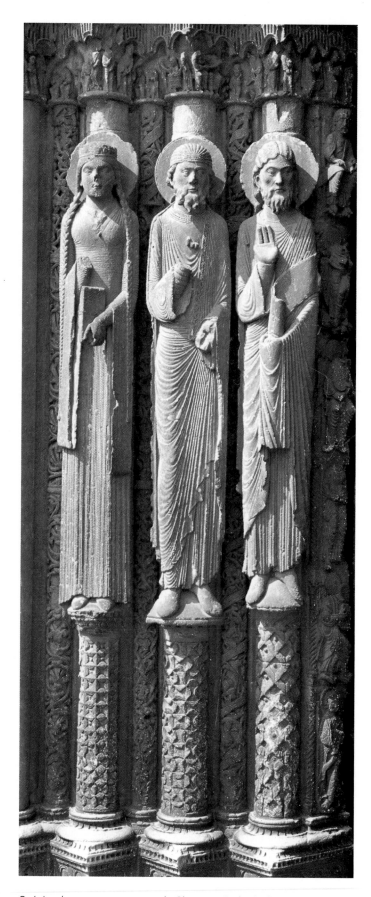

2.4 Jamb statues, west portal, Chartres Cathedral, begun 1145.

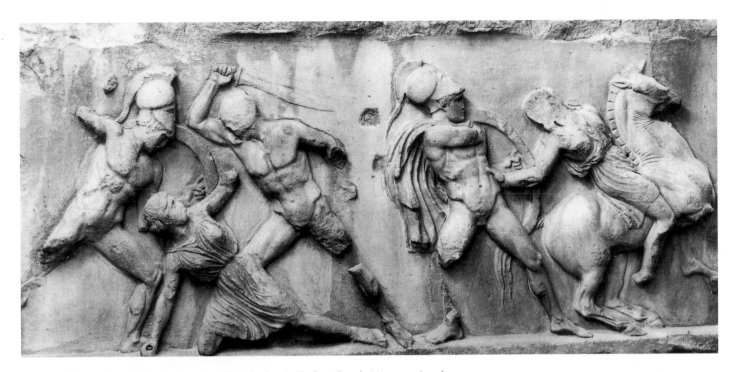

2.5 East frieze, from Halicarnassus (modern Bodrum), Turkey. British Museum, London.

only a small distance from their base, such as the Halicarnassus frieze (Fig. **2.5**) *low relief* or *bas relief* (bahruh-leef). Sculptures such as those from Chartres Cathedral that project by at least half their depth are termed *high relief* or *haut-relief* (oh-ruh-leef).

Linear

The third category of sculpture, linear sculpture, emphasizes construction with linear items such as wire or neon tubing, as we might see in a mobile such as Figure **2.6**. Artworks using linear materials and occupying three-dimensional space will occasionally puzzle us as we try to decide whether they are really linear or full-round. Here again, absolute definition is less important than the process of analysis and aesthetic experience and response.

2.6 Alexander Calder, *Spring Blossoms*, 1965. Painted metal and heavy wire, extends 4 ft 4 ins × 8 ft 6 ins (1.35 × 2.59 m). Palmer Museum of Art, Pennsylvania State University (Gift of the class of 1965).

METHODS OF EXECUTION

In general, we may say that sculptors execute their works using subtraction, construction, substitution, or manipulation techniques, or any combination of these.

Subtraction

Subtractive, or carved, works (see the Companion Website: Sculpture) usually begin with a large block, typically of wood or stone, from which the sculptor cuts away (subtracts) the unwanted material. In previous eras, and to some extent today, sculptors had to work with whatever materials were at hand. Wood carvings emanated from forested regions, soapstone carvings from the Arctic, and great works of marble from the regions surrounding the quarries of the Mediterranean. Anything that can yield to the carver's tools can be formed into a work of sculpture. However, stone, with its promise of immortality, has proven to be the most popular material.

Three types of rock hold potential for the carver. *Igneous* rock—for example, granite—has hard mass and potential immortality. However, sculptors find it difficult to carve and therefore not desirable. *Sedimentary* rock such as limestone lasts a relatively long time, carves easily, and polishes ideally. Beautifully smooth and lustrous surfaces result from sedimentary rock. *Metamorphic* rock, including marble, appears the sculptor's ideal. It lasts, carves pleasurably, and exists in a broad range of colors. Whatever the artist's choice, one requirement must be met: the material to be carved, whether wood, stone, or a bar of soap, must be free from flaws.

A sculptor who sets about carving a work does not begin simply by imagining a *Samson Slaying a Philistine* (see Fig. **2.3**) and then attacking the stone. The first step involves creating a model, usually smaller than the intended sculpture. The model, made of clay, plaster, wax, or some other material, reflects the precise details—in miniature—of the final product.

Once the likeness of the model has been enlarged and transferred, the artist begins to rough out the actual image ("knocking away the waste material," as Michelangelo put it). In this stage of the sculpting process, the artist carves to within two or three inches of the finished area,

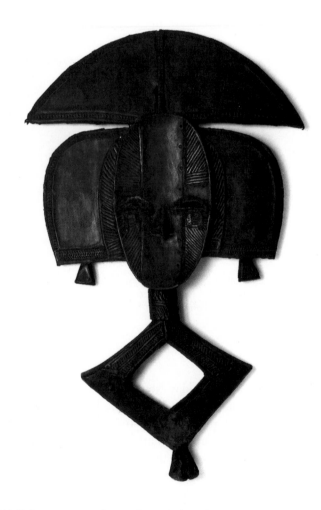

2.7 Bakota ancestor figure, from Gabon, late 19th century. Wood and copper sheeting, height 26¾ ins (68 cm). British Museum, London.

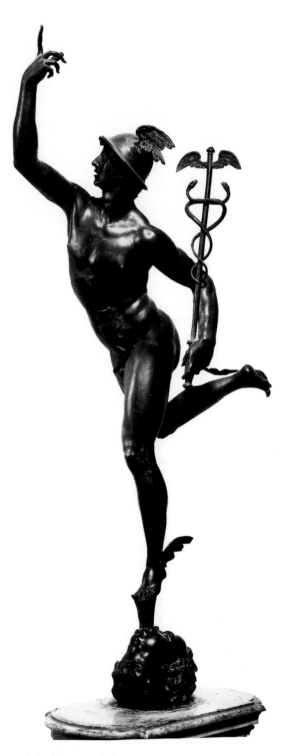

2.8 Giovanni Bologna, *Mercury*, c. 1567. Bronze, height 5 ft 9 ins (1.75 m). Museo Nazionale del Bargello, Florence.

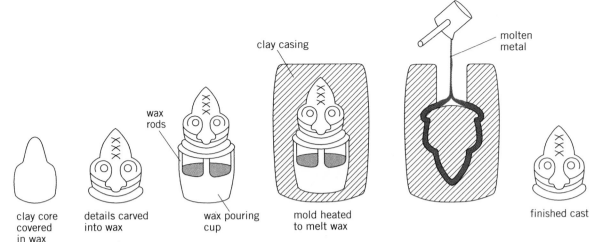

2.9 Lost-wax process.

using specific tools designed for the purpose. Then, using a different set of carving tools, she or he carefully takes the material down to the precise detail. Finishing work and polishing follow.

Construction

In contrast with carving from a large block of material, the sculptor using construction starts with a small amount of raw material and adds element to element to create the work. The term *built sculpture* often describes works executed with a constructive method. The materials employed in this process can be plastics, metals such as aluminum or steel, terracottas (clay), epoxy resins, or wood. Many times, materials are combined (Fig. **2.7**). Sculptors commonly combine methods as well. For example, built sections of metal or plastic may be combined with carved sections of stone.

Substitution

The substitution method—also called casting or replacement processes—transforms material from a plastic, molten, or fluid state into a solid state. The creation of a piece of cast sculpture always involves the use of a mold. First, the artist creates an identically sized model of the intended sculpture. This *positive* she or he then covers with a material, such as plaster of Paris, which when hardened and removed will retain the surface configurations of the positive. Called a *negative*, this form becomes the mold for the actual sculpture. The artist pours molten or fluid material into the negative and allows it to solidify. When the mold is removed, the work of sculpture emerges. Surface polishing, if desired, helps to bring the work to its final form (Fig. **2.8**).

One example of substitution is the ancient technique called "lost-wax" or *cire-perdue* (seer pair-DOO; Fig. **2.9**).

In this method of casting the artist creates the basic mold by using a wax model, which he or she then melts to leave the desired space in the mold. The artist then covers the heat-resistant "core" of clay—approximately the shape of the sculpture—with a layer of wax approximately the thickness of the final work. The sculptor carves the details in the wax. Rods and a pouring cup made of wax attach to the model, followed by thick layers of clay. When the clay dries, the artist heats the mold to melt the wax. Molten metal can then be poured into the mold. When the molten metal has dried, the clay mold is broken and removed, which means that the sculpture cannot be duplicated.

Very often sculpture is cast so it is hollow. This saves money, since it requires less material. It also results in a work less prone to crack, since it is less susceptible to expansion and contraction resulting from changes in temperature. Hollow sculpture is, naturally, lighter and thus more easily shipped and handled.

Manipulation

Manipulation—also called modeling—uses pliable materials such as clay, wax, or plaster, which the artist shapes, by skillful use of the hands or tools into a final form (see the Companion Website: Sculpture). For example, from a rough lump of clay turned on a device called a potter's wheel emerges an elegant vase.

COMPOSITION

Composition in sculpture comprises the same elements and principles as composition in two-dimensional art—line, form, color, mass, texture, repetition, balance, unity, and focal areas. Sculptors' uses of these elements and principles differ significantly from those of pictorial artists, however, since they work in three dimensions.

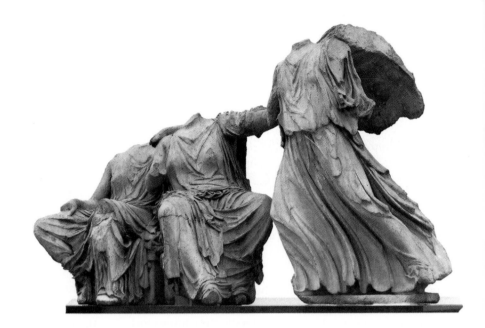

2.10 (*right and opposite*) Part of the east pediment of the Parthenon, Athens, c. 438–432 B.C.E. Left to right: Persephone, Demeter, Isis, Hestia(?), Dione, and Aphrodite ("Three Seated Goddesses"). Marble, over life-size. British Museum, London.

2.11 (*below, right*) Alberto Giacometti, *Man Pointing*, 1947. Bronze, 70½ × 40¾ × 16⅜ ins (179 × 103.4 × 41.5 cm), at base 12 × 13¼ ins (30.5 × 33.7 cm). The Museum of Modern Art, New York (Gift of Mrs. John D. Rockefeller 3rd).

Elements

Unlike a picture, a sculpture has literal *mass*. It takes up three-dimensional *space*, and its materials have *density*. Mass in pictures can be thought of as relative mass: the mass of forms in a picture has application principally in relation to other forms within the same picture. In sculpture, however, mass is literal and consists of actual volume and density. So, the mass of a sculpture 20 ft (6 m) high, 8 ft (2.5 m) wide, and 10 ft (3 m) deep, but made of balsa wood, appears less than a sculpture 10 ft (3 m) high, 4 ft (1.25 m) wide, and 3 ft (1 m) deep, made of lead. Space and density must both be considered. Later in the chapter we'll discuss what happens when an artist disguises the material of a work to look and feel like a different material.

As stated in the previous chapter, *line* and *form* are closely related. We can separate them (with some difficulty) when we discuss pictures, because in two dimensions an artist uses line to define form. In painting, line is a construction tool. In sculpture form draws our interest, and when we discuss line in sculpture, we do so in terms of how it is revealed in form.

When we view a sculpture, its elements direct our eye from one point to another, just as focal points do, via line and color, in a picture (Fig. **2.10**). Some works direct the eye through the piece and then off into space. Such sculptures have an *open* form. The sculptor of Figure **2.11** directs the eye outward from the work in the same fashion as composition that escapes the frame in painting. If, on the other hand, the work directs the eye continually back into the form, we say the form is *closed*. If we allow our eye to follow the linear detail of Figure **2.12**, we find

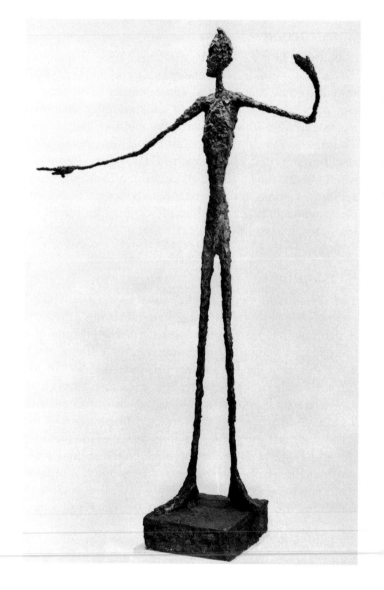

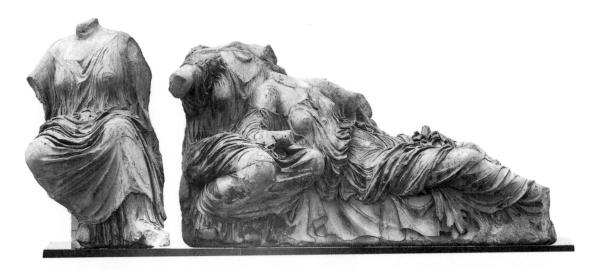

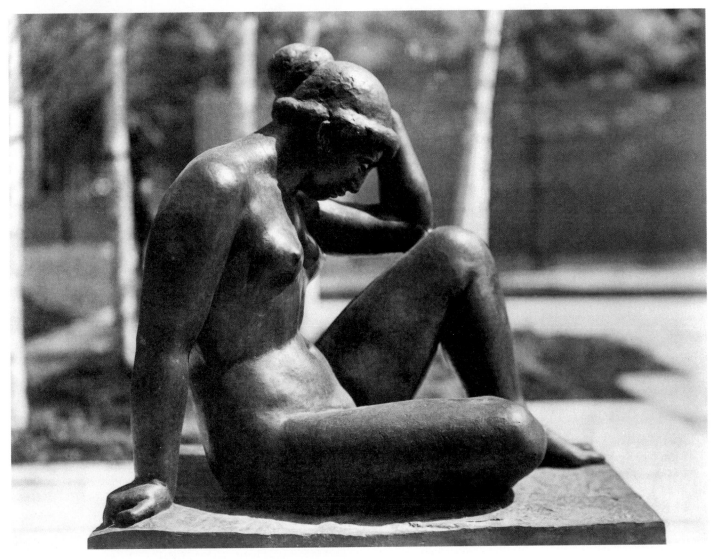

2.12 Aristide Maillol, *The Mediterranean*, 1902–5 (cast 1951–53). Bronze, 41 × 45 × 29¾ ins (104.1 × 114.3 × 75.6 cm), including base. The Museum of Modern Art, New York (Gift of Stephen C. Clark).

Sculpture and Human Reality

Michelangelo, *David*

Towering some 18 feet (5.5 m) above the floor on its base, Michelangelo's *David* (Fig. **2.13**) awesomely exemplifies *terribilità* (tay-ree-bee-lee-TAH), Michelangelo's particular tendency to create awe-inspiring characters. This nude champion exudes a pent-up energy as the body seems to exist merely as an earthly prison for the soul. The upper body moves in opposition to the lower. As the viewer's eye travels downward along the right arm and leg and then up along the left arm, a subtle thrust and counterthrust of movement emerges.

Much of the effect of *David*—the bulging muscles, exaggerated rib cage, heavy hair, undercut eyes, and frowning brow—may be due to the fact that these features were intended to be read from a distance. The sculpture was originally intended to be placed high above the ground on a buttress for Florence Cathedral. Instead, the city leaders put it in front of the Palazzo Vecchio, believing it too magnificent to be placed so high.

The political symbolism of the work was recognized from the outset. *David* stood for the valiant Florentine Republic. It also stood for all of humanity, elevated to a new and superhuman power, beauty, and grandeur. However, its "total and triumphant nudity," which reflected Michelangelo's belief in the divinity of the human body, kept it hidden from the public for two months. When it did appear, a brass girdle with twenty-eight copper leaves hung around the statue's waist.

Inspired by the Hellenistic sculptures he had seen in Rome (see pp. 235–7), Michelangelo set out in pursuit of an emotion-charged, heroic ideal. The scale, musculature, emotion, and stunning beauty and power of those earlier works became a part of Michelangelo's style. However, in contrast to the Hellenistic approach, in which the "body 'acts' out the spirit's agony" (compare the *Laocoön* (lay-AH-koh-ahn), by Hagesandrus, Polydorus, and Athenodorus, see Fig. **10.11**), *David* remains controlled, exhibiting the extraordinary action-in-repose for which Michelangelo is famous.

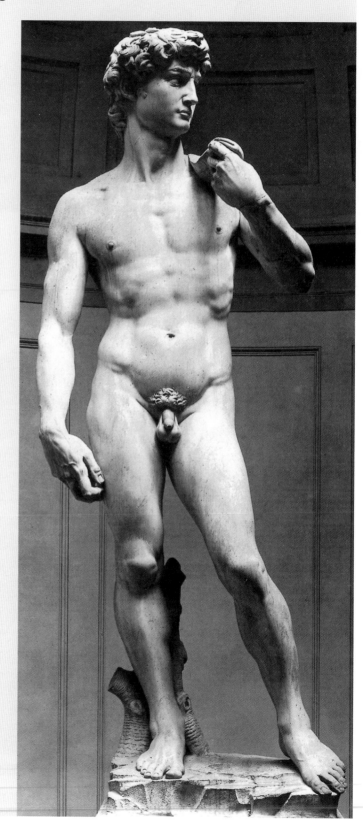

2.13 Michelangelo, *David*, 1501–4. Marble, height 13 ft 5 ins (4.08 m). Accademia, Florence.

that it continually leads our eye back into the work. This is similar to composition kept within the frame in painting and to closed forms in music, which we will discuss in Chapter 4.

Some sculptures have openings. We call any such holes in a sculpture *negative space*, and we can discuss this characteristic in terms of its role in the overall composition. In some works negative space is inconsequential; in others it is significant. We must decide which, and determine how negative space contributes to the overall piece.

Perhaps *color* does not seem particularly important to us when we think of sculpture. We tend to see ancient sculpture as white and modern sculpture as natural wood or rusty iron. But color is as important to the sculptor as it is to the painter. In some cases the material itself may be chosen because of its color; in others, such as terracottas, the sculpture may be painted. The lifelike sculptures of Duane Hanson (see Fig. **2.1**) depend on color for their effect. They are so lifelike that one could easily confuse them with real persons. Finally, still other materials may be chosen or treated so that nature will provide the final color through oxidation or weathering.

Texture, the roughness or smoothness of a surface, is a tangible characteristic of sculpture. We can actually perceive texture through our sense of touch. Even when we cannot touch a work of sculpture, we can perceive and respond to texture, which can be both physical and suggested. Sculptors go to great lengths to achieve the texture they desire. In fact, much of a sculptor's technical mastery manifests itself in that final ability to impart a surface to the work. We will examine texture more fully in our discussion of sense responses.

Principles

Proportion is the relationship of shapes. Just as we have a seemingly innate sense of balance, so we have a feeling of proportion. That feeling tells us that each form in the sculpture exists in proper relationship to the others. As any student of art history will tell us, proportion—or the ideal of relationships—has varied from one civilization or culture to another. For example, such a seemingly obviously proportioned entity as the human body has varied greatly in its proportions as sculptors over the centuries have depicted it. Study the differences in proportion in the human body among Michelangelo's *David* (Fig. **2.13**), the Chartres saints (see Fig. **2.4**), an ancient Greek kouros figure (Fig. **2.14**), and Giacometti's *Man Pointing* (see Fig. **2.11**). Each depicts the human form, but each utilizes differing proportions. This difference in proportion helps transmit the message the artist wishes to communicate about his or her subject matter.

2.14 Kouros, c. 615 B.C.E. Marble, height 6 ft 4 ins (1.93 m). Metropolitan Museum of Art, New York (Fletcher Fund, 1932).

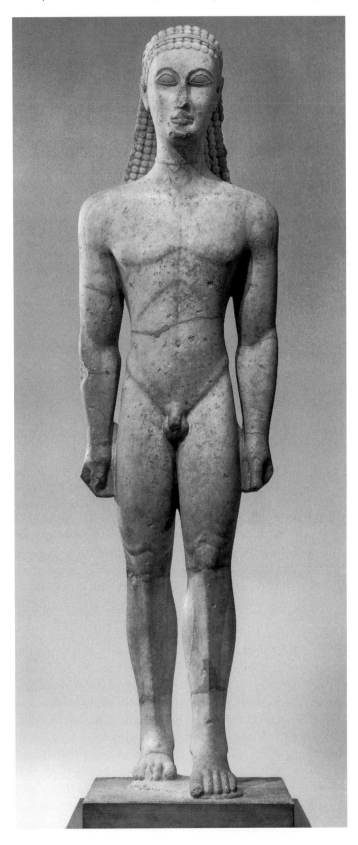

Profile

Michelangelo

Michelangelo (1475–1564) was a sculptor, painter, and architect and perhaps the greatest artist in a time of greatness. He lived during the Italian Renaissance, a period known for its creative activity, and his contemporaries included Leonardo da Vinci and Raphael (rah-fah-AYL). In art, the age's great achievement, Michelangelo led all others. He had a remarkable ability to concentrate his thoughts and energy. Often while working he would eat only a little bread, sleep on the floor or on a cot beside his unfinished painting or statue, and continue to wear the same clothes until his work was finished.

Michelangelo's birthplace, Caprese, Italy, a tiny village, belonged to the nearby city-state of Florence. He attended school in Florence, but his mind was on art, not on his studies. Even as a young child he was fascinated by painters and sculptors at work.

After gaining the patronage of Lorenzo de' Medici (MEH-dee-chee; Lorenzo the Magnificent), the young Michelangelo lived at the Medici Palace. One day Lorenzo saw him carving a marble faun's head and liked it so much that he took Michelangelo to live with him in his palace, treating the boy like a son. Lorenzo died in 1492, and Florence changed almost overnight. Savonarola (sah-voh-nah-ROHL-uh), a Dominican monk, rose to power and held the people under the spell of his sermons. Michelangelo feared Savonarola's influence and his art commissions dried up. Thus, he decided to leave Florence.

In 1496 Michelangelo traveled to Rome for the first time. There he gained a commission to carve a marble group showing the Virgin Mary supporting the dead Christ on her knees. This superb sculpture, known as the *Pietà* (pee-ay-TAH), won him wide fame. One of the few works signed by Michelangelo, it now stands in St. Peter's Basilica in Rome.

When he was twenty-six, Michelangelo returned to Florence. He was given an 18-foot (5.5-m) marble block that another sculptor had already started to carve. The block was nearly ruined. Michelangelo worked on it for more than two years. Out of its huge mass, and in spite of the difficulties caused by the first sculptor's work, he carved his youthful, courageous *David* (see Fig. 2.13).

Between 1508 and 1512 Michelangelo painted the vaulted ceiling of the Sistine Chapel in Rome (see Figs. **11.9** and **11.10**) with frescoes featuring hundreds of giant figures that made up his vision of the world's creation.

Painting and sculpture, however, did not absorb all of Michelangelo's genius. When Florence lay in danger of attack, he superintended the city's fortification. He was also an accomplished poet and wrote many sonnets (see Chapter 11). In his last years, he designed the dome of St. Peter's Basilica in Rome, which has been described as the finest architectural achievement of the Italian Renaissance. Michelangelo worked with many of the leaders of his time. He knew and competed with Leonardo da Vinci and Raphael. He died in 1564, at the age of eighty-nine, and was buried in the church of Santa Croce (kroh-chay) in Florence.

Discover more about Michelangelo at these sites: http://www.wga.hu/frames-e.html?/bio/m/michelan/biograph.html; http://graphics.stanford.edu/projects/mich/; and http://www.artcyclopedia.com/artists/michelangelo_buonarroti.html.

Rhythm, harmony, and variation constitute *repetition* in sculpture, as they did in the pictorial arts. In sculpture, though, we must look more carefully and closely to determine how the artist has employed these elements because they can occur more subtly. If we reduce a sculpture to its components of line and form, we begin to see how (as in music) rhythmic patterns—regular and irregular—occur. In Figure 2.5, for example, a regular rhythmic pattern exists in space as the eye moves from figure to figure and from leg to leg of the figures. We can also judge whether the components are consonant or dissonant. For instance, again in Figure 2.5, a sense of dynamics—action of movement—results from the dissonance of juxtaposing the strong triangles of the stances and groupings with the *biomorphic* lines of the human body. On the other hand, the unity of the curves in Figure 2.15 provides us with a consonant series of relationships. Finally, we can see how line and form appear in theme and variation. We noted the repetition of triangles in Figure 2.5. In contrast, the sculptor of Figure 2.15 varies his motif, the oval, as our eye moves from the child's face to the upper arm, the hand, and finally the cat's face.

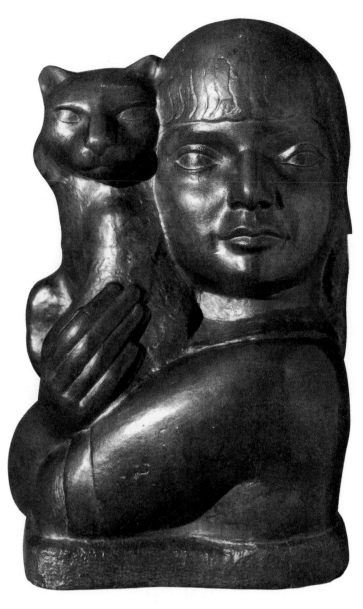

2.15 William Zorach, *Child with Cat*, 1926. Bronze, 17½ × 10 × 7½ ins (44 × 25 × 19 cm). Palmer Museum of Art, Pennsylvania State University.

OTHER FACTORS

Articulation

Important, also, in viewing sculpture is noting the manner by which we move from one element to the next. We call that manner of movement *articulation*, and it applies to sculpture, painting, photography, and all the other arts. As an example, let us step outside the arts to consider human speech. Sentences, phrases, and individual words constitute nothing more than sound syllables (vowels) articulated (joined together) by consonants. We understand what someone says because that individual articulates as he or she speaks. Let us put the five vowel sounds side by side: EH–EE–AH–O–OO. As yet we do not have a sentence. Articulate those vowels with consonants, and we have meaning: "Say, she must go too." The nature of an artwork depends on how the artist has repeated, varied, harmonized, and related its parts and how he or she has articulated the movement from one part to another— that is, how he or she indicates where one stops and the other begins.

Focal Area (Emphasis)

Sculptors, like painters or any other visual artists, must concern themselves with drawing the viewer's eye to those areas of their work central to what they wish to communicate. They must also provide the means by which the eye can move around the work. However, their task is more complicated, because they deal in three dimensions and they have little control over the direction from which one will first perceive the piece; the entire 360-degree view contributes to the total message communicated by the work.

The devices of convergence of line, encirclement, and color work for sculptors just as they do for painters. The encircling line in Figure **2.15** causes us, however we proceed to scan the work, to focus ultimately on the child's face.

One further device is available—movement, or kinesthesis. Sculptors have the option of placing moving objects in their work. Such an object immediately becomes a focal point of the sculpture. A mobile (see Fig. **2.6**) presents many ephemeral patterns of focus as it turns at the whim of the breezes.

Ephemeral

Ephemeral art has many different expressions and includes the works of the conceptualists, who insist that "art is an activity of change, of disorientation and shift, of violent discontinuity and mutability." Designed to be transitory, ephemeral art makes its statement and then, eventually, ceases to exist. Undoubtedly the largest work of sculpture ever designed was based on that concept. Christo and Jeanne-Claude's *Running Fence* (Fig. **2.16**) was an event and a process, as well as a sculptural work. In a sense such works are conceptual in that they call attention to the experience of art in opposition to its actual form. At the end of a two-week viewing period, *Running Fence* was dismantled completely.

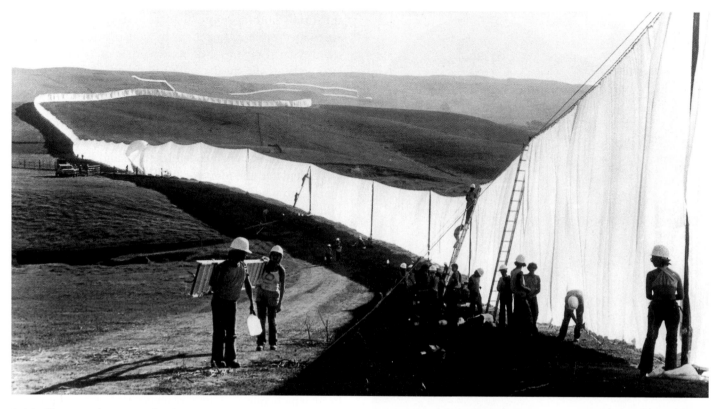

2.16 Christo and Jeanne-Claude, *Running Fence, Sonoma and Marin Counties, California*, 1972–6. Woven nylon fabric and steel cables, height 18 ft (5.49 m), length 24½ miles (39.2 km).

Found

This category of sculpture is exactly what its name implies. Very often natural objects, whether shaped by human hands or not, for some reason take on characteristics that stimulate aesthetic response. They become *objets d'art* (ahb-zheh dart) not because an artist puts them together (although an artist may combine found objects to create a work), but because an artist chooses to take them from their original surroundings and hold them up to the rest of us as vehicles for aesthetic communication. In other words, an "artist" decides that such an object says something aesthetically. As a result, it is presented in that vein.

Some may have concern about such a category, however, because it removes skill from the artistic process. As a result, objects such as driftwood and interesting rocks can assume perhaps an unwarranted place as art products or objects. Nonetheless, if a "found" object is altered in some way to produce an artwork, then the process probably falls under one of our previously noted methods, and the product can be termed an artwork in the fullest sense of the word.

SENSE STIMULI

TOUCH

We can touch sculpture and feel its roughness or its smoothness, its coolness or perhaps its warmth. Even if museum regulations prohibit us from touching a specific work, we can see the surface texture and translate the image of that texture into an imaginary tactile sensation. Any work of sculpture cries out to be touched, and tactility plays a greater role in our response to sculpture than to other arts.

TEMPERATURE AND AGE

Color in sculpture stimulates our response by utilizing the same universal symbols as it does in paintings, photographs, and prints. Reds, oranges, and yellows stimulate sensations of warmth; blues and greens, sensations of coolness. In sculpture, color can result from the conscious choice of the artist, either in the selection of mate-

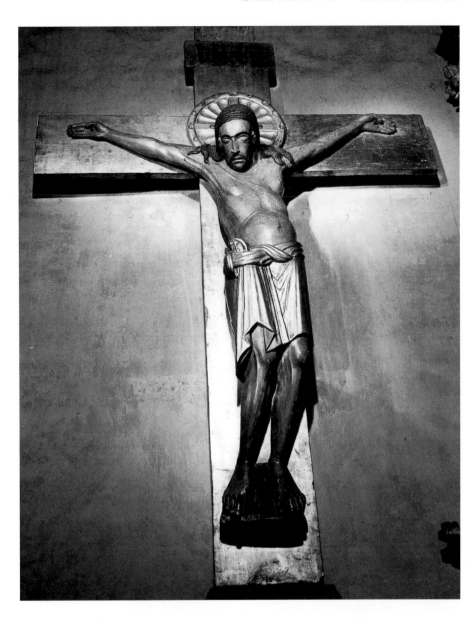

2.17 *Gero Crucifix*, Cologne Cathedral, c. 975–1000. Wood, height 6 ft 2 ins (1.87 m).

rial or in the selection of the pigment with which the material is painted. Or, as we indicated earlier, color may result from the artist's choice to let nature color the work through wind, water, sun, and so forth.

This weathering effect, of course, creates very interesting patterns, but in addition it gives the sculpture the attribute not only of space but also of time, because the work will change as nature performs its wonders. A copper sculpture early in its existence will be a different work, a different set of stimuli, from what it will be five, ten, or twenty years hence. This is not entirely accidental; artists choose copper knowing what weathering will do to it. They obviously cannot predict the exact nature of the weathering or the exact hues of the sculpture at any given time in the future, but such predictability is irrelevant.

The effects of age on a sculpture may shape our response. Ancient objects possess a great deal of charm and character. A wooden icon such as that in Figure **2.17** might have extra emotional impact because of the effects of age on its surfaces.

DYNAMICS

Line, form, and juxtaposition create dynamics in works of sculpture. The activity of a sculpture tends to be heightened because of its three-dimensionality. In addition, we experience a certain sense of dynamics as we move around them. Although we move, rather than the sculpture, we perceive and respond to what seems to be movement in the work itself.

2.18 Egyptian statuary. Metropolitan Museum of Art, New York (Gift of Edward S. Harkness).

SIZE

Because sculpture has mass—that is, takes up space and has density—our senses respond to the weight and/or the scale of a work. Egyptian sculpture, which is solid, stable, and oversized (Fig. **2.18**), has mass and proportion as well as line and form that make it appear heavier than a non-Egyptian work of basically the same size, such as Figure **2.8**. Moreover, the very same treatment of texture, lifelikeness, and subject elicits a completely different sense response if one work is 3 feet (1 m) and another 130 feet (39.6 m) tall.

Exaggerated size and anatomical form, for symbolic effect, may also be seen in a colossal bust of Emperor Constantine (see Fig. **10.14**), a gigantic representation—the head is over 8 feet (2.4 m) tall—exhibiting a stark and expressive realism countered by caricatured, ill-proportioned intensity. This likeness is not a portrait of Constantine—it represents the artist's view both of Constantine's presentation of himself as emperor and of the office of emperor itself.

Early in the chapter we mentioned the possibility of an artist's disguising the material from which she makes the work. Marble polished to appear like skin, or wood polished to look like fabric, can change the appearance of mass of a sculpture and significantly affect our response to it.

We must also consider the purpose of disguising material. For example, does the detailing of the sculpture reflect a formal concern for design, or does it reflect a concern for the greatest lifelikeness? Examine the cloth represented in *The Burghers of Calais* (see Fig. **2.2**) and the Chartres saints (see Fig. **2.4**). In both cases the sculptor has disguised the material by making stone appear to be cloth. In Figure **2.2** the cloth is detailed to reflect reality. It drapes as real cloth would drape, and as a result its effect in the composition depends upon the subtlety of line characteristic of draped cloth. However, in Figure **2.4** the sculptor has depicted cloth in such a way that its effect in the design is not dependent upon how cloth drapes, but rather upon the decorative function of line as the sculptor wishes to use it. Real cloth cannot drape as the sculptor has depicted it. Nor, probably, did the sculptor care. The main concern here was for decoration, for using line (that looks like cloth) to emphasize the rhythm of the work. When sculpture de-emphasizes lifelikeness in order to draw attention to the substance from which it is made, we call it *glyptic* (glihp-tihk). Glyptic sculpture emphasizes the material from which the work is created and usually retains the fundamental geometric qualities of that material.

LIGHTING AND ENVIRONMENT

One final factor that significantly influences our sense response to a sculpture, a factor that we very often do not consider and that remains outside the control of the artist unless he or she personally supervises every exhibition of the work, is lighting and environment. As we will see in Chapter 5, light plays a basic role in our perception of and thereby our response to three-dimensional objects. The direction and number of sources of light striking a three-dimensional work can change the entire composition of that work. Whether the work stands outdoors or indoors, the method of lighting affects the overall presentation. Diffuse room lighting allows us to see all aspects of a sculpture without external influence. However, if the work rests in a darkened room illuminated from particular directions by spotlights, it achieves greater dramatic quality and affects our response accordingly.

The question of where and how a work is exhibited also contributes to our response. The response to a sculpture placed in a carefully designed environment that screens our vision from distracting or competing visual stimuli will change if the sculpture is exhibited among other works amid the bustle of a public park, for instance.

THINKING CRITICALLY

- Examine Giacometti's *Man Pointing* (Fig. **2.11**) and compare it with the archaic Greek kouros in Figure **2.14**. What visions of humankind do you find in each work and how are they similar or different?

Do a basic analysis of a work of sculpture by using the topics in this chapter as an outline. Begin with the following:

- Reaction. Does the artist present clues in the work as to any response he or she might seek to achieve? In what ways does the artist stimulate emotional and intellectual response? What was your response and what means does the artist employ to evoke it?

Now build a comparative analysis by choosing two or more works and detailing how they reflect specific qualities described in the chapter. For example:

- Dimensionality. How does the dimensionality of Maillol's *The Mediterranean* (Fig. **2.12**) change your perception as compared with the "Three Goddesses" from the Parthenon (Fig. **2.10**)? What is the dimensionality of each work? How does that dimensionality contribute to each work's overall design and effect? Try to imagine the original location of the *Three Goddesses* as you frame your analysis.

- Method of execution. What method of execution is employed by Michelangelo (*David*; Fig. **2.13**) and Bologna (*Mercury*; Fig. **2.8**)? How do the methods of execution and materials create a final effect, and how do those considerations differ in each work?

- Focal areas. Compare the west portal jamb statues from Chartres Cathedral (Fig. **2.4**) with the *Gero Crucifix* (Fig. **2.17**) in terms of how the areas of interest work to move the eye around the sculptures. Which areas are primary and which are secondary?

CYBER STUDY

BUILT SCULPTURE:
—Mary Mead, *Advancing Slowly*
http://www.decordova.org/decordova/sculp_park/mead.html

CAST SCULPTURE:
—Magdalena Abakanowicz, *Puellae* (Girls)
http://www.nga.gov/cgi-bin/pinfo?Object=108121+0+none

CHAPTER THREE

ARCHITECTURE

IMPORTANT TERMS

Arcade Several arches placed side by side.

Bearing-wall A system of architectural structure in which the walls support themselves.

Cantilever An overhanging beam or floor supported at only one end.

Context The environment surrounding a work of architecture.

Ferroconcrete Concrete cast in place with metal reinforcement embedded in the concrete.

Function The basic purpose of a building.

Groin vault Tunnel vaults meeting at right angles.

Post-and-lintel An architectural structure consisting of horizontal beams laid across open spaces between vertical supports.

Prestressed concrete Concrete using metal rods and wires under stress or tension to cause structural forces to flow in predetermined directions.

Tunnel vault Arches placed back to back to enclose space.

Scale The relationship of the size of a building to the human form.

Skeleton frame A system of architectural structure in which a framework supports the building and the walls are attached to the frame.

FORMAL AND TECHNICAL QUALITIES

Every street in our towns represents a museum of ideas and engineering. The houses, churches, and commercial buildings we pass every day reflect appearances and techniques almost as old as the human race itself. We go in and out of these buildings, often without taking much notice of them, and yet they frequently dictate actions that we can or cannot take.

In approaching architecture as an art, we really cannot separate aesthetic properties from practical or functional ones. In other words, architects first have a particular function to achieve in their building. That function represents their principal concern. The aesthetics of the building remain important, but they must be tailored to overall practical considerations. For example, when architects set about designing a 110-story skyscraper, they are locked into an aesthetic form that will be vertical rather than horizontal in emphasis. They may attempt to counter verticality with strong horizontal elements, but the physical fact that the building will be taller than wide forms the basis from which the architects must work. Their structural design must take into account all the practical needs that are implicit in the building's use. Nonetheless, considerable room for aesthetics remains. The treatment of space, texture, line, and proportion can give us buildings of unique style and character—or of unimaginative sameness.

Architecture is often described as the art of sheltering. To consider it as such we must use the term "sheltering" very broadly. Obviously types of architecture exist within which people do not dwell and under which they cannot escape the rain. Architecture encompasses more than buildings. So, we can consider architecture as the art of sheltering people both physically and spiritually from the raw elements of the unaltered world.

In this chapter, as in previous ones, attention focuses predominantly on technical, definitional matters. Understanding these basics gives us tools to get more out of experiencing architectural structures and pleasure in communicating our reactions to others. Later in the text (Chapters 9–13), the history of architecture unfolds and some of its meaning for humankind emerges.

As well as the art of sheltering, architecture comprises design of three-dimensional space to create practical enclosure. Its basic forms include residences, places of worship, and commercial buildings. Each can take innumerable shapes, from single-family residences to the ornate palaces of kings to high-rise condominiums and apartments. The categorization of architectural forms can also be expanded to include bridges, walls, monuments, and so forth.

In examining the technical qualities of a work of architecture we will limit ourselves to ten fundamental elements: structure, building materials, line, repetition, balance, scale, proportion, context, space, and climate.

STRUCTURE

Although many systems of construction or structural support exist, the text that follows treats only a few: *post-and-lintel, arch, cantilever, bearing-wall,* and *skeleton frame.*

Post-and-Lintel

Post-and-lintel structures consist of horizontal beams (lintels) laid across the open spaces between vertical supports (posts) traditionally of stone. They are similar to *post-and-beam* structures, in which series of vertical posts

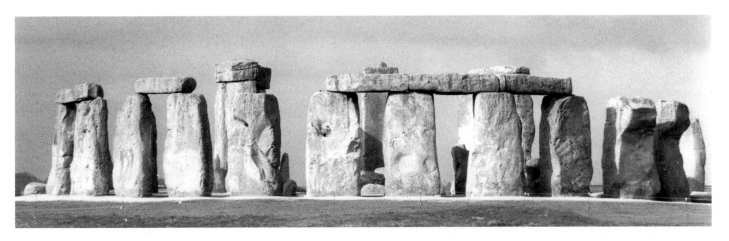

3.1 Stonehenge, Salisbury Plain, England, c. 1800–1400 B.C.E.

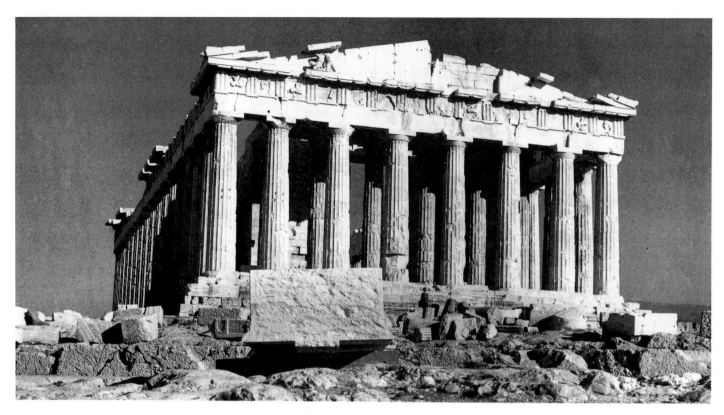

3.2 Parthenon, Acropolis, Athens, 448–432 B.C.E.

join horizontal members, traditionally of wood. Nails, pegs, or lap joints hold together the wooden members of post-and-beam structures.

The lack of *tensile strength* in their fundamental material, stone, limits post-and-lintel structures in their ability to define space. Tensile strength is the ability of a material to withstand bending. If a slab of stone that is supported at each end bridges an opening, it can span only a narrow space before it cracks in the middle and falls to the ground. However, stone has great *compressive strength*—the ability to withstand compression or crushing.

A very early example of a post-and-lintel structure is Stonehenge, that ancient and mysterious religious configuration of giant stones in Great Britain (Fig. **3.1**). The ancient Greeks refined this system to high elegance; the most familiar of their post-and-lintel creations is the Parthenon in Athens (Fig. **3.2**).

The Greek post-and-lintel structure has served as a *prototype* for buildings throughout the world and down the centuries. One of its most interesting aspects rests in the treatment of *columns* and *capitals*. Figure **3.3** shows the three basic Greek orders—*Doric*, *Ionic*, and *Corinthian*. These represent only some of the styles possible—column capitals can be as varied as the imagination of the architect who has designed them. Primarily they act as a transition for the eye as it moves from post to lintel.

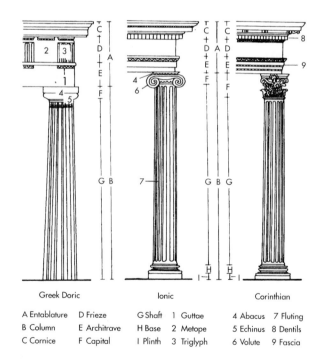

A Entablature	D Frieze	G Shaft	1 Guttae	4 Abacus	7 Fluting
B Column	E Architrave	H Base	2 Metope	5 Echinus	8 Dentils
C Cornice	F Capital	I Plinth	3 Triglyph	6 Volute	9 Fascia

3.3 Greek columns and capitals: (*left*) Doric, (*center*) Ionic, (*right*) Corinthian.

The columns themselves also vary in shape and detail. A final element, present in some columns, is *fluting*—vertical ridges cut into the column.

Arch

The arch represents a second type of architectural structure. Post-and-lintel structure limits the amount of unencumbered space it can cross, but the arch can define large spaces because its stresses transfer outward from the center (the *keystone*) to its legs (piers, columns, or door and window jambs). It does not depend solely on the tensile strength of its material.

Many different styles of arch exist, some of which appear in Figure 3.4. The characteristics of different arches may be exploited for structural as well as for decorative functions. As an example, examine St. Alban's Cathedral (Fig. 3.5), built in the English Norman style. This style of building, with its accent on rounded arches, was loosely based on the Classical architecture of Roman times. The transfer of stress from the center of an arch outward and downward dictates the need for a strong support to keep the legs from caving outward. Such a reinforcement is called a *buttress* (Figs. 3.6 and 3.7). The designers of Gothic cathedrals sought to achieve a sense of lightness. Since stone comprised their basic building material, they recognized that some system had to be developed that would overcome the bulk of a stone buttress. Therefore they developed a system of buttresses that accomplished structural ends but were light in appearance: thus *flying buttresses* (of which Fig. 3.6 shows fine examples).

Several arches placed side by side form an *arcade* (Fig. 3.8). Arches placed back to back to enclose space form a *tunnel vault* (Fig. 3.9). When two tunnel vaults intersect at right angles, they form a *groin vault* (Fig. 3.10). The protruding masonry indicating diagonal juncture of arches in a groin vault constitutes *rib vaulting* (Figs. 3.11 and 3.12).

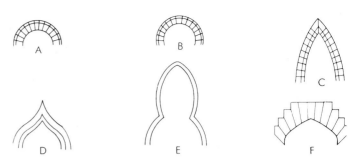

3.4 The arch: (A) round (Roman), (B) horseshoe (Moorish), (C) lancet (pointed, Gothic), (D) ogee, (E) trefoil, (F) Tudor.

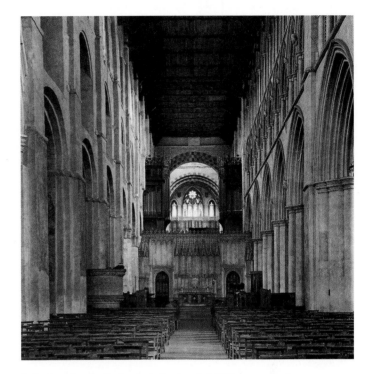

3.5 St. Alban's Cathedral, England, 1077, nave, facing east.

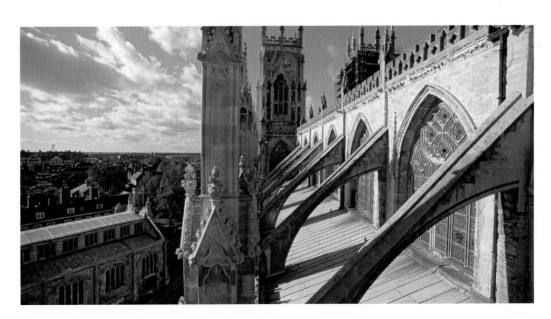

3.6 Detail of the arcs and buttresses of York Minster, the cathedral of Saint Peter, built between the 13th and 14th centuries, with work continuing into the 15th century.

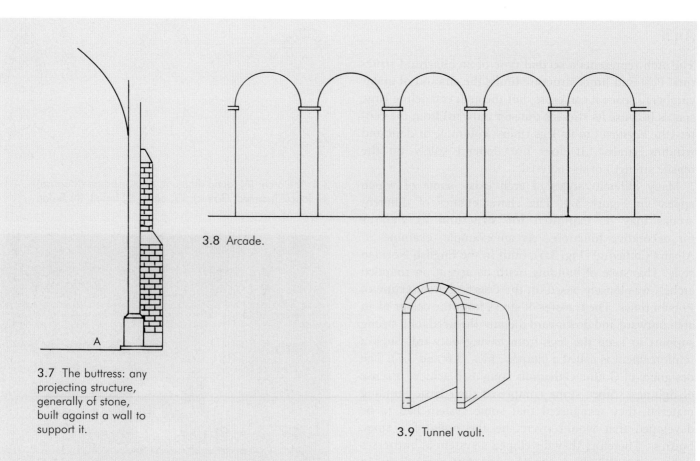

3.8 Arcade.

3.7 The buttress: any projecting structure, generally of stone, built against a wall to support it.

3.9 Tunnel vault.

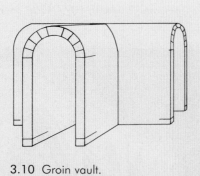

3.10 Groin vault.

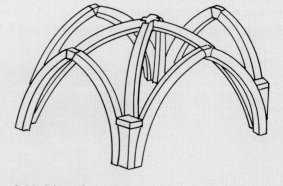

3.11 Rib vault.

When arches join at the top, with their legs forming a circle, a *dome* results (Figs. **3.13** and **3.14**). Through intersecting arches, this allows for more expansive, freer space within the structure. If the structures that support the dome form a circle, they create a circular building such as the Pantheon in Rome. To permit squared space beneath a dome, the architect needs to transfer weight and stress through the use of *pendentives* (Fig. **3.15**).

The problems architects face in utilizing one form or another for structural support are illustrated by the story of St. Paul's Cathedral, London. Its dome measures 112 feet (34 m) in diameter and stands 365 feet (110 m) tall at the top of the cross. The lantern and cross alone weigh 700 tons (711 tonnes), while the dome and its superstructure weigh in at 64,000 tons (65,000 tonnes). In designing this cathedral, Wren faced seemingly insurmountable problems of supporting such a tremendous load. His ingenious solution turns the dome into a timber shell covered in lead, with the actual weight of the dome only a fraction of what it would have been in stone. This allowed Wren to create a wonderful silhouette on the outside and to have a high ceiling in the interior (Fig. **3.16**).

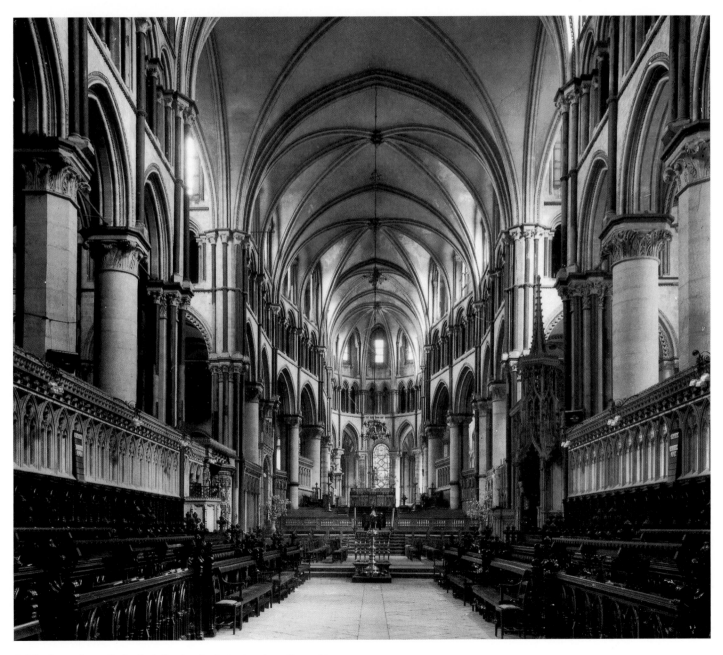

3.12 Canterbury Cathedral, England, choir showing rib vaulting.

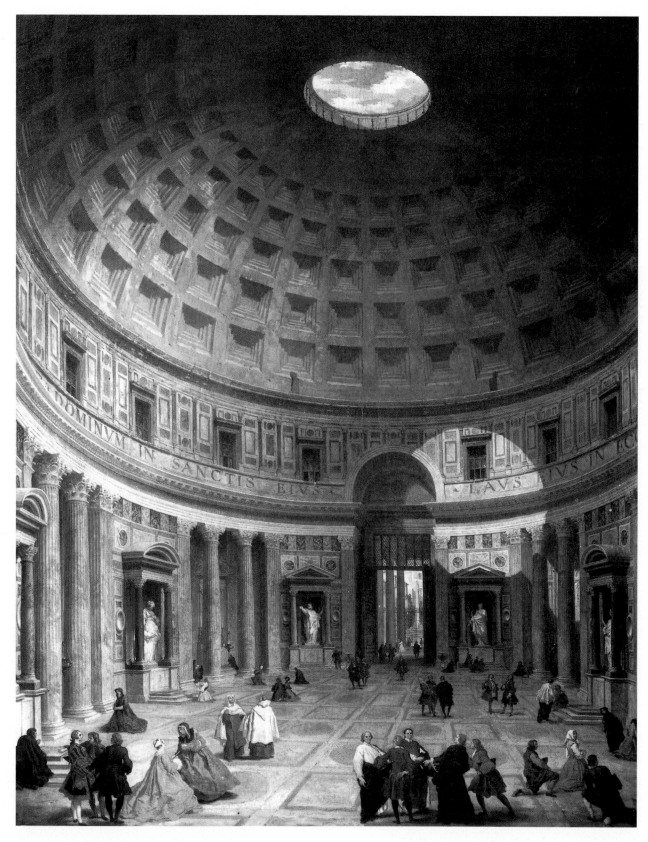

3.13 Giovanni Paolo Panini, *The Interior of the Pantheon, Rome*, c. 1734/5. Oil on canvas, 50½ × 39 ins (128 × 99 cm). National Gallery of Art, Washington, D.C. (Samuel H. Kress Collection).

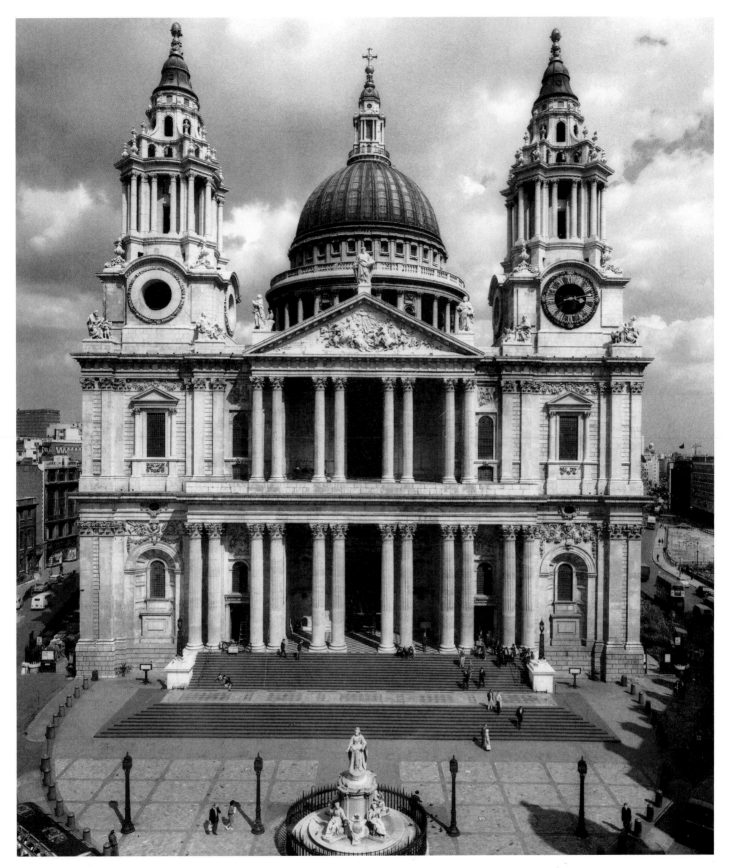

3.14 Christopher Wren, St. Paul's Cathedral, London, west façade, 1675–1710.

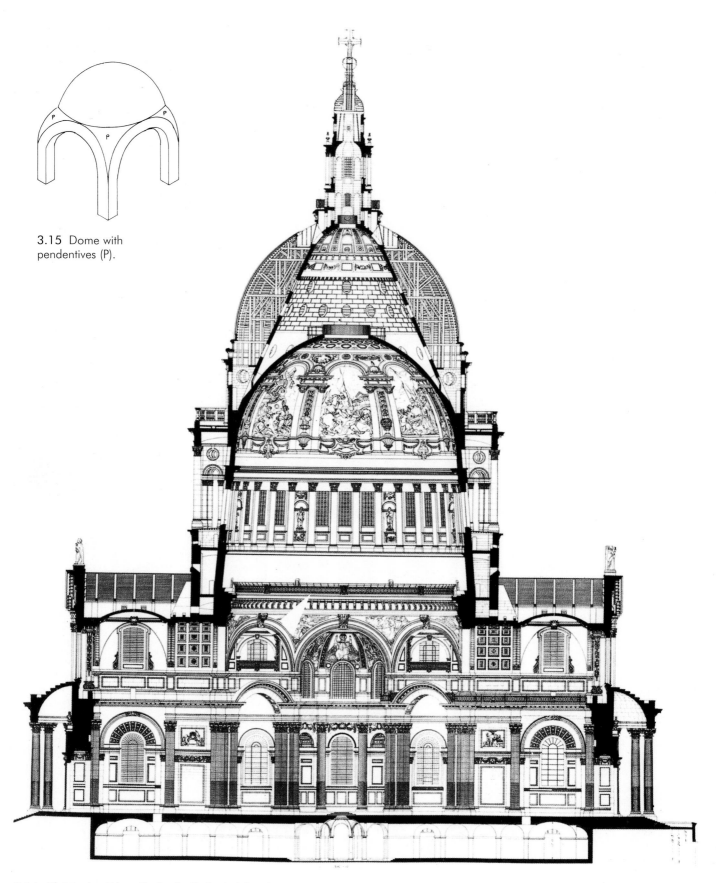

3.15 Dome with pendentives (P).

3.16 Christopher Wren, St. Paul's Cathedral, London, cross-section.

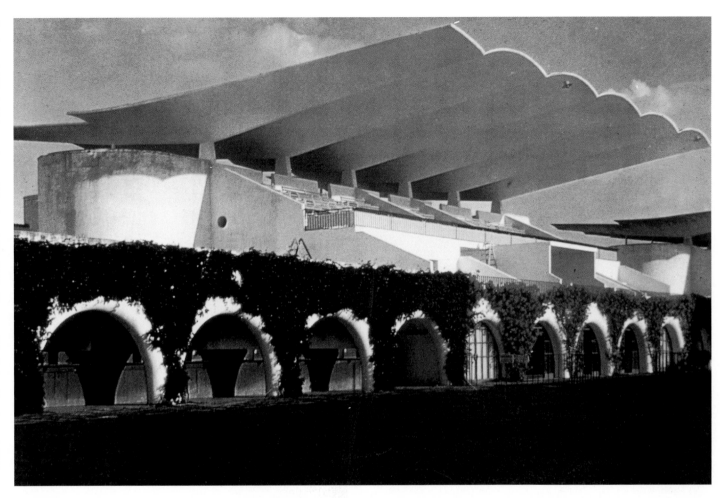

3.18 Eduardo Torroja, Zarzuela Race Track Grandstand, Madrid, 1935.

Cantilever

A cantilever is an overhanging beam or floor supported at only one end (Fig. 3.17). Although not a twentieth-century innovation—many nineteenth-century barns in the central and eastern parts of the US employed it—the cantilever emerged dramatically with the introduction of modern materials such as steel beams and *prestressed concrete*. The possibilities of cantilever as a structure reveal themselves in Eduardo Torroja's (tohr-ROH-hah) soaring Zarzuela Race Track Grandstand (Fig. 3.18). A fascinating example of this structural system emerges in Frank Lloyd Wright's Fallingwater (see Fig. 3.27). In the case of the Zarzuela Grandstand, we see structural transparency (when an architect expresses a building's structure outwardly as opposed to hiding it beneath a façade). Here, structural transparency allows the architect to sculpt a more dynamic form and, thus, to enhance our reaction to the work. In the case of Fallingwater, cantilever structure allows the architect to mimic the natural forms with which he desires the building to blend.

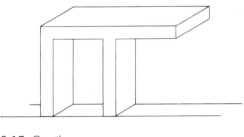

3.17 Cantilever.

Bearing-Wall

In this system, the wall supports itself, the floors, and the roof. Log cabins exemplify bearing-wall construction; so do solid masonry buildings, in which the walls are the structure. In variations of bearing-wall construction, such as Figure 3.36, the wall material is continuous—that is,

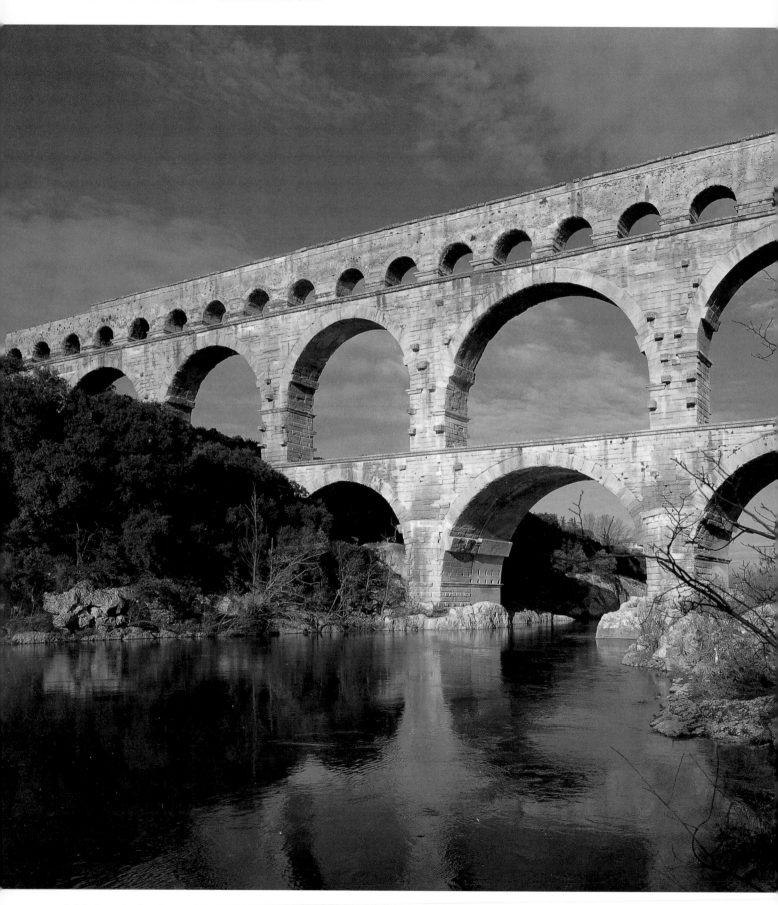

3.19 Pont du Gard, near Nîmes, France, 1st century B.C.E.

not jointed or pieced together—in a system called *monolithic construction.*

Skeleton Frame

Here a framework supports the building. The walls attach to the frame, forming an exterior skin. When skeleton framing utilizes wood, as in house construction, we call the technique *balloon construction.* When metal forms the frame, as in skyscrapers, we call it *steel-cage construction.*

BUILDING MATERIALS

Historic and contemporary architectural practices and traditions often center on specific materials, and to understand architecture further, we need to note a few.

Stone

The use of stone as a material turns us back to post-and-lintel systems and Figures **3.1** and **3.2.** When stone conjoins with mortar—for example, in arch construction—that combination results in *masonry construction.* The most obvious example of masonry, however, remains the brick wall. Masonry construction utilizes stones, bricks, or blocks joined together with mortar, one on top of the other, to provide standard, structural, weight-bearing walls (Fig. **3.19**). The pressures that play on the joints between blocks and mortar and the foundation on which they rest limit what can be accomplished with masonry. However, when one considers that office buildings such as Chicago's Monadnock Building (Fig. **3.20**) are skyscrapers and that their walls consist solely of masonry—no hidden steel reinforces the walls—it becomes obvious that this elemental combination of stone and mortar has numerous applications.

Concrete

The use of concrete stands central to much contemporary architectural practice, but it had significance as far back in the past as ancient Rome. The Pantheon (see Fig. **3.13**) comprises a masterful structure of concrete with a massive concrete dome, 142 feet (43 m) in diameter, resting on concrete walls 20 feet (6 m) thick. In contemporary architecture, we find *precast concrete* (concrete cast in place using wooden forms around a steel framework). *Ferroconcrete (reinforced concrete)* has metal reinforcement embedded in the concrete. Such a technique combines the tensile strength of the metal with the compressive strength of the concrete. *Prestressed* and *post-tensioned concrete* use metal rods and wires under stress or tension to cause structural forces to flow in predetermined directions. Both are extremely versatile building materials.

Wood

Whether in balloon framing or in laminated beaming, wood has played a pivotal role in architecture, especially in the United States. As new technologies emerge to make engineered beams from what was once scrapwood, it seems that it will remain a viable building product—and being a renewable resource, it also has a less negative impact on the environment than do many other materials. In domestic architecture dimensional lumber remains predominant as framing, even though it costs more than steel. This results largely from the conservatism of the building trade, which remains reluctant to adopt new techniques or invest in tools to employ other materials.

Steel

Steel gives almost limitless possibilities for construction. Its introduction into the nineteenth-century industrial age forever changed style and scale in architecture. We noted steel-cage and cantilever construction earlier. *Suspension construction* in structures such as bridges, superdomes, and aerial walkways has carried architects to the safe limits of space spansion—and sometimes beyond. The *geodesic dome* (Fig. **3.21**), invented by an American architect, Richard Buckminster Fuller, uses materials in a unique way. Consisting of a network of metal rods and hexagonal plates, the geodesic dome provides a light, inexpensive, yet strong and easily assembled building.

LINE, REPETITION, AND BALANCE

Line and repetition perform the same compositional functions in architecture as in painting and sculpture. In his Marin County Courthouse in California (Fig. **3.22**), Frank Lloyd Wright takes a single motif—the arc—and varies only its size, repeating it almost endlessly with dynamic and fascinating results.

Christopher Wren, the architect of St. Paul's Cathedral (see Figs. **3.14** and **3.16**), also designed one of the façades of Hampton Court Palace outside of London, England (Fig. **3.23**), in the classically oriented style of the English Baroque (see Chapter 11). Wren's use of line, repetition, and balance results in a sophisticated visual design and engaging perceptual experience. Note first the symmetrical façade. The outward wing at the far left of the photograph duplicates at the right. In the center of the building

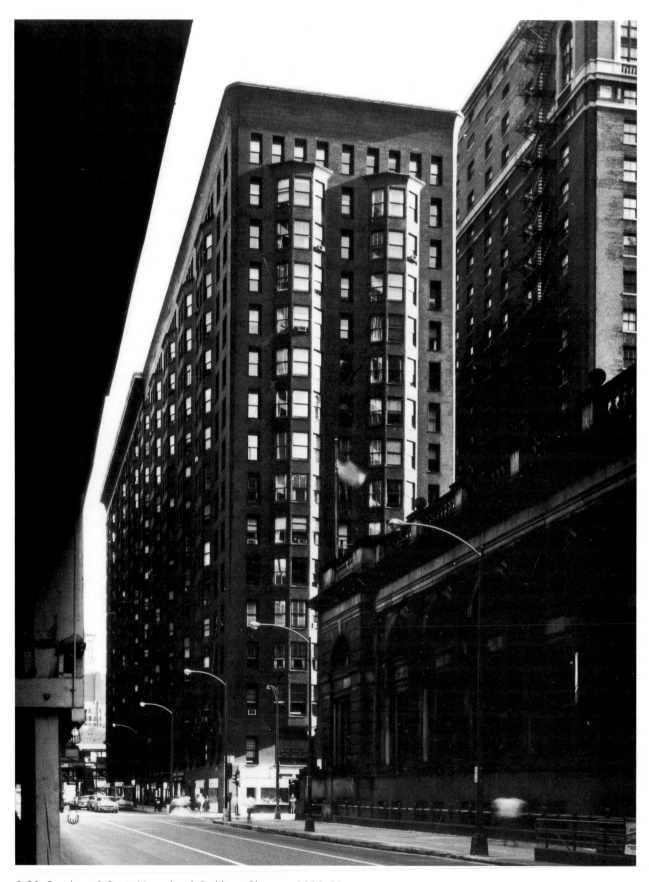

3.20 Burnham & Root, Monadnock Building, Chicago, 1889–91.

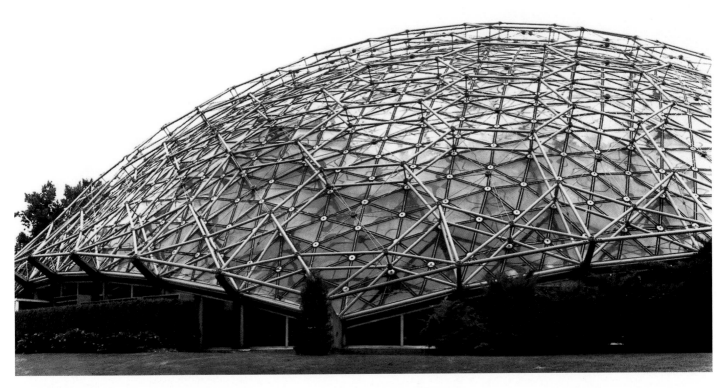

3.21 Richard Buckminster Fuller, geodesic dome, Climatron, St. Louis, Missouri, 1959.

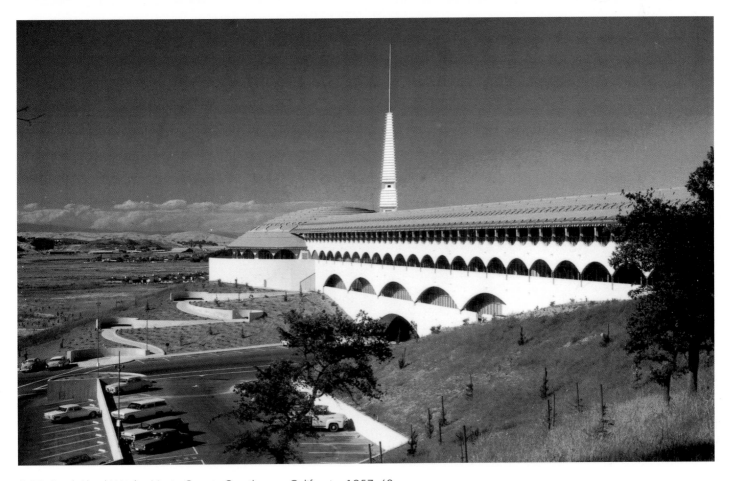

3.22 Frank Lloyd Wright, Marin County Courthouse, California, 1957–63.

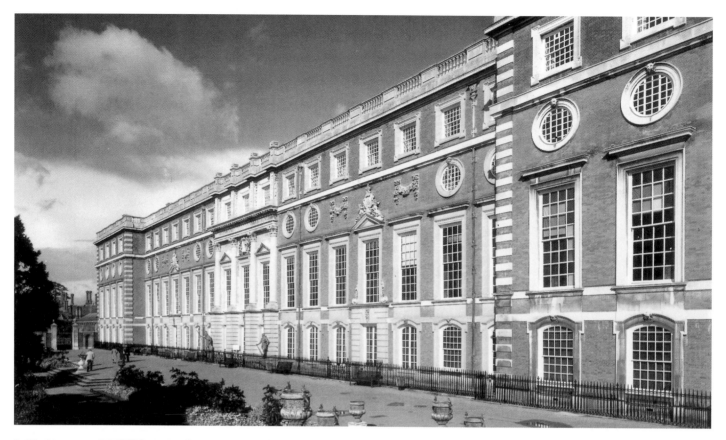

3.23 Hampton Court Palace, England, Wren façade, 1689.

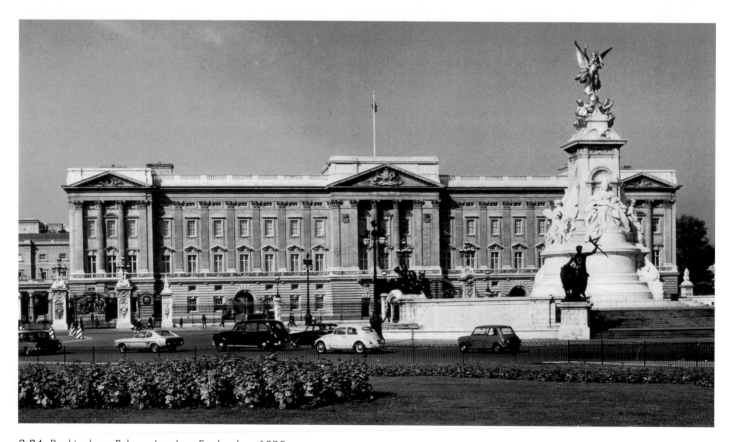

3.24 Buckingham Palace, London, England, c. 1825.

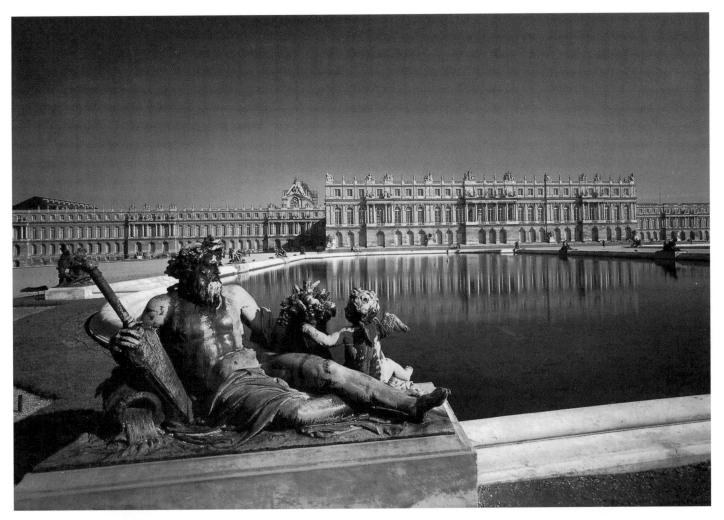

3.25 Louis Le Vau and Jules Hardouin-Mansart, Palace of Versailles, France, 1669–85.

four attached columns surround three windows. The middle window forms the exact center of the design, with mirror-image repetition on each side. Above the main windows appear a series of relief sculptures, *pediments* (triangular casings), and circular windows. Return to the main row of windows at the left border of the picture and count toward the center. The outer wing contains four windows; then seven windows, then the central three; then seven; and finally four. Patterns of threes and sevens are very popular in architecture and carry religious and mythological symbolism. Wren has established a pattern of four in the outer wing, three in the center, and then repeated it within each of the seven-window groups to create three additional patterns of three! How could he create patterns of three with only seven windows? First, locate the center window of the seven. It has a pediment and a relief sculpture above it. On each side of this window are three windows (a total of six) without pediments. So, we have two groupings of three windows each. A cir-

cular window rests above each of the outside four windows. The window on each side of the center window does not have a circular one above it. Rather, it has a relief sculpture, the presence of which joins these two windows with the center window to give us our third grouping of three. Line, repetition, and balance in this façade form a marvelous perceptual exercise and experience.

Buckingham Palace, London (Fig. **3.24**), and the Palace of Versailles (Fig. **3.25**) illustrate different treatments of line and repetition. Buckingham Palace uses straight lines almost exclusively, with repetition of rectilinear and triangular form. Like Hampton Court Palace, it exhibits *fenestration* groupings of threes and sevens, and the building itself is symmetrical and divided by three pedimented, porticolike protrusions. Notice how three major pediments break the predominantly horizontal line of the building while the window pediments and the verticality of the attached columns give interest and contrast across its full length.

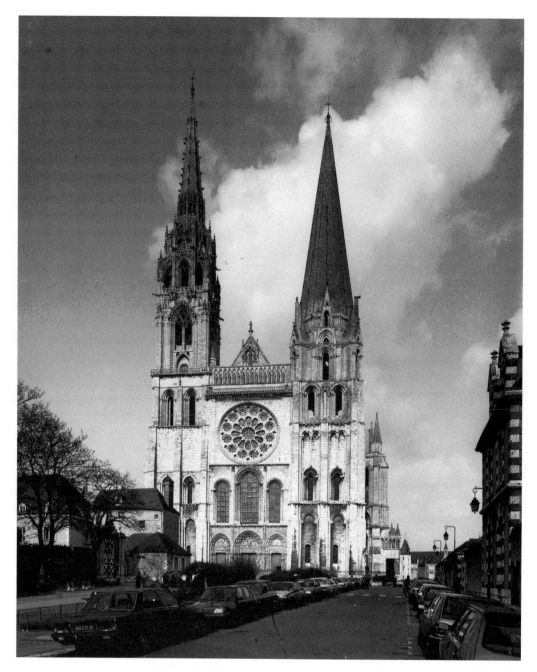

3.26 Chartres Cathedral, France, exterior, 1145–1220.

Compare Buckingham Palace with the Palace of Versailles, in which repetition occurs in groupings of threes and fives. Contrast is provided by juxtaposition and repetition of curved lines in the arched windows and Baroque statuary. Notice how the horizontal shape of the building, despite three porticoes, remains virtually undisturbed, in contrast with that of Buckingham Palace.

SCALE AND PROPORTION

Scale in architecture refers to a building's size and the relationship of the building and its decorative elements to the human form. Scale may range from the intimacy of a domestic bungalow to the towering power of a skyscraper such as the Petronas Towers (see Fig. 3.41). Proportion, or the relationship of individual elements to each other, also plays an important role in a building's visual effect.

In this case, the elements of concern are the parts of the building in juxtaposition and their intended effects—such as the relationships just discussed relative to Hampton Court Palace. Proportion and scale form tools with which the architect can create straightforward or deceptive relationships. We must decide how these elements are used and to what effect. In addition, proportion in many buildings is mathematical: the relationships of one part to another often form ratios of three to two, one to two, one to three, and so on. Discovering such relationships in a building provides one of the fascinating challenges whenever we encounter a work of architecture.

CONTEXT

An architectural design should take into account its context, or environment. In many cases context is essential to the statement made by the design. For example, Chartres Cathedral (Fig. **3.26**) sits at the center of and on the highest point in the town of Chartres. Its placement at that particular location had a purpose for the medieval arti-

sans and clerics responsible for its design. The centrality of the cathedral to the community was an essential statement of the centrality of the church in the life of the medieval community. Context also has a psychological bearing on scale. A skyscraper in the midst of skyscrapers has great mass but does not appear as massive as it would in isolation. A cathedral, alongside a skyscraper, looks relatively small in scale. However, one standing at the center of a community of small houses appears quite the opposite.

Context is also important in terms of the design of line, form, and texture relative to the physical environment. Sometimes the environment can be shaped according to the compositional qualities of the building, during or after its construction. Perhaps the best illustration of that principle is Louis XIV's palace at Versailles, whose formal symmetry reflects in the design of thousands of acres around it.

On the other hand, a building may be designed so as to reflect the natural characteristics of its environment. Frank Lloyd Wright's Fallingwater, in Pennsylvania (Fig. **3.27**), illustrates this principle. Many architects have

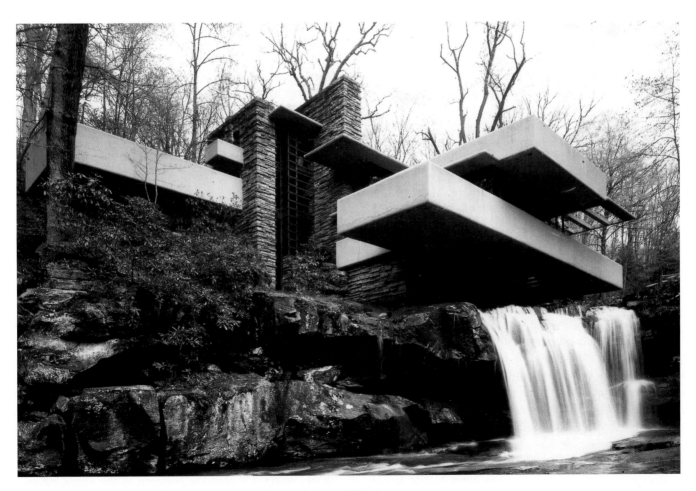

3.27 Frank Lloyd Wright, Fallingwater, Bear Run, Pennsylvania, 1936–7.

Profile

Frank Lloyd Wright

Frank Lloyd Wright (1867–1959) pioneered ideas in architecture far ahead of his time and became probably the most influential architect of the twentieth century. Born in Richland Center, Wisconsin, Wright grew up under strong influences of his clergyman father's love of Bach and Beethoven. He entered the University of Wisconsin at fifteen, forced to study engineering because the school had no architecture program.

In 1887 Wright took a job as a draughtsman in Chicago and, the next year, joined the firm of Adler and Sullivan. In short order Wright became Louis Sullivan's chief assistant. As Sullivan's assistant Wright handled most of the firm's designing of houses. Deep in debt, Wright moonlighted by designing for private clients on his own. When Sullivan objected, Wright left the firm to set up his own private practice.

As an independent architect, Wright led the way in a style of architecture called the Prairie school. Houses designed in this style have low-pitched roofs and strong horizontal lines reflecting the flat landscape of the American prairie. These houses also reflect Wright's philosophy that interior and exterior spaces blend together.

In 1904 Wright designed the strong, functional, Larkin Building in Buffalo, New York, and in 1906 the Unity Temple in Oak Park, Illinois. After traveling to Japan and Europe, he returned to America in 1911 to build a house on his grandfather's farm, Taliesin (Ta-lee-AY-zuhn), which is Welsh for "shining brow." In 1916 Wright designed the Imperial Hotel in Tokyo, floating the structure on an underlying sea of mud. As a consequence, when the catastrophic earthquake of 1923 occurred, the hotel suffered very little damage.

The Great Depression of the 1930s greatly curtailed new building projects, and Wright spent his time writing and lecturing. In 1932 he established the Taliesin Fellowship, a school in which students learned by working with building materials and problems of design and construction. In winter the school moved from Wisconsin to Taliesin West, a desert camp near Phoenix, Arizona.

The mid-1930s represented a period of intense creative output for Wright, and some of his most famous designs occurred during those years. What is perhaps his most dramatic project, the Kaufmann House—Fallingwater—in Bear Run, Pennsylvania (Fig. 3.27), emerged in 1936–7. Another famous project during this period was the S. C. Johnson and Son Administration Building in Racine, Wisconsin.

Two other significant buildings, among many, came later. The Solomon R. Guggenheim Museum (see Fig. 3.39) began in 1942 and completed in 1957, and the Marin County Courthouse, California (see Fig. 3.22), followed over the period 1957–63.

Wright's work was always controversial, and he lived a flamboyant life full of personal tragedy and financial difficulty. Married three times, he had seven children and died in Phoenix, Arizona on April 9, 1959.

Find out more about Frank Lloyd Wright at: www.pbs.org/flw/buildings/ and www.greatbuildings.com.

---

advanced such an idea, especially in residences where large expanses of glass allow us to feel a part of the outside while we are inside. The interior decoration of such houses often takes as its theme the colors, textures, lines, and forms of the environment surrounding the home. Natural fibers, earth tones, delicate wooden furniture, pictures that reflect the surroundings, large open spaces—together they form the core of the design, selection, and placement of nearly every item in the home, from walls to furniture to silverware.

SPACE

It seems almost absurdly logical to state that architecture must concern space—for what else, by definition, is architecture? However, the world teems with examples of architectural design that have not met that need. Design of space essentially means the design and flow of contiguous spaces relative to function. Take, for example, a sports arena. Of primary concern is the space necessary for the sports that are intended to occupy the building.

Will it play host to basketball, hockey, track, football, or baseball? Each of these sports places a design restriction on the architect, and curious results occur when functions not intended by the design move into its parameters. When the Brooklyn Dodgers moved to Los Angeles, they played for a time in the Los Angeles Coliseum, a facility designed for the Olympic Games and track and field, and reasonably suited to the addition of football. However, the imposition of baseball created ridiculous effects; the left-field fence rose only slightly over 200 feet (61 m) from home plate!

In addition to the requirements of the game, a sports arena must accommodate the requirements of the spectators. Pillars that obstruct the spectator's view do not create goodwill and discourage the purchase of tickets. Likewise, attempting to put too many seats in a confined space can create severe discomfort. It is not easy to deter-mine where to drawn the line between more seats and fan comfort. The old Montreal Forum, in which anyone over the height of 5 feet 2 inches (1.58 m) sat with their knees under their chin, did not harm ticket sales for the Montreal Canadiens hockey team. However, such space design might be disastrous for a franchise in a less hockey-oriented city.

Finally, the design of space should take into account various needs peripheral to the primary functions of the building, such as rest rooms and concession stands.

Once functional concerns have been met, the architect can start to consider aesthetic aspects of space design. Eero Saarinen's Trans-World Airline Terminal in New York City (Fig. 3.28) takes the dramatic shape of flight in curved lines and carefully designed spaces, which accommodate large masses of people and channel them to and from waiting aircraft. (Such shapes can be executed only

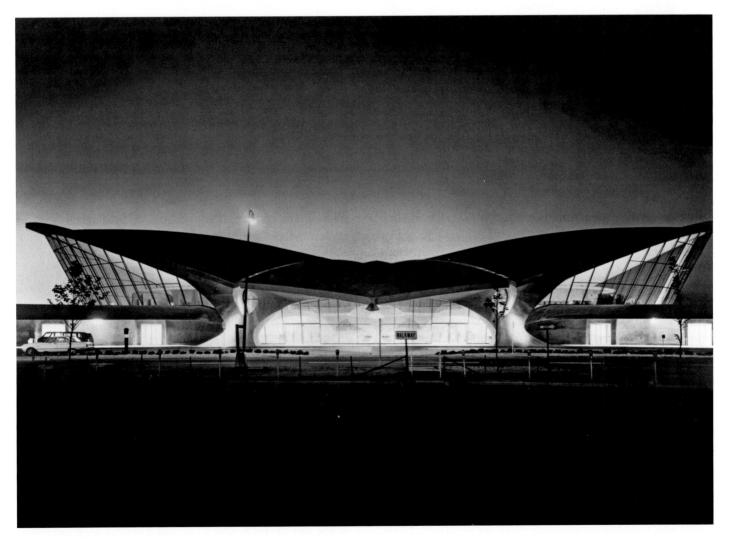

3.28 Eero Saarinen, TWA terminal, Kennedy Airport, New York, 1962.

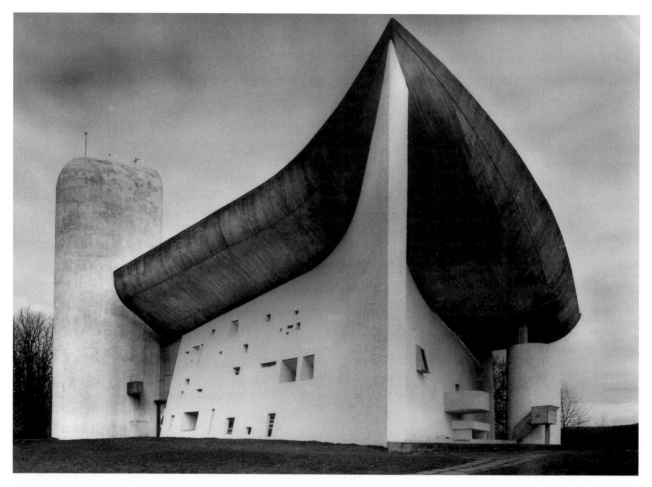

3.29 Le Corbusier, Notre-Dame-du-Haut, France, from the southeast, 1950–4.

using modern construction techniques and materials such as reinforced concrete.) Flight has also been suggested by Le Corbusier's dynamic church Notre-Dame-du-Haut (nah-truh-dahm-doo-OH; Fig. **3.29**). However, this pilgrimage church appears more like a work of sculpture than a building. Here the building's function cannot be surmised from its form. Rather, the juxtaposed *rectilinear* windows and *curvilinear* walls and the overwhelming roof nestled lightly on thin pillars above the walls all appear as a "pure creation of the spirit."

CLIMATE

Climate has always been a factor in architectural design in zones of severe temperature, either hot or cold. As the world's energy supplies diminish, this factor will grow in importance. In the temperate climate of much of the United States, solar systems and designs that make use of the moderating influence of the earth are common. These are *passive* systems—their design accommodates natural phenomena rather than adding technological devices such as solar collectors.

For example, in the colder areas of the United States an energy-efficient building can be made by creating a design with no glass, or minimal glass, on its north-facing side. Windows looking south can be covered in the summer and then uncovered to catch sunlight in midwinter, when it still provides considerable warmth.

Since temperatures at the shallow depth of 5 feet (1.6 m) below the earth's surface rarely go above or below 50°F (10°C), regardless of season, the earth presents a gold mine of potential for design. Houses that are built into the sides of hills or recessed below the earth's surface require much less heating or cooling than those standing fully exposed—whatever the extremes of climate. Even in zones of uniform and moderate temperature, design must consider climate. The "California lifestyle," for example, requires design that accommodates easy access to the out-of-doors and large, open spaces with free-flowing traffic patterns.

Architecture and Human Reality

Le Corbusier, Villa Savoye

Art and architecture of the early twentieth century began to exhibit a simple, straightforward, and practical approach. That quality found an exponent in the Swiss painter–architect Charles-Edouard Jeanneret (1887–1965), known by his pseudonym Le Corbusier (luh kohr-boo-SYAY). Le Corbusier defined a house as "a machine for living." By that he did not mean that a house ought to be an artless, empty mechanical environment fit only for robots to inhabit. Rather, and fairly typical of his time, he saw machines as beneficial to human needs. Le Corbusier believed that a house should be conceived, designed, and produced in the same rational manner as are tools, cars, and airplanes. He thought that traditional houses were irrational in design and frustrated the promise of the new age and the good life that machines would bring.

As a result, Le Corbusier attempted to design simple buildings whose structure and inner logic were clear and void of any surface decoration. The function of a building was to be clearly recognizable in the relation of its forms. Le Corbusier's realization of his philosophy came in the Villa Savoye, just outside Paris (Fig. 3.31). Villa Savoye uses ferroconcrete, which exploits the possibilities offered by skeleton framing to create free and open spaces in the interior. The cube on pillars of reinforced concrete called pilotis (Fig. 3.30) was a favorite device of Le Corbusier because it allowed space to flow under and through the building and enhanced its sense of volume. Hollowed out on three sides, Villa Savoye allows sunlight to flood the center of the building. Without load-bearing walls in the interior, free space abounds. The building has no "front" or "back" because it is open on every side. Thus it achieves Le Corbusier's objective of total interpenetration of outer and interior space.

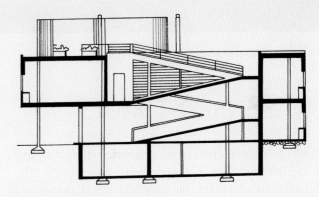

3.30 Section of the Villa Savoye.

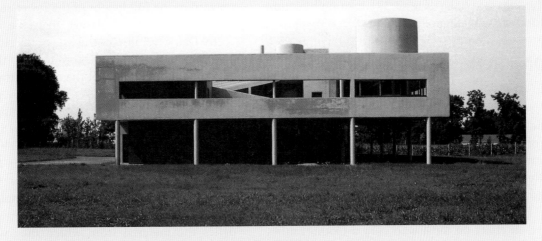

3.31 Le Corbusier, Villa Savoye, Poissy, France, 1928–30.

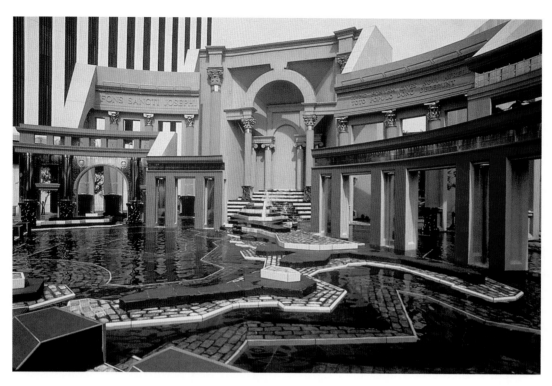

3.32 Charles Moore, Piazza d'Italia, New Orleans, 1978–9.

SENSE STIMULI

As should be clear by this point, sensual response to aesthetic design constitutes a composite experience. The individual characteristics we have discussed previously provide the stimuli for our response. Lately, color has become an especially important tool for the Postmodern architect in stimulating sense responses. The effects of color in the Piazza d'Italia (Fig. 3.32) turn architecture into an exotic sensual experience.

CONTROLLED VISION AND SYMBOLISM

The Gothic cathedral has been described as the perfect synthesis of intellect, spirituality, and engineering. The upward, striving line of the Gothic arch makes a simple yet powerful statement of medieval people's striving to understand their earthly relation to the spiritual unknown. Even today the simplicity and grace of that design have an effect on most who view a Gothic cathedral such as Notre Dame, Paris (Fig. 3.33).

The cathedral at Amiens (Fig. 3.34) has a similar basic composition to Notre Dame, but rather than creating a sense of foursquare power, it gives an impression of delicacy. Amiens Cathedral illustrates a late development of

Gothic style. The differences between Amiens and Notre Dame provide an important lesson in the ways design can elicit a response. At Amiens, greater detail, as opposed to flat stone, focuses our attention. Both cathedrals divide into three obvious horizontal and vertical sections of roughly the same proportion. Notre Dame appears to rest heavily on its lowest section, whose proportions are diminished by the horizontal band of sculptures above the portals. Amiens, on the other hand, carries its portals upward to the full height of the lower section. In fact, the central portal, much larger than the central portal of Notre Dame, reinforces the line of the side portals to form a pyramid whose apex penetrates into the section above. The roughly equal size of the three portals of Notre Dame reinforces its horizontal sense, thereby giving it stability. Similarly, each use of line, form, and proportion in Amiens reinforces lightness and action, as compared with stability and strength in Notre Dame. This does not imply that one design is better than the other. Each exists on its own terms and simply displays a different approach.

Together with the grandeur of simple vertical line in Gothic cathedrals emerges an ethereal lightness that defies the material from which they were constructed. The medieval architect created in stone not the heavy yet elegant composition of the early Greeks, which focused upon treatment of stone, but rather a construction that focuses on space—the ultimate mystery. Inside the cathedrals, the stained glass high above the worshipers' heads

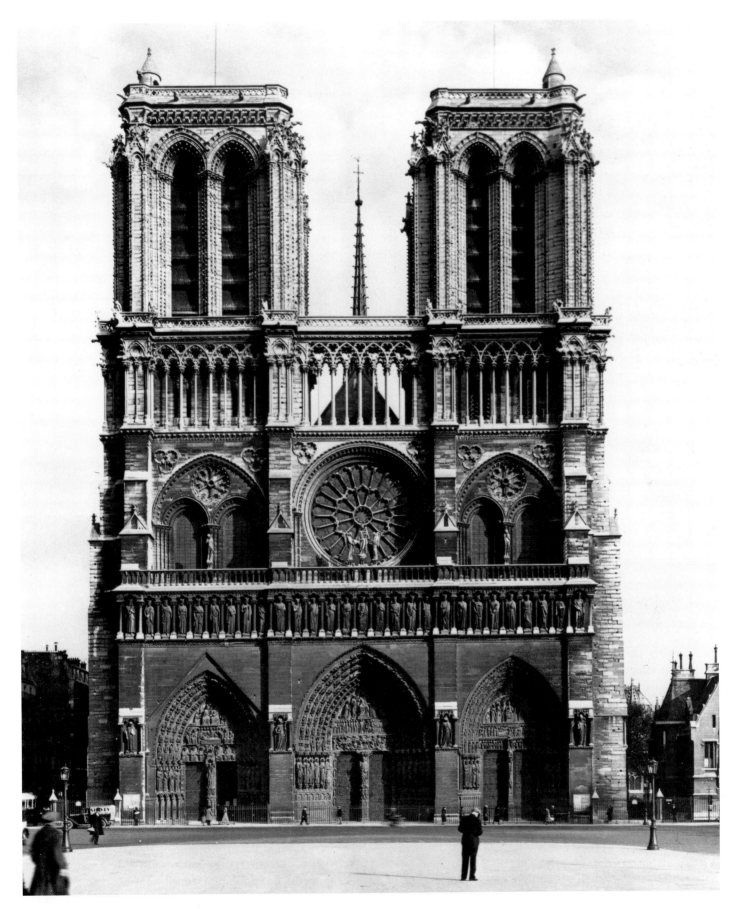

3.33 Notre Dame, Paris, west front, 1163–1250.

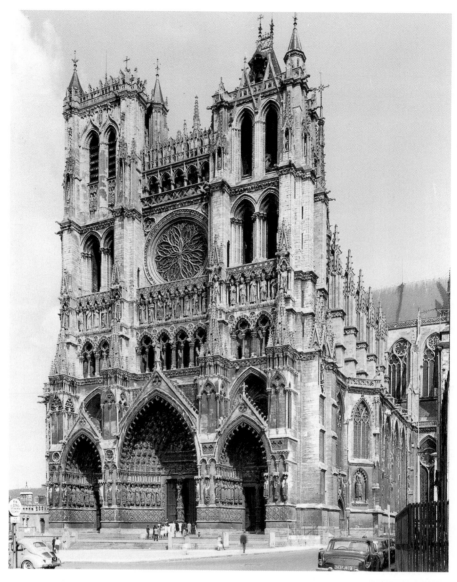

3.34 Amiens Cathedral, France, west front, c. 1220–59.

so controls the light entering as to produce an over-whelming effect of mystery. Line, form, scale, color, structure, balance, proportion, context, and space all combine to form unified compositions that have stood for hundreds of years as symbols of the Christian experience.

A totally different appeal to the emotions emerges from the ornate German Baroque Kaisersaal Residenz in Würzburg (Fig. 3.35), wherein line and form, materials and color convey a message of opulence.

STYLE

The Christian experience also determines the design of Conrad & Fleishman's the Holy Family Church in Parma, Ohio (Fig. 3.36). However, despite the upward-striving power of its composition linking it with its medieval predecessors, this church has a modern clarity of line and sophistication, which perhaps speaks more of our own conception of space as less unknowable and more conquerable. The juxtaposing of straight and curved lines creates an active and dynamic response in a modern style that prompts abruptness rather than mystery. The composition is cool, and its material calls attention to itself by starkness and lack of decoration.

Each part of the church remains distinct and not quite subordinate to the totality of the design. This building perhaps represents a philosophy and style intermediate between that underlying Chartres Cathedral, whose entire design reduces to a single motif—the Gothic arch—and that of the Baroque, as seen in the Hall of Mirrors of the Palace of Versailles (Fig. 3.37). No single part of the

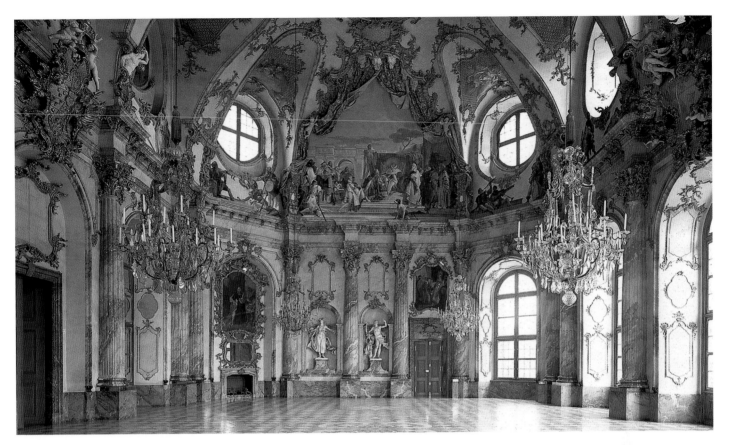

3.35 Balthasar Neumann, Kaisersaal Residenz, Würzburg, Germany, 1719–44.

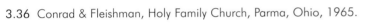

3.36 Conrad & Fleishman, Holy Family Church, Parma, Ohio, 1965.

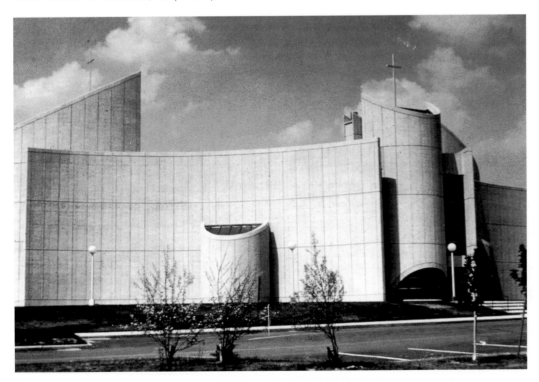

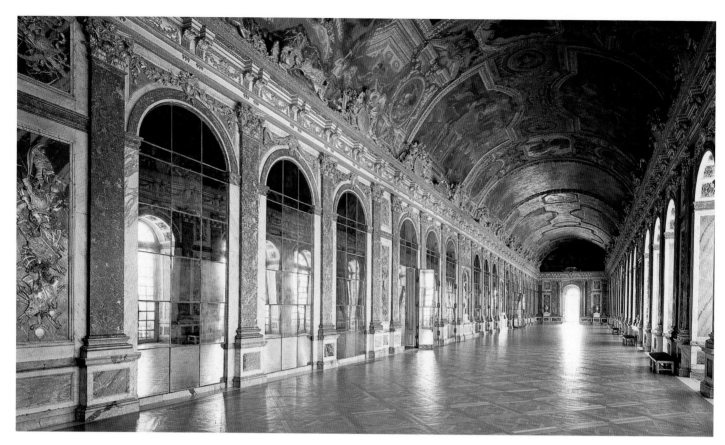

3.37 Jules Hardouin-Mansart and Charles Le Brun, Palace of Versailles, France, Hall of Mirrors, 1680.

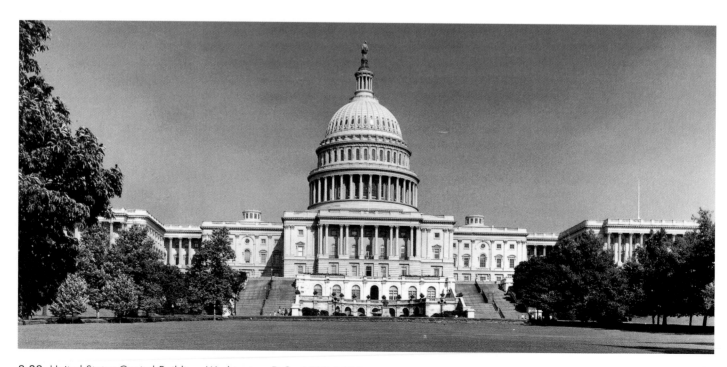

3.38 United States Capitol Building, Washington, D.C., 1792–1856.

design of this hall epitomizes the whole, yet each part subordinates to the whole. Ornate complexity calls for involvement and investigation and intends to overwhelm with opulence. Here, as in most art, the expression and stimuli reflect the patron. Chartres Cathedral reflects the medieval church; the Church of the Holy Family, the contemporary church; and Versailles, King Louis XIV. Versailles is complex, highly active, and yet warm. The richness of its textures, the warmth of its colors, and its curvilinear softness create a certain kind of comfort despite its scale and formality.

In the United States Capitol, a Neoclassical house of government (Fig. **3.38**), formality creates a foursquare, solid response. The symmetry of its design and the weight of its material give us a sense of impersonal power, heightened by the crushing weight of the dome. No longer do we see the upward-striving spiritual release of the Gothic arch, or even the powerful elegance of the Greek post-and-lintel. The Capitol Building, based on a Roman prototype, elicits a sense of struggle. This effect results from upward columnar thrust (heightened by the context provided by Capitol Hill) and downward thrust (of the dome), focused toward the interior.

APPARENT FUNCTION

The architect Louis Sullivan (of whom Frank Lloyd Wright was a pupil) is credited with the concept that form follows function. This means that the form or shape or design of any building must grow from the function the building serves. When someone looks at a building, they should recognize at the outset the purpose of that building. Sullivan here inadvertently edges against one of art's great debates: should art serve a purpose, or exist out of its own needs exclusively? By his maxim "form follows function," Sullivan meant that purpose should be the first (but not the only) consideration in design. This principle, which also implied that beauty resides in the purity of unornamented form, was applied in a great deal of modernist design in the period following World War I (see Chapter 13).

This philosophy stood in contrast to aestheticism, an artistic movement characterized by the slogan "art for art's sake." Those who championed this cause reacted against Victorian notions that a work of art must be uplifting, educational, or otherwise socially or morally beneficial. They argued that artworks stand independent and self-justifying and need no reason for being, other than the fact of being beautiful. This represents the championing of form over function or purpose.

To a degree we have seen that concept in the previous examples, even though, with the exception of the Church of the Holy Family, they all precede Sullivan in time. A worthy question concerning the Guggenheim Museum in New York City (Fig. **3.39**) might be how well Wright followed his teacher's philosophy. A story exists that Wright hated New York City because of unpleasant experiences he had had with the city fathers during previous projects.

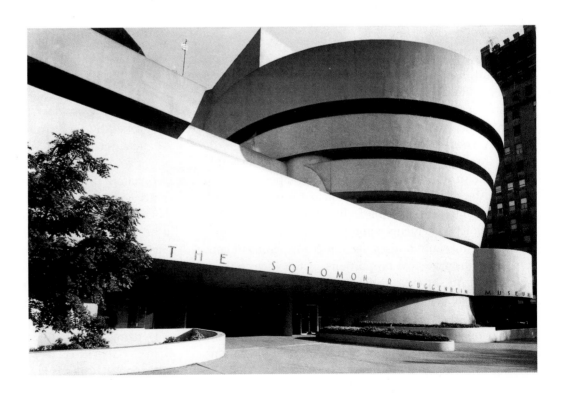

3.39 Frank Lloyd Wright, Guggenheim Museum, New York, 1942–59.

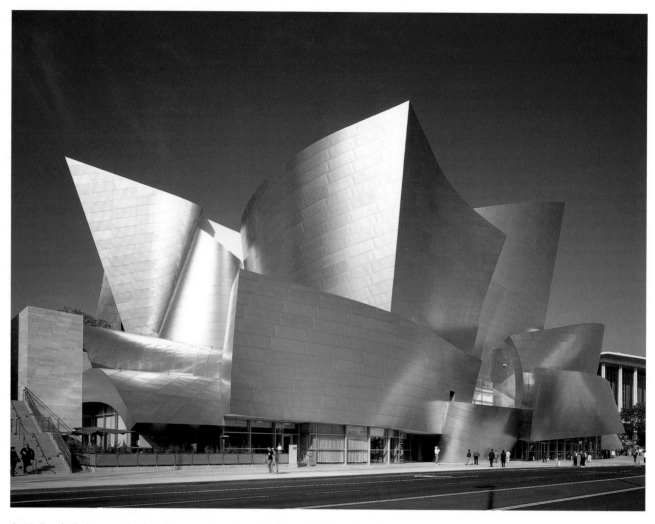

3.40 Frank Gehry, south elevation of Walt Disney Concert Hall, Los Angeles, 2003.

As a result, the Guggenheim Museum, which he designed late in his life, became his final gesture of derision to the city. This center of contemporary culture and art, with its single, circular ramp from street level to roof, emerged (so the story goes) from the plans for a parking garage. Be that as it may, its line and form create a simple, smoothly flowing, leisurely, upward movement juxtaposed against another stark and dynamic rectilinear form. The building's line and color and the feeling they produce make contemporary statements appropriate to the contemporary art the museum houses. Its modernity stands in contrast with the Classical proportions of the Metropolitan Museum of Art, just down the street, which houses great works of ancient and modern art. The Guggenheim expresses its interior design outwardly in the ramp, and one can argue whether its slowly curving, unbroken line reinforces the manner and pace that one should pursue when going through a museum.

DYNAMICS

Leisurely progress does not represent the sense of stimulus evoked by the cantilevered roof of the grandstand at Zarzuela Race Track in Spain (see Fig. 3.18). Speed, power, and flight form its preeminent concerns. The sense of dynamic instability inherent in the structural form—cantilever—and this particular application of it mirror the dynamic instability and forward power of the race horse at full speed. However, despite the form and strong diagonals, this design remains controlled. The architect has created unity by repeating the track-level arcade in the arched line of the cantilevered roof. The design evokes dynamism humanized in the softness of its curves and control of its scale.

Dynamics also defines Canadian-born architect, Frank Gehry's (GHAIR-ee; b. 1929) Walt Disney Concert Hall in Los Angeles, California (Fig. 3.40). His architectural theory creates functional works of sculpture rather than buildings in the traditional sense. His early works witnessed an architectural language of plywood and corrugated metal. Later, these evolved into distorted but lucid concrete and metal. They reflect an aesthetic that appears somewhat disjointed, as if attempting to belong to a social context likewise disjointed. Disney Hall suggests to some the sails of a ship. It also can suggest the turmoil of our times in its "visual chaos." This building, along with Gehry's Guggenheim Museum building in Bilbao, Spain, attempts to change the language of architecture. These buildings stand like immense works of sculpture against the background of the city and continue a curvaceous, free-form style that has become the architect's signature. He utilized similar abstract, free-form components in other works such as the Gehry House and the Fishdance Restaurant, which employ a similarly sleek curvaceous cladding. The forms of the building take on sculptured dimensions so complex that they required an advanced aerospace computer program to allow the contractor to build the building in a reasonable way.

SCALE

Nothing symbolizes the technological achievement of modern humans more nor its overpowering sense of control than the skyscraper. Also, nothing symbolizes the subordination of humans to their technology more than the scale of this monumental type of building (Fig. **3.41**).

The 88-story Petronas Twin Towers was developed as an integral part of the Kuala Lumpur City Center in Malaysia. Designed by Cesar Pelli and Associates, the Twin Towers symbolize strength and grace, using geometric principles typified in Islamic architecture. The 1,483-foot (451.9-m) Twin Towers, until recently the world's tallest buildings, are linked by a 192-foot (58.4-m) double-decker skybridge at levels 41 and 42, 574 feet (174 m) above the street level. The sense of scale expressed in this building gains extra power from the twin tower concept, with increased visual height emerging from the taper—exaggerating its linear perspective.

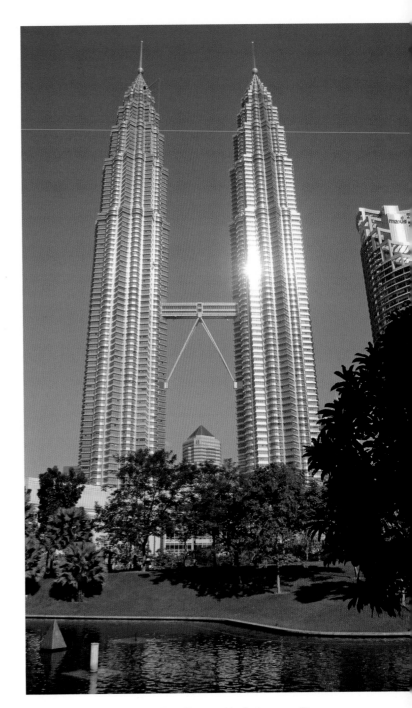

3.41 Cesar Pelli, Petronas Twin Towers, Kuala Lumpur City, Malaysia, 1997. Glass and steel, 1,483 ft (451.9 m) high.

THINKING CRITICALLY

As mentioned in the opening of this chapter, understanding terms and concepts brings experience to more confident and pleasurable levels. You can enhance your response and build a basic critical analysis of a work of architecture by using the topics in this chapter as an outline. Pick an example such as St. Paul's Cathedral (Fig. **3.14**) and ask yourself how it reflects the qualities appropriate to the specific topics. Begin with the following approaches:

• Reaction. This building was designed to create a reaction. What elements discussed in the chapter combine to create your reaction? What are your intellectual and emotional responses to the architectural work, and what causes them?

Now build a comparative analysis by choosing two or more works and detailing how they reflect specific qualities described in the chapter. For example:

• Structure. Describe the structures basic to the Monadnock Building (Fig. **3.20**) and Fallingwater (Fig. **3.27**). How do the elements you can see suggest how the building is supported and how do the two examples differ in the way they use their structures to form their visual appeal?

• Scale and proportion. Using the same two examples, how do the sizes of the examples relate to the human form? Describe and compare how proportion works in each example.

• Context. How does the Palace of Versailles (Fig. **3.25**) explore its context? What is the environment in which the example stands?

CYBER STUDY

ARCHITECTURAL EXAMPLES INDEXED BY ARCHITECT:
—With dates and nation
http://www.artcyclopedia.com/media/Architect.html
—With cross-index of date and period
http://www.bluffton.edu/~sullivanm/index/index2.html#B
www.greatbuildings.com

CHAPTER FOUR

MUSIC AND OPERA

OUTLINE

FORMAL AND TECHNICAL QUALITIES

FORMS
  Mass
  Cantata
  Oratorio
  Fugue
  Symphony
  Concerto
COMPOSITION
  Sound
  Rhythm
  Melody

Harmony
Profile: Wolfgang Amadeus
  Mozart
  Tonality
  Texture

SENSE STIMULI

OUR PRIMAL RESPONSES
THE MUSICAL
  PERFORMANCE

OPERA
  Types of Opera
  The Opera Production
Music and Human Reality:
  Bizet, Carmen
Thinking Critically
Cyber Study

IMPORTANT TERMS

Concerto A composition for one or more solo instruments, accompanied by an orchestra, typically in three movements.

Fugue A musical composition in a fixed form in which a theme is developed by counterpoint.

Homophony A type of musical texture in which chords accompany one main melody.

Melody A succession of sounds with rhythmic and tonal organization.

Monophony A type of musical texture using a single musical line without accompaniment

Opera A staged, musical/theatrical work in which music predominates.

Oratorio A large choral work for soloists, chorus, and orchestra, developed in the Baroque period.

Polyphony A type of musical texture utilizing two or more melodic lines of relatively equal interest performed at the same time.

Symphony A lengthy orchestral composition, usually in four movements.

FORMAL AND TECHNICAL QUALITIES

We all have favorite forms of music: tejano, reggae, rock, rhythm and blues, rap, gospel, or Classical. Occasionally we are surprised to find that our favorite tune or musical form was once something else: a rock tune that first was an operatic aria, or an ethnic style that combines styles from other ethnic traditions. Whatever the case, all music comprises rhythms and melodies—they differ only in the ways they are put together. In this chapter we shall concentrate first on some traditional forms, but after that we discuss qualities that apply to all music.

Music has often been described as the purest of the art forms because it is free from the physical restrictions of space that apply to the other arts. However, the freedom enjoyed by the composer becomes a constraint for us listeners because music places significant responsibility on us. That responsibility is especially critical when we try to learn and apply musical terminology, because we have only a fleeting moment to capture many of the characteristics of music. A painting or a sculpture stands still for us; it does not change or disappear, despite the length of time it takes us to examine and appreciate. Our attempt to grasp musical terminology appears more challenging because many of the concepts seem technical and most of the terminology foreign: specifically Italian. Nonetheless, music plays such a natural and ever-present role in our lives that we undoubtedly know and can perceive more than we suspect at both a formal and a technical level.

FORMS

At a formal level, our experience of a musical work begins with its type, or form. The term *form* is a very broad one. In addition to the forms we identify momentarily, all of which are associated with what we call "classical" (serious, or "high" art) music, we can also identify broader "forms" of music of which "classical" is only one—for example, the musical forms of jazz, pop/rock, and so on (see the Companion Website: Music, Musical Forms). As we will see in Chapter 11, the term Classical also refers to a specific style of music within this broad "classical" form.

The basic form of a music composition shapes our initial encounter by providing us with some specific parameters for understanding. Unlike our experience in the theatre, we usually find an identification of the musical composition, by type, in the concert program. Here are a few of the more common forms: three vocal forms and three instrumental forms. We will encounter a few more

in Part II of the text, and will define them within their historical contexts.

Mass

The mass is a sacred choral composition consisting of five sections: Kyrie, Gloria, Credo, Sanctus, and Agnus Dei (KEE-ree-ay; KRAY-doh; SAHNK-toos; AHN-yoos-day-ee). These also form the parts of the mass ordinary—the Roman Catholic church texts that remain the same from day to day throughout most of the year. The Kyrie text implores, "Lord, have mercy upon us. Christ, have mercy upon us. Lord, have mercy upon us." The Gloria text begins, "Glory be to God on High, and on earth peace, good will towards men." The Credo states the creed: "We believe in one God, the Father, the Almighty, maker of heaven and earth," and so on. The Sanctus confirms, "Holy, holy, holy, Lord God of Hosts: Heaven and earth are full of thy glory. Glory be to thee, O Lord Most High." The Agnus Dei (Lamb of God), implores, "O Lamb of God, that takest away the sins of the world, have mercy upon us. O Lamb of God, that takest away the sins of the world, have mercy upon us. O Lamb of God, that takest away the sins of the world, grant us thy peace." (Listen to "Kyrie" from the *Pope Marcellus Mass* by Palestrina [Pa-leh-STREE-nah], music CD track 7.) The requiem mass, which often comprises a musical program, is a special mass for the dead.

Cantata

A cantata is usually a choral work with one or more soloists and an instrumental ensemble. Written in several movements, and typified by the church cantata of the Lutheran church of the Baroque period, it often includes chorales and organ accompaniment. The word "cantata" originally meant a sung piece. The Lutheran church cantata (exemplified by those of Johann Sebastian Bach) uses a religious text, either original or drawn from the Bible or based on familiar hymns—chorales. In essence, it served as a sermon in music, drawn from the lectionary (prescribed Bible readings for the day and on which the sermon is based). A typical cantata might last twenty-five minutes and include several different movements—choruses, recitatives, arias, and duets.

Oratorio

An oratorio is a large-scale composition using chorus, vocal soloists, and orchestra. Normally an oratorio sets a narrative text (usually biblical), but does not employ acting, scenery, or costumes. The oratorio was a major achievement of the Baroque period. This type of musical composition unfolds through a series of choruses, arias, duets, recitatives, and orchestral interludes. The chorus of an oratorio has special importance and can comment on or participate in the dramatic exposition. Another feature of the oratorio is the use of a narrator, whose recitatives (vocal lines imitating the rhythms and inflections of normal speech) tell the story and connect the various parts. Like operas, oratorios can last more than two hours. (Listen to Handel's "Hallelujah Chorus" from the oratorio *Messiah*, music CD track 9.)

Fugue

The fugue is a polyphonic (see p. 127) composition based on one main theme. It can be written for a group of instruments or voices or for a single instrument like an organ or harpsichord. Throughout the composition, different melodic lines, called "voices," imitate the subject. The top melodic line is the soprano and the bottom line the bass. A fugue usually includes three, four, or five voices. The composer's exploration of the subject typically passes through different keys and combines with different melodic and rhythmic ideas. Fugal form is extremely flexible: the only constant feature is the beginning, in which a single, unaccompanied voice states the theme. The listener's task, then, is to remember that subject and follow it through the various manipulations that follow.

Symphony

An orchestral composition, usually in four movements, a symphony typically lasts between twenty and forty-five minutes. In this large work, the composer explores the full dynamic and tonal range of the orchestral ensemble. The symphony came from the Classical period of the late eighteenth century and evokes a wide range of carefully structured emotions through contrasts of tempo and mood. The sequence of movements usually begins with an active fast movement, changes to a lyrical slow movement, moves to a dancelike movement, and closes with a bold fast movement. The opening movement almost always takes a specific shape—sonata form—in which a theme is introduced, alternated, and repeated. In most Classical symphonies, each movement is self-contained with its own set of themes. Unity in a symphony occurs partly from the use of the same key in three of the movements and also from careful emotional and musical complement among the movements. (Listen to Haydn's *Symphony No. 94 in G Major*, "Surprise", music CD track 11; also Beethoven's *Symphony No. 5 in C Minor*—first movement, music CD track 14. In the Haydn, listen for

the theme's mood. In the Beethoven, listen for repetition of the theme.)

Concerto

A solo concerto (kahn-CHAIR-toh) is an extended composition for an instrumental soloist and orchestra. Reaching its zenith during the Classical period of the eighteenth century, it typically contains three movements, in which the first is fast, the second slow, and the third fast. Concertos join a soloist's virtuosity and interpretive skills with the wide-ranging dynamics and tonal colors of an orchestra. The concerto thus provides a dramatic contrast of musical ideas and sound in which the soloist is the star. Typically, concertos present a great challenge to the soloist and a great reward to the listener, who can delight in the soloist's meeting of the technical and interpretive challenges of the work. Nonetheless, the concerto balances the orchestra and soloist, which act as partners, focusing on the interplay between them. Concertos can last from twenty to forty-five minutes (listen to *Brandenburg Concerto No. 2 in F Major*, music CD track 8). Typically, during the first movement, and sometimes the third, of a Classical concerto, the soloist has an unaccompanied showpiece called a cadenza.

Common in the late Baroque period of the seventeenth century (see Chapter 11), the *concerto grosso* is a composition for several instrumental soloists and small orchestra (in contrast to the solo concerto—see above). In the Baroque style, contrast between loud and soft sounds and large and small groups of performers was typical. In a concerto grosso, a small group of soloists (two to four) contrasts a larger group called the *tutti* consisting of between eight and twenty players. Most often a concerto grosso contains three movements contrasting in tempo and character. The first movement is fast; the second, slow; and the third, fast. The opening movement, usually bold, explores the contrasts between *tutti* and soloists. The slow movement tends to be more lyrical, quiet, and intimate. The final movement is lively, lighthearted, and sometimes dancelike.

COMPOSITION

Understanding vocabulary and being able to identify its application in a musical composition helps us to comprehend communication using the musical language, and thereby to understand the creative communicative intent of the composer and the musicians who bring the composition to life. The ways in which musical artists shape the characteristics that follow bring us experiences that can challenge our intellects and excite our emotions.

As in all communication, meaning depends upon each of the parties involved; communicators and listeners must assume responsibility for facility in the language utilized.

Among the basic elements by which music is composed, we discuss six: (1) Sound; (2) Rhythm; (3) Melody; (4) Harmony; (5) Tonality; and (6) Texture.

Sound

Musical composers design sounds and silences. In the broadest sense, sound is anything that excites the auditory nerve: sirens, speech, crying babies, jet engines, falling trees, and so on. We might even call such sources noise. Musical composition, although it can employ even "noise," usually depends on controlled and shaped sound, consistent in quality. We distinguish music from other sounds by recognizing four basic properties: (1) pitch; (2) dynamics; (3) tone color; and (4) duration.

PITCH Pitch is a physical phenomenon measurable in vibrations per second. Therefore, when we describe differences in pitch we describe recognizable and measurable differences in sound waves. A pitch has a steady, constant frequency. A faster frequency produces a higher pitch; a slower frequency produces a lower pitch. Making a sounding body—a vibrating string, for example—smaller makes it vibrate more rapidly. Musical instruments designed to produce high pitches, such as the piccolo, therefore tend to be small. Instruments designed to produce low pitches tend to be large—for instance, bass viols and tubas. In music, we call a sound that has a definite pitch a *tone*.

In Chapter 1 we discussed color. It comprises a range of light waves within a visible spectrum. Sound also comprises a spectrum, whose audible pitches range from 16 to 38,000 vibrations per second. We can perceive 11,000 different pitches! That exceeds practicality for musical composition. Therefore, by convention musicians traditionally divide the sound spectrum into at least ninety equally spaced frequencies comprising seven and a half *octaves*. A piano keyboard consists of eighty-eight keys (seven

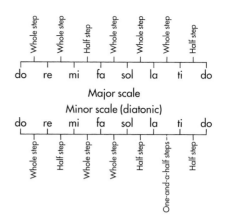

4.2 The major and minor scales.

octaves plus two additional notes), which represents the same number of equally spaced pitches (Fig. 4.1).

A *scale*—an arrangement of pitches played in ascending or descending order—is a conventional organization of the frequencies of the sound spectrum. The thirteen equally spaced pitches in an octave comprise a *chromatic scale*. However, the scales that sound most familiar to us are the major and minor scales, each of which consists of an octave of eight pitches. The distance between any two pitches is an *interval*. Intervals between two adjacent pitches are half steps. Intervals of two half steps are whole steps. The major scale—*do re mi fa sol la ti do* (recall the song, "Doe, a deer . . ." from *The Sound of Music*)—has a specific arrangement of whole and half steps (Fig. 4.2). Lowering the third and sixth notes of the major scale gives us the harmonic (the most common) minor scale.

Not all music conforms to the conventions of Western scales. European music prior to approximately 1600 C.E. does not, nor does Eastern music, which makes great use of quarter tones. In addition, some contemporary Western music departs completely from the conventions of *tonality*. Listen, for example to tracks 1 and 2 on the music CD. These examples represent cultures whose music does not conform to the Western conventions of pitch, scale, and tonality.

DYNAMICS We call degrees of loudness or softness in music *dynamics*. Any tone can be loud, soft, or anywhere in between. Dynamics describe the loudness or softness of the tones, measured in decibels, and depend upon the physical phenomenon of amplitude of vibration. Employing greater force in the production of a tone creates wider sound waves and causes greater stimulation of the auditory nerves. This means that the size of the sound wave, not its number of vibrations per second, changes.

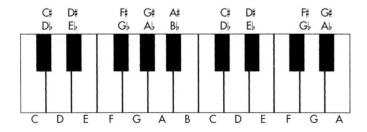

4.1 Part of the piano keyboard, with pitches.

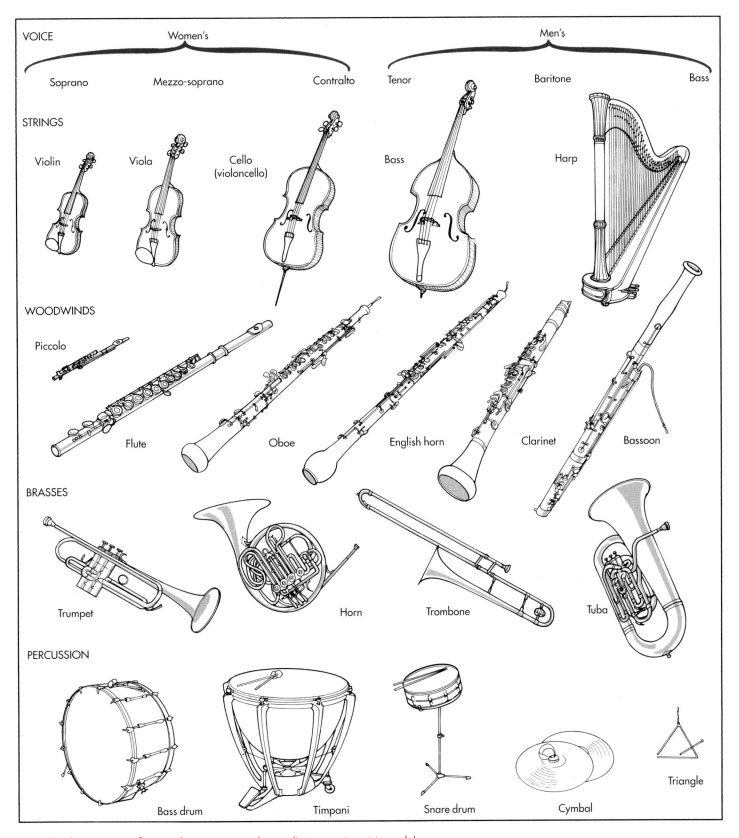

VOICE

Women's

Men's

Soprano   Mezzo-soprano   Contralto   Tenor   Baritone   Bass

STRINGS

Violin   Viola   Cello (violoncello)   Bass   Harp

WOODWINDS

Piccolo   Flute   Oboe   English horn   Clarinet   Bassoon

BRASSES

Trumpet   Horn   Trombone   Tuba

PERCUSSION

Bass drum   Timpani   Snare drum   Cymbal   Triangle

4.3 The key sources of musical tone in an orchestra (instruments not to scale).

Composers indicate dynamic level with a series of specific notations:

pp	pianissimo (pee-yah-NEE-see-moh)	very soft
p	piano	soft
mp	mezzo (MEHT-zoh) piano	moderately soft
mf	mezzo forte (FOR-tay)	moderately loud
f	forte	loud
ff	fortissimo	very loud

The notations of dynamics that apply to an individual tone, such as *p, mp,* and *f,* may also apply to a section of music. Changes in dynamics may be abrupt, gradual, wide, or small.

As we listen to and compare musical compositions we can consider the use and breadth of dynamics in the same sense that we consider the use and breadth of palette in painting. Compare the different dynamic treatments of music CD track 1, "Han Ya Xi Shui," particularly the ending, with music CD track 19, Debussy's "Clair de Lune."

TONE COLOR Tone color, or timbre (TAM-ber), is the characteristic of tone that allows us to distinguish a pitch played on a violin, for example, from the same pitch played on a piano. In addition to identifying characteristic differences among sound-producing sources, tone color can also refer to differences in quality of tones produced by the same source. Here the analogy of "tone color" is particularly appropriate. We describe a tone produced with an excess of air—for example, by a breathy human voice—as "white." Figure 4.3 illustrates some of the various sources that produce musical tone and account for its variety of tone colors (see the Companion Website: Music, Instruments).

In the keyboard family, the piano could be considered either a stringed or a percussion instrument since it produces its sound by vibrating strings struck by hammers. The harpsichord sets strings in motion by plucking, and the organ makes sound by air.

Electronically produced music, available since the development of the RCA synthesizer at the Columbia-Princeton Electronics Music Center in the 1950s, has become a standard source in assisting contemporary composers. Originally electronic music fell into two categories: (1) the electronic altering of acoustically produced sounds, which came to be labeled as *musique concrète,* and (2) electronically generated sounds. However, advances in technology have blurred those differences over the years.

DURATION Another characteristic of sound is duration: the length of time vibration continues without interruption. Duration in musical composition uses a set of con-

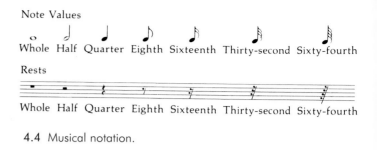

4.4 Musical notation.

ventions called notation (Fig. 4.4). This system consists of a series of symbols (notes) by which the composer indicates the relative duration of each tone. The system is progressive—each duration notation uses a symbol either double or half the duration of the other notes. Musical notation also includes a series of symbols that denote the duration of silences in a composition. These symbols, called *rests,* have the same values as the symbols for duration of tone.

Rhythm

Rhythm comprises recurring pulses and accents that create identifiable patterns. Without rhythm we have only an aimless rising and falling of tones. Composing music means placing each tone into a time or rhythmical relationship with every other tone. As with the dots and dashes of the Morse code we can "play" the rhythm of a musical composition without reference to its tones. Each symbol of the musical notation system denotes a duration relative to each other symbol in the system. Rhythm consists of: (1) beat; (2) meter; and (3) tempo (see the Companion Website: Music, Rhythm).

BEAT The individual pulses we hear are called *beats.* Beats may be grouped into rhythmic patterns by placing accents every few beats. Beats form basic units of time and the background against which the composer places notes of various lengths.

METER Normal musical practice groups clusters of beats into units called *measures.* When these groupings are regular and reasonably equal they comprise *simple* meters. When the number of beats in a measure equals three or two it constitutes *triple* or *duple* meter. We, as listeners, can distinguish between duple and triple meters because of their different *accent* patterns. In triple meter we hear an accent every third beat—ONE two three, ONE two three—and in duple meter the accent is every other beat—ONE two, ONE two. If four beats occur in a meas-

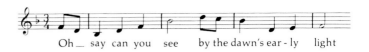

Oh __ say can you see   by the dawn's ear-ly   light

4.5 "The Star-Spangled Banner" (excerpt).

ure (sometimes called quadruple meter), the second accent is weaker than the first—ONE two THREE four, ONE two THREE four.

Listen to music CD track 3, a sample of Ghanaian drumming. Here we find a definite triple meter, as contrasted with the duple meter in music CD track 6, "As Vesta Was Descending." When accent occurs on normally unaccented beats, we have *syncopation*, as also occurs in the Ghanaian drumming piece. Sometimes repetitive patterning or strict metrical development does not occur. The free-flowing rhythm of music CD track 4, "O Viridissima Virga," by Hildegard of Bingen (see Chapter 10) illustrates the lack of strict metrical development.

TEMPO *Tempo* is the rate of speed of the composition. A composer may notate tempo in two ways. The first method is by a *metronome marking*, such as ♩ = 60 means that the piece should be played at the rate of sixty quarter notes (♩) per minute. Such notation is precise. The other method is less precise and involves more descriptive terminology in Italian:

Largo (broad) Grave (grahv) (grave, solemn)	Very slow
Lento (slow) Adagio (ah-DAH-zhee-oh) (leisurely)	Slow
Andante (at a walking pace) Moderato (moderate)	Moderate
Allegro (cheerful)	Fast
Vivace (vee-VAH-chay) (vivacious) Presto (very quick)	Very fast

Melody

Melody comprises a succession of sounds with rhythmic and tonal organization. We can visualize melody as linear and essentially horizontal. Two other terms, *tune* and *theme*, relate to melody as parts to a whole. For example, the tune in Figure 4.5 is a melody.

However, a melody is not always a tune. In general, the term tune implies singability, and many melodies cannot be considered singable. A theme is also a melody. However, in musical composition theme specifically means a central musical idea, which may be restated and varied throughout a piece. Thus a melody is not necessarily a theme.

Related to theme and melody is the *motif* (moh-TEEF), or *motive*, a short melodic or rhythmic idea around which

a composer may design a composition. For example, in Beethoven's *Symphony No. 5 in C Minor* (music CD track 14) the first movement develops around a motif of four notes.

In listening for how a composer develops melody, theme, and motif we can use two terms to describe what we hear: *conjunct* and *disjunct*. Conjunct melodies comprise notes close together, stepwise, on the musical scale. For example, the interval between the opening notes of the soprano line of J. S. Bach's chorale "Jesu Joy of Man's Desiring" from *Cantata 147* (Fig. 4.6) never exceeds a whole step. Disjunct melodies contain intervals of two steps or more. However, no formula exists for determining disjunct or conjunct characteristics; no line marks where a melody ceases to be disjunct and becomes conjunct. These constitute relative, descriptive terms. For example, the opening melody of "The Star-Spangled Banner" (see Fig. 4.5) is more disjunct than the opening melody of "Jesu Joy of Man's Desiring"—or the latter is more conjunct than the former.

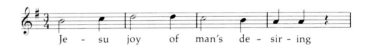

Je - su   joy   of   man's   de - sir - ing

4.6 "Jesu Joy of Man's Desiring" (excerpt).

Harmony

When two or more tones sound at the same time, we have harmony. This is essentially a vertical arrangement, in contrast with the horizontal arrangement of melody. However, harmony also has a horizontal property: movement forward in time. In listening for harmony we listen for how simultaneous tones sound together.

Two tones played simultaneously constitute an interval; three or more form a *chord*. When we hear an interval or a chord we respond first to its *consonance* or *dissonance*. Consonant harmonies sound pleasant and stable in their arrangement, while dissonant harmonies sound tense and unstable. Consonance and dissonance, however, are not absolute properties. Essentially they derive from convention and, to a large extent, culture. Dissonance to our ears may be consonance to someone else's, and vice versa. We

Profile

Wolfgang Amadeus Mozart

Wolfgang Amadeus Mozart (MOHT-zahrt; 1756–91) is often considered the greatest musical genius of all time. His output—especially in view of his short life—was enormous and included sixteen operas, forty-one symphonies, twenty-seven piano and five violin concertos, twenty-five string quartets, nineteen masses, and other works in every form popular in his time. Perhaps his greatest single achievement is in the characterization of his operatic figures.

Mozart was born on January 27, 1756, in Salzburg, Austria. His father, Leopold Mozart, held the position of composer to the archbishop and was a well-known violinist and author of a celebrated theoretical treatise on playing the instrument. When Wolfgang was only six years old, his father took him and his older sister, Maria Anna (called Nannerl) on tours throughout Europe during which they performed as harpsichordists and pianists—separately and together. They gave public concerts and played at the various courts. In Paris in 1764, Wolfgang wrote his first published works, four violin sonatas. In London he came under the influence of Johann Christian Bach. In 1768 young Mozart became honorary concertmaster for the archbishop of Salzburg.

In 1772, however, a new archbishop came to power, and the cordial relationship Mozart enjoyed with the previous archbishop came to an end. By 1777 the situation became so strained that the young composer asked to be relieved of his duties, and the archbishop grudgingly agreed.

In 1777 Mozart traveled with his mother to Munich and Mannheim, Germany, and to Paris, where she died. During this trip alone, Mozart composed seven violin sonatas, seven piano sonatas, a ballet, and three symphonic works, including the *Paris Symphony*.

The final break between Mozart and the archbishop occurred in 1781, but before that time Mozart had unsuccessfully sought another position. Six years later, in 1787, Emperor Joseph II finally engaged him as chamber composer—at a salary considerably smaller than that of his predecessor. Mozart's financial situation worsened steadily, and he incurred significant debts that hounded him until his death.

Meanwhile, his opera *The Abduction from the Seraglio* (suh-RAH-lee-oh) enjoyed great success in 1782; in the same year he married Constanze Weber, the daughter of friends. He composed his great *Mass in C Minor* for her, and she was the soprano soloist in its premiere.

During the last ten years of his life, Mozart produced most of his great piano concertos; the four horn concertos; the *Haffner*, *Prague*, *Linz*, and *Jupiter* symphonies; the six string quartets dedicated to Haydn; five string quintets; and the major operas, *The Marriage of Figaro*, *Don Giovanni*, *Cosi Fan Tutte*, *La Clemenza di Tito*, and *The Magic Flute*. Mozart could not complete his final work, the *Requiem*, because of illness. He died in Vienna on December 5, 1791, and was buried in a mass grave. Although the exact nature of his illness is unknown, no evidence exists that Mozart's death was deliberately caused (as the popular movie, *Amadeus*, implies). Learn more at www.mozartproject.org.

---

need, above all, to determine *how* the composer utilizes these two properties. Most Western music sounds primarily consonant. Dissonance, on the other hand, can be used for contrast, to draw attention to itself, or as a normal part of *harmonic progression*.

As its name implies, harmonic progression involves the movement forward in time of harmonies. In discussing pitch we noted the convention of the major and minor scales—the arrangement of the chromatic scale into a system of *tonality*. When we play or sing a major or minor scale we note a particular phenomenon: our movement

from *do* to *re* to *mi* to *fa* to *sol* to *la* is smooth and seems natural. But when we reach the seventh tone of the scale, *ti*, something happens. It seems as though we *must* continue back to *do*, the *tonic* of the scale. Try it! Sing a major scale and stop at *ti*. You feel uncomfortable. Your mind tells you that you must resolve that discomfort by returning to *do*. That same sense of tonality—that sense of the tonic—applies also to harmony. Within any scale a series of chords may be developed on the basis of the individual tones of the scale. Each of the chords has a subtle relationship to each of the other chords and to the tonic. That relationship creates a sense of progression that leads back to the chord based on the tonic.

Tonality

Utilization of tonality or key has taken composers in various directions over the centuries. Conventional tonality, employing the major and minor scales and keys, forms the basis for most sixteenth- to twentieth-century Western music, as well as traditionally oriented music of the twentieth century.

In the early twentieth century, some composers abandoned traditional tonality. Atonal compositions sought the freedom of any combination of tones without the necessity of having to resolve chordal progressions. Typically compositions using traditional tonality begin in a home key, modulate away, and return at the end.

Texture

Texture in painting and sculpture denotes surface quality—roughness or smoothness. Texture in weaving denotes the interrelationship of the warp and the woof—the horizontal and vertical threads in fabric. The organization in Figure 4.7 would be described as open or loose texture; that in Figure 4.8, closed or tight. No single musical arrangement corresponds to either of these spatial concepts. The characteristic called *sonority* describes the relationship of tones played at the same time. A chord with large intervals between its members would have a more open, or thinner, sonority (or texture) than a chord with small intervals between its tones; that chord would have a tight, thick, or close sonority or texture. Traditionally, however, musical texture refers to the way in which composers use melodic lines in their pieces. Three basic musical textures comprise monophony, polyphony, and homophony.

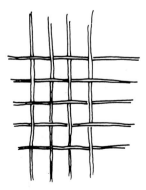
4.7 Open (loose) texture.

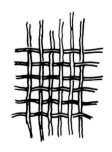
4.8 Closed (tight) texture.

MONOPHONY When a single musical line exists without accompaniment, the piece has a monophonic texture. Many voices or instruments may play at the same time, as in the Gregorian chant illustrated on music CD track 4, but as long as they sing the same notes at the same time—in unison—the texture remains monophonic. In Handel's "Hallelujah Chorus" (music CD track 9), there occur instances in which men and women sing the same notes in different octaves. This still represents monophony.

POLYPHONY Polyphony means "many-sounding," and it occurs when two or more melodic lines of relatively equal interest perform at the same time. This combining technique, also called counterpoint, appears in Palestrina's "Kyrie" from the *Pope Marcellus Mass* (music CD track 7). When the counterpoint uses an immediate restatement of the musical idea, as in the Desprez, then the composer utilizes *imitation*.

HOMOPHONY When chords accompany one main melody, we have homophonic texture. Here the composer focuses attention on the melody by supporting it with subordinate sounds. In a Bach chorale, for example, all four voices sing together simultaneously. The main melody occurs in the soprano, or top, part. The lower parts sing melodies of their own, which differ from the main melody, but, rather than being independent as would be the case in polyphony, they support the soprano melody and move with it in a progression of chords related to the syllables of the text.

SENSE STIMULI

OUR PRIMAL RESPONSES

We can find no better means of illustrating the sensuous effect of music than to contrast two totally different musical pieces. Debussy's "Clair de Lune" (music CD track 19) provides us with an example of how musical elements can combine to give us a relaxing and soothing experience. Here, the tone color of the piano, added to the elements of a constant beat in triple meter, consonant harmonies, subtle dynamic contrasts, and extended duration of the tones combine in a richly subdued experience that engages us but lulls us at the same time. In contrast, Stravinsky's "Auguries of Spring: Dance of Youths and Maidens" from *The Rite of Spring* (music CD track 21) has driving rhythms, strong syncopation, dissonant harmonies, wildly contrasting dynamics, and the broad tonal palette of the orchestra to rivet us and ratchet up our excitement level. We cannot listen to this piece or the frantic pulsations of Leonard Bernstein's (1918–90; BURN-stine) "Mambo" (music CD track 23) without experiencing a rise in pulse rate. In all cases, our senses have responded at an extremely basic level over which we have, it would seem, little control.

Music contains a sensuous attraction difficult to deny. At every turn it causes us to tap our toes, drum our fingers, or bounce in our seats in a purely physical response. This involuntary motor response perhaps represents the most primitive aspect of our sensuous involvement—as primitive as the images in Stravinsky's *The Rite of Spring*. If the rhythm is irregular and the beat divided or syncopated, as in this piece of music, we may find one part of our body doing one thing and another part doing something else. Having compared the Debussy and Stravinsky pieces, do we have any doubt that a composer's choices have the power to manipulate us sensuously?

From time to time throughout this chapter, we have referred to certain historical conventions that permeate the world of music. Some of these have a potential effect on our sense response. Some notational patterns can form a kind of musical shorthand, or perhaps mime, that conveys certain kinds of emotion to the listener. This, of course, has little meaning for us unless we take the time and effort to study music history. Some of Mozart's string quartets, for example, indulge in exactly this kind of communication—another illustration of how expanded knowledge can increase the depth, value, and enjoyment of the aesthetic experience.

THE MUSICAL PERFORMANCE

A certain part of our sense response to music occurs as a result of the nature of the performance itself. As we suggested earlier in the chapter, the scale of a symphony orchestra gives a composer a tremendously variable canvas on which to paint. Let's pause, momentarily, to familiarize ourselves with this fundamental aspect of the musical equation. As we face the stage in an orchestral concert, we note perhaps as many as one hundred instrumentalists facing back at us. Their arrangement from one concert to another is fairly standard, as illustrated in Figure 4.9.

A large symphony orchestra can overwhelm us with diverse timbres and volumes; a string quartet cannot. Our expectations and our focus change as we perceive the performance of one or the other. Because, for example, we know our perceptual experience with a string quartet will not involve the broad possibilities of an orchestra, we tune ourselves to seek the subtler, more personal messages within that particular medium. The difference between listening to an orchestra and listening to a quartet is similar to the difference between viewing a museum painting of monumental scale and the exquisite technique of a miniature.

Programmatic suggestion can have much to do with sensual response to a musical work. Debussy's *Prelude to the Afternoon of a Faun* elicits images of Pan frolicking through the woodlands and cavorting with the nymphs on a sunny afternoon. Of course, much of what we imagine has been stimulated by the title of the composition. Our perception is heightened further if we know the poem by Mallarmé (mah-lahr-MAY) on which the symphonic poem is based. This piece represents *program music*, which comprises instrumental music associated with a story, poem, idea, or scene. *Absolute music* comprises instrumental music without a program. Titles, and especially text, in musical compositions may be the strongest devices a composer has for communicating directly with us. Images are triggered by words, and they can stimulate our imaginations and senses to wander freely "in tune" with the musical development. Johannes Brahms called a movement in his *German Requiem* "All Mortal Flesh is as the Grass"; we certainly receive a philosophical and religious communication from that title. Moreover, when the chorus ceases to sing and the orchestra plays alone, the instrumental melodies stimulate images of fields of grass blowing in the wind.

Harmony and tonality both have considerable importance in stimulating our senses. Just as paintings and sculpture stimulate sensations of rest and comfort or action and discomfort, so harmonies create a feeling of repose and stability if consonant and a sensation of restlessness and instability if dissonant. Harmonic progression that leads to a full cadential resolution leaves us feeling fulfilled; unresolved cadences puzzle and perhaps irritate us. Major or minor tonalities have significantly differing effects: major sounds positive; minor, sad or mysterious. The former seems close to home, and the latter exotic. Atonal music sets us adrift to find the unifying thread of the composition.

Melody, rhythm, and tempo have close parallels to the use of line in painting, and the term *melodic contour* could be seen as a musical analogue to this element of painting. At this point we should consider enhancing and expressing our responses in all the arts by noting the shared terminology among the arts disciplines—for example, line, form, color, rhythm, repetition, and harmony—and grasping the nuances of how that terminology applies across disciplinary lines. When the tones of a melody are conjunct and undulate slowly and smoothly, they trace a pattern having the same effect as their linear visual counterpart—sensuous, soft, comfortable, and placid.

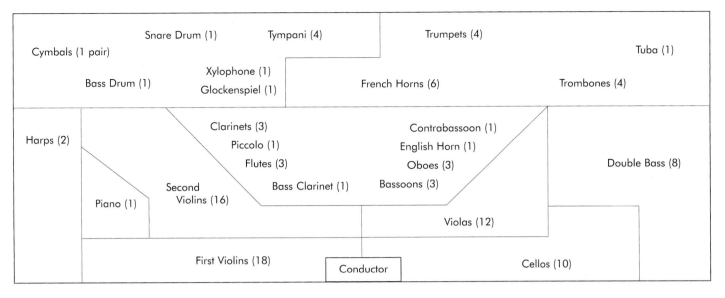

4.9 Typical seating plan for a large orchestra (about 100 instrumentalists), showing the placement of instrumental sections.

When melodic contours are disjunct and tempos rapid, the pattern and response change:

In conclusion, it remains for us as we respond to music to analyze how each of the elements available to the composer has in fact become a part of the channel of communication, and how the composer (consciously or unconsciously) has put together a work that elicits sensory responses from us. The "Thinking Critically" section at the end of this chapter offers some suggestions on effective listening.

OPERA

The composer Pietro Mascagni (mahs-KAH-nyee) reportedly said, "In my operas do not look for melody or beauty . . . look only for blood."

Mascagni represented a style of late-nineteenth-century opera called *verismo* (vay-REEZ-moh), a word with the same root as verisimilitude, meaning "true to life." *Verismo* opera treated themes, characters, and events from life in a down-to-earth fashion. In Mascagni's operas and the operas of other composers of the *verismo* style, we find plenty of blood, but we also find fine drama and music, and the combination of drama and music into a single artistic form constitutes opera. In basic terms, opera is a dramatic work sung to orchestral accompaniment. In opera, the music comprises the predominant element, but the addition of a story line, scenery, costumes, and staging makes opera significantly different from other forms of music.

In one sense, we could describe opera as the purest integration of all the arts. It contains music, drama, poetry, and visual arts. It even includes architecture, because an opera house constitutes a particular architectural entity with very specific requirements for orchestra, audience, and stage space, as well as stage machinery. In its wide variety of applications, opera ranges from tragedies of spectacular proportions, involving several hundred people, to intimate music dramas and comedies with two or three characters (Figs. **4.10–4.12**).

In an opera, unlike theatre, the production reveals character and plot through song rather than speech. This convention removes opera from the lifelikeness we might expect in the theatre and asks us to suspend our disbelief, sometimes incredibly, so that we can enjoy magnificent music and the heightening of dramatic experience that music's contribution to mood, character, and dramatic action affords us.

Central to an opera are performers who can sing and act simultaneously. These include major characters played by star performers as well as secondary solo singers and chorus members plus supernumeraries—"supers" or "extras"—who do not sing but merely flesh out crowd scenes (see Figs. **4.10–4.12**).

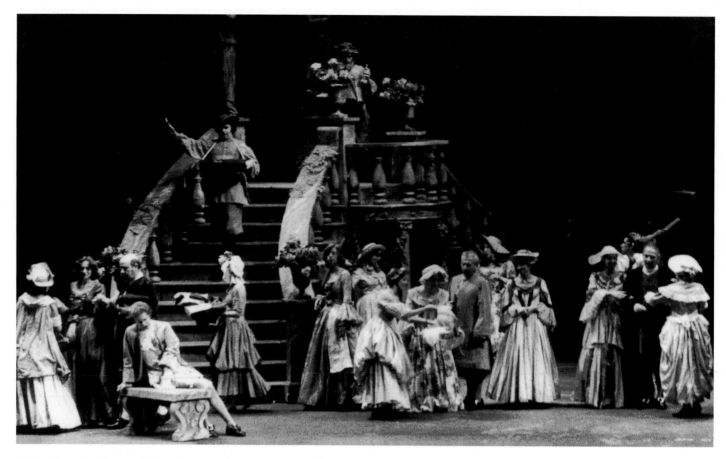

4.10 Giacomo Puccini, *Manon Lescaut*. Opera Company of Philadelphia. Photo by Trudy Cohen.

Types of Opera

In Italian, the word opera means "work." In Florence, Italy, in the late sixteenth century, artists, writers, and architects eagerly revived the culture of ancient Greece and Rome. Opera was an attempt by a group known as the *camerata* (Italian for fellowship or society) to re-create the effect of ancient Greek drama, in which, scholars believed, the words were chanted or sung as well as spoken. Through succeeding centuries, various applications of the fundamental concept of opera have arisen, and among these applications stand four basic types of opera: (1) grand opera; (2) opéra comique; (3) opera buffa; and (4) operetta.

Grand opera, used synonymously with "opera," refers to serious or tragic opera, usually in five acts. Another name for this type of opera is *opera seria* (oh-pay-RAH SAY-ree-ah) (serious opera), which treats heroic subjects usually in a highly stylized manner—for example, the gods and heroes of ancient times.

Opéra comique (oh-pay-RAH coh-MEEK) is opera, regardless of subject matter, that has spoken dialogue. This type of opera must not be confused with comic opera.

Opera buffa (oh-pay-RAH BOO-fah) is comic opera (again, not to be confused with opéra comique), which usually does not have spoken dialogue. It usually uses satire to treat a serious topic with humor—for example, Mozart's *The Marriage of Figaro*.

Operetta also has spoken dialogue, but it has come to refer to a light style of opera characterized by popular themes, a romantic mood, and often a humorous tone. It is frequently considered more theatrical than musical, and its story line is usually frivolous and sentimental. Listen to an example from the American standard, *Porgy and Bess*, on the music CD track 22.

The Opera Production

Like theatre, opera is a collaborative art, joining the efforts of a composer, a dramatist, a stage director, and a musical director. At its beginnings, an opera emerges when a composer sets to music a text, called a *libretto* (and written by a *librettist*). As suggested earlier, the range of subjects and characters in opera may be extremely broad, from mythological to everyday. All characters come to life through performers who combine singing and acting. Opera includes the basic voice ranges of soprano, alto, tenor, and bass, but divides them more precisely. Below are some of the categories.

Coloratura soprano	Very high range; capable of executing rapid scales and trills.
Lyric soprano	Fairly light voice; cast in roles requiring grace and charm.
Dramatic soprano	Full, powerful voice, capable of passionate intensity.
Lyric tenor	Relatively light, bright voice.
Dramatic tenor	Powerful voice, capable of heroic expression.
Basso buffo	Cast in comic roles; can sing very rapidly.
Basso profundo	Extremely low range capable of power; cast in roles requiring great dignity.

Since the majority of operas in the contemporary repertoire do not have American origin, the American respondent usually has to overcome a language barrier to understand the dialogue and thereby the plot. A desire for snobbery or exclusivity does not cause the lack of English-translation performances; much of it is pure practicality. For example, performing operas in their original language makes it possible for the best singers to be heard around the world. Imagine the complications if a great singer had to learn a single opera in the language of every country in which he or she performed it. In addition, opera loses much of its musical character in translation. We spoke of tone color, or timbre, earlier in this chapter. Timbre characteristics implicit in the Russian, German, and Italian languages vanish when translated into English. In addition, inasmuch as opera is in a sense the Olympic Games of the vocal-music world—the demands made on the human voice by the composers of opera call for the highest degree of skill and training of any vocal medium—tone, placement, and the vowels and consonants requisite

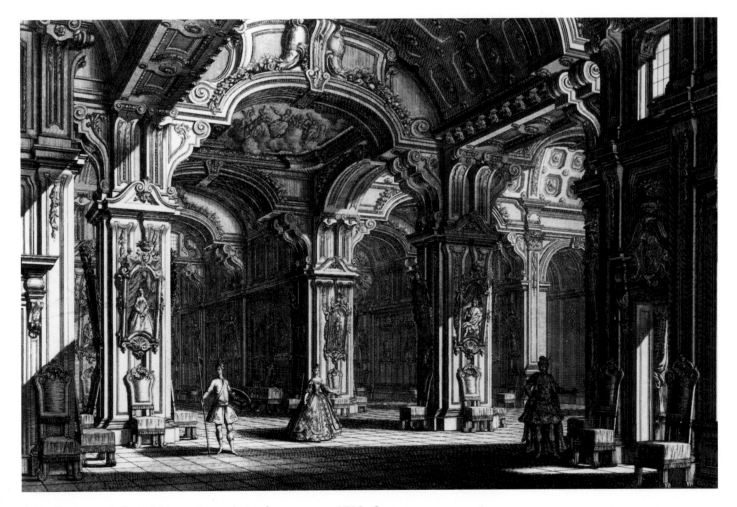

4.11 Giuseppe Galli da Bibiena, Scene design for an opera, 1719. Contemporary engraving. Metropolitan Museum of Art, New York (Elisha Whittelsey Fund).

Music and Human Reality

Bizet, *Carmen*

George Bizet's (bee-ZEH) opera *Carmen* takes its libretto from a literary classic, a story by Prosper Mérimée. Its heroine, Carmen, is a seductive employee in a cigarette factory in nineteenth-century Seville. She flirts with Don Jose, a soldier, and completely enraptures him to the point where he deserts his service to follow her first to her haunt, a disreputable tavern, and then to a mountain pass where gypsy smugglers have made their hideout. But Carmen soon tires of Don Jose and becomes interested in the great toreador Escamillo (ehs-kah-MEEL-yoh). On the day of a bullfight in Seville, Carmen arrives with Escamillo, the latter welcomed as a hero. After Escamillo enters the bullring, Don Jose appears, dishevelled and distraught. In vain he pleads with Carmen to return to him. When she refuses, he stabs her fatally with a dagger. Emerging from the bullfight, Escamillo finds Don Jose weeping over Carmen's dead body.

Carmen began as *opéra comique*. When Bizet first wrote his score, he used spoken dialogue, and this is the way *Carmen* was heard at the Opéra Comique in Paris on March 3, 1875. Incidentally, it still plays that way at that house. But elsewhere, dialogue was replaced by recitatives, sung dialogues prepared not by the composer himself but by Ernest Guiraud.

Today a number of ballet sequences are interpolated (using background music from other Bizet compositions). *Carmen* had no ballets.

As a character and as a woman, Carmen fascinates. Bizet uses her as a symbol of "woman." Every passage Carmen sings is a new mask, mirroring the man she is addressing. Her receptive nature is portrayed with uncanny realism in her change of tone as she addresses the passers-by, Jose, Zuniga, the smugglers, and Escamillo. For each of the men, she alters the sound of her voice, the character of her melody, her mood, her tempo.

Much in *Carmen* disturbed audiences in 1875. The vivid portrayal of such an immoral character caused shock. Never before had an opera presented women onstage smoking cigarettes. Some listeners objected to the music, thinking it too much like Wagner, because Bizet assigned such importance to the orchestra and on random occasions used a leading-motif (*leitmotif*) technique. Nevertheless, *Carmen* was by no means the total failure that some of Bizet's early biographers suggested. As a matter of fact, some critics hailed it, a publisher paid a handsome price for the publication rights, and the opera company kept it in its repertory the following season—a great compliment to the composer.

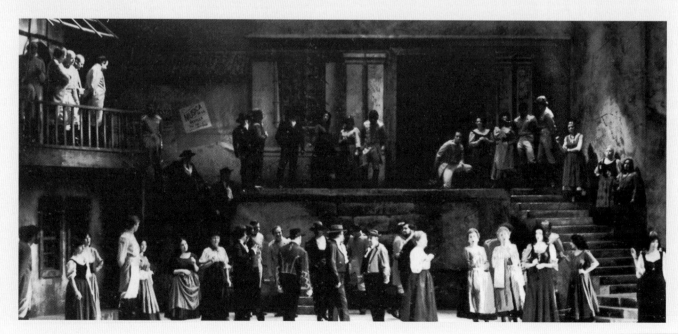

4.12 Georges Bizet, *Carmen*. Opera Company of Philadelphia. Composite photo by Trudy Cohen.

to that placement, become very important to the singer. It is one thing for a tenor to sing the vowel "eh" on high B-flat in the original Italian. If the translated word to be sung on the same note employs an "oo" vowel, the technical demand changes considerably. So, the translation of opera from its original tongue into English causes more difficult and complex problems than simply providing an accurate translation for a portion of the audience that does not know the text—as important as that may seem. Translation must concern itself with tone quality, color, and the execution of tones in the *tessitura*, or normal range, of the human voice.

Experienced operagoers may study the score before attending a performance. However, every concert program contains a plot synopsis (even when the production is in English), so that everyone can follow what happens. Opera plots, unlike mysteries, have few surprise endings, and knowing the plot ahead of time does not diminish the experience of responding to the opera. To assist the audience, often opera companies project the translated lyrics on a screen above the stage, much like subtitles in a foreign film.

The opening element in opera is the *overture*. This orchestral introduction may have two characteristics. First, it may set the mood or tone of the opera. Here the composer works directly with our sense responses, putting us in the proper frame of mind for what follows. In his overture to *I Pagliacci* (ee pahl-YAH-chee), for example, Ruggiero Leoncavallo creates a tonal story foretelling comedy, tragedy, action, and romance, using only the orchestra. Listening to this overture, we can identify these elements, and in so doing understand the relative unimportance of English to comprehension of the work. Add to the "musical language" the language of body and mime, and we can understand even complex ideas and character relationships—*without* words. In addition to this type of introduction, an overture may provide melodic introductions—passages introducing the *arias* and *recitatives* (reh-sih-tah-TEEV) that will follow.

The plot of an opera unfolds through recitative, or sung dialogue. Recitative moves the plot along from one section to another; it usually has little emotional content, and the words are more important than the music. There are two kinds of recitative. In the first, *recitativo secco*

(ray-chee-tah-TEE-voh say-koh), the singer has very little musical accompaniment, or sometimes none at all. Any accompaniment usually occurs in the form of light chording under the voice. The second type, *recitativo stromento* (ray-chee-tah-TEE-voh stroh-MEHN-toh), has full musical accompaniment.

The real emotion and poetry of an opera lie in its arias. Musically and poetically, an aria reflects high dramatic feeling. The great opera songs that we know consist of arias such as "Dido's Lament" (music CD track 10) from the opera *Dido and Aeneas* by Henry Purcell (1659?–95; PUR-suhl or pur-SEHL). The passage comes from the end of the tragic opera when Dido, resigned to her fate, sings this powerful aria whose text, translated, says:

> "When I am laid in earth,
> May my wrongs create
> No trouble in thy breast.
> Remember me!
> But ah! forget my fate!"

Every opera contains ensemble pieces such as duets, trios, and quartets, as well as chorus sections in which everyone gets into the act. In addition, ballet or dance interludes appear frequently. These may have nothing to do with the development of the plot, but add more life and interest to the dramatic production, and in some cases provide a link from one scene into another.

Bel canto, as its name implies, is a style of singing emphasizing the beauty of sound. Its most successful composer, Gioacchino Rossini, had a great sense of melody and sought to develop the *art song* to its highest level. In *bel canto* singing the melody is the focus.

In the nineteenth century, Richard Wagner (REE-kahrd VAHG-nuhr) (music CD track 18) gave opera and theatre a prototype that still continues to influence theatrical production—*organic unity*. Every element of his productions integrated to create a *Gesamtkunstwerk* (geh-ZAHMT-koonst-vairk), a work of total unity. Wagner also used *leitmotif* (lite-moh-TEEF), a common element in contemporary film. A leitmotif is a musical theme associated with a particular person or idea. Each time that person appears or is thought of, or each time the idea surfaces, we hear the leitmotif.

THINKING CRITICALLY

When listening to music, guide your listening, sharpen your perceptions, associate what you hear with musical terms, and critically analyze the selection by asking yourself the following questions. (As an example, listen to Bach's *Prelude and Fugue No. 1 in C*, BWV 846 at www.classicalarchives.com/main/.)

- Subject. Does the composition try to convey a subject or does it represent only that which is pure (absolute music)? Does the title of the piece suggest something (program music)?

- Function. Was the piece composed with any particular purpose in mind (march, lullaby, serenade, waltz)? Was it composed for some particular occasion? Does the piece introduce something or set the mood for some activity (prelude, overture)?

- Form. Does the title of the piece identify its form? How does it follow the characteristics of the form?

- Sound. How does the piece explore dynamics? Using the specific musical terms—for example, pianissimo, forte—describe the progression of the piece from beginning to end. In what ways does the music explore tone color?

- Rhythm. What is the meter? Do any changes occur? If so, where and how?

- Tempo. In what ways does the tempo of the piece affect your response? Using the specific musical terms—for example, largo, andante—describe the progression of speeds from beginning to end.

- Texture. What textures does the music explore? Where do changes, if any, in texture occur?

CYBER STUDY

SONATA:
—Franz Joseph Haydn, *Piano Sonata No. 20 in C Minor*, 1. Allegro Moderato
www.classicalarchives.com/main/

SYMPHONY:
—Ludwig van Beethoven, *Symphony No. 3 in E flat Major*, "*Eroica,*" Op. 55, 1. Allegro con brio
www.classicalarchives.com/main/

CONCERTO:
—George Frederick Handel, *Concerto Grosso Op. 6, No. 12 in B Minor*
www.classicalarchives.com/main/

SUITE:
—Johann Sebastian Bach, *Orchestral Suite No. 2 in B Minor*, BWV 1067
www.classicalarchives.com/main/

CHAPTER FIVE

THEATRE

IMPORTANT TERMS

Aesthetic distance The mental and physical separation of the audience from the performance.

Comedy A genre of complex qualities involving humor. Comedy may or may not involve laughter and may or may not end "happily."

Complication A part of plot containing a series of conflicts and decisions by the characters.

Dénouement A part of plot containing the final resolution.

Exposition A part of plot containing necessary background information.

Melodrama A genre characterized by stereotyped characters, implausible plots, and an emphasis on spectacle.

Performance art A theatrical-type performance that combines elements from fields in the humanities and the arts.

Protagonist The main character of a play.

Script A written document containing the words of the play.

Tragedy A serious drama or other literary work in which conflict between a protagonist and a superior force (often fate) concludes in disaster for the protagonist.

FORMAL AND TECHNICAL QUALITIES

Of all the arts, theatre comes the closest to personalizing the love, rejection, disappointment, betrayal, joy, elation, and suffering that we experience in our daily lives. It does so because theatre uses live people acting out situations that very often look and sound like real life. Theatre once functioned in society like television and movies do today. Many of the qualities of all three forms are identical. We shall find in this chapter the ways that theatre, which frequently relies on *drama* (a written script), takes lifelike circumstances and compresses them into organized episodes. The result, although looking like reality, goes far beyond it in order to help us find in its characters pieces of ourselves.

The word *theatre* comes from the Greek *theatron*—the part of the Greek theatre where the audience sat. Its literal meaning is "a place for seeing," but for the Greeks this implied more than the sense experience of vision (which, indeed, is an important part of the theatrical production). To the ancient Greeks, "to see" also might include comprehension and understanding. Thus, witnessing—seeing and hearing—a theatrical production was felt with the emotions and mediated by the intelligence of the mind, leading to an understanding of the importance of the play. Further, for the ancient Greeks, *theatron*, while a physical part of the theatre building, implied a nonphysical place—a special state of being of those who together watched the lives of the persons of the drama.

Like the other performing arts, theatre is an interpretive discipline. Between the playwright and the audience stand the director, the designers, and the actors. Although each functions as an individual artist, each also serves to communicate the playwright's vision to the audience. Sometimes the play becomes subordinate to the expressive work of its interpreters; sometimes the concept of director as master artist places the playwright in a subordinate position. Nonetheless, a theatrical production always requires the interpretation of a concept through spectacle and sound by theatre artists.

Theatre represents an attempt to reveal a vision of human life through time, sound, and space. It gives us flesh-and-blood human beings involved in human action—we must occasionally remind ourselves that the dramatic experience is not reality: it is an imitation of reality, acting as a symbol to communicate something about the human condition. Theatre is make-believe: through gesture and movement, language, character, thought, and spectacle, it imitates action. However, if this were all theatre that consisted of, we would not find it as captivating as we do, and as people have for more than 2,500 years.

GENRES

At the formal level, theatre comprises *genre*—or type of play—from which the production evolves. Some of the genres of theatre are *tragedy, comedy, tragicomedy, melodrama*, and *performance art*. Some are products of specific periods of history, and illustrate trends that no longer exist; others are still developing and as yet lack definite form. Our response to genre differs from our formal response or identification in music, for example, because we seldom find generic identification in the theatre program. Some plays are well-known examples of a specific genre, for example, the tragedy *Oedipus the King* by Sophocles. In these cases, as with a symphony, we can see how the production develops the conventions of genre. Other plays, however, are not well known or may be open to interpretation. As a result, we can draw our conclusions only after the performance has finished.

Tragedy

We commonly describe tragedy as a play with an unhappy ending. Aristotle treats this subject in detail in *The Poetics*. The playwright Arthur Miller describes tragedy as "the consequences of a man's total compulsion to evaluate himself justly; his destruction in the attempt posits a wrong or an evil in his environment." In the centuries since its inception, tragedy has undergone many variations as a means by which the playwright makes a statement about human frailty and failing.

Typically, tragic heroes make free choices that bring about suffering, defeat, and, sometimes, triumph as a result of defeat. The protagonist often undergoes a struggle that ends disastrously. In Greek Classical tragedy of the fifth century B.C.E. (see Chapter 10), the hero or heroine was generally a larger-than-life figure who gained a moral victory amid physical defeat. Classical heroes usually suffer from a tragic flaw—some defect that causes them to contribute to their own downfall. In a typical Classical tragedy, the climax occurs as the hero or heroine recognizes his or her role and accepts destiny. In the years from ancient Greece to the present, however, writers have employed many different approaches. Arthur Miller argues the case for tragic heroes of "common stuff," suggesting that "the tragic right is a condition of life, a condition in which the human personality is able to flower and realize itself." Refer to the Cyber Study at the end of the chapter for examples.

Comedy

The word "comedy" comes from the Greek *komoidia* (koh-mee-DEE-ah), which is a derivative of the Greek word for a singer in a revel, from *kômos* (KOH-mohs), meaning "a band of revelers." Comedy deals with light or amusing subjects or with serious and profound subjects in a light, familiar, or satirical manner. As a consequence, it is more complex than tragedy and more complicated to define precisely. The genre dates to the fifth century B.C.E., when it was associated with the revelry linked to worship of the god Dionysus (dy-uh-NY-suhs). The first period of Greek comedy, known as Old Comedy, is represented by the comedies of Aristophanes (air-ih-STAH-fuh-neez; see Chapter 10, p. 232). These were mostly satires of public officials. By Roman times, comedy shifted its focus to ordinary citizens portrayed as stock characters. It also had formularized plots. For the most part disappearing until the Middle Ages, comedy reappeared as simply a story with a happy ending. In more recent times, the genre has taken divergent paths, depending on the attitude of its authors toward their subject matter. As a result, we find, for example, satirical comedy, in which the author intends to ridicule. When the ridicule focuses on individuals, we have *comedy of character*. When the satire is on social conventions, *comedy of manners* results. This genre was especially popular and well developed in the eighteenth century in England. Satire of conventional thinking produces *comedy of ideas*. A few more types include: *romantic comedy* (the progress from troubles to triumphs in love) and *comedy of intrigue* (amusement and excitement through an intricate plot of reversals with artificial, contrived situations—for example, the Spanish comedies of Lope de Vega (vay gah) and Tirso de Molina (moh-LEE-nah)). *Sentimental comedy* entails exploitation of potentially serious issues without approaching the truly tragic aspects of the subject or examining its underlying significance. See Cyber Study for examples.

Tragicomedy

As the name suggests, tragicomedy mixes forms and, like the other types, has been defined in different terms in different periods. Until the nineteenth century, the ending defined this form. Traditionally, characters reflect diverse social standings—kings (as in tragedy) and common folk (as in comedy)—and reversals go from bad to good and good to bad. The genre also includes language appropriate to both tragedy and comedy. Early tragicomedies were serious plays that ended, if not happily, then at least by avoiding catastrophe. In the past century-and-a-half, the term has been adapted to describe plays in which the mood may shift from light to heavy, or in which endings are neither exclusively tragic nor comic. See Cyber Study for an example.

Melodrama

Melodrama is another mixed form. It takes its name from the terms *melo* (Greek for "music") and "drama." Melodrama first appeared in the late eighteenth century, when dialogue took place against a musical background. In the nineteenth century, the term was applied to serious plays without music. Melodrama uses stereotypical characters involved in serious situations in which suspense, pathos, terror, and occasionally hatred are aroused. It portrays the forces of good and evil battling in exaggerated circumstances. As a rule, the issues involved are simplified and uncomplicated: good is good and evil is evil; there are no ambiguities.

Geared largely for a popular audience, the form concerns itself primarily with situation and plot. Conventional in its morality, melodrama tends toward optimism—good always triumphs in the end. Typically, the hero or heroine is placed in life-threatening situations by the acts of a villain and then rescued at the last instant. The forces against which the characters struggle are external ones—caused by an unfriendly world rather than by inner conflicts. Probably because melodrama took root in the nineteenth century, at a time when spectacular scenic effects were in vogue, many melodramas depend on sensation scenes for much of their effect. The popular nineteenth-century adaptation of Harriet Beecher Stowe's novel *Uncle Tom's Cabin* reflects this fondness for spectacle, as Eliza and the baby, Little Eva, escape from the plantation and are pursued across a raging, ice-filled river. These effects taxed the capacities of theatres to their maximum, but gave the audience spectacle. Not all melodramas use such extreme scenic devices, but their use was so frequent that they have become identified with the type.

Performance Art

The late twentieth century produced a form of theatrical presentation called Performance Art. Performance Art pushes the limits of traditional theatre in a variety of directions, some of which deny traditional concepts of theatrical production itself. It constitutes a type of performance that combines elements from fields in the humanities and arts, from urban anthropology to folklore, and dance to feminism. Performance Art pieces called *Happenings* grew out of the Pop Art movement of the 1960s and were designed as critiques of consumer culture. European performance artists, influenced by the early twentieth-century movement of Dadaism, tended toward politics more than their American counterparts. Many Happenings focused on the idea that art and life should be connected.

Because of its hybrid and diverse nature, we can study no "typical" performance artist or work as an illustration. We can, however, note three brief examples, which, if they do not typify, at least illumine this movement. The Hittite Empire, an all-male performance art group, performs *The Undersiege Stories*, which focuses on nonverbal communication and dance and includes confrontational scenarios. Performance artist Kathy Rose blends dance and film animation in unique ways. In one performance in New York, she creatively combined exotic dances with a wide variety of styles that included German Expressionism (see p. 363) and science fiction. The *New York Times* called her performance "visual astonishments." Playwright Rezo Abdoh's *Quotations from a Ruined City*, an intense and kinetic piece, features ten actors who act out outrage in fascinating, energetic fashion. The complicated, overlapping scenes, tableaux, and dances are punctuated by the sound of loud but unintelligible prerecorded voices. The piece combines elements depicting brutality, sadism, and sexuality. In the 1990s, Performance Art saw some difficult times because many people viewed it as being rebellious and controversial for its own sake.

THE PRODUCTION

Theatre consists of a complex combination of elements that form a single entity called a performance or a production. Understanding theatre production as a work of art can be enhanced if we have some tools for approaching it. The following come to us from the distant past.

Writing 2,400 years ago in the *Poetics*, Aristotle argued that tragedy consisted of plot, character, diction, music, thought, and spectacle. We can use and expand upon Aristotle's terminology to describe the basic parts of a production. These six parts—and their descriptive terminology—still cover the entire theatrical product. We shall reshape Aristotle's terms into language more familiar to us, explain what they mean, and learn how we can use them to understand how a theatrical production works—things to look and listen for in a production. First, we will examine the script, and include in that discussion Aristotle's concept of diction, or language. Next, we will examine plot, thought—themes and ideas—character, and spectacle, which we shall call the visual elements. That will be followed by a brief discussion of what Aristotle called music but which, to avoid confusion, we will call aural elements.

Script

A playwright creates a written document called a script, which contains the dialogue used by the actors. Aristotle called the words written by the playwright *diction;* we will refer to this part of a production as its *language.* The playwright's language tells us at least part of what we can expect from the play. For example, if everyday speech has been used, we generally expect the action to resemble everyday truth, or reality. In the play *Fences* (1986), playwright August Wilson uses everyday language to bring the characters to life in the context of the period:

(*Act I, scene iii. Troy is talking to his son.*)

Like you? I go out of here every morning . . . bust my butt . . . putting up with them crackers everyday . . . cause I like you? You about the biggest fool I ever saw.
  (Pause)
    It's my job. It's my responsibility! You understand that? A man got to take care of his family. You live in my house . . . sleep you behind on my bedclothes . . . fill you belly up with my food . . . cause you my son.[1]

Poetic language, on the other hand, usually indicates less realism and perhaps stronger symbolism. Compare the language of *Fences* with the poetry used by Pierre Corneille (kohr-NAY), a seventeenth-century dramatist, in *Le Cid* (luh seed) to create a mythical hero who is larger than life:

(*Act III, scene iv*)

Rodrigue: I'll do your bidding, yet still do I desire
To end my wretched life, at your dear hand.
But this you must not ask, that I renounce
My worthy act in cowardly repentance.
The fatal outcome of too swift an anger
Disgraced my father, covered me with shame.[2]

In both plays, we use language and its tone to aid us in determining the implication of the words. Language helps to create the overall tone and style of the play. It can also reveal character, theme, and historical context.

Plot

Plot is the structure of the play, the skeleton that gives the play shape, and on which the other elements hang. The nature of the plot determines how a play works: how it moves from one moment to another, how conflicts are structured, and how the experience ultimately comes to an end. We can examine the workings of plot by seeing

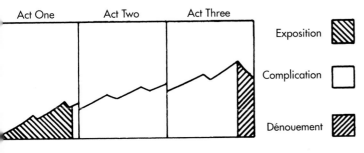

5.1 Hypothetical dynamic and structural development of a three-act play.

the play somewhat as a timeline, beginning as the script or production begins, and ending at the final curtain, or the end of the script. In many plays, plot tends to operate like a climactic pyramid (Fig. **5.1**). In order to keep our attention, the dynamics of the play rise in intensity until they reach the ultimate crisis—the *climax*—after which they relax, through a resolution called the *dénouement* (day-noo-MAWN; French for "untangling"), to the end of the play.

Depending on the playwright's purpose, plot may be shaped with or without some of the features described below. Sometimes plot may be so de-emphasized that it virtually disappears. However, as we try to evaluate a play critically, the elements of plot give us things to look for—if only to note that they do not exist in the play at hand.

EXPOSITION Exposition provides necessary background information. Through it the playwright introduces the characters—their personalities, relationships, backgrounds, and present situation. Exposition frequently forms a recognizable section at the beginning of a play. It can be presented through dialogue, narration, setting, lighting, costume—or any device the playwright or director chooses. The amount of exposition in a play depends very much on where the playwright takes up the story, called the *point of attack*. A play told chronologically may need fairly little expositional material, while others require a good bit of prior summary.

COMPLICATION Drama centers on conflict. Although not every play fits that definition, conflict of some sort provides a fundamental dramatic device in order to interest an audience. At some point in the play, someone or something frustrates the expected course of events, giving the audience reason to be interested in what transpires. At a specific moment, an action someone takes or a decision someone makes upsets the current state of affairs. Sometimes called the *inciting incident*, it opens the middle part of the plot—the *complication*. The complication con-

tains the meat of the play, and it comprises a series of conflicts and decisions, called crises (from the Greek *krisis*, meaning "to decide"), that rise in intensity until they reach a turning point—the climax—that constitutes the end of the complication section.

DÉNOUEMENT The dénouement is the final resolution of the plot: the period of time during which the audience senses that the action is ending—a period of adjustment, downward in intensity, from the climax. Ideally, the dénouement brings about a clear and ordered resolution.

Exposition, complication, and dénouement comprise a timeframe in which the remaining parts of the play operate. This structural picture is not always so neat, though. Some plays do not conform to this kind of plot structure, yet that does not make them poorly constructed or of inferior quality. Nor does it mean that these concepts cannot generally be used as a means for describing and analyzing how a play is put together.

FORESHADOWING Preparation for subsequent action—foreshadowing—provides credibility for future action, keeps the plot logical, and avoids confusion. It builds tension and suspense: the audience senses that something is about to happen, but because they do not know exactly what or when, anticipation builds suspense and tension. In the movie *Jaws*, a rhythmic musical theme foreshadows the presence of the shark. Just as the audience becomes comfortable with that device, the shark suddenly appears—without the music. As a result, uncertainty as to the next shark attack heightens immensely. Foreshadowing also moves the play forward by pointing toward events that will occur later.

DISCOVERY Discovery is the revelation of information about characters, their personalities, relationships, and feelings. Hamlet discovers from his father's ghost that his father was murdered by Claudius, and is urged to avenge the killing—a discovery without which the play cannot proceed. The skill of the playwright in structuring the revelation of such information in large part determines the overall impact of the play on the audience.

REVERSAL Reversal is any turn of fortune; for example, Oedipus falls from power and prosperity to blindness and exile; Shakespeare's King Lear goes from ruler to victim of disaster. In comedy, reversal often changes the roles of social classes, as peasants jump to the upper class, and vice versa. In *Tartuffe* (see p. 27), as the play begins, Orgon can see nothing negative about Tartuffe, regardless of others' pleading. At the climax, however, Orgon sees clearly, and Tartuffe suffers his warranted reversal.

Character

Character is the psychological motivation of the people in the play. In most plays, the audience focuses on why individuals do what they do, how they change, and how they interact with other individuals, as the plot unfolds.

Plays reveal a wide variety of characters—both persons and motivating psychological forces. Every play has characters who fulfill major functions and on whom the playwright wishes to focus. Minor characters also exist. They may interact with the major characters, and their actions constitute subordinate plot lines. Much of the interest created by the drama lies in the exploration of how people with specific character motivations react to circumstances. For example, when Rodrigue in *Le Cid* discovers that his father has been humiliated, what in his character makes him decide to avenge the insult, even though it means killing the father of the woman he loves, thereby jeopardizing that love? Such responses, driven by character, drive plays forward.

Protagonist

Inside the structural pattern of a play some kind of action must take place. We must ask ourselves how the play works. How do we get from the beginning to the end? Most of the time, we take that journey via the actions and decisions of the *protagonist*, or central personage. Deciding on the protagonist of a play often poses challenging choices. However, understanding the play requires ascertaining the central character. In Terence Rattigan's *Cause Célèbre* three different responses emerge, depending upon whom the director chose as the protagonist. There are two central female roles. A good case could be made for either as the central personage of the play. Or they could be equal.

Often in drama a character appears in order to accentuate or contrast qualities in another character, particularly the protagonist. We call such a contrasting character a *foil*. One of the best and best-known examples is Dr. Watson in Sir Arthur Conan Doyle's Sherlock Holmes stories. Here, Dr. Watson's obtuseness makes Holmes's deductions appear all the more brilliant.

Themes

Themes and ideas comprise the intellectual content of a play (Aristotle used the term "thought"). In Lanford Wilson's *Burn This* (1987), for example, a young dancer, Anna, lives in a Manhattan loft with two gay roommates, Larry and Robby. As the play opens, we learn that Robby has been killed in a boating accident. Anna has just returned from the funeral and a set of bizarre encounters with Robby's family. Larry, a sardonic advertising executive, and Burton, Anna's boyfriend, maintain a constant animosity. Into the scene bursts Pale, Robby's brother and a threatening, violent figure. Anna is both afraid of and irresistibly attracted to Pale; the conflict of their relationship drives the play forward to its climax.

The above brief description summarizes the *plot* of a play. However, what the play is about—its *themes*—remains for us to discover and develop. Some might say it is about loneliness, anger, and the way not belonging is manifested in human behavior. Others might focus on abusive relationships, and others on how it deals with hetero- and homosexual conflicts and issues. The process of coming to conclusions about meaning involves several layers of interpretation. One involves the playwright's interpretation of the ideas through the characters, language, and plot. A second lies in the director's decisions about what the playwright has in mind, which is balanced by what the director wishes to communicate because, or in spite, of the playwright. Finally, we interpret what we actually see and hear in the production.

Visual Elements

The director takes the playwright's language, plot, and characters and translates them into action by using, among other things, what Aristotle called "spectacle," or what the French call *mise-en-scène* (meez-ahn-sehn), but which we can simply call the visual elements. The visual elements of a production include, first of all, the physical relationship established between actors and audience. The actor–audience relationship can take any number of shapes. For example, the audience might sit surrounding, or perhaps on only one side of, the stage. The visual elements also include stage settings, lighting, costumes, and properties, as well as the actors and their movements. Whatever the audience can see contributes to this aspect of the theatrical production.

THEATRE TYPES Part of our response to a production is shaped by the design of the space in which the play is produced. The earliest and most natural arrangement, the theatre-in-the-round, or *arena* theatre (Fig. 5.2), puts the audience around the playing area on all sides. Whether the stage is circular, square, or rectangular remains irrelevant. Some argue that the closeness of the audience to the actors in an arena theatre provides the most intimate kind of theatrical experience. A second possibility, the *thrust*, or three-quarter, theatre (Fig. 5.3), has the audience around the playing area on three sides. The most familiar example of this type of theatre is what we understand to

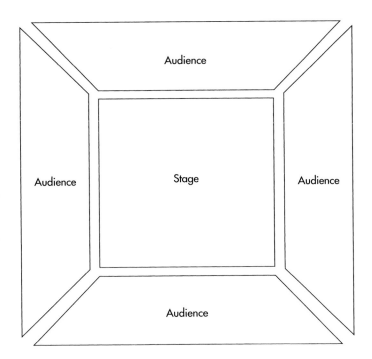

5.2 Ground plan of an arena theatre.

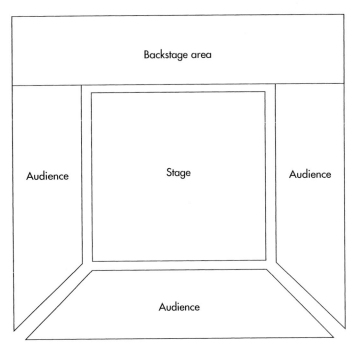

5.3 Ground plan of a thrust theatre.

have been the theatre of the Shakespearean period. The third arrangement, and the one most widely used in contemporary productions, the *proscenium* theatre, places the audience on only one side, viewing the action through a frame (Fig. 5.4).

Various experimental arrangements of audience and stage space also exist. Sometimes acting areas stand in the middle of the audience, creating little island stages. In certain circumstances, these small stages create quite an interesting set of responses and relationships between actors and audience.

Common experience indicates that the physical relationship of the acting area to the audience has an effect on the depth of audience involvement. It has also been found that some separation is necessary for certain kinds of emotional responses. We call this mental and physical separation *aesthetic distance*. The proper aesthetic distance allows us to become involved in what we know is fictitious and even unbelievable.

The visual elements may or may not have independent communication with the audience; this provides one option for the director and designers. Before the nineteenth century, no coordination of the various elements of a theatre production occurred. This, of course, had all kinds of curious, and in some cases catastrophic, consequences. However, for the past century, most theatre productions have adhered to the *organic theory* of play production: everything, visual and aural, is designed with a single purpose. Each production has a specific goal in terms of audience response, and all of the

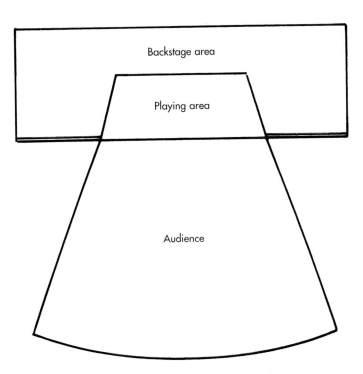

5.4 Ground plan of a proscenium theatre.

elements in the production attempt to achieve this. See the Companion Website: Theatre.

SCENE DESIGN Simply stated, scene design in the theatre seeks to create an environment suitable for achieving the aims of the production. Scene designers use the same tools of composition—line, form, mass, color, repetition,

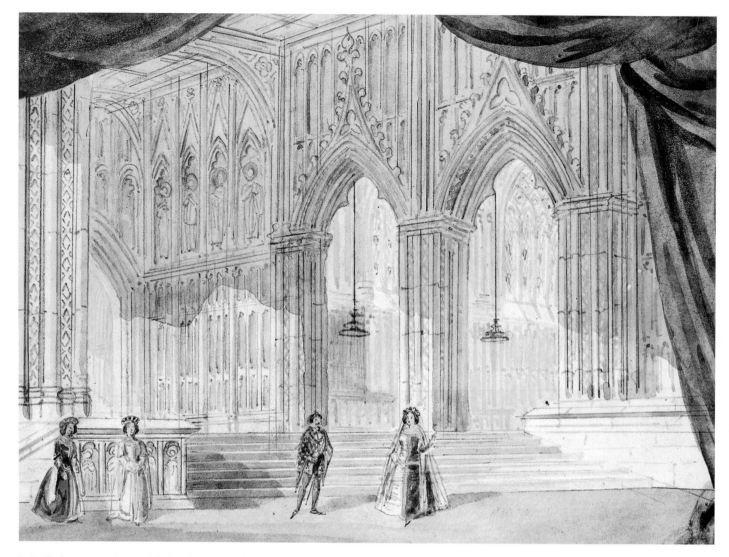

5.5 Shakespeare, *Richard II*, Act II, scene ii (entrance into St. Stephen's Chapel). Producer: Charles Kean, London, 1857. Scene designer: Thomas Grieve. Victoria & Albert Museum, London.

and unity—as painters. In addition, since a stage design occupies three-dimensional space and must allow for the movement of the actors in, on, through, and around the elements of scenery, the scene designer becomes a sculptor as well. Figures 5.5 and 5.6 illustrate how emphasis on certain elements of design highlights different characteristics in the production. Thomas Grieve's *Richard II* (Fig. 5.5) is formal, but light and spacious. His regular rhythms and repetition of arches create a completely different feeling from that elicited by Robert Burroughs's design for *Peer Gynt* (peer ghihnt; Fig. 5.6), where the zigzagging diagonals juxtaposed among verticals create a sense of action. Scene designers are limited by the stage space, the concepts of the director, the amount of time and budget available for the execution of the design, and elements of practicality—for example, can the design withstand the wear and tear the actors will cause? Scene

designers are also limited by the talent and abilities of the staff available to execute the design. A complex setting requiring sophisticated painting and delicate carpentry, complex construction, and intricate computerization may prove difficult to execute and upset the production schedule even in the professional theatre.

A *scenic environment* occurs wherever theatre takes place: any physical surrounding for a production constitutes a scenic design because someone makes an artistic choice in its selection. In contemporary theatre, scene designers are creative partners who determine the direction and appearance of a production. Scene design must have something of its own to say to the audience. Stage design is first and foremost a visual art, and the fundamental artistic tools of the scene designer consist of those of the visual artist we studied in Chapter 1: the elements and principles of composition, such as line and color.

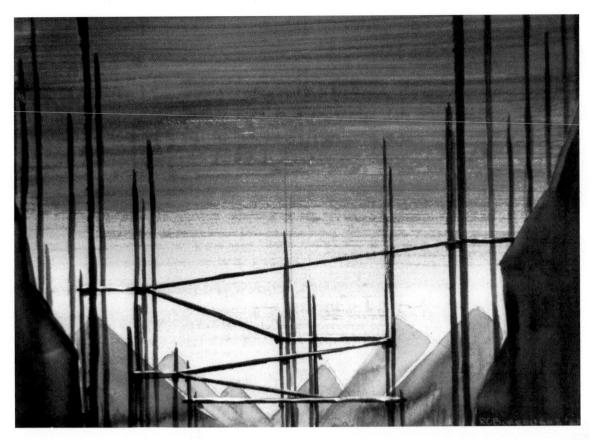

5.6 Scenic design for Ibsen, *Peer Gynt*, University of Arizona Theatre. Director: Peter R. Marroney. Scene designer: Robert C. Burroughs.

LIGHTING DESIGN Lighting designers are perhaps the most crucial of all the theatre artists in modern productions. Without their art, nothing done by the actors, the costume designer, the property master or mistress, the director, or the scene designer would be seen by the audience. Yet lighting designers work in an ephemeral medium. They must sculpt with light and create shadows that fall where they desire them to fall; they must "paint" over the colors provided by the other designers. In doing so, they use lighting instruments with imperfect optical qualities. Lighting designers, even with the availability of computer assistance, essentially do their work in their minds, unlike scene designers, who can paint a design mock-up and then calculate the end product in feet and inches. Lighting designers must imagine what their light will do to an actor, to a costume, and to a set. They must enhance the color of a costume, accent the physique of an actor, and reinforce the plasticity of a setting. They also try to reinforce the dramatic structure and dynamics of the play. They work within the framework of light and shade. Without shadows and highlights, the human face and body become imperceptible: a human face without shadows cannot be seen clearly more than a few feet away. In a theatre, such small movements as the raising of an

eyebrow must be seen clearly as much as 100 feet (30.5 m) away. The lighting designer helps to make this possible. In contemporary theatre productions, with computerized movement of lighting instruments a reality, stage lighting has assumed an even more important role in theatrical presentations.

In summary, lighting design serves four functions or purposes: (1) *selective visibility*; lighting helps us see what the production requires of us, with proper focus on actors and settings, and enhancement of our perception of forms and depth; (2) *rhythm and structure*; changes in lighting help move the play and indicate the rises and falls in action from which we perceive the play's meaning; (3) *mood*; lighting is, arguably, our most important clue to the atmosphere of the play; (4) *illusion and motivation*; by creating sunlight, lamplight, moonlight, and other sources of light, lighting helps us experience the time and place of the action.

COSTUME DESIGN Perhaps we think of theatrical costumes merely as clothing that has to be researched to reflect a particular historical period and constructed to fit particular actors. But costuming goes beyond that. Costume designers work with the entire body of the actor.

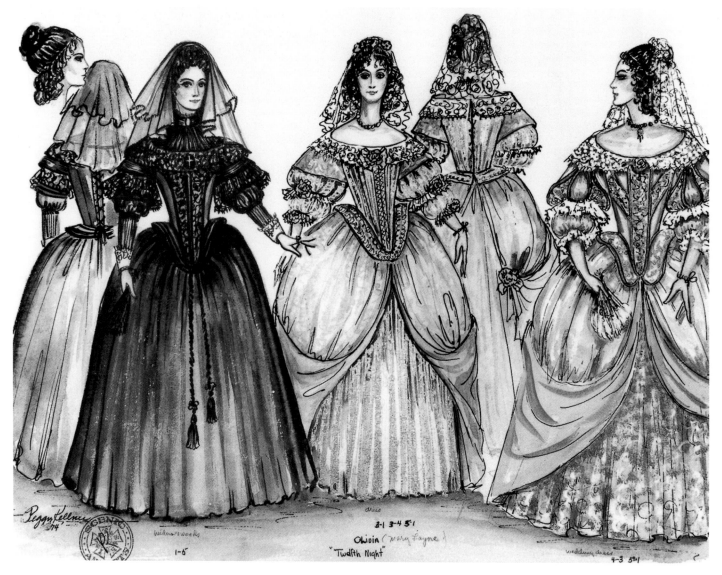

5.7 Costume designs for Shakespeare, *Twelfth Night*, Old Globe Theatre, San Diego, California. Director: Craig Noel. Costume designer: Peggy J. Kellner.

They design hairstyles and clothing and sometimes makeup to suit a specific person or occasion, a historical era, a character, a locale.

Stage costuming has three functions. First, it *accents*— it shows the audience which personages are the most important in a scene, and it shows the relationship between people.

Second, it *reflects*—a particular era, time of day, climate, season, location, or occasion. The designs in Figure 5.7 reflect a historical period. We recognize different eras primarily through silhouette, or outline. Costume designers may merely suggest full detail or may actually provide it, as is the case in Figure 5.7. Evident here is the designer's concern not only for the period but also for character in her choice of details, color, texture, jewelry, and hair-

style. Notice the length to which the designer goes to indicate detail, providing both front and back views of the costume, as well as a head study showing the hair without a covering.

Third, stage costuming *reveals* the characters of the personages as well as their social position, profession, cleanliness, age, physique, and health. In Figure 5.8 the principal concern of the designer clearly lies less with historical period than with production style and character. This costume design reveals the high emotional content of the particular scene, and we see at first glance the deteriorated health and condition of King Lear as he goes mad on the heath. The contrast provided by the king in such a state heightens the effect of the scene, and details such as the bare feet, the winter furs, and the storm-ravaged cape

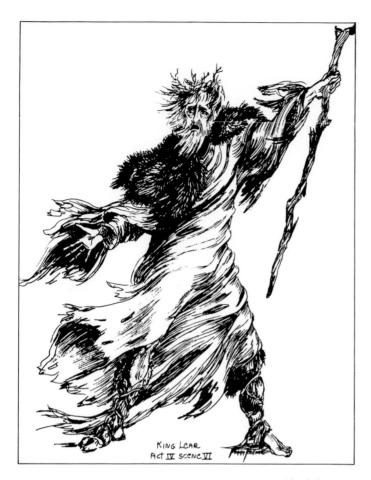

5.8 Costume design for Shakespeare, *King Lear*, Old Globe Theatre, San Diego, California. Director: Edward Payson Call. Costume designer: Peggy J. Kellner.

are precise indicators of the pathos that we find and respond to. Costume designers work, as do scene and lighting designers, with the same general elements as painters and sculptors: the elements of composition. A stage costume is an actor's skin: it allows her to move as she must, and occasionally it restricts her from moving as she should not.

PROPERTIES Properties fall into two general groups: *set props* and *hand props*. Set properties are part of the scene design: furniture, pictures, rugs, fireplace accessories, and so on. Along with the larger elements of the set, they identify the mood of the play and the tastes of those who inhabit this world. Hand properties used by the actors in stage business—cigarettes, papers, glasses, and so forth—also help to portray characters. The use of properties reveals significant information toward our understanding of a play. For example, if at the opening curtain all properties appear to be neat and in order, but as the play develops the actors disrupt them, so that at the end the entire scene is in disarray, that simple transition illustrates and

enhances what has happened in the play. As in all artworks, details make important statements.

Aural Elements

What we hear contributes to our understanding and enjoyment of a production. The aural elements, whether the actors' voices, the background music, or the clashing of swords, function importantly in a theatrical production. How a production sounds represents a series of conscious choices on the part of all the artists involved: playwright, director, actors, and designers. Just as a composer of a musical piece creates harmonies, dynamics, rhythms, and melodies, the director, working with the actors and sound designer, makes the production develop in an aural sense so the audience has the proper mood, moves in the appropriate emotional direction, and focuses on meaningful attention points.

Dynamics

Every production has its own dynamic patterns, which we can chart (as in Fig. 5.1). They make the structural pattern of a play clear, and help to hold the interest of the audience. Scientific studies indicate that attention or interest functions intermittently; human beings can concentrate on specific items only for very brief periods. Therefore, holding audience attention over the two-hour span of a production requires employing devices whereby from time to time interest or attention can peak and then relax. The peaks must be carefully controlled. A production should build to a high point of dramatic interest—the climax. However, each scene or act has its own peak of development—again, to maintain interest. Thus the path from the beginning of the play to the high point of dramatic interest is not a steady rise, but a series of peaks and valleys. Each successive peak rises closer to the ultimate one. The director controls where and how high these peaks occur by controlling the dynamics of the actors—volume and intensity, both bodily and vocal.

Actors

Although we cannot always determine easily which functions in a production are the playwright's, which the director's, and which the actor's, the main channel of communication between the playwright and the audience remains the actors. Through their movements and speech an audience perceives the play.

Looking for two elements among many in an actor's portrayal of a role enhances our understanding and response. The first is *speech*. Language should be under-

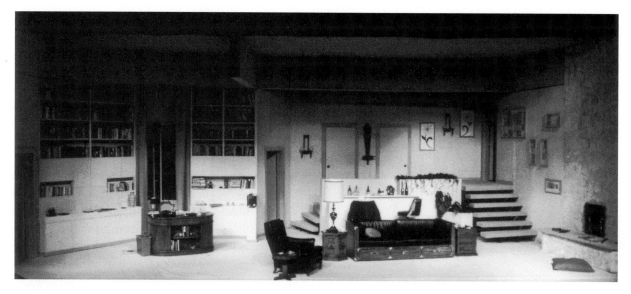

5.9 Proscenium setting for Jean Kerr, *Mary, Mary*, University of Arizona Theatre. Director: H. Wynn Pearce. Scene and lighting designer: Dennis J. Sporre.

stood as the playwright's words, and speech the manner in which the actor delivers those words. Speech, like language, can range from high lifelikeness to high theatricality. If an actor's speech adheres to normal conversational rhythms, durations, and inflections, we respond in one way. If it utilizes extended vowel emphasis, long, sliding inflections, and dramatic pauses, we respond quite differently—even though the playwright's words remain identical in both cases.

The second element of an actor's portrayal that aids our understanding is the physical reinforcement he or she gives to the character's basic motivation. Most actors try to identify a single basic motivation for their character. That motivation is called a *spine*, or *superobjective*. Everything that pertains to the decisions the person makes remains consistent because it all stems from this basic drive. Actors will translate the drive into something physical that they can do throughout the play. For example Blanche, in Tennessee Williams's *A Streetcar Named Desire*, is driven by an immense desire to clean everything she encounters, because of the way she regards herself and the world around her. Ideally, the actress playing Blanche will discover that element of Blanche's personality as she reads the play and develops the role. But to make that spine clear to us in the audience, she will need to translate it into physical action. Therefore, we will see Blanche constantly smoothing her hair, rearranging and straightening her dress, cleaning the furniture, brushing imaginary dust from others' shoulders, and so forth. Nearly every physical move she makes will relate somehow to the act of cleaning. Of course, these movements will be subtle; if we are attentive, we will notice

them, but even if we do not pick them up we are likely to perceive them subconsciously and so understand the nature of the character portrayed. See the Companion Website: Theatre, The Director.

Lifelikeness

In describing the relationship of the visual elements to the play, we have noted the designers' use of compositional elements. The use of these elements relative to life can be placed on a continuum, on one end of which rests theatricality and the other lifelikeness. Items high in lifelikeness are those with which we deal in everyday life: language, movements, furniture, trees. As we progress toward theatricality, the elements of the production express less and less relationship to everyday life. They become distorted, exaggerated, and perhaps even nonobjective. Poetry, as we noted, is high in theatricality; everyday speech is high in lifelikeness. The position of the various elements of a production on this continuum suggests the style of the play, in the same sense that brushstroke, line, and palette indicate style in painting.

Figures 5.9–5.14 illustrate the range between lifelikeness and theatricality. Figure 5.9 is a proscenium setting high in lifelikeness—including a full ceiling over the setting. When we examine the detail comprising the setting, we see nothing that we would not see in any "real" room, with the exception that the "fourth wall" of the room has been removed to allow the audience to perceive the play's action set therein. Figure 5.10 is an arena setting high in lifelikeness; it reflects the style of the presentation. However, the requirement of the arena configuration that

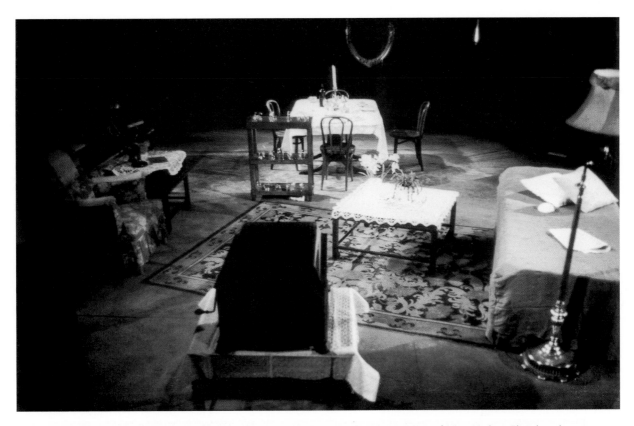

5.10 Arena setting for Tennessee Williams, *The Glass Menagerie*, State University of New York at Plattsburgh. Director: H. Charles Kline. Scene and lighting designer: Dennis J. Sporre.

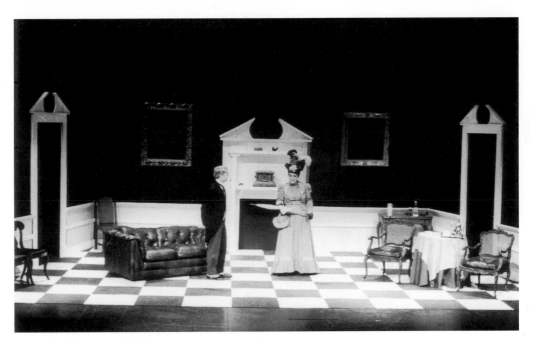

5.11 Proscenium setting for Oscar Wilde, *The Importance of Being Earnest*, University of Arizona Theatre. Director: William Lang. Costume designer: Helen Workman Currie. Scene and lighting designer: Dennis J. Sporre.

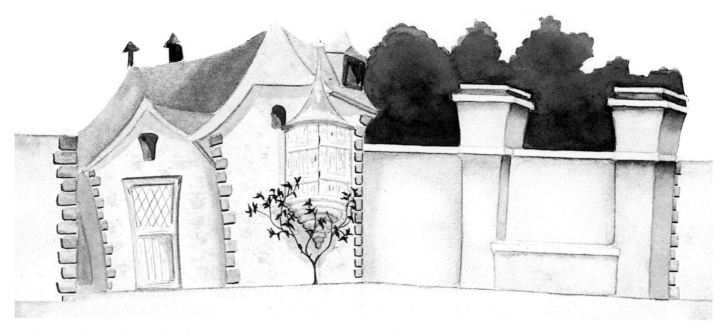

5.12 Scene design for Jerry Devine and Bruce Montgomery, *The Amorous Flea*, University of Iowa Theatre. Director: David Knauf. Scene and lighting designer: Dennis J. Sporre.

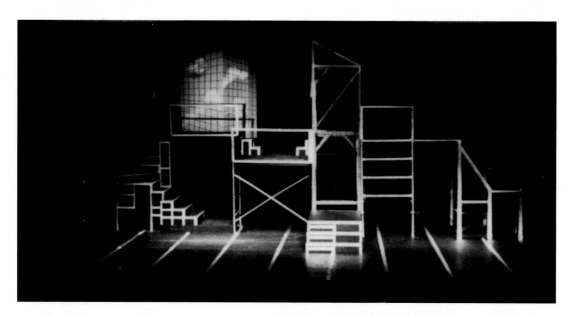

5.13 Proscenium setting for Stephen Sondheim musical, *Company*, University of Arizona Theatre. Director: Peter R. Marroney. Scene and lighting designer: Dennis J. Sporre.

there be no walls moves the production away from life-likeness. Note that some theatricality—specifically, the empty picture frame—occurs in the decoration of this set. Further, although every item of the set appears as if it might furnish our own living room, lifelikeness takes a significant step down because, rather than seeing a room with its fourth wall removed, we can see through the first, second, and third walls as well—to the point that other members of the audience face us and their reactions can sometimes supersede the reality of the stage space itself. In Figure 5.11, although the set props have high lifelike-ness and the setting is representational, the designer has

Profile

William Shakespeare

William Shakespeare (1564–1616) was one of the world's greatest literary geniuses. Most of his work was for the theatre, but he left a remarkable sequence of sonnets in which he pushed the resources of the English language to breathtaking extremes. In his works for the theatre, Shakespeare represents the Elizabethan love of drama, and the theatres of London were patronized by lords and commoners alike. They sought and found, usually in the same play, action, spectacle, comedy, character, and intellectual stimulation deeply reflective of the human condition. Thus it was with Shakespeare, the preeminent Elizabethan playwright. His appreciation of the Italian Renaissance—which he shared with his audience—can be seen in the settings of many of his plays. With true Renaissance breadth, Shakespeare went back into history, both British and Classical, and far beyond, to the fantasy world of *The Tempest*. Like most playwrights of his age, Shakespeare wrote for a specific professional company of which he became a partial owner. The need for new plays to keep the company alive from season to season provided much of the impetus for his prolific output.

We know only a little about Shakespeare's life. Playwrights were not highly esteemed people in England in the sixteenth century, and there was virtually no reason to write about them. We do, however, know more about Shakespeare than we do about most of his contemporaries. The principal facts of his life are well established. He was baptized in the parish church of Stratford-upon-Avon on April 26, 1564, and probably attended the local grammar school. We next learn of him in his marriage to Ann Hathaway in 1582, when a special action was necessary to allow the marriage without delay. The reason is clear—five months later, Ann gave birth to the couple's first daughter, Susanna. The next public mention comes in 1592, when Shakespeare's reputation as a playwright was sufficient to warrant a malicious comment from another playwright, Robert Greene. From then on, there are many records of his activities as dramatist, actor, and businessman. In addition to his steady output of plays, he also published a narrative poem entitled *Venus and Adonis*, which was popular enough to have nine printings in the next few years. His standing as a lyric poet was established with the publication of 154 sonnets in 1609.

In 1594 he helped found a theatrical company called the Lord Chamberlain's Company, in which he functioned as shareholder, actor, and playwright. In 1599, the company built its own theatre, the Globe, which came directly under the patronage of James I when he assumed the throne in 1603. (A faithful reproduction of Shakespeare's Globe Theatre was completed in London in 1998.) Shakespeare died in 1616, shortly after executing a detailed will. His will, still in existence, bequeathed most of his property to Susanna and her daughter. He left small mementoes to friends. He mentioned his wife only once, leaving her his "second best bed" with its furnishings.

Read more about Shakespeare at www. shakespeare.com and www-tech.mit.edu/Shakespeare/.

---

attempted to heighten the theatrical nature of the production by using open space where one might expect solid walls in this proscenium production.

The setting in Figure 5.12 moves further toward theatricality, and indicates clearly through exaggerated detail and two-dimensionality the whimsical nature of the production. The design in Figure 5.13 creates a purely formal environment. Various areas of the set serve as locations and have realistic furniture, and this use of representational detail keeps the setting tied to the overall approach of the actors. Finally, in Figure 5.14, the designer suggests neither time nor place. Here the emphasis reinforces the high action of the production. The steep ramps throughout the set make it impossible for the actors to walk from one level to the next; the setting forces them to run.

In most arts the artist tries to develop a unique style—a recognizable mark. Some artists change their style, but they do so by their own choice. Interpretive artists such as costume, scene, and lighting designers, and to a degree conductors as well, must submerge their personal style in favor of that of the work with which they are involved. Playwrights or directors set the style, and scene designers adapt to it and make their design reflect it.

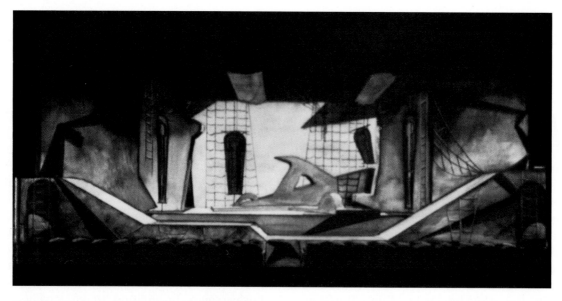

5.14 Scene design for Euripides, *The Bacchae*, University of Illinois at Chicago Circle. Director: William Raffeld. Scene and lighting designer: Dennis J. Sporre.

SENSE STIMULI

In each of the elements just discussed, the production stimulates our senses in a particular manner. We respond to the play's structure and how it works; we respond to dynamics. We are stimulated by the theatricality or life-likeness of the language of the playwright and the movements and speech of the actors. We find our response shaped by the relationship of the stage space to the audience, and by the sets, lights, properties, and costumes. All of these elements bombard us simultaneously with complex visual and aural stimuli. How we respond, and how much we can respond, determines our ultimate understanding of and reaction to a production.

The theatre is unique in its ability to stimulate our senses, because only the theatre makes a direct appeal to our emotions through the live portrayal of other individuals involved directly in the human condition. Being in the presence of live actors gives us more of life in two hours than we could experience outside the theatre in that same time span. The term we use to describe our reaction to and involvement with what we experience in a theatrical production is *empathy*. Empathy causes us to cry when individuals whom we know are only actors become involved in tragic or emotional situations. Empathy makes us wince when an actor slaps the face of another one, or when two football players collide at full speed. Empathy is our mental and physical involvement in situations in which we are not direct participants.

Now let us examine a few of the more obvious ways in which a production can appeal to our senses. In plays that deal in conventions, *language* may act as virtually the entire stimulant of our senses. Through language the playwright sets the time, place, atmosphere, and even small details of decoration. We become our own scene, lighting, and even costume designer, imagining what the playwright tells us ought to be there. In the opening scene of *Hamlet* we find Bernardo and Francisco, two guards. The hour is midnight; it is bitter cold; a ghost appears, in "warlike form." How do we know all of this? In a modern production we might see it all through the work of the costume and set designers. But such need not be the case, because the playwright gives us all of this information in the dialogue. Shakespeare wrote for a theatre that had no lighting save for the sun. His theatre (such as we know of it) probably used no scenery. As costumes, the actors wore the street clothes of the day. The theatrical environment remained the same whether the company played *Hamlet, Richard III,* or *The Tempest*. So what needed to be seen needed to be imagined. The play's language provided the stimuli for the audience.

We also respond to what we *see*. A sword fight performed with flashing action, swift movements, and great intensity sets us on the edge of our chair. Although we know the action is staged and the incident fictitious, the excitement of the moment captures us.

Theatre and Human Reality

David Rabe, *Hurly-Burly*

David Rabe (b. 1940; Fig. **5.15**) is one of America's foremost contemporary playwrights. A Vietnam veteran, Rabe has treated themes of physical and emotional violence—sometimes controversially—in plays that use war as a backdrop. *Hurly-Burly* (1984) is about drug- and people-abuse in Hollywood. As in many of his plays, the male hero, Eddie, has a hoodlumlike, demented quality. Such treatment suggests that Rabe likes to create a world in which people are defined by a particular "lingo." He has a very "masculine" vision of his heroes. The way they speak makes them who they are. That is Rabe's dramatic strategy, as he puts it: a choice.

In *Hurly-Burly* the characters speak the language of high tech and Hollywood. Rabe uses the language as a kind of stage poetry, metaphorically and stylistically, rather than trying to reflect reality. Eddie rants against television, and Rabe wants the audience to see Eddie's distress—the brilliance of his mind, and the waste of it. Rabe wants the audience to be drawn to Eddie, to recognize Eddie's ideas, and to develop a sympathetic chord in Eddie's sensibility. Eddie has a kind of innocence and gullibility. He is a very open person.

From Eddie's character and from the play, David Rabe tries to point out to the audience that, although somewhat off-centered, the people of *Hurly-Burly* can be found anywhere—not just in Hollywood. They could be from Wall Street, from Washington, D.C., or they could be professional athletes. From Rabe's point of view, everybody is addicted: "Cocaine and TV are both drugs."

For Rabe, human reality lies not in where a play's setting or whether the language appears contemporary. Rather, it is defined by the cause-and-effect at work in human events. "Realism is sane—everybody is sane in realism, no matter how crazy they are."[3]

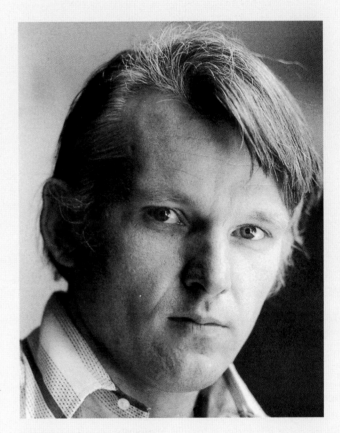

5.15 David Rabe in 1972.

Events of a quite different dynamic quality can grip and manipulate us. In many plays we witness character assassination, as one life after another bares before us. The intense but subtle *movements* of the actors—both bodily and vocal—can pull us here and push us there emotionally, and perhaps cause us to leave the theatre feeling emotionally drained. Part of our response results from subject matter, part from language—but much of it results from careful manipulation of *dynamics*.

Mood plays an important factor in theatrical communication. Before the curtain rises, our senses are tickled by stimuli designed to put us in the mood for what follows. The houselights in the theatre may be very dim, or we may see a cool or warm light on the front curtain. Music fills the theatre. We may recognize the raucous tones of a 1930s jazz piece, or a melancholy ballad. Whatever the stimuli, they all carefully prepare us for the way the director wishes us to react. Once the curtain rises, the assault on our senses continues. The palette utilized by the scene, lighting, and costume designers helps communicate the mood of the play and other messages about it. The rhythm and variation in the visual elements capture our

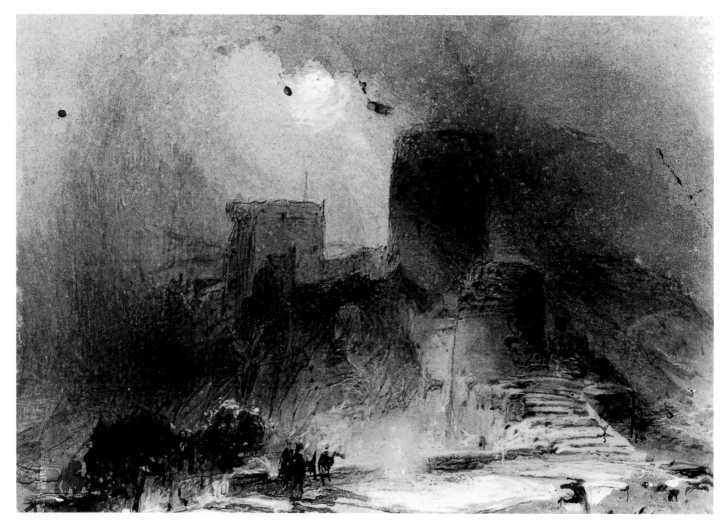

5.16 Scene design (probably an alternative design) for Charles Fechter's revival of Shakespeare, *Hamlet*, Lyceum Theatre, London, 1864. Designer: William Telbin. Victoria & Albert Museum, London.

interest and reinforce the rhythmic structure of the play. For example, in Figure **5.6**, the use of line and form as well as color provides a formal atmosphere reflecting the epic grandeur of Ibsen's *Peer Gynt*.

The degree of plasticity or three-dimensionality created by the lighting designer's illumination of the actors and the set causes us to respond in many ways. If the primary lighting instruments hang directly in front of the stage, plasticity diminishes and the actors appear washed out or two-dimensional. We respond quite differently to the maximum plasticity and shadow that results from lighting coming nearly from the side.

A play's audience also reacts to the mass of a setting. Scenery that towers over the actors and appears heavy differs in effect from scenery that seems minuscule relative to the human form. The settings in Figures **5.11** and **5.16**, for example differ from one another in scale, and each places the actors in a different relationship with their surroundings.

Finally, focus and line work upon our senses. Careful composition can create sharp movement, outlines, and shadows. Or it can create soft, or blurred images. Each of these devices acts as a stimulant; each has the potential to elicit a relatively predictable response. Perhaps in no other art are such devices so available and full of potential for the artist. We, as audience, benefit through nearly total involvement in the life situation that comes to us over the footlights.

THINKING CRITICALLY

Create a basic analysis of a theatre production by using the following outline of concepts from the text as a guide.

- Genre. In what genre was the play? How did it exhibit the characteristics of tragedy, comedy, melodrama, etc.?

- Plot. How did the plot work? Where in the play would you say the exposition ended? Where was the climax? Where were the crises? What instances of foreshadowing, discovery, and reversal were present? Was the plot a significant part of the play or not? Why?

- Protagonist. Who was the protagonist? How did his or her actions and decisions move the plot? Was the protagonist active or passive?

- Character. How did the playwright draw the characters? Were they three-dimensional? Did you find any of them identifiable with your own life and feelings?

- Themes. What ideas did the play pursue? In what ways did the playwright or the production make you aware of the point of view being presented?

- Theatre form. In what theatre form was the play produced? What effect on your response to the play did the form create? Would you have had a different response if the production had utilized a different physical arrangement—for example, thrust, arena, or proscenium?

- Visual elements. In what ways did the settings, costumes, and lighting reinforce the message and style of the play? How did the visual elements provide historical or structural information to the audience?

- Language. How did the playwright's language and the actors' speech create meaning for you?

- Reaction. How did the previous elements combine to create a reaction in you? In other words, what drew your attention? What was your emotional response to the production, and what caused that reaction?

CYBER STUDY

TRAGEDY:
—Sophocles, *Oedipus the King.*
http://etext.lib.virginia.edu/toc/modeng/public/SopOedi.html
—William Shakespeare, *King Lear.*
http://www.infomotions.com/etexts/literature/english/1600-1699/shakespeare-king-45.txt

TRAGICOMEDY:
—Henrik Ibsen, *The Wild Duck.*
http://etext.lib.virginia.edu/toc/modeng/public/IbsWild.html

COMEDY:
—Aristophanes, *Lysistrata.*
http://www.gutenberg.org/etext/7700
—William Shakespeare, *Comedy of Errors.*
http://etext.lib.virginia.edu/toc/modeng/public/HulCome.html
—Richard Brinsley Sheridan, *The School for Scandal.*
http://www.bartleby.com/18/2/

CHAPTER SIX

CINEMA

IMPORTANT TERMS

Absolute film Film that exists for its own aesthetic sake.

Crosscutting An alternation between two separate actions that are related by theme, mood, or plot but occur at the same time.

Cutting within the frame A method of shooting the film that avoids the necessity of editing.

Direct address A technique whereby the actors appear to address the audience directly.

Dissolve A means of ending a scene.

Documentary film Film that records actual events.

Editing The process of assembling the various pieces or shots of a film.

Master shot A single shot of an entire piece of action, taken to facilitate the assembly of the film in the editing process.

Narrative film Film that tells a story.

Structural rhythm The manner in which various shots in a film are joined together and juxtaposed with other cinematic images, visual and aural.

FORMAL AND TECHNICAL QUALITIES

Like theatre, but without the spontaneity of "live" performers, cinema can confront us with life very nearly as we find it on our streets. On the other hand, through the magic of sophisticated special effects, films can take us to new worlds that are open to no other form of art. Film, also, because of its status in popular culture, possesses a unique ability to fulfill the function of art, discussed in the Introduction, as a social and political weapon. In this regard, film reminds us of how we can be influenced by works of art, sometimes subtly, and sometimes blatantly. For example, director James Cameron has admitted that he made his movie *Titanic* (1997) as a Marxist-Socialist critique of America. Consequently, we need to reflect on the meanings and implications of the works we encounter and enjoy. Part of our task in developing critical perception of works of art includes identifying how they can not only entertain us but can create changes in our culture as well.

Cinema is the most familiar and most easily accessible art form. We usually accept it almost without conscious thought, at least in terms of the story line or the star image presented or the basic entertainment value of the product. Yet all these elements are carefully crafted out of editing techniques, camera usage, juxtaposition of image, and structural rhythms. These details of cinematic construction can enhance our viewing and raise film from mere entertainment into the realm of serious art. Bernard Shaw once observed, "Details are important; they make comments." It is not as easy as it might seem to perceive the details of a film because, while we search them out, the entertainment elements of the film draw our attention away from the search.

Cinema is aesthetic communication through the design of time and three-dimensional space compressed into a two-dimensional image. If we examine a strip of film, we see only a series of still pictures running the length of the strip. Each of these pictures, or *frames*, is about ⅞ inch (22 mm) wide and ⅝ inch (16 mm) high. If we study the frames in relation to one another, we see that even though each may seem to show exactly the same scene, the position of the object differs slightly. This film contains sixteen frames per foot (30 cm). When the film runs on a projecting device and passes before a light source at the rate of twenty-four frames per second (sixteen to eighteen frames per second for silent films), a magnifying lens enlarges the frames printed on it. Projected onto a screen, the images appear to move. However, the motion picture,

as film is popularly called, does not really move but only seems to, due to an optical phenomenon called *persistence of vision*, which according to legend was discovered by the astronomer Ptolemy in the second century C.E. The theory states that the eyes take a fraction of a second to record an impression of an image and send it to the brain. Once the impression has been received, the eye retains it on the retina for about one-tenth of a second after the actual image has disappeared.

The film projector pulls the film between the light source and a lens in a stop-and-go fashion, the film pausing long enough at each frame to let the eye take in the picture. Then a shutter on the projector closes, the retina retains the image, and the projection mechanism pulls the film ahead to the next frame. Perforations along the right-hand side of the filmstrip enable the teeth on the gear of the driving mechanism to grasp the film and not only move it along frame by frame but also hold it steady in the gate (the slot between the light source and the magnifying lens). This stop-and-go motion gives the impression of continuous movement. If the film did not pause at each frame, the eye would receive a blurred image.

The motion picture originally served as a device for recording and depicting motion. But once they realized that goal, filmmakers then quickly discovered that the projector could also record and present stories—in particular, stories that made use of the unique qualities of the medium of film.

CLASSIFICATIONS

Our formal response to film recognizes three basic classifications of films: narrative, documentary, and absolute (avant garde).

Narrative

Narrative (also called fictional) film tells a story; in many ways it uses the technique of theatre. It follows the rules of literary construction in that it begins with expository material, adds levels of complications, builds to a climax, and ends with a resolution of all the plot elements. As in theatre, the personages in the story are portrayed by professional actors under the guidance of a director. The action of the plot takes place within a setting designed and constructed primarily for the action of the story but allowing the camera to move freely in photographing the action. Many narrative films are *genre* films, constructed out of familiar literary styles—the western, the detective story, and the horror story, among others. In these films, the story elements are so familiar to the audience that they usually know the outcome of the plot before it

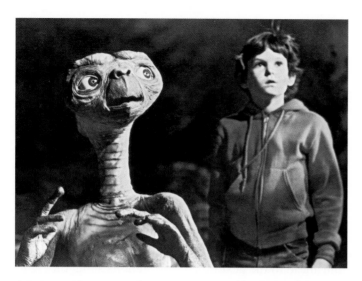

6.1 Henry Thomas as Elliott and his friend E.T., *E.T.*, 1982. Director: Steven Spielberg.

begins. The final showdown between the "good guy" and the "bad guy," the destruction of a city by an unstoppable monster, and the identification of the murderer by the detective are all familiar plot elements that have become clichés or stereotypes within the genre; their use fulfills audience expectations. Film versions of popular novels and stories written especially for the screen are also part of the narrative-film form, but since film comprises a major part of the mass entertainment industry the narrative presented usually consists of material that will attract a large audience and thus assure a profit. In a film of this genre the narrative can also be interpreted symbolically. Regardless of the story, principles of universality apply. *E.T.: The Extra-Terrestrial* (1982; Fig. **6.1**), for example, tells a story of fantasy that also symbolizes the innocence and beauty of childhood. E.T. says goodbye to his friend Elliott, and Elliott will likewise outgrow his childhood. The memories, however, remain. Narrative films may also include elements from documentary and absolute film (see discussion below).

Documentary

Documentary film attempts to record actuality using primarily either a sociological or a journalistic approach. It normally does not use professional actors and is often shot as the event occurs—at the time and place of its occurrence. The film may use a narrative structure, and some of the events may be ordered or compressed for dramatic reasons, but its presentation gives the illusion of reality. The footage shown on the evening television news,

programming concerned with current events or problems, and full coverage either by television or film companies of a worldwide event, such as the Olympics, are all kinds of documentary film. All convey a sense of reality as well as a recording of time and place. A classic example of documentary film is Leni Riefenstahl's (REE-fehn-shtahl; 1902–2003) *Olympia* (1936).

Riefenstahl's *Triumph of Will* (1935), commissioned by Adolf Hitler, celebrated the Nazi party's first convention at Nuremberg in 1934, and Hitler staged the event carefully to take full advantage of the cameras. In this documentary, Riefenstahl shows virtuosity in style and compelling aesthetics. Her dazzling portrayal of Hitler as a charismatic leader of a master race caused the Allies to ban the film for several years after the defeat of Nazi Germany in World War II. After the war, Riefenstahl served four years in prison for her contribution to Nazi propaganda.

Absolute (Avant-garde)

Absolute film exists for its own sake, for its record of movement or form. It does not use narrative techniques, although documentary techniques can be used in some instances. Created neither in the camera nor on location, absolute film is built carefully, piece by piece, on the editing table or through special effects and multiple-printing techniques. It tells no story but exists solely as movement or form. Absolute film rarely exceeds twelve minutes (one reel) in length, and is not usually created for commercial intent but meant only as an artistic experience. Narrative or documentary films may contain sections that can be labeled absolute, and these can be studied either in or out of the context of the whole film.

THE PRODUCTION

Mise-en-scène

Mise-en-scène means the same in cinema as in theatre and dance. It encompasses the entirety of the visual space of the production. In film, however, *mise-en-scène* can be more complicated. Once the physical space of the *mise-en-scène* transfers to film, it becomes a picture or image of the original and separates the audience from the space that with theatre and dance would be shared with the audience. So, in film, we define *mise-en-scène* as "how the visual materials are staged, framed, and photographed" (Louis Giannetti, *Understanding Movies* p. 44). *Mise-en-scène* in cinema has a kinship with painting in that the filmmaker creates an image consisting (as in theatre and dance) of formal patterns and shapes presented on a flat surface (like painting) and enclosed in a frame.

Director

In film, the director has the function of converting the *mise-en-scène* from three-dimensional to two-dimensional space. Film directors have a great deal of control over the final product—more than a theatre director. In the theatre, as suggested in Chapter 5, the director functions as an interpreter between the playwright and the actors and designers. Theatre directors also may control the movements and interpretations of the actors, but essentially the theatre production leads us to an understanding of the playwright's script. We focus on the actors—the main channel of communication—and when we leave the theatre, we rarely discuss the director. Quite the contrary situation occurs in cinema. When we discuss a film, we usually do so in terms of the director, because, unlike a stage director, who typically has strong control up to the rise of the curtain and very little thereafter, the film director has significant control over the final product which, once "in the can," varies not at all from what the director intended. That degree of directorial precision and control occurs only in cinema.

In the mid-1950s, a term emerged in the French journal *Cahiers du Cinéma* (kah-YAY-doo-see-nay-MAH) that described what its proponents considered directorial dominance in film art: the *auteur* (oh-TUHR) theory. According to this theory, whoever controls the *mise-en-scène* is the true "author" of the film.

Techniques

EDITING Film is rarely recorded in the order of its final presentation. It is filmed in bits and pieces and put together, after all the photography is finished, as one puts together a jigsaw puzzle or builds a house. The force or strength of the final product depends upon the editing process, the manner in which the camera and the lighting are handled, and the movement of the actors before the camera. Naturally, the success of a film depends equally on the strength of the story presented and the ability of the writers, actors, directors, and technicians who have worked on the film. However, this level of success depends on the personal taste of the audience and the depth of perception of the individual, and therefore does not lie within the boundaries of this discussion.

Perhaps the greatest difference between film and the other arts discussed within this volume is *plasticity*—the quality of film that enables it to be cut, spliced, and ordered according to the needs of the film and the desires of the filmmaker. If twenty people were presented with all the footage shot of a presidential inauguration and asked to make a film commemorating the event, we would probably end up with twenty completely different films. Each filmmaker would order the event according to his or her own views and artistic ideas. This concept of plasticity, then, constitutes one of the major advantages of the use of the machine in consort with an artform.

The filmmaker must synthesize a product out of many diverse elements. The editing process creates or builds the film, and within that process are many ways of joining shots and scenes to make a whole. Let's examine some of these basic techniques. *Cutting* is simply joining together shots during the editing process. A *jump cut* is a cut that breaks the continuity of time by moving forward from one part of the action to another that is obviously separated from the first by an interval of time, location, or camera position. This is often used for shock effect or to call attention to a detail, as in commercial advertising on television. The *form cut* cuts from one image to another—a different object that has a similar shape or contour; it is used primarily to make a smoother transition from one shot to another. For example, in D.W. Griffith's silent film *Intolerance*, attackers use a battering ram to smash in the gates of Babylon. The camera shows the circular frontal area of the ram as it advances toward the gate. The scene cuts to a view of a circular shield, placed in the framing of the shot in exactly the same position as the front view of the battering ram.

Montage (mahn-TAHZH) can be considered the most aesthetic use of the cut in film. Filmmakers handle it in two basic ways: first, as an indication of compression or elongation of time and, second, as a rapid succession of images to illustrate an association of ideas. Montage also allows the filmmaker to depict complex ideas or draw a metaphor visually. Sergei Eisenstein, the Russian film director (see p. 158), presents a shot in one of his early films of a Russian army officer walking out of the room, his back to the camera and his hands crossed behind him. Eisenstein cuts immediately to a peacock strutting away from the camera and spreading its tail. These two images are juxtaposed, and the audience is allowed to make the association that the officer is as proud as a peacock.

CAMERA VIEWPOINT Camera position and viewpoint are equally as important to the structure of the film as the editing process. In the earliest days of the silent film the camera was merely set up in one basic position; the actors moved before it as if they were performing before an audience on a stage in a theatre. However, watching all the action from one position became dull, and thus the early filmmakers moved the camera in order to add variety. Out of this emerged the many angle *shots* that open up a range of possible comments on the subject being filmed.

Cinema and Human Reality

Sergei Eisenstein, *Battleship Potemkin*

Sergei M. Eisenstein's (eye-zehn-stine) 1925 film *Battleship Potemkin* remains one of the most influential films ever made. It is a great classic of film art. When released, it brought instant fame both to Eisenstein and to a newly emerging film industry in the former Soviet Union. Among other things, it added a new dimension to film language: montage editing.

After the Bolshevik Revolution in 1917, the Soviet government took control of the country's film industry and decreed that film would serve the purpose of education and propaganda to indoctrinate the Russian masses and promote class consciousness throughout the world. Originally designed to celebrate the twentieth anniversary of the unsuccessful 1905 Revolution against the Czar, *Battleship Potemkin* was limited by Eisenstein to narrating a single episode in the struggle—the mutiny of the *Potemkin* and the subsequent massacre of civilians on the steps leading down to the harbor in Odessa (Fig. **6.2**).

The film has a number of qualities that give it the appearance of a documentary. Eisenstein engaged non-professionals who looked like the type of character he wished to portray. The film was shot on location. Its collective hero is the Russian people—represented by the people of Odessa, the mutineers, and the sailors on other ships who rebelled against Czarist oppression.

Eisenstein's use of montage, featuring juxtaposing shots and lighting, camera angle, and subject movement, creates meaning by incorporating shots within shots. His cuts between shots were intentionally jarring and designed to create shock and agitation in the audience. Eisenstein identified five types of montage and used each in the film: (1) *metric montage*—conflict caused by the length of shots; (2) *rhythmic montage*—conflict generated by the rhythm of movement within the shots; (3) *tonal montage*—arrangement of shots by their "tone" or "emotional sound"; (4) *overtonal montage*—a synthesis of the previous three types; and (5) *intellectual montage*—the juxtaposition of images to create visual metaphor.

In the Soviet Union, the film did not immediately gain favor. Eisenstein was accused of being overly formal—that is, being concerned with aesthetic form rather than ideological content. Once they noted that it received universal acclaim outside the Soviet Union, the Soviet authorities changed their tune and supported the film enthusiastically.

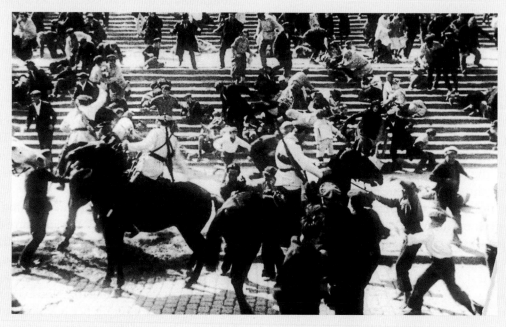

6.2 *Battleship Potemkin*, still from the "Odessa steps" sequence, 1925. Director: Sergei M. Eisenstein.

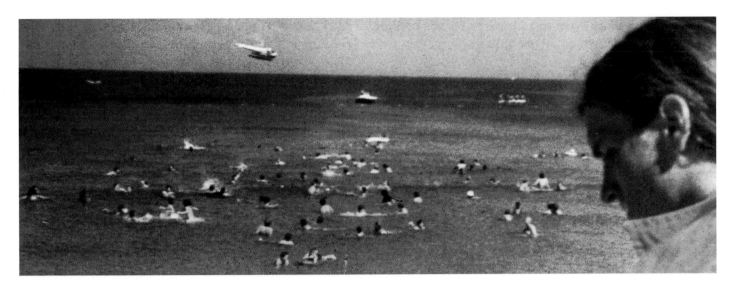

6.3 *Jaws*, 1975. Universal Pictures. Director: Steven Spielberg.

The *shot* is what the camera records over a particular period of time and forms the basic unit of filmmaking. The *master shot* comprises a single shot of an entire piece of action, taken to facilitate the assembly of the component shots of which the scene will finally be composed. The *establishing shot* is a long shot (see below) introduced at the beginning of a scene to establish the interrelationship of details, a time, or a place.

The *long shot* places the camera a considerable distance from the subject; the *medium shot* moves nearer to the subject; and the *close-up* even nearer. We call a close-up of two people within the frame a *two-shot*, and a *bridging shot* is one inserted in the editing of a scene to cover a brief break in continuity.

An equally important variable of camera viewpoint consists of whether the scene has an objective or subjective viewpoint. The *objective viewpoint* takes the form of an omnipotent viewer, roughly analogous to the technique of third-person narrative in literature. In this way, filmmakers allow their audience to watch the action through the eyes of a universal spectator. However, those who wish to involve their audience more deeply in a scene may use the *subjective viewpoint*: the scene unfolds as if the audience were actually participating in it, and we see the action from the filmmaker's perspective. This is analogous to the first-person narrative technique.

CUTTING WITHIN THE FRAME *Cutting within the frame* avoids the editing process. It can be created by actor movement, camera movement, or a combination of the two. It allows the scene to progress smoothly and is used most often on television. In a scene in John Ford's classic *Stagecoach*, the coach and its passengers have just passed through hostile territory without being attacked; the driver and his passengers all express relief. Ford cuts to a long shot of the coach moving across the desert and *pans*, or follows, it as it moves from right to left on the screen. This movement of the camera suddenly reveals in the foreground, and in close-up, the face of a hostile warrior watching the passage of the coach. In other words, the filmmaker has moved smoothly from a long shot to a close-up without needing the editing process. He has also established a spatial relationship.

In a scene from *Jaws* (Fig. 6.3) the camera also moves from distant objects to the face in the foreground, finally including them both in the frame; the pan across the scene occurs without editing of the film. Directors choose to cut or to cut within the frame because the results of each option create psychological overtones that cause responses in the viewer. In the arena scene from *Gladiator* (DreamWorks Pictures, 2000), Russell Crowe's gladiator character confronts another gladiator and a tiger. Director Ridley Scott cuts back and forth from Russell Crowe to the tiger and the other gladiator to create suspense. When he combines them all in one shot, however, he produces the maximum sense of danger.

DISSOLVES During the printing of the film negative, transitional devices can be worked into a scene. Filmmakers generally use them to indicate the end of one scene and the beginning of another. The camera can cut or jump to the next scene, but the transition stays smoother if the scene fades out into black and the next scene fades in. This is called a *dissolve*. A *lap dissolve* occurs when the fade-out and the fade-in occur simultaneously and the scene momentarily overlaps. A *wipe* is a form of optical transition in which an invisible line moves across the screen, eliminating one shot and revealing the next, much in the way a windshield wiper moves across the windshield of a car. In silent film the transition could also be created by closing or opening the aperture of the lens: this is called an *iris-out* or an *iris-in*.

FOCUS Even the manner in which the lens focuses can add to the meaning of the scene. If both near and distant objects appear clearly at the same time, the camera uses *depth of focus*. In Figure 6.3 foreground and background appear in focus. In this situation actors can move without necessitating a change of camera position. Many television shows recorded before an audience use this kind of focus.

If the main object of interest stays clear while the remainder of the scene blurs out of focus, the camera portrays *rack* or *differential focus*. With this technique the filmmaker can draw the audience's attention to one element within a shot.

MOVEMENT The movement of the camera as well as its position can add variety or impact to a shot or scene. Many kinds of physical (as opposed to apparent) camera movement exist. The *track* is a shot taken as the camera moves in the same direction, at the same speed, and in the same place as the object being photographed. A *pan* is taken by rotating the camera horizontally while keeping it fixed vertically. It is usually employed in enclosed areas, particularly television studios. The *tilt* moves the camera vertically or diagonally, and adds variety to a sequence. Moving the camera toward or away from the subject is known as a *dolly shot*. Modern sophisticated lenses can achieve the same effect by changing the focal length—this negates the need for camera movement and is known as a *zoom shot*.

LIGHTING The camera cannot photograph a scene without light, whether it be natural or artificial. Most television productions shot before a live audience require a flat, general illumination pattern. For close-ups, stronger and

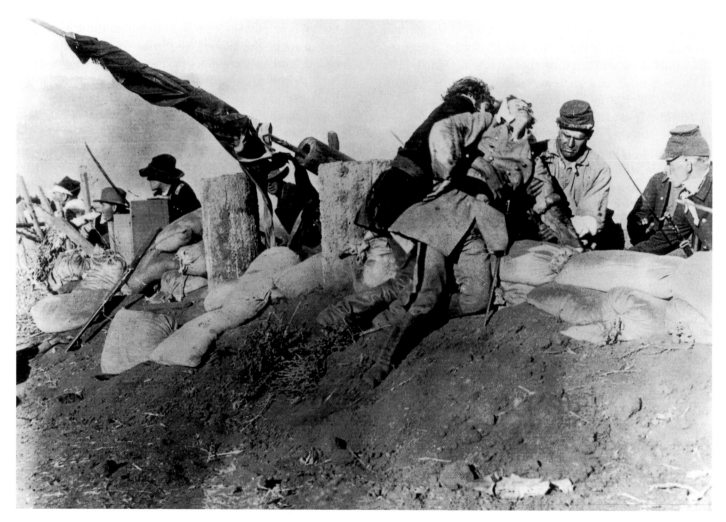

6.4 *The Birth of a Nation*, 1915. Director: D. W. Griffith.

Profile

D.W. Griffith

David Lewelyn Wark Griffith (1875–1948) was the first giant of the motion-picture industry and a genius of film credited with making film an artform. As a director, D. W. Griffith never needed a script. He improvised new ways to use the camera and to cut the celluloid, which redefined the craft for the next generation of directors.

D. W. Griffith was born on January 22, 1875, in Floydsfork, Kentucky, near Louisville. His aristocratic Southern family had been impoverished by the American Civil War, and much of his early education came either in a one-room schoolhouse or at home. His father, a former Confederate colonel, told him battle stories that may have affected the tone of Griffith's early films.

When Griffith was seven, his father died and the family moved to Louisville. He quit school at sixteen to go to work as a bookstore clerk. In the bookstore he met some actors from a Louisville theatre. This acquaintanceship led to work with amateur theatre groups and to tours with stock companies. He tried playwriting, but his first play failed on opening night in Washington, D.C. He also attempted writing screenplays, but his first scenario for a motion picture also met with rejection. While acting for New York studios, however, he did sell some scripts for one-reel films, and when the Biograph Company had an opening for a director in 1908, Griffith was hired.

During the five years he spent with Biograph, Griffith introduced or refined all the basic techniques of filmmaking. His innovations in cinematography included the close-up, the fade-in and fade-out, soft focus, high- and low-angle shots, and panning (moving the camera in panoramic long shots). In film editing, he invented the techniques of flashback and crosscutting—interweaving bits of scenes to give an impression of simultaneous action.

Griffith also expanded the horizon of film with social commentary. Of the nearly 500 films he directed or produced, his first full-length work was his most sensational. *The Birth of a Nation* (first shown as *The Clansman* in 1915; see Fig. 6.4) was hailed for its radical technique but condemned for its racism. As a response to censorship of *The Birth of a Nation*, he produced *Intolerance* (1916), an epic integrating four separate themes.

After *Intolerance*, Griffith may have turned away from the epic film because of the financial obstacles involved, but his gifted performers more than made up for this loss, for they were giants in their own right. Among the talented stars that he introduced to the industry were Dorothy and Lillian Gish, Mack Sennett, and Lionel Barrymore.

In 1919 Griffith formed a motion picture distribution company called United Artists with Mary Pickford, Charlie Chaplin, and Douglas Fairbanks.

Griffith's stature within the Hollywood hierarchy was one of respect and integrity. He became one of the three linchpins of the ambitious Triangle Studios, along with Thomas Ince and Mack Sennett.

View excerpts of Griffith's films at www.uno.edu/~dream/Griffith/home.html.

---

more definitely focused lights are required to highlight features, eliminate shadows, and add a feeling of depth. Cast shadows or atmospheric lighting (in art, chiaroscuro) are often used to create a mood, particularly in black-and-white films (Fig. 6.4). Lighting at a particular angle can heighten the feeling of texture, just as an extremely close shot can. These techniques add visual variety to a sequence.

If natural or outdoor lighting is used and the camera is hand-held, the film appears unsteady; this technique and effect is called *cinéma vérité*. Such camera work and natural lighting are found most often in documentary films or sequences photographed for newsreels or television news programming. It comprises one of the conventions of current-events reporting and adds to the sense of reality and immediacy suitable for this kind of film recording. Contemporary portrayals of war such as *Saving Private Ryan* (1998) and *We Were Soldiers* (2002) utilize the techniques of *cinéma vérité* masterfully, in addition, ironically, to applying computer-generated scenography.

These techniques and many others are used to ease technical problems, to make films smoother or more static, depending upon the needs of the story line, or to add an element of commentary. One school of cinematic thought believes that camera technique is best when not noticeable; another, more recent, way of thinking asserts that the obviousness of all the technical aspects of film adds meaning to the concept of cinema. In any case, camera technique adds variety and commentary, meaning and method, to the shot, the scene, and the film.

SENSE STIMULI

Film aims, as does any art, to involve the audience in its product, either emotionally or intellectually. Nothing surpasses a good plot with well-written dialogue delivered by trained actors to create audience interest. But filmmakers can enhance their final product in other ways as well—techniques that manipulate the audience toward a deeper involvement or a heightened intellectual response.

Perception is most important in the area of technical detail. We should begin to cultivate the habit of noticing even the tiniest details in a scene, for often these add a commentary that the average member of an audience misses. For example, in Hitchcock's *Psycho*, when the caretaker of the motel (played by Anthony Perkins) wishes to spy upon the guests in cabin 1, he pushes aside a picture that hides a peephole. The picture is a reproduction of Giovanni Bologna's statue *Rape of the Sabine Woman*—Hitchcock's irony is obvious. Thus, perception becomes the method through which viewers of film find its deeper meanings as well as its basic styles.

CROSSCUTTING

The most familiar and most easily identified filmmaking technique used to heighten feeling is *crosscutting*. Crosscutting alternates between two separate actions related by theme, mood, or plot, but that usually occur at the same time. Its most common function is to create suspense. Consider this familiar cliché. Pioneers going west in a wagon train are besieged by hostile warriors. The settlers hold them off, but ammunition runs low. The hero has been able to find a cavalry troop, and they ride to the rescue. The film alternates between pioneers fighting for their lives and soldiers galloping across the countryside toward them. The film continues to cut back and forth, the pace of cutting increasing until the sequence builds to a climax—then the cavalry arrives in time to save the wagon train. The famous chase scene in *The French Connection*, the final sequences in *Wait Until Dark*, and the sequences of the girl entering the fruit cellar in *Psycho* each helps to build suspense through crosscutting techniques.

A more subtle case of crosscutting—*parallel development*—occurs in *The Godfather, Part I*. At the close of that film Michael Corleone acts as godfather for his sister's son; at the same time his men destroy all his enemies. The film alternates between views of Michael at the religious service and sequences showing violent death. This parallel construction draws an ironic comparison; the juxtaposition allows the audience to draw their own inferences and added meaning.

TENSION BUILD-UP AND RELEASE

If the plot of a film is believable, the actors competent, and the director and film editor talented and knowledgeable, a feeling of tension can occur. If this tension becomes too great, the audience will seek some sort of release, and an odd-sounding laugh, a sudden noise, or a loud comment from a member of the audience may cause the rest of the viewers to laugh, thus breaking the tension and in a sense destroying the atmosphere so carefully created. Wise filmmakers therefore build into their film a *tension release* that deliberately draws laughter from the audience, but at a place in the film where they wish them to laugh. This can be engineered by a comical way of moving, a gurgle as a car sinks into a swamp, or merely a comic line. It does not have to be too obvious, but it should be present in some manner. After a suspenseful sequence the audience needs to relax; once the tension release does its job, they can be drawn into another exciting situation.

Sometimes, to shock the audience or maintain their attention, a filmmaker may break a deliberately created pattern or convention of film. In *Jaws*, for example, each time the shark is about to appear, a four-note musical motif is played. The audience thereby grows to believe that they will hear this warning before each appearance, and so they relax. However, toward the end of the film the shark suddenly appears without benefit of the motif, shocking the audience. From that point until the end of the film they can no longer relax, and their full attention is directed to it.

DIRECT ADDRESS

Another method used to draw attention is *direct address*. In most films, the actors rarely look at or talk directly to the audience. However, in *Tom Jones*, while Tom and his landlady are arguing over money, Tom suddenly turns to the audience and says, "You saw her take the money." The audience's attention focuses on the screen more strongly than ever after that. This technique has been effectively adapted by television for use in commercial messages. For

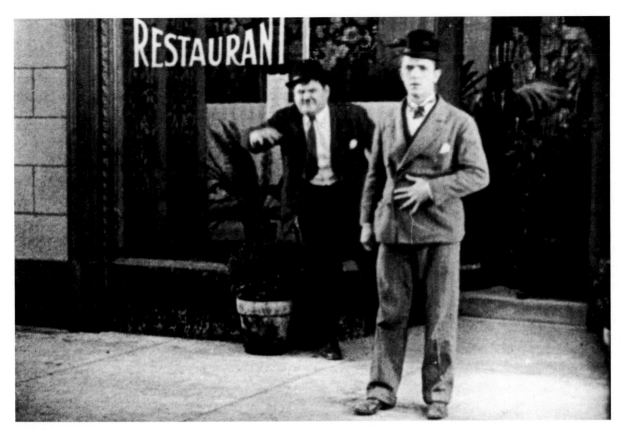

6.5 *Your Darn Tootin'*, 1928. A Hal Roach Production for Pathé Films. Director: Edgar Kennedy.

example, a congenial man looks at the camera (and you) with evident interest and asks if you are feeling tired, run-down, and sluggish. He assumes you are and proceeds to suggest a remedy. In a sense, the aside of nineteenth-century melodrama and the soliloquy of Shakespeare were also ways of directly addressing an audience and drawing them into the performance.

In silent films, where this type of direct address to the audience could not be used, the device of titles was substituted. However, some of the silent comedians felt that they should have direct contact with their audience, and so they developed a *camera look* as a form of direct address. After an especially destructive moment in his films, Buster Keaton would look directly at the camera, his face immobile, and stare at the audience. When Charlie Chaplin achieved an adroit escape from catastrophe he might turn toward the camera and wink. Stan Laurel would look at the camera and gesture helplessly (Fig. **6.5**), as if to say, "How did all this happen?" Oliver Hardy, after falling into an open manhole, would register disgust directly to the camera and the audience. These all created ways of letting the audience know that the comedians knew they were there. Some sound comedies adapted this technique too. In the "road" pictures of Bob Hope

and Bing Crosby both stars, as well as camels, bears, fish, and anyone else who happened to be around, would comment on the film or the action directly to the audience. However, this style may have been equally based on familiarity with radio programs in which the performer usually spoke directly to the home audience.

MAGNITUDE AND CONVENTION

In considering the magnitude of a film we must be aware of the means by which the film is to be communicated. In other words, was the film made for a television showing or for projection in a large theatre? Due to the size of the television screen, large panoramas or full-scale action sequences are not entirely effective on television—they become too condensed. To be truly effective, television films should be built around the close-up and around concentrated action and movement, because the television audience is closer to the screen than are the viewers in a large theatre. Scenes of multiple images with complex patterns of movement, or scenes of great violence, will become confusing because of the intimacy of television, and will seem more explicit than they really are. On the other hand, when close shots of intimate details are enlarged through projection in a theatre they may appear somewhat ridiculous. The nuance of a slightly raised eyebrow that is so effective in the living room will appear either silly or overly dramatic when it is magnified on a 60-foot (18-m) screen.

Film, as theatre, has certain conventions or customs that the viewer accepts without hesitation. When an exciting chase scene takes place, no one wonders about the location of the orchestra playing the music that enhances the sequence. They merely accept the background music as part of the totality of the film. A film photographed in black-and-white is accepted as a recording of reality, even though the viewers know that the real world has color. The conventions of the musical film are equally acceptable to an audience that has been conditioned to accept them: when a performer sings and dances in the rain in the middle of a city street, none of the audience wonders whether the performer will be arrested for creating a public spectacle.

This consideration of convention is especially important to the acceptance of the silent film as a form of art. The silent film should not be thought of as a sound film without sound, but as a separate entity with its own special conventions. These revolve around the methods used to indicate sound and dialogue without actually using them. The exaggerated pantomime and acting styles, the use of titles, character stereotyping, and visual metaphors all constitute conventions that were accepted during the silent era but can appear ludicrous today, because of changes in style and taste and improvements in the devices used for recording and projecting film. The action in the silent film was recorded and presented at a speed of sixteen to eighteen frames per second; when presented today on a projector that operates at twenty-four frames per second, the movement becomes too fast and appears jerky and disconnected. However, once we learn to accept these original conventions, we may find that the silent film is an equally effective form of cinematic art.

Visual metaphor, just mentioned, works the same as verbal metaphor (see p. 193); it uses a visual image to transfer an idea to another circumstance by inference. Metaphorical comparisons also create a kind of shock. For example, in *The Mission*, the priest's (Robert De Niro) entire ascent up the mountain while carrying the soldier's armor works as a visual metaphor for the internal awareness of guilt that the De Niro character feels; when he is forgiven and freed of his guilt, the weaponry is cut from him and it tumbles down the mountain, offering him relief—both from the weight of the armor and from his own guilt.

STRUCTURAL RHYTHM

Much of the effectiveness of a film relies on its success as a form as well as a style. Filmmakers create rhythms and patterns based on the way they choose to tell their stories or that indicate deeper meanings and relationships. The manner in which the various shots join together and juxtapose with other cinematic images, both visual and aural, we call *structural rhythm*.

Symbolic images in film range from the very obvious to the extremely subtle, but they are all useful in directing the attention of the audience to the ideas inherent in the philosophical approach underlying the film. This use of symbolic elements can be found in such clichés as the hero dressed in white and the villain dressed in black, in the more subtle use of water images in Fellini's *La Dolce Vita*, or even in the presence of an X whenever someone is about to be killed in *Scarface*. Symbols certainly imply additional meanings apparent to sensitive viewers.

Sometimes, symbolic references can be enhanced by form cutting—for example, cutting directly from the hero's gun to the villain's gun. Or the filmmaker may choose to repeat a familiar image in varying forms, using it as a composer would a motif in music. In *Fort Apache*, John Ford uses clouds of dust as a curtain to cover major events; the dust indicates the ultimate fate of the cavalry troop. Grass, cloud shapes, windblown trees, and patches of color have appeared symbolically and as motifs. For example, George Lucas uses form cutting with obviousness in *Star Wars, Episode I: The Phantom Menace*.

Another part of structural rhythm is the repetition of certain visual patterns throughout a film. A circular image positioned against a rectangular one, a movement from right to left, an action repeated regularly throughout a sequence—all can become observable patterns or even thematic statements. The silent film made extreme use of thematic repetition. In *Intolerance*, D.W. Griffith develops four similar stories simultaneously and continually cross-cuts among them. This particular use of form enabled him to develop the ideas of the similarity of intolerance throughout the ages. In their silent films Laurel and Hardy often built up a pattern of "You do this to me and I'll do that to you"; they called it "tit for tat." Their audience would be lulled into expecting this pattern, but at a certain point the film would present a variation on the familiar theme (a process quite similar to the use of theme and variation in musical composition). The unexpected breaking of the pattern would surprise the audience into laughter.

Parallel development, discussed earlier, can also create form and pattern throughout a film. For example, Edwin S. Porter's *The Kleptomaniac* alternates between two stories: a wealthy woman caught shoplifting a piece of jewelry, and a poor woman who steals a loaf of bread. Each sequence alternately shows crime, arrest, and punishment; the wealthy woman's husband bribes the judge to let her off, while the poor woman goes to jail. Porter's final shot shows the statue of justice holding her scales, one weighted down with a bag of gold. Her blindfold is raised over one eye, looking at the money. In this case, as in others, the form is the film.

AUDIO

When sound films became practicable, filmmakers found many ways of using the audio track creatively in addition to just recording dialogue. It could be used for symbolism, for motifs that reinforced the emotional quality of a scene, or for stronger emphasis or structural rhythm.

Some filmmakers believe that a more realistic feeling occurs if film is cut rather than dissolved. Abrupt cuts from scene to scene give the film a staccato rhythm that approaches the reality they hope to achieve. Dissolves, on the other hand, create a slower pace and tend to make the film's transitions smooth and thus more romantic. If the abrupt cutting is done to the beat of the sound track, a pulsating rhythm is created for the film sequence; this in turn adds a sense of urgency.

In Fred Zinnemann's *High Noon*, the sheriff waits for the midday train to arrive. The sequence, in montage, shows the townspeople, as well as the sheriff, waiting. Every eight beats of the musical track the shot changes. Then as noon approaches, the shot changes every four beats. Tension mounts. The feeling of rhythm is enhanced by images of a clock's pendulum swinging to the beat of the sound track. Tension continues to build. The train's whistle sounds. A series of rapid cuts of faces turning and looking follows, but the sound track has only silence, which serves as a tension release. This last moment of the sequence also serves as transition between the music and silence. In other films the track may shift from music to natural sounds and back to music again. Or a pattern may be created of natural sound, silence, and a musical track. All depends on the mood the filmmaker tries to create. Hitchcock often uses music as a tension release or an afterthought, as he usually relies on the force of his visual elements to create structural rhythm.

Earlier in this chapter we mentioned the use of motif in *Jaws*. Many films opt for an audio *motif* to introduce visual elements or to convey meaning symbolically. Walt Disney, particularly in his pre-1940 cartoons, often uses his sound track in this manner. For example, Donald Duck tries to catch a pesky fly, but the fly always manages to elude him. In desperation Donald sprays the fly with insecticide. The fly coughs and falls to the ground. But on the sound track we hear an airplane motor coughing and sputtering, and finally diving to the ground and crashing. In juxtaposing these different visual and audio elements, Disney uses his track symbolically.

John Ford often underlines sentimental moments in his films by accompanying the dialogue of a sequence with traditional melodies. As the sequence comes to a close the music swells and then fades away to match the fading out of the scene. In *The Grapes of Wrath*, when Tom Joad says goodbye to his mother, "Red River Valley" plays on a concertina; as Tom walks over the hill the music becomes louder, and when he disappears from view it fades out. Throughout the film, this familiar folk song serves as a thematic reference to the Joads' home in Oklahoma and also boosts the audience's feelings of nostalgia.

A pivotal step in the use of music in film occurred with George Lucas's first film of the *Star Wars* trilogy (1977). Lucas revived the use of bold symphonic accompaniment to heighten the dramatic effect of the scenes. As Louis Giannetti notes in *Understanding Movies* (p. 224), "John Williams's score is brassy, powerful, and richly orchestrated, very much in the manner of the lushly romantic and full-bodied scores of Hollywood's golden age. Critic Frank Spotnitz noted that 'the score is like a second screenplay, commenting on and enriching the first.'" Indeed, the recollection of older cinematic traditions recurs repeatedly in *Star Wars*' visual and dialogue allusions.

Voiceover narration can change the fundamentals of a film. Technically, voiceover is a nonsynchronous spoken commentary often used to convey a character's thoughts. Nonsynchronous means that the sound does not derive from an obvious source in the visuals. A voiceover often provides a useful device for filmmakers to establish a tone different than what would occur in a strictly objective presentation. For example, in *Dances with Wolves* (1990), director Kevin Costner uses voiceover narration to create a sympathetic tone. In a more abstract sense, voiceover narration can change the very nature of the communicative model of the film. Specifically, who is the message sender? Films often comprise multiple authors, and the use of a voiceover narrator gives the film authorship a further layer for the message receiver (us) to unravel. Usually the narrator is a character in the film who helps us interpret the events. But, as Louis Giannetti points out (*Understanding Movies,* p. 337), "A film's narrator is not necessarily neutral. Nor is he or she necessarily the filmmaker's mouthpiece."

THINKING CRITICALLY

Create a basic analysis of a work of film by using the following outline of concepts from the text as a guideline.

- Genres. What was the genre of the film? If it was a narrative film, how did the elements of plot work? Where did the crises, climax, and dénouement occur? If it was an absolute film, what artistic elements such as composition were evident, and how did the filmmaker use them to create specific effects? If the film was a documentary, what characteristics of that genre did the filmmaker explore?

- Editing. What elements of editing were utilized, and how did those elements control viewer response or affect the rhythm and pace of the film?

- Shots. What shots did the filmmaker seem to emphasize? How did that emphasis create a basic sense of spectacle in the film?

- Cutting. How did the editor make use of cutting to create rhythmic flow in the film? What specific effects did the cutting techniques have on the mood, structure, and meaning of the film?

- Dissolves. Did the filmmaker use any particular types of dissolve for specific effects? If so, what were they?

- Focus. How did the use of focus seek to control your attention? Was it successful?

- Camera movement. In what ways did camera movement contribute to the overall effect of the film?

- Reaction. How did the previous elements combine to create a reaction in you? In other words, what drew your attention? What was your emotional response to the film, and what caused that reaction?

CYBER STUDY

GREAT FILMS BY DECADE:
http://www.filmsite.org/pre20sintro.html
http://www.filmsite.org/20sintro.html
http://www.filmsite.org/30sintro.html
http://www.filmsite.org/40sintro.html
http://www.filmsite.org/50sintro.html
http://www.filmsite.org/60sintro.html
http://www.filmsite.org/70sintro.html
http://www.filmsite.org/80sintro.html
http://www.filmsite.org/90sintro.html

CHAPTER SEVEN

DANCE

OUTLINE

FORMAL AND TECHNICAL QUALITIES

FORMS
  Ballet
  Modern Dance
  World Concert/
    Ritual Dance
  Folk Dance
  Jazz Dance
CHOREOGRAPHY
  Formalized Movement
  Line, Form, and Repetition

Rhythm
Mime and Pantomime
Theme, Image, and Story
  Line
Music
Mise-en-scène
Profile: Martha Graham
  Lighting

SENSE STIMULI

Dance and Human Reality:
  Martha Graham,
    Appalachian Spring
MOVING IMAGES
FORCE
SIGN LANGUAGE
COLOR
Thinking Critically
Cyber Study

IMPORTANT TERMS

Ballet "Classical" or formal dance.

Choreographer The artist who creates a dance work.

First position The basic position for all movements in ballet. The heels are together and the toes "open" and out to the side.

Folk dance A body of group dances performed to traditional music.

Jazz dance A variety of styles of movement originating in the African American experience.

Mime Bodily movement that suggests the actions of people or animals.

Mise-en-scène The visual elements supporting a dance work, including settings, lighting, and costumes.

Modern dance Highly individualized twentieth-century dance works essentially antiballetic in philosophy.

Pantomime The acting out of dramatic action without words.

Plié A bending of the knees with the feet in first position.

World concert/ritual dance Concert and ceremonial dances specific to a country or culture.

FORMAL AND TECHNICAL QUALITIES

Every December, Tchaikovsky's *Nutcracker* ballet rivals Handel's *Messiah* and television reruns of the Jimmy Stewart movie *It's a Wonderful Life* as a holiday tradition. Dance is one of the most natural and universal of human activities. In virtually every culture, regardless of location or level of sophistication, we find some form of dance. Dance appears to have sprung from humans' religious needs. For example, scholars are relatively certain that the theatre of ancient Greece developed out of that society's religious tribal dance rituals. It is without doubt that dance is part of human communication at its most fundamental level. We can see this expression even in little children who, before they begin to paint, sing, or imitate, begin to dance.

Carved and painted scenes dating from antiquity to the beginning of the era of film give us only the scantiest means by which to study the history of dance, an ephemeral art of movement—something we will notice as we move through Chapters 9–13 of this book. Dance is also a social activity and, although this text takes a fairly relativistic view of what comprises art, discussion of dance in this text is limited to what may be called "theatre dance"—dance that involves a performer, a performance, and an audience.

FORMS

Dance focuses on the human form in time and space. It can follow numerous directions and traditions, including ballet, modern, world concert/ritual, folk, jazz, tap, and musical comedy. The discussion that follows treats five of these: ballet, modern, world concert/ritual, folk, and jazz dance.

Ballet

Ballet comprises what can be called "classical" or formal dance. Its rich tradition rests heavily upon a set of prescribed movements and actions. In general, ballet is a highly theatrical dance presentation consisting of solo dancers, duets, and choruses, or the *corps de ballet* (cohr-duh-bah-LAY). According to Anatole Chujoy in the *Dance Encyclopedia*, the basic principle in ballet is "the reduction of human gesture to bare essentials, heightened and developed into meaningful patterns." George Balanchine saw the single steps of a ballet as analogous to single frames in a motion picture. Ballet, then, became a fluid succession of images, existing within specialized codes of

movement. As with all dance and indeed all the arts, ballet expresses basic human experiences and desires. See the Companion Website: Dance, Ballet.

Modern Dance

Modern dance is a label given to a broad variety of highly individualized dance works beginning in the twentieth century, American in derivation, and antiballetic in philosophy. It began as a revolt against the stylized and tradition-bound elements of ballet. The basic principle of modern dance could be stated as an exploration of natural and spontaneous or uninhibited movement, in strong contrast with the conventionalized and specified movement of ballet. The earliest modern dancers found stylized ballet incompatible with their need to communicate in twentieth-century terms. As Martha Graham characterized it, "There are no general rules. Each work of art creates its own code." Nonetheless, in its attempts to be non-balletic, it has accrued certain conventions and characteristics. While there are narrative elements in many modern dances, there may be less emphasis on them than in traditional ballet. There also exist differences in the use of the body (particularly in the angularity of line expressed in modern dance), use of the dance floor (which in modern dance becomes more interactive with the dancer rather than being just a surface from which to spring and then return), and interaction with the visual elements. See the Companion Website: Dance.

World Concert/Ritual Dance

Out of a plethora of scholarly arguments about how to label and define certain types of dance emerged the term "world dance." This name describes dances specific to a particular country. Within or alongside the category of world dance exists another label: *ritual dance*. In other words, among the dances classified as "world" there exist dances based in ritual—dances having ceremonial functions, formal characteristics, and particular prescribed procedures—that pass from generation to generation. Perhaps complicating the definition further, some of the dances falling in to such a category have public presentation as their objective, and some have both ritualistic and public performance aims. Further, some ritual dances would never be performed in front of an audience because of their sacredness.

World concert/ritual dances typically center around topics important to single cultures—for example, "religion, moral values, work ethics or historical information relating to a culture" (Nora Ambrosio, *Learning About Dance*, p. 94). Some of the dances involve cultural com-

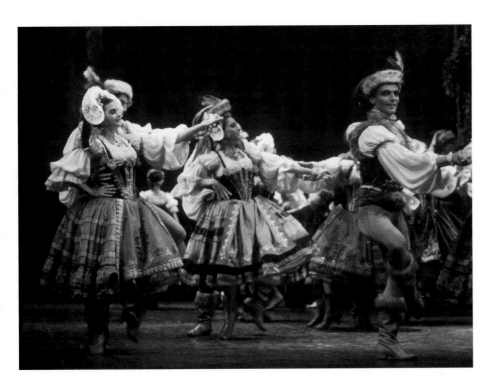

7.1 The Csárdás, a traditional Hungarian folk dance.

munication, and others—such as those in the Japanese *Noh* and *Kabuki* traditions—are theatrical. World concert/ritual dance is an important element of many African and Asian cultures. At least in general terms, world concert/ritual dance can be differentiated from the next category, *folk dance*, although the boundaries often blur.

Folk Dance

Folk dance, somewhat like folk music, is a body of group dances performed to traditional music. Similar to folk music, we do not know the artists who developed it. Folk dances began as a necessary or informative part of certain societies, and their characteristics always identify stylistically with a given culture. They developed over a period of years, passing from one generation to another. They have prescribed movements, prescribed rhythms, and prescribed music and costume. At one time or another they may have become formalized—committed to some form of record. But they form part of a heritage, and usually do not represent the creative result of an artist or a group of interpretive artists, as do forms of dance. Likewise, they exist more to involve participants than to entertain an audience (Fig. **7.1**).

Folk dancing establishes an individual sense of participation in society, the tribe, or a mass movement. "The group becomes one in conscious strength and purpose, and each individual experiences a heightened power as part of it . . . [a] feeling of oneness with one's fellows which is established by collective dancing."[1]

Jazz Dance

Jazz dance traces its origins to Africa prior to the arrival of African slaves on the American continent. Today it exists in a variety of forums including popular theatre, concert stage, movies, and television. The rhythms of African music found their way into dances performed for enjoyment and entertainment. The foundations they provided led to the Minstrel shows, in which dances were performed by white entertainers in blackface. By the late twentieth century, jazz dance had evolved into a variety of styles of movement, lacking a precise definition other than that of a vital, theatrical dance rooted in jazz and the African heritage. Jazz dance relies heavily on improvisation and syncopation.

CHOREOGRAPHY

Dance is an art of time and space that utilizes many of the elements of the other arts. In the setting and in the line and form of the human body it involves many of the compositional elements of pictures, sculpture, and theatre. Dance also relies heavily on the elements of music—whether or not music accompanies the dance presentation. However, the essential ingredient of dance remains the human body and its varieties of expression.

Formalized Movement

The most obvious repository of formalized movement in dance is ballet. All movement in ballet stems from five

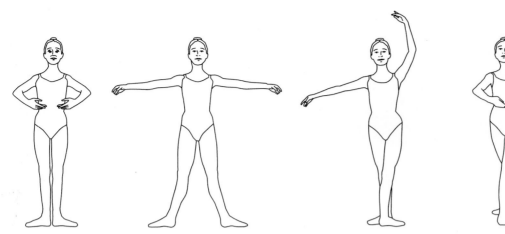

7.2A First position. 7.2B Second position. 7.2C Third position. 7.2D Fourth position. 7.2E Fifth position.

7.2 The five ballet positions.

basic leg, foot, and arm positions. In the *first position* (Fig. 7.2A) the dancer stands with weight equally distributed between the feet, heels together, and toes open and out to the side. In ballet all movements evolved from this basic "open" position; the feet are never parallel to each other with both pointing straight forward. The *second position* (Fig. 7.2B) is achieved by opening the first position the length of one's foot, again with the weight placed evenly on both feet. In the *third position* (Fig. 7.2C) the heel of the front foot touches the instep of the back foot; the legs and feet must be well turned out. The heel of the front foot is opposite the toe of the back foot in the *fourth position* (Fig. 7.2D). The feet are parallel and separated by the length of the dancer's foot; again, the weight is placed evenly on both feet. The *fifth position* (Fig. 7.2E) is the most frequently used of the basic ballet positions. The feet stay close together with the front heel touching the toe of

the back foot. The legs and the feet must be well turned out to achieve this position correctly, and the weight rests evenly on both feet. As is clear from Figure 7.2, each position changes the attitude of the arms as well as that of the legs and feet. From these five basic positions a series of fundamental movements and poses develops, and form the core of every movement of the human body in formal ballet.

Many variations can be made upon the five basic positions. For example, the *grande seconde* (Fig. 7.3) varies second position with one leg elevated to full height. One leg also elevates in the *demi-hauteur* (deh-mee-oh-TUHR), or "half-height" (Fig. 7.4). Full height requires extension of the leg at a 90-degree angle to the ground; half height requires a 45-degree extension.

Movements carry the same potential for variety. For example, in the *ronds de jambe à terre* (ruhn duh zhamb ah tair; Fig. 7.5) the leg from the knee to and including

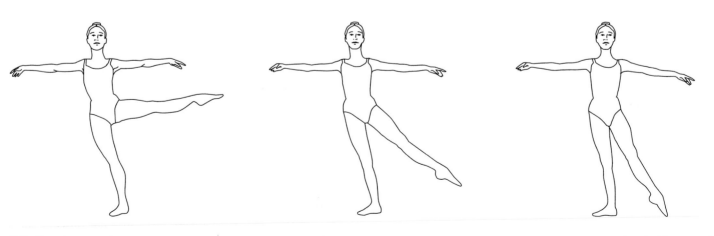

7.3 *Grande seconde.* 7.4 *Demi-hauteur.* 7.5 *Ronds de jambe à terre.*

the foot rotates in a semicircle. As we develop expertise in perceiving dance, it becomes obvious in watching formal ballet (and, to a lesser degree, modern dance) that we see a limited number of movements and poses, turns and leaps, done over and over again. Thus these bodily compositions form a kind of theme with variations, and in that respect they are interesting in themselves.

In addition, we can find a great deal of excitement in the bodily movements of formal ballet if for no other reason than the physical skills required for their execution. Just as in gymnastics or figure skating, the strength and grace of individuals in large part determine their qualitative achievement. Yet ballet encompasses far more than just a series of gymnastic exercises.

Perhaps the most familiar element of ballet is the female dancer's toe work or dancing *on point* (Fig. 7.6). Requiring special kind of footgear (Fig. 7.7), dancing on point is a fundamental part of the female dancer's development, but it usually takes a minimum of two years of thorough training and development before a dancer can begin. Certain kinds of turns are not possible without toeshoes—for example, spinning on point or being spun by a partner.

We have focused on ballet in this discussion of formalized movement because it is the most familiar of the traditional, formalized dance forms. Ballet, however, is not alone in adhering to formalized patterns of movement. Formalized movement allows us to distinguish folk and other dances, such as the *pavane*, the *galliard*, the *waltz*, and the *mambo*. All have formal or conventional patterns of movement. Perhaps only modern dance resists formal movement, and even then not completely.

Line, Form, and Repetition

The compositional elements of line, form, and repetition apply to the use of the human body in exactly the same sense that they apply to painting and sculpture—the latter especially. We can analyze the body of the dancer as a sculptural, three-dimensional form that reflects the use of line, even though the dancer moves continually. The body as a sculptural form moves from one pose to another, and if we were to take a stop-action movie of a dance, we could analyze, frame by frame or second by second, the compositional qualities of the human body. The human form in every illustration in this chapter, including those that show groupings of dancers, can be analyzed as a composition of line and shape. Dance, therefore, can be seen at two levels: first, as a type of pictorial communication employing symbols that occur only for a moment and, second, as the design of transition with movement between those moments.

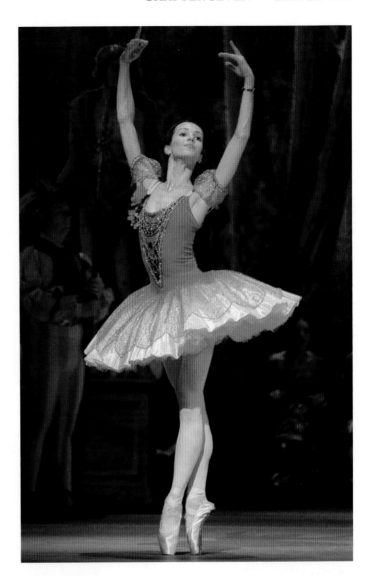

7.6 On point.

7.7 On point, detail.

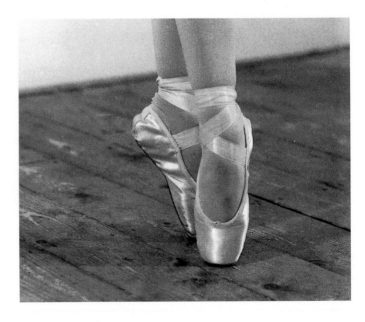

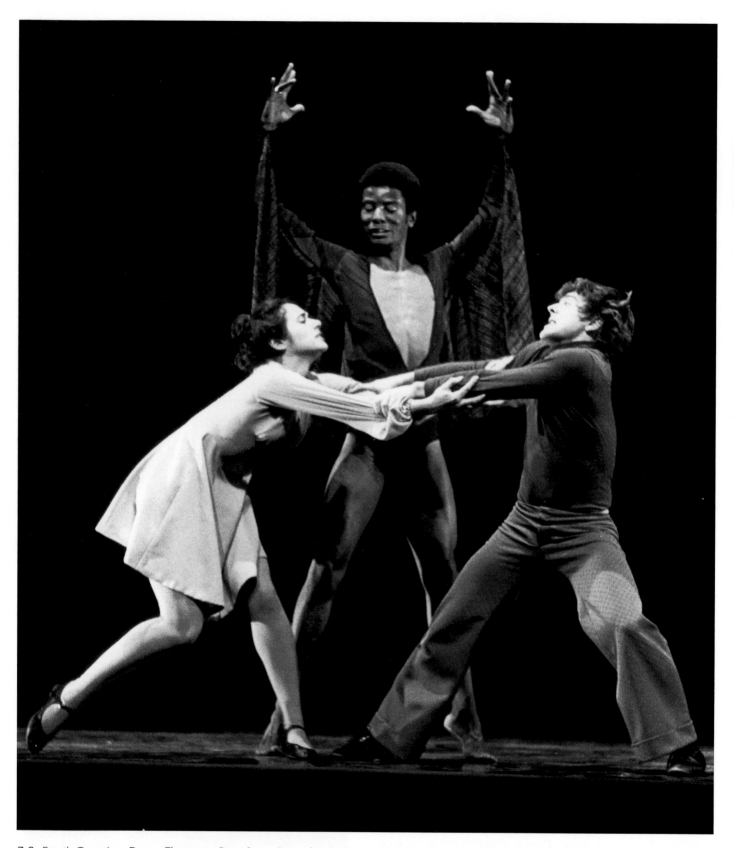

7.8 *Family Tree*, Jazz Dance Theatre at Penn State, Pennsylvania State University. Choreographer: Jean Sabatine.

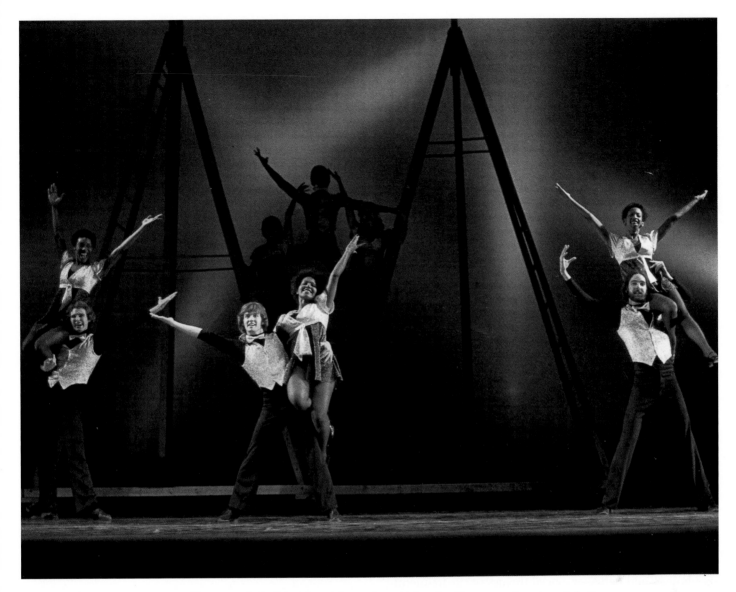

7.9 *Nameless Hour*, Jazz Dance Theatre at Penn State, Pennsylvania State University. Choreographer: Jean Sabatine.

Because dancers move through time, the concept of repetition becomes an important consideration in analyzing how a dance work is put together. The relationship of the movements to each other as the dance progresses shows us a repetitional pattern that is very similar to theme and variation in music. *Choreographers* plan these patterns using individual dancers' bodies as well as combinations of dancers in duets, trios, or the entire *corps de ballet* (Figs. 7.8 and 7.9). Watching a dance should focus on how movements, ensembles, scenery, and individual bodies explore diagonal, curved, or asymmetric lines, just in the same way that responding to a painting or work of sculpture involves perceiving and evaluating how those same elements of composition have been explored by the artist.

Rhythm

As we watch a dance we can see that the steps relate coherently. Dance phrases hold together by their rhythm, in the same sense as in musical rhythm. Sequences of long and short motions occur that are highlighted by accents. In a visual sense, dance rhythms occur in spatial arrangements, up and down, back and forth, curved and linear, large and small. We can also perceive rhythmic relationships in the ebb and flow of dancers' energy levels. Energy, of course, calls to mind dynamics in the sense the term is used in music and theatre, and the rhythm of dynamics often creates a pyramidal form rising to a peak and tapering to a resolution. See the Companion Website: Music and Dance, Rhythm.

Mime and Pantomime

Any dance form may contain elements of bodily movement that we call *mime* and *pantomime*. Bodily movement is mimetic whenever it suggests the kinds of movements we associate with people or animals or if it employs any of the forms of conventional sign language, such as the Delsarte system. And if narrative elements occur in the dance and the dancer actually portrays a character in the theatrical sense, we also may have pantomimetic action. Pantomime is the "acting out" of dramatic action without words. In the romantic style of ballet, for example, pantomime helps to carry forward the story line. We sense the emotions and character relationship in the dancers' steps, gestures, movements, and facial expressions. Only when the movement of the dance creates purely an emotional expression of the dancer can we say that it has no mime or pantomime.

Theme, Image, and Story Line

Our consideration of the presence or absence of mime leads us to a consideration of how dance communicates its idea content. Three general possibilities exist. First, the dance may contain *narrative* elements—it may tell a story. Romantic ballet usually has strong narrative elements. Second, the dance may communicate through *abstract* ideas. It has a specific theme to communicate but no story line—the ideas relate to some aspect of human emotion or the human condition. Modern ballet—twentieth-century ballet—has dealt increasingly with abstract ideas. Modern dance, especially, tends to explore human psychology and behavior. Social themes occur frequently, as do impressions or expressions from plays, poems, and novels. Religious and folk themes can be found too.

A variation of abstract idea content in dance is ethnic influence. It is interesting to note how elements of dance reflect sociocultural background. Jazz dance, for example, may stimulate us to consider the African American heritage in the United States. The third possibility is the absence of any narrative or abstract communication in a work. The piece may be a divertissement (dee-vair-TEES-mawn; French for "diversion")—some ballets are divertissements.

Participating as an audience member for dance requires active involvement, and determining the meaning involved in the themes, images, and story line of a dance requires evaluation of the feeling the choreographer tries to establish. In addition, we should attempt to discover what the choreographer tries to say through the elements of the dance. Do the dancers portray a character, transmit an emotion, or some combination?

Music

Dance associates with music as a matter of course. Music usually serves as a basis for the bodily movement of the work we perceive, although it is not absolutely necessary for dance to be accompanied by music. However, it is impossible to have dance without one element of music—rhythm. Every action of a dancer's body has some relationship in time to every other movement, and those relationships establish rhythmic patterns that are musical regardless of the presence or absence of sound.

When we hear music accompanying a dance we can respond to the relationship of the dance to the musical score. The most obvious link we see and hear comes between the gestures and footfalls of the dancer and the beat of the music. In some cases the two occur in strict accord—a one to one beat-for-beat relationship—and in other cases not.

The *dynamics* of the dance also relate to those of the music. Here, intensity, or force, of the dance plays the primary role. Moments of great intensity can manifest themselves in rapid movement and forceful leaps. Or they may reflect in other qualities. We can use the same kind of analysis in dance as we used in theatre to plot dynamic levels and overall structure. For maximum interest variety of intensity must occur. If we chart the relationship of the peaks and valleys of dynamics, we may conclude that the dynamic structure of a dance is similar to the dynamic structure of a play: it tends to be pyramidal, building to a high point and then relaxing to a conclusion. This applies whether or not narrative elements are present.

Mise-en-Scène

Because dance is essentially a visual and theatrical experience, we respond partly to those theatrical elements of dance manifested in the environment of the presentation. In other words, we can respond to the *mise-en-scène* of the dance (see Figs. 7.9 and 7.11). We can note elements of lifelikeness and how they reflect or otherwise relate to the aural and visual elements of the dance. A principal consideration here is the interrelationship of the dance with properties, settings, and the floor of the theatrical environment. Some dances employ massive stage designs. Others have no setting at all; they occur in a neutral environment. A principal difference between formal ballet and modern dance lies in the use of the *dance floor*. In formal ballet the floor acts principally as an agent from which dancers spring and to which they return. But in modern dance the floor assumes an integral role in the performance, and we are likely to see the dancers sitting on the floor, rolling on it—in short, *interacting* with the floor.

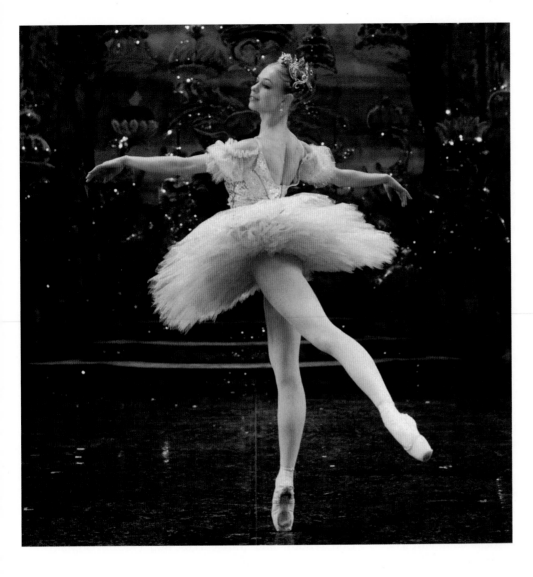

7.10 Traditional tights and tutu.

Consideration of the floor in dance also concerns how its use relates to the themes and images of the dance.

How the choreographer utilizes space plays a critical role in transmitting meaning. Changing levels, directions, shapes, and floor patterns form a fundamental part of how dance works, and understanding a dance and responding to it involves active perception and evaluation of how the entirety of the physical space and the dancers' space interact and communicate.

In discussing the relationship of *costume* to dance, we would do well to return to the section on costume design in Chapter 5 to note the purposes of costume, because they apply equally to dance as to theatrical productions. Some dances use traditional, conventional, and neutral costumes. Little representation of story line or character reflects in the tights and *tutu* of the female dancer shown in Figure 7.10. However, in many dances we see costumes high in lifelikeness. They may help portray character, locality, and other aspects of the dance (see Figs. 7.8 and 7.9).

Costumes should allow dancers to do whatever the choreographer expects of them. In fact, costume may become an integral part of the dance itself. For example, Martha Graham's *Lamentation* casts a single dancer costumed in what we could best describe as a tube of fabric— no arms, no legs, just a large envelope of cloth. Every movement of the dancer stretches the cloth so that the line and form is not that of a human body but rather of a human body enveloped in a moving fabric.

The final element of the dance costume to consider, and one of great significance, is footgear. Dancers' footgear ranges from the simple, soft, and supple ballet slipper to the specialized toeshoe of formal ballet, with street shoes, character Oxfords, and a variety of representational or symbolic footwear in between. Modern dance often occurs barefoot. The fundamental requirements of footgear are comfort and enough flexibility to allow the dancer to dance. Footgear must be appropriate to the surface of the stage floor, whether toeshoe, ballet slipper, or character Oxford. Great care must be taken to ensure that

Profile

Martha Graham

Martha Graham (1893–1991), arguably, contributed more to the art of modern dance as an innovative choreographer and teacher than any other individual. Her techniques were rooted in the muscular and nerve-muscle responses of the body to inner and outer stimuli. She created the most demanding body-training method in the field of modern dancing.

Born in Pittsburgh on May 11, 1893, Graham spent her early years there and in Santa Barbara, California. As a teenager she began studying dance at Denishawn, a dance company founded by Ruth St. Denis and Ted Shawn. Her dance debut came in *Xochitl* (ZOH-chee-tuhl), a ballet choreographed by St. Denis and based on an Aztec theme. It proved a great success both in vaudeville and concert performances.

Graham left Denishawn in 1923 to become a featured dancer in the Greenwich Village Follies. She also taught for a time at the Eastman School of Music in Rochester, N.Y. She debuted in New York City as an independent artist in 1926. One year later, her program included the dance piece *Revolt*, probably the first dance of protest and social comment in the United States.

Graham became interested in social comment as a legitimate theme in the arena of the arts, and combined it with her attraction to the early history of America. Her most famous ballet, *Appalachian Spring*, in which Graham herself danced the principal role of The Bride, resulted. Other roles included The Revivalist, The Husbandman, The Pioneering Woman, and The Followers. Perhaps the best loved of Graham's works, and the one with the finest score, *Appalachian Spring* takes as its pretext a wedding on the American frontier. The dance is like no actual ceremony or party, however. The movement not only expresses individual character and emotion, but it has a clarity, spaciousness, and definition that relate to the open frontier, which must be fenced and tamed. During the dance, the characters emerge to make solo statements; the action of the dance is suspended while they reveal what is in their hearts. The Bride's two solos suggest not only joy but trepidation for the future. (See box opposite.)

In a career spanning seventy years, Martha Graham created 180 dance works. Some of these were based on Greek legends: *Night Journey*, first performed in 1947, about Jocasta, the mother of Oedipus; *Clytemnestra* (kly-tehm-NEH-struh; 1958); and *Cave of the Heart* (1946), about the tragedy of Medea. *Letter to the World* (1940) was based on the life of poet Emily Dickinson. *Seraphic Dialogue* (1955) dealt with Joan of Arc, and *Embattled Garden* (1962) took up the Garden of Eden legend. Among her other works were *Alcestis* (1960); *Acrobats of God* (1960); and *Maple Leaf Rag* (1990). Graham announced her retirement in 1970, but she continued to create new dances until her death from cardiac arrest in New York City on April 1, 1991.

Find more about Martha Graham at www.pbs.org/wnet/americanmasters/database/graham_m.html.

---

the dance floor is not too hard, too soft, too rough, too slippery, or too sticky. The floor is so important that many touring companies take their own floor with them to ensure that they will be able to execute their movements properly. There have been cases in which professional dance companies have refused to perform in local auditoriums because the floor was dangerous for the dancers.

Lighting

Inasmuch as the entire perception of a dance relies on viewing the human body as a three-dimensional form, the work of the lighting designer stands critical in impor-

tance. How we perceive the human form in space depends on how that body is lit. Certainly our emotional and sense response is highly shaped by the nature of the lighting that plays on the dancer and the dance floor.

SENSE STIMULI

The complex properties of dance make possible diverse and intense communicative stimuli. We can respond at different levels to an artwork. To some extent we can respond even at a level of total ignorance. There will be

Dance and Human Reality

Martha Graham, *Appalachian Spring*

Social criticism as an artistic message came into vogue in the United States during the Great Depression of the 1930s. During the same period, modern dance pioneer Martha Graham began to pursue topical themes in her dances. Her interest in the shaping of America led to a now renowned dance piece set to the music of Aaron Copland, *Appalachian Spring* (1944; Fig. **7.11**). It deals, among other things, with the triumph of love and common sense over the fire-and-brimstone of American puritanism at that time.

Appalachian Spring came about as a result of a commission funded by Elizabeth Sprague Coolidge and had its première on October 30 at the Library of Congress as part of its concert series. Its story deals with a pioneer frontier marriage. The characters are a young bride, a young groom, an older woman who is their advisor and protector, and a preacher—a fire-and-brimstone frontier evangelist who prophesies hellfire and damnation for all who do not agree with him. Around the preacher flock a group of young spinsters who worship him and whom Martha Graham used as a source of comedy in the dance. She treated the young couple and their taking over of a new house and a new farm with moving and sensitive simplicity. Overall, the work read like a "love letter, a dance of hope, budding, fresh, and beautiful."[2] *Appalachian Spring* has become perhaps the most admired work in the Graham company repertoire. Its music has become an American classic, and the stunning set by sculptor Isamu Noguchi (see p. 370) a benchmark in theatrical design.

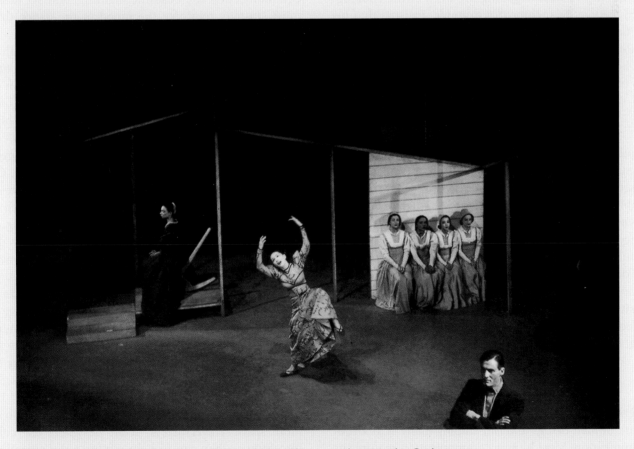

7.11 *Martha Graham in Appalachian Spring*, 1954. Choreographer: Martha Graham.

levels of understanding, levels of meaning, levels of potential response for the uninitiated as well as the thoroughly sophisticated viewer. The more sophisticated a *balletomane* one becomes, the fuller one's understanding and response will be.

MOVING IMAGES

Like every other artwork that exists in space, dance appeals to our senses through the compositional qualities of line and form. These exist not only in the human body but in the visual elements of the *mise-en-scène*. Essentially, horizontal lines stimulate a sense of calm and repose. Vertical lines suggest grandeur and elegance. Diagonal lines stimulate a feeling of action and movement (see Figs. 7.8 and 7.9), and curved lines, grace. As we react to a dance work we respond to how the human body expresses line and form—when standing still and when moving through space. If alert and perceptive, we can recognize not only how lines and forms appear but also how they repeat from dancer to dancer and from dancer to *mise-en-scène*.

Often, the kind of line created by the body of a dancer forms the key to understanding the work of the choreographer. George Balanchine, for example, insisted that his dancers be almost skin and bone; you would not see a corpulent or overly developed physique in his company. Thus bodies, too, affect our perception, and choreographers capitalize on that in their dance conceptions.

FORCE

We noted in Chapter 4 that the beat of music makes a fundamental appeal to our senses. Beat is the aspect of music that sets our toes tapping and our fingers drumming. Probably our most basic responses to a dance come from the dynamics expressed by the dancers and in the music. A dancer's use of vigorous and forceful action, high leaps, graceful turns, or extended pirouettes appeals directly to us, as does the tempo of the dance. Variety in dynamics—the louds and softs and the highs and lows of bodily intensity as well as musical sound—create the dancer's and choreographer's means of providing interest, just as in acting, directing, and painting.

SIGN LANGUAGE

Dancers, like actors, can stimulate us directly because they are human beings and can employ many symbols of communication. Most human communication requires us to learn a set of symbols—we can respond to dance at this level only when we have mastered its language. Systems of sign language, such as the Delsarte, use the positions of the arms, hands, and head to transmit meaning. Likewise, each of the hand movements of the hula dance communicates an idea, and we should concentrate on these, not the vigorous hip movements.

However, a set of universal body symbols exists to which all of us respond (so psychologists tell us), regardless of our level of familiarity or understanding. For example, the gesture of acceptance in which the arms are held outward with the palms up has the same meaning universally. Rejection is shown by holding the hands in front of the body with the palms out as if to push away. When dancers employ universal symbols we respond to their appeal to our senses just as we would to the nonverbals or body language in everyday conversation.

COLOR

Although dancers use facial and bodily expressions to communicate some aspects of the human condition, we do not receive as direct a message from them as we do from the words of actors. So, to enhance the dancer's communication the costume, lighting, and set designers must strongly reinforce the mood of the dance through the *mise-en-scène* they create.

The principal means of expression of mood is through color. Because lifelikeness is not as important in dance as it is in the theatre, lighting designers can work in much more obvious ways with color. They may not have to worry if the face of a dancer appears red or blue or green—which would be a disaster in a play. So we often see much stronger, more colorful, and more suggestive lighting in dance performances than in the theatre. Colors are more saturated, intensity much higher, and the qualities of the human body, as form, explored much more strongly by light from various directions. The same adheres to costumes and settings. Because dancers do not portray roles with high lifelikeness, their costumes can communicate in an abstract way.

On the other hand, scene designers must utilize color so as to focus attention on the dancer in the stage environment—that is, unless the choreographer intends a synthesis of the dancer with the environment, as in the case, for example, of some works by choreographer Merce Cunningham. In any but the smallest of stage spaces it is very easy for the human body to be overpowered by the elements of the setting, since the latter occupies so much more space. Nevertheless, scene designers use color as forcefully as they can to help reinforce the overall mood of the dance.

THINKING CRITICALLY

Create a basic analysis of a dance work by using the following outline of concepts from the text as a guide.

- Genre. In what ways did the dance piece pursue the characteristics of a particular genre—for example, ballet, modern, world concert/ritual, folk, or jazz dance?

- Formalized movement. In what ways did elements of formalized movement shape the piece? What recognizable explorations of first, second, third, fourth, and fifth positions occurred?

- Line, form, and repetition. How did the dancers, individually and as a group, create visual forms and repetitions? What were these forms—for example, were they rounded, angular, vertical, horizontal—and how did they create an emotional or intellectual impact?

- Rhythm. What was the rhythmic structure of the piece?

- Mime and pantomime. What, if any, elements of mime and pantomime were in the dance? What, if any, was the story line or symbolism of the dancers' movements?

- Theme, image, and story line. What kind of message or experience was the dance trying to communicate? Did it succeed; why or why not?

- Music. How did the dance relate to the music that accompanied it? If there was no musical accompaniment, what effect did that have on your experience of the work?

- Mise-en-scène. What role did the elements of the mise-en-scène play in the dance? How did the settings, lighting, and costumes work in conjunction with the movements of the dancers to create a total experience? In what ways did changes in lighting enhance or detract from your experience of the piece?

- Reaction. How did the previous elements combine to create a reaction in you? What drew your attention, and why? What were your emotional and intellectual responses to the dance piece, and what caused them?

CYBER STUDY

BALLET:
www.ccs.neu.edu/home/yiannis/dance/history.html

MODERN:
www.infoplease.com/ce6/ent/A0833540.html

CHAPTER EIGHT

LITERATURE

OUTLINE

FORMAL AND TECHNICAL QUALITIES

FORMAL DIVISIONS
Fiction
Saki (H. H. Munro),
"The Blood-feud of
Toad-Water:
a West-country Epic"
Literature and Human Reality:
Alice Walker, "Roselilly"
Poetry
Geoffrey Chaucer, *The*
Canterbury Tales, "The
Cook's Prologue" and
"The Cook's Tale"
Petrarch Sonnet CCXXV
William Shakespeare,
Sonnet XIX

Nonfiction
John Wesley, *God*
Brought Me Safe
Oliver Goldsmith, "The
Benefits of Luxury, in
Making a People More
Wise and Happy"
Drama
Profile: Toni Morrison
TECHNICAL DEVICES
Fiction
Poetry
William Shakespeare,
"The Seven Ages of
Man"

Robert Frost, "Stopping
by Woods on a Snowy
Evening"
Christina Rossetti,
"Uphill"
Nonfiction

SENSE STIMULI

PICTURES
SOUNDS
EMOTIONS
Thinking Critically
Cyber Study

IMPORTANT TERMS

Anecdotes Stories or observations about moments in a biography.

Fiction A work of literature created from the author's imagination rather than from fact.

Figures The use of language to take words beyond their literal meaning.

Imagery A verbal representation of a sensory experience.

Lyric poetry A brief, subjective work employing strong imagination, melody, and feeling.

Metaphors Figures of speech that give new implications to words; they are implied comparisons.

Meter The type and number of rhythmic units in a line of poetry.

Narrative poetry Poetry that tells a story.

Plot The structure of a work of literature.

Point of view The perspective of a work of fiction: first person, epistolary, third person, stream of consciousness.

FORMAL AND TECHNICAL QUALITIES

Read any good books lately? Ever tried to write poetry? From the earliest of times, cultures have been defined by their literature, whose medium comprises language. Today, before a movie or soap opera comes to the screen, we must have a story and, usually, a script. Such things constitute literature, whose greatest characteristic is the arousal of the imagination and the emotions by means of speech and writing.

Traditionally, literature falls into two categories: utilitarian and creative. Creative literature has a different approach than utilitarian literature. The approach determines the category—creative or utilitarian—in the same sense that one picture (composed of line, form, and color) can be termed "art," whereas another picture composed of those same elements, but that seeks only to present a visual copy, can be termed "illustration." This text focuses on creative literature—literature pursuing excellence of form or expression and presenting ideas of permanent or universal interest.

People read creative literature because they expect it to hold their interest and provide pleasure—for the same reasons they watch athletic contests or go to movies. Common experience maintains that reading creative literature is good for us, but, in all honesty, we read for the immediate reward of the pleasure it provides. Some rewards of reading may lie in the future, but immediate rewards come from the experience of participating. Creative literature takes us out of ourselves while we engage in it.

This chapter, like the preceding ones, focuses on fundamentals. History comes later. It helps to know the categories of literature and how literature is put together in order to get the most out of reading and to share experiences with others using the proper descriptive terminology. As do artists in all the arts, writers utilize the formal and technical details discussed here to shape their material in order to effect responses in their readers. They choose their words very carefully to provide maximum impact. Our initial response (What is it?) to works of literature, made up of those carefully chosen words and devices, begins, as it does in the other arts, with formal divisions, or genres. The formal divisions of literature are fiction, poetry, nonfiction, and drama. First, however, we need a few words of clarification. In this section we divide literature as just noted—in four genres. Later, as we discuss technical devices, we will view that section—again—through the prism of the four formal divisions.

FORMAL DIVISIONS

Fiction

Works of fiction emanate from the author's imagination rather than from fact. Normally, it takes one of two approaches to its subject matter: realistic—the appearance of observable, true-to-life details; or nonrealistic—fantasy. Fictional elements can appear in narrative poetry, drama, and even biography and epic poetry. Traditionally, however, we divide fiction into two broad categories: novels and short stories.

NOVELS The novel, a fictional prose narrative of considerable length, has a plot that unfolds from the actions, speech, and thoughts of the characters. Normally novels treat events within the range of ordinary experience and draw upon original subject matter rather than traditional or mythic subjects. Novels typically have numerous characters and employ normal, everyday speech. Their subject matter falls into two general categories: sociological-panoramic, covering a wide-ranging story of many years and various settings; and dramatic-intimate, covering a restricted time and setting.

Often novels fall into classification by subject matter, including the following:

epistolary Told through the medium of letters written by one or more of the characters, for example, Samuel Richardson, *Pamela* (1740).

Gothic Pseudo-medieval fiction with a prevailing atmosphere of mystery and terror, for example, Ann Radcliffe, *The Mysteries of Udolpho* (1794).

historical Set in a period of history and attempting to portray the spirit, manners, and social conditions of the time with realistic detail and faithfulness to historical fact, for example, Robert Graves, *I, Claudius* (1934).

manners Finely detailed observations of the customs, values, and mores of a highly developed and complex society, for example Jane Austen, *Pride and Prejudice* (1813).

picaresque The adventures of a rogue or lowborn adventurer, for example, Thomas Nash, *The Unfortunate Traveller* (1594).

psychological Depicting the thoughts, feelings, and motivations of the characters as equal to or greater than the external action of the narrative. The internal states of the characters are influenced by and in turn trigger external events, for example, Leo Tolstoy, *War and Peace* (1864–9).

sentimental Exploiting the reader's capacity for tenderness, compassion, or sympathy to a disproportionate degree by presenting an unrealistic view of its subject, for example, once again, Samuel Richardson, *Pamela* (1740).

As we noted in other chapters about categories of art, often we find that we can fit a work into more than one category. For example, we might place contemporary novelist Toni Morrison's (see p. 191) novel, *Love* (2003) in both historical and psychological categories. The work typifies Morrison's style with its scope and complexity. On a large scale, it explores the consequences of desegregation: Is assimilation good or bad? Should black people have kept what they had? Where does racial uplift end and nationalism begin? Nonetheless, the novel also has a small and intimate level focusing on love: parental love, unbridled love, lust, celibacy, and the deepest of friendships. In Morrison's universe, even hate constitutes a form of love. All these themes wrap around a story about Bill Cosey, a charismatic black entrepreneur who ran a chic seaside resort for wealthy African Americans during segregation. When segregation ended and black people could spend their money in wider circles, the business faltered and ultimately failed. At the beginning of the novel, two feuding women now reside at the long-closed resort: Cosey's widow and his granddaughter. They set the current action in motion.

SHORT STORIES As the name implies, short stories are short prose fictional works focusing on unity of characterization, theme, and effect, as differentiated from more expansive narrative forms such as the novel. Short stories typically concern only a single effect portrayed in a single, significant episode or scene and utilizing a limited number of characters. In short stories we find very concise narration and character that lacks full development. Although as a specific literary form, the short story did not develop until the nineteenth century, it has a historical precedent, and we can consider as part of the short story genre the *fables* of ancient times: narratives designed to enforce a useful truth, particularly in which animals or inanimate objects speak and act like human beings. A fable differs from a folktale in that it has a moral woven into the story; for example, Aesop's fables. Perhaps the best-known poet of ancient Greece, Aesop's (EE-sahp; 6th century B.C.E.?) existence, however, probably consists only in legend. Various citations and traditions surround him, and attempts occurred even in ancient Greece to establish him as an actual person. Editors ascribe approximately 200 fables to him: fables such as the turtle and the hare and the fox and the grapes. Aesop marks the onset of the Western fable tradition. Fables like the fox and the grapes provide us with examples of *accismus* (ak-SIHZ-

muhs), a form of irony in which a person feigns indifference to or pretends to refuse, something he or she really desires, for example, the fox's dismissal of the grapes: One hot summer's day a Fox was strolling through an orchard till he came to a bunch of Grapes just ripening on a vine which had been trained over a lofty branch. "Just the things to quench my thirst," quoth he. Drawing back a few paces, he took a run and a jump, and just missed the bunch. Turning around again with a One, Two, Three, he jumped up, but with no greater success. Again and again he tried after the tempting morsel, but at last had to give it up, and walked away with his nose in the air, saying, "I am sure they are sour."

"IT IS EASY TO DESPISE WHAT YOU CANNOT GET."

In the short story "The Blood-feud of Toad-Water: a West-country Epic," the Scottish writer H. H. Munro (1870–1916), who wrote under the pseudonym of Saki, describes a scene of Edwardian England. He uses the tools of flippancy, wit, and invention to satirize social pretension, unkindness, and stupidity.

The Blood-feud of Toad-Water:
a West-country Epic
Saki (H. H. Munro)
1870–1916

The Cricks lived at Toad-Water; and in the same lonely upland spot Fate had pitched the home of the Saunderses, and for miles around these two dwellings there was never a neighbour or a chimney or even a burying-ground to bring a sense of cheerful communion or social intercourse. Nothing but fields and spinneys and barns, lanes and wastelands. Such was Toad-Water; and, even so, Toad-Water had its history. Thrust away in the benighted hinterland of a scattered market district, it might have been supposed that these two detached items of the Great Human Family would have leaned towards one another in a fellowship begotten of kindred circumstances and a common isolation from the outer world. And perhaps it had been so once, but the way of things had brought it otherwise. Indeed, otherwise. Fate, which had linked the two families in such unavoidable association of habitat, had ordained that the Crick household should nourish and maintain among its earthly possessions sundry head of domestic fowls, while to the Saunderses was given a disposition towards the cultivation of garden crops. Herein lay the material, ready to hand, for the coming of feud and ill-blood. For the grudge between the man of herbs and the man of live stock is no new thing; you will find traces of it in the fourth chapter of Genesis. And one sunny afternoon in late spring-time the feud came—came, as such things mostly do come, with seeming aimlessness and triviality. One of the Crick

Literature and Human Reality

Alice Walker, "Roselilly"

Wit and irony are tools used by the African American author Alice Walker (Fig. 8.1) in her novels, poetry, and critical writings. The battles she fights are for rights for blacks and women. However, she is prone to satirize political activists just as much as their opponents. Her life and writing reflect the tensions and ideals of a "womanist"—a word she has coined for a black feminist. The "twin afflictions" of the civil rights and black power movements and the women's movement are the focus of her work.

Walker came from a family of Georgia sharecroppers and was one of eight children. Because a childhood accident left her blind in one eye, she was able to attend Spelman College, a prestigious black women's college in Atlanta, on a state rehabilitation scholarship. She continued her education at Sarah Lawrence in New York and graduated in 1965. Her identity as a black and a woman was challenged by an unwanted pregnancy, an abortion, and a trip to South Africa. She returned to the South and married a Jewish civil rights leader, from whom she was divorced in 1976.

Her short stories indicate a preoccupation with "the oppressions, the insanities, the loyalties, and the triumphs of black women." Her technique is subtle and experimental, and we can see some of that in the way that she weaves together the ritual of the marriage ceremony and the thoughts of her female character in "Roselilly" as a counterpoint to her theme of the distance between promise and fulfillment.

Roselilly
Alice Walker
(b. 1944)

Dearly Beloved.
She dreams; dragging herself across the world. A small girl in her mother's white robe and veil, knee raised waist high through a bowl of quicksand soup. The man who stands beside her is against this standing on the front porch of her house, being married to the sound of cars whizzing by on highway 61.

We are gathered here
Like cotton to be weighed. Her fingers at the last minute busily removing dry leaves and twigs. Aware it is a superficial sweep. She knows he blames Mississippi for the respectful way the men turn their heads up in the yard, the women stand waiting and knowledgeable, their children held from mischief by teachings from the wrong God. He glares beyond them to the occupants of the cars, white faces glued to promises beyond a country wedding, noses thrust forward like dogs on a track. For him they usurp the wedding.

in the sight of God
Yes, open house. That is what country black folks like. She dreams she does not already have three children. A squeeze around the flowers in her hands chokes off three and four and five years of breath. Instantly she is ashamed and frightened in her superstition. She looks for the first time at the preacher, forces humility into her eyes, as if she believes he is, in fact, a man of God. She can imagine God, a small black boy, timidly pulling the preacher's coattail.

to join this man and this woman
She thinks of ropes, chains, handcuffs, his religion. His place of worship. Where she will be required to sit apart with covered head. In Chicago, a word she hears when thinking of smoke, from his description of what a cinder was, which they never had in Panther Burn. She sees hovering over the heads of the clean neighbors in her front yard black specks falling, clinging from the sky. But in Chicago. Respect, a chance to build. Her children at last from underneath the detrimental wheel. A chance to be on top. What a relief, she thinks. What a vision, a view, from up so high.

in holy matrimony
Her fourth child she gave away to the child's father who had some money. Certainly a good job. Had gone to Harvard. Was a good man but weak because good language meant so much to him he could not live with Roselilly. Could not abide TV in the living room, five beds in three rooms, no Bach except from four to six on Sunday afternoons. No chess at all. She does not forget to worry about her son among

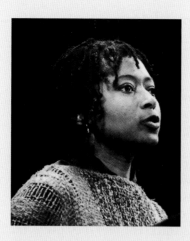

8.1 Alice Walker reading excerpts from her Pulitzer Prizewinning novel *The Color Purple* in 1985.

his father's people. She wonders if the New England climate will agree with him. If he will ever come down to Mississippi, as his father did, to try to right the country's wrongs. She wonders if he will be stronger than his father. His father cried off and on throughout her pregnancy. Went to skin and bones. Suffered nightmares, retching and falling out of bed. Tried to kill himself. Later told his wife he found the right baby through friends. Vouched for, the sterling qualities that would make up his character.

It is not her nature to blame. Still, she is not entirely thankful. She supposes New England, the North, to be quite different from what she knows. It seems right somehow to her that people who move there to live return home completely changed. She thinks of the air, the smoke, the cinders. Imagines cinders big as hailstones; heavy, weighing on the people. Wonders how this pressure finds its way into the veins, roping the springs of laughter.

If there's anybody here that knows a reason why
But of course they know no reason why beyond what they daily have to know. She thinks of the man who will be her husband, feels shut away from him because of the stiff severity of his plain black suit. His religion. A lifetime of black and white. Of veils. Covered head. It is as if her children are already gone from her. Not dead, but exalted on a pedestal, a stalk that has no roots. She wonders how to make new roots. It is beyond her. She wonders what one does with memories in a brand-new life. This had seemed easy, until she thought of it. "The reasons why . . . the people who" . . . she thinks, and does not wonder where the thought is from.

these two should not be joined
She thinks of her mother, who is dead. Dead, but still her mother. Joined. This is confusing. Of her father. A gray old man who sold wild mink, rabbit, fox skins to Sears, Roebuck. He stands in the yard, like a man waiting for a train. Her young sisters stand behind her in smooth green dresses, with flowers in their hands and hair. They giggle, she feels, at the absurdity of the wedding. They are ready for something new. She thinks the man beside her should marry one of them. She feels old. Yoked. An arm seems to reach out from behind her and snatch her backward. She thinks of cemeteries and the long sleep of grandparents mingling in the dirt. She believes that she believes in ghosts. In the soil giving back what it takes.

together
In the city. He sees her in a new way. This she knows, and is grateful. But is it enough? She cannot always be a bride and virgin, wearing robes and veil. Even now her body itches to be free of satin and voile, organdy and lily of the valley. Memories crash against her. Memories of being bare to the sun. She wonders what it will be like. Not to have to go to a job. Not to work in a sewing plant. Not to worry about learning to sew straight seams in workingmen's overalls, jeans, and dress pants. Her place will be in the home, he has said, repeatedly, promising her rest she had prayed for. But now she wonders. When she is rested, what will she do? They will make babies—she thinks practically about her fine brown body, his strong black one. They will be inevitable. Her hands will be full. Full of what? Babies. She is not comforted.

let him speak
She wishes she had asked him to explain more of what he meant. But she was impatient. Impatient to be done with sewing. With doing everything for three children, alone. Impatient to leave the girls she had known since childhood, their children growing up, their husbands hanging around her, already old, seedy. Nothing about them that she wanted, or needed. The fathers of her children driving by, waiving, not waving; reminders of times she would just as soon forget. Impatient to see the South Side, where they would live and build and be respectable and respected and free. Her husband would free her. A romantic hush. Proposal. Promises. A new life! Respectable, reclaimed, renewed. Free! In robe and veil.

or forever hold

She does not even know if she loves him. She loves his sobriety. His refusal to sing just because he knows the tune. She loves his pride. His blackness and his gray car. She loves his understanding of her *condition*. She thinks she loves the effort he will make to redo her into what he truly wants. His love of her makes her completely conscious of how unloved she was before. This is something; though it makes her unbearably sad. Melancholy. She blinks her eyes. Remembers she is finally being married, like other girls. Like other girls, women? Something strains upward behind her eyes. She thinks of the something as a rat trapped, cornered, scurrying to and fro in her head, peering through the windows of her eyes. She wants to live for once. But doesn't know quite what that means. Wonders if she has ever done it. If she ever will. The preacher is odious to her. She wants to strike him out of the way, out of her light, with the back of her hand. It seems to her he has always been standing in front of her, barring her way.

his peace

The rest she does not hear. She feels a kiss, passionate, rousing, within the general pandemonium. Cars drive up blowing their horns. Firecrackers go off. Dogs come from under the house and begin to yelp and bark. Her husband's hand is like the clasp of an iron gate. People congratulate. Her children press against her. They look with awe and distaste mixed with hope at their new father. He stands curiously apart, in spite of the people crowding about to grasp his free hand. He smiles at them all but his eyes are as if turned inward. He knows they cannot understand that he is not a Christian. He will not explain himself. He feels different, he looks it. The old women thought he was like one of their sons except that he had somehow got away from them. Still a son, not a son. Changed.

She thinks how it will be later in the night in the silvery gray car. How they will spin through the darkness of Mississippi and in the morning be in Chicago, Illinois. She thinks of Lincoln, the president. That is all she knows about the place. She feels ignorant, *wrong*, backward. She presses her worried fingers into his palm. He is standing in front of her. In the crush of well-wishing people, he does not look back.[1]

hens, in obedience to the nomadic instincts of her kind, wearied of her legitimate scratching-ground, and flew over the low wall that divided the holdings of the neighbours. And there, on the yonder side, with a hurried consciousness that her time and opportunities might be limited, the misguided bird scratched and scraped and beaked and delved in the soft yielding bed that had been prepared for the solace and well-being of a colony of seedling onions. Little showers of earth-mould and root-fibres went spraying before the hen and behind her, and every minute the area of her operations widened. The onions suffered considerably. Mrs. Saunders, sauntering at this luckless moment down the garden path, in order to fill her soul with reproaches at the iniquity of the weeds, which grew faster than she or her good man cared to remove them, stopped in mute discomfiture before the presence of a more magnificent grievance. And then, in the hour of her calamity, she turned instinctively to the Great Mother, and gathered in her capacious hands large clods of the hard brown soil that lay at her feet. With a terrible sincerity of purpose, though with a contemptible inadequacy of aim, she rained her earth bolts at the marauder, and the bursting pellets called forth a flood of cackling protest and panic from the hastily

departing fowl. Calmness under misfortune is not an attribute of either hen-folk or womenkind, and while Mrs. Saunders declaimed over her onion bed such portions of the slang dictionary as are permitted by the Nonconformist conscience to be said or sung, the Vasco da Gama fowl was waking the echoes of Toad-Water with crescendo bursts of throat music which compelled attention to her griefs. Mrs. Crick had a long family, and was therefore licensed, in the eyes of her world, to have a short temper, and when some of her ubiquitous offspring had informed her, with the authority of eye-witnesses, that her neighbour had so far forgotten herself as to heave stones at her hen—her best hen, the best layer in the countryside—her thoughts clothed themselves in language "unbecoming to a Christian woman"—so at least said Mrs. Saunders, to whom most of the language was applied. Nor was she, on her part, surprised at Mrs. Crick's conduct in letting her hens stray into other body's gardens, and then abusing of them, seeing as how she remembered things against Mrs. Crick—and the latter simultaneously had recollections of lurking episodes in the past of Susan Saunders that were nothing to her credit. "Fond memory, when all things fade we fly to thee," and in the paling light of an April afternoon the two women confronted each other from their respective sides of the party wall, recalling with shuddering breath the blots and blemishes of their neighbour's family record. There was that aunt of Mrs. Crick's who had died a pauper in Exeter workhouse—every one knew that Mrs. Saunders' uncle on her mother's side drank himself to death—then there was that Bristol cousin of Mrs. Crick's! From the shrill triumph with which his name was dragged in, his crime must have been pilfering from a cathedral at least, but as both remembrancers were speaking at once it was difficult to distinguish his infamy from the scandal which beclouded the memory of Mrs. Saunders' brother's wife's mother—who may have been a regicide, and was certainly not a nice person as Mrs. Crick painted her. And then, with an air of accumulating and irresistible conviction, each belligerent informed the other that she was no lady—after which they withdrew in a great silence, feeling that nothing further remained to be said. The chaffinches clinked in the apple trees and the bees droned round the berberis bushes, and the waning sunlight slanted pleasantly across the garden plots, but between the neighbour households had sprung up a barrier of hate, permeating and permanent. The male heads of the families were necessarily drawn into the quarrel, and the children on either side were forbidden to have anything to do with the unhallowed offspring of the other party. As they had to travel a good three miles along the same road to school every day, this was awkward, but such things have to be. Thus all communication between the households was sundered. Except the cats. Much as Mrs. Saunders might deplore it, rumour persistently pointed to the Crick he-cat as the presumable father of sundry kittens of which the Saunders she-cat was indisputably the mother. Mrs. Saunders drowned the kittens, but the disgrace remained. Summer succeeded spring, and winter summer, but the feud outlasted the waning seasons. Once, indeed, it seemed as though the healing influences of religion might restore to Toad-Water its erstwhile peace; the hostile families found themselves side by side in the soul-kindling atmosphere of a Revival Tea, where hymns were blended with a beverage that came of tea-leaves and hot water and took after the latter parent, and where ghostly counsel was tempered by garnishings of solidly fashioned buns—and here, wrought up by the environment of festive piety, Mrs. Saunders so far unbent as to remark guardedly to Mrs. Crick that the evening had been a fine one. Mrs. Crick, under the influence of her ninth cup of tea and her fourth hymn, ventured on the hope that it might continue fine, but a maladroit allusion on the part of the Saunders good man to the backwardness of garden crops brought the Feud stalking forth from its corner with all its old bitterness. Mrs. Saunders joined heartily in the singing of the final hymn, which told of peace and joy and archangels and golden glories; but her thoughts were dwelling on the pauper aunt of Exeter. Years have rolled away, and some of the actors in this wayside drama have passed into the Unknown; other onions have arisen, have flourished, have gone their way, and the offending hen has long since expiated her misdeeds and

lain with trussed feet and a look of ineffable peace under the arched roof of Barnstaple market. But the Blood-feud of Toad-Water survives to this day.[2]

Poetry

Poetry is designed to convey a vivid and imaginative sense of experience. It uses condensed language selected for its sound, suggestive power, and meaning, and employs specific technical devices such as meter, rhyme, and metaphor. Poetry can be divided into three major types: *narrative, dramatic,* and *lyric.*

NARRATIVE Narrative poetry tells a story. *Epic* poetry is narrative poetry of substantial length and elevated style. It uses strong symbolism, and has a central figure of heroic proportions. A *ballad* is a sung or recited narrative, and a *metrical romance* is a long narrative, romantic tale in verse. Geoffrey Chaucer's *The Canterbury Tales* illustrate narrative poetry.

The Canterbury Tales
Geoffrey Chaucer
c. 1340–1400

THE COOK'S PROLOGUE

The cook from London, while the reeve yet spoke,
Patted his back with pleasure at the joke.
"Ha, ha!" laughed he, "by Christ's great suffering,
This miller had a mighty sharp ending
Upon his argument of harbourage!
For well says Solomon, in his language,
'Bring thou not every man into thine house';
For harbouring by night is dangerous.
Well ought a man to know the man that he
Has brought into his own security.
I pray God give me sorrow and much care
If ever, since I have been Hodge of Ware,
Heard I of miller better brought to mark.
A wicked jest was played him in the dark.
But God forbid that we should leave off here;
And therefore, if you'll lend me now an ear,
From what I know, who am but a poor man,
I will relate, as well as ever I can,
A little trick was played in our city."
    Our host replied: "I grant it readily.
Now tell on, Roger; see that it be good;
For many a pasty have you robbed of blood,
And many a Jack of Dover have you sold
That has been heated twice and twice grown cold.
From many a pilgrim have you had Christ's curse,
For of your parsley they yet fare the worse,

Which they have eaten with your stubble goose;
For in your shop full many a fly is loose.
Now tell on, gentle Roger, by your name.
But yet, I pray, don't mind if I make game,
A man may tell the truth when it's in play."

    "You say the truth," quoth Roger, "by my fay!
But 'true jest, bad jest' as the Fleming saith.
    And therefore, Harry Bailey, on your faith,
Be you not angry ere we finish here,
If my tale should concern an inn-keeper.
Nevertheless, I'll tell not that one yet.
But ere we part your jokes will I upset."
    And thereon did he laugh, in great good cheer,
And told his tale, as you shall straightway hear.

Thus ends the prologue of the cook's tale

THE COOK'S TALE

There lived a 'prentice, once, in our city,
And of the craft of victuallers was he;
Happy he was as goldfinch in the glade,
Brown as a berry, short, and thickly made,
With black hair that he combed right prettily.
He could dance well, and that so jollily,
That he was nicknamed Perkin Reveller.
He was as full of love, I may aver,
As is a beehive full of honey sweet;
Well for the wench that with him chanced to meet.
At every bridal would he sing and hop,
Loving the tavern better than the shop.
    When there was any festival in Cheap,
Out of the shop and thither would he leap,
And, till the whole procession he had seen,
And danced his fill, he'd not return again.
He gathered many fellows of his sort
To dance and sing and make all kinds of sport.
And they would have appointments for to meet
And play at dice in such, or such, a street.
For in the whole town was no apprentice
Who better knew the way to throw the dice
Than Perkin; and therefore he was right free
With money, when in chosen company.
His master found this out in business there;
For often-times he found the till was bare.
For certainly a revelling bond-boy
Who loves dice, wine, dancing, and girls of joy—
His master, in his shop, shall feel the effect,
Though no part have he in this said respect;
For theft and riot always comrades are,
And each alike he played on gay guitar.
Revels and truth, in one of low degree,
Do battle always, as all men may see.
    This 'prentice shared his master's fair abode
Till he was nigh out of his 'prenticehood,
Though he was checked and scolded early and late
And sometimes led, for drinking, to Newgate;

But at the last his master did take thought,
Upon a day, when he his ledger sought,
On an old proverb wherein is found this word:
"Better take rotten apple from the hoard
Than let it lie to spoil the good ones there."
So with a drunken servant should it fare;
It is less ill to let him go, apace,
Than ruin all the others in the place.
Therefore he freed and cast him loose to go
His own road unto future care and woe;
And thus this jolly 'prentice had his leave.
Now let him riot all night long, or thieve.
    But since there's never thief without a buck
To help him waste his money and to suck
All he can steal or borrow by the way,
Anon he sent his bed and his array
To one he knew, a fellow of his sort,
Who loved the dice and revels and all sport,
And had a wife that kept, for countenance,
A shop, and whored to gain her sustenance.

Of this cook's tale Chaucer made no more. [3]

DRAMATIC Dramatic poetry utilizes dramatic form or technique. Typically, it involves a portrayal of life or character or the telling of a story usually involving conflicts and emotions through action and dialogue (drama can also utilize prose). The major form of dramatic poetry, the dramatic monologue, takes the form of a poem written as a speech of an individual character to an imaginary audience. It develops a narrative sense of the speaker's history and psychological insights into his or her character in a single vivid scene, for example, Robert Browning's "My Last Duchess."

LYRIC Lyric poetry, originally intended to be sung and accompanied by a lyre, comprises a brief, subjective work employing strong imagination, melody, and feeling to create a single, unified, and intense impression of the personal emotion of the poet. The sonnet represents the most finished form of lyric poetry. It has two types: Petrarchan (Italian) and Shakespearean (English). Petrarch (PEE-trahrk or PEH-trahrk; 1304–74) developed the sonnet form to its highest expression, to the degree that we now call this form the Petrarchan (sometimes, Italian) sonnet. A fixed verse form, it contains fourteen lines. Typically the sonnet treats a variety of moods and subjects, but particularly the poet's intense psychological reactions to his beloved. The fourteen lines divide into eight lines rhymed *abbaabba* and six lines with a variable rhyme scheme. Usually the first eight lines present the theme or problem in the poem, and the final six present a change in thought or resolution of the problem. The following sonnet proved the most popular love poem in the European Renaissance. It portrays a lover's ambivalence in a series of paradoxes:

Sonnet CCXXV
Canzone XXI
Petrarch

I find no peace and all my war is done,
I fear and hope, I burn and freeze like ice;
I fly above the wind yet can I not arise,
And nought I have and all the world I sesan. [seize]
That loseth nor locketh holdeth me in prison
And holdeth me not, yet can I escape nowise;
Nor letteth me live or die at my devise,
And yet of death it giveth me occasion.
Without eyes, I see, and without tongue I plain, [complain]
I desire to perish, and yet I ask health,
I love an other, and thus I hate myself,
I feed me in sorrow and laugh at all my pain,
Likewise displeaseth me both death and life,
And my delight is cause of this strife.

The sonnet form developed in Italy in the thirteenth century, and, as we have said, reached its highest form of expression in Petrarch. Imported into England, it was adapted to create the form now called a Shakespearean sonnet. Shakespearean sonnet adapts the Petrarchan sonnet and has fourteen tines grouped into three quatrains (four tines) and a couplet, with a rhyme scheme of *abab cdcd efef gg*, as Sonnet XIX illustrates.

In this poem, Shakespeare employs some intriguing imagery to address the effects of aging: blunting the lion's paws; making the earth devour her own sweet brood; plucking keen teeth from the fierce tiger's jaws; burning the phoenix in her blood (the phoenix was an Egyptian mythological creature that consumed itself by fire after 500 years, and rose renewed from its ashes); and creating age lines with an antique pen. Shakespeare solves the dilemma by countering time with the ageless nature of literature.

Sonnet XIX
William Shakespeare
1564–1616

Devouring Time, blunt thou the lion's paws,
And make the earth devour her own sweet brood;
Pluck the keen teeth from the fierce tiger's jaws,
And burn the long-lived phoenix in her blood.

Make glad and sorry seasons as thou fleets,
And do whate'er thou wilt, swift-footed Time,
To the wide world and all her fading sweets;
But I forbid thee one most heinous crime:

O, carve not with thy hours my love's fair brow,
Nor draw no lines there with thine antique pen;
Him in thy course untainted do allow
For beauty's pattern to succeeding men.

Yet, do thy worst, old Time: despite thy wrong,
My love shall in my verse ever live young.[4]

Nonfiction

Nonfiction consists of literary works based mainly on fact rather than on the imagination, although nonfictional works may contain fictional elements. Biography, essays, and speeches comprise the major forms of nonfiction. Traditionally, the essay consists of a short literary composition on a single subject, usually presenting the personal views of the author. Speeches such as Abraham Lincoln's "Gettysburg Address" and Martin Luther King's "I have a Dream" mark an important category of nonfiction, as do historical articles and texts such as political legislation and newspaper articles.

BIOGRAPHY A biography undertakes a written account of an individual's life. Over the centuries, it has taken many forms and has witnessed many techniques and inventions, including literary narratives, catalogues of achievement, and psychological portraits. We call accounts of the lives of saints and other religious figures hagiographies (ha-ghee-AHGH-ruh-fee or hay-jee-AHGH-ruh-fee).

John Wesley (1703–91), the Anglican clergyman who founded the Methodist Church, provides a sample of the elements of biography in *God Brought Me Safe*.

God Brought Me Safe
John Wesley
1703–91

[Oct. 1743]

Thur. 20.—After preaching to a small, attentive congregation, I rode to Wednesbury. At twelve I preached in a ground near the middle of the town to a far larger congregation than was expected, on "Jesus Christ, the same yesterday, and to-day, and for ever." I believe every one present felt the power of God; and no creature offered to molest us, either going or coming; but the Lord fought for us, and we held our peace.

I was writing at Francis Ward's in the afternoon when the cry arose that the mob had beset the house. We prayed that God would disperse them, and it was so. One went this way, and another that; so that, in half an hour, not a man was left. I told our brethren, "Now is the time for us to go"; but they pressed me exceedingly to stay; so, that I might not offend them, I sat down, though I foresaw what would follow. Before five the mob surrounded the house again in greater numbers than ever. The cry of one and all was, "Bring out the minister; we will have the minister." I desired one to take their captain by the hand and bring him into the house. After a few sentences interchanged between us the lion became a lamb. I desired him to go and bring one or two more of the most angry of his companions. He brought in two, who were ready to swallow the ground with rage; but in two minutes they were as calm as he. I then bade them make way, that I might go out among the people. As soon as I was in the midst of them I called for a chair, and, standing up, asked, "What do any of you want with me?" Some said, "We want you to go with us to the Justice." I replied, "That I will with all my heart." I then spoke a few words, which God applied; so that they cried out with might and main, "The gentleman is an honest gentleman, and we will spill our blood in his defence." I asked, "Shall we go to the Justice to-night, or in the morning?" Most of them cried, "To-night, to-night"; on which I went before, and two or three hundred followed, the rest returning whence them came.

The night came on before we had walked a mile, together with heavy rain. However, on we went to Bentley Hall, two miles from Wednesbury. One or two ran before to tell Mr. Lane they had brought Mr. Wesley before his Worship. Mr Lane replied, "What have I to do with Mr. Wesley? Go and carry him back again." By this time the main body came up, and began knocking at the door. A servant told them Mr. Lane was in bed. His son followed, and asked what was the matter. One replied, "Why an't please you, they sing psalms all day; nay, and make folks rise at five in the morning. And what would your Worship advise us to do?" "To go home," said Mr Lane, "and be quiet."

Here they were at a full stop, till one advised to go to Justice Persehouse at Walsall. All agreed to do this; so we hastened on, and about seven came to his house. But Mr. P. likewise sent word that he was in bed. Now they were at a stand again; but at last they all thought it the wisest course to make the best of their way home. About fifty of them undertook to convoy me. But we had not gone a hundred yards when the mob of Walsall came, pouring in like a flood, and bore down all before them. The Darlaston mob made what defense they could; but they were weary, as well as outnumbered; so that in a short time, many being knocked down, the rest ran away, and left me in their hands.

To attempt speaking was vain, for the noise on every side was like the roaring of the sea. So they dragged me along till we came to the town, where, seeing the door of a large house open, I attempted to go in; but a man, catching me by the hair, pulled me back into the middle of the mob. They made no more stop till they had carried me through the main street, from one end of the town to the other. I continued speaking all the time to those within hearing, feeling no pain or weariness. At the west end of the town, seeing a door half open, I made toward it, and would have gone in, but a gentleman in the shop would not suffer me, saying they would pull the house down to the ground. However, I stood at the door and asked, "Are you willing to hear me speak?" Many cried out, "No, no, knock his brains out; down with him; kill him at once." Others said, "Nay, but we will hear him first." I began asking, "What evil have I done? Which of you all have I wronged in word or deed?" and continued speaking for above a quarter of an hour, till my voice suddenly failed. Then the floods began to lift up their voice again, many crying out, "Bring him away! Bring him away!"

In the meantime my strength and my voice returned, and I broke out aloud into prayer. And now the man who had just before headed the mob turned and said, "Sir, I will spend my life for you: follow me, and not one soul here shall touch a hair of your head." Two or three of his fellows confirmed his words, and got close to me immediately. At the same time, the gentleman in the shop cried out, "For shame, for shame! Let him go." An honest butcher, who was a little farther off, said it was a shame they should do thus; and pulled back four or five, one after another, who were running on the most fiercely. The people then, as if it had been by common consent, fell to the right and left; while those three or four men took me between them, and carried me through them all. But on the bridge the mob rallied again: we therefore went on one side over the mill-dam, and thence through the meadows, till, a little before ten, God brought me safe to Wednesbury, having lost only one flap of my waistcoat and a little skin from one of my hands.[5]

ESSAY The essay is a nonfictional literary composition on a single subject, usually presenting the personal views of the author.

The word "essay" comes from the French, meaning "to try" and the vulgar Latin, meaning "to weigh." Essays include many subforms and a variety of styles, but they uniformly present a personal point of view with a conscious attempt to achieve a certain grace of expression. Characteristically, the best essays show clarity, good humor, wit, urbanity, and tolerance. For the most part, essays are brief, but occasionally they are much longer works, such as *The Federalist Papers* by Alexander Hamilton, John Jay, and James Madison (1787). Traditionally, essays fall into two broad categories: *informal* or *formal*.

INFORMAL Informal essays tend to be brief, conversational in tone, and loose in structure. They can be categorized as *familiar* (or *personal*) and *character*. The personal essay presents an aspect of the author's personality as he or she reacts to an event. Character essays describe individuals, isolating and portraying their dominant traits, for example.

FORMAL Formal essays, which are generally longer and more tightly structured than informal ones, tend to focus on impersonal subjects and place less emphasis on the personality of the author. Oliver Goldsmith provides an example below.

The Benefits of Luxury, in Making a People More Wise and Happy
Oliver Goldsmith
1730?–74

From such a picture of nature in primeval simplicity, tell me, my much respected friend, are you in love with fatigue and solitude? Do you sigh for the severe frugality of the wandering Tartar, or regret being born amidst the luxury and dissimulation of the polite? Rather tell me, has not every kind of life vices peculiarly its own? Is it not a truth, that refined countries have more vices, but those not so terrible; barbarous nations few, and they of the most hideous complexion? Perfidy and fraud are the vices of civilized nations, credulity and violence those of the inhabitants of the desert. Does the luxury of the one produce half the evils of the inhumanity of the other? Certainly those philosophers who declaim against luxury have but little understood its benefits; they seem insensible, that to luxury we owe not only the greatest part of our knowledge, but even of our virtues.

It may sound fine in the mouth of a declaimer, when he talks of subduing our appetites, of teaching every sense to be content with a bare sufficiency, and of supplying only the wants of nature; but is there not more satisfaction in indulging those appetites, if with innocence and safety, than in restraining them? Am not I better pleased in enjoyment than in the sullen satisfaction of thinking that I can live without enjoyment? The more various our artificial necessities, the wider is our circle of pleasure; for all pleasure consists in obviating necessities as they rise; luxury, therefore, as it increases our wants, increases our capacity for happiness.

Examine the history of any country remarkable for opulence and wisdom, you will find they would never have been wise had they not been first luxurious; you will find poets, philosophers, and even patriots, marching in luxury's train. The reason is obvious: We then only are curious after knowledge, when we find it connected with sensual happiness. The senses ever point out the way, and reflection comments upon the discovery. Inform a native of the desert of Kobi, of the exact measure of the parallax of the moon,

he finds no satisfaction at all in the information; he wonders how any could take such pains, and lay out such treasures, in order to solve so useless a difficulty: but connect it with his happiness, by showing that it improves navigation, that by such an investigation he may have a warmer coat, a better gun, or a finer knife, and he is instantly in raptures at so great an improvement. In short, we only desire to know what we desire to possess; and whatever we may talk against it, luxury adds the spur to curiosity, and gives us a desire to becoming more wise.

But not our knowledge only, but our virtues are improved by luxury. Observe the brown savage of Thibet, to whom the fruits of the spreading pomegranate supply food, and its branches are habitation. Such a character has few vices, I grant, but those he has are of the most hideous nature; rapine and cruelty are scarcely crimes in his eye; neither pity nor tenderness, which ennoble every virtue, have any place in his heart; he hates his enemies, and kills those he subdues. On the other hand, the polite Chinese and civilized European seem even to love their enemies. I have just now seen an instance where the English have succoured those enemies, whom their own countrymen actually refused to relieve.

The greater the luxuries of every country, the more closely, politically speaking, is that country united. Luxury is the child of society alone; the luxurious man stands in need of a thousand different artists to furnish out his happiness; it is more likely, therefore, that he should be a good citizen who is connected by motives of self-interest with so many, than the abstemious man who is united to none.

In whatsoever light, therefore, we consider luxury, whether as employing a number of hands naturally too feeble for more laborious employment; as finding a variety of occupation for others who might be totally idle; or as furnishing out new inlets to happiness, without encroaching on mutual property; in whatever light we regard it, we shall have reason to stand up in its defence, and the sentiment of Confucius still remains unshaken: *that we should enjoy as many of the luxuries of life as are consistent with our own safety, and the prosperity of others; and that he who finds out a new pleasure is one of the most useful members of society.*[6]

Drama

Drama consists of a composition in prose or poetry intended to portray life or character or to tell a story usually involving conflicts and emotions through action and dialogue. Typically, dramas are intended for theatrical production, and, as such, we treat them in this text within the category of theatre (see Chapter 5). However, we can classify many dramas in literature as "closet dramas"—dramas written for reading (not acted or performed on a stage).

Profile

Toni Morrison

Toni Morrison (b. 1931) was born in Lorain, Ohio, as Chloe Anthony Wofford. She was the second of four children of George Wofford, a shipyard welder, and Ramah Willis Wofford. Her parents moved to Ohio from the South to escape racism and to find better opportunities in the North. At home, Chloe heard many songs and tales of Southern black folklore. The Woffords were proud of their heritage. Lorain was a small industrial town populated with immigrant Europeans, Mexicans, and Southern blacks who lived next to each other. Chloe attended an integrated school. In her first grade, she was the only black student in her class and the only child who could read. She was friends with many of her white schoolmates and did not encounter discrimination until she started dating. In college at Howard University in Washington, D.C., she majored in English, and because many people couldn't pronounce her first name correctly, she changed it to Toni, a shortened version of her middle name.

Later she taught at Howard, where she joined a small writers' group as refuge from an unhappy marriage to a Jamaican architect, Harold Morrison. Today, Toni Morrison is one of America's most celebrated authors. Her major novels, *The Bluest Eye* (1969), *Sula* (1973), *Song of Solomon* (1977), *Tar Baby* (1981), *Beloved* (1987), *Jazz* (1992), *Paradise* (1998), and *Love* (2003) have received extensive national acclaim. She received the National Book Critics Circle Award in 1977 for *Song of Solomon* and the 1988 Pulitzer Prize for *Beloved.* In 1993 Morrison was awarded the Nobel Prize for literature. She is an editor at Random House and a visiting lecturer at Yale University.

Morrison is noted for her spare but poetic language, emotional intensity, and sensitive observation of African American life. Her novel *Jazz* is intended to follow *Beloved* as the second volume of a projected trilogy, although *Jazz* does not extend the story told in *Beloved* in a conventional way. The characters are new, and so is the location of the novel. Even the narrative approach is different. In terms of chronology, however, *Jazz* begins roughly where *Beloved* ended and continues the greater story. Morrison wishes to tell the story of her people passing through their American experience, from the days of slavery in the 1900s to the present. The individuals struggle to establish and sustain a personal identity without abandoning their own history, while individual and community interests clash. *Jazz* reads almost like a blues ballad from the musical age it suggests.

Learn more about Toni Morrison at www.distinguishedwomen.com/biographies/morrison.html and www.pbs.org/newshour/bb/entertainment/jan-june98/morrison_3-9.html.

TECHNICAL DEVICES

Fiction

POINT OF VIEW In simplest terms, point of view represents the perspective from which an author tells a story to the reader. Point of view has three main types: first person, third person singular, and third person omniscient. When an author uses first person singular, she tells the story using a narrative from the "I" point of view. For example, in Charlotte Brontë's (BRAHN-tee or BRAHN-tay; 1816–55) *Jane Eyre* we see the story through the eyes and narration of one of the characters. Third person gives us a story told by a narrator, not one of the characters in the story. It has two forms: singular and omniscient. In the first case—first person singular—the narrator writes from the viewpoint of a single character, describing or seeing only what that character sees, hears, and knows, but not in the voice of that character. In the latter form—third person omniscient—the narrator may take the viewpoint of any or all characters, or stand outside the characters, thus capable of commenting on any aspect of the story. Authors may vary or combine these forms of point of view to suit their own purposes. Thus, point of view serves as one means by which fiction is put together, allowing authors to communicate meaning.

APPEARANCE AND REALITY Fiction claims to be true to actuality, but it builds on invented sequences of events. It refers back on itself, layering the fictional and the factual.

TONE Tone, or the atmosphere of the story, represents, essentially, the author's attitude toward the story's literal facts. In reading, much like listening to conversation, the words carry meaning, but the way in which the speaker or author says or presents them—their tone—shapes meaning much more than we realize. In addition, the atmosphere of the story sometimes includes the setting or the physical environment. In many stories, atmosphere holds psychological as well as physical characteristics, and when all of these characteristics of tone merge, they provide subtle and powerful suggestions leading to fuller understanding of the work.

CHARACTER Literature appeals through its people, but not just people alone. It draws our interest because we see a human character struggling with some important problem. Authors write to that potential interest and usually strive to focus our attention, and to achieve unity, by drawing a central character with whose actions, decisions, growth, and development we can identify, and in whom we can find an indication of some broader aspect of the human condition. As we noted in Chapter 5, the term character goes beyond the mere identification of a "person." Character means the psychological spine of individuals; the driving force that makes them respond the way they do when faced with a given set of circumstances. Character interests us: given a set of troubling or challenging circumstances, what does the character of the individual lead him or her to do?

In developing character, an author has numerous choices, depending, again, on purpose. Character may be fully three-dimensional and highly individual—as complex as the restrictions of the medium allow. Novels, because of their length and the fact that the reader can go back to double-check a fact or description, allow much more complex character development or individuality than do plays, whose important points must be found by the audience almost at the moment they are presented. Also, a change of narrative viewpoint, appropriate to a novel but not to a play (unless the play uses a narrator, as in *Our Town*, or a chorus, as in Greek classical tragedy), can give the reader aspects of character in a more efficient manner than can revelation through action or dialogue.

On the other hand, the author's purpose may be served by presenting character not as a fully developed individual but as a type. Whatever the author's choice, the nature of character development tells us much about the meaning of the work.

PLOT Plot, the structure of the work, embodies more than the story line or the facts of the piece. In literature, as in the theatre, we find our interest dependent upon action. The action of a literary work dramatizes a fully realized theme, situation, or character. Plot brings that action into coherency. It creates unity in the work and thereby helps us to find meaning. Plot forms the skeleton that determines the ultimate shape of the piece, once the elements of flesh have been added to it.

Plot may be the major or subordinate focus in a work, and it can be open or closed. Closed plots rely on the Aristotelian model of pyramidal action with an exposition, complication, and denouement. An open plot has little or no resolution. We merely leave the characters at a convenient point and imagine them continuing as their personalities dictate.

THEME Most good stories have an overriding idea or theme that shapes the other elements. Quality in works of art rest at least partly on artists' ability to utilize the tools of their medium, as well as on whether they have something worthwhile to say. Some critics argue that the quality of a theme has less importance than what the author does with it. Yet the conclusion seems inescapable: the best artworks are those in which the author has taken a meaningful theme and developed it exceptionally. The theme or idea of a work consists, then, of what the author has to say. Theme may mean a definite intellectual concept, or it may indicate a highly complex situation. Clues to understanding the idea can come as early as our exposure to the title. Beyond that, the author usually reveals the theme in small pieces as the work moves from beginning to conclusion.

SYMBOLS As we discussed in the Introduction, symbols stand for or suggest something else by reason of relationship, association, convention, or accidental resemblance. They often comprise a visible manifestation of something invisible (for example, the lion as a symbol for courage and the cross as a symbol of Christianity). In this sense, all words function as symbols. The symbols used in literature are often private or personal in that their significance emerges only in the context of the work in which they appear. For example, the optician's trade sign of a huge pair of spectacles in F. Scott Fitzgerald's *The Great Gatsby* (1925) functions as a piece of scenic detail, but we can also understand it as a symbol of divine nearsightedness. A symbol can have more than one meaning. It can be hidden, profound, or simple. Symbols function in literature, as in all art, as devices that expand the content of a work beyond specifics to universals. In literature, symbols give a work its richness and much of its appeal. When we realize that a character in a story, for example, represents a symbol, regardless of how much of an individual the writer may have portrayed, the story takes on

CHAPTER EIGHT ♦ LITERATURE 193

new meaning because the character symbolizes us—some aspect of our complex and often contradictory natures.

Poetry

LANGUAGE In discussing the language of poetry, we focus on eight factors: rhythm, imagery, personification, figures, metaphor, symbols, allegory, and hyperbole.

Rhythm in poetry consists of the flow of sound through accents and syllables. For example, in Robert Frost's "Stopping by Woods on a Snowy Evening" (see below) each line contains eight syllables with an accent on every other syllable. We call rhythms like Frost's, which depend on a fixed number of syllables per line, accentual-syllabic. Contrast that with the freely flowing rhythm of Shakespeare's "The Seven Ages of Man," from Act II of *As You Like It*, in which rhythmic flow uses naturally occurring stresses in the words. This use of stress to create rhythm we call accentual.

The Seven Ages of Man
William Shakespeare
1564–1616

All the world's a stage,
And all the men and women merely players.
They have their exits and their entrances,
And one man in his time plays many parts,
His acts being seven ages. At first the infant
Mewling[i] and puking in the nurse's arms.
Then the whining schoolboy, with his satchel
And shining morning face, creeping like snail
Unwillingly to school. And then the lover,
Sighing like furnace, with a woeful ballad[ii]
Made to his mistress' eyebrow. Then a soldier,
Full of strange oaths and bearded like the pard,[iii]
Jealous in honor,[iv] sudden and quick in quarrel,
Seeking the bubble reputation[v]
Even in the cannon's mouth. And then the justice,
In fair round belly with good capon lined,[vi]
With eyes severe and beard of formal cut,
Full of wise saws[vii] and modern instances,[viii]
And so he plays his part. The sixth age shifts
Into the lean and slippered Pantaloon,[ix]
With spectacles on nose and pouch on side;
His youthful hose, well saved, a world too wide
For his shrunk shank, and his big manly voice,
Turning again toward childish treble, pipes
And whistles in his sound. Last scene of all,
That ends this strange eventful history,
Is second childishness and mere oblivion,
Sans[x] teeth, sans eyes, sans taste, sans everything.[7]

---

i   Whimpering.
ii Poem.
iii Leopard.
iv Sensitive about honor.
v   As quickly burst as a bubble.
vi Magistrate bribed with a chicken.
vii Sayings.
viii Commonplace illustrations.
ix The foolish old man of Italian comedy.
x   Without.

Imagery, a verbal representation of objects, feelings, or ideas can be *literal* or *figurative*. The former involves no change or extension in meaning; for example, "green eyes" means simply eyes that are a green color. The latter, figurative, involves a change in literal meaning; for example, green eyes might become "green orbs."

Figures, like images, take words beyond their literal meaning. Much of poetic meaning comes in comparing objects in ways that go beyond the literal. For example, in Robert Frost's "Stopping by Woods on a Snowy Evening," snowflakes are described as "downy," which endows them with the figurative quality of soft, fluffy feathers on a young bird. In the same sense, Frost uses "sweep" and "easy" to describe the wind.

Stopping by Woods on a Snowy Evening
Robert Frost
1874–1963

Whose woods these are I think I know.
His house is in the village though;
He will not see me stopping here
To watch his woods fill up with snow.

My little horse must think it queer
To stop without a farmhouse near
Between the woods and frozen lake
The darkest evening of the year.

He gives his harness bells a shake
To ask if there is some mistake.
The only other sound's the sweep
Of easy wind and downy flake.

The woods are lovely, dark and deep.
But I have promises to keep.
And miles to go before I sleep.
And miles to go before I sleep.[8]

Metaphors are figures of speech by which new implications are given to words. Thus the expression "the twilight of life" applies the word "twilight" to the concept of life to create an entirely new image and meaning. Metaphors are implied but not explicit comparisons.

Symbols are also often associated with figures of speech, but not all figures are symbols, and not all symbols are figures. Symbolism is critical to poetry, which uses compressed language to express, and carry us into, its meanings. In poetry "the whole poem helps to determine the meaning of its parts, and in turn, each part helps to determine the meaning of the whole poem."[9] See the Companion Website: Literature.

Personification is a figure of speech in which abstract qualities, animals, or inanimate objects take on human characteristics. This device finds its way into many forms of literature, particularly allegories (see below), and has occurred since the ancient Greek poet, Homer (see Chapter 10).

Hyperbole (hy-PUHR-boh-lee) constitutes an intentional exaggeration for emphasis or comic effect. The device occurs frequently in love poetry.

The *allegory* constitutes a work in which related symbols work together, with characters, events, or settings that represent ideas or moral qualities. Often the characters of an allegory personify abstractions such as Fellowship and Good Deeds in the fifteenth-century English morality play *Everyman*. In the following poem, *Uphill* (1858) Christina Rossetti (1830–94) uses the road, the hill, the inn, the darkness at end of day, the traveler, and the other wayfarers as parts of the poet's allegorical vision of our spiritual journey to our ultimate destination.

Uphill
Christina Rossetti

Does the road wind uphill all the way?
    Yes, to the very end.
Will the day's journey take the whole long day?
    From morn to night, my friend.

But is there for the night a resting place?
    A roof for when the slow dark hours begin.
May not the darkness hide it from my face?
    You cannot miss that inn.

Shall I meet other wayfarers at night?
    Those who have gone before.
Then must I knock, or call when just in sight?
    They will not keep you standing at that door.

Shall I find comfort, travel-sore and weak?
    Of labor you shall find the sum.
Will there be beds for me and all who seek?
    Yea, beds for all who come.

STRUCTURE Form or structure in poetry derives from fitting together lines of similar structure and length tied to other lines by end rhyme. For example, the sonnet, as we discussed earlier, has fourteen lines of iambic pentameter rhymed 1-3, 2-4, 5-7, 6-8, 9-11, 10-12, 13-14 (see "Meter" below). In contrast to the highly structured sonnet, examine the loose rhyme scheme that was employed by Langston Hughes in his poem "Theme for English B" (see p. 394).

SOUND STRUCTURES Sound structures give poetry its ear. We note four of them: rhyme, alliteration, assonance, and consonance.

Rhyme—the coupling of words that sound alike—constitutes the most common sound structure in poetry. It ties the sense together with the sound. Rhyme can be masculine, feminine, or triple. Masculine rhyme uses single-syllable vowels such as "hate" and "mate." Feminine rhyme uses sounds forming accented and unaccented syllables, for example, "hating" and "mating." Triple rhyme has a correspondence over three syllables, such as "despondent" and "respondent."

Alliteration, a second type of sound structure, repeats an initial sound for effect: for example "fancy free."

Assonance uses a similarity among vowels but not consonants, for example, "quite like."

Consonance repeats or involves recurrence of identical or similar consonants, as in Shakespeare's song "The ousel cock so black or hue." Poets often combine consonance with assonance and alliteration.

METER Meter refers to the type and number of rhythmic units in a line. We call rhythmic units feet. Four common kinds of feet are iambic, trochaic, anapestic, and dactylic. Iambic meter alternates one unstressed and one stressed syllable; trochaic alternates one stressed and one unstressed syllable; anapestic alternates two unstressed and one stressed syllable; and dactylic alternates one stressed and two unstressed syllables.

Line, also called verse, determines the basic rhythmic pattern of the poem. Lines take their names from the number of feet they contain: one foot—monometer; two—dimeter; three—trimeter; four—tetrameter; five—pentameter; six—hexameter; seven—heptameter; and eight—octameter.

Nonfiction

Writers use any number of elements to compose nonfictional works, including the basic matters of facts and anecdotes.

FACTS Facts, the verifiable details around which writers shape biographies, often have a way of becoming elusive when they go beyond the simple matters of birth, death, marriage, and other date-related occurrences. Facts can turn out to be observations filtered through the personality of the observer. Incontrovertible facts may comprise a chronological or skeletal framework for a biography, but they may well not create much interest. Frequently they do not provide much of a skeleton either. In truth, many individuals of interest to us may have few facts recorded about them.

On the other hand, the lives of other important individuals have been chronicled in such great detail that almost too many facts exist. Artistry entails selection and composition, and many facts require omission from the narrative in order to maintain the reader's interest. Another issue concerns what the author should actually do with the facts. If they constitute injurious material, should the author use them? In what context? Whatever the situation, facts alone prove highly insufficient for an artistic or interesting biography.

ANECDOTES Anecdotes, stories or observations about moments in a biography, take the basic facts and expand them for illustrative purposes, thereby creating interest. Either true or untrue, anecdotes serve the purpose of creating a memorable generalization. They sometimes also generate debate or controversy.

Quotations form part of anecdotal experience. Authors use quotations to create interest by changing the presentational format to that of dialogue. In the sense that dialogue creates the impression that we are part of the scene, as opposed to being third parties listening to someone else describe a situation, dialogue brings us closer to the subjects of the biography.

SENSE STIMULI

Literature, like all the arts, appeals to our senses by the way in which the writer uses the tools of the medium. Specifically, literature uses words. What we see and hear in literature results from the skill of the writer in turning words into sense-stimulating images.

PICTURES

Skillful wordplay opens many sensual vistas, and any of the excerpts in this chapter can bring us to those vistas. The very words of the title of Saki's short story—Toad-water—conjure pictures. Perhaps the image of this place depends on our having had some experience of toads, so for those who have not, toad-water brings to mind a soggy primeval place hovering somewhere around the level of squalor. Toads, with their warts and other unlovely features, constitute denizens of dank, unlovely places. Likewise, William Shakespeare's "Seven Ages of Man" conjures vivid pictures of an infant mewling and puking in its mother's arms, or an old person "sans teeth, sans eyes, sans taste, sans everything."

SOUNDS

We hear real sounds stimulated by words. Shakespeare, again creates sounds through words as he describes a "big manly voice,/ Turning again toward childish treble, pipe/ And whistles in his sound," and we hear the sibilance of a toothless octogenarian and picture puckered lips caving inward over exposed gums. Even John Wesley's straightforward description of anger, brought to life by quotations, evokes the raucous belligerency of the mob, brought to life by images of rioting mobs of our day crashing into our rooms via television news. A writer's choice of words causes sounds to well up in our heads, often as real as if we were there ourselves.

EMOTIONS

The mood evoked by a piece of literature can turn us in on ourselves, stimulating sensations traveling from pleasure to pain. We may not understand why we react as we do, but we understand vividly the power of words to invade our personal world and move us. When Langston Hughes writes "Nor do I often want to be a part of you./ But we are, that's true," this poem, written many years ago cannot help but raise an emotion. The emotion may differ depending on whether we are black, white, yellow, or some combination, liberal or conservative, but the emotion strikes home in one way or another nonetheless. Visceral reactions, arguably, form the top layer of the onion comprising our response to literary stimuli. When we peel the top layer away and delve into those layers beneath, real pleasure and sense of accomplishment result. Examining the whats of artistic stimulation provides significant challenge. Determining the whys multiplies the reward exponentially. Finally, what better place than to close a chapter on literature can we have the opportunity to stress a vital survival note: words matter! They create meaning and clarity. Our ability to use and understand them makes us intelligible and knowledgeable—or not.

THINKING CRITICALLY

Build a basic critical analysis of a work of literature by using the topics in this chapter as an outline: pick an example and ask yourself hard questions about the work's performance and significance.

- Reaction. What purpose does the author have in mind in this work? How do you react? Does the work probe a significant subject?

- Genre. Is the work fictional, poetic, narrative, dramatic, lyric, or biographical? What characteristics lead you to that conclusion?

- Fiction. If the work is one of fiction, is it a novel or short story? Explain how point of view, appearance and reality, tone, character, plot, theme, and symbols are developed.

- Poetry. If the work is poetic, describe the use of rhythm, imagery, figures, metaphors, structure, sound structures, and meter.

- Biography. If the work is biographical, how has the author utilized facts and anecdotes?

- Essay. If the work is an essay, explain how either formality or informality is expressed.

CYBER STUDY

LITERATURE INDEXED BY GENRE:
—Fiction
Louisa May Alcott's *Little Women*, Jane Austen's *Pride and Prejudice*, Mariano Azuela's *The Underdogs*, Emily Bronte's *Wuthering Heights*, James Joyce's *Dubliners*, and Virginia Woolf's *Night and Day*
—Poetry
Samuel Taylor Coleridge's, *The Rime of the Ancient Mariner*, Dante Alighieri's *The Divine Comedy*, T. S. Eliot's *The Wasteland*, Homer's *The Iliad*, Amy Lowell's *Sword Blades and Poppy Seed*, Naidu Sarojini's *The Golden Threshold*, William Shakespeare's *Sonnets*, Sara Teasdale's *Rivers to the Sea*, and William Butler Yeats's *A Poet to His Beloved*.
http://www.lib.umd.edu/ETC/ReadingRoom/

LITERATURE INDEXED BY AUTHOR AND/OR TITLE:
http://www.infomotions.com/alex/

LITERATURE INDEXED BY AUTHOR, TITLE, OR SUBJECT:
http://digital.library.upenn.edu/books/titles.html

LITERATURE INDEXED BY AUTHOR, TITLE, OR DEWEY DECIMAL CLASSIFICATION:
http://www.ipl.org/reading/books/

PART II

THE STYLES OF THE ARTS

How Artists Portray "Reality"

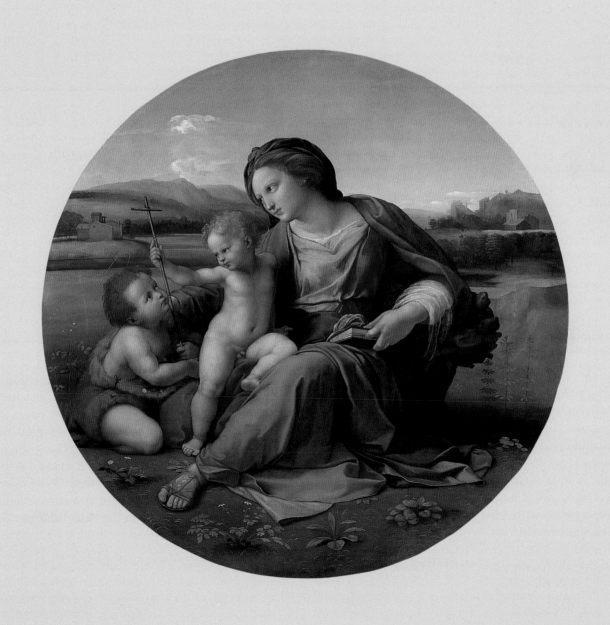

CHAPTER NINE

ANCIENT APPROACHES

c. 30,000 to c. 480 B.C.E

IMPORTANT TERMS

Archaic style A style of Greek vase painting and sculpture dating to the sixth century B.C.E.

Bible From the Greek word for books, and referring to the town of Byblos.

Doric style A style of Greek architecture marked by heavy, slanted columns with a flat slab for a capital.

Kouros Referring to Archaic sculpture of Greek youth.

Pao-chia system The ancient Chinese system of mutual responsibility.

Pre-Columbian Native American art that predates the arrival of Columbus in 1492.

Psalm From the Psalter, the hymnal of ancient Israel.

Stylized A type of depiction in which lifelikeness has been altered for artistic effect.

Torah The Hebrew Bible's book of the Law, comprising the books of Genesis, Exodus, Leviticus, Numbers, and Deuteronomy.

Venus figure A feminine figurine from the Paleolithic period.

THE CONTEXT

THE STONE AGE

The Old **Stone Age**, the Paleolithic Age (pay-lee-oh-LITH-ihk), reaches back beyond one million years B.C.E. Toward the end of the period, humans probably began to think in artistic and religious terms. The second stage of human culture, the Neolithic period or *New Stone Age*, stretched between approximately 8000 B.C.E. and 3000 B.C.E. In the New Stone Age humans began domesticating some of the animals they had been accustomed to chasing and killing. We cannot reconstruct how humans lived during the latter half of the Old Stone Age, when the artistic achievements we study momentarily occurred. Some evidence exists to suggest that perhaps as early as 100,000 B.C.E. people had some sort of religion. By 50,000 B.C.E. Neanderthal people buried their dead with ceremony and care, behavior suggesting a belief in the hereafter. At this time humankind began to grasp the notions of selfhood and individuality and began to use symbols. This occurrence formed the final link from our earliest known ancestors, who emerged from the darkness of prehistory into the light of history and civilization.

When villages evolved into cities, a stage of cultural development occurred, called civilization. To meet the definition of civilization, a culture involves five things: (1) urban centers; (2) a written language (implying a common language); (3) trade or commerce; (4) a common religion; and (5) a centralized government.

THE MIDDLE EAST

In the **Middle East** around 6000 B.C.E., *Sumer* became the earliest recognizable culture to emerge in this area. Sumerians (soo-MEER-ee-uhnz) lived in villages and organized themselves around several religious centers, which grew rapidly into cities. Religion and government shared a close relationship in Sumer. Religion permeated the social, political, and ethical life of society. Sumerians had a large number of gods and by about 2250 B.C.E. worshiped a well-developed and generally accepted pantheon (PAN-thee-ahn), to which the Sumerians gave human and animal attributes.

By the year 1000 B.C.E. a new power had replaced the Sumerians: The *Assyrians*. Peoples from Ashur on the River Tigris, the Assyrians had both military power and skill that enabled them to maintain supremacy over the region, including Syria, the Sinai peninsula, and as far as lower Egypt. For nearly 400 years they appear to have engaged in almost continuous warfare, ruthlessly destroying their enemies and leveling the cities that they conquered. Finally, they too felt the conqueror's sword and were utterly destroyed.

At approximately the same time that Sumerian society reached its height, another civilization developed in *Egypt*. From the beginning, Egyptian civilization identified the king with a god who represented a direct link between the royal line and the creator sun god. Religion played a central role in an Egyptian's personal and social life as well as in civil organization. Egyptians considered death a doorway to an afterlife, in which the departed could cultivate his or her own portion of the netherworlds with water supplied by the gods.

We know the people who wrote and collected the books of the Old Testament, the offspring of the Patriarchs, variously as *Hebrews*, Israelites, and Jews. They began as an identifiable group around 1200 B.C.E., and they described themselves as both a religious and national entity. The word "Hebrew" refers to Abraham's ethnic group. Eventually Abraham's descendents came to be called "Israel" (after Abraham's grandson). The terms Jew and Jewish refer to the religion of Judaism and emerge from the Southern Kingdom, Judah, of a divided Israel after the highpoint of the kingships of Saul, David, and Solomon. Perhaps the height of the kingdom of Israel came in the time of King David and his son, King Solomon (c. tenth century B.C.E.), when the twelve tribes of Israel united and the kingdom extended from Phonecia in the west to the Arabian Desert in the east.

ASIA

In **Asia** at a time just slightly prior to the Israelites' enslavement in Egypt, verifiable history began in *China*, in the Shang Dynasty (c. 1400–c. 1100 B.C.E.). From the earliest times, China witnessed the crowding of populations into tight-walled villages. The family—as opposed to the individual, state, or religious group—formed the most significant social unit. This was reinforced by the practice of ancestor worship. The family also formed the basic political unit. A scheme of mutual responsibility called the *Pao-chia* (pow-CHEE-uh) system made individuals belonging to the same household answerable for each other's actions.

AMERICA

In **America**, these same time parameters witnessed the rise of the first Mesoamerican civilization, the *Olmec*. The Olmecs lived along the Gulf coast of Mexico in the current states of Veracruz and Tabasco. They drained swamps, cleared farmland, and raised earth mounds on which they built political and religious centers. They also engaged in long-distance trade. The principal center of Olmec culture flourished between 1200 and 900 B.C.E. and had been abandoned by 400 B.C.E.

EUROPE

In **Europe**, the time from approximately 800 to 480 B.C.E. saw the *Archaic Greek* period. Archaic Greek culture consisted of a collection of city-states, or *poleis* (*singular—polis*; POH-lays/POH-lihs) of self-governing people. Each polis had its own sense of self. Some, like Athens, had high esteem for the arts and philosophy; others, like Sparta, were militaristic and seemingly indifferent to high culture. Nonetheless, a strong unifying spirit ran among these independent poleis of Greek derivation—they saw themselves as "Hellenes" (HEHL-eenz) and shared a common language and calendar, which dated to the first Olympic games in 776 B.C.E.

The conditions just described, from the Stone Age, Middle East, Asia, America, and Europe formed the context for the arts that we now examine from each of these settings and cultures.

THE ARTS

THE STONE AGE

Humankind's first known sculpture dates from the period from approximately 30,000 to 15,000 B.C.E.[1] The head and body of a man carved from mammoth ivory emerged from a burial site at Brno in the Czech Republic (Fig. **9.1**). Although the work has many body parts missing, the head reveals an apparent attention to anatomical details with closely cropped hair, low brow, and deeply set eyes.

Stone Age art probably began approximately 25,000 to 30,000 years B.C.E. and, at its earliest, consisted of simple lines scratched in damp clay. The people making these scratchings lived in caves and seem, eventually, to have elaborated them into the outlines of animals. This development—from what appears to be idle doodling into sophisticated art—seems to have come in three phases. Black outline drawings of animals with a single colored filler mark the first. Next came the addition of a second color within the outline, to create a sense of light and shade, or modeling (chiaroscuro). These depictions often incorporated projecting portions of the cave walls to add a sense of three-dimensionality and, thereby, lifelikeness.

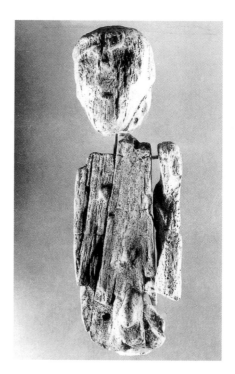

9.1 Man from Brno, c. 27,000–20,000 B.C.E. Ivory, height 9 ins (20 cm). Moravian Museum, Brno, Czech Republic.

In many cases it appears as though the artist picked a specific rock protrusion or configuration for the animal drawing. The third phase in the development of early art consists of exciting multicolored paintings in impressive realistic style. In this category fall the well-known paintings at Altamira in Spain (Fig. **9.2**). Here the artists captured detail, essence, mass, and a remarkable sense of movement, using only earth colors and charcoal.

The earliest artists seem to have shied away from the difficulties of drawing three-dimensionality, keeping their subjects in profile (as, much later, the Egyptians did). Only an occasional turning of head or antlers tests the artist's skill at portraying depth.

So-called Venus figures (Fig. **9.3**) have been found on burial sites in a band stretching approximately 1,100 miles (1,833 km) from western France to the central Russian plain. Many scholars believe that these figures are the first works in a representational style. They share certain stylistic features and have remarkably similar overall composition. They may be symbolic fertility figures—hence modern scholars have named them after the Roman goddess of love and beauty—or they may be no more than objects for exchange or recognition. Whatever the case, each figure has the same tapering legs, wide hips, and tapering shoulders and head, forming a diamond-shaped silhouette.

The Woman from Willendorf (see Fig. **9.3**), the best-known example of a Venus figure, emphasizes swollen thighs and breasts and prominent genitals, implying that the image represents fertility. Some have gone so far as to suggest that these works reveal their makers' obsessions

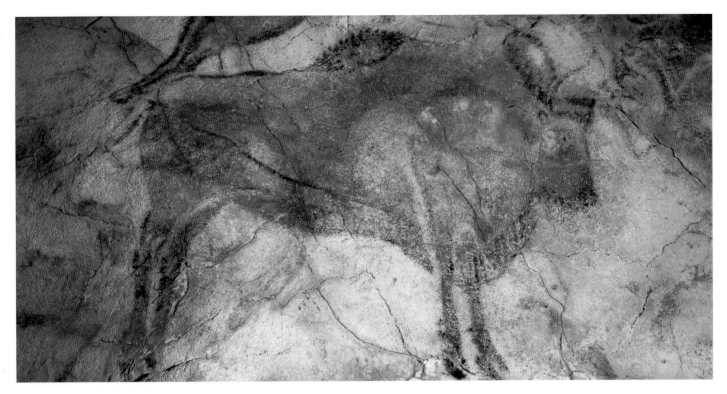

9.2 Bison, from Altamira, Spain, c. 14,000–10,000 B.C.E. Paint, length 8 ft 3 ins (2.51 m).

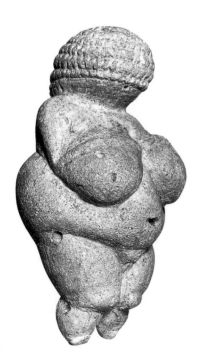

9.3 Woman from Willendorf, Lower Austria, c. 30,000–25,000 B.C.E. Limestone, height 4⅓ ins (11 cm). Naturhistorisches Museum, Vienna.

with sexual ideas. Carved from limestone, the Woman from Willendorf, originally colored red—the color of blood—perhaps symbolizes life itself. Many early peoples painted corpses red.

Although faceless, Venus figures usually have hair, often wear bracelets, beads, aprons, or a waist band, and sometimes show markings that may represent tattoos. Although a male hunting ethos dominated the culture that made them, only women appear in the statuary that survives. Emphasis on their sexuality, the mystery and apparent miracle of birth, and the uniquely female role therein clearly influenced the carvers' perception and portrayal of reality.

The cave of Lascaux (lah-SKOH) lies slightly over a mile from the little French town of Montignac, in the valley of the Vézère river. A group of children, investigating a tree uprooted by a storm, scrambled down a fissure into a world undisturbed for thousands of years and discovered the cave. Hundreds of paintings were found there, as elsewhere in France, Spain, and other parts of Europe. The significance of the Lascaux works lies in the quantity and the quality of an intact group.

An overwhelming sense of power emerges from the main hall or "Hall of Bulls" (Fig. 9.4). The thundering herd moves below a sky of rolling contours formed in the stone ceiling. At the entrance of the hall an 8-foot (2.5-m) unicorn begins a monumental montage of bulls,

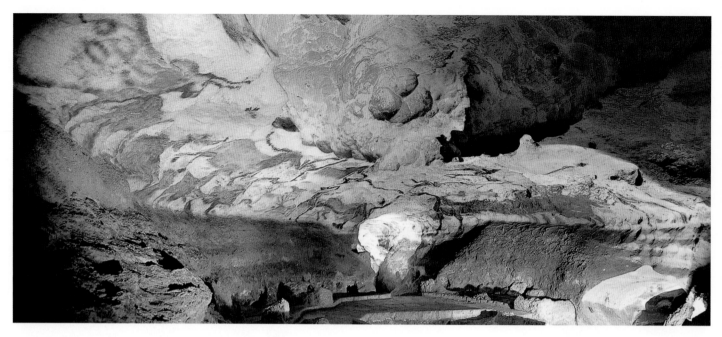

9.4 Main hall, or Hall of Bulls, Lascaux, France. Paint on limestone, 30 × 100 ft (9 × 30 m).

horses, and deer, whose shapes intermingle and whose colors radiate warmth and power, with heights of up to 12 feet (3.5 m). Although the paintings in the main hall were created over a long period and by a succession of artists, the cumulative effect of this 30- by 100-foot (9- × 30-m) domed gallery seems to make it a single work, carefully composed for maximum impact utilizing lively color, interestingly unified shapes or forms, active line, and, to a degree, chiaroscuro.

THE MIDDLE EAST

Sumerian Art

Some time around 6000 B.C.E. the first recognizable civilization appeared in that part of the Near East we call Mesopotamia—the region between the Tigris and Euphrates rivers (in present-day Iraq)—and the earliest recognizable culture to emerge in this area was Sumer (soo-muhr). Sumerians lived in villages and organized themselves around several important religious centers, which grew rapidly into cities. Sumerian mathematics employed a system of counting based on sixty and that system was used to measure time (we still have sixty minutes in one hour) and circles, divided into 360 degrees. The wheel appeared in Sumer as early as 3000 B.C.E.

The majority of surviving artworks from Mesopotamia prior to 3000 B.C.E. are painted pots and stamp seals, all of which reflect a similar style involving conventionalized forms and devices. Abstract decoration of pottery served to satisfy the creative urge while providing functional objects. Stamp seals, although clearly functional, went beyond tool status. Sumerian artisans regarded stamp seal surfaces as ideally suited to exercise creative ingenuity. Early seals were round or rectangular; later, for reasons unknown to us, cylindrical ones came into being. Sumerians applied a carved wooden roller to wet clay to produce a ribbonlike design of indefinite length. The creative possibilities inherent in cylinder seal design appeared far greater than in the other shapes. The way that intricate design can be repeated infinitely seems to have fascinated the Sumerians. Scenes of sacrifice, hunting, and battle all appear in the examples of cylinder seal art that have survived. Figure **9.5** combines two Sumerian fertility symbols: the lioness and the intertwined snake. This motif appears repeatedly in Sumerian art.

In the *low-relief* art of the early Sumerians such as Figure **9.6** we find a preoccupation with ritual and the gods. This large alabaster vase celebrates the cult of E-anna, goddess of fertility and love. Divided into four bands, or *registers*, it commemorates the marriage of the goddess, which was re-enacted to ensure fertility. The bottom band has alternating stalks of barley and date palms; above it appear rams and ewes. In the second band, naked worshipers carry baskets of fruit and other offerings. At the top the goddess herself stands before her shrine—two coiled bundles of reeds—to receive a worshiper or priest, also nude, whose tribute basket brims with fruit. The composition exhibits an alternating flow of movement: from left to right in the rams and ewes, and right to left in

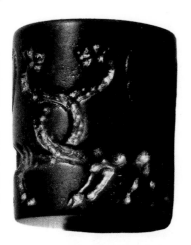
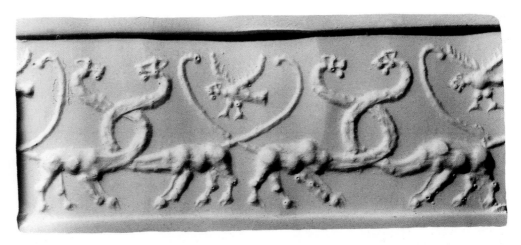

9.5 Cylinder seal and impression, showing snake-necked lions, from Mesopotamia, c. 3300 B.C.E. Green jasper, height 1¾ ins (4 cm). Louvre, Paris.

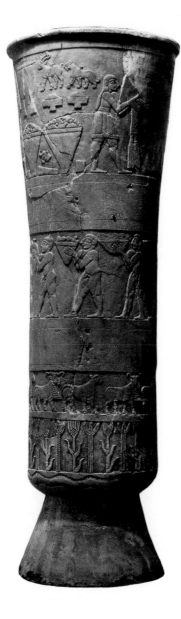

9.6 Vase with ritual scene, from E-anna, Uruk (modern Warka), Iraq, c. 3500–3100 B.C.E. Alabaster relief, height 36 ins (91 cm). Iraq Museum, Baghdad.

the worshipers. Conventions of figure portrayal are similar to but not as rigid as those in Egyptian art (see pp. 207–16).

Other works from this period such as Figures **9.7** and **9.8** illustrate the splendor of the Sumerian court. Inlaid in gold and laden with the symbolism of masculine fertility, the dazzling golden goat from the royal graves at Ur (Fig. **9.9**) manifests the basic Sumerian belief in a pantheon of gods personifying nature. The elegantly depicted goat represents Tammuz, one of the gods of vegetation.

Various primitive peoples had used picture writing to convey messages. Sumerian writing, however, initiated the use of qualitatively different pictorial symbols: the Sumerians (and later the Egyptians) used pictures to indicate the syllabic sounds that occurred in different words rather than simply to represent the objects themselves. Sumerian language consisted of monosyllables used in combination. Writing materials consisted of an unbaked clay tablet and a reed stylus that, when pressed into the soft clay, produced a wedge-shaped mark. Wedges and combinations of wedges make up Sumerian writing, called "cuneiform" (kyoo-NEE-ih-fawnn), from the Latin *cuneus* (KYOO-nee-uhs), meaning "wedge."

Writing leads to literacy and literacy leads to literature. The oldest known story in the world comes to us from Sumer, although its most complete version dates to as late as the seventh century B.C.E. The *Gilgamesh* epic, an episodic tale, tells the story of Gilgamesh (probably a real person) who ruled at Uruk (OO-ruhk) during the first half of the third millennium B.C.E., although no historical evidence documents that. One part of this epic describes a flood, which parallels that in the story of Noah's Ark in the Bible book of Genesis. *Gilgamesh* represents a quest

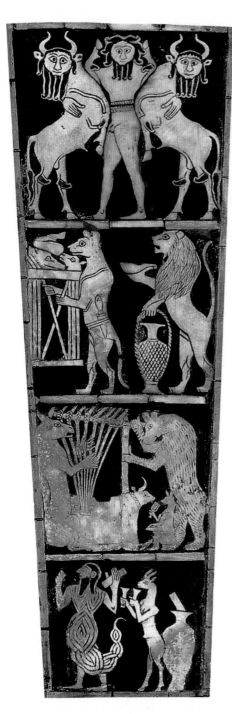

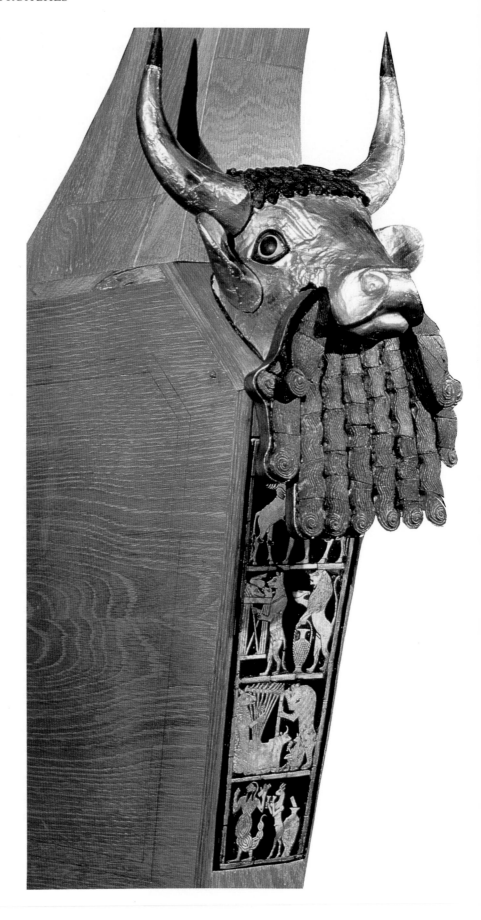

9.7 (*above*) Soundbox panel of the royal lyre, from the tomb of Queen Puabi, Ur, Iraq, 2650–2550 B.C.E. Shell inlay set in bitumen, height 13 ins (33 cm). University of Pennsylvania Museum, Philadelphia.

9.8 (*right*) Royal lyre, from the tomb of Queen Puabi, Ur. Wood with gold, lapis lazuli, and shell inlay. University of Pennsylvania Museum, Philadelphia.

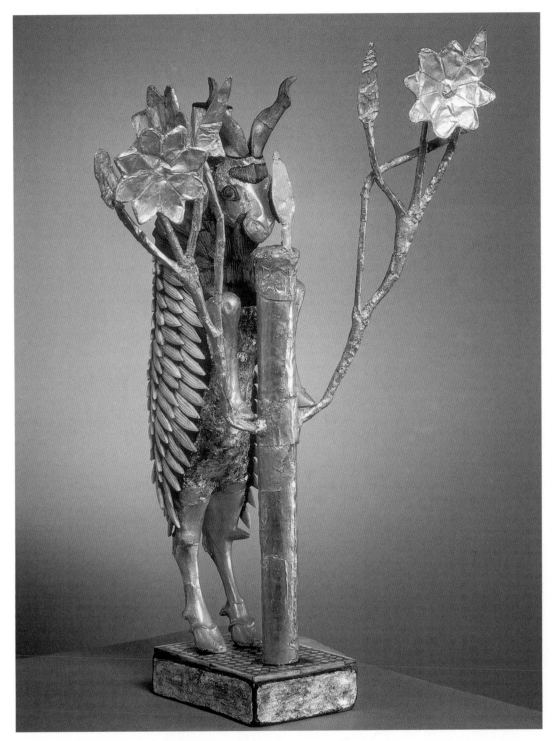

9.9 He-goat, from Ur, c. 2600 B.C.E. Wood with gold and lapis lazuli overlay, height 20 ins (51 cm). University of Pennsylvania Museum, Philadelphia.

against nature, man, and the gods, and we can find numerous themes in its twelve tablets, including the role of women, who, while subservient to men, appear both compassionate and wise. The epic also deals with the issues of worlds beyond this one—we encounter both a world of the dead and a place of the gods. *Gilgamesh* also treats the theme of the responsibilities of leaders and the responsibilities of the gods. The short excerpt that follows comes from a kind of prologue that opens the epic and introduces us to the character of Gilgamesh.

Masterworks

The Tell Asmar Statues

Undoubtedly the most striking features of these Sumerian votive figures (made as an act of worship to the gods) are their enormous, staring eyes, with their dramatic exaggeration (Fig. 9.10). Arguably representing Abu, the quasi-divine king (the large figure), a goddess assumed to be his spouse, and a crowd of worshipers, the statues occupied places around the inner walls of an early temple, in prayer, awaiting the divine presence. The figures have great dignity, despite the stylization and somewhat crude execution. In addition to the staring eyes, our attention is drawn to the distinctive carving of the arms, which are separate from the body. The composition is closed and self-contained, reflecting the characteristics of prayer.

Certain geometric and expressive qualities characterize these statues. In typical Sumerian style, each form is based on a cone or cylinder, and as stylized arms and legs and pipelike, rather than lifelike, depictions of the subtle curves of human limbs. They are made of gypsum, a very fragile material.

The god Abu and the mother goddess may be distinguished from the rest by their size and by the large diameter of their eyes. The meaning in these statues clearly bears out what we know of Mesopotamian religious thought. The gods were believed to be present in their images. The statues of the worshipers were substitutes for the real worshipers, even though there appears to have been no attempt to make the statues look like any particular individual: every detail is simplified, focusing attention on the remarkable eyes constructed from shell, lapis lazuli, and black limestone.

Large and expressive eyes appear a basic convention of Sumerian art—although a convention that is found in other ancient art as well. We do not know its basis, but the idea of the eye as a source of power permeates ancient folk-wisdom. The eye could act as a hypnotizing, controlling force, for good or for evil—hence the expression "evil eye," which is still in use today. Symbolic references to the eye range from "windows of the soul" to the "all-seeing" vigilance of the gods.

The Sumerians used art, like language, to communicate through conventions. Sumerian art took life-likeness, as perceived by the artist, and reduced it to a few conventional forms. These statues also established social hierarchy and, to those who understood the conventions, communicated larger truths about the world.

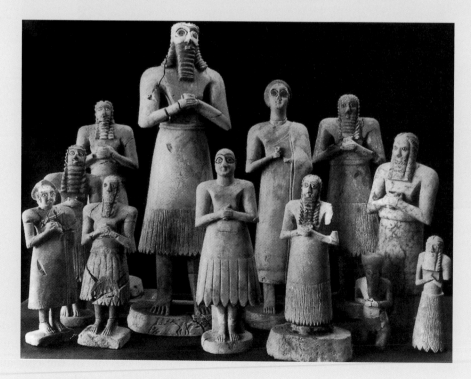

9.10 Statues of worshipers and deities from the Square Temple at Tell Asmar, Iraq, c. 2750 B.C.E. Gypsum, tallest figure 30 ins (76 cm). Iraq Museum, Baghdad, and Oriental Institute, University of Chicago.

The Epic of Gilgamesh
Tablet I

He who has seen everything, *I will make known* (?) to the
   lands.
I will teach (?) about him who experienced all things, ...
   alike,
Anu granted him the totality of knowledge of *all*.
He saw the Secret, discovered the Hidden,
he brought information of (the time) before the Flood.
He went on a distant journey, pushing himself to
   exhaustion,
but then was brought to peace.
He carved on a stone stela all of his toils,
and built the wall of Uruk-Haven,
the wall of the sacred Eanna Temple, the holy sanctuary.
Look at its wall which gleams like *copper* (?),
inspect its inner wall, the likes of which no one can equal!
Take hold of the threshold stone—it dates from ancient
   times!
Go close to the Eanna Temple, the residence of Ishtar,
such as no later king or man ever equaled!
Go up on the wall of Uruk and walk around,
examine its foundation, inspect its brickwork thoroughly.
Is not (even the core of) the brick structure made of kiln-
   fired brick,
and did not the Seven Sages themselves lay out its plans?
One league city, one league palm gardens, one league
   lowlands, the
open area (?) of the Ishtar Temple,
three leagues and the open area (?) or Uruk it (the wall)
   encloses.

   ...

Take and read out from the lapis lazuli tablet
how Gilgamesh went through every hardship

Supreme over other kings, lordly in appearance,
he is the hero, born of Uruk, the goring wild bull.
He walks out in front, the leader,
and walks at the rear, trusted by his companions.
Mighty net, protector of his people,
raging flood-wave who destroys even walls of stone!

Assyrian Art

Under Sargon II, who came to power in 722 B.C.E., the
high priests regained many of the privileges they had lost
under previous kings, and the Assyrian Empire reached
the peak of its power. Early in his reign he founded the
city of Dur Sharrukin (door shah-ROO-kihn; on the site
of modern Khorsabad), about 9 miles (15 km) northeast
of Nineveh. His vast royal citadel, occupying an area of
some quarter of a million square feet, reflected an image
not only of his empire but of the cosmos itself. The reconstruction of the citadel in Figure **9.11** shows the style of
architecture at the time and illustrates the priorities of
Assyrian civilization. Clearly, in Sargon's new city, secular
architecture took precedence over temple architecture.
The rulers seem to have been far more preoccupied with
building fortifications and pretentious palaces than with
erecting religious shrines. Dur Sharrukin was built, occupied, and abandoned within a single generation.

The citadel, representing the ordered world, rises like
the hierarchy of Assyrian gods, from the lowest levels of
the city, through a transitional level, to the king's palace,
which stands on its own elevated terrace. Two gates connect the walled citadel to the outside world. The first was
undecorated; the second was adorned with and guarded
by winged bulls and genii (Fig. **9.12**).

Remarkably, excavations at the site have revealed fairly
inadequate construction methods. In addition, buildings
have haphazard arrangement, and within the inner walls
five minor palaces crowd with obvious difficulty into the
available space.

The main palace comprises an arrangement of ceremonial apartments around a central courtyard. Winged bulls
and other figures guarded entrances to the throne room.
The walls of the room itself, decorated with floor-to-ceil-
ing murals, stood approximately 40 feet (12 m) high.
Three small temples adjoined the palace and beside these
rose a *ziggurat* (zih-goo-RAT) with successive stages
painted in different colors, connected by a spiral staircase.
True masonry structure used mud brick, laid without
mortar while still damp and pliable, and dressed and
undressed stone. Some roof structures used brick barrel
vaulting, although the majority appear to have had flat
ceilings with painted beams.

Corresponding to the vast scale of the buildings,
the great guardian figures seen in Figure **9.12** guard the
gate. Undoubtedly symbolizing the supernatural powers
of the king, these colossal hybrids reflect majestic power
in stature and scale. Carved partly in relief and partly in
the round, they are rationalized to be seen from front or
side. The sculptor has provided each figure with a fifth
leg, with the result that the viewer can always see four.
Each of these monoliths was carved from a single block of
stone upward of 15 feet (4.5 m) square.

Egyptian Art

Egypt, protected by deserts and confined to the narrow
Nile valley, remained relatively isolated for thousands of
years. It had a unified civilization, under the control of an
absolute monarch (pharaoh). As a rural society, it depended uniquely upon the regular annual flooding of its single
river, the Nile.

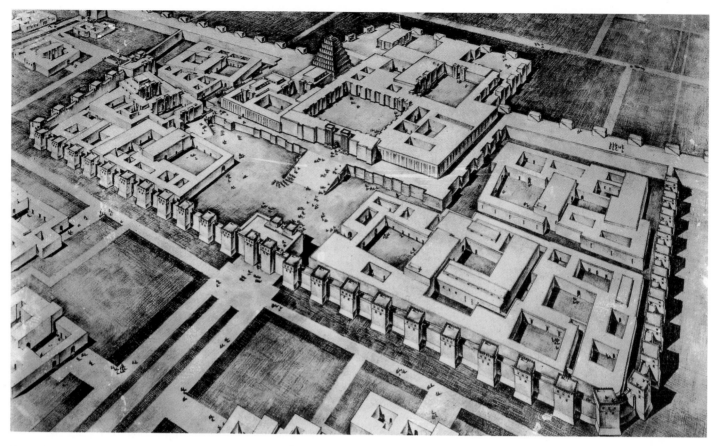

9.11 Sargon II's citadel, Dur Sharrukin (modern Khorsabad), Iraq, reconstruction.

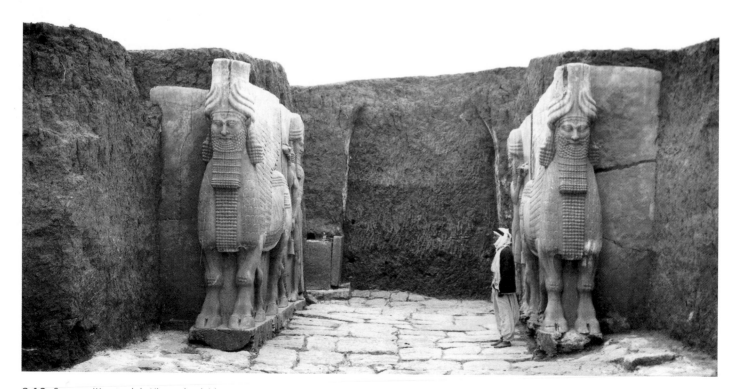

9.12 Sargon II's citadel, Khorsabad (during excavation), gate with pair of winged and human-headed bulls, 8th century B.C.E. Limestone.

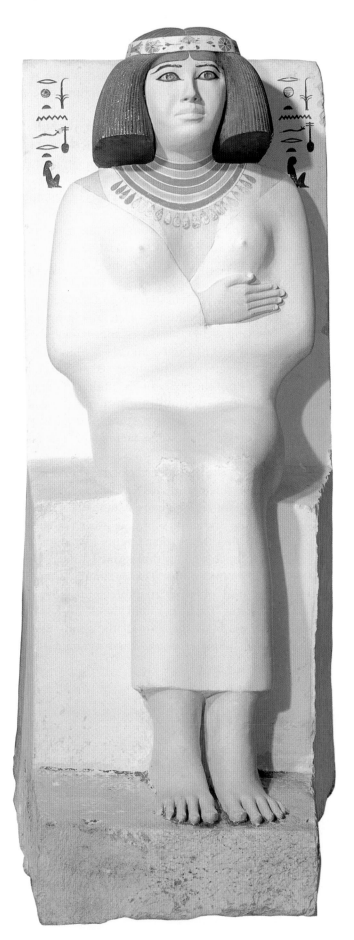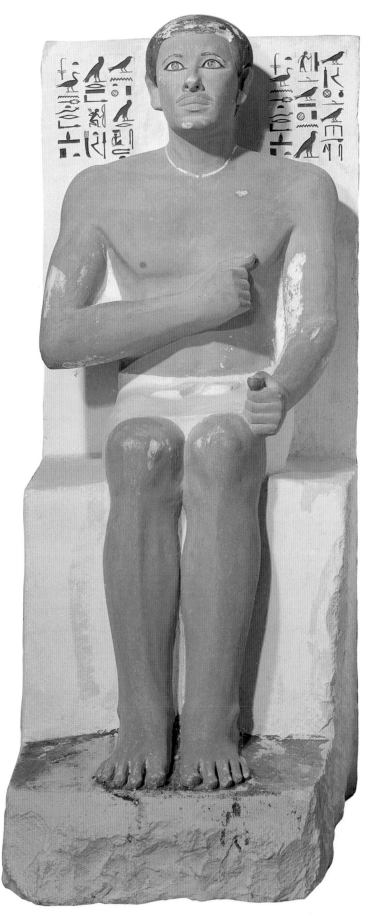

9.13 Prince Rahotep and his wife Nofret, from Medum, Egypt, c. 2580 B.C.E.
Painted limestone, height 3 ft 11½ ins (1.2 m). Egyptian Museum, Cairo.

Death—or, rather, everlasting life in the hereafter—provided the focus of much of the art of the Egyptians. Appearing mostly in the service of the cult of a god or to glorify the power and wealth of a pharaoh, art and architecture centered on the provision of an eternal dwelling-place for the dead.

Sculpture formed the major art form of the Egyptians. It not only furnished the "other self" for the tomb of the deceased, to provide immortality, but also stood in temples. By c. 2800–c. 2400 B.C.E., sculptors had overcome many of the technical difficulties that plagued their predecessors. Possibly, religious tenets had also confounded sculptors during earlier times. (Many so-called primitive peoples throughout history have regarded the lifelike portrayal of the human figure as inviting danger—they thought that making a likeness of an individual captured the soul.)

Sculpture from this period shows technical mastery and strong artisanship. Life-size pieces capture the human form in exquisite detail. At the same time, certain conventions idealize royalty. Egyptian belief in the divinity of the pharaoh dictated a dignified and majestic portrayal. Although rigidity of treatment lessened as time went on, softening and human-centered qualities never completely divested the pharaonic statue of its divine repose.

The dual sculpture of Prince Rahotep and his wife Nofret (Fig. 9.13) comes from the tomb of the prince. The stylized posture represents a trademark of Egyptian art, with its intellectual or conceptual, as opposed to lifelike or visual, nature. The statues' striking colors exemplify the Egyptian tendency to use paint to provide a decorative surface for sculpture. The eyelids of both figures are painted black, with dull eyes of light-colored quartz. In line with convention, the skin tones of the woman are several shades lighter in value than those of the man. A woman's skin was traditionally creamy yellow, whereas a man's ranged from light to dark brown.

Probably for the first time in Egyptian art, we find full development of the three-dimensional female body. Nofret wears the typical gown of the period, cut to reveal voluptuous breasts. The artist has meticulously observed and depicted detail here, as in all the details of the upper portion of both statues.

The years around 2700 B.C.E. brought forth the most remarkable edifices of Egyptian civilization—the pyramids of Giza. In addition to the three most obvious pyramids, the area comprises burial places for almost all of the important individuals of Dynasties IV and V. Each pyramid complex has four buildings. The largest pyramid, that of Cheops (Fig. 9.14), measures approximately 750 feet (228 m) square (440 cubits) and rises at an angle of approximately 51 degrees to a height of 481 feet (146 m). The burial chamber of the pharaoh lay hidden in the middle (Fig. 9.15). True masonry construction consisted of irregularly placed, rough-hewn stone blocks covered by a carefully dressed limestone facing approximately 17 feet (5 m) thick.

Egypt's pyramids are the oldest existing buildings in the world. These ancient tombs are also among the world's largest structures. The largest stands taller than a forty-story building and covers an area greater than that of ten football fields. More than eighty pyramids still exist, and their once-smooth limestone surfaces hide secret passageways and rooms. The pyramids of ancient Egypt served a vital purpose: to protect the pharaohs' bodies after death. Each pyramid held not only a pharaoh's preserved body but also all the goods that he would need in his life after death. Their pyramidal form

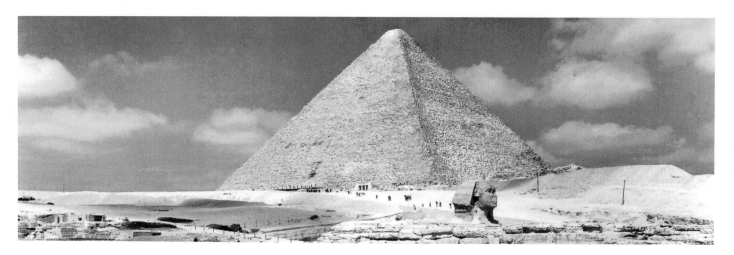

9.14 Great Pyramid of Cheops (Khufu), Giza, Egypt, 2680–2565 B.C.E.

comprises active line on the diagonal and yet a solidly stable composition, as discussed in Chapter 1.

Less than a century later and just to the southeast of the site of the Great Pyramid of Cheops, Egyptian sculptors carved from the native rock a Great Sphinx (Fig.

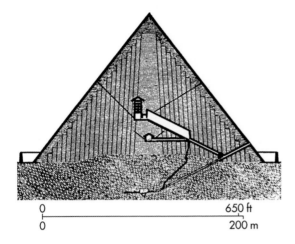

9.15 Longitudinal south–north section of the Great Pyramid of Cheops.

9.16). Here, as in the pyramids, we find an impressive symbol of the Egyptian belief in the divine kingship of the pharaoh and his embodiment of the sun god. The royal head rises from the body of a lion to a height of 65 feet (20 meters; equivalent to a six-story building). The features of the face probably reflected those of Pharaoh Chephren, whose pyramid sits behind the Great Sphinx and adjacent to the Great Pyramid of Cheops. Damaged in later times, the Great Sphinx marks the apex of pharaonic power.

Around c. 1575–c. 1100 B.C.E. another building of great luxury and splendor arose: the temple at Luxor (Fig. 9.17). It approaches more nearly the modern conception of architecture—as a useful place for humankind to spend the present, rather than eternity. Built by Amenhotep III, the temple is dedicated to the Theban Triad of Amun, Mut, and Chons. It served two purposes. First, it was the place of worship for Amun, Mut, and Chons. Second, during the great feast of the middle of the flood, the barques of these gods were anchored there for several days.

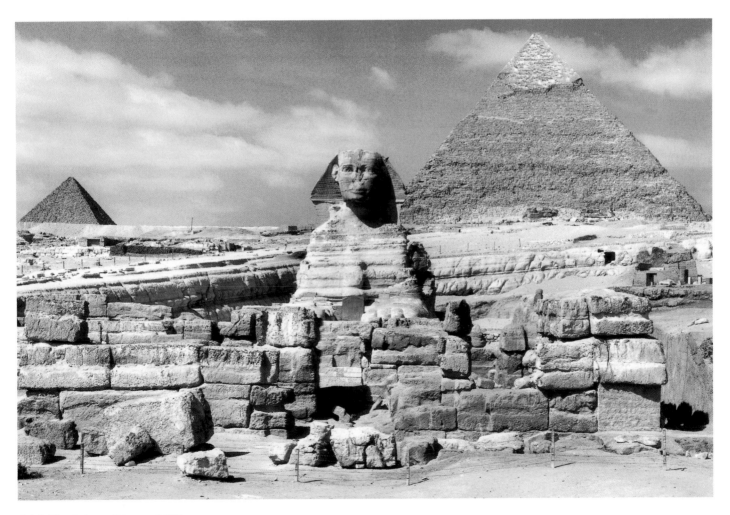

9.16 The Sphinx, Giza, c. 2650 B.C.E.

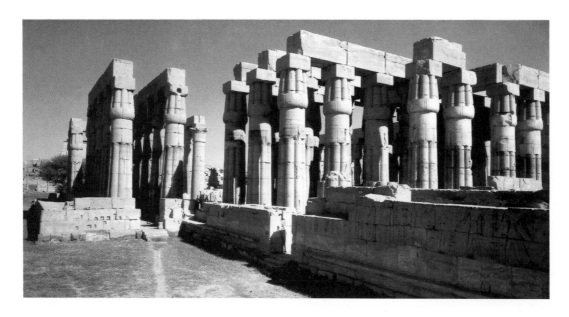

9.17 Temple at Luxor, Egypt, 1417–1397 B.C.E.

Amenhotep III was a great builder and his taste for splendid buildings drew sustenance from a number of excellent architects. Notable among these was Athribis, whose likeness at age eighty we find preserved in a magnificent statue showing that he retained his intellectual and physical abilities and that he expected to reach the age of 110, which the Egyptians considered to be the natural human life span.

People entered the post-and-lintel temple structure through a vestibule full of giant pillars with palm-shaped capitals. From the vestibule they then progressed to a huge courtyard surrounded by bunched columns, then to the *hypostyle* room, and, finally, the Holy of Holies. We cannot escape the loveliness of the columns. The balance between the open spaces and the mass of the columns creates a beautiful play of light and shade. The proportions were massive: the seven pairs of central pillars in the Hall of Pillars rise nearly 52 feet (15.8 m) high. Surviving the centuries, the temple grew when Rameses II added a forecourt ringed with columns and covered walkways as well as containing two colossal statues of the king and a pair of obelisks. The walls of the courtyard present relief sculptures of Rameses and his family. Later, the inner enclosure served as a sanctuary for Alexander the Great, while in early Christian times it served as a Christian church.

Tomb paintings and low-relief carvings functioned to furnish the dead with an "eternal castle" and thus to establish the status they had attained on earth, which they would continue to have in the hereafter. Most of what we now know about Egyptian painting of this period comes from the Theban rock tombs. Ceiling decorations are common and elaborate. The paintings portray the vivacity and humor of daily life.

The tomb of Queen Nefertari-mi-en-Mat (c. 1290–1229 B.C.E.—one of the four principal wives of King Rameses II and his favorite—lies in the Valley of Queens in western Thebes (now the west bank at Luxor), by precipitous cliffs at the end of the gloomy valley of Biban el Harin. The paintings adorning the walls of Nefertari's tomb exemplify a style of painting done in low relief,

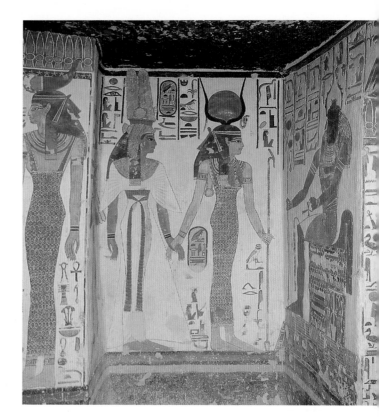

9.18 *Queen Nefertari Guided by Isis*, from the First Room of the tomb of Queen Nefertari, Thebes.

Profile

Nefertiti

Nefertiti (neh-fuhr-TEE-tee; c. 1372–1350 B.C.E.; Fig. 9.19) was Akhenaton's (ah-keh-NAH-tuhn) Great Royal Wife. Scholars debate whether she was a princess from another land or an Egyptian. Those believing her to be of Egyptian origin are also divided. One group claims she was the daughter of Aye and Tiy, and the other claims her as the oldest daughter of Amenhotep III and another wife, possibly Sitamun. Whatever her parentage, Nefertiti was married to Akhenaton and while living in Memphis gave birth to six daughters. Possibly she also had sons, although no record has been found of this. Egyptians did not portray the male heirs as children. Possibly she was Tutankhamun's mother. Nefertiti achieved a prominence unknown to other Egyptian queens. In fact, more statues and drawings exist of her than of Akhenaton. Some experts have even claimed that Nefertiti, not Akhenaton, instigated the monotheistic religion of Aton. Around year 15 of Akhenaton's reign, Nefertiti mysteriously disappeared from public view. Perhaps she died, but no indication of this can be found. Some scholars think that she was banished for some reason, and lived the rest of her years in the northern palace, raising Tutankhamun. Whatever may have happened, she was replaced by her oldest daughter, Meritaten, and disappeared from history.

Akhenaton's own words describe Nefertiti: "The Hereditary Princess, Great of Favor, Mistress of Happiness, Gay with the two feathers, at hearing

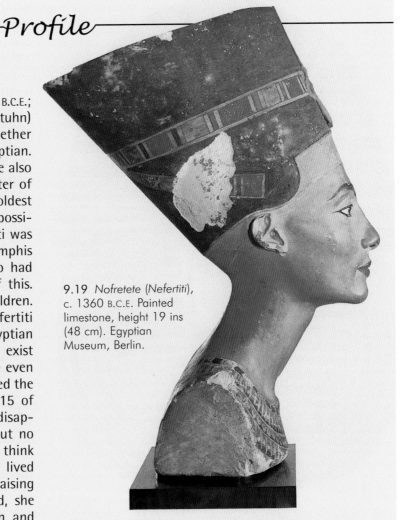

9.19 *Nofretete (Nefertiti)*, c. 1360 B.C.E. Painted limestone, height 19 ins (48 cm). Egyptian Museum, Berlin.

whose voice one rejoices, Soothing the heart of the king at home, pleased at all that is said, the Great and Beloved Wife of the King, Lady of the Two Lands, Neferu-aton Nefertiti, living forever."

and show great elegance, charm, and vivacious color. The tomb houses a vibrant painting showing the goddess Selkis on the extreme left, with a scorpion on her head (Fig. 9.18). On the extreme right appears the goddess Maat. Her hieroglyph, the feather, rests on her head. Over the door to the Main Room is the vulture goddess Nekhbet of El-Kab (partly visible in the top right corner of the illustration). Her claws hold the shen-sign, which symbolizes eternity and sovereignty. The rear wall of the recess depicts Queen Nefertari led by the goddess Isis toward the beetle-headed Khepri—a form assumed by the sun god implying his everlasting resurrection. On her crown Isis wears the horns of a cow, surrounded by the sun-disc from which hangs a cobra. In her left hand she carries the divine scepter. Queen Nefertari dresses according to the fashion of the time, and over the vulture hood she wears the tall, feathered crown of the Divine Consort.

Rich, warm, and elegant, the paintings reveal high stylization. The limited palette uses four hues, which never change in value throughout the work. Yet the overall effect of this wall decoration reflects great variety. The human form appears in flat profile—the conventionalized style of the eyes, hands, head, and feet show no attempt at lifelikeness. Quite the contrary: the fingers become extenuated designs, elongating the arms to balance the elegant and sweeping lines of legs and feet. The matching figures of Selkis and Maat (extreme left and right) even have arms of unequal length and proportion.

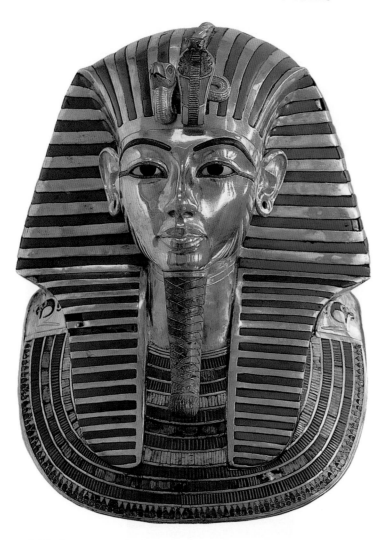

9.20 Funerary mask of King Tutankhamun, c. 1340 B.C.E. Gold inlaid with enamel and semiprecious stones, height 21¼ ins (54 cm). Egyptian Museum, Cairo.

The reign of Akhenaton (c. mid-1400s B.C.E.) marks a break in the continuity of artistic style in Egypt. Stiff poses disappear in favor of a more natural form of representation. Moreover, the pharaoh appears in intimate scenes of domestic life as well as in the formal ritual or military acts previously expected. He no longer appears with the traditional human and animal gods of Egypt. Rather, he and his queen are depicted worshiping the disc of the sun, Aton, whose rays end in hands that either bless the royal pair or hold to their nostrils the *ankh*, the symbol of life. What accounts for this revolution is not certain.

Sculpture at Amarna departed from tradition. It moved away from the strong emphasis on tombs and temples and became more a form of secular art. Amarna sculptors sought to represent the uniqueness and individuality of humankind through the human face. In one sense their

sculptures are highly lifelike, and yet, in another, they depart into the realm of spirituality. The bust of Queen Nefertiti (see Fig. 9.19) illustrates these characteristics. Of course, we have no way of knowing how Queen Nefertiti actually looked, but the figure shows such anatomical correctness that it could be a lifelike representation. Nonetheless, the line and proportions of the neck and head appear elongated, probably to increase her spiritual appearance.

One of the most popular artifacts from the succeeding period is an exquisite funerary mask from the tomb of Akhenaton's son Tutankhamun (Fig. 9.20), discovered in the Valley of Kings near Thebes. The mask of solid beaten gold inlaid with semiprecious stones and colored glass was designed to cover the face of the king's mummy and contains the royal *nemes* headdress with two flaps hanging down at the sides. A ribbon holds his braid at the back. The hood formed by the headdress reveals two symbolic creatures: the uraeus serpent and the vulture goddess Nekhbet of El-Kab, divinities who protected Lower and Upper Egypt.

Egyptian funerary art extended to literature as well, and we find in *The Book of the Dead*, or more accurately, "Book of Going Forth by Day," a collection of ancient Egyptian mortuary texts (probably compiled and re-edited during the sixteenth century B.C.E.) comprising spells or magic formulas placed in tombs to protect and serve the deceased in the afterlife. These texts include works called the Coffin Texts that date to c. 2100 B.C.E., Pyramid Texts, dating to c. 2350 B.C.E., and other writings. Later compilations added other materials. In total, *The Book of the Dead* contains 200 chapters, but no single source contains them all. The title, *The Book of the Dead*, came from a German Egyptologist who published the first collection of the texts in 1842.

A brief excerpt entitled "Hymn to Osiris" illustrates:

The Egyptian Book of the Dead
The Papyrus Of Ani
Hymn to Osiris

Homage to thee, Osiris, Lord of eternity, King of the Gods, whose names are manifold, whose forms are holy, thou being of hidden form in the temples, whose Ka is holy. Thou art the governor of Tattu (Busiris), and also the mighty one in Sekhem (Letopolis). Thou art the Lord to whom praises are ascribed in the name of Ati, thou art the Prince of divine food in Anu. Thou art the Lord who is commemorated in Maati, the Hidden Soul, the Lord of Qerrt (Elephantine), the Ruler supreme in White Wall (Memphis). Thou art the Soul of Ra, his own body, and hast thy place of rest in Henensu (Herakleopolis). Thou art the beneficent one, and art praised in Nart. Thou makest thy soul to be raised up. Thou art the Lord of the Great House in Khemenu (Hermopolis). Thou art the mighty one of victories in Shas-hetep, the Lord of eternity, the Governor of Abydos. The path of his throne is in Ta-tcheser (a part of Abydos). Thy name is established in the mouths of men. Thou art the substance of Two Lands (Egypt). Thou art Tem, the feeder of Kau (Doubles), the Governor of the Companies of the gods. Thou art the beneficent Spirit among the spirits. The god of the Celestial Ocean (Nu) draweth from thee his waters. Thou sendest forth the north wind at eventide, and breath from thy nostrils to the satisfaction of thy heart. Thy heart reneweth its youth, thou producest the ... The stars in the celestial heights are obedient unto thee, and the great doors of the sky open themselves before thee.

The reign of Akhenaton gave rise to a lovely poem, *The Hymn to the Aton*, the sun god. It pays testament to the omniscience of the one god in Akhenaton's pantheon. It expresses reverence and awe from a pharaoh still considered to be a divine representative of the god himself. Note the mention of Akhenaton's wife Nefer-iti (Nefertiti).

The Hymn to the Aton
Accredited to Pharaoh Akhenaton

At daybreak, when thou arisest on the horizon,
When thou shinest as the Aton by day,
Thou drivest away the darkness
and givest thy rays.
The Two Lands are in festivity every day,
Awake and standing upon (their) feet,
For thou hast raised them up.
Washing their bodies, taking (their) clothing,
Their arms are (raised) in praise
at thy appearance.
All the world, they do their work.

All beasts are content with their pasturage;
Trees and plants are flourishing.
The birds which fly from their nests,
Their wings are (stretched) out
in praise to thy Ka.
All beasts spring upon (their) feet. . .
Whatever flies and alights,
They live when thou hast risen (for) them.
The ships are sailing north and south as well,
For every way is open at thy appearance.
The fish in the river dart before thy face;
Thy rays are in the midst of the great green sea.

Creator of seed in women,
Thou who makest fluid into man,

Who maintainest the son in the womb of his mother,
Who soothest him with that which
stills his weeping,
Thou nurse (even) in the womb,
Who givest breath to sustain all that he has made!
When he descends from the womb to breathe
On the day when he is born,
Thou openest his mouth completely,
Thou suppliest his necessities.
When the chick in the egg
speaks within the shell,
Thou givest him breath within it to maintain him.
When thou hast made him his fulfillment
within the egg, to break it,
He comes forth from the egg to speak
at his completed (time);
He walks upon his legs
when he comes forth from it.

How manifold it is, what thou hast made!
These are hidden from the face (of man).
O sole god, like whom there is no other!
Thou didst create the world according to thy desire,
Whilst thou wert alone;
All men, cattle and wild beasts,
Whatever is on earth, going upon (its) feet,
And what is on high, flying with its wings.

The countries of Syria and Nubia, the land of Egypt,
   Thou settest every man in his place,
Thou suppliest their necessities:
Everyone has his food, and his time of life
is reckoned.
Their tongues are separate in speech,
And their natures as well.
Their skins are distinguished,
As thou distinguishest the foreign peoples.
Thou makest a Nile in the underworld,
Thou bringest it forth as thou desirest
To maintain the people (of Egypt)
According as thou madest them from thyself,
The lord of all of them, wearying (himself)
with them,
The lord of every land, rising for them,
the Aton of the day, great of majesty.

All distant foreign countries,
thou makest their life (also),
For thou hast set a Nile in heaven,
That it may descend for them and make waves
upon the mountains,
Like the great green sea,
To water their fields in their towns.
How effective they are, thy plans,
O lord of eternity!
The Nile in heaven, it is for the foreign peoples

And for the beasts of every desert
that go upon (their) feet;
(While the true) Nile comes from the underworld
    for Egypt.

Thy rays suckle every meadow.
When thou risest, they live, they grow for thee.
Thou makest the seasons in order to rear
all that thou hast made,
The winter to cool them,
And the heat that they may taste thee.
Thou hast made the distant sky
in order to rise therein,
In order to see all that thou dost make.
Whilst thou wert alone,
Rising in the form as the living Aton,
Appearing shining, withdrawing or approaching,
Thou madest millions of forms of thyself alone.
Cities, town, fields, road, and river—

Every eye beholds thee over against them,
For thou art the Aton of the day
over the earth ...

Thou art in my heart,
And is no other that knows thee
Save thy son Nefer-kheperu-Re Wa-en-Re,
For thou hast made him well-versed in thy plans and in
    the strength.

The world came in to being by thy hand,
According as thou hast made them.
When thou hast risen they live,
When thou settest they die.
Thou art lifetime thy own self,
For one lives (only) through thee.
Eyes are (fixed) on beauty until thou settest.
All work is laid aside
when thou settest in the west.
(But) when (thou) risest (again),
[Everything is] made to flourish
for the king,... .
Since thou didst found the earth
And raise them up for thy son,
Who came forth from thy body:
the King of Upper and Lower Egypt, ...
Akh-en-Aton, ... and the Chief Wife
of the King ... Nefer-iti,
    living and youthful forever and ever.

Hebrew Art

The Temple in Jerusalem symbolized Hebrew faith as early as its third king, Solomon (c. 1000 B.C.E.). Described in the Bible in I Kings 5–9, the Temple of Solomon served primarily as the house of the Lord God, rather than being a place for the common people to come to worship.

The temple itself, as reconstructed in Figure 9.21, stood on a platform with a dominating entrance of huge wooden doors flanked by two bronze pillars about 18 feet (5.5 m) tall. The doors were decorated with carved palms, flowers, and cherubim (guardian winged beasts sometimes shown with human or animal faces). The entrance hall, or vestibule, measured approximately 15 by 30 feet (4.5 m × 9 m). Inside the temple proper existed a Holy Place, or *Hekal*, about 45 feet (13.5 m) high, 60 feet (18 m) long, and 30 feet (9 m) wide. The paneled walls, made from cedars of Lebanon and carved in rich floral designs, were pierced at the top by small rectangular windows that allowed light to enter the temple. The room itself had various sacred furnishings: ten large lampstands, an inlaid table for priestly offerings, and a cedarwood altar covered with gold.

From a staircase behind the altar the High Priest entered the Holy of Holies, the most sacred part of the Temple, a windowless cubicle 30 feet (9 m) square. It contained the Ark of the Covenant, the symbol of God's presence, which the Jews had carried with them from the wilderness. Two large cherubim flanked the Ark.

The word "bible" comes from the Greek word for book, and it refers to the town of Byblos, which exported the papyrus reed used in the ancient world for making books. The Jews compiled the history of their culture and religion into a collection of sacred writings called scriptures. The compilation grew from the oral traditions of the Hebrew people and took shape over a period of years as it was assembled, transcribed, and verified by state officials and scholars. The Bible has been handed down in a variety of forms. The Hebrew Bible, often called the Masoretic Text (MT), is a collection of twenty-four books written in Hebrew, with a few passages in Aramaic.

The earliest written Bible probably dates to the United Monarchy of King David in the tenth century B.C.E. It comprises an assemblage of history, songs, stories, and prophecy. The current Hebrew Bible, canonized by the Council of Jamnia in 90 C.E., contains three parts: the Law (Torah), the Prophets, and the Writings. Briefly, the Torah comprises the books of Genesis, Exodus, Leviticus, Numbers, and Deuteronomy. The Prophets include Joshua, Judges, Samuel, Kings, Isaiah, Jeremiah, Ezekiel, and the twelve minor prophets. The Writings, which contain a variety of literary forms, including poetry and apocalyptic visions, comprise the biblical books of Psalms, Proverbs, Job, Song of Songs, Ruth, Lamentations, Ecclesiastes, Esther, Daniel, Ezra, Nehemiah, and Chronicles.

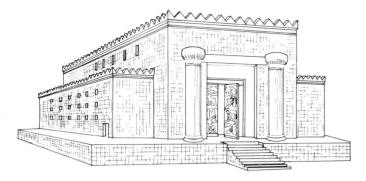

9.21 Reconstruction drawing of Solomon's Temple, Jerusalem. The significance of the two bronze pillars is uncertain, but some scholars suggest that they may have represented the twin pillars of fire and smoke that guided the Israelites during their wanderings in the desert after the Exodus from Egypt.

The Psalter forms the hymnal of ancient Israel. Most of the Psalms were probably composed to accompany worship in the temple. They can be divided into various categories such as hymns, enthronement hymns, songs of Zion, laments, songs of trust, thanksgiving, sacred history, royal psalms, wisdom psalms, and liturgies. Here we include Psalm 22 (a psalm of David), and Psalms 130 and 133 (Songs of Ascent).[2]

Psalm 22

My God, my God, why hast thou forsaken me?
    Why art thou so far from helping me, from the words of
    my groaning?
2 O my God, I cry by day, but thou dost not answer;
    and by night, but find no rest.
3 Yet thou art holy,
    enthroned on the praises of Israel.
4 In thee our fathers trusted;
    they trusted, and thou didst deliver them.
5 To thee they cried, and were saved;
    in thee they trusted, and were not disappointed.
6 But I am a worm, and no man;
    scorned by men, and despised by the people.
7 All those who see me mock at me,
    they make mouths at me, they wag their heads;
8 "He committed his cause to the LORD; let him deliver him,
    let him rescue him, for he delights in him!"

9 Yet thou art he who took me from the womb;
    thou didst keep me safe upon my mother's breasts.
10 Upon thee was I cast from my birth,
    and since my mother bore me thou hast been my God.
11 Be not far from me,
    for trouble is near
    and there is none to help.

12 Many bulls encompass me,
    strong bulls of Bashan surround me;
13 they open wide their mouths at me,
    like a ravening and roaring lion.
14 I am poured out like water,
    and all my bones are out of joint;
    my heart is like wax,
    it is melted within my breast;
15 my strength is dried up like a potsherd,
    and my tongue cleaves to my jaws;
    thou dost lay me in the dust of death.

16 Yea, dogs are round about me;
    a company of evildoers encircle me;
    they have pierced my hands and feet—
17 I can count all my bones—
    they stare and gloat over me;
18 They divide my garments among them,
    and for my raiment they cast lots.

19 But thou, O LORD, be not far off!
    O thou my help, hasten to my aid!
20 Deliver my soul from the sword,
    my life from the power of the dog!
21 Save me from the mouth of the lion,
    my afflicted soul from the horns of the wild oxen!
22 I will tell of thy name to my brethren;
    in the midst of the congregation I will praise thee:
23 You who fear the LORD, praise him!
    all you sons of Jacob, glorify him,
    and stand in awe of him, all you sons of Israel!
24 For he has not despised or abhorred
    the affliction of the afflicted;
    and he has not hid his face from him,
    but has heard, when he cried to him.

25 From thee comes my praise in the great congregation;
    my vows I will pay before those who fear him.
26 The afflicted shall eat and be satisfied;
    those who seek him shall praise the LORD!
    May your hearts live for ever!

27 All the ends of the earth shall remember
    and turn to the LORD;
    and all the families of the nations
    shall worship before him.
28 For dominion belongs to the LORD,
    and he rules over the nations.

29 Yea, to him shall all the proud of the earth bow down;
    before him shall bow all who go down to the dust,
    and he who cannot keep himself alive.
30 Posterity shall serve him;
    men shall tell of the LORD to the coming generation,
31 And proclaim his deliverance to a people yet unborn,
    that he has wrought it.

Psalm 130

Out of the depths I cry to thee, O LORD!
    Lord, hear my voice!
2 Let thy ears be attentive
    to the voice of my supplications!

3 If thou, O LORD, shouldst mark iniquities,
    Lord, who could stand?
4 But there is forgiveness with thee,
    that thou mayest be feared.

5 I wait for the LORD, my soul waits,
    and in his word I hope;
6 My soul waits for the LORD
    more than watchmen for the morning,
    more than watchmen for the morning.

7 O Israel, hope in the LORD!
    For with the LORD there is steadfast love,
    and with him is plenteous redemption.
8 And he will redeem Israel from all his iniquities.

Psalm 133

Behold, how good and pleasant it is
    when brothers dwell in unity!
2 It is like the precious oil upon the head,
    running down upon the beard,
    upon the beard of Aaron,
    running down on the collar of his robes!
3 It is like the dew of Hermon,
    which falls on the mountains of Zion!
    For there the LORD has commanded the blessing,
    life for evermore.

ASIA

China's earliest dynasty, the Shang (c. 1400–1100 B.C.E.), produced two types of bronzes: weapons and ceremonial vessels. Both are frequently covered with elaborate designs, either incised or in high-relief. Each line has perfectly perpendicular sides and a flat bottom, meeting at a precise 90-degree angle; this contrasts, for example, with incised decoration, which forms a groove. The bronze ritual vessel in a shape called *hu* (Fig. **9.22**) has subtle symmetrical patterns and delicate craftsmanship. Deftly placed ridges and gaps break the graceful curves and although the designs are delicate, the overall impression is one of solidity and stability.

Another innovation of the Shang culture was stone sculpture in high-relief or in the round. The most numerous objects to survive are small-scale images in jade. These occur in a broad range: from fish, owls, and tigers as single units to metamorphoses such as the elephant head of Figure **9.23**. This design combines simplicity with subtle detail. Its feline head has large, sharp teeth, an elephant's trunk, and bovine horns.

AMERICA

We label American Indian art as either *pre-Columbian*—before Columbus, which we shall examine here,—or *post-Columbian* and encompasses weaving, metalsmithing, pottery, and architecture. Like all others, American Indian artists developed their own set of conventions or ground rules. Some of these differ significantly from the artistic conventions of Western culture. Those who do not come from the culture themselves may never—probably cannot ever—fully engage a work of art from this tradition, with all its subtleties, comprehending what it comprises in the understanding of its creators.

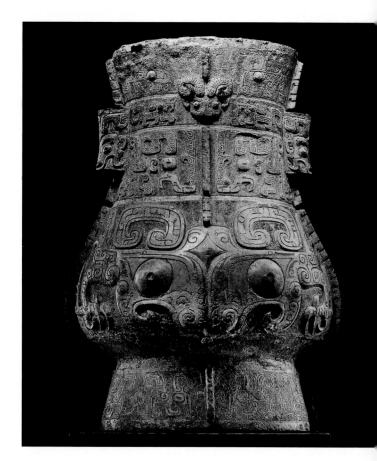

9.22 Ritual wine vessel or *hu*, c. 1300–1100 B.C.E. Bronze, height 16 ins (40.6 cm), width 11 ins (27.9 cm). Nelson Atkins Museum of Art, Kansas City (Purchase: Nelson Trust).

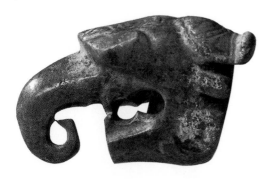

9.23 Elephant feline head, from China, c. 1200 B.C.E. (Shang Dynasty). Jade, length 1⅝ ins (4 cm). Cleveland Museum of Art (Anonymous gift).

In many respects, however, American Indian art remains the same as Western, Asian, or any other art: human, and containing visual, emotional, and psychological qualities. It represents a vision of some form of reality and has a primary intention of sharing that vision with other people. Art from any culture addresses the fundamental qualities (purposes and functions) we addressed in the Introduction.

Among many American Indian groups no specific term equivalent to the word "art" exists. In American Indian culture in general, however, art consists of anything technically well done or that has a well-conceived end result. The effect could be magical or thought to bring power. In essence, an "artist" was merely one person who possessed greater skill at something than another. Only a few Indian tribes—for example the Northwest Coast, Mayan, and Inca—had a group of professionals who earned a living by producing art. Within American Indian culture exists a wide variety of expressions, approaches to materials,

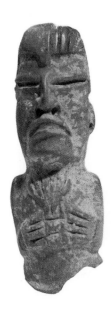

9.24 Olmec-style head with trace of red paint inlay, from Xochipala, Guerrero, Mexico, 1250–750 B.C.E. Fragment of carved stone figurine, 3 × 1 ins (7.6 × 2.5 cm). National Museum of the American Indian, Smithsonian Institution, Washington, D.C.

and general styles. The earliest identifiable art in Mexico comes from the Olmecs—the word means "dwellers in the land of rubber"—and dates to approximately 1000 B.C.E. The Olmecs constituted a major civilization, which traded extensively with parts of Mesoamerica at a considerable distance from the Olmec territory along the Gulf of Mexico. They carved a number of animal subjects, including jaguars and figures called were-jaguars that combined human and jaguar features. Their human carvings often have a characteristic turned-down mouth (Fig. 9.24). Even though much of the body of the tiny figure is missing, we can see the care with which details were carved on this green-gray stone effigy.

Olmec artists also carved on a colossal scale, producing stone heads some 8 feet (2.4 m) in diameter, again with turned-down mouths. These were crafted from basalt boulders moved to the gulf coast from the Tuxtla Mountains more than 60 miles (97 km) inland. Scholars believe they represent portraits of rulers.

Olmec architecture includes the Great Pyramid at La Venta, Mexico, an earth mound rising to a height of around 100 feet (30 m). Whether its rounded form has resulted from erosion or was intended to replicate a volcano remains unknown.

EUROPE

In ancient Greece, the time from approximately 800 to 480 B.C.E. is called the "Archaic period," and by the middle of the sixth century B.C.E. Greek artists tried to portray the human body in a three-quarter position, between profile and full frontal. A new feeling for three-dimensional space emerged, and artists began to depict eyes more accurately. Fabric began to assume the drape and folds of real cloth. All these characteristics mark vase painting in a style called Archaic (Fig. 9.25).

Most of the freestanding statues in the Archaic style are of nude youths, known as *kouroi* (koo-roy). The term means, simply, "male youth," and the singular form is *kouros* (koo-rohs; Fig. 9.26). These statues focus on physicality and athleticism, and all exhibit a stiff, fully frontal pose. Most of the kouroi were sculpted as funerary and temple art. Many of them were signed by the artist: "So-and-so made me." In addition, the sculpture attempts to indicate movement. The left foot extends forward, giving a greater sense of motion than if both feet were side by side in the same plane. Compare this approach to that expressed in the Egyptian statuary of Figure 9.13.

In the Archaic period, temples exhibited a new adaptation of post-and-lintel structure. The style of these temples was called Doric after one of the Hellenic peoples, the Dorians. We can sense the qualities and details of the

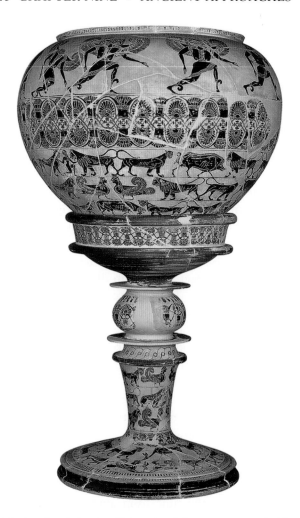

9.25 Attic bowl showing Perseus and the gorgons, early 6th century B.C.E. Height 36½ ins (93 cm). Louvre, Paris.

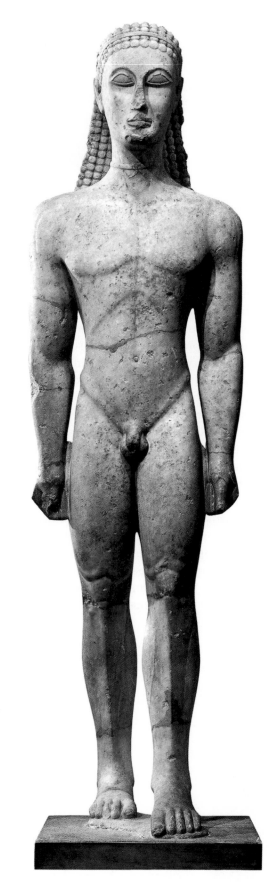

9.26 Kouros, c. 615 B.C.E. Marble, height 6 ft 4 ins (1.93 m). Metropolitan Museum of Art (Fletcher Fund, 1932).

Doric order by examining a reconstruction drawing of the west front of the Temple of Artemis at Corfu (Fig. **9.27**) and by referring to the drawing of the parts of the order in Figure **9.28**. We note especially the tapering columns that sit directly on the stylobate. The column shafts have flutes (vertical grooves), and the capital consists of a simple slab.

Although we cannot play any Greek music, because we simply do not know how to interpret the surviving records, we do know that music played a fundamental role in Greek life and education, and in Greek mythology, music had tremendous power to influence behavior. The gods themselves invented musical instruments, and the deities and heroes of Greek legend played them to remarkable effect. Apollo played the lyre (Fig. **9.29**), and Athena, the flute. Achilles, Homer's great hero of the *Iliad*, played proficiently.

Surviving records tell us that Greek music consisted of a series of modes, the equivalent of our scales. Each

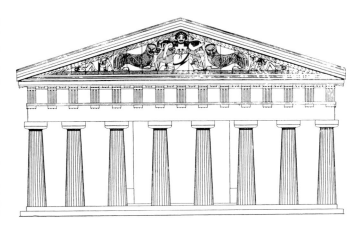

9.27 Reconstruction drawing of the west front of the Temple of Artemis, Corfu [after Rodenwaldt].

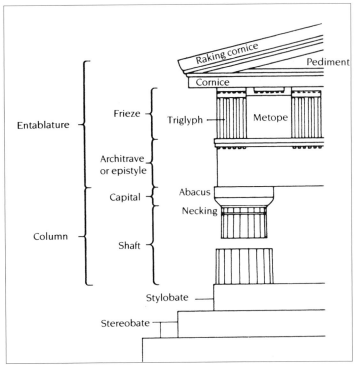

9.28 The Doric order.

mode—for example, the Dorian and Phrygian—had a name and a particular characteristic sound, not unlike the difference between our major and minor scales, and the Greeks attributed certain behavioral outcomes to each mode. Just as we say that minor scales sound sad or exotic, the Greeks held that the Dorian mode exhibited strong, even warlike, feelings, while the Phrygian elicited more sensual emotions.

Each mode had a referent planet, day of the week, and guardian or patron deity:

Mode	Planet	Day	Patron deity
Mixolydian	Mercury	Wednesday	Hermes
Lydian	Venus	Friday	Zeus and Apollo
Phrygian	Sun	Sunday	Demeter and Aphrodite
Dorian	Mars	Tuesday	Hephaistos
Hypolydian	Jupiter	Thursday	Ares and Poseidon
Hypophrygian	Saturn	Saturday	Artemis and Hera
Hypodorian	Moon	Monday	Hestia

Attaching the days of the week to various musical modes represented a practice that we can trace back to Babylonia and Sumeria of ancient Mesopotamia (see Chapter 1).

The ancient Greeks attributed various ethical powers to music and claimed that music could affect character. We call this the Greek doctrine of *ethos*. Music in ancient Greece permeated society and embodied cultural values. For the ancient Greek, music, poetry, and dancing were inseparable. Music thus constituted an integrated artform, and Greek philosophers recognized its power and influence in their society, which led to the development of the doctrine of ethos. Although most of the major Greek philosophers believed in music's influence, they disagreed about the manner in which it worked and how it influ-

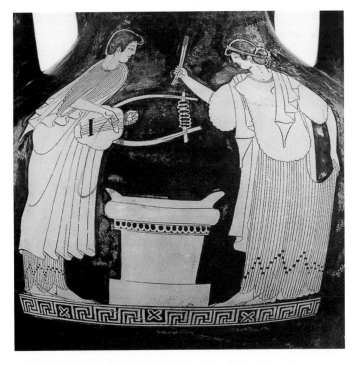

9.29 Attributed to the Eucharides Painter, amphora showing Apollo playing a lyre and Artemis holding an aulos before an altar, c. 490 B.C.E. Height 18½ ins (47 cm). Metropolitan Museum of Art, New York (Rogers Fund, 1907).

enced people, as can be seen in the divergent opinions of Plato and Aristotle on the matter. Plato insisted that artistry fueled the passions and misled the seeker of truth. Aristotle, by contrast, believed that the arts repaired deficiencies in nature and made a moral contribution.

We have a fairly good picture of what Greek musical instruments looked like from their depictions in vase paintings. Figure 9.29 illustrates the aulos, a double-reed instrument, and the lyre, a stringed instrument. The Greeks were particularly fond of vocal music, and instruments principally accompanied vocal music. The lyrics of songs have survived, and these include songs to celebrate acts by the various gods, from whom some mortal had gained special favor.

Homer is probably the best-known of the ancient Greek poets, but he was by no means the only one. By the end of the seventh century B.C.E. poets appeared who tell us their names, and sing of themselves, their travels, military adventures, homesickness, drinking parties, poverty, hates, and loves.

The poet Sappho (born around 615 B.C.E.) lived all her life on the island of Lesbos. She gathered around her a coterie of young women interested in poetry. Many of Sappho's poems are written in honor of one or other of these young women. Sappho was called a lyrist or lyric poet because, in the custom of the time, she wrote her poems to be performed with the accompaniment of a lyre. One of the first poets to write in the first person, she described love and loss as they affected her personally, in a sensual and melodic style.

Homer's *Iliad* and *Odyssey* created the mythical history that later Greeks accepted as their historic heritage. They took the dark and unknown past and created in a literary, originally oral, form a cultural foundation for an entire people. They told of heroes and described the gods. They depicted places and events and did so in a form that represented a significant artistic achievement: *epic poetry* (see Chapter 8).

Both poems deal with minor episodes in the story of the battle of Troy, which ended, with the destruction of the city, in about 1230 B.C.E. Divided into twenty-four books, the *Odyssey* tells the story of Odysseus, king of Ithaca, as he travels home from the Trojan War to recover his house and kingdom. Also set in twenty-four books, the *Iliad* explores the heroic ideal with all its contradictions. Homer develops events on the battlefield and behind the lines of both adversaries. From his descriptions, an elaborate evocation emerges of the splendor and tragedy of war and the inconsistencies of mortals and gods. The heroes are types, not real people, and legend established their characters long before Homer described them in this epic poem. Here is a brief extract:

The Iliad
Book XX
Homer
8th century B.C.E.

How Achilles made havoc among the men of Troy.

So by the beaked ships around thee, son of Peleus, hungry for war, the Achaians armed; and over against them the men of Troy, upon the high ground of the plain.

But Zeus bade Themis call the gods to council from many-folded Olympus' brow; and she ranged all about and bade them to the house of Zeus. …
Thus gathered they within the doors of Zeus; nor was the Earthshaker heedless of the goddess' call, but from the salt sea came up after the rest, and set him in the midst, and inquired concerning the purpose of Zeus: "Wherefore, O Lord of the bright lightning, hast thou called the gods again to council? Say, ponderest thou somewhat concerning the Trojans and Achaians? for lo, the war and the fighting of them are kindled very nigh."

And Zeus, who gathered the clouds, answered him, saying: "Thou knowest, O Earthshaker, the purpose within my breast, wherefor I gathered you hither; even in their perishing have I regard unto them. But for me I will abide here, sitting within a fold of Olympus, where I will gladden my heart with gazing; but go all ye forth that ye come among the Trojans and Achaians and succour these or those, howsoever each of you hath a mind. For if Achilles alone shall fight against the Trojans, not even a little while shall they hold back the son
of Peleus, the fleet of foot. Nay, but even aforetime they trembled when they looked upon him; now therefore that his wrath for his friend is waxen terrible I fear me lest he overleap the bound of fate, and storm the wall."

Thus spake the son of Kronos, and roused unabating war.[3]

We close this discussion with a brief look at perhaps the best-known poet from the culture of ancient Greece, whose existence, however, probably consists only of legend: Aesop. Various citations and traditions surround this writer, and attempts occurred even in ancient Greece to establish his identity as an actual person. Editors ascribe approximately 200 fables to him, such as those of the turtle and the hare and the fox and the grapes (see Chapter 8). Aesop marks the onset of the Western fable tradition, but the Aesop fable of the hawk and the nightingale appeared in Hesiod's work, and in the work of another Greek poet, Archilochus (ahr-KIHL-loh-kuhs), a seventh-century B.C.E. warrior-poet often considered the greatest poet after Homer.

THINKING CRITICALLY

- Identify the fundamental characteristics of Egyptian, Assyrian, and Archaic Greek art. Choose one example from each period, and compare the examples by noting how they exemplify the characteristics of their time and how they are like or different from each other.

- From the evidence presented in the chapter, and from any other material you can find, evaluate the statement that the art of the Stone Age indicates that human beings were as fully developed in their humanity as current humans are.

- Drawing on notions of aesthetics as Western culture has developed them (see p. 19), develop a comparison with American Indian concepts of "art."

- Employing the concepts of line, form, mass, and articulation, do a comparative, formal analysis of the Tell Asmar statues (Fig. 9.10) and the Archaic Greek kouros in Figure 9.26.

CYBER STUDY

PREHISTORIC ART:
http://witcombe.sbc.edu/ARTHprehistoric.html#general

MESOPOTAMIA:
http://witcombe.sbc.edu/ARTHancient.html#AncNearEast

ANCIENT EGYPT:
http://witcombe.sbc.edu/ARTHancient.html#AncEgypt

AMERICAN INDIAN:
http://doaks.org/PCWebSite/Gallery%20Tour/Gallery%20HTML%20pages/02gallery.html

ARCHAIC GREECE:
http://library.thinkquest.org/26264/art/periods/site004.htm

CHAPTER TEN

ARTISTIC REFLECTIONS IN THE PRE-MODERN WORLD

c. 480 B.C.E to c. 1400 C.E.

─────────── OUTLINE ───────────

THE CONTEXT

EUROPE
  Greece
  Rome
  The Middle Ages
THE MIDDLE EAST
  Byzantium
  Islam
ASIA
  China
  India
  Japan
AFRICA
AMERICA

THE ARTS

EUROPE
  Greek Classicism and
    Hellenism
  Masterworks: Myron, **Discus**
  Thrower
  Imperial Roman Classicism
  Medieval Music
  Profile: Hildegard of Bingen
  Romanesque Style
  Medieval Literature
  Gothic Style
  Medieval Theatre

THE MIDDLE EAST
  Byzantine Style
  Islamic Art
ASIA
  Chinese Art
  Japanese Art
AFRICA
  Nok Style
  Igbo-Ukwu Style
  Ife Style
  Djenne Style
AMERICA
  Thinking Critically
  Cyber Study

───────────── IMPORTANT TERMS ─────────────

Aryballus A shape in Inca pottery containing a wide base and tall, flanged neck.

Classicism An artistic style dating to fifth-century-B.C.E. Greece and exhibiting simplicity, clarity of structure, and appeal to the intellect.

Contrapposto stance In sculpture, the arrangement of body parts so that the weight-bearing leg is apart from the free leg, thereby shifting the hip/shoulder axis.

Diptych Two panels hinged together.

Gothic style A style of visual arts and architecture most closely associated with the pointed arch and a sense of light and space.

Hieratic style A style in Byzantine art presenting formalized, almost rigid, depictions to inspire reverence and meditation.

Plainchant Also called chant and plainsong (and sometimes, Gregorian chant). A body of sacred Christian monophonic music.

Organum Polyphony developed through the addition of melodic lines to plainchant.

Romanesque style A broad style of visual art and architecture referring to vaulted medieval architecture preceding the Gothic style.

THE CONTEXT

EUROPE

Greece

In Europe the *Athenian Greeks* defeated the Persians at the battle of Marathon in 490 B.C.E. Claiming to be the saviors of Greece in the Persian Wars, the Athenians also had a ruined city to rebuild after its destruction by the Persians. A thriving commerce, unique religion, and inquisitive philosophies including Sophistry, Stoicism, and Epicureanism, combined with a spirit of victory and heroics caused Athens to rise, under the leadership of the city-state's ruler Pericles (PAIR-ih-kleez; ruled 450–429 B.C.E.), to heights that would create the foundations of Western culture. The "Golden Age" of Athens, however, lasted less than a century, and after its defeat by Sparta in the Peloponnesian Wars, Athens remained a cultural center, but its political sphere had been eclipsed. Peace finally came to the Greek peninsula after the Macedonian conquest of Philip II. Philip's son, Alexander (the Great; 356–323 B.C.E.) ushered in the *Hellenistic* era in which Greek ideas and culture spread throughout the Mediterranean and Middle East, from Spain in the west to the Indus River in India in the east. The Peloponnesian Wars and the Hellenistic age witnessed the lasting philosophies and aesthetics of Plato and Aristotle.

Rome

Roman civilization developed in parallel to that of Greece and progressed from Etruscan origins through a Republican form of government to an empire. When Hellenistic culture waned after the death of Alexander the Great, the Romans emerged as the masters of the Mediterranean region and, eventually, over most of Europe. By 70 C.E. the Romans had destroyed the Temple of Solomon in Jerusalem (see p. 217) and colonized Britain, spreading their pragmatic and pluralistic version of Hellenistic Mediterranean civilization to peoples of northern and western Europe. Under Augustus, the first Roman emperor (63 B.C.E.–14 C.E.), Roman culture turned to Greek Classicism for inspiration, and in that spirit glorified Rome, the emperor, and empire. Inventive and utilitarian, Roman culture left us roads, fortifications, viaducts, planned administration, and a sophisticated and robust legal system.

The Middle Ages

The fall of Rome moved Europe into what we call the Middle Ages, or the *Medieval* Period—that period beginning with the fall of Rome and closing with the Renaissance in Italy. The years from around 200 C.E. to the middle of the sixth century we often call the Early Christian period. Some people occasionally use the term "Dark Ages" to describe the years between 550 and 750.

The Carolingian and Ottonian period (referring to the reigns of Charlamagne and the Ottonian Emperors) occurred from 750 to 1000; the *Romanesque*, from 1000 to 1150. The High Middle Ages included the High *Gothic*, from 1150 to 1400, and the late Gothic period from 1300 to around 1450, which overlaps High Gothic and formed a time of transition when the flower of the Renaissance began to bloom. People of the Renaissance called the thousand years between the fifth and the fifteenth centuries the Middle Ages or Medieval Period on the theory that nothing—or worse than nothing—happened between the classical perfection of Greece and Rome and the revival of classical humanism in the fifteenth century. The Middle Ages were dominated by the Christian Church and a strong papacy, whose concepts ranged from a harsh, judgmental God in the early years to a softer, beneficent Jesus in the Gothic period. Socially, the structure ranged from feudalism, a system of military service and land ownership that created a pyramid of political and military power—a masculine, "men-at-arms" code of behavior—to chivalry, a softer, more feminine, point of view in ethics and personal conduct. The early Middle Ages witnessed monasticism, mysticism, and asceticism. The Gothic era saw the plague, the Hundred Years' War between England and France, and the Crusades with their military, religious, and political objectives. As strong as the medieval Christian Church might have been, the time saw an increasing secularism, what some call the Gothic dualism (the conflict between mystical religion and secularism often appearing in the same context).

THE MIDDLE EAST

Byzantium

At the same time in the Middle East two cultures flourished: *Byzantium* and *Islam*, until the former fell victim to the latter in the middle of the fifteenth century. Byzantium stood astride the main land route from Europe to Asia and its riches. Byzantium possessed tremendous potential as a major metropolis. In addition, the city had a defensible deep-water port and controlled the passage between the Mediterranean and the Black Sea. Blessed with fertile agricultural surroundings, it formed the ideal "New Rome." For this was the objective of the Emperor Constantine when he dedicated his new capital in 330 C.E. and changed its name to Constantinople (literally, "city of Constantine"). It prospered and became the center of Orthodox Christianity and mother to a unique and intense style in the visual arts and architecture. When Rome fell to the Goths in 476 C.E. it had long since handed the torch of civilization to Constantinople. Here the arts and learning of the Classical world were preserved and nurtured, along with an Eastern orientation, while western Europe underwent the turmoil and destruction of barbarian invasion.

Islam

Elsewhere in the Middle East, the Arabian peninsula of the seventh century C.E. watched the rise of the third great monotheistic religions of the region, *Islam*. When Muhammad (c. 570–632 C.E.), the prophet of Islam, started to preach, conditions included great suffering among the poor in southwestern Arabia. Muhammad began preaching in Mecca around 610 C.E., but his teaching did not immediately meet acceptance. A period of conflict followed in which forces loyal to Muhammad physically conquered those opposed to him. By the time of his death, his message and governance reigned supreme on the Arabian peninsula, and his followers acknowledged him as Prophet. Islam spread rapidly throughout the Middle East, and the Muslims threatened to overrun Europe until Charles Martel (sharl mahr-TEHL) defeated them in 732. During the period of the Middle Ages in Europe, Muslims assumed responsibility for transmitting much of the classical knowledge of the ancient world. They excelled in mathematics and science, and produced proficient artists, writers, and artisans.

Islam believes in one absolute and all-powerful God, known as Allah, the just and merciful creator of the universe. Islam requires all believers to perform five religious duties, known as the Five Pillars of Islam. First, believers must confirm their faith by reciting the *shahadah*: "I witness that there is no god but the God (Allah) and that Muhammad is his prophet." This affirmation must be made before witnesses and constitutes the only requirement for conversion to Islam. Second, Muslims must perform canonical worship five times a day. Third, Muslims must fast during the holy month of Ramadan. Fourth, believers must make a yearly payment of *zalaat*, a set percentage of each adult's wealth, to help the poor. Fifth, at least once in their lifetime, if possible, a believer must perform the *hajj*, the annual pilgrimage to Mecca.

ASIA

China

In **Asia** (almost one thousand years before Muhammad, and at the time just reaching the Classical Greek culture of Europe) lived the first and greatest professional teacher and philosopher in *China*: Confucius (551–479 B.C.E.). His teaching is contained in five classical works (not all of which were actually written by him). His thought rests more on a pragmatic level than an intellectual one. His primary interest lay in politics. He proposed a return to the ancient way, in which persons must play their proper, assigned roles subject to authority. But he saw government primarily as an ethical challenge. A ruler's virtue rather than power brought contentment to the people. Confucius aimed to convince rulers to pursue ethical principles. Thus, he became China's first moralist and founder of a great ethical tradition.

India

In India, also in the sixth century B.C.E., rose Buddhism, a system of philosophy and ethics founded by Gautama Siddartha, the Buddha (563–483 B.C.E.). Buddhism found its way to China shortly thereafter and formed a cornerstone of Chinese culture. The Four Noble Truths of Buddha comprise: (1) existence is suffering; (2) the origin of suffering is desire; (3) suffering ceases when desire ceases; and (4) the way to reach the end of desire is to follow the Eightfold Path. This comprises right belief, right resolve (to renounce carnal pleasure, harm no living creature, and so on), right speech, right conduct, right occupation or living, right effort, right contemplation or right-mindedness, and right ecstasy. The final goal of the religious person is to gain enlightenment and so escape from existence into blissful nonexistence—*nirvana*. Buddhists believe that the substance of all objects is illusion, and that greed, hatred, and delusion separate people from reality and keep them tied to the cycle of earthly existence. Religious living allows them to escape this cycle.

Japan

Across the Sea of Japan from China lies *Japan*, whose early history, religion, and artistry reflect strong Chinese influences. Chinese chronicles mention Japan for the first time in the first century C.E. By that time, Japan had entered the Metals Age and had developed a major rice-growing economy. The first development of any major political center appears to have occurred in the fourth century.

Between the sixth and eighth centuries Japan passed from what historians call "protohistory" into civilization. The Yamato rulers created a state centered on the Chinese model. Buddhism was introduced and adopted by the Japanese ruling class some time in the sixth century, although Shinto, Japan's ancient polytheistic nature cult, remained strong. Over the next 200 years, the constitution of Japan took shape on the model of Confucian ethics, and land reform transformed the aristocracy into a bureaucracy paid by the state. The Japanese also adopted legal and penal codes and developed historical chronicles. An official break with China occurred in 894 C.E. Japanese aesthetics matured as well. As in Europe, a new middle class made a significant impact on Japanese culture. Zen gardens proliferated and the tea ceremony emerged.

AFRICA

In Africa, while Islamic culture spread across northern Africa and into Europe, the cultures of Sub-Saharan Africa continued traditions that had existed for thousands of years, over which time African artists and craftspeople created objects of sophisticated vision and masterful technique. We know that the cultures of Sub-Saharan Africa traded with the Middle East and Asia as early as 600 C.E. Chinese Tang Dynasty coins found along the coast of East Africa document this fact. The ravages of time and the lack of written language, however, prohibit our deeper understanding of the cultures. We do know that climate, materials, and the nature of tribal culture doomed many African cultural artifacts to extinction; only a small number remain. Nonetheless, what has survived traces a rich vision that varies from culture to culture. Its purposes range from magical to utilitarian.

AMERICA

In America, native peoples populated the entirety of North, Central, and South America, and we will examine art from each of these areas shortly. In Central America, however, the city of Teotihuacan (tay-oh-TEE-whah-kahn) arose in the area just northeast of present-day Mexico City. By the year 200 C.E. it constituted a major metropolis and center of manufacturing and commerce. In fact, it constitutes the very first large city-state in the Americas. When it reached its zenith between 350 and 650 B.C.E. it had a population of around 200,000, which made it one of the largest cities in the world. Teotihuacans traded their manufactured goods throughout Central America in exchange for luxury items such as feathers and jaguar skins. Farmers in the surrounding areas drained swamps, terraced hillsides, and grew staples such as corn, squash, and beans.

The pantheon of Teotihuacan gods proved prototypical to the gods of subsequent Mesoamerican cultures such as the Aztecs, whom we study in the next chapter. Teotihuacans worshiped, among others, a Rain God and the Feathered Serpent. By the end of the eighth century Teotihuacan had fallen into permanent decline, and its ceremonial center had burned. Nonetheless, the city remained a legendary pilgrimage site until the arrival of the Spanish in the fifteenth century.

THE ARTS

EUROPE

Greek Classicism and Hellenism

CLASSICISM Classicism is an artistic style and cultural perspective based on principles associated with the art and thought of ancient Greece and Rome. Specifically, this means a striving for harmony, order, reason, intellect, objectivity, and formal discipline. It contrasts with, for instance, Romanticism (see Chapter 12) and other "anti-classical" styles and directions such as the Baroque and Rococo (Chapter 11), which emphasize imagination, emotion, and free expression. Artworks in the Classical style—for example, Myron's *Discus Thrower* (see p. 230)—represent idealized perfection rather than real life. This embodies an ideal of beauty, sculpted according to the aesthetic principles of proportion, balance, and unity of form. Classicism is also an ideological viewpoint that reflects the idea of ancient Greece as the fount of civilization, later expanded to view western European culture as its ultimate fulfillment.

Style generally relates to treatment of form rather than content or subject matter, but often form and content cannot be separated. When Classicism modified to a more individualized and lifelike treatment of form, its subject matter broadened to include the mundane.

Such expression, particularly in painting, reflected a technical advance as well as a change in attitude. Many of the problems of foreshortening—the perceivable diminution of size as the object recedes in space—had been solved and, as a result, figures have a new sense of depth. By the end of the fifth century B.C.E. the convention typified in Egyptian and Mesopotamian art—of putting all the figures along the baseline on the front plane of the design—gives way to suggestions of depth. By the end of the fourth century B.C.E. the problems of depth and foreshortening were fully overcome. Impressions of lifelikeness are also heightened in some cases by the use of light and shadow.

SCULPTURE The fifth century saw many of the most talented artists turn to sculpture and architecture. The age of Greek Classical style in sculpture probably begins with the sculptors Myron and Polyclitus (pah-lih-KLY-tuhs) in the middle of the fifth century B.C.E. Both contributed to the development of *cast* sculpture (see Chapter 2). Polyclitus reportedly achieved the ideal proportions of the male athlete (Fig. **10.1**). Note that the *Lance Bearer* by Polyclitus represents *the* male athlete, and not *a* male ath-

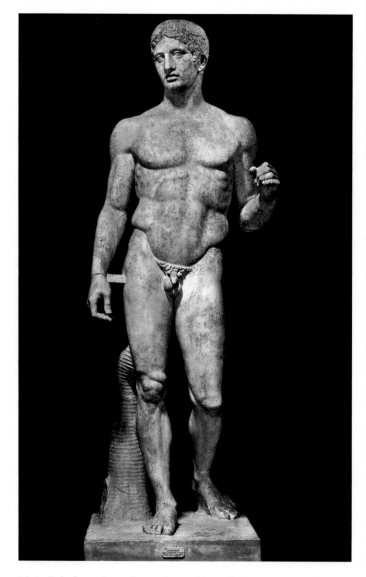

10.1 Polyclitus, *Doryphorus* (*Lance Bearer*), Roman copy after an original of c. 450–440 B.C.E. Marble, height 6 ft 6 ins (1.98 m). Museo Archeologico Nazionale, Naples.

lete. In this work the body's weight rests on one leg in the *contrapposto* stance. This simple but important new posture, characteristic of Greek Classical style, results in a sense of relaxation and controlled dynamics and a subtle play of curves.

Polyclitus developed a set of rules for constructing the ideal human figure that he laid out in his treatise *The Canon* (*kanon* is the Greek word for "rule" or "law"). The *Lance Bearer* supposedly illustrates his theory, but because neither the treatise nor the original statue has survived, we do not know what set of proportions Polyclitus thought ideal. Probably, he used ratios between some basic unit and the length of some body part or parts. For Myron's work see the *Discus Thrower* in the Masterworks feature (see p. 230).

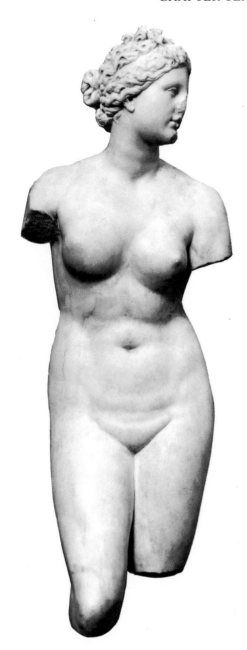

copy; the original has never been found.) Aphrodite's body bends to the left in the famous Praxitelean S-curve. Originally, she rested her weight on one foot. Strain on the ankle was minimized by attaching the arm to drapery and a vase.

The late fourth century found in the sculpture of Lysippus (a favorite of Alexander the Great) a dignified naturalness and a new concept of space. In the *Scraper* (Fig. **10.3**) he attempts to put the figure into motion, in contrast to the posed figures at rest of earlier periods. The sculpture has a mundane theme—an athlete scraping dirt and oil from his body. The proportions of the figure reflect greater lifelikeness than those of Polyclitus. Style had moved a long way from earliest Classicism, but Classical influence remained.

10.2 Praxiteles, *Cnidian Aphrodite*, probably Hellenistic copy of 4th-century B.C.E. bronze original. Marble, height 5 ft ½ in (1.54 m). Metropolitan Museum of Art, New York (Fletcher Fund).

Classical Greek statuary may be portraiture, but the features are always idealized. Man may be the measure of all things, as the Greek philosopher Protagoras argued, but Greek Classical artists raised him above human reality to the state of perfection found only in the gods.

Sculpture of the fourth century B.C.E. illustrates the change in emphasis reflected in late Classical styles. Famous for his *individualism* and delicacy in choice of themes, Praxiteles created in the *Cnidian Aphrodite* (Fig. **10.2**) an inward-looking style different from the formal detachment of earlier sculpture. (Note that this is a

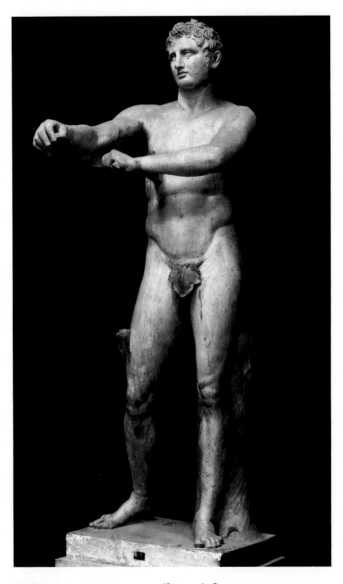

10.3 Lysippus, *Apoxyomenus (Scraper)*, Roman copy, probably after a bronze original of c. 330 B.C.E. Marble, Height 6 ft 9 ins (2.05 m). Musei Vaticani, Rome.

Masterworks

Myron, *Discus Thrower*

Myron's *Discus Thrower* (or *Discobolus*) (Fig. **10.4**) exemplifies the Classical concern for restraint in its subdued vitality and subtle suggestion of movement coupled with balance. But it also expresses the sculptor's interest in the flesh of the idealized human form. This example of the *Discus Thrower* is a much later marble copy. Myron's bronze original (cast sculpture, see Chapter 2), allowed more flexibility of pose than marble. A statue, as opposed to a relief sculpture, must stand on its own, and supporting the weight of the marble on a small area, such as one ankle, poses a significant structural problem. Metal has greater tensile strength (the ability to withstand bending and twisting), and thus this problem does not arise.

In *Discovery of the Mind: The Greek Origins of European Thought*, Bruno Snell writes: "If we want to describe the statues of the fifth century in the words of their age, we should say that they represent beautiful or perfect men, or, to use a phrase employed in the early lyrics for the purposes of eulogy: 'god-like' men. Even for Plato the norm of judgment still rests with the gods, and not with men."

Myron's representation of this young athlete contributes a sense of dynamism to Greek sculpture. Here Myron tackles a vexing problem for the sculptor: how to condense a series of movements into a single pose without making the sculpture appear static or frozen. His solution dramatically intersects two opposing arcs: one created by the downward sweep of the arms and shoulders; the other by the forward thrust of the thighs, torso, and head.

Typical of Greek freestanding statues, the *Discus Thrower* is designed to be seen from one direction only. It represents thus a sort of freestanding, three-dimensional "super-relief." The beginnings of Classical style celebrate the powerful nude male figure. The suggestions of moral idealism, dignity, and self-control in the statue express all qualities inherent in Classicism. However, the *Discus Thrower* marks a step forward, in the increasing vitality of figure movement. Warm, full, and dynamic, Myron's human form achieves a new level of expressiveness and power. Fully controlled and free of the unbridled emotion of later sculpture, Myron's work focuses on balanced composition, and form takes precedence over feeling.

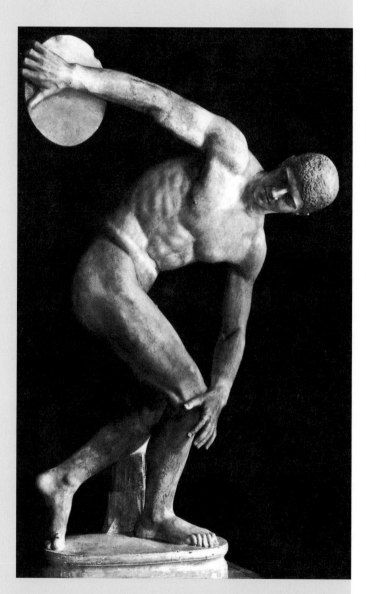

10.4 Myron, *Discobolus* (*Discus Thrower*), Roman copy after a bronze original of c. 450 B.C.E. Marble, life-size. Museo Nazionale Romano, Rome.

THEATRE The classical theatre of Periclean Athens was a theatre of convention, and the term convention, as it applies here, takes on a new meaning. Every era and every style have their conventions—those underlying, accepted expectations and/or rules that influence artists subtly or overtly. "Theatre of convention" implies a style of production lacking in illusion or stage realism. Theatre of convention to a large extent leaves the artists freer to explore the ideal than theatre of illusion (in which scenic details are portrayed representationally) because dependence upon stage mechanics and historically accurate costume does not hamper the playwright. An audience simply accepts a poetic description in theatre of convention and does not demand to see it. Thus in imagination rests the key to theatre of convention.

Greek dramatists pursued lofty moral themes fundamental to their perception of the universe. Although some plays from the classical era have survived, and indicate what and how playwrights wrote, we do not know specifically how those works became theatre—that is, how they became a production. Nevertheless, we can build a picture of production from descriptions in the plays themselves, from other literary evidence, and from a few archeological examples.

Theatre productions in ancient Greece comprised part of religious festivals that were held three times a year: the City Dionysia, Rustic Dionysia, and Lenaea. The first of these was a festival of tragic plays and the last of comic ones. The City Dionysia occurred in the theatre of Dionysus in Athens. Our knowledge of Greek theatre grows somewhat through the fact that, although most of these plays have not survived, we do at least know the titles and the names of the authors who won these contests from the earliest one, held in 534 B.C.E., through to the final one.

The records, inscribed in stone, show that three playwrights figured prominently and repeatedly as winners in the contests of the era:[1] Aeschylus, Sophocles, and Euripides (EH-skih-luhs; SAH-foh-kleez; yoo-RIH-pih-deez). All the complete tragedies to survive are by these three playwrights: seven by Aeschylus, seven by Sophocles, and eighteen by Euripides.

A playwright entering the contests for tragedy or comedy was required to submit the work to a panel of presiding officers, who selected just three authors for actual production. Early plays in the Classical style had only one actor together with a chorus, and at selection time the playwright was assigned the chief actor plus a *choregus*—a patron who paid for all the production expenses. The playwright functioned as author, director, choreographer, and musical composer. He often also played the leading role.

AESCHYLUS (525–456 B.C.E.) Aeschylus was the most famous poet of ancient Greece. Clearly fitting the Classical mold, he wrote magnificent tragedies of high poetic language and lofty moral themes. In *Agamemnon*, the first play in the *Oresteia* (ohr-eh-STY-uh) trilogy, Aeschylus's chorus warns us that success and wealth are insufficient without goodness.

> Justice shines in sooty dwellings
> Loving the righteous way of life,
> But passes by with averted eyes
> The house whose lord has hands unclean.
> Be it built throughout of gold.
> Caring naught for the weight of praise
> Heaped upon wealth by the vain, but turning
> All alike to its proper end.[2]

Aeschylus probed questions that we still ask: How responsible are we for our own actions? How much are we controlled by the will of the gods (or God)? His characters are larger than life; they are types rather than individuals, in accordance with the idealism of the time. Yet they are also human. Aeschylus's early plays consist of the traditional single actor, plus a chorus of fifty. Later, he is credited with the addition of a second actor, and by the end of his career a third actor had been added and the chorus reduced to twelve.

Aeschylus's plays make a strong appeal to the intellect. He lived through the Persian invasions, witnessed the great Athenian victories, and fought at the battle of Marathon (490 B.C.E.). His plays reflect this experience and spirit.

SOPHOCLES (496?–406 B.C.E.) Sophocles' career overlapped that of Aeschylus, and he reached his peak at the zenith of the Greek Classical style with works such as *Oedipus the King*. But he lived well beyond the death of Pericles in 429 B.C.E., therefore experiencing the shame of Athenian defeat.

Sophocles' plays illustrate a trend toward increasing realism. Sophocles was a less formal poet than Aeschylus. His themes are more humane and his characters more subtle, although his exploration of the themes of human responsibility, dignity, and fate matches the intensity and seriousness of Aeschylus. His plots show increasing complexity, but within the formal restraints of the Classical spirit. Classical Greek theatre was mostly discussion and narration. Themes often dealt with bloodshed, but, though the play led up to violence, blood was never shed on stage. The results often appeared in a tableau typically on a wagon rolled out from the *skene* (see p. 232).

EURIPIDES (480?–406 B.C.E.) Euripides was younger than Sophocles, although both men died in 406 B.C.E. They competed with each other but differed in approach. Euripides' plays carry realism to the furthest extent we see in Greek tragedy. They deal with individual emotions rather than great events, and his language, though still basically poetic, comes closer to normal speech with much less formality than that of his predecessors.

Euripides experimented with, and ignored, many of the conventions of Greek theatre. He explored the mechanics of scene painting and depended less on the chorus than his rivals.[3] Sometimes he questioned the religion of his day. Strictly speaking, his plays are tragicomedies rather than pure tragedies. Some critics have described many of them as melodramas (see Chapter 5).

Plays such as *The Bacchae* reflect the changing Athenian spirit and dissatisfaction with contemporary events. Euripides was not particularly popular in his time, perhaps because his audience expected a more idealistic, formal, and conventional treatment of dramatic themes and characters.

ARISTOPHANES (448?–380? B.C.E.) Tragedies and satyr plays were not the only works produced in the theatre of the Classical era in Athens. The Athenians were extremely fond of comedy; unfortunately no examples survive from the Periclean period. Aristophanes, the most gifted of the comic poets of the post-Classical period, wrote highly satirical, topical, sophisticated, and often sexually suggestive plays such as *Lysistrata*. Eleven of his plays survive, and we still see translated productions. As the personal and political targets of his invective remain unknown to us, these modern productions are mere shadows of what took the stage at the turn of the fourth century B.C.E. As we noted in the Introduction, in *Lysistrata* Aristophanes creates a plot in which the women of Athens go on a sex strike to rid the city of war and warmongers.

THEATRE DESIGN The form of the Greek theatre owes much to the choral dances associated with the worship of Dionysus from which it originated. In 534 B.C.E. Thespis reportedly introduced a single actor to these dances, or dithyrambs. In 472 B.C.E., Aeschylus added a second actor, and in 458 B.C.E., Sophocles added a third.

Throughout its history the Greek theatre comprised a large circular *orchestra*—an acting and dancing area—with an altar at its center, and a semicircular *theatron*—an auditorium or viewing place—usually cut into or occupying the slope of a hill. Since the actors played more than one role, they needed somewhere to change costume, and so a *skene* (skee-nay)—a scene building or retiring place—was added. The gradual development of the *skene*

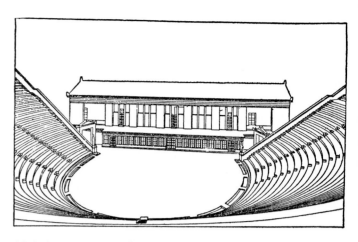

10.5 Reconstruction of the Hellenistic theatre at Ephesus, Turkey, c. 280 B.C.E., rebuilt c. 150 B.C.E.

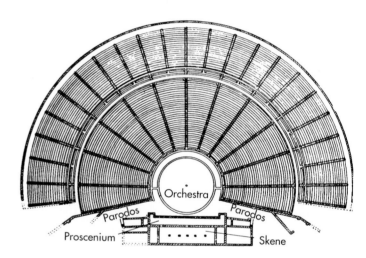

10.6 Polyclitus the Younger, Theatre at Epidaurus, Greece, c. 350 B.C.E., plan.

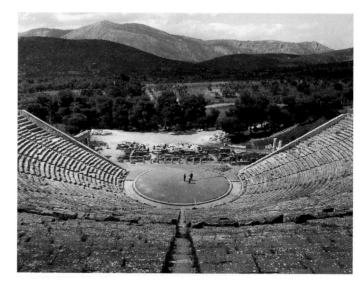

10.7 Theatre at Epidaurus. Diameter 373 ft (114 m), orchestra 80 ft (24 m) across.

to include a raised stage is somewhat obscure, but clearly, by Hellenistic times it had emerged, and the building had become a rather elaborate affair with projecting wings at each end (Fig. **10.5**).

The earliest surviving theatre, dating from the fifth century B.C.E., the Theatre of Dionysus sits on the south slope of the Acropolis in Athens. It witnessed the plays of Aeschylus, Sophocles, Euripides, and Aristophanes. Its current form dates back to a period of reconstruction work around 338–326 B.C.E.

The theatre at Epidaurus (Figs. **10.6** and **10.7**) is the best-preserved ancient theatre. Built by Polyclitus the Younger about 350 B.C.E., 100 years after the end of the Classical period, it demonstrates by sheer size the monumental character the theatre had assumed by that time. The *orchestra* has a diameter of 80 feet (24 m) and an altar to Dionysus in the center. The auditorium—slightly more than a semicircle—is divided by an *ambulatory*, or covered walkway, about two-thirds of the way up, and by radiating stairways. All the seats were of stone with the first or lowest row reserved for the dignitaries of Athens. Here the seats had backs and arms. Some were decorated with relief sculptures.

Undoubtedly variation existed in the design of theatres in different locations but, again, time has removed most examples from our grasp. The many theories of how Greek theatre productions worked, how scenery was or was not used, and when a raised stage appeared make fascinating reading.

ARCHITECTURE The arts of the Western world have returned over the past 2,400 years to the style of Classical Greek architecture, and nothing brings that style so clearly to mind as the Greek temple. Most people have an amazingly accurate concept of its structure and proportions. The art historian H. W. Janson suggests that the crystallization of the characteristics of a Greek temple is so complete that when we think of one Greek temple, we basically think of all Greek temples.

The Classical Greek temple, as seen in Figure **10.8**, has a structure of horizontal blocks of stone laid across vertical columns. This *post-and-lintel construction* is not unique to Greece, but certainly the Greeks refined it to its highest aesthetic level.

Greek temples consist of three principal *orders*: Doric, Ionic, and Corinthian (see Fig. **3.3**). These are not just decorative and elevational conventions, but systems of proportion. The first two are Classical; the third, though of Classical derivation, belongs to the later, Hellenistic, style. The contrasts between these types make an important, if subtle, stylistic point. Simplicity was an important characteristic of the Greek Classical style, and the Doric and Ionic orders maintain clean and simple lines. The Corinthian order features more ornateness and complexity. Differences also exist in column bases and the configuration of the lintels, as well as in the columns and capitals.

Perched atop the Acropolis at Athens, the Parthenon (see Fig. **10.8**) stands as the greatest temple built by the

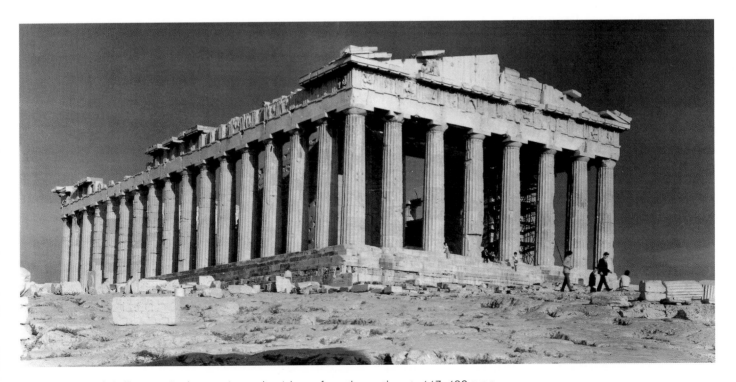

10.8 Ictinus and Callicrates, Parthenon, Acropolis, Athens, from the northwest, 447–438 B.C.E.

Greeks and the prototype for all Classical buildings thereafter. When the Persians sacked Athens in 480 B.C.E., they destroyed the then existing temple and its sculpture. Pericles rebuilt the Acropolis in the late fifth century B.C.E. Athens was at its zenith, and the Parthenon was its crowning glory.

In plan the Parthenon is a peripteral temple—columns surround the interior room, or *cella*, and the number of columns on the sides equals twice the number across the front, plus one. The inside, divided into two parts, housed the 40-foot (12-m)-high ivory and gold statue of the goddess Athena Parthenos. The Parthenon typifies every aspect of Greek Classical style in architecture. Doric in character and geometric in configuration, it achieves balance through symmetry, and the clean, simple line and plan hold the composition together perfectly.

The internal harmony of the design lies in the regular repetition of virtually unvaried form. Each column is alike and equidistant from its neighbor, except at the corners, where the spacing lessens in subtle, aesthetic adjustment. A great deal has been written about the so-called "refinements" of the Parthenon—the elements that intentionally depart from strict geometric regularity. According to some scholars, the slight outward curvature of horizontal elements compensates for the tendency of the eye to perceive downward sagging if all elements are actually parallel. Each column swells about 7 inches (17 cm)—called *entasis*—supposedly to compensate for the tendency of vertical parallel lines to appear to curve inward. The columns also tilt inward at the top so as to appear upright. The *stylobate* (the foundation immediately below the row of columns) rises toward the center so as not to appear to sag under the immense weight of the stone columns and roof.

The white marble, which in other circumstances might appear stark, may have been chosen to harmonize with and reflect the intense Athenian sunlight. However, some parts of the temple and its statuary would originally have been brightly painted.

Here we have the perfect embodiment of Classical characteristics: *convention, order, balance, idealization, simplicity, grace,* and *restrained vitality*—of this earth but mingled with the divine. See the Companion Website: Architecture, Classicism.

LITERATURE Arguably the greatest lyric poet of ancient Greece, Pindar (PIHN-duhr or PIHN-dahr; 518–c. 438 B.C.E.) wrote choral odes to celebrate victories in the various official games throughout Greece. He enjoyed a high reputation in his lifetime throughout the Greek world. Pindar wrote seventeen volumes of choral lyric poetry of every genre, only four of which survived complete.

An ode celebrates an occasion of public or private dignity employing a blending of emotion and general meditation. In ancient Greece, the word *ōidé* (ee-deh) or ode referred to a choric song usually accompanied by a dance. Choral odes also formed an integral part of Greek drama. Pindar's odes divide into Olympian, Pythian, Isthmian, and Nemean—named for the games from which the victories he celebrated arose.

In a Pindaric ode we find a particular kind of three-part structure that contains a *strophe* (STROH-fee; two or more lines repeated as a unit), followed by a metrically similar *antistrophe* (an-TIH-stroh-fee). In the choral odes of Greek drama, each of these parts corresponded to a specific movement of the chorus as it performed that part. In the strophe they moved from right to left; in the antistrophe, they moved from left to right. The third part of the structure, the *epode* (EH-pohd) or summary, exhibited a different meter. In the *Isthmian Odes* that follow, the translator has indicated each of these parts. (The figures in square brackets within the text indicate line numbers in the Greek original.)

Isthmian Odes
Pindar

Isthmian 1
For Herodotus of Thebes, Chariot Race, ?458 B.C.E.

[str. 1]
My mother, Thebe of the golden shield, I shall place your interests above my lack of leisure. May rocky Delos, in whose praises I have poured myself out, not be indignant at me. [5] What is dearer to good men than their noble parents? Yield, island of Apollo; indeed, with the help of the gods I shall accomplish the end of both graceful songs,

[ant. 1]
honoring in the dance both Phoebus with the unshorn hair, in wave-washed Ceos with its mariners, and the sea-dividing reef of the Isthmus. [10] Since the Isthmus gave to the people of Cadmus six garlands from her games, the glory of triumph for my fatherland, where Alcmena bore her fearless

[epode 1]
son, before whom the bold hounds of Geryon once trembled. But I, while I frame for Herodotus a prize of honor for his four-horse chariot, [15] and for managing the reins with his own hands and not another's, want to join him to the song of Castor or of Iolaus, for of all heroes they were the strongest charioteers, the one born in Sparta and the other in Thebes.

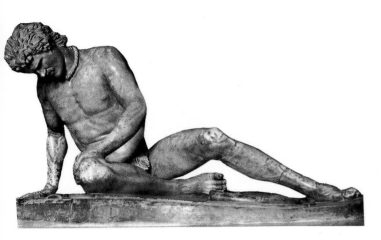

10.9 *Dying Gaul*, Roman copy of a bronze original from Pergamon, Turkey, of c. 230–220 B.C.E. Marble, life-size. Museo Capitolino, Rome.

HELLENISTIC STYLE As the age of Pericles gave way to the Hellenistic period, the dominant characteristics of Classicism gradually modified to form a less formal, more realistic, and more emotional style reflecting a diversity of approaches.

Hellenistic style in sculpture dominated the Mediterranean world for several centuries until the first century B.C.E. As time progressed, style changed to reflect an increasing interest in individual human differences. Hellenistic sculptors often turned to pathos, banality, trivia, and flights of individual virtuosity. The *Dying Gaul* (Fig. **10.9**) provides powerful expression of emotion and pathos, depicting a noble warrior on the verge of death. Representing a Gallic casualty in the wars between Pergamon and barbarian invaders, the man slowly bleeds to death from a chest wound. The figure sits on a stage, as if to act out a drama. The *Nike of Samothrace* (Fig. **10.10**), or *Winged Victory*, displays a dramatic, dynamic technical virtuosity. Symbolizing a triumph of one of Alexander's successors, the victory figure seems to defy its heavy marble material and rise weightless, at the same time presenting a sense of great strength and power. The sculptor has treated stone almost as if the work were a painting. As a result, a full, awesome reality of wind and sea emerges.

The common Hellenistic theme of suffering dominates the Laocoön (lay-AH-koh-ahn) group (Fig. **10.11**). The sculpture depicts the Trojan priest Laocoön and his sons strangled by sea serpents. Based on Greek myth, the subject reflects Laocoön's punishment for defying Poseidon, god of the sea, and warning the Trojans of the Greek strategy of the Trojan horse. Emotion and movement burst all restraint; muscles strain and veins bulge in stark realism.

The temple of the Olympian Zeus (Fig. **10.12**) illustrates Hellenistic modification of Classical style in architecture. Temple architecture in this style sought to produce an overpowering emotional experience. The product of an empire rather than a reflection of the aspirations of a free people in a city-state, its scale and complexity have increased, but order, balance, moderation, and consonant harmony remain. In these huge ruins we see a change in proportions from the Parthenon, and slender and ornate Corinthian columns replace the Doric ones. The first major Corinthian temple, begun by the architect Cossutius for King Antiochus IV of Syria, it was not completed until the second century C.E., under the Roman emperor Hadrian. The cause was its elaborate detail. The remaining ruins only vaguely suggest the scale and richness of the original building, which was surrounded by an immense, walled precinct.

Imperial Roman Classicism

SCULPTURE Some Roman art appears merely to imitate Greek prototypes, but much of it displays vigorous, uniquely Roman creativity.

Hellenistic influence grew in the late first century B.C.E. Greek Classical influence dominated, but always with a Roman—a more practical and individual—character. By the first century C.E., Classical influence had returned sculpture to the idealized style of Periclean Athens. Greek Classical form was duplicated, recast, and translated into vital forms of the present. It was also a common practice to copy the idealized body of a well-known Greek statue and add to it a portrait head of a contemporary Roman (Fig. **10.13**). The aesthetics of sculptural depiction thus remained Greek, with Roman clothing added: the pose, rhythm, and movement of the body originated in the past. Much sculpture at this time portrayed the emperor, raising him to the status of a god, perhaps because a far-flung empire required assurances of stability and suprahuman characteristics in its leaders.

The reality that men are men and not gods was not long in returning to Roman consciousness, however, and third-century sculpture exhibits an expressive starkness. In the fourth century a new and powerful emperor took the throne, and his likeness (Fig. **10.14**)—part of a gigantic sculpture (the head is over 8 feet [2.5 m] tall)—shows an exaggerated, ill-proportioned intensity comparable with Expressionist works of the early twentieth century (see pp. 363–4). This work is not an actual likeness of Constantine. Instead, it is the artist's view of Constantine's perception of himself as emperor, and of the office of emperor itself. The exaggerated features of this work,

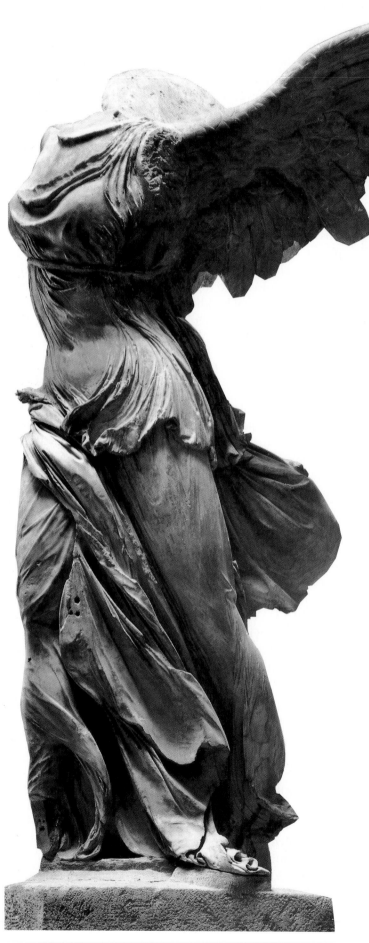

however, do not reach the level of stylization witnessed, for example, in the bearded male figure from Djenne (see Fig. 10.57), but do show similarities to the approach taken in the head from Jemaa, Nigeria (see Fig. 10.55).

LITERATURE At the time when literature became reasonably acceptable to the practical Romans, it was nurtured chiefly through the contributions of Greek slaves. At first, it imitated Greek literature and was written in Greek. Latin was initially seen as a peasant language with few words capable of expressing abstract notions. Credit for developing a Latin prose style and vocabulary for the expression of philosophical ideas probably comes from Cicero (106–43 B.C.E.).

During the reign of Augustus, the poets Horace (65–8 B.C.E.) and Virgil (70–19 B.C.E.) wrote verses glorifying the emperor, the origins of Rome, the simple honesty of rural life, patriotism, and the glory of dying for one's country. Horace was an outstanding Latin lyric poet and satirist. The most frequent themes of his Odes and verse Epistles include love, friendship, philosophy, and the art of poetry. The Horatian odes, short lyric poems written in stanzas of two to four lines, give us a contrast with the odes of Pindar that we just studied. Whereas Pindar's odes contain lofty, heroic subjects and style, Horace's odes remain intimate and reflective. Nonetheless, Horace's work has discipline, elegance, and dignity. Horace uses a serious and serene tone with irony and melancholy frequent visitors, as well as gentle humor.

10.10 *Nike of Samothrace (Winged Victory)*, c. 190 B.C.E. Marble, height 8 ft (2.43 m). Louvre, Paris.

Odes
Book 1, Poem 1
Horace

Maecenas, born of monarch ancestors,
The shield at once and glory of my life!
There are who joy them in the Olympic strife
And love the dust they gather in the course;

The goal by hot wheels shunn'd, the famous prize,
Exalt them to the gods that rule mankind;
This joys, if rabbles fickle as the wind
Through triple grade of honours bid him rise; ...
To me the artist's meed, the ivy wreath
Is very heaven: me the sweet cool of woods,
Where Satyrs frolic with the Nymphs, secludes
From rabble rout, so but Euterpe's breath

Fail not the flute, nor Polyhymnia fly
Averse from string new the Lesbian lyre.
O, write my name among that minstrel choir,
And my proud head shall strike upon the sky!

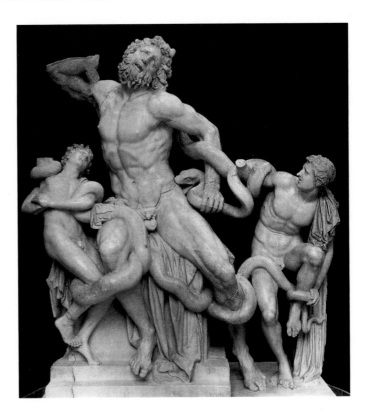

Virgil's *Aeneid* (ee-NEE-ihd) tells the story of the founding of Rome, in an epic account of the journey of Aeneas from the ruins of Troy to the shores of Italy. A section of Book 1 follows.

The Aeneid
Book 1
Virgil
70–19 B.C.E.

ARMS and the man I sing, who first made way
Predestined exile, from the Trojan shore
To Italy, the blest Lavinian strand.
Smitten of storms he was on land and sea
By violence of Heaven, to satisfy
Stern Juno's sleepless wrath; and much in war.
He suffered, seeking at the last to found
The city, and bring o'er his fathers' gods
To safe abode in Latium; whence arose
The Latin race, old Alba's reverend lords,
And from her hills wide-walled, imperial Rome.

10.11 (*above right*) Hagesandrus, Polydorus, and Athenodorus, *Laocoön and his Two Sons*, 1st century C.E. Marble, height 5 ft (1.52 m). Musei Vaticani, Rome.

10.12 (*right*) Temple of Olympian Zeus, Athens, 174 B.C.E.–130 C.E.

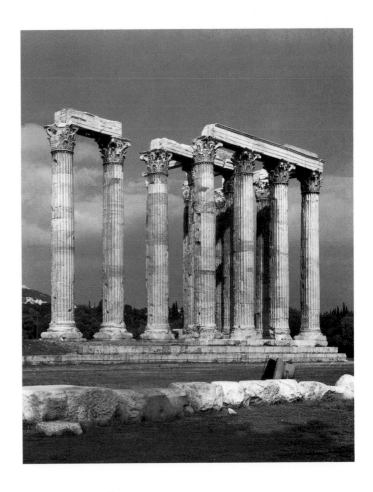

O Muse, the causes tell! What sacrilege,
Or vengeful sorrow, moved the heavenly Queen
To thrust on dangers dark and endless toil
A man whose largest honor in men's eyes
Was serving Heaven? Can gods such anger feel?

In ages gone an ancient city stood—
Carthage, a Tyrian seat, which from afar
Made front on Italy and on the mouths
Of Tiber's stream; its wealth and revenues
Were vast, and ruthless was its quest of war.
'T is said that Juno, of all lands she loved,
Most cherished this—not Samos' self so dear.
Here were her arms, her chariot; even then
A throne of power o'er nations near and far,
If Fate opposed not, 't was her darling hope
To 'stablish here; but anxiously she heard
That of the Trojan blood there was a breed
Then rising, which upon the destined day
Should utterly o'erwhelm her Tyrian towers;
A people of wide sway and conquest proud
Should compass Libya's doom;—such was the web
The Fatal Sisters spun.
                        Such was the fear
Of Saturn's daughter, who remembered well
What long and unavailing strife she waged
For her loved Greeks at Troy. Nor did she fail
To meditate th' occasions of her rage,
And cherish deep within her bosom proud
Its griefs and wrongs: the choice by Paris made;
Her scorned and slighted beauty; a whole race
Rebellious to her godhead; and Jove's smile
That beamed on eagle-ravished Ganymede.
With all these thoughts infuriate, her power
Pursued with tempests o'er the boundless main
The Trojans, though by Grecian victor spared
And fierce Achilles; so she thrust them far
From Latium; and they drifted, Heaven-impelled
Year after year, o'er many an unknown sea—
O labor vast, to found the Roman line.[4]

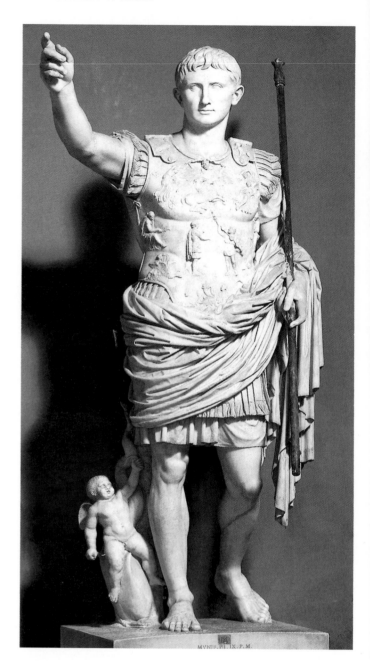

10.13 *Augustus of Primaporta*, early 1st century C.E. Marble, height 6 ft 8 ins (2.03 m). Musei Vaticani, Rome.

Throughout the literature of the Augustan period runs a moralizing Stoicism. This Greek philosophy held that God was the basis of the universe, that human souls were sparks of the divine fire, and that virtue was all-important. The most remarkable product of Stoicism in poetry was satire, which allowed writers to advocate morality with great popular appeal.

Although Constantine cleared the way for Christianity to proceed without overt persecution in the Roman Empire, St. Paul undoubtedly made it palatable to the more logical inclinations of a heritage that had its origins in Classicism.

Rooted in Judaism's post-exilic Messianic hopes, Christianity arose in what its central personage and its later believers professed was God's intervention in human history to establish a new covenant to supplant the covenant established with Moses. Jesus of Nazareth was the Christ—Messiah. The Apostle Paul, the most effective missionary of early Christianity, its first theologian, and sometimes called the "second founder" of Christianity, wrote more than one-fourth of the New Testament and translated Christianity into terms acceptable to Greek-thinking people of the Roman Empire. His theology

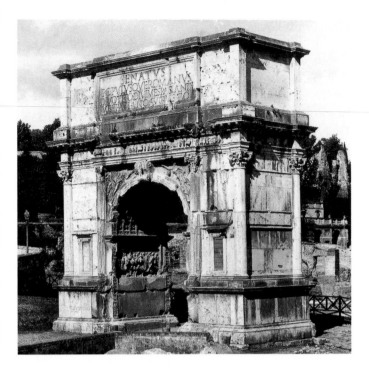

10.18 Arch of Titus, Roman Forum, Rome, 81 C.E. Marble.

10.19 (*below left*) Pantheon, Rome, c. 118–28 C.E.

10.20 (*below right*) Pantheon, plan and section.

Placed in the center of the city of Rome, the Colosseum housed gladiatorial games, including the martyrdom of Christians by turning lions loose on them as a gruesome "spectator sport." Emperors competed with their predecessors to produce the most lavish spectacles here. Originally a series of poles and ropes supported awnings to provide shade for the spectators. The space below the arena contained animal enclosures, barracks for gladiators, and machines for raising and lowering scenery.

Roman triumphal arches comprised another type of impressive architectural monument. In the Arch of Titus (Fig. **10.18**), the Roman Classical style survives in a memorial to the emperor Titus (reigned 79–81 C.E.) raised by his younger brother, Domitian (reigned 81–96 C.E.). It records accomplishments that Titus shared with his father, Vespasian (reigned 69–79 C.E.), in the conquest of Jerusalem. The sculptural reliefs on the arch show Titus riding in his chariot in triumph. The reliefs form allegories of political reverence rather than illustrations of historical events. Accompanying Titus in them we find figures such as the *Genius Senatus* and the *Genius Populi Romani*—embodiments of the spirit of the Senate, or governing body, and the general populace. This work illustrates the contrast of external appearance—the richly and delicately ornamented façade—with the massive internal

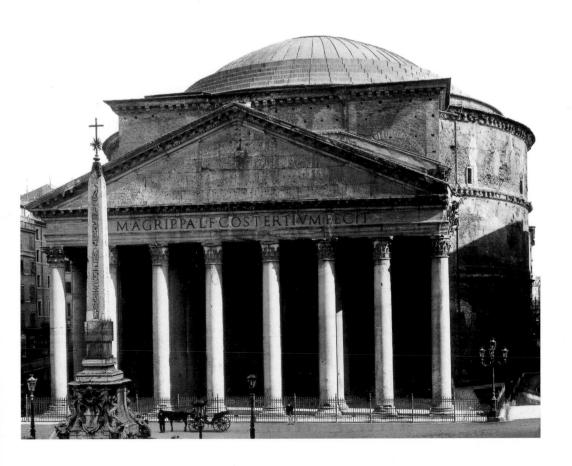

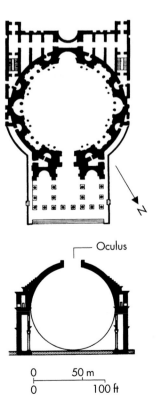

structure of the arch, a characteristic that reappeared in Renaissance architecture.

The Pantheon (Figs. **10.19** and **10.20**; see also Fig. **3.13**) fuses Roman engineering, practicality, and style in a domed temple of unprecedented scale, dedicated, as its name indicates, to all the gods.

In both plan and section the Pantheon is round. From the exterior we glimpse a cella comprising a simple, unadorned cylinder capped by a gently curving dome. The entrance is a Hellenistic porch with huge Corinthian columns. Originally it was approached by a series of steps and attached to a rectangular forecourt, so we see only part of a more complex design.

Inside (see Fig. **3.13**), the scale and detail are overwhelming. The drum and dome consist of solid monolithic concrete reinforced with bands of vitrified tile. The vertical gravity loads are collected and distributed to the drum by arches incorporated in the concrete. The wall of the 20-foot-thick drum has alternating rectangular and curved niches cut into it, thus forming a series of massive radial buttresses. Originally, statues of the gods occupied these niches carved out of the massive walls. Corinthian columns add grace and lightness to the lower level, and heavy horizontal moldings accentuate a feeling of open space made possible by the huge dome. It is 143 feet (43 m) in both diameter and height (from the floor to the *oculus* [AH-kyoo-luhs; Latin for "eye"], the round opening at the top of the dome). The circular walls supporting the dome stand 20 feet (6 m) thick and 70 feet (21 m) high. Recessed square *coffers* on the underside of the dome give an added sense of lightness and reflect the framework into which concrete was poured. Originally the ceiling was gilded to create a suggestion of the golden dome of heaven.

How could the Romans have built such a colossal structure? Historians have argued that the key lies in a novel form of concrete containing a specific kind of cement developed near Naples. The secret, however, may rest with the mysterious rings around the dome, as suggested by a Princeton University study: "Probably they perform a function similar to the buttresses of a Gothic cathedral . . . The extra weight of the rings . . . helps stabilize the lower portion of the dome: rather than functioning like a conventional dome, the Pantheon behaves like a circular array of arches, with the weight of the rings holding the end of each arch in place."[6]

Medieval Music

By around the year 500 C.E., a body of sacred—religious—music called chant, *plainchant*, or *plainsong* had developed for use in Christian worship services. (The terms, along with Gregorian chant, are commonly used as synonyms, although detailed study reveals differences.) Chant was vocal and took the form of a single melodic line (*monophony*) using notes relatively near each other on the musical scale. The haunting, undulating character of early chant possibly points to Near Eastern origins. Chants were sung in a flexible tempo with unmeasured rhythms following the natural accents of normal Latin speech. In one type of chant setting, called *syllabic*, each syllable of the chant took one note. In another, called *melismatic* (mehl-iz-MAT-ik), each syllable spread over several notes.

The selection "Kyrie" (music CD track 7) lets us sense the flavor of the undulating and ethereal melody of the melismatic type. Kyrie is one of the five parts of the *mass ordinary* (see Chapter 4). These sections, sung by the choir, alternate with the affirmation, "*Hodie Christus Resurrexit*" ("Today Christ is Risen"), sung by a soloist, which gives the piece an ABABA structure.

Plainchant is often called Gregorian chant because Pope Gregory I (540–604 C.E.) supposedly supervised the selection of melodies and texts he thought most appropriate and compiled them for church services. Although Pope Gregory did not invent plainchant, his contributions of selection and codification were apparently such that the form acquired his name.

At some time between the eighth and tenth centuries, monks in monastery choirs began to add a second melodic line to the chant. Improvised at first, the additional line paralleled the original note for note at the interval of a fourth or a fifth. We call medieval music that consists of Gregorian chant and an additional melodic line (or lines) *organum* (OHR-guh-nuhm). Between the tenth and thirteenth centuries organum reached a state of true *polyphony*. As time progressed, the independent melodies became increasingly independent of each other and differed rhythmically as well as melodically.

From the eleventh to the end of the thirteenth century, chiefly in southern France, northern Italy and northern Spain, a class of lyric poet-musicians appeared. These troubadors or troubadours (TROO-buh-dawr), as we know them, often held knightly rank and utilized a lyric poetry that had intricate meter and rhyme and usually embraced a romantic strain. One of the greatest of the troubadour poets, Bernart de Ventadorn (van-tah-DAWRN; d. 1194/5) or Bernard de Ventadour, has given us an excellent example in "Quan vei la lauzeta mover" (music CD track 5). His lyrics convey emotional power, delicacy, lyricism, and simplicity. From it we get not only the sentiments of the poem, but also the timbres and rhythms of the period. The lyrics begin by describing a lark, its wings "faced with the sun," which opens the

Profile

Hildegard of Bingen

One of the significant musical and literary figures of the time, the German nun Hildegard of Bingen (1098–1179) was educated at the Benedictine cloister of Disibodenberg and became prioress there in 1136. Having experienced visions since a child, at age forty-three she consulted her confessor, who reported the matter to the archbishop of Mainz. A theological committee confirmed the authenticity of her visions, and a monk was appointed to help her record them in writing. The finished work, *Scivias* (1141–52), consisted of twenty-six visions, prophetic, symbolic, and apocalyptic in form. About 1147 Hildegard left Disibodenberg to found a convent at Rupertsberg, where she continued to prophesy and to record her visions in writing.

She is the first composer whose biography we know. She founded a convent, where her musical plays were performed. She wrote music and texts to her songs, mostly liturgical plainchant honoring saints and the Virgin Mary. She believed that music provided the means of recapturing the original joy and beauty of paradise and that music was invented and musical instruments made in order to worship God appropriately. She wrote in the plainchant tradition of a single vocal melodic line that we just discussed. She wrote seventy-seven chants and the first musical drama in history, which she entitled "The Ritual of the Virtues."

Hildegard of Bingen wrote her music for performance by the nuns of the convent she headed. She combined all her music into a cycle called *The Symphony of the Harmony of the Heavenly Revelations*. Illustrative of Hildegard's composition, *O Viridissima Virga* (music CD track 4) moves in monophonic texture and undulating, free rhythm common to chant as we discussed it earlier. The text praises the Virgin Mary using the metaphor of the "greenest branch" (*virdissima virga*). The opening stanza salutes the Virgin: "O greenest branch, I greet you, you who budded in the winds of the questioning of the saints."

Hildegard believed that many times a day, humans fall out of sorts and lose their way. Music formed the sacred technology that could best redirect human hearts toward heaven. It could integrate mind, heart, and body and heal discord.

Hildegard's numerous other writings include a morality play, a book of saints' lives, two treatises on medicine and natural history, and extensive correspondence, in which we find further prophecies and allegorical treatises. Her lyrical poetry, gathered in *The Symphony of the Harmony of the Heavenly Revelations* (*Symphonia armonie celestium revelationum*), consists of seventy-seven poems (all with music), and these works together form a liturgical cycle.

Learn more about Hildegarde at http://www.fordham.edu/halsall/med/hildegarde.html and http://www.staff.uni-mainz.de/horst/hildegard/music/music.html.

---

heart and melts it in love. The poet ceases to know how to control himself. He loses himself, "Ladies, I give way to despair." It is a sorrowful expression of love's destructive power (according to some commentators, Bernart was a confirmed misogynist).

Romanesque Style

At the beginning of the new millennium (1001) a new and radical style in architecture emerged. The Romanesque style took hold throughout Europe in a relatively short period. Originally meaning "debased Roman," it takes its name from the Roman-style round arches and columns of its doorways and windows. The term, invented in the early nineteenth century, described medieval vaulted architecture that preceded the Gothic pointed arch. In addition to arched doorways and windows, this style characteristically has a massive, static quality—a further reflection of the barricaded mentality and lifestyle generally associated with the Middle Ages.

The Romanesque style nonetheless exemplified the power and wealth of the Church Militant and Triumphant. If the style mirrored the social and intellectual system that produced it, it also reflected a new religious fervor and a turning of the Church toward its growing flock. Romanesque churches were larger than their predecessors—Figures **10.21** and **10.22** give some impression of their scale. St.-Sernin, an example of southern French Romanesque, reflects a heavy elegance and complexity. The church plan forms a *Roman cross*, and the side aisles

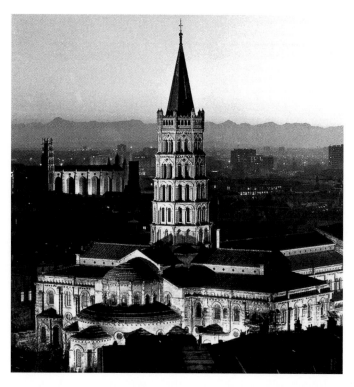

10.21 St.-Sernin, Toulouse, France, c. 1080–1120. (The top part of the tower was added in the 13th century.)

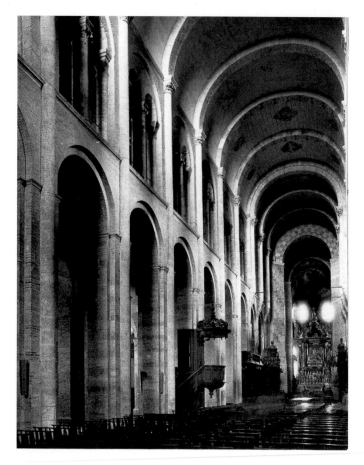

10.22 St.-Sernin, interior.

extend beyond the crossing to create an ambulatory. Here pilgrims, mostly on their way to Spain, could walk around the altar without disturbing the service.

Significantly, this church has a stone roof, whereas earlier buildings had wooden roofs. As we view the magnificent vaulted interior we wonder how the architect reconciled the conflicting forces of engineering, material, and aesthetics. Given the properties of stone and the increased force of added height, did he try to push his skills to the brink of practicality in order to create an interior of breathtaking scale? Did his efforts reflect the glory of God or the abilities of humankind?

Returning to the exterior view, we can see how some of the stress of the high tunnel vaulting was diffused. In a complex series of vaults, the tremendous weight and outward thrust of the central vault transferred to the ground, leaving a high and unencumbered central space. If we compare this structural system with that of post-and-lintel and consider the compressive and tensile properties of stone, we can easily see the superiority of the arch as a structural device for creating open space. See the Companion Website: Architecture, Romanesque and Gothic styles.

In the case of sculpture, Romanesque refers more to an era than to a style. Examples remain so diverse that if most sculptural works did not decorate Romanesque architecture, we probably could not group them under a stylistic label. However, we can draw some general conclusions. First, it is associated with Romanesque architecture. Second, it is heavy and solid. Third, its medium is usually stone. Fourth, it is monumental. These last two characteristics represent a distinct departure from previous sculptural style. Monumental stone sculpture had all but disappeared in the fifth century. Its reemergence across Europe in such a short time was remarkable, indicating at least a beginning of an outward dissemination of knowledge from the cloistered world of the monastery to the general populace—for it was applied to the exterior of the building, where it could appeal to the lay worshiper. This artistic development almost certainly led to an increase in religious zeal among the laity.

The Last Judgment tympanum (TIHM-puh-nuhm) created at Autun in France (Fig. 10.23), presents its message clearly. In the center of the composition, framed by a Roman-style arch, we see an awe-inspiring figure of Christ. Beside him appear a series of disproportional figures. The inscription of the artist, Gislebertus (zheez-lay-BAIR-tuhs), tells us that their purpose was "to let this horror appal those bound by earthly sin." The idea of death remained central to medieval thought, and devils shared the stage, gleefully pushing the damned into the flaming pit.

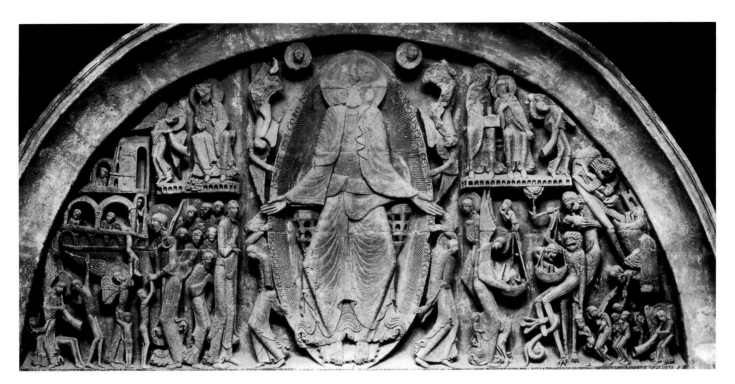

10.23 Gislebertus, Last Judgment tympanum, Autun Cathedral, France, c. 1130–5.

Medieval Literature

In the early Middle Ages, with the notable exception of the court of Charlemagne in the late eighth and early ninth centuries, the politically powerful cared little for culture, and for the most part could neither read nor write. Thanks to the efforts of the monastic community, and particularly Benedictine monks, important books and manuscripts were carefully preserved and copied.

Literature flourished in Spain, where Muslim contact with Greek scholarship led to the setting up of schools in Córdoba. Aristotle, Plato, and Euclid shared the curriculum alongside the Koran. Toledo and Seville were also centers of learning. Biblical literature, however, remained the central focus of the Middle Ages in Christian Europe.

In addition, there existed poems of traveling minstrels and court poets, popular throughout Europe. These professional storytellers produced fantastic legends and romances, such as the *Song of Roland* from France. In the *Song of Roland*, an unknown poet with fine but simple dramatic skills tells the story of a great battle between the emperor Charlemagne (742–814 C.E.) and the Saracens of Saragossa in Spain, which took place in the year 778 C.E. Charlemagne, deceived by the Saracens, draws his main army back into France, and leaves Roland with a rearguard to hold the mountain pass. The Saracens, aided by recreant Christian knights, kill Roland and his entire army after a furious struggle. Our extract describes the battle between Roland's army and the Saracens.

The Song of Roland

King Marsilion comes along a valley
with all his men, the great host he assembled;
twenty divisions, formed and numbered by the King,
helmets ablaze with gems beset in gold,
and those bright shields, those hauberks sewn with brass.
Seven thousand clarions sound the pursuit,
and the great noise resounds across that country.
Said Roland then: "Oliver, Companion, Brother,
that traitor Ganelon has sworn our deaths:
it is treason, it cannot stay hidden,
the Emperor will take his terrible revenge.
We have this battle now, it will be bitter,
no man has ever seen the like of it.
I will fight here with Durendal, this sword,
and you, my companion, with Halteclere—
we've fought with them before, in many lands!
how many battles have we won with these two!
Let no one sing a bad song of our swords." AOI.[7]

• • •

The battle is fearful and vast,
the men of France strike hard with burnished lances.
There you would have seen the great pain of warriors,
so many men dead and wounded and bleeding,
one lies face up, face down, on another.
The Saracens cannot endure it longer.
Willing and unwilling they quit the field.
The French pursue, with all their heart and strength. AOI.

• • •

Roland the Count calls out to Oliver:
"Lord, Companion, now you have to agree
the Archbishop is a good man on horse,
there's none better on earth or under heaven,
he knows his way with a lance and a spear."
The Count replies: "Right! Let us help him then."
And with these words the Franks began anew,
the blows strike hard, and the fighting is bitter;
there is a painful loss of Christian men.
To have seen them, Roland and Oliver,
these fighting men, striking down with their swords,
the Archbishop with them, striking with his lance!
One can recount the number these three killed:
it is written—in charters, in documents;
the Geste tells it: it was more than four thousand.
Through four assaults all went well with our men;
then comes the fifth, and that one crushes them.
They are all killed, all these warriors of France,
all but sixty, whom the Lord God has spared:
they will die too, but first sell themselves dear. AOI.

Count Roland sees the great loss of his men,
calls on his companion, on Oliver:
"Lord, companion, in God's name, what would you do?
All these good men you see stretched on the ground.
We can mourn for sweet France, fair land of France!
a desert now, stripped of such great vassals.
Oh King, and friend, if only you were here!
Oliver, Brother, how shall we manage it?
What shall we do to get word to the King?"
Said Oliver: "I don't see any way.
I would rather die now than hear us shamed." AOI.[8]

Another major literary accomplishment of the early Middle Ages, one with a completely different subject matter, was the German *Nibelungenlied* (nee-buh-LUHN-guhn-leed; "Song of the People of the Mists," meaning the dead). These early hero-stories of northern peoples, which took their final shape in southeast Germany c. 1200, are a rich mixture of history, magic, and myth.

The favorite Old English epic *Beowulf* (BAY-oh-wuhlf) is the earliest extant poem in a modern European language. Composed by an unknown author, it falls into separate episodes that incorporate old legends. Its three folk stories center on the hero Beowulf, and his exploits against the monster Grendel, Grendel's mother—a hideous water hag—and a fire-breathing dragon.

From the period of the Middle Ages corresponding to the Gothic style, we study momentarily the Italian poet Dante (DAHN-tay), perhaps the greatest poet of the age. The major work of his life was *The Divine Comedy*. Its description of heaven, hell, and purgatory forms a vision of the state of souls after death told in an allegory—a dramatic device in which the superficial sense accompanies a deeper or more profound meaning. It works on several levels to demonstrate the human need for spiritual illumination and guidance. On a literal level, it describes the author's fears as a sinner and his hopes for eternal life. On deeper levels, it represents the quandaries and character of medieval society faced with, for example, balancing Classicism and Christianity. Here is a sample:

The Divine Comedy
(Circle Two) Canto V
The Carnal
Dante
1265–1321

So we went down to the second ledge alone;
  a smaller circle of so much greater pain
  the voice of the damned rose in a bestial moan.

There Minos sits, grinning, grotesque, and hale.
  He examines each lost soul as it arrives
  and delivers his verdict with his coiling tail.

That is to say, when the ill-fated soul
  appears before him it confesses all,
  and that grim sorter of the dark and foul

decides which place in Hell shall be its end,
  then wraps his twitching tail about himself
  one coil for each degree it must descend.[9]

This Gothic period also witnessed the English poet Geoffrey Chaucer, a sample of whose work we read in Chapter 8, and Christine de Pisan (c. 1365–c. 1463), a prolific and versatile French poet and author whose diverse writings include numerous poems of courtly love and several works championing women. Her works include *The Book of the City of Ladies* (1405), in which she described women known for their heroism and virtue.

Decameron, by Giovanni Boccaccio (boh-KAH-choh; 1313–75), uses a *frame-tale* in which ten young people flee the plague in Florence in 1348 to sit out the danger in the countryside. To amuse themselves, they tell one hundred stories. The *Decameron* extols the virtue of humankind, proposing that to be noble, one must accept life as one finds it, without bitterness. Above all, the work suggests, one must accept the responsibility for, and consequences of, one's actions.

Despite a growing secularization in society, the mysticism of the earlier Middle Ages remained very much alive, as Joan of Arc demonstrated. We can see it clearly in the works of Marguerite Porète, Margery Kempe, Catherine of Siena, and Julian of Norwich.

Marguerite Porète (d. 1306) wrote *Le Miroir des simples âmes* (*Mirror of Simple Souls*) sometime between 1296 and 1306. Her verse and commentary form a dialogue between Love, Reason, and the Soul and suggest that the individual moves through seven stages of spiritual growth as it progresses toward union with God. Porète argues that in the last stage the soul need not concern itself with Masses, penance, sermons, fasts, or prayer. Her book was condemned in 1306 and was burned in her presence.

Two years later, accused of continuing to make copies of her book available to others, she was imprisoned in Paris, tried for heresy, and burned at the stake.

The Mirror of Simple Souls, sprawling and episodic, changes quickly from narrative to dialogue. The main speakers, personifications of "Love," "Reason," and "the Soul," discuss sublime matters as one might hear lively discussions on the street: "Oh, for god's sake, love, what are you saying?"; "Reason, you'll always be half-blind"; "Oh, yon sheep, how crude is your understanding!" This excerpt is taken from the introduction.

The Mirror of Simple Souls
Marguerite Porète

Introduction

You who would read this book,
if you indeed wish to grasp it,
think about what you say,
for it is very difficult to comprehend;
humility, who is keeper of the treasury of knowledge
and the mother of the other Virtues,
Most overtake you.

Theologians and other clerks,
you will not have the intellect for it,
no matter how brilliant your abilities,
if you do not proceed humbly
and make Love and faith, together,
cause you to rise above Reason
[since] they are the ladies of the house.
…
Humble, then your wisdom
which is based on Reason,
and place all your fidelity
in those things which are given
by Love, illuminated through Faith.
And thus you will understand this book
which makes the Soul live by love.

Gothic Style

TWO-DIMENSIONAL ART In the twelfth to the fifteenth centuries, traditional paintings in the form of frescoes and altar panels returned to prominence. The characteristics of Gothic style in two-dimensional art include the beginning of three-dimensionality in figure representation and a striving to give figures mobility and life within three-dimensional space. Space emerges as the essence of Gothic style. Gothic painters and illuminators had not mastered perspective, and their compositions do not have the spatial rationality of later works, but if we compare them with their predecessors of the earlier medieval eras, we discover that they have more or less broken free from the static, frozen two-dimensionality of earlier styles.

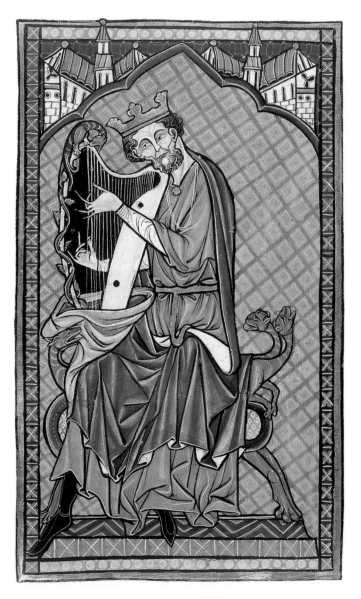

10.24 *David Harping*, from the Oscott Psalter, c. 1270. 7½ × 4¾ ins (20 × 11.1 cm). British Library, London.

Gothic painting also shows spirituality, lyricism, and a new humanism (mercy, as opposed to the irrevocable judgment of the past) with less crowding.

The Gothic style of two-dimensional art found magnificent expression in manuscript illumination. The courts of France and England produced some truly exquisite works. In *David Harping* (Fig. **10.24**) the curious proportions of the face and hands of David, and the awkward linear draping of fabric juxtaposed against the curves of the harp and chair, create a sense of unease and nervous tension. Something like carelessness exists in the layout of the background screen, and yet the repetition of the diamond forms (compare with Picasso's *Girl Before a Mirror*, Fig. **1.26**) provides a captivating counterpoint to the "X" shapes in the blue, orange, and beige border. The upward curving arcs at the top intended symmetry, and their hand-drawn quality reinforces the imprecision of the repetition of diamond shapes. A touch of realism appears in the curved harp string David plucks, and rudimentary use of highlight and shadow gives basic three-dimensionality to cloth and skin. While unbalanced in the interior space, the figure, nonetheless, does not crowd the borders.

ARCHITECTURE Gothic style in architecture took many forms, but is best exemplified in the Gothic cathedral. The cathedral, in its synthesis of intellect, spirituality, and engineering, perfectly expresses the medieval mind. Gothic architectural style developed initially in a very localized way on the Île de France in the late twelfth century and spread outward to the rest of Europe. It had died as a style in some places before it was adopted in others.

Cathedrals were church buildings whose purpose was the service of God. However, civic pride as well as spirituality inspired their construction. Various local guilds contributed their services in financing or in the actual building work, and guilds were often memorialized in special chapels and stained-glass windows. Gothic cathedrals occupied the central, often elevated, area of the town or city. Their physical centrality and context symbolized the dominance of the universal Church over human affairs, both spiritual and secular. Probably no other style has exercised such an influence across the centuries or played such a central role, even in twentieth-century Christian architecture.

We can pinpoint the beginnings of Gothic architecture between 1137 and 1144 in the rebuilding of the royal Abbey Church of St.-Denis near Paris. Ample evidence exists that the Gothic style was a physical extension of philosophy, rather than a practical response to the structural limitations of the Romanesque style—Gothic theory preceded its application. Abbot Suger, advisor to Louis VI and a driving force in the alteration of St.-Denis, held that harmony—the perfect relationship of parts—forms the source of beauty, that Light Divine is a mystic revelation of God, and that space symbolizes God's mystery. The composition of St.-Denis and subsequent Gothic churches expressed that philosophy and, as a result, Gothic architecture shows more unification than Romanesque. Both in exterior spires and the pointed arch, Gothic cathedrals use refined, upward-striving line to symbolize humanity's striving to escape from earth into the mystery of space.

The pointed arch constitutes the most easily identifiable characteristic of this style, and it represents not only a symbol of Gothic spirituality but also an engineering practicality. Compared with the round arch, it redistributes the thrust of downward force into more equal and controllable directions. The round arch places tremendous pressure on its *keystone*, which then transfers thrust outward to the sides and requires massive external buttressing, whereas the pointed arch controls thrust into a downward path through its legs. The pointed arch also makes design more flexible. Space encompassed by a round arch is limited to the radius of specific semicircles, whereas dimensions around a pointed arch can be adjusted to any desired practical and aesthetic parameters.

Engineering advances implicit in the new form made possible larger *clerestory* (KLEER-stoh-ree; see Glossary) windows (hence more light) and more slender ribbing (hence a greater emphasis on space as opposed to mass). Outside, practical and aesthetic flying buttresses carry the outward thrust of the vaults through a delicate balance of ribs, vaults, and buttresses gracefully and comfortably to the ground. The importance of stained-glass windows in Gothic cathedrals cannot be overemphasized. Now that space and light replace bulky Romanesque walls, windows take the place of frescoes in telling the story of the gospels and the saints. They carefully control light entering the sanctuary, reinforcing a marvelous sense of mystery.

With the exception of St. Paul's Cathedral in London, Salisbury (Fig. **10.25**) is the only English cathedral whose entire interior structure was built to the design of a single architect and completed without a break, in 1265. However, the cathedral took another fifty-five years to complete, and the famous spire, built between 1285 and 1310, added an additional 404 feet (123 m) to a squat tower that rose only a few feet above the nave. The spire thus became the highest in England and the second highest in Europe. Unfortunately, the piers and foundations could not carry the additional 6,400 tons, and the masons were forced to add a strong stone vault at the crossing of the nave below the tower.

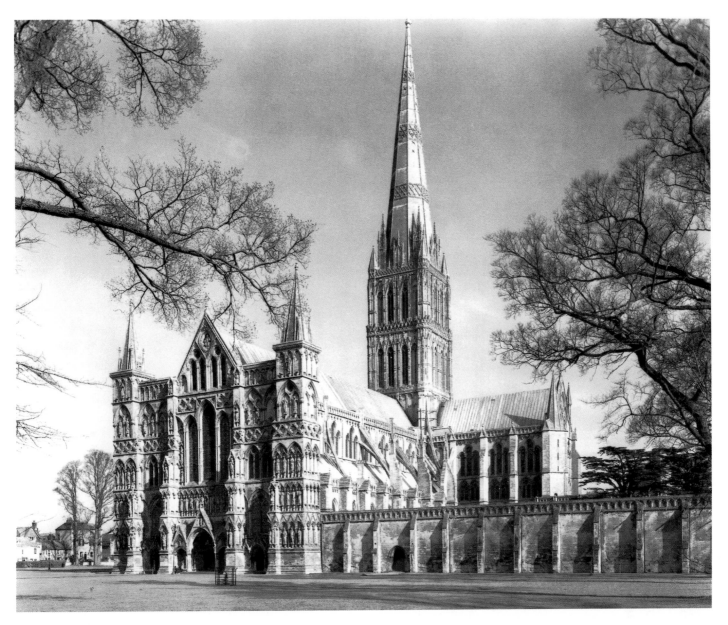

10.25 Salisbury Cathedral, England, from the southwest, begun 1220.

Compared to the soaring vertical cathedrals of France such as Notre Dame, Paris, and Amiens (see Figs. **3.33** and **3.34**), Salisbury seems long, low, and sprawling. The west front, wider than the nave, functions almost as a screen wall. Its horizontal bands of decoration emphasize the horizontal thrust of the building. The plan of the cathedral (Fig. **10.26**), with its double *transept*, retains features of the Romanesque style. The same emphasis on the horizontal appears in the interior, where the nave wall is made up of a succession of arches and supports. Watch the Companion Website: Architecture, Romanesque and Gothic styles.

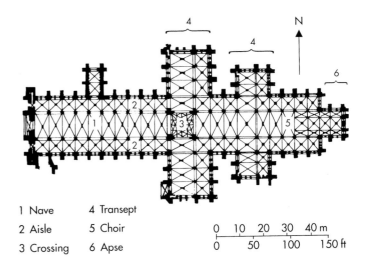

1 Nave	4 Transept
2 Aisle	5 Choir
3 Crossing	6 Apse

10.26 Salisbury Cathedral, plan.

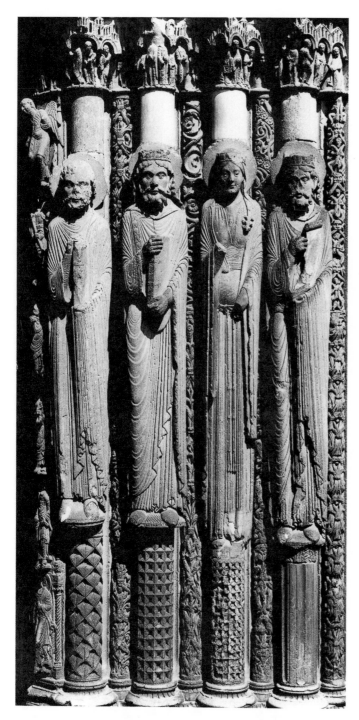

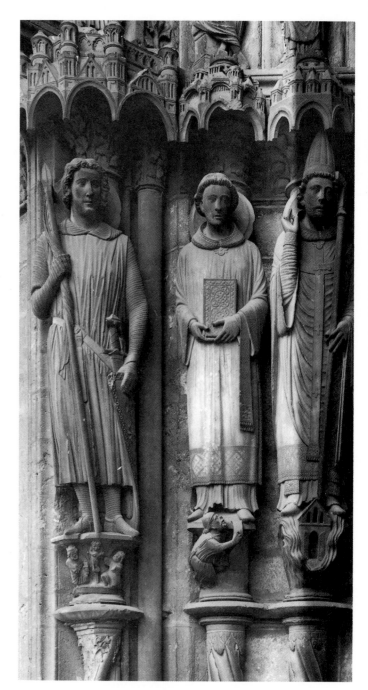

10.27 Chartres Cathedral, France, jamb statues on west portal, c. 1145–70.

10.28 Chartres Cathedral, jamb statues on south portal, c. 1215–20.

SCULPTURE Gothic sculpture again reveals the changes in attitude of the period. It portrays serenity and idealization. Like Gothic painting, it has a human quality. Conceptions of Christ as a benevolent teacher and of God as beautiful replace the vale of tears, death, and damnation typical of earlier in the Middle Ages. This style has a new order, symmetry, and clarity. Its visual images carry with distinctiveness over a distance. The figures of

Gothic sculpture stand away from their backgrounds (Fig. **10.27**).

Compositional unity changed from Early to Late Gothic. Early architectural sculpture was subordinate to the overall design of the building, but later work lost much of that integration as it gained in emotionalism (Fig. **10.28**).

The sculptures of Chartres Cathedral, which bracket nearly a century, illustrate clearly the transition from

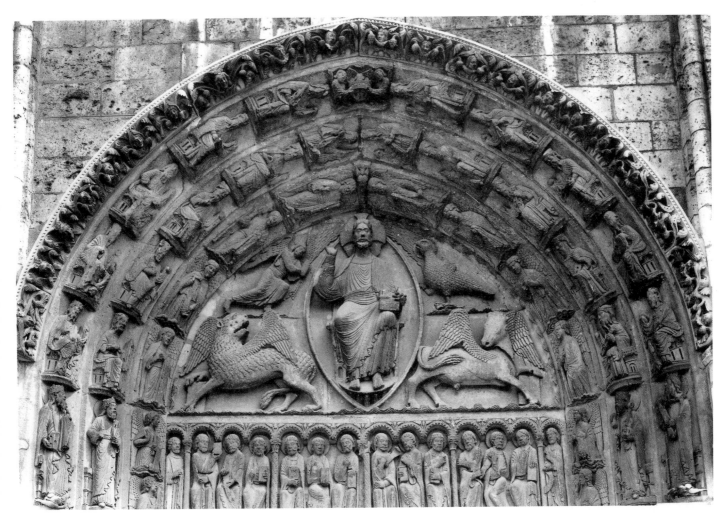

10.29 Chartres Cathedral, central tympanum of west portal, c. 1145–70.

Early to Late Gothic. The attenuated figures of Figure 10.27 display a relaxed tranquillity, idealization, and simple realism. Although an integral part of the portal columns, they emerge from them, each statue in its own space. Detail is somewhat formalized and shallow, but we now see the human figure beneath the fabric—in contrast to previous uses of fabrics as mere compositional decoration.

Lifelikeness is even more pronounced in the figures of 100 years later (Fig. 10.28). Here we can see the characteristics of the High Gothic style. Proportion appears more lifelike, and the figures have only the most tenuous connection to the building. Figures are carved in subtle S-curves rather than as rigid perpendicular columns. Fabric drapes are much more naturally depicted, with deeper and softer folds. In contrast to the idealized older saints, these figures have the features of specific individuals expressing qualities of spirituality and determination.

The content of Gothic sculpture, like most church art, was didactic, or designed to teach. Many of its lessons are

fairly straightforward and can be appreciated by anyone with a basic knowledge of the Bible. Christ appears as a ruler and judge of the universe above the main doorway of Chartres Cathedral (Fig. 10.29), with a host of symbols of the apostles and others. Also decorating the portals appear sculptures of the prophets and kings of the Old Testament, who proclaim the harmony of secular and spiritual rule by implying that the kings of France represent the spiritual descendants of biblical rulers.

Other lessons of Gothic cathedral sculpture stay more hidden. According to some scholars, specific conventions, codes, and sacred mathematics are involved. These factors relate to positioning, grouping, numbers, symmetry, and recognition of subjects. For example, the numbers three, four, and seven (often found in compositions of later periods) symbolize the Trinity, the Gospels, the sacraments, and the deadly sins. The positioning of the figures around Christ shows their relative importance—the place on his right is the most important. These codes and symbols are used on highly complex levels. All of this is consistent with the mysticism of the period, which held to strong beliefs in allegorical and hidden meanings in holy sources.

Medieval Theatre

As the Middle Ages progressed, drama became associated with the Church. Its progression from sacred to secular began with the earliest church drama, which consisted of simple elaborations and illustrations of the mass (called tropes). Later drama included bible stories (mystery plays), lives of the saints (miracle plays), and didactic allegories (morality plays).

Mystery plays take their name from the Latin word meaning "service" or "occupation" rather than from the word for "mystery." The designation probably refers to the production of religious plays by the occupational guilds of the Middle Ages rather than from the "mysteries" of revelation. Dating from the twelfth century, *The Representation of Adam* is the oldest known French mystery play. It had three parts, each with written dialogue: the Fall of Adam and Eve, the Murder of Abel, and the Prophecies of Christ. Latin instructions, which indicated scenery, costumes, and even actors' gestures, were written into the play: "Paradise shall be situated in a rather prominent place, and is to be hung all around with draperies and silk curtains."

Miracle plays presented a real or fictitious account of the life, miracles, or martyrdom of a saint. Almost all the surviving miracle plays concern either the Virgin Mary or St. Nicholas, the fourth-century bishop of Myra in Asia Minor, both of whom had active cults during the Middle Ages. The Mary plays consistently involve her coming to the aid of all who invoke her, be they worthy or wanton. The Nicholas plays are similar in content, usually chronicling the deliverance of a crusader or the conversion of a Saracen king.

Morality plays used allegorical characters such as Sloth, Gluttony, Lust, Pride, and Hatred to communicate their message. The most famous morality play (one which is still performed) is *Everyman*. In its story, Death summons Everyman to his final judgment. Everyman then seeks, as companions on his journey to judgment, the qualities (characters) of Fellowship, Kindred, Cousin, and Goods. Each refuses to join him. He finally asks Good Deeds, but Good Deeds is too weak from neglect to make the journey. Seeking advice from Knowledge, Everyman is told to do penance—an act that revives Good Deeds, who then takes up the journey with Everyman. Along the way, Five Wits also deserts him as he nears the grave. Good Deeds, however, stays with him until the end. So he is welcomed to Heaven.

THE MIDDLE EAST

Byzantine Style

A fundamental characteristic of Byzantine visual art is the concept that art has the potential to interpret as well as to represent. Byzantine art and literature were both conservative and mainly anonymous and impersonal. Much Byzantine art remains undated, and questions concerning derivation of styles lie unresolved. Yet the development of narrative Christian art, with its relatively new approach, can be dated to the mid-fifth century, and early attempts at *iconography* (the pictorialization of sacred personages) can be traced to the third and fourth centuries.

The content and purpose of Byzantine art was always religious, although the style of representation underwent numerous changes. The period of Justinian (reigned 527–65 C.E.) marks an apparently deliberate break with the past. What we now describe as the Byzantine style, with its antinaturalistic character, began to take shape in the fifth and sixth centuries, although the Classical Hellenistic tradition seems to have survived as an undercurrent. Throughout the seventh century, Classicism and decorative abstraction intermingled in Byzantine art.

By the eleventh century Byzantine style had adopted a *hierarchical* formula in wall painting and mosaics. The Church represented the kingdom of God: moving up the hierarchy, figures changed in form from human to divine. Thus placement in the composition depended upon religious, not spatial, relationships. A strictly two-dimensional, flat style appeared—elegant and decorative, and without any perspective.

Stylization and dramatic intensity characterize twelfth-century Byzantine art; approaches further intensified in the thirteenth century with turbulent movement, architectural backdrops, and elongated figures. The fourteenth century produced small-scale, crowded works with narrative content. They use confused space and irrational perspective. Figures are distorted, with small heads and feet, which produces a more intense spirituality.

We can draw a few general conclusions with regard to Byzantine art (which encompasses nearly 1,000 years of history, and, thereby, several shifts in style). First, the *content* of Byzantine art focuses on human figures. Those figures reveal three main elements: (1) *holy figures*—Christ, the Virgin Mary, the saints, and the apostles with bishops and angels portrayed in their company; (2) *the emperor*—believed divinely sanctioned by God; (3) *the Classical heritage*—images of cherubs, mythological heroes, gods and goddesses, and personifications of virtues. In addition, the *form* of Byzantine two-dimensional art increasingly reflected a consciously derived spirituality.

ARCHITECTURE The church of San Vitale in Ravenna, Italy (Figs. **10.30–10.32**), the major Justinian monument in the West, probably was built as a testament to Orthodox Christianity. The structure consists of two concentric octagons (Fig. **10.31**). The hemispherical dome rises 100 feet (30.5 m) above the inner octagon, and floods the interior with light. Eight large piers alternate with columned niches to define the central space. The *narthex* (porch) sits at an odd angle, with two possible explanations—one practical and one spiritual: (1) the narthex paralleled a street that existed when the building was under construction, and (2) it was designed in order to make worshipers reorient themselves on entering the complex arrangement of spaces, so that they would experience a notable transition from the outside world to the spiritual one.

On the second level of the *ambulatory* a special gallery reserved for women existed—a standard feature of Byzantine churches. The aisles and galleries contrast strikingly with the calm area under the dome. Clerestory light reflects off the mosaic tiles with great richness. In fact, new construction techniques in the vaulting allow for windows on every level and open the sanctuary to much more light than previously possible, or found in the West until the end of the Romanesque style and the advent of the Gothic. The view seen in Figure **10.32** reveals delicate design with symmetrical (regular) repetitive elements. Three large arches rise two stories and provide niches in which appear six (three over three) smaller arches—three symbolizes the Christian Trinity.

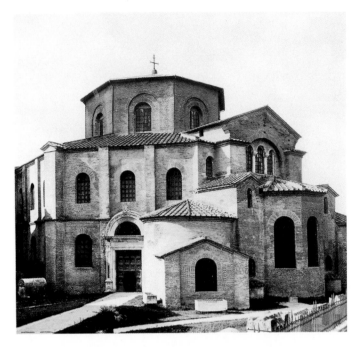

10.30 San Vitale, Ravenna, Italy, 526–47 C.E.

10.31 (*below*) San Vitale, plan and transverse section.

10.32 (*below right*) San Vitale, interior.

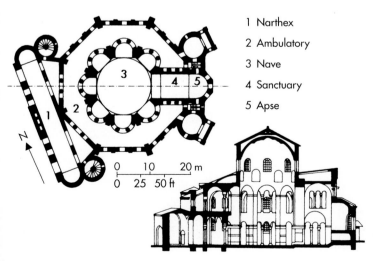

1 Narthex
2 Ambulatory
3 Nave
4 Sanctuary
5 Apse

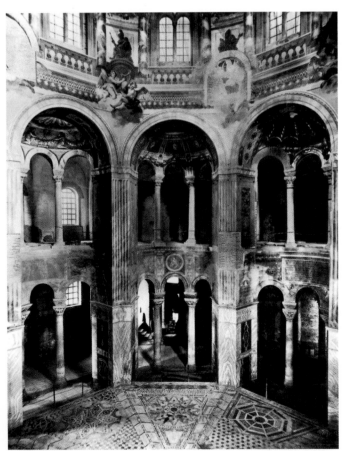

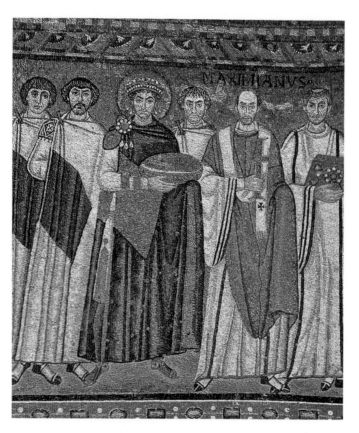

10.33 *Emperor Justinian and His Court*, San Vitale, Ravenna, c. 547 C.E. Wall mosaic.

The sanctuary itself comes alive with mosaics of the imperial court and sacred events. Figure 10.33 provides a vivid picture of the emperor. Particularly fascinating here is the stylistic contrast of two mosaics in the same church. *Abraham's Hospitality and the Sacrifice of Isaac* (Fig. 10.34) demonstrates a relaxed lifelikeness, whereas the mosaic depicting Justinian and his court demonstrates stylization, more typically Byzantine, with the figures posed rigidly and frontally rather than realistically. The emperor has a golden halo with a red border, wears a regal purple robe, and presents a golden bowl to Christ, pictured in the semidome above. The mosaics link the church to the Byzantine court, reflecting the connection of emperor to the faith, of Christianity to the state, and, indeed, the concept of the "Divine Emperor." Justinian and the empress, Theodora, are portrayed as analogous to Christ and the Virgin.

The church of San Vitale praises the emperor and Orthodox Christianity in the West; the church of Hagia Sophia (Holy Wisdom) in Constantinople (modern Istanbul) represents a crowning memorial in the East (Figs. 10.35–10.38). Characteristic of Justinian Byzantine

10.34 *(below) Abraham's Hospitality and the Sacrifice of Isaac*, San Vitale, Ravenna. Wall mosaic.

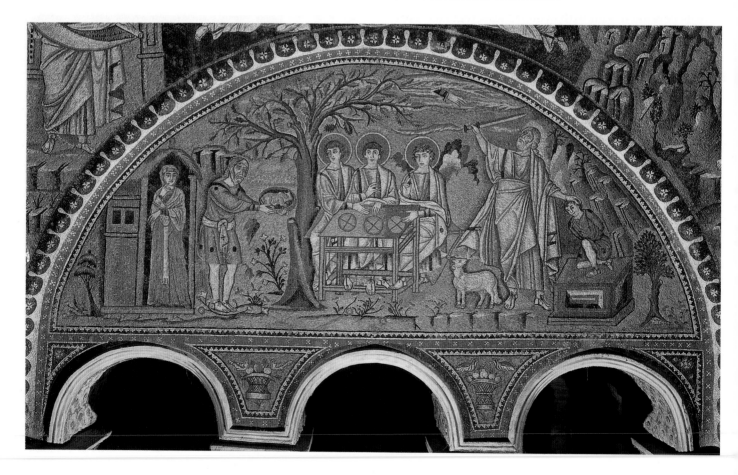

style, Hagia Sophia uses Roman vaulting techniques with Hellenistic design and geometry, resulting in a richly colored building in an Eastern antique style. Basic to the conception, the elevated central area with its domed image of heaven creates large, open, and functional spaces.

Its architect, Anthemius (am-THEEM-ee-uhs), was a natural scientist and geometer from Tralles in Asia Minor, who built the church to replace an earlier basilica. For a long time this constituted the largest church in the world, yet it was completed in only five years and ten months. It uses Byzantine masonry techniques, in which courses of brick alternate with courses of mortar equally thick as or thicker than the bricks. Given the speed of construction, this placed great weight on insufficiently dry mortar. As a result, arches buckled and buttresses had to be erected almost at once. The eastern arch and part of the dome fell in 557 C.E., after two earthquakes. No one has since constructed such a large, flat dome. The delicate proportioning of the vaults that support such great weight suggests an intense spirituality; it creates a transcendental environment, where thoughts and emotions waft to a spiritual sphere. "It seemed as if the vault of heaven were suspended above one," wrote the sixth-century Byzantine historian Procopius.

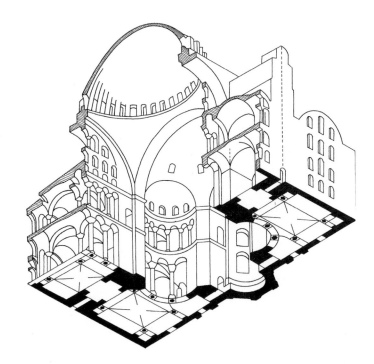

10.35 Hagia Sophia, axonometric section (bird's eye view).

10.36 (below) Anthemius of Tralles and Isidorus of Miletus, Hagia Sophia, 532–7 C.E.

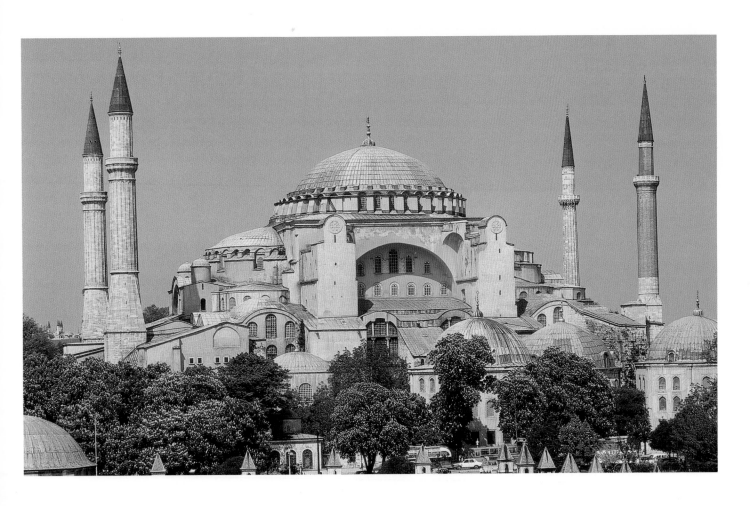

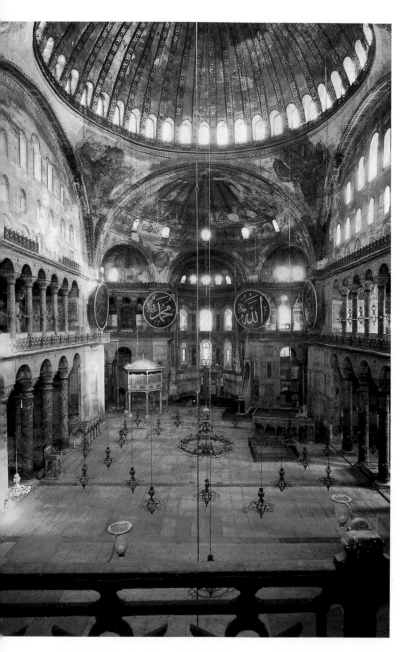

10.37 Hagia Sophia, interior.

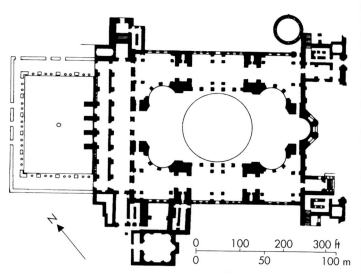

10.38 Hagia Sophia, plan.

Justinian's reign thus inaugurated the style called Byzantine, blending together previous styles—Eastern and Western—to create something new. Forms and relationships took on a spiritual essence built on Classical models but shaped uniquely. The works from the reign of Justinian synthesize the relationships between God, the State, philosophy, and art. The emperor was the absolute monarch and also defender of the faith, seen to govern by and for the will of God. Reality was therefore spiritualized and was reflected in works of art that depicted earthly habitation in a *hieratic* ("holy" or "sacred") style.

MOSAICS AND IVORIES By about the year 500 C.E. the *hieratic* style of Byzantine art presented formalized, almost rigid depictions intended not so much to represent people as to inspire reverence and meditation (see Fig. **10.33**). (Do not confuse this style with the hierarchical formula discussed earlier. The hierarchical arrangement dealt with figure placement top to bottom. Hieratic style deals with figure proportion.) One formula of the hieratic style ordained that an individual should measure nine heads (seven heads would be our modern measurement). The hairline had to be a nose's length above the forehead. "If the man is naked, four noses' lengths are needed for half his width." By the thirteenth century, mosaics returned to more lifelike depictions, but still with a clear sense of spirituality.

Ivory, traditionally a luxury material, stayed consistently popular in Byzantium. Many, but not all, Byzantine ivories are *diptychs* (DIHP-tick)—on two hinged panels. Ivories from the tenth century show delicate elegance and high finish. The Harbaville Triptych (Fig. **10.39**) has been described as the most beautiful of all Byzantine ivories. Called a *triptych* because of its three sections (*tri*), it was probably intended as a portable altar or shrine. Each of the two wings folded shut across the center panel. In the top center Christ is enthroned and flanked by John the Baptist and the Virgin Mary. They plead for mercy on behalf of all humanity. Five of the apostles appear below. An ornament, repeated with the addition of rosettes at the bottom border and three heads in the top border, divides the two *registers* (recall Sumerian and Egyptian art) of the central panel. On either side of Christ's head appear medallions depicting angels holding the symbols of the sun and the moon. The Harbaville Triptych exhibits the

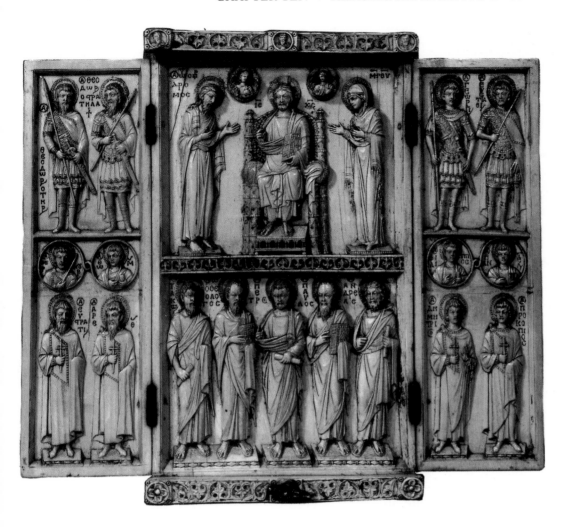

10.39 *The Harbaville Triptych*, interior, late 10th century. Ivory, height 9½ ins (24 cm); width of central panel 5⅜ ins (14 cm). Louvre, Paris.

frontal pose, formality, solemnity, and slight elongation of form that typify the Byzantine hieratic style. Here it produces a sense of detachment from the world and evokes a deep spirituality. Byzantium remained the stronghold of Orthodox Christianity until the middle of the fifteenth century when it fell to the forces of Islam.

Islamic Art

TWO-DIMENSIONAL ART Theoretically, Islam prohibits all human and animal figures from art because of the Scriptural command against making images. In reality, images are widespread: the only prohibition seems to have been on objects intended for public display. In the courts of the caliphs, images of living things were commonplace. They were considered harmless if they did not cast a shadow, were small in scale, or appeared on everyday objects.

In the early years of Islam, there seems to have been some continuity in the visual arts. The Arabs obtained manuscripts from Byzantium and were tremendously interested in Greek science. A plethora of illustrated texts translated into Arabic resulted. Typical of this type of Arab illustration is a pen-and-ink sketch perhaps from a Mesopotamian manuscript of the fourteenth century (Fig. **10.40**). The drawing has a clear presentation, with many of the strokes seeming to act as accents. The lines flow freely in subtle curving movements to establish a comfortable rhythm across the page. In very simple line, the artist is able to capture human character, thus showing strong observational ability. The witty flavor of the drawing goes far beyond mere illustration.

LITERATURE Probably the most familiar Islamic literature, besides the Qur'an, consists of a collection of tales called *The Arabian Nights* or *The Thousand and One Nights*. These accumulated during the Middle Ages, and as early as the tenth century they formed part of the oral traditions of Islam in the Near East. Over the years more tales were added, including a unifying device called a *frame-tale*, which places all of the separate stories within a large framework. By around 1450 the work had assumed its final form.

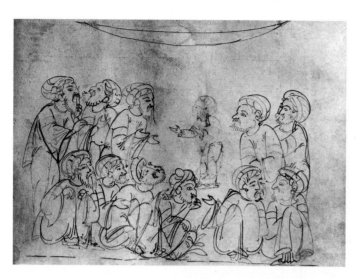

10.40 Al-Qasim ibn 'Ali al-Hariri, *Maqamat al-Hariri* (a book of stories), 1323. Mesopotamian manuscript. British Library, London (Oriental Collection).

The frame-tale recounts the story of a jealous Sultan who, convinced that all women were unfaithful, married a new wife each evening and put her to death the following morning. A new bride, Shaharazad, gained a reprieve by beginning a story on her wedding night and artfully maintaining the Sultan's curiosity. She gained a reprieve for 1,001 nights—during which time she produced three male heirs. After this the Sultan abandoned his original practice. The tales capture the spirit of Islamic life, its exotic setting, and its sensuality, as well as reflecting a moral code.

The Qur'an (Arabic, "the Recital") comprises the sacred scripture of Islam, and Muslims regard it as the infallible Word of God: a flawless record of an eternal tablet preserved in Heaven, revealed over a period of twenty years to the Prophet Muhammad. At first, Muhammad's followers memorized the intermittent revelations and recited them in ritual prayers. Although some verses were written down in Muhammad's lifetime, they did not achieve their present, authoritative, form until the reign of the third caliph. For the Muslim community, the Qur'an forms the ultimate source of knowledge and continuing inspiration for life.

Consisting of 114 *surahs* or chapters of unequal length, the entire Qur'an has a length somewhat shorter than the Christian New Testament. The earliest surahs belong to the Meccan period and comprise the shortest chapters. They exhibit a dynamic rhymed prose. Later surahs are longer and more prosaic. In the current version of the Qur'an, the arrangement falls according to length, with the shortest surahs placed last in the text. In essence, the current order reverses the chronological order of the original text. The early surahs issue a call to moral and reli-gious obedience in view of the coming Day of Judgment. The later, Medina surahs give directions for the establishment of a social order agreeable to the moral life called for by God. The Qur'an presents a forceful vision of a single, all-powerful, and merciful God. Muslims believe it to comprise God's final revelation, which is given in a vivid language capable of being fully understood only in the original Arabic.

The Qur'an places God as the absolute creator and sustainer of an ordered universe that mirrors his absolute power, wisdom, and authority. It details the consequences of God's ultimate judgment on each individual: the joys of the gardens of Paradise and the punishment and horrors of Hell.

Interpreting the Qur'an properly remains central to all schools of Islamic thought. *Tafsir*, a special branch of learning, focuses on the Qur'an. Translations have traditionally been forbidden, and any translations are still viewed as paraphrases to assist in understanding the actual scripture. We include below an excerpt from *Surah 4* ("Women"), which addresses issues pertinent to Arabic society at the time of Muhammad: that of a code of conduct protecting the legal rights of women and assuring care for the poor and unfortunate.

Surah 4, 1–4
"The Women"

In the name of Allah, the Beneficent, the Merciful.

4.1: O people! be careful of (your duty to) your Lord, Who created you from a single being and created its mate of the same (kind) and spread from these two, many men and women; and be careful of (your duty to) Allah, by Whom you demand one of another (your rights), and (to) the ties of relationship; surely Allah ever watches over you.

4.2: And give to the orphans their property, and do not substitute worthless (things) for (their) good (ones), and do not devour their property (as an addition) to your own property; this is surely a great crime.

4.3: And if you fear that you cannot act equitably towards orphans, then marry such women as seem good to you, two and three and four; but if you fear that you will not do justice (between them), then (marry) only one or what your right hands possess; this is more proper, that you may not deviate from the right course.

4.4: And give women their dowries as a free gift; but if they of themselves be pleased to give up to you a portion of it, then eat it with enjoyment and with wholesome result.

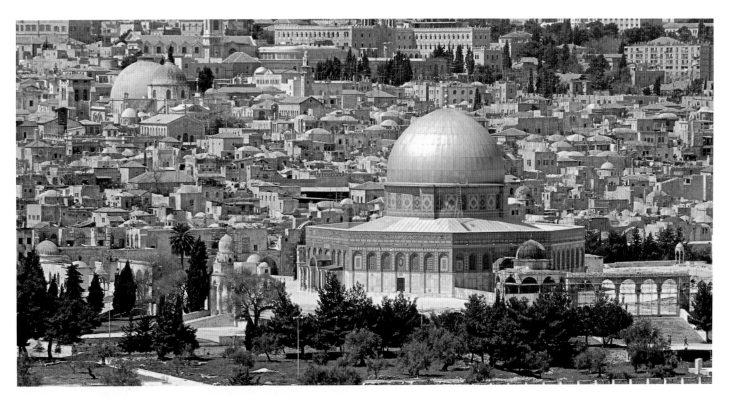

10.41 Dome of the Rock, Jerusalem, late 7th century C.E.

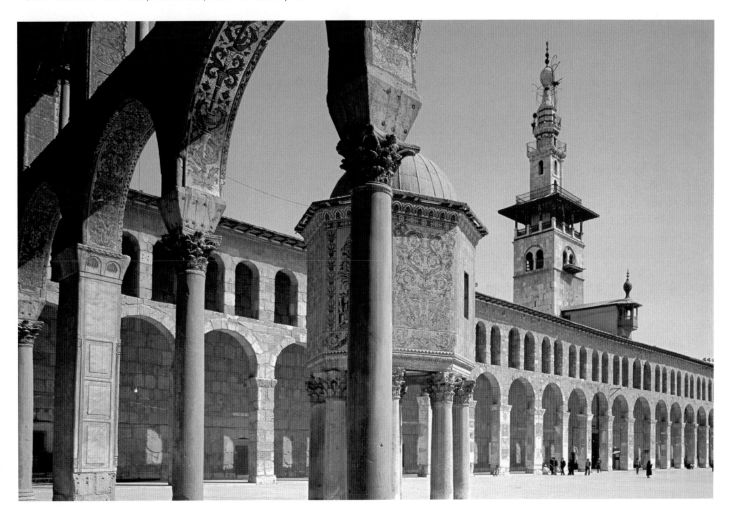

10.42 Great Mosque, Damascus, Syria, courtyard looking west, c. 715 C.E.

ISLAMIC STYLE IN ARCHITECTURE Work on the first major example of Islamic architecture—the Dome of the Rock in Jerusalem (Fig. **10.41**)—was begun in 685 C.E. by Islamic emperors who were direct descendants of the Prophet's companions. Built near the site of the Temple of Solomon (see p. 217), it was designed as a special holy place—not an ordinary mosque. Its location is revered by Jews as the tomb of Adam and the place where Abraham prepared to sacrifice Isaac. According to Muslim tradition, it also is the place from which Muhammad ascended into heaven. Written accounts suggest its purpose was to overshadow a Christian church of similar construction on the other side of Jerusalem—the Holy Sepulchre. Caliph Abd al-Malik wanted a monument that would outshine the Christian churches of the area, and, perhaps, the Ka'ba in Mecca.

The Dome of the Rock is shaped as an octagon, and inside it contains two concentric ambulatories (walkways) surrounding a central space capped by the dome. The exterior was later decorated with the glazed blue tiles that give the façade its dazzling appearance; the interior glitters with gold, glass, and mother-of-pearl multicolored mosaics.

Undoubtedly, the Dome of the Rock was intended to speak to Christians as well as Muslims, distracting the latter from the splendor of Christian churches. Inside the mosque is an inscription: "The Messiah Jesus Son of Mary is only an apostle of God, and His Word which he conveyed into Mary, and a Spirit proceeding from Him. Believe, therefore in God and his apostles and say not 'Three.' It will be better for you. God is only one God. Far be it from his glory that He should have a son."

Another excellent example of Islamic architecture is the Great Mosque in Damascus, Syria (Fig. **10.42**). When the Muslims captured Damascus in 635 C.E., they adapted the precinct of a pagan temple, which had meanwhile been converted into a Christian church, into an open-air mosque. Seventy years later, Caliph al-Walid demolished the church and set about building Islam's largest mosque. The only feature of the original buildings left standing was the Roman wall, though the four original towers were metamorphosed into the first minarets, from which the faithful were called to prayer. Unfortunately, the centuries have not been kind to the Great Mosque. Sacked a number of times, the mosque lost much of the splendor of its lavish decorations. However, some of its grandeur remains in the arcaded courtyard, with fine, gold-inlaid detailing visible in the returns of the arches (Fig. **10.42**). Inside, colorful mosaics (Fig. **10.43**) express great subtlety of detail and texture. These works rank among the most accomplished of mosaics and were probably produced by Byzantine artisans.

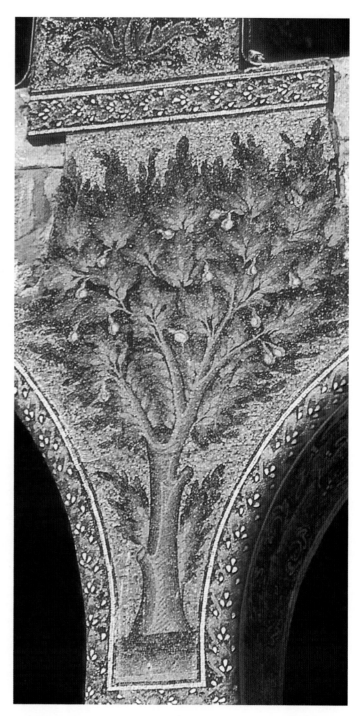

10.43 Great Mosque, Damascus, details of mosaic decoration, c. 715 C.E.

ASIA

Chinese Art

SCULPTURE By the third century B.C.E., the Chinese had reached a high level of technical accomplishment in the field of sculpture. They had developed scientific manufacturing processes for pottery and knew how to control firing temperatures.

We know this because Emperor Qin Shihuangdi, who reigned for almost the whole of the Qin Dynasty (221–206 B.C.E.), spent most of his time preparing his palace and mausoleum. In March 1974, during the digging of a well at Lintong, some life-size and lifelike pottery figures were unearthed. Pits were found containing terracotta warriors, horses, and bronze chariots. In one vault alone (measuring 760 × 238 feet [231 × 72 m]), 6,000 terracotta warriors and horses were found. A total of three vaults contain over 8,000 figures (Fig. 10.44).

The warriors have various expressions. Some are dignified; others, vigorous; some are cheerful; others, debonair. Some appear lost in brooding, while still others look witty and handsome. Each figure displays an almost knowable character, as if some living form had been miraculously frozen in time through the consummate skill of the artists. Precise detailing reveals temperament, rank, and home province of these warriors. Common soldiers, for example, appear in short battle tunics or laceless armored suits. Their heads are covered by small round caps, and they wear square-toed sandals on their feet.

The horses appear well bred, and all look muscular and vigorous. Their proportions are perfect (Fig. 10.45) and even their expressions indicate the artists' strong insight, understanding, and skill. The eyes stare ahead intensely and the necks stretch in graceful curvature, reflecting energy and power. The hardness of the figures and their almost flaw-free condition testify to the superior clay-making technology (manipulation; see Chapter 2) of the Qin Dynasty.

The demand for Buddhist images in the sixth century C.E. made the period one of significant sculptural output. Probably the one great age of Chinese sculpture, it shows deep spirituality, reflecting stiff, austere abstraction (Fig. 10.46). In this stone carving of Guanyin, the Goddess of Mercy, we see a female Bodhisattva (bah-dih-SAHT-vah), or person who is going to attain enlightenment. The gentle curving flow of line from all points in the image directs the eye upward to the serene face. Repetition of deep curves unifies the composition, giving it grace, harmony, and softness. In this later feminine form, the Bodhisattva stays in this world to help others achieve salvation before passing onto *nirvana* herself; she becomes a gentle and compassionate protectress.

ARCHITECTURE Very little has survived of early Chinese architecture, partly because most of it was constructed of wood, and partly because a mass destruction of Buddhist monasteries, temples, and shrines occurred in 845 C.E. We can capture a sense of its style, however, by examining a reconstruction drawing of the main hall of the ninth-century Fo-kuang-ssu (Monastery of the Buddha's Halo) on

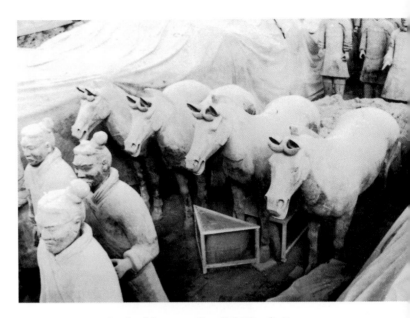

10.44 Warriors, Tomb of Emperor Qin Shihuangdi, Lintong, near Xi'an (Shaanxi), China, c. 221–209 B.C.E. (Qin Dynasty). Terracotta, life-size figures.

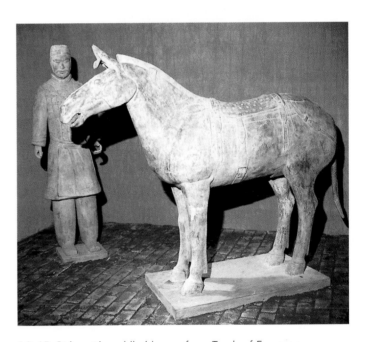

10.45 Rider with saddled horse, from Tomb of Emperor Qin Shihuangdi, Lintong. Terracotta, life-size.

Mount Wu-t'ai (Fig. 10.47). Dating to the Tang Dynasty (618–906 C.E.), this represents China's oldest wooden building. The curved roof lines, deep overhangs, and ornate decoration represent Asian style.

Also typical is the Liurong Temple or Six Banyan Pagoda of Guangzhou (Fig. 10.48). Built in its final form in approximately 989 C.E., in the early years of the Song Dynasty (960–1279), the pagoda rises 188 feet (57 m) in nine exterior stories. On the inside it contains seventeen stories. Richly painted in red, green, gold, and white, it was at one time called the Flowery Pagoda. The current name comes from the famous writer and calligrapher Su Dong-po, who visited it in 1100 and admired the six banyan trees surrounding it. The upward curving lines of the eaves and the colorful glazed roof tiles became characteristic of Chinese architecture from this time onward.

PAINTING Our quick survey gives us two examples of Chinese painting style in the period covered by this chapter separated by more than one thousand years. In the first, from the Han Dynasty (206 B.C.E.–220 C.E.), we find movement and lively depictions of, for example, mythical beings, dragons, and rabbits: the painted tile in Figure 10.49 exhibits skillfully rendered figures whose brushstroke suggests liveliness and movement. They appear in three-quarter poses, which gives the painting a sense of depth and action, and the diagonal sweep of line adds to the sense of motion. The poses of the personages suggest

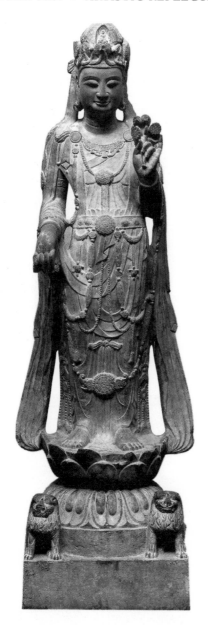

10.46 *Guanyin, The Bodhisattva of Compassion*, from the Ku Shihto Ssu monastery, Sion, Shensi Province, China (Northern Chou-sui Dynasty). Limestone, height 6⅜ ins (16.2 cm).

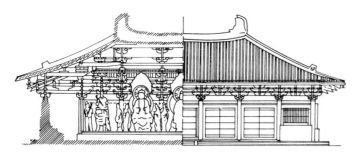

10.47 Fo-kuang-ssu (Monastery of the Buddha's Halo), Mount Wu-t'ai, northern Shansi, China, front elevation and cross section of main hall, 9th century (Tang Dynasty).

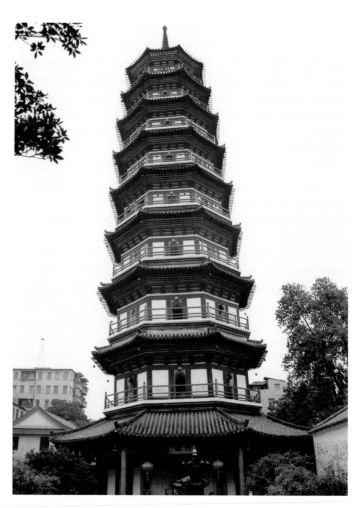

10.48 Liurong Temple (Six Banyan Pagoda), Guangzhou, China, c. 989 C.E. (Song Dynasty).

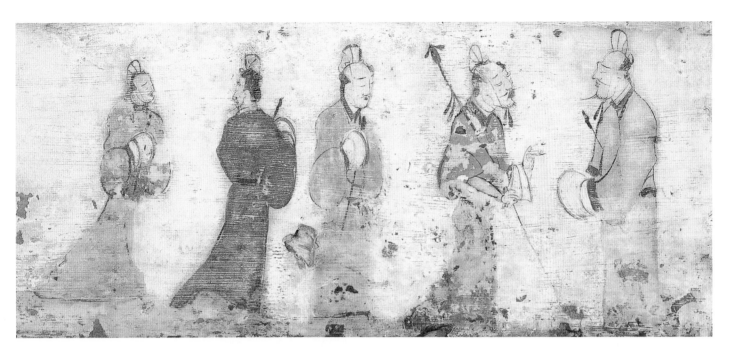

10.49 Lintel and pediment of tomb, from China, 1st century B.C.E. (Han Dynasty). Gray earthenware; hollow tiles painted in ink and colors on a whitewashed ground, 29 × 80½ ins (73.8 × 204.7 cm). Museum of Fine Arts, Boston (Denman Waldo Ross Collection, and Gift of C. T. Loo).

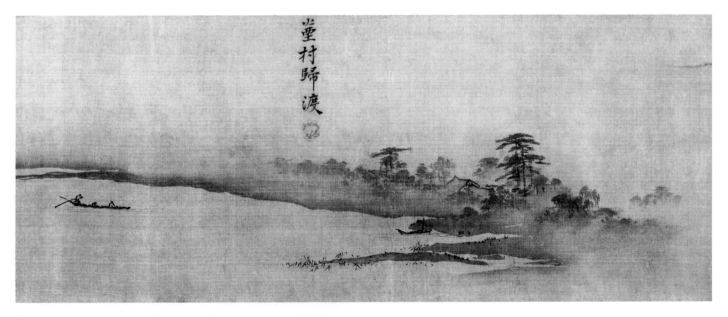

10.50 Xia Gui, *Twelve Views from a Thatched Cottage* (detail), c. 1200–30. Handscroll, ink on silk, height 11 ins (28 cm). Nelson Atkins Museum of Art, Kansas City (Purchase: Nelson Trust).

individual character—the psychology of the figure portrayed. Although the use of pose and direction reflects a sophisticated approach and technique, the figures stand on the same baseline, with no sense of placement in deeper space.

Since the Song Dynasty of the thirteenth century, the Chinese have regarded painting as their greatest art. The basic conventions were established then and painting reached a height that has probably never been surpassed. Buddhist influence remained strong, although secular art grew in prominence too. Secular painting emphasized landscapes, as opposed to human events and images. Figure 10.50, in a soft and atmospheric style, forms part of a larger scroll entitled *Twelve Views from a Thatched*

Cottage by Xia Gui (c. 1180–1230). This work depicts a mountain range and a lake with boats. Each of the sections of the scroll carries an inscription—for example, "Distant Mountains and Wild Geese." Taken as a whole, the scroll reveals time as well as space as it moves from daylight to dusk.

Subtle artistic technique merges soft washes with firm brushstrokes, and images move from sharp focus to indistinct suggestion utilizing atmospheric perspective. The detailing gives the subject a degree of lifelikeness, but it goes beyond that to give a "sense" of nature. The images are impressions rather than depictions. The artist selects details carefully and concentrates on essences.

In the eleventh century, color mattered little. Most Chinese painting was monochromatic. For the Chinese, landscapes represent nature as a whole: each small detail symbolizes the larger universe. In this painting an overriding mysticism emerges, probably reflecting the Daoist belief system.

Japanese Art

ARCHITECTURE Buddhism made a significant impact on Japan during the Jogan or Early Heian (hy-ahn) period (794–897). Esoteric Buddhism, or the Mikkyo, emphasized secrecy and mystery, and we can see its precepts in a monastery (Fig. **10.51**) in a remote part of Nara prefecture. The secluded location of Muroji (-ji means "temple") removes the temple from "distractions and corruptions." The design of the *kondo* (kahn-doh), or main hall, is asymmetrical, with a close relationship to its context—the natural site. Rising above a terrace and surrounded on the upper level by a porch, it has an almost modern contextual relationship. Its shingled roof sets it apart from the tiled-roof structures of Chinese influence (see Figs. **10.47** and **10.48**).

PAINTING AND SCULPTURE In the thirteenth century, Japanese sculpture turned to a simple style that stressed strength and virility. A series of civil wars had led to the military dictatorship of the shoguns and their samurai (warriors) and to a broadly based feudal regime. This reflected in the works of sculptors such as Unkei, whose demonic and colossal wooden Buddhist deities (Fig. **10.52**) guard the entrance to the Todaiji at Nara, one-time capital of Japan. The statue suggests power, expressed in the fierce facial expression and forbidding hand, and simplicity, through the clean lines of the swirling fabrics.

In the late thirteenth century, Japanese painting expanded its subject matter from individual portraiture to include landscape (Fig. **10.53**). The Kumano Mandala

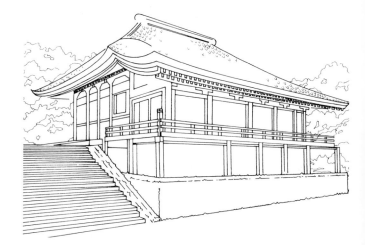

10.51 Kondo of Muroji, Nara prefecture, Japan, 9th century (Early Heian period).

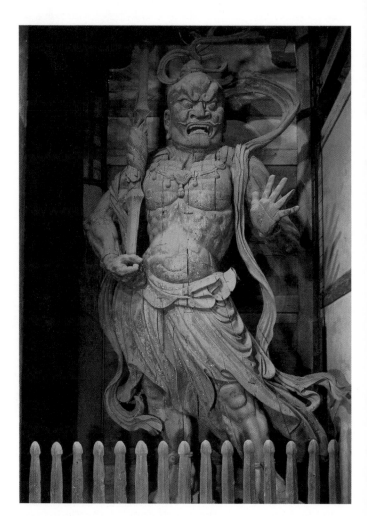

10.52 Unkei, *Nio*, Todaiji, Nara, 1203. Wood, height 26 ft 6 ins (8 m).

draws into close proximity three Shinto shrines geographically many miles apart. Above them appear *mandalas* (MAN-dah-lah) containing Buddhist deities. A *man-*

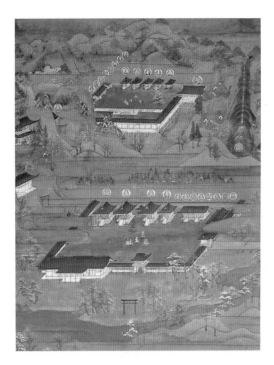

10.53 Kumano Mandala, c. 1300 (Kamakura period). Color on silk. Cleveland Museum of Art (John L. Severance Fund).

dala is a circular diagram of the cosmos used for meditation, ceremonial incantation, or magic. The presence of Buddhist deities in portrayals of Shinto shrines attests to the dominance of Buddhism at the time. Around and between the depiction of the shrines appears a delicately rendered landscape. The presentational style creates a shorthand of ideas and a beautiful design of delicate and active line, holding the entire work together and leading the eye from section to section. Notice that although the buildings seem to represent three dimensions, no convergence of lines toward vanishing points, as in true linear perspective, appears (see Chapter 1).

In contrast to the Kumano Mandala, with its mysticism, the Heiji Monogatari scroll (Fig. 10.54) depicts a dramatic fire scene replete with crowds and emotion. As the Sanjo Palace burns, figures and flames explode from the right border to the left. The artist creates a masterful stylized scene so tightly controlled compositionally that it could be a study for any painter of any age. The forceful diagonals and the powerful, horizontal, dark thrust of the palace roof meet to form an arrow shooting across the paper. In a design as intricate and powerful as any Baroque painting (see p. 294), this work builds detailed individual pieces, stimulating in their own right, into a large and complicated unity of contrasting colors, values, and textures. Straight and curved lines combine to create further conflict and dramatic tension.

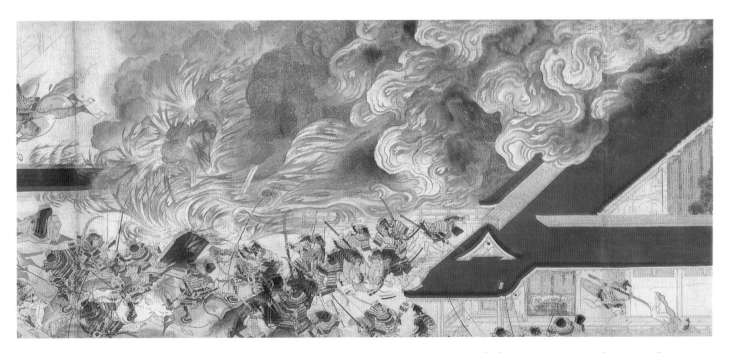

10.54 *Night Attack on the Sanjo Palace*, from the Heiji Monogatari scroll, detail, second half of 13th century (Kamakura period). Handscroll, ink and colors on paper, 16¼ ins × 23 ft (41.3 cm × 7 m). Museum of Fine Arts, Boston (Fenollosa-Weld Collection; © 2002 Museum of Fine Arts, Boston).

THEATRE AND LITERATURE Japan's two great dramatic forms, Noh and the later Kabuki (kah-BOO-kee; see p. 316), both originated from religious rituals dating to the late eighth and early ninth centuries, when drama functioned as a teaching tool for Buddhist monks. The dramatizing of religious ritual in Buddhism slowly grew more and more secularized, found its way out of the sanctuary, and gained in popularity, much as did miracle, mystery, and morality plays in medieval Europe (see p. 252). The results emerged as dramatic forms performed in markets as well as places of worship.

Noh drama matured during the fourteenth century into an original literary and performing art. Highly conventionalized, it emerged from two sources: simple dramas based on symbolic dances performed to music at the imperial court, and mimes popular with the common people. Its final form is credited to a Shinto priest named Kan'ami (1333–84) and his son Seami (1363–1443). They also founded one of the hereditary lines of Noh performers, the Kanze (kahn-zay), who still perform today.

Noh drama is performed on a simple, almost bare stage and, like early Classical Greek tragedy, uses only two actors. Also, as in Classical Greek drama, the actors wear elaborate masks and costumes, and a chorus functions as a narrator. Actors chant highly poetic dialogue to an orchestral accompaniment. All their actions suggest rather than depict, which gives the drama its stylization and conventionality; symbolism and restraint characterize both acting and staging.

Subjects range from stories of Shinto gods to Buddhist secular history. The tone of Noh plays tends toward seriousness—appealing to the intellect—with a focus on the spirit of some historical person who wishes for salvation but is tied to this earth by worldly desires. The plays tend to be short, and an evening's performance encompasses several, interspersed with comic burlesques called Kyogen ("Crazy Words").

In general, Noh plays fall into five types, according to subject: (1) gods; (2) warriors; (3) women; (4) spirits or mad persons; and (5) demons. Traditionally, an evening's performance included all five types, performed in the order noted.

At a time falling between two European literary works studied later in this chapter, the *Song of Roland* (see p. 245) and Dante's *Divine Comedy* (see p. 246) a significant writer arose in Japan: Lady Murasaki Shikibu (born c. 978 C.E.), part of a minor branch of a powerful family. Her name came partly from the title of the office her father held (Shikibu) and partly from a character in her book (Murasaki). Influenced by her father's strong scholarly abilities, although hampered by her expected role as a femininely ignorant woman, she developed tremendous

knowledge but needed to hide it because it exceeded what a woman properly should know. After the death of her husband, Lady Murasaki became an attendant to the Empress Akiko, tutoring her in Chinese and reading Chinese poetry to her. Lady Murasaki kept a detailed diary of customs, court dress, and her own thoughts. Perhaps at the bequest of the Empress for something more entertaining than traditional stories, Lady Murasaki wrote the novel *The Tale of Genji*. The task took her perhaps as many as twenty years to complete.

The Tale of Genji, an intricate and detailed description of court life, tells the story of the son of the Emperor by his favorite consort. The Emperor tries to protect his son, who has no backing at court, by making him a Genji, a member of the nonroyal clan—one who cannot be Emperor and, thus, poses no threat to anyone. Genji turns into the most handsome, talented, and charming person at court ("the shining Genji"). The book works its way through Genji's life. The story continues into the next generation after Genji's death.

The book modeled its characters on actual persons at court and made it a particularly biting criticism. It reveals tremendous detail about the life of Heian Japan.

AFRICA

Nok Style

During the first millennium B.C.E., on the Jos plateau of northern Nigeria, a nonliterate culture of farmers entered the Iron Age and developed an accomplished artistic style. Named the "Nok style" after the village of Nok where the first sculptures were discovered, it appeared in terracotta figures comparable to the Qin Dynasty warriors of China (see Fig. **10.44**). The sculptures had bold design; some represent animals realistically and others portray life-sized human heads (Fig. **10.55**). Although stylized, for example, with segmented lower eyelids, each work reveals individualized character. Facial expressions and hair styles differ and "it is this unusual combination of human individuality and artistic stylization which gives them their peculiar power."[10] These heads represent probably portraits of ancestors of the ruling class. The technique and medium of execution seem to have been chosen to ensure permanence, for magical rather than artistic reasons. The Nok style appears to have influenced several West African styles.

Igbo-Ukwu Style

The level of skill achieved by the ninth and tenth centuries C.E. appears in a ritual war pot from the village of

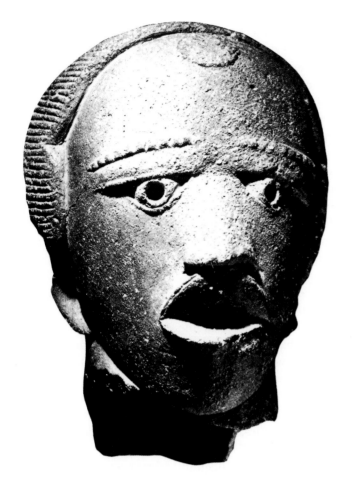

10.55 Head from Jemaa, Nigeria, c. 400 B.C.E. Terracotta, height 10 ins (25 cm). National Museum, Lagos.

come to life. The full mouth and expressive eyes suggest extreme sensitivity. In fact, the depiction has such sensitivity that we seem fully capable of reading this individual's mood. The high brow and minutely detailed headdress complete this portrait and bring to its surface the innermost qualities of the individual in almost photographic lifelikeness.

Djenne Style

At Djenne, in Mali, comes a small, fourteenth-century terracotta figure of a bearded male (Fig. 10.57). This example of manipulation technique (see Chapter 2) reveals a striking and stylized thrusting chin. The lower and upper jaws protrude grotesquely from a platelike appendage—probably a stylized beard—where the jaw would normally be. Lightly incised into the conical surface of the head are the man's eyes. The torso's proportions pinch inward, as if compressed by the undetached arms, and details of what could be armor show careful technique. The sophisticated rendering of the entire form suggests that the artist intended to reflect internal psychological or spiritual qualities.

Igbo-Ukwu in eastern Nigeria (see Fig. 0.5). Cast using the *cire-perdue* or lost-wax process (see Chapter 2), this leaded bronze artifact is amazing in its virtuosity. The graceful design of the pot's curved lines and flaring base in itself is exquisite, but the addition of a delicate and detailed rope overlay reflects sophistication of both technique and vision.

Ife Style

A link between the Nok culture and that of Ife, also in Nigeria, may have existed to draw these two cultures together in their art across the centuries. Ife formed an important cultural and religious center in the southwest. The accomplishments of its artists—their mastery of the terracotta medium, their rendering skills, and the depth of their vision—suggest to some scholars a long developmental period, culminating in twelfth- to thirteenth-century works such as Figure 10.56. This terracotta head represents a mature artistic style with precise anatomical detail and textures that make the figures seem ready to

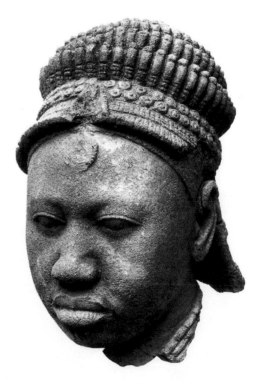

10.56 Head of a queen, from Ife, Nigeria, 12th–13th century. Terracotta, height 10 ins (25 cm). Museum of Ife Antiquities, Ife.

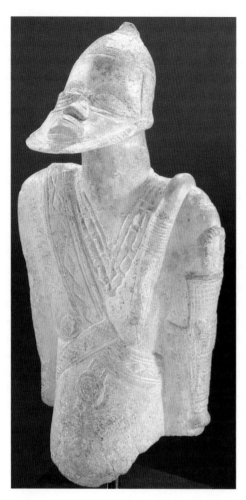

10.57 Bearded male figure from Djenne, Mali, 14th century. Terracotta, height 15 ins (38 cm). Detroit Institute of Arts (Eleanor Clay Ford Fund for African Art).

AMERICA

In America native peoples had developed significant civilizations. In the last chapter we discussed the Olmecs of Mexico, one of many indigenous peoples. Their art conformed to some general characteristics. In general, American Indian art tended to be portable and functional because the people were primarily nomadic, and practicality demanded that possessions be kept to a minimum and provide maximum utilization. If works of art—objects of beauty—were necessary, then they should fulfill their aesthetic functions as well as some domestic function. There were, nonetheless, some works of art designed for their own sake—for example, Figure 10.58, an openwork vessel with a design representing a bird. This ceramic object, with cutout areas precluding it as a container, appears to be only aesthetic in function. In cultures such as those of the Plains Indians, Aztecs, and Incas, which were strongly militaristic, artistic expression found its way into ceremonial objects as well as costumes and weaponry.

In addition to following broad, general characteristics, American Indian works of art also can reflect specific tribal characteristics. For example, a pottery shape called the *aryballus* (uh-RIH-buh-luhs), shown in Figure 10.59. Delicate in design, this multicolored ceramic urn features carefully painted small geometric patterns arranged symmetrically. The insect appended to the bowl creates an intriguing focal point and provides a visual counterpoint to the smooth and lustrous surface. The neck of the urn rises in a graceful curve and then splays outward into a disclike lip, divided symmetrically by underhung

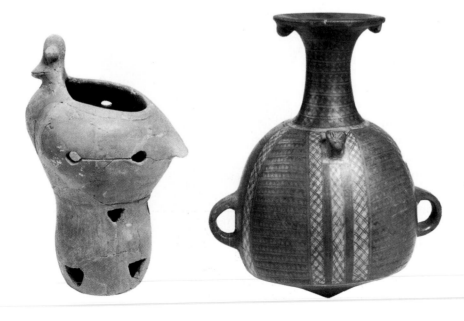

10.58 (far left) Openwork bird jar, from Ocklockonee Bay, Florida. Redware, with pre-fired "kill" hole in base, height 10½ ins (26.7 cm). National Museum of the American Indian, Smithsonian Institution, Washington, D.C.

10.59 (left) Arybal-shaped Inca vessel, from Bolivar, Ecuador, 10½ × 8¾ ins (26.7 × 22.2 cm). National Museum of the American Indian, Smithsonian Institution, Washington, D.C.

droplets. Aesthetic sensitivity and sophistication can be seen in the treatment of the lip. The asymmetrical handles placed below the centerline of the bowl give it a dynamic force and create additional interest for the viewer.

In the center of the city of Teotihuacan stands the Ciudadela (see-you-dah-DAY-lah), a large sunken plaza in the midst of temple platforms. The Ciudadela functioned as a political and religious center and could accommodate crowds in excess of 60,000 people. The Temple of the Feathered Serpent in the Ciudadela (Fig. **10.60**) reveals the sloping walls typical of Teotihuacan architectural style as well as a stairway balustrade with painted reliefs of the Feathered Serpent, the goggle-eyed Rain God (or Fire God), and aquatic shells and snails. The style of these Teotihuacan figures stands in strong contrast to the Olmec statuary we saw in Chapter 9. The latter style showed a three-dimensional and curvilinear essence, whereas this exhibits a flat, angular, and more abstract style. Some people suggest that the juxtaposition of figures here as representing the alternating wet and dry seasons or, perhaps, as the cycle of regeneration. We do not know for sure.

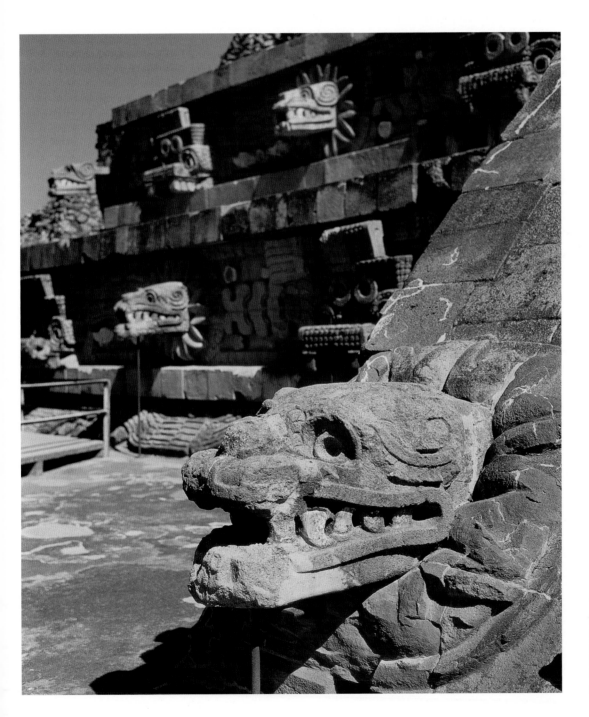

10.60 Serpent head at the base of a stairway of the Temple of the Feathered Serpent, the Ciudadela, Teotihuacan, Mexico. Teotihuacan culture, c. 350 C.E. (?)

THINKING CRITICALLY

- Identify the basic characteristics of Greek Classicism and explain how the Parthenon (Fig 10.8) and two architectural examples from your own city or town exemplify those characteristics. In what ways are the local examples like or different from the Parthenon?

- Using line, form, mass, articulation, and your own personal, emotional reaction as points of comparison, analyze the *Scraper* (Fig. 10.3), the *Bodhisattva of Compassion* (Fig. 10.46), and the bearded figure from Djenne (Fig.10.57).

- Using your personal reaction and at least two characteristics of poetry (see Chapter 8), compare the excerpts from the *Aeneid* and the *Song of Roland*.

- Enumerate and compare the ways in which the Chinese painting *Twelve Views from a Thatched Cottage* (Fig. 10.50) and the Byzantine mosaic *Emperor Justinian and His Court* (Fig. 10.33) change what we would call photographic reality (lifelikeness) into something else. How do those changes from lifelikeness affect the ways in which you respond to the works?

- Explain the basic characteristics of Romanesque and Gothic art using illustrations from this chapter as examples. What kind of world do you think would have evoked the characteristics of each of these styles?

CYBER STUDY

CLASSICAL GREECE:
http://library.thinkquest.org/26264/art/periods/site100.htm
http://witcombe.sbc.edu/ARTHgreecerome.html#Greek

ROME:
http://witcombe.sbc.edu/ARTHgreecerome.html#Roman

AFRICA:
http://artnetweb.com/guggenheim/africa/south.html

CHINA:
http://www.chinapage.com/paint1.html

JAPAN:
http://www.bergerfoundation.ch/wat1/frameset?pg=
   japon&ref=First_japan82&babel=en

BYZANTINE STYLE:
http://witcombe.sbc.edu/ARTHmedieval.html#Byzantine

ISLAMIC STYLE:
http://witcombe.sbc.edu/ARTHmedieval.html#Islamic

ROMANESQUE STYLE:
http://witcombe.sbc.edu/ARTHmedieval.html#Romanesque

GOTHIC STYLE:
http://witcombe.sbc.edu/ARTHmedieval.html#Gothic
http://witcombe.sbc.edu/ARTHmedieval.html#LateGothic

CHAPTER ELEVEN

ARTISTIC STYLES IN THE EMERGING MODERN WORLD

c. 1400 to c. 1800

— OUTLINE —

IMPORTANT TERMS

Absolute music Music that presents purely musical ideas.

Baroque style A diverse seventeenth-century style in the visual and performing arts generally typified by largeness, ornateness, and emotional appeal.

High Renaissance The period between 1495 and 1527 encapsulated by the genius of Leonardo da Vinci, Michelangelo, and Raphael.

Madrigal A musical setting of lyric poetry for four or five voices.

Mass The most important rite of the Roman Catholic liturgy. A musical form reflecting the parts of the mass.

Program music Music written to illustrate an external idea.

Renaissance The period from approximately 1400 to 1527 that was seen as a rebirth of understanding after the Middle Ages.

Rococo style An eighteenth-century style typified by intricacy, grace, charm, and delicacy.

Word painting A musical technique in which the music attempts to enhance the meaning and emotion of a written text.

THE CONTEXT

EUROPE

The Renaissance

In Europe the period from around 1400 to 1550, or the Renaissance, was explicitly seen as a rebirth of our understanding of ourselves as social and creative beings. "Out of the sick Gothic night our eyes are opened to the glorious touch of the sun," was how the writer Rabelais (RAB-uh-lay, 1494?–1553) expressed what most of his educated contemporaries felt. Florence, the crucible of the Renaissance in Italy, was called the "New Athens," and here the fine arts, or "liberal arts," were first redefined as art, in contrast to their status as crafts in the Middle Ages. Now accepted among the intellectual disciplines, the arts became an essential part of learning and literary culture. Artists, architects, composers, and writers gained confidence from their new status and from the technical mastery they were achieving. For the first time, it seemed possible not merely to imitate the works of the Classical world, but to surpass them.

Definitions of the Renaissance have been debated for centuries. The word certainly describes a new sense of self and self-awareness felt by Western European people, who had come to see themselves as no longer part of the "Middle Ages." But deciding where and how the Renaissance began, and what specifically it comprised, is as difficult as answering the question of where and how it ended—if it ended at all.

Renaissance scholars sought the answers to all questions, and they took empirical approaches to their inquiry rather than using the tools of faith and philosophy. As a result, forward-looking science and backward-looking traditional values commonly clashed. Spirited inquiry often raised more questions than it could answer, and the questions and conflicts that flowed from this inquiry had unsettling and destabilizing effects.

A significant concept of the Renaissance, humanism, did not, as some have ventured, deny God or faith. Rather, it attempted to discover humankind's own earthly fulfillment, perfectly expressed in the biblical idea: "O Adam, you may have whatever you shall desire." The medieval view of life as a vale of tears, with no purpose other than preparing for salvation and the afterlife, gave way to a more liberating ideal of people playing important roles in this world.

Further, in July 1497, Vasco da Gama sailed from Lisbon, Portugal and rounded the African Cape of Good Hope. By May of 1498, he had reached India. After Christopher Columbus had shown the way, the rate of exploration of the world increased rapidly. Among those who descended on the Americas came restless men and ex-soldiers looking for easy wealth and fame. In a few short years, therefore, curiosity and individual self-confidence had taken humankind to the furthest reaches of the planet to explore and exploit it for the benefit of the kingdoms of Europe. The sixteenth century in Spain, called the *siglo de oro* ("golden century"), owed much of its glitter to the Americas—although it was silver, not gold, that underlay its richness.

The fifteenth century proved an important crucible for Renaissance thought and activity, but the apex of the Renaissance came in the late fifteenth and early sixteenth centuries, as a newly established papal authority called artists to Rome. We describe this time (approximately 1495–1527) as the High Renaissance because the term "high" when applied to artistic styles or movements signifies an advancement toward an acme or fullest extent, specifically a late, fully developed, or most creative stage or period.

The Reformation and Counter-Reformation

In Northern Europe the late fifteenth and sixteenth centuries witnessed a confluence of economic, political, and religious conflicts that, for ease of reference, we call the Reformation. It took place during the "Renaissance" and represented the most shattering and lasting blow the Christian Church has perhaps ever experienced outside the East/West split of the early Church. Of course, it did not just appear out of the blue. It was, rather, the climax of centuries of sectarian agitation—in the fourteenth century, for example, English cries for reform and resentment of papal authority led to an English translation of the Bible. But reform and separation stand worlds apart, and we must realize that the Reformation did not begin as an attempt to start a new branch of Christianity, but as a sincere attempt to reform serious religious problems in the Roman Catholic Church.

The desire for spiritual regeneration in the Roman Catholic Church in the late fifteenth and early sixteenth centuries eventually led to internal reform. This process, often called the Counter-Reformation, took shape in the 1540s and 1550s in loyalty to the pope and in opposition to Protestant doctrines and practices. In addition, however, a Catholic Reformation existed that comprised more than a reaction against Protestantism, but for the impulse for renovation, purification, and an internal rebirth of Catholic sensibility.

One further important aspect of political life in the seventeenth and early eighteenth centuries, absolutism, revolved around the absolute monarch, who received a mandate from God, according to "divine right." Strong dynasties controlled Europe, and the first half of the seventeenth century saw the consolidation of secular control over religious affairs in the European states. Absolutism made it difficult to envisage a society that did not follow the religion of its sovereign and it proved politically advantageous for rulers to clothe themselves with divine right. Protestant movements, which taught that truth and sovereignty lay in the Bible alone, continued nonetheless to defy the state Churches. In states where royal power proved strongest, dissent went underground or into asylum elsewhere.

The Enlightenment

The eighteenth century has often been called the "Age of Enlightenment," but century marks prove arbitrary boundaries that tell us very little about history or art. Styles, philosophies, and politics come and go for a variety of reasons. We can say that eighteenth-century enlightenment grew out of various seventeenth-century ideas that fell on more or less fertile soil at different times in different places.

Seventeenth- and eighteenth-century thought saw people as rational beings living in a universe governed by some systematic natural law. Some believed that law an extension of God's law. Others held that natural law stood by itself. Natural law extended to include international law, and accords emerged in which sovereign nations, bound by no higher authority, could work together for the common good.

Enlightenment, reason, and progress are secular ideas, and the age grew increasingly secular. Politics and business superseded religion, wresting leadership away from the Church, of whatever denomination. Toleration increased and persecution and the imposition of corporal punishment for religious, political, or criminal offenses grew less common as the era progressed. Enlightened thought led to an active desire, called humanitarianism, to raise the downtrodden from the low social circumstances into which ignorance and tyranny had cast them. All men and women had a right, as rational creatures, to dignity and happiness. This desire to elevate the social circumstances of all people led to an examination and questioning of political, judicial, economic, and ecclesiastical institutions.

ASIA

In Asia, Chinese society of the fifteenth to eighteenth centuries marked a period of change. The Ming Dynasty ruled China and produced a stable foundation for prosperity through public works such as irrigation, reforestation, and the building of dams. Simultaneously, the Ming established a strict policy for population control, including a massive program of resettlement. China witnessed a tremendous period of prosperity under the Ming Dynasty. The Ming Dynasty came to an end in 1644. In India, the sixteenth to eighteenth centuries saw the subcontinent under the rule of the Mughals—Muslim descendants of Mongols, Turks, Iranians, and Afghans—who invaded India in the early sixteenth century. The height of Mughal rule came under Akbar (r. 1556–1605). A brilliant ruler who liked the challenges of governing a vast empire, Akbar introduced a number of worthwhile policies, including the reconciliation and assimilation of Hindus, who comprised a majority of the Indian population. He also encouraged marriages between Mughal and Rajput aristocracy. He allowed new Hindu temples to be built, and personally attended Hindu festivals. By the end of Akbar's reign, the Mughal Empire covered most of India north of the Godavari River. By the time of the reign of Shah Jahan (r. 1628–58), India enjoyed significant political stability, economic activity, and a flourishing artistic climate. Shah Jahan attempted to expand the empire beyond the Khyber Pass, but the attempt accomplished little other than emptying the royal treasury. The state turned into a gigantic military machine with an out-of-control, expanding nobility. This burgeoning aristocracy placed tremendous burdens on the peasantry.

Seventeenth-century Japan witnessed impressive economic growth and a tripling of the population to more than 30 million. Samurai (warriors) were forced to live in towns near their masters. Sharply divided from other classes by their superior status, they became an administrative class responsible for managing the revenue of the shogun (commander of the Japanese army). They attended special schools where they learned Neo-Confucianism, among other subjects. Japanese society became increasingly urban through the eighteenth century, and a strong middle class of merchants and artisans developed. The arts flourished; the puppet theatre and Kabuki theatre emerged (see p. 316). The reign of the Tokugawa shoguns (1603–1867) stood at its peak.

AFRICA

In Africa between 1450 and 1600, Europeans traveled to the African coasts, but their presence remained limited and their influence marginal until the nineteenth century. This period saw the rise of a number of states throughout the continent. It also witnessed the clash of Christian and Muslim kingdoms of Ethiopia. On the east coast, the Portuguese dismantled the existing trading network between cities, and replaced it with one of their own. The east coast of Africa also saw a significant traffic in slaves. In the long term, slave trading proved detrimental to the economic health of East Africa. West Africa, however, experienced the opposite effect. States in that area used the slave trade and adapted it to their own ends without becoming totally dependent on it.

The Kingdom of Benin constituted a large empire that flourished from the fourteenth to the nineteenth centuries. We know it today from its large trove of bronze, iron, and ivory artifacts, particularly life-sized bronze heads of its kings. Portuguese explorers reached Benin in the late fifteenth century and developed a commercial relationship, increasingly involving the slave trade.

AMERICA

In America, the Spanish conquistadors landed in force during the *siglo de oro*. When they came to the South Central region of present-day Mexico, they encountered the Aztecs, who lived in the highlands in an area of basins that were separated by eroded volcanic peaks and broken mountain ranges. According to their own records, the Aztecs migrated from the north, probably around the early thirteenth century. Finding an island in a saltwater lake, the Aztecs built their future city and capital, Tenochtitlan (tay-NAWK-teet-lan) there. Aztec leaders refused permanent friendship with other tribes because they believed they were the chosen people of their principal god and that he had forbidden alliances. This fostered a commitment to war that played a significant role in the rise of the Aztec Empire.

The Incas ruled the largest native empire of the Americas, eventually including an estimated 12 million people in much of what is now Peru and Ecuador as well as in large parts of Chile, Bolivia, and Argentina. Near the end of the fourteenth century, the empire began to expand from its initial base in the Cuzco region of the southern Andes mountains of South America. The empire ended with the Spanish invasion led by Francisco Pizarro (pee-ZAH-roh) in 1532. The term *Inca* refers to the ruler himself as well as to the people of the valley of Cuzco, the capital of the empire. The Inca Empire probably began as a small kingdom, similar to many others in the Andes during the fourteenth century. How the Incas came to power remains unknown, nor can scholars determine for certain if Manco Capac (MAHN-koh KAH-pahk), supposedly the founding ruler, was a historical personage. In the early sixteenth century, the death of the Inca ruler plunged the empire into civil war. No system of succession had been determined. Atahualpa (ah-tah-WHAHL-pah) finally won the disastrous war and was on his way to Cuzco in 1532 to claim the whole kingdom when the Spanish conquistador Pizarro arrived. The Incas allowed Pizarro and a contingent of about 150 soldiers to enter the regional capital where Atahualpa and his army had camped. The invading Spaniards took Atahualpa captive and, thus, assured the collapse of the empire.

THE ARTS

EUROPE

The Early Renaissance

PAINTING In Italy, the early Renaissance found its artistic spark and heart in about 1400 in the wealthy city-state of Florence.

During the first two decades of the fifteenth century, sculpture reigned as the premier visual art of the time. Painters, for the most part, kept busy painting altarpieces for Florentine churches—generally in a variation of Gothic style. Unlike sculpture, painting showed little concern for the human spirit or for the stylistic problems that occupied sculptors. But ideas were developing, and came to fruition in the work of Masaccio (mah-ZAH-koh or mah-ZAHT-choh; Tommaso di Giovanni, 1401–29). The hallmark of Masaccio's invention and development of a "new" style concerns the way he employs deep space and rational foreshortening or perspective in his figures. Rational use of linear perspective, determined by Brunelleschi (broo-nuh-LEHS-kee; see p. 280) from his Classical models, proved to be one of the great inventions of the Renaissance. In collaboration with the artist Masolino, Masaccio was summoned in 1425 to create a series of frescoes for the Brancacci Chapel of the Church of Santa Maria del Carmine in Florence. See the Companion Website: Visual Art, Perspective.

The most famous of Masaccio's frescoes in the Brancacci family chapel, *The Tribute Money* (Fig. **11.1**), makes full use of the new discovery of linear perspective, as the rounded figures move freely in unencumbered deep space. It employs a technique called "continuous narration," unfolding a series of events across a single canvas—here the New Testament story from Matthew (17:24–7).

The figures in this fresco are remarkably accomplished. In the first place, Masaccio dresses them in fabric that falls like real cloth. Next, each figure stands in Classical *contrapposto* stance. The painting establishes little sense of motion, but the accurate rendering of the feet makes these figures seem to stand on real ground. Masaccio uses light to reveal form and volume. He establishes a source for the light that strikes the figures and then renders the objects in the painting so that all highlights and shadows occur as if caused by that single light source.

Masaccio's figures form a circular and three-dimensional grouping rather than a flat line across the surface of the work, as in *La Primavera* by Botticelli (bah-tih-CHAY-lee) (Fig. **11.2**). Even the haloes of the apostles appear in the new perspective and overlap at odd angles. Compositionally, the single vanishing point, which controls the linear perspective, sits at the head of Christ—we see this device for achieving focus again in Leonardo da Vinci's *Last Supper* (see Fig. **11.8**). In addition,

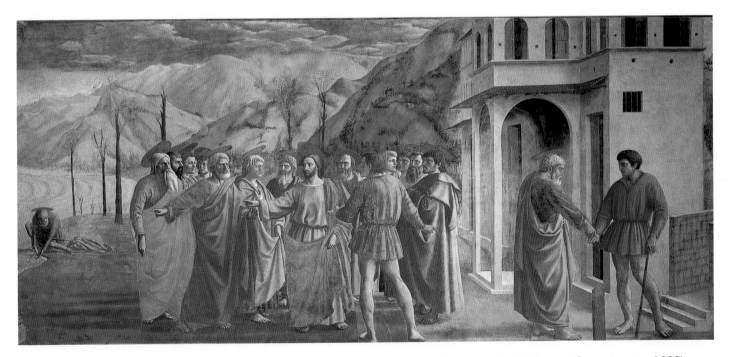

11.1 Masaccio, *The Tribute Money*, Brancacci Chapel, Santa Maria del Carmine, Florence, c. 1427. Fresco (after restoration 1989), 8 ft 4 ins × 19 ft 8 ins (2.54 × 5.9 m).

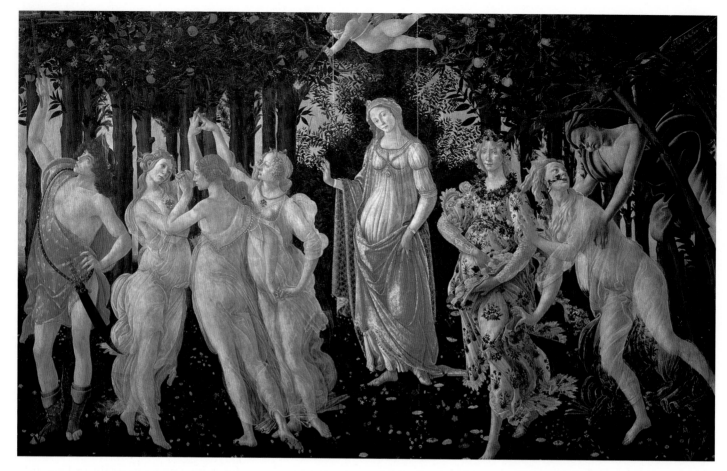

11.2 Sandro Botticelli, *La Primavera* (*Spring*), c. 1478. Tempera on panel, 6 ft 8 ins × 10 ft 4 ins (2.03 × 3.15 m). Galleria degli Uffizi, Florence.

Masaccio utilizes atmospheric perspective, in which he achieves distance through diminution of light and blurring of outlines. This not only enhances dimensionality but provides a unifying device.

By the last third of the fifteenth century, most of the originators of Renaissance art had died. The essences of the new art were well known and well established; it proved a time for further exploration in other avenues. One of these turned inward toward the life of the spirit, and in its search created a lyrical expression, much more poetic than anything we have seen thus far. Outward reality was often ignored in favor of more abstract values. We see this tradition best expressed in the paintings of Sandro Botticelli (Alessandro Filipepi, c. 1445–1510). The linear quality of *La Primavera*, or *Spring* (Fig. **11.2**), suggests an artist apparently unconcerned with deep space or subtle plasticity in light and shade. Rather, forms emerge through outline. The composition moves gently across the picture through a lyrical combination of undulating curved lines, with focal areas in each grouping. Mercury, the Three Graces, Venus, Flora, Spring, and Zephyrus— each part of this human, mythical composition carries its

own emotion: contemplation, sadness, or happiness. Note the apparently Classical and non-Christian subject matter. But, in fact, the painting uses *allegory* to equate Venus with the Virgin Mary. Beyond the immediate qualities, deeper symbolism relates also to the Medici family, the patron rulers of Florence.

Anatomically, Botticelli's figures are quite simple. He shows little concern for detailed musculature. Although he renders figures three-dimensionally and shades them subtly, they seem almost weightless, floating in space without anatomical definition.

SCULPTURE An attempt to capture the essence of European sculpture in the Early Renaissance can, again, best be served by looking to fifteenth-century Florence, where sculpture also enjoyed the patronage of the Medici. The early Renaissance sculptors developed the skills to create images of high lifelikeness. Their goal, however, differed from that of the Greeks, with their idealized reality of human form. Rather, Renaissance sculptors found their ideal in individualism. The ideal was the glorious— even if not quite perfect—individual. Sculpture of this style presented an uncompromising and stark view of humankind—complex, balanced, and full of action. Freestanding statuary, long out of favor, returned to dominance. The human form built up layer by layer upon its skeletal and muscular framework, reflecting scientific inquiry and interest in anatomy. Even when clothed, fifteenth-century sculpture revealed the body under the garments, quite unlike medieval works. And relief sculpture caught onto the new means of representing deep space through systematic, scientific perspective.

Notable and typical among fifteenth-century Italian sculptors were Lorenzo Ghiberti (ghee-BAIR-tee; 1378–1455) and Donatello (Donato de' Bardi, 1386–1466). Ghiberti's *Gates of Paradise*, from the doors of the Baptistery in Florence, show the same concern for rich detail, humanity, and feats of perspective evident in Florentine painting. Ghiberti, who trained as a goldsmith and painter, creates beautiful surfaces with delicate detail. He also conveys a tremendous sense of space in each of the ten panels. In *The Story of Jacob and Esau* (Fig. **11.3**), for example, he uses receding arcades to create depth and perspective. The bold relief of these scenes took Ghiberti twenty-one years to complete.

The greatest masterpieces of fifteenth-century Italian Renaissance sculpture came from the unsurpassed master of the age, Donatello (doh-nah-TAY-loh or dahn-uh-TEHL-oh). He had a passion for antiquity. His magnificent *David* (Fig. **11.4**) was the first freestanding nude

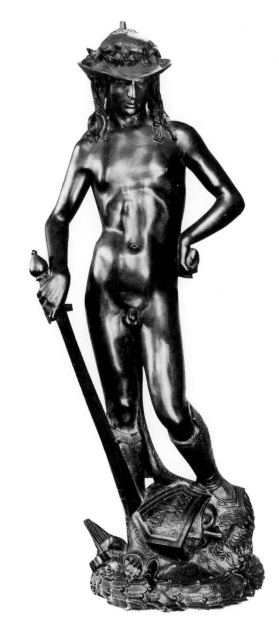

11.4 Donatello, *David*, dated variously 1430–40. Bronze, height 5 ft 2¼ ins (1.58 m). Museo Nationale del Bargello, Florence.

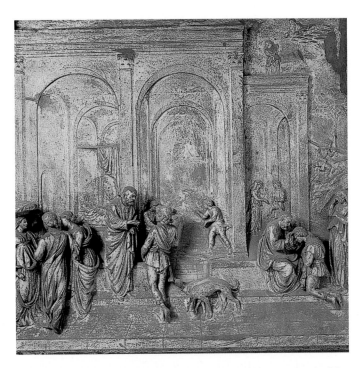

11.3 Lorenzo Ghiberti, *The Story of Jacob and Esau*, panel of the *Gates of Paradise*, Baptistery, Florence, c. 1435. Gilt bronze, 31¼ ins (79 cm) square.

sculpture since Classical times, but, unlike Classical nudes, David stands partially clothed. His armor and helmet, along with his bony elbows and adolescent character, invest him with high individualization. Donatello has returned to the Classical *contrapposto* stance, but the carefully executed form expresses a new humanity suggesting a statue almost capable of movement. The work symbolizes Christ's triumph over Satan. The laurel crown on the helmet and laurel wreath on which the work stands allude to the Medici family, in whose palace the statue was displayed in 1469.

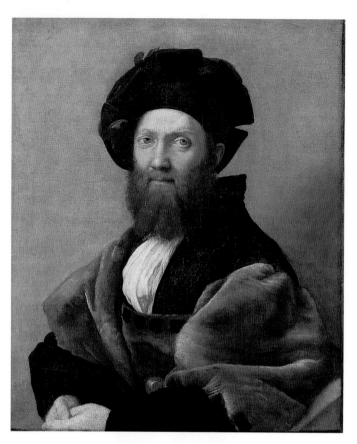

11.5 Raphael, *Count Baldassare Castiglione*, 1514. Oil transferred from wood to canvas, 2 ft 9¾ ins × 2 ft 3½ ins (82 × 66 cm). Louvre, Paris.

for all of Europe. In this influential work, Castiglione suggests, through an imagined dialogue, a picture of an artistically ordered society, in which cultivated Italians regard social living as a fine art.

The particular character of *The Courtier* lies in the realistic style of the conversations. Above all, *The Courtier* propounds the humanist's ultimate ideals—of men and women of intellectual refinement, cultural grace, moral stability, spiritual insight, and social consciousness. It provided a model of the ideal Renaissance society, but its values remain timeless: true worth is determined "by character and intellect rather than by birth." The excerpt that follows, although brief, illustrates both the context of the time and the content of Castiglione's work.

The Courtier
On Women
Baldassare Castiglione
1478–1529

Leaving aside, therefore, those virtues of the mind which she must have in common with the courtier, such as prudence, magnanimity, continence and many others besides, and also the qualities that are common to all kinds of women, such as goodness and discretion, the ability to take good care, if she is married, of her husband's belongings and house and children, and the virtues belonging to a good mother, I say that the lady who is at Court should properly have, before all else, a certain pleasing affability whereby she will know how to entertain graciously every kind of man with charming and honest conversation, suited to the time and the place and the rank of the person with whom she is talking. And her sense and modest behavior, and the candor that ought to inform all her actions, should be accompanied by a quick and vivacious spirit by which she shows her freedom from boorishness; but with such a virtuous manner that she makes herself thought no less chaste, prudent and benign than she is pleasing, witty and discreet. Thus she must observe a certain difficult mean, composed as it were of contrasting qualities, and take care not to stray beyond certain fixed limits. Nor in her desire to be thought chaste and virtuous, should she appear withdrawn or run off if she dislikes the company she finds herself in or thinks the conversation improper. For it might easily be thought that she was pretending to be straitlaced simply to hide something she feared others could find out about her; and in any case, unsociable manners are always deplorable.[1]

LITERATURE The sixteenth century witnessed the climax and close of what amounted to an Italian monopoly in Renaissance literature. The influence of the Italian Renaissance spread to the rest of Europe, reaching France in the middle third of the century and England in the last third of the century. The common factor everywhere was imitation of the classics. In Italy the writers of the High Renaissance were apparently indifferent to the tragic social and political events to which they bore witness. Most, like Castiglione, chose to ignore what was going on.

In essence, the Renaissance state was monarchical. In fact, the whole movement of the Renaissance skewed toward monarchical government. In Italy, it may have seemed less so than in France and Spain, but it was nonetheless the case in the petty duchies and principalities, and the gentlemen and ladies of the Renaissance were courtiers. The Count Baldassare Castiglione (kah-stee-lee-YOH-nee; 1478–1529) was himself the perfect courtier (Fig. **11.5**), and his book *Il Cortegiano* or *The Courtier* became a universal guide to "goodly manners" and "civil conversation" of the court of the duchy of Urbino. In effect, he was the arbiter of courtly behavior

A second major literary figure of the time was Ludovico Ariosto (ah-ree-OH-stoh; 1474–1533). Ariosto was a courtier of the house of Este (EH-stay) at Ferrara, and was employed as a civil servant and diplomat as well as a court poet. Classically trained, he wrote most of his work in Latin until he was twenty-five years old. Ariosto's father died when he was twenty-six, and he assumed responsibility for providing for his four brothers and five sisters. He spent fourteen years as confidential secretary to Cardinal d'Este, and during this time he traveled throughout Italy on a number of political missions. In 1518, he entered the service of the cardinal's brother, the duke of Ferrara, eventually becoming the duke's director of entertainment. Under Ariosto's supervision, the court enjoyed pageants and dramatic productions, Ariosto himself designing the theatre and scenery and writing a number of the plays. As early as 1505 he began his masterpiece, *Orlando Furioso*, forty cantos (sections) of which appeared in 1516. For nearly thirty years he continued to revise the work, which became one of the most influential poems of the Renaissance. *Orlando Furioso* ("Roland in a Mad Fury") is a romantic epic—its forty-six cantos total over 1,200 pages—of "Loves and Ladies, Knights and Arms . . . Of Curtesies, and many a Daring Feat." Ariosto depended heavily on the Greco-Roman tradition of Homer and Virgil, and borrowed incidents, character types, and rhetorical devices, such as the catalogue of troops and extended simile. Designed for a sophisticated audience, the work employs an ottava rima (a stanza of eight lines rhyming *abababcc*), and is written in a polished and graceful style. It became a bestseller throughout Europe.

Orlando Furioso captivated its sixteenth-century readers with its elements of supernatural trips to the moon, allegorical incidents that taught modesty and chastity, and romantic adventure. However, the characters are shallow and two-dimensional, for Ariosto made no attempt to probe the depths of human behavior or to tackle important issues. Nonetheless, he works out individual incidents with care and carries them through to a climax, after which he takes up the next, and ties all the loose threads together at the end. *Orlando Furioso* served the Renaissance as a model of the large-scale narrative poem written with technical skill, smoothness, and the gracefulness typical of the classics. Ariosto spent most of his adult life writing and revising this masterpiece.

Amidst the poets of the time we find the man Michelangelo, who wrote more than 300 sonnets to add to his work as a sculptor, painter, architect, and musical composer. His sonnets comprise a remarkable autobiography. They make us a spectator to the struggles of his life and his passions. He wrote a number of letters that reveal something about himself, but not usually anything profound: a few quarrels about money and commissions. His sonnets, however, reveal more of the man, and we find

them jotted down at odd moments, sometimes in the margins of his sketches, and revealing some particular relevant feeling or spontaneous idea. The following sonnet, which illustrates his poetry, forms one of a set of seven sonnets by Michelangelo set to music by the twentieth-century English composer Benjamin Britten. The musical work uses the sonnets in their original Italian, and so we present the Italian first, followed by an English translation. Notice that the Italian employs the form and rhyme scheme of the Petrarchan sonnet we studied in Chapter 8. The English version does not.

Sonnet XVI
Michelangelo
c. 1340–1400

Taken from Benjamin Britten's
Seven Sonnets of Michelangelo, no. 1, Op. 22.

Sì come nella penna e nell'inchiostro
È l'alto e 'l basso e 'l mediocre stile,
E ne' marmi l'immagin ricca e vile,
Secondo che 'l sa trar l'ingegno nostro;
Così, signor mie car, nel petto vostro,
Quante l'orgoglio, è forse ogni atto umile:
Ma io sol quel c'a me proprio è e simile
Ne traggo, come fuor nel viso mostro.

Chi semina sospir, lacrime e doglie,
(L'umor dal ciel terreste, schietto e solo,
A vari semi vario si converte),
Però pianto e dolor ne miete e coglie;
Chi mira alta beltà con sì gran duolo,
Dubbie speranze, e pene acerbe e certe.

English translation:

Just as in pen and ink
there is a high, low, and medium style,
and in marble are images rich and vile,
according to the art with which we fashion it,
so, my dear lord, in your heart,
along with pride, are perhaps some humble thoughts:
but I draw thence only what is proper for myself
in accordance with what my features show.

Who sows sighs, tears and lamentations
(dew from heaven on earth, pure and simple,
converts itself differently to varied seeds)
will reap and gather tears and sorrow;
he who gazes upon exalted beauty with such pain
will have doubtful hopes and bitter, certain sorrows.

The sonnet as a poetic form found great popularity in the High Renaissance, and we also find it among the poets of the Golden Age of Spain. Gutierre de Cetina (thay-TEE-nah; 1520?–1557?) draws on classical and Italian poetry, using the Italianate meters of the Petrarchan sonnet. Cetina freely translated from Petrarch in his poetry, but his sonnets, considered his finest work, show an elegance and facile meter all their own. Again, we present the poem in its original Spanish, utilizing the Petrarchan rhyme scheme followed by a loose English translation not employing the form.

Soneto

Gutierre de Cetina

c. 1340–1400

"Como al pastor que en la ardiente hora estiva
la verde sombra, el fresco aire agrada,
y como a la sedienta su manada
alegra alguna fuente de agua viva,

así a mi árbol do se note o escriba
mi nombre en la corteza delicada
alegra, y ruego a Amor que sea guardada
la planta porque el nombre eterno viva.

Ni menos se deshace el hielo mío,
Vandalio, ante tu ardor, cual suele nieve
a la esfera del sol ser derretida."

Así decía Dórida en el río
mirando su beldad, y el viento leve
llevó la voz que apenas fue entendida.

English translation:

"Like a shepherd who amidst the fiery heat of day
delights in leafy shadows or fresh breezes
or when his thirsty flocks have joy
in finding fonts of water pure and sweet;

So my tree rejoices when my name is writ
in letters plain or symbols in its fragile bark.
God of Love keep this tree safe
so that the name may live eternally.

And yet my heart of ice will not melt down
howe'er you burn, Vandalio;
I am no melting snow neath Phoebus' rays!"

So spoke proud Dorida as in the stream
she gazed upon her beauty, but her voice,
caught by the wind, grew fainter than a dream.

ARCHITECTURE Early Renaissance architecture centered in Florence and departed from medieval architecture in three significant ways: (1) its concern with the revival of Classical models along technical lines. Ruins of Roman buildings were measured carefully and their proportions became those of Renaissance buildings. Rather than seeing Roman arches as limiting factors, Renaissance architects saw them as geometric devices by which a formally derived design could be composed; (2) the application of decorative detail—nonstructural ornamentation—to the façade of the building; and (3) a radical change in the outer expression of structure. The outward form of a building previously related closely to the structural support of the building—for example, post-and-lintel, masonry, and the arch. In the Renaissance, these supporting elements were hidden from view and the external appearance no longer sacrificed to structural concerns.

Early architecture of the period, such as the dome of Florence Cathedral (Fig. 11.6), imitated Classical form appended to medieval structures. This curious design by Filippo Brunelleschi (1377–1446) was added to a fourteenth-century building in the fifteenth century. The soaring dome rises 180 feet (55 m) into the air, and its height is apparent from both outside and within.

Compared with the Pantheon (see Figs. 10.19 and 10.20), Brunelleschi's departure from traditional practice becomes clear. The dome of the Pantheon is impressive only from the inside of the building, because its exterior supporting structure is so massive that it clutters the visual experience. On the exterior of Brunelleschi's dome, though, the supporting elements such as stone and timber girdles and lightweight ribbings are hidden, resulting in an aesthetic statement where visual appearance rivals structural considerations. Unlike most domes up until that time (for example, the Pantheon and the Hagia Sophia—see Fig. 10.36) the dome of Florence Cathedral takes a pointed rather than semicircular shape. Scholars call that shape *quinto acuto* or "pointed fifth." The dome actually consists of a "cloister vault" system, wherein a series of interpenetrating barrel vaults (see Chapter 3) comprise the dome. The design came from Neri di Fioravanti (fl. 14th century; fee-oh-rah-VAHN-tee). Filippo Brunelleschi, a goldsmith and clockmaker, however, figured out how to solve the puzzles inherent in the dome's construction. It became Brunelleschi's life work.

Classical ornamentation also marks Brunelleschi's Pazzi Chapel (Fig. 11.7). It uses its walls as a plain background for surface decoration. Concern for proportion and geometric design emerge clearly, but the overall com-

11.6 (*opposite*) Filippo Brunelleschi, Florence Cathedral, dome, 1420–36.

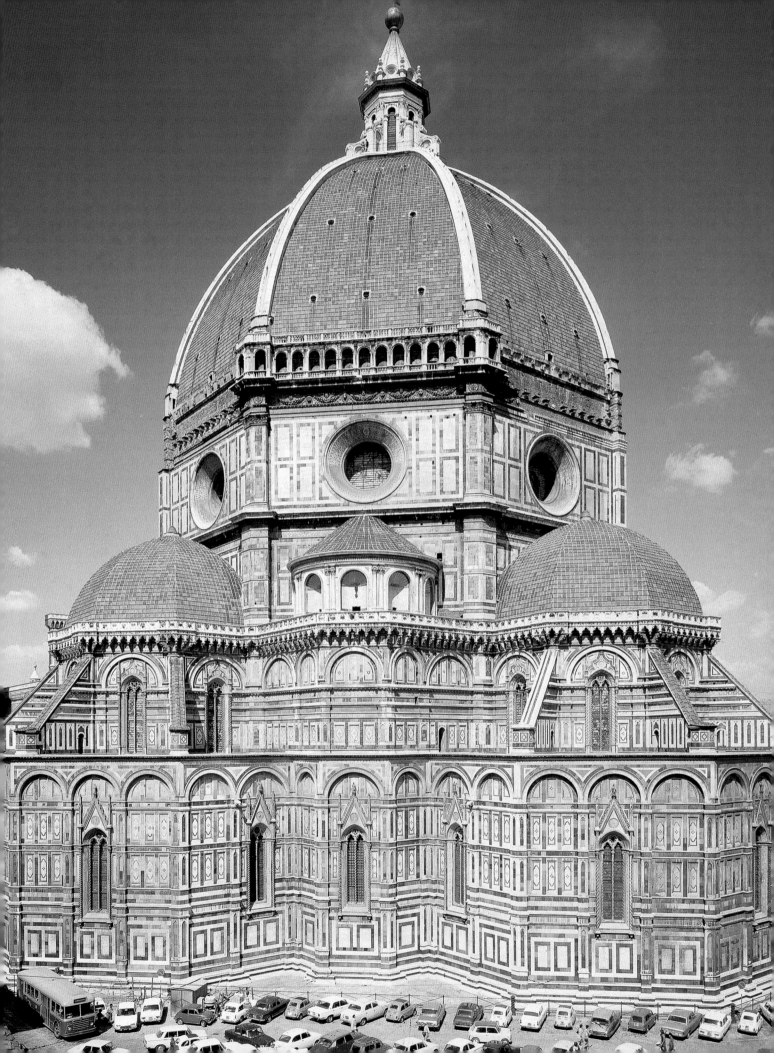

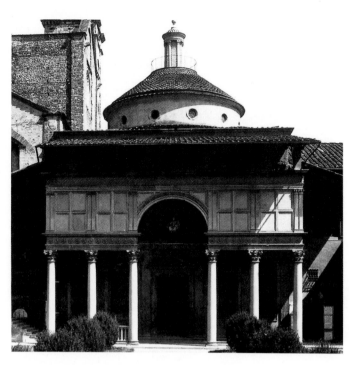

11.7 Filippo Brunelleschi, Pazzi Chapel, Santa Croce, Florence, c. 1440–61.

position is not a slave to pure arithmetical considerations. Rather, the Pazzi Chapel reflects Brunelleschi's sense of Classical aesthetics. Brunelleschi had profound influence in the first half of the fifteenth century, and he served as a model and inspiration for later Renaissance architects.

The High Renaissance

The high point of the Renaissance came in the early sixteenth century. Its importance as the apex of Renaissance art has led scholars to call this period in the visual arts the High Renaissance. Painters of the High Renaissance included the masters of Western visual art: Leonardo da Vinci, Michelangelo, Raphael, and Titian.

A concept of particular importance to our overview of visual art in the High Renaissance style is that of genius. Genius was implicit in the humanistic exploration of the individual's earthly potential and fulfillment. In Italy between 1495 and 1520 everything in visual art was subordinate to the overwhelming genius of two men, Leonardo da Vinci and Michelangelo Buonarroti. Their impact has led many to debate whether the High Renaissance of visual art was a culmination of earlier Renaissance style or a new departure.

High Renaissance painting sought a universal ideal achieved through impressive art, as opposed to overemphasis on anatomy or tricks of perspective. Figures became types again, rather than individuals—godlike human beings in the Greek Classical tradition. Artists and writers of the High Renaissance sought to capture the essence of Classical art and literature without resorting to copying, which would have captured only the externals. They tried to emulate, and not to imitate. As a result, High Renaissance art idealizes all forms and delights in

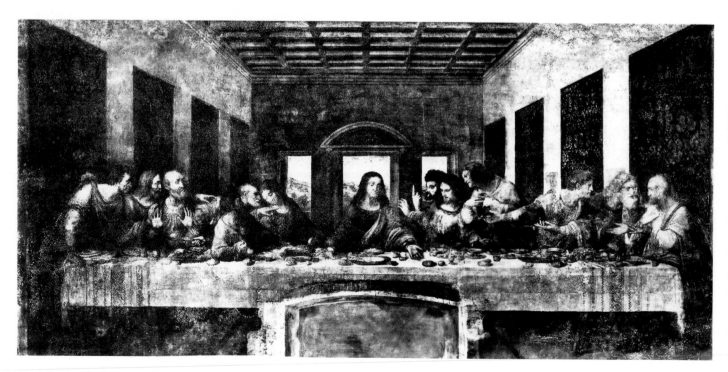

11.8 Leonardo da Vinci, *The Last Supper*, Santa Maria delle Grazie, Milan, c. 1495–8. Wall painting, 15 ft 2 ins × 28 ft 10 ins.

composition. It is stable without being static, varied without confusion, and clearly defined without dullness.

High Renaissance artists carefully observed how the ancients borrowed motifs from nature, and they then set out to develop a system of mathematically defined proportion and compositional beauty. Such faith in harmonious proportions reflected a belief among artists, writers, and composers that a harmonious universe and nature possessed perfect order. High Renaissance style departed from previous styles in its meticulously arranged composition, based almost exclusively on geometric devices, such as a central triangle or an oval. Composition was closed—line, color, and form kept the viewer's eye continually redirected into the work, as opposed to leading off the canvas.

LEONARDO DA VINCI The work of Leonardo da Vinci (1452–1519) contains an ethereal quality that he achieved by blending light and shadow. He considered color of lesser importance than volume, which he accomplished through light and shade. In order to unify his compositions, he covered his paintings with a thin, lightly tinted varnish, giving them a hazy or smoky quality called *sfumato* (sfoo-MAH-toh), literally "smoked," from the Italian. His figures hover between reality and illusion as one form disappears into another, and only highlighted portions emerge. *The Last Supper* (Fig. **11.8**) captures the drama of Christ's prophecy, "One of you shall betray me," at the moment when the apostles respond with disbelief. Leonardo's choice of medium proved most unfor-

tunate because his mixture of oil, varnish, and pigments (as opposed to fresco) did not suit the damp wall. The painting began to flake and was reported to be perishing as early as 1517. Since then it has been clouded by retouching, defaced by a door cut through the wall at Christ's feet, and bombed during World War II. Miraculously, it survives.

In *The Last Supper*, human figures and not architecture form the focus. The figure of Christ dominates the center of the painting. All line, actual and implied, leads outward from his face, pauses at various subordinate focal areas, directs back into the work, and returns to the central figure. Various postures, hand positions, and groupings of the disciples direct the eye from point to point. Figures emerge from the gloomy architectural background in strongly accented relief; nothing anchors them to the floor of the room where they sit. This typically geometric composition expresses much drama within a mathematical format. Yet, despite the drama, the mood in this work and others remains calm, belying the conflict of Leonardo's own life and times.

MICHELANGELO Perhaps the most dominant figure of the High Renaissance was Michelangelo Buonarroti (bwoh-nuh-ROH-tee; 1475–1564). While Leonardo was a skeptic, Michelangelo was a man of great faith. Leonardo was fascinated by science and natural objects; Michelangelo, by contrast, showed little interest in anything other than the human form. Michelangelo's Sistine Chapel ceiling (Figs. **11.9** and **11.10**) shines as an exam-

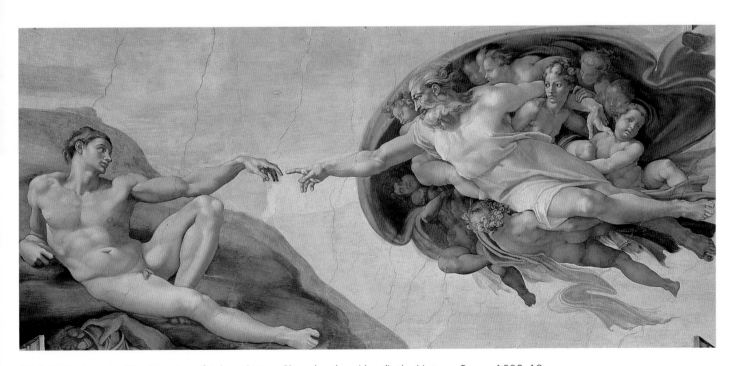

11.9 Michelangelo, *The Creation of Adam*, Sistine Chapel ceiling (detail), the Vatican, Rome, 1508–12.

ple of the ambition and genius of the era of the High Renaissance and its philosophies. In each of the triangles along the sides of the chapel the ancestors of Christ await the Redeemer. Between them, amidst painted pillars, rest the sages of antiquity. In the corners, Michelangelo depicts various biblical stories, and across the center of the ceiling he unfolds the episodes of the first book of the Bible, Genesis. The center of the ceiling captures the Creation of Adam (Fig. 11.9) at the moment of fulfill-ment, and does so in sculpturesque human form and beautifully modeled anatomical detail. God, in human form, stretches outward from his matrix of angels to a reclining but dynamic Adam, awaiting the divine infu-sion, the spark of the soul. The figures do not touch, and we get a supreme feeling of anticipation of what we imag-ine will be the power and electricity of God's physical contact with mortal man.

Michelangelo believed that the image from the artist's hand must spring from the idea in his or her mind. The idea is the reality, and it is revealed by the genius of the artist. The artist does not create the ideas, but finds them in the natural world, which reflects the absolute idea: that of beauty.

PAPAL SPLENDOR: THE VATICAN Rome was the city of the arts in the fifteenth and sixteenth centuries. The Renaissance—and particularly the High Renaissance, when the papacy called all great artists to Rome—con-tributed most of the splendor of Vatican art and architec-ture. The papacy as a force and the Vatican as the symbol of that force represent a synthesis of Renaissance ideas and reflections. St. Peter's and the Vatican have earthly and heavenly qualities that reflect the reality of the Church on earth and the mystery of the spiritual church of Christ (Fig. 11.11). The Church sponsored art on a grand scale to give glory to God and to draw the general populace closer to God.

Plans for replacement of the original basilica of Old St. Peter's were made by Nicholas V (reigned 1447–55) in the fifteenth century, but it was Pope Julius II (reigned 1503–13) who decided to put them into effect. Julius commissioned Donato Bramante (brah-MAHN-tay; 1444–1514) to construct the new basilica. Bramante's design called for a building in the form of a Greek cross. The work was planned as "an harmonious arrangement of architectural forms" in an "image of bright amplitude and picturesque liveliness." But Bramante died before his plans were carried out, and was succeeded by two of his assistants and by Raphael (see p. 286). Changes were made, partly because the designs were then severely criti-cized by Michelangelo. Eventually Pope Paul III (reigned 1534–49) convinced Michelangelo to become chief archi-

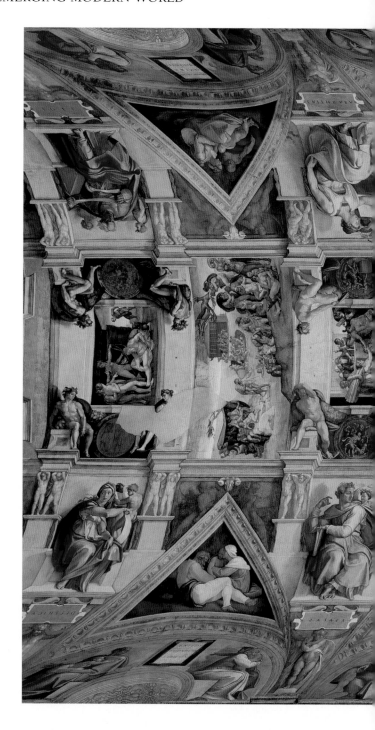

11.10 Michelangelo, Sistine Chapel ceiling, the Vatican, Rome, 1508–12.

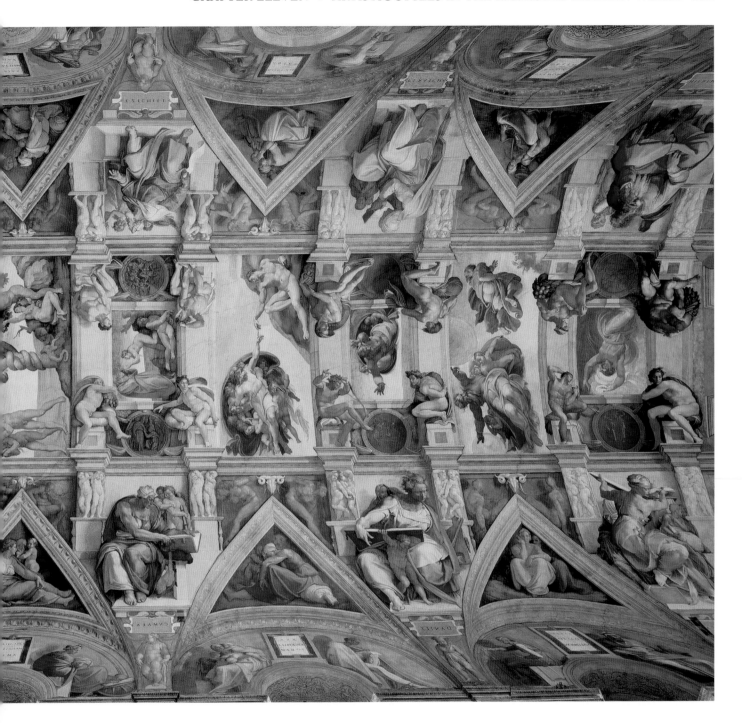

tect. Michelangelo set aside liturgical considerations and returned to Bramante's original conception, which he described as "clear and pure, full of light . . . whoever distances himself from Bramante, also distances himself from the truth." Michelangelo's project was completed in May of 1590 as the last stone was added to the dome and a High Mass was celebrated. Work on thirty-six columns continued, however, and was completed by Giacomo della Porta (c. 1522/3–1602) and Domenico Fontana (1543–1607) after Michelangelo's death. Full completion of the basilica as it stands today was under the direction

of yet more architects, including Carlo Maderno (1556– 1629). He was forced to yield to the wishes of the cardinals and change the original form of the Greek cross to a Latin cross. As a result, the Renaissance design of Michelangelo and Bramante, with its central altar, was rejected. It was replaced by Maderno's design, including a *travertine* façade of gigantic proportions and sober elegance. His extension of the basilica was influential in the development of Baroque architecture. The project was completed in 1614, more than 150 years after the first plans were laid.

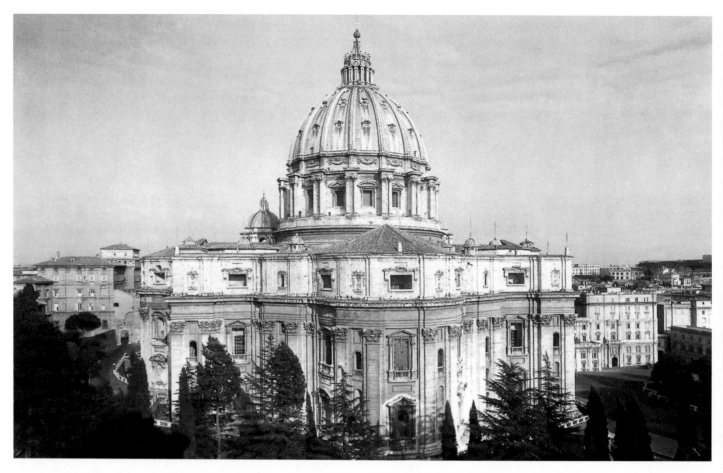

11.11 Michelangelo, St. Peter's, Rome, from the west, 1546–64 (dome completed by Giacomo della Porta, 1590).

RAPHAEL Raphael (rah-fah-EL; 1483–1520), generally regarded as the third painter in the High Renaissance triumvirate, did not reach the same level of genius and accomplishment as Leonardo and Michelangelo. In *The Alba Madonna* (Fig. **11.12**), the strong central triangle appears within the geometric parameters of a tondo, or circular shape. Strong, parallel horizontal lines counteract the tendency of a circle to roll (visually). The solid baseline of the central triangle emerges in the leg of the infant John the Baptist (left), the foot of the Christ Child, the folds of the Madonna's robes, and the rock and shadow at the right. The left side of the central triangle comprises the eyes of all three figures and carries along the back of the infant John to the border. The right side of the triangle runs along the edge of the Madonna's robe, joining the horizontal shadow at the right border.

Within this formula, Raphael depicts a comfortable, subtly modeled, and idealized Mary and Christ Child with soft and warm textures. Raphael's treatment of skin creates an almost tactile sensation—we can almost discern the warm blood flowing beneath it, a characteristic relatively new to two-dimensional art. Raphael's figures express lively power, and his mastery of three-dimensional form and deep space is unsurpassed.

THE HIGH RENAISSANCE IN VENICE Tiziano Vecelli, known in English as Titian (TISH-uhn; 1488?–1576), made one of the most crucial discoveries in the history of art. The art historian Frederick Hartt describes it this way: "He was the first man in modern times to free the brush from the task of exact description of tactile surfaces, volumes, and details, and to convert it into a vehicle for the direct perception of light through color and for the unimpeded expression of feeling."[2] This new type of brushwork exists in the *Assumption of the Virgin* (Fig. **11.13**) but remains in the background. Long before he died, he used the technique on entire paintings, and so did most other painters in Venice.

Part of Titian's unique technique lay in the way in which he built up pigment from a reddish ground through many layers of glaze, which lent warmth to all the colors of the painting. The glazes toned down colors that the artist believed too demanding and gave depth and richness to the work. Glazing made many of the colors and

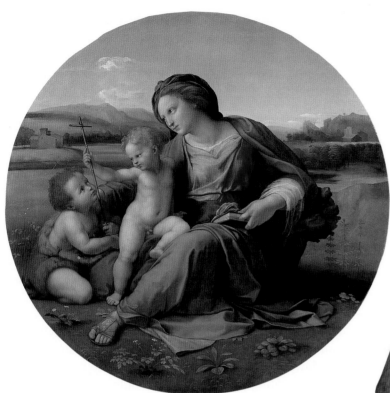

11.12 *(above)* Raphael, *The Alba Madonna*, c. 1510. Canvas (originally oil on panel), 37¼ ins (94.5 cm) in diameter. National Gallery of Art, Washington D.C. (Andrew W. Mellon Collection). Image © 2005 Board of Trustees, National Gallery of Art, Washington.

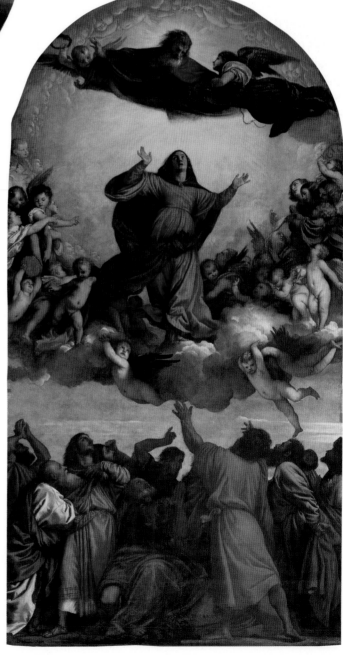

11.13 Titian, *Assumption of the Virgin*, 1516–18. Panel, 22 ft 6 ins × 11 ft 10 ins (6.9 × 3.6 m). Santa Maria Gloriosa dei Frari, Venice, Italy.

shadows seem "miraculously suspended." Titian may have used as many as thirty or forty layers of glaze on a single painting.

Assumption of the Virgin exudes an almost fiery glow from the underpainting, and our eyes move upward from the base of the picture, forming eye level, to a hovering Madonna lifted on a cloud by a host of putti or cherubs. Above her, emerging from a flaming yellow and orange sky, boiling in undulating brushstrokes and angelic faces, rests the figure of God. The circular sweep of the painting's arched top and the encircling angels separate the Virgin from the outstretched hands of the apostles by compositional psychology as well as space, almost breached by the raised arm of the foreground figure.

Northern Europe

TWO-DIMENSIONAL ART In the north of Europe lies a small area known as the Low Countries where, in the fifteenth century, Flemish painters and musicians forged new approaches amid a dominant culture of Late Gothic architecture and sculpture. Here in Flanders they formed a link with their contemporaries in northern Italy—the heart of the Early Renaissance in art; they were to influence European painters and musicians for the next century. However, many scholars see early-fifteenth-century Flemish arts as remaining part of the Late Gothic style, despite the contact with Italy, and despite Italian admiration of Flemish painting.

Flemish painting of this period was revolutionary. Whereas painters of the Gothic style essentially retained a certain two-dimensional feeling, and little continuity in their perspective, Flemish painters achieved pictorial reality and rational perspective. The sense of completeness and continuity marks a new and clearly different style. Line, form, and color are painstakingly controlled to compose subtle, varied, three-dimensional, clear, and logically unified statements.

Part of the drastic change in Flemish painting stemmed from a new development in painting media—oil paint. Oil's versatile characteristics gave Flemish painters new opportunities to vary surface texture and brilliance, and to create far greater subtlety of form. Oil paint allowed blending of color areas, because it could be worked wet on the canvas, whereas egg tempera, the previous painting medium, dried almost immediately upon application. Gradual transitions between color areas made possible by oils allowed fifteenth-century Flemish painters to use *atmospheric perspective* and control this most effective indicator of deep space better than had previously been possible. Blending between color areas also enhanced chiaroscuro, by which all objects assume three-dimensionality, for without highlight and shadow the illusion of depth is lost. Early-fifteenth-century Flemish painters explored light and shade not only to heighten three-dimensionality of form but also to achieve rational unity in their compositions, for example, by having consistent light sources and natural shadows on surrounding objects. This new unity and realistic three-dimensionality separated the fifteenth-century Flemish style from Gothic art and tied it to the Renaissance.

The Arnolfini Marriage, or *Giovanni Arnolfini and His Bride* (Fig. 11.14), by Jan van Eyck (fahn YK; c. 1390–1441) illustrates the qualities of Flemish painting and also stimulates a marvelous range of aesthetic responses. Van Eyck used the full range of values from darkest darks to lightest lights and blended them with extreme subtlety to achieve a soft and lifelike appearance. His colors are rich, varied, and predominantly warm in feeling. All forms achieve three-dimensionality through subtle color blending and softened shadow edges. Natural highlights and shadows emanate from obvious sources, such as the windows, and tie the figures and objects together.

The painting depicts a young couple taking a marriage vow in the sanctity of the bridal chamber, and the painting is thus both a portrait and a marriage certificate. The artist has signed the painting in legal script above the mirror "Johannes de Eyck fuit hic. 1434" (Jan van Eyck was here. 1434). In fact, we can see the artist and another witness reflected in the mirror.

As early as the late Middle Ages, southern Germany stood positioned at the center of a thriving trade axis that connected the Netherlands with Italy. Throughout Europe, much of the wealth created in centers such as the Netherlands and Germany encouraged arts and letters. By the late fifteenth century important artists such as Albrecht Dürer (DYOO-ruhr; 1471–1528) followed the trade routes back and forth to Italy, helping to bring the Renaissance to northern Europe.

Dürer shared Leonardo's deep curiosity about the natural world. He expressed this curiosity especially in his drawings, which explore the human figure and physiognomy, and animals, plants, and landscapes. Unlike Leonardo, however, Dürer worked principally as an engraver and was tortured by religious problems during this time of the Protestant Reformation. We can see Dürer's skill as a printmaker and his remarkable artistic and religious insight in the woodcut *The Four Horsemen of*

11.14 (*opposite*) Jan van Eyck, *The Arnolfini Marriage* (*Giovanni Arnolfini and His Bride*), 1434. Oil on panel, 33 × 22½ ins (84 × 57 cm). National Gallery, London.

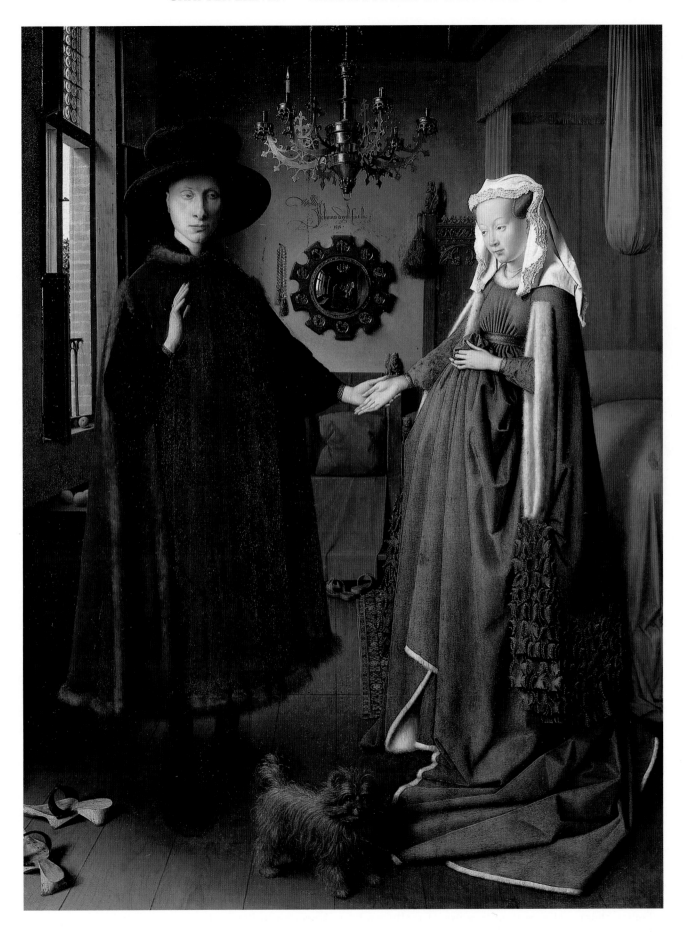

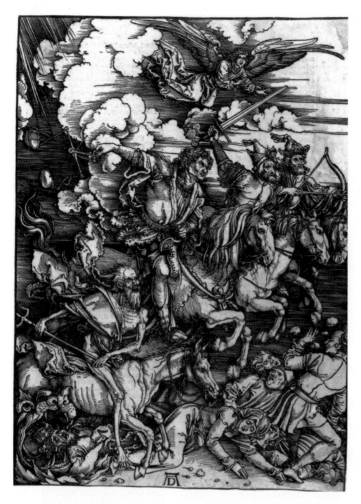

11.15 Albrecht Dürer, *The Four Horsemen (Apocalypse)*. c. 1497–8. Woodcut, 15½ × 11 ins (39.4 × 28.1 cm). Museum of Fine Arts, Boston (Bequest of Francis Bullard; © 2002 Museum of Fine Arts, Boston).

the Apocalypse (Fig. **11.15**; see also Fig. **1.9**). Here we find the tensions that were evident in northern Europe at the end of the fifteenth century. The emotions of *The Four Horsemen of the Apocalypse* exhibit a medieval preoccupation with superstition, famine, fear, and death that typify German art of this period and place Dürer at a pivot point between medieval and Renaissance styles. This woodcut presents a frightening vision of doomsday and the omens leading up to it, as described in the Revelation of St. John, the last book of the Bible. In the foreground, Death tramples a bishop, and working toward the background, Famine swings a scales, War brandishes a sword, and Pestilence draws a bow. Underneath, trampled by the horses' hoofs, lies the human race. The perspective foreshortening and three-dimensionality of figures reflect the influence of the Italian Renaissance. We can read human character and emotion in the faces of the figures, which individualize them and give them a sense of reality and

a proximity to life that adds depth to the meaning of the work. The technique of the woodcut gives the work its particular quality; Dürer creates lines of delicacy that combine into a poignantly complex picture.

THEATRE While Late Renaissance Italy prepared the way for our modern theatre building and certain acting techniques, sixteenth-century England produced a new theatre of convention, and history's foremost playwright.

England's drama in the mid- to late sixteenth century had a national character, influenced by the severance of Church and state under Henry VIII. Nevertheless, strong Italian literary influences existed in England at this time, and the theatre reflected them. The Elizabethans loved drama, and the theatres of London saw prince and commoner together among their audiences. Elizabethan plays have found universal appeal through the centuries since their first production.

SHAKESPEARE We gain perspective on the Renaissance world's self-perception when we compare the placid, composed reflections of Italian painting with Shakespeare's tragic portraits of intrigue in Renaissance Italy. William Shakespeare (1564–1616; see Profile, p. 149) wrote 154 sonnets, published in 1609, that expressed strong feeling held within precisely crafted artistic form. He also wrote two heroic narratives. We, however, remember him mostly as the pre-eminent Elizabethan playwright, often called the English national poet. Many people consider him the greatest playwright of all time. We do not know for sure the exact order in which he wrote his plays or the chronology of their appearance on the stage. His earliest plays date to the 1590s. The early years of the seventeenth century witnessed his greatest tragedies, such as *Hamlet* (see the Masterworks feature). His last plays (*The Winter's Tale* and *The Tempest*) date to the years 1610–11 and combine romance, comedy, and tragedy in an experimental style that takes the tragic form and applies light-hearted and fanciful elements. There is a robust, peculiarly Elizabethan and Renaissance quality in Shakespeare's plays. His ideas have universal appeal because of his understanding of human motivation and character and his ability to probe deeply into emotion. Shakespeare's plays reflect life and love, action and nationalism; and they present those qualities robustly, in magnificent poetry that explores the English language in unrivaled fashion. Shakespeare's use of tone, color, and complex or new word meanings gives his plays a musical as well as a dramatic quality that appeals to every generation.

We know about the theatres that Shakespeare played in than about his life. They may have looked like the reconstruction in Figure **11.16**.

Masterworks

William Shakespeare, *Hamlet*

Hamlet, Shakespeare's most famous play, was first performed in 1601 and published in 1603. Shakespeare's source for the play may have been Belleforest's *Histoires Tragiques* (1559). Shakespeare's play may also have used as a source a lost play supposedly by Thomas Kyd, usually referred to as the *Ur-Hamlet. Hamlet*, however, has its own unique central element in Hamlet's tragic flaw: his hesitation to avenge his father's murder.

At the beginning of the play, Hamlet mourns the death of his father, who has been murdered, and also laments his mother's marriage to his uncle Claudius within a month of his father's death. Hamlet's father's ghost appears to Hamlet, telling him that he was poisoned by Claudius and asking him to avenge his death. Hamlet hesitates, requiring further evidence of foul play. His uncertainty and hesitancy make him increasingly moody, and everyone believes that Hamlet is going mad. The pompous old courtier Polonius believes that Hamlet is lovesick over his daughter Ophelia.

Despite Claudius's apparent guilt, Hamlet still cannot act. Nevertheless, he terrorizes his mother and kills the eavesdropping Polonius. Fearing for his life, Claudius sends Hamlet to England with his friends Rosencrantz and Guildenstern, who have orders to have Hamlet killed. Discovering the orders, Hamlet arranges to have his friends killed instead. Returning to Denmark, Hamlet learns that Ophelia has killed herself, and that her brother Laertes has vowed vengeance on Hamlet for Polonius's death. Claudius happily arranges the duel. Both Hamlet and Laertes are struck by the sword that Claudius has had dipped in poison. Gertrude mistakenly drinks from the cup of poison intended for Hamlet. Before Hamlet dies, he fatally stabs Claudius.

In the play, Shakespeare appears to suggest that traditional beliefs about revenge are oversimplified, arguing that revenge does not solve evil if evil lies in a complex situation: "The time is out of joint; O cursed spite/That ever I was born to set it right" (V.i.189–90). He also seems to maintain that revenge itself is morally wrong. In *Hamlet*, as well as the other tragedies (*Othello, King Lear,* and *Macbeth*), Shakespeare explores with great psychological subtlety how the personality flaws in the protagonist lead almost inevitably to his own destruction and the destruction of those around him.

Hamlet
Act III, scene i
William Shakespeare
1564–1616

Hamlet:

To be, or not to be: that is the question:
Whether 'tis nobler in the mind to suffer
The slings and arrows of outrageous fortune,
Or to take arms against a sea of troubles,
And by opposing end them? To die: to sleep:
No more; and by a sleep to say we end
The heartache and the thousand natural shocks
That flesh is heir to,—'tis a consummation
Devoutly to be wish'd. To die, to sleep;
To sleep: perchance to dream: ay, there's the rub:
For in that sleep of death what dreams may
    come,
When we have shuffled off this mortal coil,
Must give us pause: there's the respect
That makes calamity of so long life;
For who would bear the whips and scorns of
    time,
The oppressor's wrong, the proud man's
    contumely,
The pangs of despised love, the law's delay,
The insolence of office and the spurns
That patient merit of the unworthy takes,
When he himself might his quietus make
With a bare bodkin? Who would fardels bear,
To grunt and sweat under a weary life,
But that the dread of something after death,
The undiscover'd country from whose bourn
No traveller returns, puzzles the will
And makes us rather bear those ills we have
Than fly to others that we know not of?
Thus conscience does make cowards of us all;
And thus the native hue of resolution
Is sicklied o'er with the pale cast of thought,
And enterprises of great pith and moment
With this regard their currents turn awry,
And lose the name of action.[3]

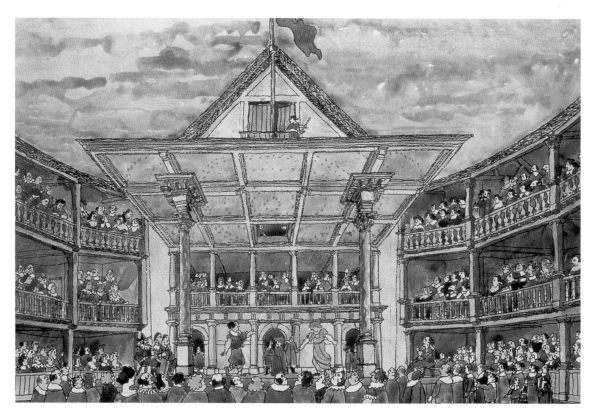

11.16 The second Globe Theatre, London, as reconstructed, c. 1614.

Shakespeare's plays fall into three distinct genres: comedies (including *Love's Labour's Lost*, *A Midsummer Night's Dream*, and *Much Ado About Nothing*), tragedies, and histories. His history plays are large-scale dramatizations and glorifications of events that took place between 1200 and 1550. His greatest tragedy is *Hamlet* (first performed in 1601 and published in 1603). The Hamlet story was a widespread legend in northern Europe.

Shakespeare was not the only significant playwright of the English Renaissance stage. The plays of Christopher Marlowe (1564–93) and Ben Jonson (1573–1637) still captivate theatre audiences.

Marlowe's love of sound permeates his works, and if his character development is weak, his heroic grandeur has the Classical qualities of Aeschylus and Sophocles (see p. 231). His most famous play, *Doctor Faustus* (*The Tragical History of the Life and Death of Doctor Faustus*), first published in 1604, resembles the plot of a medieval morality play, using richly poetic language to narrate a man's temptation, fall, and damnation. His language was a breakthrough in drama of the time. His flexible use of blank verse and the brilliance of his imagery combine to stimulate emotion and rivet his audience's attention. The imagery of terror in the final scene stands among the most powerful in all drama. In addition, Marlowe's language

and imagery unify the play: the patterns in Faust's references to heaven subtly imply the force he cannot escape and yet which he must, at the beginning, deny. "He cannot escape from a world order and from responsibility, nor can he escape from a dream of unfettered domination. That is his tragedy."[4]

MUSIC Renaissance music differed from medieval style particularly in features such as greater melodic and rhythmic integration, a more extended range, broader texture, and subjection to harmonic principles of order. In the sixteenth century this integrated style produced distinct vocal and instrumental idioms, and vocal music, under the influence of humanism, became increasingly intent on expressing a text. In fact, vocal music, because of the humanistic interest in language, was a more important musical idiom than instrumental music. Renaissance composers tried to enhance the meaning and emotion of the written text. In doing so, they often used what we call *word painting*—for example, if a text described a descent, then the music might utilize a descending melodic line. In sum, however, and despite the increased sense of emotion, Renaissance music remained restrained and balanced, avoiding extreme contrasts in dynamics, tone color, or rhythm.

The texture of Renaissance music was mostly polyphonic, with imitation among the voices being fairly common. Homophony also appeared, especially in light music such as dance. In addition, the musical texture of a piece might vary, with the contrast used to highlight the particular emotion of the composition. Its qualities applied across Europe, including Italy, although we discuss it here in the Northern Europe section as a convenience.

SACRED MUSIC In the Renaissance centre of Rome, the papal chapel ranked as one of the central musical forces in Europe. There, the career of composer Giovanni Pierluigi da Palestrina (pah-lehs-TREE-nuh; 1526?–94) flourished; he became the most celebrated composer of his time. Palestrina enjoyed the grace and favor of popes and cardinals. Director of the Julian Chapel Choir from 1551 to 1555, he became a singer in the pontifical choir in the latter year and composed for the papal chapel. Because he was married, however, he was forced to leave his post when Pope Paul IV imposed a stricter discipline in choral appointments. Palestrina's works are exclusively vocal and almost totally liturgical; the only exception is a single book of madrigals and a collection of spiritual madrigals. He wrote 105 masses, of which the *Pope Marcellus Mass* is the most famous. It was dedicated to Pope Marcellus II, who reigned briefly in 1555, when Palestrina sang in the papal choir. The mass uses six voice parts (*a cappella*—without accompaniment): soprano, alto, two tenors, and two basses. Let's examine the "Kyrie" from this mass (music CD track 7). This piece has a rich, polyphonic texture in which the six voices imitate each other. The melodic contours are rounded, evoking images of the Gregorian chant. The melody is in the top voice, the cantus or soprano line. The Kyrie is in three sections:

1. *Kyrie eleison*   (Lord, have mercy upon us).

2. *Christe eleison*   (Christ, have mercy upon us).

3. *Kyrie eleison*   (Lord, have mercy upon us).

The words of this brief text repeat with different melodic treatments and express calm supplication. Each section ends with all voices coming together on sustained chords.

Another important form of Renaissance sacred music is the *motet*, which is like the mass in style, but shorter than the mass. The Renaissance motet is a polyphonic choral work set to a Latin text other than the ordinary of the mass. Its most significant proponent was Flemish composer Josquin Desprez (day-pray; c. 1440–1521), whose four-voice motet, *Ave Maria . . . virgo serena*, contains delicate and serene music.

SECULAR MUSIC The sixteenth century witnessed development of previous forms into the *madrigal*, a setting of lyric poetry for four or five voices. The term madrigal applies to two important types of secular vocal music. One type appeared exclusively in fourteenth-century Italy; the other developed anew and flourished in Italy during the sixteenth century amid an explosion of Italian poetry. The sixteenth-century madrigal normally comprises a text of from three to fourteen lines (of seven and eleven syllables in no particular order) arranged in a rhyme scheme of the poet's choosing. The musical setting emphasizes the mood and meaning of individual words and phrases of the text rather than formal structure.

Madrigals employed as few as three and as many as eight parts, although, in general, before 1650 a four-part texture was preferred. After that, a five-part composition predominated. Madrigals were often performed by solo voices, one per part, but with instruments substituting for some of the voices or doubling the various parts. By the second half of the sixteenth century, the madrigal formed the dominant form of secular music in Italy and the rest of Europe.

Baroque Style

The seventeenth century brought an age of intellectual, spiritual, and physical action. Along with the new age came a tremendously diverse new style, the Baroque. (The word itself originally referred to a large, irregularly shaped pearl of the kind often used in the extremely fanciful jewelry of the post-Renaissance period.) In many cases, the Baroque meant opulence, intricacy, ornateness, and appeal to the emotions, and outdid previous styles in reflecting the grandiose expectations of its patrons. In other cases, it was intellectual and more subdued. The idea of proving one's position to one's peers using overwhelming art took hold of the aristocracy, the bourgeoisie (middle classes), and even the Roman Catholic Church. Its strategy for coping with the Reformation and the spread of Protestantism included attracting worshipers back into the Church with magnificent art, architecture, and music.

Systematic rationalism sprang forth as a means of explaining the universe in secular and scientific terms, and as an organizational concept for works of art. Thus in all Baroque art a sophisticated organizational scheme subordinates a multitude of single parts to the whole and carefully merges one part into the next to create an exceedingly complex but highly unified design. The world became more and more secularized as power shifted from the Church to more worldly institutions. Over all of them reigned the absolute or all-powerful monarch.

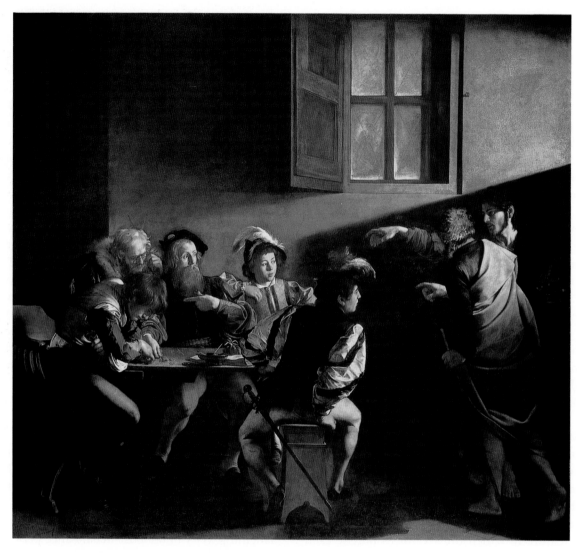

11.17 Caravaggio, *The Calling of St. Matthew*, c. 1596–8. Oil on canvas, 11 ft 1 in × 11 ft 5 ins (3.38 × 3.48 m). Contarelli Chapel, Santo Luigi dei Francesi, Rome.

The idea of absolutism dominated individual as well as collective psychology in the baroque age, each man governing his life like an absolute monarch. Balthasar Gracian advises the courtier: "Let all your actions be those of a king, or at least worthy of a king in due proportion to your estate." Every man was inwardly a king. The ego, or the superego, became an entity which recognized no limits beyond itself. . . . The baroque artist exercises this sovereignty "in due proportion to his estate" as Balthasar Gracian would have any man do; that is, his art. The seventeenth century produced artists who, if not solitaries, were at least independent men . . . who considered their art, even if it depended upon commissions, as a personal activity, allowing no limits to be placed on their creative power.[5]

The Baroque emphasized color and grandeur, while dramatic use of lights and darks carry the viewer's eye off

the canvas. Baroque art takes Renaissance clarity of form and recasts it into intricate patterns of geometry and fluid movement. Open composition symbolizes the notion of an expansive universe and a wider reality. The human figure, as an object or focus in painting, can be monumental in full Renaissance fashion, but can also now be a minuscule figure in a landscape—part of, but subordinate to, an overwhelming universe. Above all, Baroque style characterizes intensely active compositions that emphasize feeling rather than form, and emotion rather than intellect. Paintings exhibit clear individuality. Virtuosity emerged as artists sought to establish a style distinctly their own.

PAINTING Baroque painting is identifiable as a general style, although its uses were diverse and pluralistic, not conforming to a simple mold. It spread throughout

Europe with examples in every area between 1600 and 1725. Our examination encompasses three important painters in the Baroque style: Caravaggio (kah-rah-VAHD-joh), Rubens, and Rembrandt. There were many others, whose inclusion space does not permit, including Jan Vermeer (see Fig. 1.39) and the Spanish painter Diego Velázquez, whose well-known and intriguing painting *Las Meninas* (*The Maids of Honor*) can be studied at http://www.artchive.com/meninas.htm.

CARAVAGGIO In Rome—the center of early Baroque—papal patronage and the Catholic Reformation spirit brought artists together to make Rome the "most beautiful city of the entire Christian world." Caravaggio (Michelangelo Merisi, 1569–1609) was probably the most significant of the Roman Baroque painters. His extraordinary style carries lifelikeness to new heights. In *The Calling of St. Matthew* (Fig. 11.17) highlight and shadow create a dynamic portrayal of the moment when the future apostle is touched by divine grace. Here a religious subject emerges in contemporary terms. Turning away from idealized Renaissance form, Caravaggio uses realistic imagery and an everyday setting. The call from Christ streams, in dramatic chiaroscuro, across the two groups of figures. This painting expresses central themes of Catholic Reformation belief: faith and grace are open to all who have the courage and simplicity to transcend intellectual pride, and spiritual understanding is a personal, mysterious, and overpowering emotional experience.

RUBENS Peter Paul Rubens (1577–1640) is noted for his vast, overwhelming paintings and fleshy female nudes. In 1622–5, he painted a series of works as a commission from Maria de' Medici, a Florentine princess, the widow of the French king Henri IV, and regent during the minority of her son Louis XIII. *Henry IV Receiving the Portrait of Maria de' Medici* (Fig. 11.18) is one of twenty-one canvases that portray an allegorical version of the queen's life. In this painting, we see Rubens's ornate curvilinear composition, lively action, and complex color. The corpulent cupids (*putti*) and female flesh give it a sense of softness and warmth found in the work of few other artists. Rubens uses warm colors, along with deep rich blues, throughout the picture. Strong contrast makes for enhanced dynamics between lights and darks and between lively and more subdued tones. The composition sweeps from upper left to lower right and circles around the rectangular frame of Maria's portrait at the juncture of the vertical, horizontal, and diagonal axes. The painting seems to swirl before the viewer's eyes. Rich in detail, each finely rendered part subordinates to the whole. Rubens leads the eye around the painting, upward, downward,

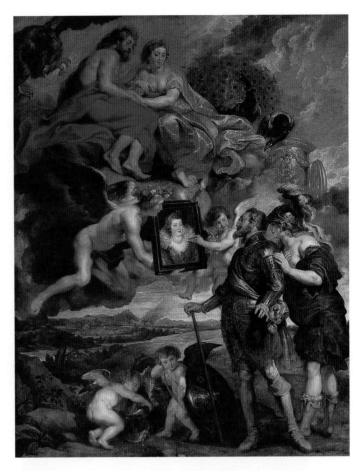

11.18 Peter Paul Rubens, *Henry IV Receiving the Portrait of Maria de' Medici*, 1622–5. Oil on canvas, 13 ft × 9 ft 8 ins (3.96 × 2.95 m). Louvre, Paris.

inward, and outward, occasionally escaping the frame altogether. Nevertheless, the sophisticated composition beneath all this complexity holds the base of the painting solidly in place and leads the eye to the smiling face of Maria. The overall effect creates a sense of richness, glamor, and optimism. It appeals directly to the emotions rather than the intellect.

The Classical allegory of the painting shows Minerva, the Roman goddess of wisdom, advising the aging King Henry IV (whose helmet and shield are being stolen by the cupids) to accept the Florentine princess as his second bride. Maria's portrait is presented by Mercury, god of commerce, while Juno and Jupiter, the principal Roman gods, look on approvingly. The painting depicts happy promises of divine intervention, radiant good health, and grandeur.

Rubens produced works at a prolific rate, primarily because he ran what was virtually a painting factory where he employed numerous artists and apprentices to assist in his work. He priced his paintings on the basis of their size and depending on how much actual work he,

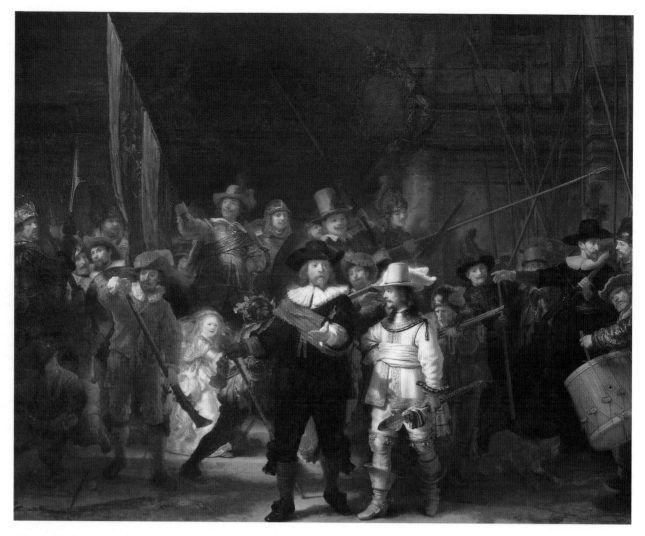

11.19 Rembrandt van Rijn, *The Night Watch* (*The Company of Captain Frans Banning Cocq*), 1642. Oil on canvas, 12 ft 2 ins × 14 ft 6 ins (3.7 × 4.44 m). Rijksmuseum, Amsterdam.

personally, had done on them. We should not be overly disturbed by this, especially when we consider the individual qualities and concepts expressed in his work. His unique Baroque style emerges from every painting, and many untrained observers can recognize a Rubens with relative ease. Clearly artistic value here lies in the conception, not merely in the handiwork.

REMBRANDT Rembrandt van Rijn (1606–69), in contrast to Rubens, could be called a middle-class artist. Born in Leiden in the Netherlands, he trained under local artists and then moved to Amsterdam. His early and rapid success gained him many commissions and students. Rembrandt became what can only be called a capitalist artist. He believed that art had value not only in itself but also in its market worth. He reportedly spent huge sums of money buying his own works so as to increase their value.

Rembrandt's genius lay in depicting human emotions and characters. He suggests rather than depicts great detail, as seen in *The Night Watch*, which is one of his greatest works (Fig. **11.19**). He concentrates here on atmosphere and shadow, implication and emotion. As in most Baroque art, the artist invites the viewer to share in an emotion, to enter into an experience rather than to observe as an impartial witness.

The huge canvas now in the Rijksmuseum in Amsterdam represents only a portion of the original, which was cut down in the eighteenth century to fit into a space in Amsterdam Town Hall. It no longer shows the bridge that members of the watch were about to cross. Group portraits, especially of military units, were popular at the time. They usually showed the company in a social setting such as a gathering around a banquet table. Rembrandt chose to break with the norm and portrayed the company as if on duty. It resulted in a scene of greater vigor and dramatic intensity, true to the Baroque spirit—but it displeased his patrons.

A recent cleaning has revealed the vivid color of the original, making it a good deal brighter than its previous state. However, it has not explained its dramatic highlights and shadows—no analysis of light can solve the problem of how these figures are illuminated, for no natural light whatsoever occurs in the scene.

Another problem lies in the title of the work. It has been suggested that this is, in fact, a "Day Watch," so that the intense light found at the center of the work can be explained as morning sunlight. But it seems that Rembrandt has made his choice of highlights for dramatic purposes only. While the figures show a fair degree of lifelikeness, no such claim can be made for the light sources.

SCULPTURE The Baroque style was particularly suited to the medium of sculpture. Sculptors charged form and space with energy, carrying beyond the limits of actual physical confines. As with painting, sculpture appealed to the emotions by inviting participation rather than neutral observation. Feeling was the focus. Baroque sculpture also treated space pictorially, almost like a painting, to describe action scenes rather than creating single sculptural forms. The best examples we can draw upon belong to the sculptor Gianlorenzo Bernini (bair-NEE-nee; 1598–1680).

David (Fig. **11.20**) exudes dynamic power, action, and emotion as he curls to unleash his stone at an imagined Goliath standing some distance away. Our eyes sweep upward along a diagonally curved line and are propelled outward by the concentrated emotion of David's expression. Throughout the work the curving theme repeats in deep, rich, and fully contoured form. A wealth of elegant and ornamental detail occupies the composition. Again the viewer participates emotionally, feels the drama, and responds to the sensuous contours of dramatically articulated muscles. Bernini's *David* flexes and contracts in action, rather than repressing pent-up energy as does Michelangelo's giant-slayer (see Fig. **2.13**).

ARCHITECTURE Probably no monarch better represents the *absolutism* of the Baroque era than the French King Louis XIV, known as the Sun King (reigned 1643–1715). And no artwork better represents the magnificence and grandeur of the Baroque style than does the Palace of Versailles (see Fig. **3.25**), near Paris, and its sculpture and grounds—a grand design of buildings and nature to reflect systematic rationalism. The great Versailles complex grew from the modest hunting lodge of Louis XIII into the grand palace of the Sun King over a number of

years, involving several architects, and amid curious political and religious circumstances.

The Versailles *château* (French for "castle") was rebuilt in 1631 by Philibert Le Roy. The façade was decorated by Louis Le Vau with bricks and stone, sculpture, wrought iron, and gilt lead. In 1668 Louis XIV ordered Le Vau to enlarge the *château* by enclosing it in a stone envelope containing the king's and queen's apartments. Jules Hardouin-Mansart expanded the *château* into a palace whose west façade extends over 2,000 feet (609 m). It became Louis XIV's permanent residence in 1682. French royalty was at the height of its power and Versailles was the symbol of the Divine Right of Kings—the absolute authority of the monarch.

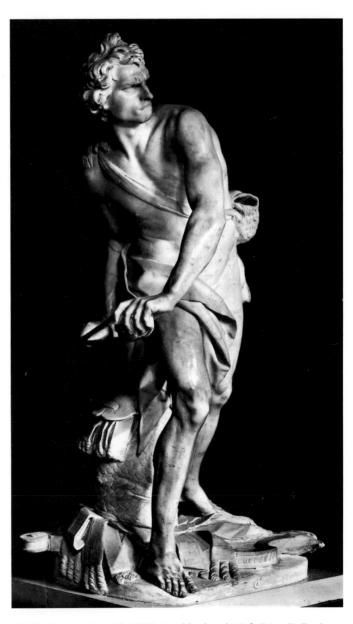

11.20 Bernini, *David*, 1623. Marble, height 5 ft 7 ins (1.7 m). Galleria Borghese, Rome.

As a symbol and in practical fact, Versailles played a fundamental role in keeping France stable. Its symbolism as a magnificent testament to royal centrality and to France's sense of nationalism is fairly obvious. As a practical device, Versailles served the purpose of pulling the aristocracy out of Paris where they could foment discontent, and isolated them where Louis XIV could keep his eye on them and keep them busy. Versailles further served as a giant economic engine to develop and export French taste and the French luxury trades.

MUSIC Baroque music did not differ from its visual cousins in that in many cases it was shaped by the needs of churches, which used its emotional and theatrical qualities to make worship more attractive and appealing. The term "Baroque" refers to music written during the period extending approximately from 1600 to 1750.

Baroque composers began to write for specific instruments, or for voices, in contrast to earlier music that might be equally well sung or played. They also brought to their music new kinds of action and tension, for example, quick, strong contrasts in tone color or volume, and strict rhythms juxtaposed against free rhythms. The Baroque era was crucial to the development of modern musical language.

INSTRUMENTAL MUSIC As Baroque composers began to write specifically for individual voices and instruments, instrumental music assumed a new importance, and musical instruments underwent technical development. A new system of "equal temperament," in which each half-step in the musical scale is equidistant from the preceding or following, was established and illustrated in a series of two sets of preludes and fugues in all possible keys (*The Well-Tempered Clavier* [klah-VEER]) by Johann Sebastian Bach, in 1722 and 1740. In this keyboard music, the fugue (see Chapter 4), with its formal structure and strict imitation, illustrates the complexity and virtuosity of Baroque composition.

The word *sonata* (suh-NAH-tuh) is one of the most elastic terms in music and has been used to refer to many different musical forms. The name itself comes from the Italian *sonare* (to sound) and came into use during the Baroque era to indicate any piece played on instruments, as distinct from the vocal *cantata*, which means "sung." Its most popular treatment during the seventeenth century became known as the trio sonata, with two high, intertwining parts for violins, flutes, or oboes played above a bass part for cello or bassoon. Usually an organist or harpsichordist played along to reinforce the bass and fill in harmonies indicated by numerals written in the bass part (a practice called "figured bass").

The concerto (see Chapter 4) was one of the forms that was contributed to Western music by the Baroque age. One of the masters of the concerto Antonio Vivaldi (vee-VAHL-dee; 1675?–1741) composed for specific occasions and usually for a specific company of performers. Probably his most familiar solo concerto is "Spring," one of four works in opus 8 (1725), *The Four Seasons*. *The Four Seasons*, an early example of *program music*, illustrates an external idea, in contrast with *absolute music*, which presents purely musical ideas. In "Spring," a series of individual pieces interlock to form an ornate whole. In the first movement (allegro) Vivaldi alternates an opening theme (A) with sections that depict bird song, a flowing brook, a storm, and the birds' return (ABACADAEA).

VOCAL MUSIC As we just noted, the Italian word *cantata* denotes "sung" (see Chapter 4). It comprises vocal compositions with instrumental accompaniment, with several movements based on related text segments. It developed from monody, or solo singing with a predominant vocal line, centering on a text to which the music was subservient. These works, which consisted of many short, contrasting sections, were far less spectacular than opera, and they were designed to be written for solo soprano voice, although many used other voices and groups of voices. Two types of cantatas existed during the Baroque era: secular and religious.

In Germany, the cantata was a sacred work that grew out of the Lutheran chorale. The master of the sacred cantata was J. S. Bach who, under obligation as a choirmaster, composed a new cantata weekly; he wrote more than 200 between 1704 and 1740. His cantatas were primarily contrapuntal (polyphonic) in texture, usually scored for up to four soloists and a four-part chorus. An excellent example, with a well-known theme, is *Cantata No. 80*: "Ein feste Burg ist unser Gott" ("A Mighty Fortress is Our God," Fig. **11.21**). Martin Luther wrote the chorale on which the cantata is based (Luther probably wrote both words and music), and the chorale represents a centerpiece of Protestant hymnology. Luther's words and melody appear in the first, second, fifth, and last movements. Salomo Franck, Bach's favorite librettist, wrote the remainder of the text. The first movement, a choral fugue, states the familiar theme and text:

> A mighty fortress is our God,
> A good defense and weapon;
> He helps free us from all the troubles
> That have now befallen us.
> Our ever evil foe,
> In earnest plots against us,

Profile

Johann Sebastian Bach

Although currently considered one of the giants of music, Johann Sebastian Bach (1685–1750) was considered old-fashioned during his lifetime, and his works lay virtually dormant after his death. Not until the nineteenth century did he gain recognition as one of the greatest composers of the Western world. Bach was born in Thuringia, in what is now Germany, and when he was ten years old both his parents died. His oldest brother, Johann Christoph, took responsibility for raising and teaching him, and Johann Sebastian became a choirboy at the Michaelskirche in Luneburg when he was fifteen. He studied the organ and was appointed organist at Neukirche in Arnstadt, where he remained for four years. Then he took a similar post at Muhlhausen at about the same time as he married his cousin, Maria Barbara Bach. One year later, he took the position of court organist at Weimar, remaining there until 1717, when Prince Leopold of Kothen hired him as his musical director. While he was serving as musical director to Prince Leopold, Bach completed the Brandenberg Concertos in 1721.

In 1720 Bach's wife died, and one year later he married Anna Magdalena Wilcken. In 1723 he moved to Leipzig as the city's musical director at the school attached to St Thomas's Church, and among his responsibilities to the city was the supply of performers for four churches. In 1747 he played at Potsdam for Frederick II the Great of Prussia but shortly thereafter his eyesight began to fail, and he went blind just before his death in 1750.

Bach had a prodigious output as a composer but this also represents a requirement as part of his responsibilities, especially at Leipzig. Over his career, he wrote more than 200 cantatas, the *Mass in B Minor*, and three settings of the Passion story, works that illustrate Bach's deep religious faith. His sacred music allowed him to explore and communicate the profound mysteries of the Christian faith and to glorify God. His cantatas typify the Baroque exploration of wide-ranging emotional development. They range from ecstatic expressions of joy to profound meditations on death. The Passions, of which the *St. Matthew Passion* is typical, tell the story of the trial and crucifixion of Jesus. Written in German rather than the traditional Latin, the Passions express Bach's devotion to Lutheranism.

In addition to his sacred works, Bach wrote a tremendous amount of important music for harpsichord and organ, including the forty-eight Preludes and Fugues, called *The Well-Tempered Clavier*, and the *Goldberg Variations*. In the fugues, he develops a single theme, which is then imitated and polyphonically developed among the voices of the composition. His many instrumental pieces include twenty concertos and twelve unaccompanied works—six for violin and six for cello. Learn more at www.jsbach.org/.

With great strength and cunning
He prepares his dreadful plans.
Earth holds none like him.

The final movement of the work rounds off the cantata. Luther's chorale is now sung in Bach's own four-part harmonization. Instruments double each voice, and the simple, powerful melody stands out against the lower parts:

Das Wort, sie sollen lassen stahn
    und kein Dank dazu haben.
Er ist bei uns wohl auf dem Plan
    mit seinem Geist und Gaben.
Nehmen sie uns den Leib,

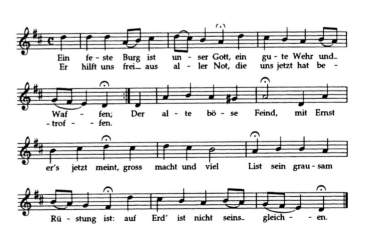

11.21 J. S. Bach, "Ein feste Burg ist unser Gott" from Cantata No. 80.

Gut, Her, Kind und Weib,
    lass fahren dahin
    sie habens kein Gevinn
das Reich muss uns doch bleiben.

Now let the Word of God abide
    without further thought.
He is firmly on our side
    with His spirit and strength.
Though they deprive us of life,
Wealth, honor, child and wife,
    we will not complain,
    It will avail them nothing
For God's kingdom must prevail.

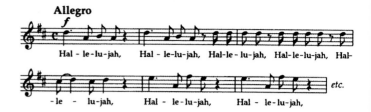

11.22 G. F. Handel, "Hallelujah Chorus" from the *Messiah*.

Baroque operas (see Chapter 4) grew out of late fifteenth-century madrigals. Many of these madrigals—some called "madrigal comedies" and some called *intermedi*—were written to be performed between the acts of theatre productions. They were fairly dramatic, and included pastoral scenes, narrative reflections, and amorous adventures. They gave rise to a new style of solo singing. The first surviving opera, *Euridice* (yoo-RID-ih-see), written by Jacopo Peri (YAH-koh-poh PAY-ree; 1561–1633), took up a contemporary pastoral drama and used characters from Greek mythology. By the second half of the seventeenth century, opera had become an important art form, especially in Italy, but also in France, Germany, and England.

Henry Purcell's *Dido and Aeneas* (1689) (music CD track 10; "Dido's Lament"), which we noted in Chapter 4, is the first opera of significance composed by an Englishman. Purcell composed it for a girls' school. The English poet laureate Nahum Tate wrote the libretto which tells a classical tale of passion and death based on the fourth book of Virgil's *Aeneid*.

Another major development in the same vein, the oratorio, had a broad scale like an opera, combining a sacred subject with a poetic text. Like a cantata, the oratorio was designed for concert performance, without scenery or costume. However, many oratorios could be staged and have highly developed dramatic content with soloists portraying specific characters.

Oratorio began in Italy in the early seventeenth century, but its greatest master was George Frederick Handel (1685–1759). Although German by birth, he lived in England and wrote oratorios in English. Most of his oratorios have highly dramatic structures and contain exposition, conflict or complication, and dénouement or resolution sections. Many could be staged in full operatic tradition (except for two outstanding examples, *Israel in Egypt* and *Messiah*). Handel's oratorios rely strongly on the chorus. The choral numbers are most frequently polyphonic, with soprano, alto, tenor, and bass parts each taking a turn with the same melody, although Handel employs homophonic sections, too. Most of the solo arias can stand on their own as performance pieces. They also fit magnificently together in a systematic development, usually following a portion of recitative, where the story-line is progressed.

Handel's works continue to enjoy wide popularity, and each year *Messiah* has thousands of performances around the world. Written in 1741 in twenty-four days, the work is made up of three parts: the birth of Jesus; Jesus' death and resurrection; and the redemption of humanity. The music comprises an overture, choruses, recitatives, and arias, and is written for small orchestra, chorus, and soloists. The choruses provide some of the world's best-loved music, including the famous, jubilant, "Hallelujah Chorus."

The "Hallelujah Chorus" (music CD track 9) provides the climax of the second part of the work. The text proclaims a victorious Lord whose host is an army with banners. Handel creates infinite variety by sudden changes of texture among monophony, polyphony, and homophony. Words and phrases are repeated over and over again (Fig. **11.22**). In unison the voices and instruments proclaim, "for the Lord God omnipotent reigneth." Polyphony marks the repeated exclamations of "Hallelujah" and yields to homophony in the hymnlike "The kingdom of this world."

LITERATURE Throughout the fifteenth century, medieval forms continued to dominate literature in Europe. The sixteenth century witnessed a true renaissance of national literatures. These were influenced in Protestant countries by the Reformation. For Roman Catholics, especially in Spain, the Counter-Reformation gave literature a deep religious emotion. Illustrative of the times, Miguel de Cervantes' (sur-VAHN-tayz; 1547–1616) *Don Quixote* (dahn kee-HOH-tay) drew a composite picture of the Spanish people that captured their mixed philosophies of realism and idealism. Written in two parts (1605 and 1615), this work has become one of the most widely read classics in Western literature.

The novel has a realistic style that satirizes the chivalric romances popular at the time. Don Quixote, Cervantes' hero, has a head full of fantasies from reading romances as he sets off to seek adventure on his old horse Rosinante with his faithful and pragmatic squire Sancho Panza. Along the way, he finds love in the person of the peasant Dulcinea (duhl-sih-NAY-uh). Cervantes uses irony as a literary device throughout the work.

After the golden age of the late sixteenth century, the mood in England darkened noticeably with the death of Queen Elizabeth in 1603. Political instability and economic difficulties threatened, and the finest writing of the time turned away from love—almost the exclusive theme of the Elizabethans—to an often anguished inner questioning.

This turn in mood led to the rise of the metaphysical poets, who wrote in a highly intellectualized, bold, ingenious, complex, and subtle style—again, typical of the baroque. The metaphysical poets utilized paradox, deliberate harshness or rigidity of expression, and probed into the analysis of emotion. Metaphysical poetry blended emotion and intellectualism, characterized by the sometimes forced juxtaposition of seemingly unconnected ideas intended to startle the reader to think through the argument of the poem. Bold literary devices, especially irony and paradox, reinforced a dramatic directness of the language employed, which followed the natural rhythms of everyday speech.

Metaphysical poetry's most notable work came from John Donne (duhn; 1573–1631). Donne's early love sonnets rank among the most urgently erotic poems in the language, but the work of his later years relentlessly explores the meaning of an intelligent person's relationship with the soul and with God. We perhaps know him best from his poem, "Death, Be Not Proud."

Death, Be Not Proud
John Donne

Death, be not proud, though some have called thee
Mighty and dreadful, for thou art not so;
For those whom thou think'st thou dost over throw
Die not, poor Death, nor yet canst thou kill me.
From rest and sleep, which but thy pictures be,
Much pleasure; then from thee much more must flow,
And soonest our best men with thee do go,
Rest of their bones, and soul's delivery.
Thou'rt slave to fate, chance, kings, and desperate men,
And dost with poison, war, and sickness dwell;
And poppy or charms can make us sleep as well
And better than my stroke; why swell'st thou then?
One short sleep past; we wake eternally,
And death shall be no more: Death, thou shalt die.

Notice that Donne retains the classical form we have now seen so often. He chides death as ineffectual, no more effective than drugs, subject to all sorts of vagaries, and subject to the ultimate defeat of the Resurrection (Donne was Dean of St. Paul's Cathedral in London).

During this era, writers in both France and England began to experiment with a versatile new form, which, because of its extended length and realistic language, seemed ideally suited to the treatment of contemporary and everyday themes. The Englishman Daniel Defoe (dee-FOH; 1660–1731) set the direction that the European novel would take. His *Robinson Crusoe* remains widely read to this day, and his *Moll Flanders* defined the novel's voice and audience for the age. Subsequent novels involved imaginary biographies or autobiographies set in contemporary society. The central figure would be a man or, more commonly, a woman, with whom the reader (usually female) would identify.

Aphra Behn (1640–89) was the first Englishwoman known to have earned her living by writing—thereby winning praise from the modern writer Virginia Woolf in *A Room of One's Own*. Behn's novel *Oroonoko* (1688) tells the story of an enslaved African prince whom Behn knew in South America. This work proved highly influential in the development of the English novel. She also wrote poetry and plays, among which is *The Forc'd Marriage* (1677). Her comedies—for example, *The Rover* (two parts—1677 and 1681) were witty, vivacious, full of social satire focused on sexual relations, and highly successful. She wrote many popular novels and, due to her charm and generosity, had a wide circle of friends. Her relative freedom as a female professional writer, however, and her use of lewd language and daring themes made her the object of scandal.

The Enlightenment

ROCOCO STYLE In the eighteenth century, the aristocracy of Europe found itself in decline, and the *Rococo* (roh-coh-COH) style reflected their increasingly superficial and delicate condition.

Among other characteristics, the Rococo satirized the customs of the age, but criticized with humor. Its intimate grace, charm, and delicate superficiality reflect the social ideals and manners of the period. Informality replaced formality in both life and painting. The logic and academic character of the Baroque style seemed lacking in feeling and sensitivity; its overwhelming scale and grandeur too ponderous. In Rococo art, deeply dramatic action gives way to lively effervescence and melodrama. Love, sentiment, pleasure, and sincerity become predominant themes. None of these characteristics conflicts with

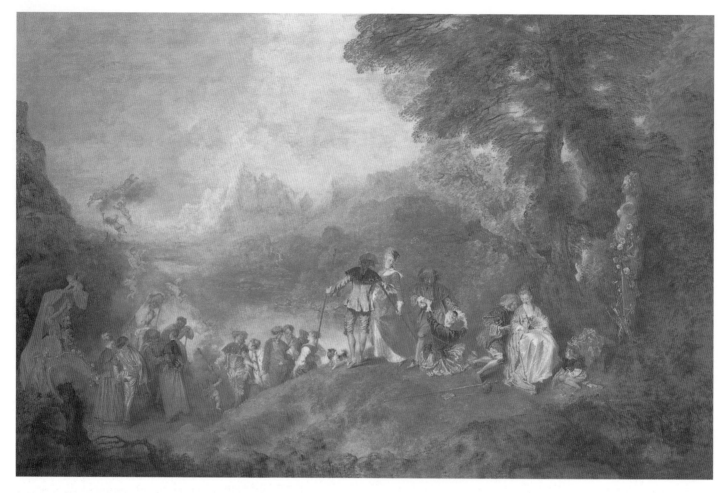

11.23 Antoine Watteau, *Embarkation for Cythera*, 1717. Oil on canvas, 4 ft 3 ins × 6 ft 4½ ins (1.3 × 1.94 m). Louvre, Paris.

the overall tone of the Enlightenment, which sought refinement of humankind. The arts of the period dignified the human spirit through social consciousness and bourgeois social morality, as well as through the graceful gamesmanship of love. Delicacy, informality, lack of grandeur, and lack of action did not always imply superficiality or limp sentimentality.

The quandary of the declining aristocracy is reflected in the Rococo paintings of Antoine Watteau (wah-TOH; 1683–1721). Although largely sentimental, Watteau's work avoids frivolity. *Embarkation for Cythera* (SIH-theh-ruh; Fig. 11.23) gives an idealized picture of aristocratic social graces. Cythera is a mythological land of enchantment—the island of Venus, Roman goddess of love. Watteau portrays aristocrats waiting to depart, idling away their time in amorous pursuits. The fantasy quality of the landscape emerges through fuzzy color areas and hazy atmosphere. A soft, undulating line underscores the human figures, all posed in slightly affected attitudes. Watteau's fussy details and decorative treatment of clothing stand in contrast to the diffused quality of the back-

ground. Each grouping of couples engages in graceful conversation and love games typical of the age. Delicacy pervades the scene, over which an armless bust of Venus presides. The doll-like figurines, which are only symbols, engage in sophisticated and elegant pleasure, but their usefulness is past, and the softness and affectation of the work counterbalance gaiety with languid sorrow.

THE ENGLISH SCHOOL The Enlightenment brought forth in England several directions of approach. For our purposes, we illustrate just one—landscape painting—and mention a second: portraiture. Portraiture and landscape painting became increasingly popular during the eighteenth century. One of the most influential English artists of the time was Thomas Gainsborough (1727–88), whose landscapes bridge the gap between Baroque and Romantic style and whose portraits range from Rococo lightheartedness to sensitive elegance.

The Market Cart (Fig. 11.24) reminds us of Watteau and other Rococo painters from mainland Europe in its delicate use of color. Gainsborough's exploration of tonal-

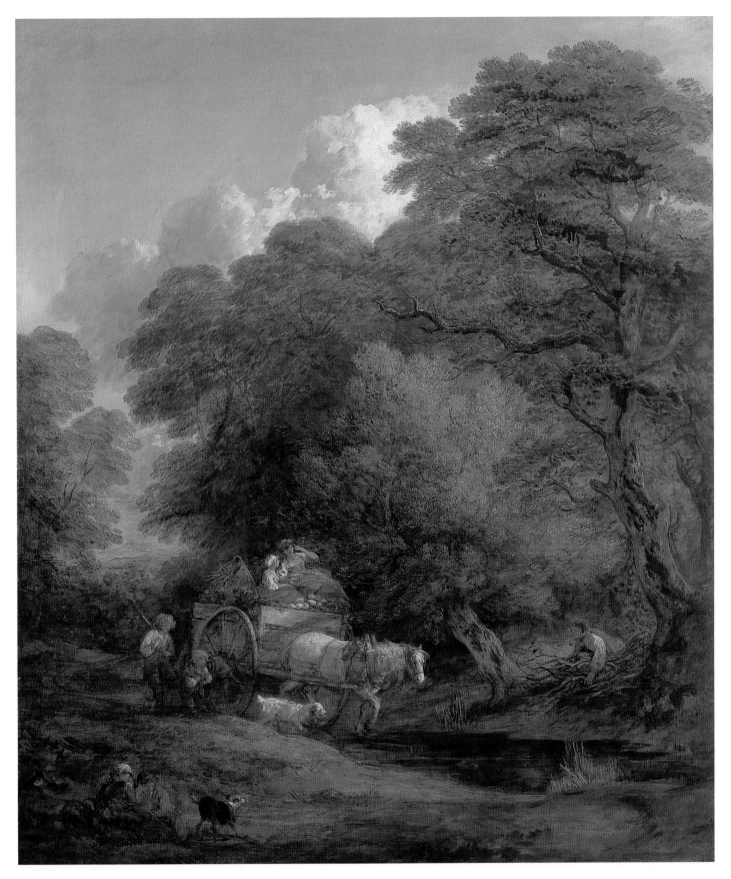

11.24 Thomas Gainsborough, *The Market Cart*, 1786–7. Oil on canvas, 6 ft ½ in × 5 ft ¼ in (1.84 × 1.53 m). Tate Gallery, London.

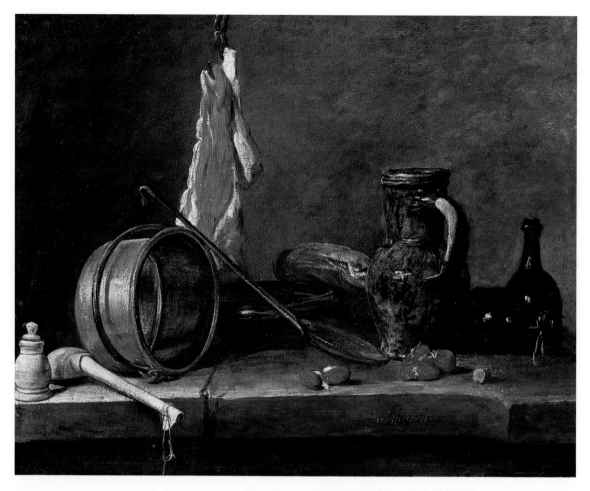

11.25 Jean-Baptiste Siméon Chardin, *Menu de Gras*, 1731. Oil on canvas, 13 × 16⅛ ins (33 × 41 cm). Louvre, Paris.

ities and shapes expresses a deep and almost mystical response to nature. Although pastoral, the composition derives energy from its diagonal character. The tree forms on the right border are twisted and gnarled. The foremost tree leads the viewer's eye up and to the left, to be caught by the downward circling line of the trees and clouds in the background and returned on the diagonal. Gainsborough does not wish us to become too interested in the humans in the picture—they are warmly rendered, but not as specific individuals. Their forms remain indistinct, suggesting that they are subordinate to the forces of nature that ebb and flow around and through them.

GENRE A new bourgeois flavor inhabits the mundane (genre) subjects of France's Jean-Baptiste Siméon Chardin (1699–1779). He was the finest still-life and genre painter of his time, on a par with Dutch masters of the previous century such as Jan Vermeer, whose technique we looked at in Chapter 1 (see Fig. 1.39). His early works are almost exclusively still lifes. *Menu de Gras* (Fig. 11.25) illustrates how the everyday can be imbued with interest. With

gentle insight, the artist invests cooking pot, ladle, pitcher, bottles, cork, a slab of meat, and other small items with significance. Richness of texture and color combined with sensitive composition and the use of chiaroscuro make these humble items somehow noble. The eye moves slowly from point to point, carefully directed by shapes and angles, color and highlight. The work controls the speed of our viewing: each new focus demands that we pause and savor its richness. There is pure poetry in Chardin's brush. We are subtly urged to go beyond the surface impression of the objects themselves into a deeper reality.

NEOCLASSICAL PAINTING The late eighteenth century went whirling back to antiquity, and in particular to nature, in the light of the discovery of the ruins of Pompeii, the art historian Winckelmann's interpretation of Greek Classicism, the philosopher Rousseau's concept of the Noble Savage, and the philosopher Baumgarten's invention of the term "aesthetics." Theoreticians of the eighteenth century saw history as a series of compartments—Antiquity, Middle Ages, Renaissance, and so on—

Jacques-Louis David, *The Oath of the Horatii*

David's famous painting *The Oath of the Horatii* (Fig. **11.26**) concerns the conflict between love and patriotism. In legend, the leaders of the Roman and Alban armies, on the verge of battle, decided to resolve their conflicts by means of an organized combat between three representatives from each side. The three Horatius brothers represented Rome; the Curatius sons represented the Albans. A sister of the Horatii was the fiancée of one of the Curatius brothers. David's painting depicts the Horatii as they swear on their swords to win or die for Rome, disregarding the anguish of their sister.

The work captures a directness and intensity of expression that were to play an important role in Romanticism. But the starkness of outline, the strong geometric composition (which juxtaposes straight line in the men and curved line in the women), and the smooth color areas and gradations hold it to the more formal, Classical tradition. The style represents academic Neoclassicism. The scene takes place in a shallow picture box, defined by a severely simple architectural framework. The costumes are historically correct. The musculature, even the arms and legs of the women, has a surface devoid of warmth or softness, like the drapery.

Ironically, David's work was admired and purchased by King Louis XVI, against whom David's revolutionary cries were later directed and whom David, as a member of the French Revolutionary Convention, would sentence to death. Neoclassicism increased in popularity and continued through the Napoleonic era and into the nineteenth century.

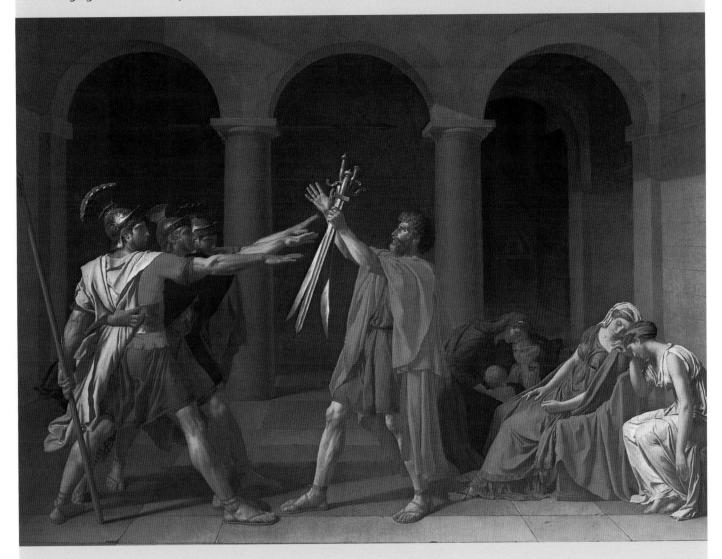

11.26 Jacques-Louis David, *The Oath of the Horatii*, 1784–5. Oil on canvas, approx. 14 × 11 ft (4.27 × 3.35 m). Louvre, Paris.

rather than as a single, continuous cultural stream broken by a medieval collapse of Classical values.

One of the principal Neoclassical painters, Jacques-Louis David (dah-VEED; 1748–1825), illustrates the newly perceived grandeur of antiquity and its reflection in subject matter, composition, depiction, and historical accuracy. They show a Roman two-dimensionality and have a strong, classically simple compositional unity. But Classical detail and principles are treated selectively and adapted—the Neoclassicism of David and others does not copy ancient works. David sought to inspire patriotism and democracy, and so some of his works are propagandist in tone (see Fig. **11.26**).

NEOCLASSICAL ARCHITECTURE In the mid-eighteenth century architecture changed entirely, embracing the complex philosophical concerns of the Enlightenment. Three important concepts emerged as a result. The first, the archeological concept, viewed the present as continually enriched by persistent inquiry into the past—the idea of *progress*. The second, *eclecticism*, allowed artists to choose among styles or, more importantly, to combine elements of various styles. The third, *modernism*, viewed the present as unique and, therefore, possible of expression in its own terms. These concepts fundamentally changed the basic premises of art from that time forward. Basic to Neoclassicism in architecture are the identifiable forms of Greece and Rome. The revival of Classicism in architecture acted in many quarters as a revolt against the frivolity of the Rococo with a serious and moral art.

The designs of colonial architects like Thomas Jefferson (1743–1826) reflect the complex interrelationships of this period. Jefferson's philosophy of architecture professed that the architecture of antiquity embodied indisputable natural principles. He was highly influenced, too, by the Italian architect Andrea Palladio (1508–80), who enjoyed popularity in a significant revival in English villa architecture between 1710 and 1750. Jefferson felt that a theory of architecture could be built on a Palladian-style reconstruction of the Roman temple. Monticello (Fig. **11.27**) has at its center superimposed Doric and Ionic *porticos* (porches). Short, low wings are attached by continuing Doric *entablatures*. The simplicity and refinement of Jefferson's building go beyond reconstruction of Classical prototypes and appeal directly to the intellect.

NEOCLASSICAL MUSIC Neoclassicism also appeared in music, which, having no "classical" antecedents, we call, simply, "Classical." It had, among others, five basic characteristics, discussed below:

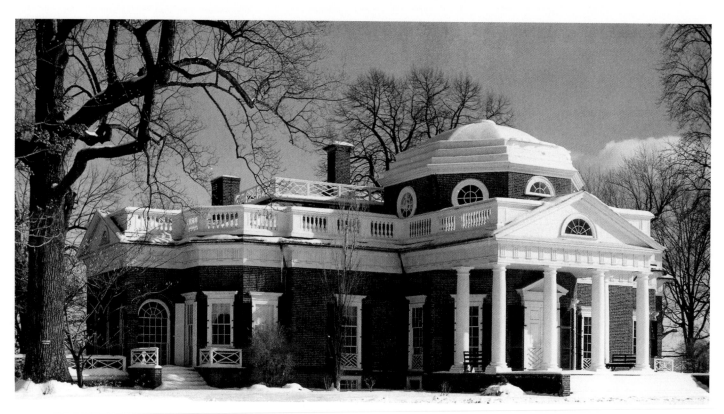

11.27 Thomas Jefferson, Monticello, Charlottesville, Virginia, 1770–84 (rebuilt 1796–1800).

1 Variety and contrast in *mood*. In contrast to Baroque style, which typically dealt with a single emotion, Classical pieces typically explore contrasts between moods. They may contrast moods within movements and also within themes. Changes in mood may be gradual or sudden; they are, however, as one might expect of a style called "Classical," well controlled, unified, and logical.

2 Flexibility of *rhythm*. Classical music explores a wide variety of rhythms, utilizing unexpected pauses, syncopations, and frequent changes from long to shorter notes. As in mood, changes in rhythm may be sudden or gradual.

3 A predominantly homophonic *texture*. Nonetheless, texture remains flexible, with sudden and gradual shifts from one texture to another. In general, the texture of Classical pieces is simpler than that of Baroque ones. However, a work may begin homophonically, with a melody and simple accompaniment, and then shift to complex polyphony featuring two or more simultaneous melodies or melodic fragments imitated among the instruments.

4 Memorable *melody*. The themes of Classical music often have a folk or popular flavor. Classical melodies tend toward balance and symmetry, again what one would expect of "Classical" works as we have seen them since the Athenian Greeks. Frequently Classical themes have two phrases of equal length. The second phrase often begins like the first but ends more decisively.

5 Gradual changes in *dynamics*—in contrast to Baroque music, which employs sudden changes in dynamics (*step dynamics*). One of the consequences of this direction in composition was the replacement of the harpsichord with the piano, an instrument more capable of handling the subtlety of Classical dynamic patterns.

THE CLASSICAL SONATA AND SONATA FORM As we noted earlier, "sonata" has been used to refer to many different musical forms, from a short piece for a single instrument to complex works in many sections or movements for a large ensemble. By the middle of the eighteenth century, however, the sonata for one or two keyboard instruments, or for another instrument accompanied by keyboard, was utilized as an instrumental genre comparable to the symphony, which we discuss in a moment. These genres share a flexible multi-movement design that music analysts call the *sonata cycle*. The term *sonata form* refers to the form of a *single movement* and

should not be confused with the term *sonata*, which describes a composition made of several movements. The sonata form, the most important musical structure of the Classical period, was used in symphonies, sonatas, and other genres mostly in the first movement.

THE CLASSICAL SYMPHONY Franz Josef Haydn (Hy-duhn; see below) began composing symphonies in the Classical sense about 1757. In his long life he solidified and enriched symphonic style. Haydn wrote 104 symphonies (some scholars put the number higher), which were widely performed and imitated during his lifetime. Wolfgang Amadeus Mozart wrote forty-one symphonies, and his last six—No. 35 in D (*Haffner*), No. 36 in C (*Linz*), No. 38 in D (*Prague*), No. 39 in E-flat, No. 40 in G Minor, and No. 41 in C (*Jupiter*)—are complex in design and rich in orchestration, wedding formal perfection and expressive depth. Ludwig van Beethoven wrote only nine symphonies (1800–24), but in them he greatly increased the form's weight and size.

The Classical orchestra, which performed the Classical symphony, typified by the supreme orchestra of the time, the court orchestra at Mannheim, Germany, had approximately thirty string players and helped to standardize the remaining instrumental complement, specifically, two flutes, two oboes, two bassoons, two horns, two trumpets, two kettledrums, and a new instrument, the clarinet. Beethoven increased the technical demands on every Classical orchestra by writing parts for piccolo, trombones, and contrabassoon. The finale of his *Symphony No. 9* also requires triangle, cymbals, and bass drum (in addition to choral voices).

HAYDN Austrian-born Franz Joseph Haydn (1732–1809) pioneered the development of the symphony from a short, simple work into a longer, more sophisticated one. Haydn's symphonies are diverse and numerous. Many of the early ones use the pre-Classical three-movement form. His middle symphonies, dating from the early 1770s, have more emotion and entail a larger scale than the earlier works. In particular, the development sections of the first movements are dramatic and employ sudden and unexpected changes of dynamics. The slow movements contain great warmth, and in the third movements Haydn frequently drew on Austrian folk songs and Baroque dance music. His changes of tonality contain great dramatic power.

Among Haydn's late works the most famous is *Symphony No. 94 in G Major* (1792), commonly known as the "Surprise Symphony" (Fig. **11.28**). The surprise is a very loud chord played by the full orchestra when it is least expected.

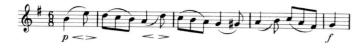

11.28 Haydn, *Symphony No. 94 in G major*, first theme.

MOZART Wolfgang Amadeus Mozart (1756–91), also an Austrian, was a child prodigy—he performed at the court of Empress Maria Theresa at the age of six. Throughout the Classical period, aristocratic patronage remained essential for musicians to earn a living, although the middle classes provided a progressively larger portion of commissions, pupil fees, and concert attendance. Mozart's short career (he died at the age of thirty-five) was dogged by financial insecurity.

Mozart's early symphonies are simple and relatively short, like those of Haydn, while his later works are longer and more complex. The last three represent his greatest symphonic masterpieces, and musicologists often call *Symphony No. 40 in G Minor* (Fig. 11.29) the typical Classical symphony (music CD track 13). This work and Nos. 39 and 41 have clear order and yet exhibit tremendous emotional urgency, which many scholars cite as the beginning of the Romantic style.

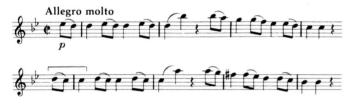

11.29 Mozart, *Symphony No. 40 in G Minor*, first movement (excerpt).

Mozart is also well known for his operas, and was especially skilled in *opera buffa*. *The Marriage of Figaro* is fast and humorous, with slapstick action in the manner of farce, but has great melodic beauty. In this quotation from the beginning of the opera (Fig. 11.30) the main character, Figaro, is measuring the new bedroom his employer has allocated to him for his married life (music CD track 12).

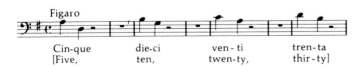

11.30 Mozart, *The Marriage of Figaro*, first theme of "Cinque . . . dieci" duet.

In a totally different vein, the final movement of Mozart's *Sonata No. 11 for Piano in A* has always been a public favorite. Called the *Rondo alla Turca* or "Turkish Rondo," it has an exotic or "Turkish" character underlined by the main theme in A minor (Fig. 11.31) that reappears throughout the rondo, softly:

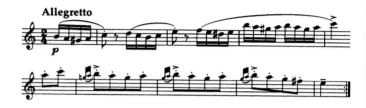

11.31 W. A. Mozart. *Sonata No. 11 for Piano in A* (K. 331) "Turkish Rondo."

BEETHOVEN Ludwig van Beethoven (1770–1827) stands somewhat apart from the Classical period, often regarded as a singular transitional figure between Classicism and Romanticism. Beethoven wanted to expand the Classical symphonic form to accommodate greater emotional character. The typical Classical symphony moves through contrasting movements; Beethoven continued that but began to work toward using a single theme throughout, thereby unifying the work.

Beethoven's symphonies differ significantly from those of Haydn and Mozart. They are more dramatic and use changing dynamics more often for emotional effects. Silence, too, emerges as a device in pursuit of dramatic and structural ends. Beethoven's also lengthened both the development section of sonata form and the coda.

He also changed traditional numbers and relationships among movements. In Symphony No. 5, no break occurs between the third and fourth movements. Beethoven's symphonies draw heavily on imagery, for example heroism in Symphony No. 3 and pastoral settings in Symphony No. 6. The famous *Symphony No. 5 in C Minor*, for example, begins with a motif that Beethoven described as "fate knocking at the door." The first movement (allegro con brio) develops according to typical sonata form (music CD track 14).

LITERATURE Jonathan Swift represents the enlightened spirit in literature. An Anglo-Irish satirist and churchman, he wrote *Gulliver's Travels*, which mocks pomposity and woolly-headed idealism equally. His other famous work in prose, *A Modest Proposal*, took satire to the very edge of horror with its chillingly deadpan suggestion that the English should solve the "Irish Problem" by eating the babies of the poor. Our excerpt here has been severely abridged to fit our space.

A Modest Proposal
Jonathan Swift
1667–1745

For Preventing the Children of Poor People in Ireland from Being a Burden to Their Parents or Country, and for Making Them Beneficial to the Public

It is a melancholy object to those who walk through this great town or travel in the country, when they see the streets, the roads and cabin doors, crowded with beggars of the female sex, followed by three, four, or six children, all in rags and importuning every passenger for an alms. These mothers, instead of being able to work for their honest livelihood, are forced to employ all their time in strolling to beg sustenance for their helpless infants, who, as they grow up, either turn thieves for want of work, or leave their dear native country to fight for the Pretender in Spain, or sell themselves to the Barbadoes.

I think it is agreed by all parties that this prodigious number of children in the arms, or on the backs, or at the heels of their mothers, and frequently of their fathers, is in the present deplorable state of the kingdom a very great additional grievance; and therefore whoever could find out a fair, cheap, and easy method of making these children sound, useful members of the commonwealth would deserve so well of the public as to have his statue set up for a preserver of the nation.

But my intention is very far from being confined to provide only for the children of professed beggars; it is of a much greater extent, and shall take in the whole number of infants at a certain age who are born of parents in effect as little able to support them as those who demand our charity in the streets.

• • •

The number of souls in this kingdom being usually reckoned one million and a half, of these I calculate there may be about two hundred thousand couples whose wives are breeders; from which number I subtract thirty thousand couples who are able to maintain their own children, although I apprehend there cannot be so many under the present distresses of the kingdom; but this being granted, there will remain an hundred and seventy thousand breeders. I again subtract fifty thousand for those women who miscarry, or whose children die by accident or disease within the year. There only remain an hundred and twenty thousand children of poor parents annually born. The question therefore, is, how this number shall be reared and provided for, which, as I have already said, under the present situation of affairs, is utterly impossible by all the methods hitherto proposed. For we can neither employ them in handicraft or agriculture; we neither build houses (I mean in the country) nor cultivate land. They can very seldom pick up a livelihood by stealing till they arrive at six years old, except where they are of towardly parts; although

I confess they learn the rudiments much earlier, during which time they can however be looked upon only as probationers, as I have been informed by a principal gentleman in the county of Cavan, who protested to me that he never knew above one or two instances under the age of six, even in a part of the kingdom so renowned for the quickest proficiency in that art.

I am assured by our merchants that a boy or a girl before twelve years old is no salable commodity; and even when they come to this age they will not yield above three pounds, or three pounds and half a crown at most on the Exchange; which cannot turn to account either to the parents or the kingdom, the charge of nutriment and rags having been at least four times that value.

I shall now therefore humbly propose my own thoughts, which I hope will not be liable to the least objection.

I have been assured by a very knowing American of my acquaintance in London, that a young healthy child well nursed is at a year old a most delicious, nourishing, and wholesome food, whether stewed, roasted, baked, or boiled; and I make no doubt that it will equally serve in a fricassee or a ragout.

I do therefore humbly offer it to public consideration that of the hundred and twenty thousand children, already computed, twenty thousand may be reserved for breed, whereof only one fourth part to be males, which is more than we allow to sheep, black cattle, or swine; and my reason is that those children are seldom the fruits of marriage, a circumstance not much regarded by our savages, therefore one male will be sufficient to serve four females. That the remaining hundred thousand may at a year old be offered in sale to the persons of quality and fortune through the kingdom, always advising the mother to let them suck plentifully in the last month, so as to render them plump and fat for a good table. A child will make two dishes at an entertainment for friends; and when the family dines alone, the fore or hind quarter will make a reasonable dish, and seasoned with a little pepper or salt will be very good boiled on the fourth day, especially in winter.

I have reckoned upon a medium that a child just born will weigh twelve pounds, and in a solar year if tolerably nursed increaseth to twenty-eight pounds.

I grant this food will be somewhat dear, and therefore very proper for landlords, who, as they have already devoured most of the parents, seem to have the best title to the children.

• • •

Those who are more thrifty (as I must confess the times require) may flay the carcass; the skin of which artificially dressed will make admirable gloves for ladies, and summer boots for fine gentlemen.

As to our city of Dublin, shambles may be appointed for this purpose in the most convenient parts of it, and butchers we may be assured will not be wanting; although I rather recommend buying the children alive, and dressing them hot from the knife as we do roasting pigs.

• • •

Some persons of a desponding spirit are in great concern about that vast number of poor people who are aged, diseased, or maimed, and I have been desired to employ my thoughts what course may be taken to ease the nation of so grievous an encumbrance. But I am not in the least pain upon that matter, because it is very well known that they are every day dying and rotting by cold and famine, and filth and vermin, as fast as can be reasonably expected. And as to the younger laborers, they are now in almost as hopeful a condition. They cannot get work and consequently pine away for want of nourishment to a degree that if at any time they are accidentally hired to common labor, they have not strength to perform it; and thus the country and themselves are happily delivered from the evils to come.

I have too long digressed, and therefore shall return to my subject. I think the advantages by the proposal which I have made are obvious and many, as well as of the highest importance.

• • •

Many other advantages might be enumerated. For instance, the addition of some thousand carcasses in our exportation of barreled beef, the propagation of swine's flesh, and improvement in the art of making good bacon, so much wanted among us by the great destruction of pigs, too frequent at our tables, which are no way comparable in taste or magnificence to a well-grown, fat, yearling child, which roasted whole will make a considerable figure at a lord mayor's feast or any other public entertainment. But this and many others I omit, being studious of brevity.

Supposing that one thousand families in this city would be constant customers for infants' flesh, besides others who might have it at merry meetings, particularly weddings and christenings, I compute that Dublin would take off annually about twenty thousand carcasses, and the rest of the kingdom (where probably they will be sold somewhat cheaper) the remaining eighty thousand.

• • •

After all, I am not so violently bent upon my own opinion as to reject any offer proposed by wise men, which shall be found equally innocent, cheap, easy, and effectual. But before something of that kind shall be advanced in contradiction to my scheme, and offering a better, I desire the author or authors will be pleased maturely to consider two points. First, as things now stand, how they will be able to find food and raiment for an hundred thousand useless mouths and backs. And secondly, there being a round million of creatures in human figure throughout this kingdom, whose sole subsistence put into a common stock would leave them in debt two millions of pounds sterling, adding those

who are beggars by profession to the bulk of farmers, cottagers, and laborers, and their wives and children who are beggars in effect; I desire those politicians who dislike my overture, and may perhaps be so bold to attempt an answer, that they will first ask the parents of these mortals whether they would not at this day think it a great happiness to have been sold for food at a year old in the manner I prescribe, and thereby have avoided such a perpetual scene of misfortunes as they have since gone through by the oppression of landlords, the impossibility of paying rent without money or trade, the want of common sustenance, with neither house nor clothes to cover them from the inclemencies of the weather, and the most inevitable prospect of entailing the like or greater miseries upon their breed forever.

I profess, in the sincerity of my heart, that I have not the least personal interest in endeavoring to promote this necessary work, having no other motive than the public good of my country, by advancing our trade, providing for infants, relieving the poor, and giving some pleasure to the rich. I have no children by which I can propose to get a single penny; the youngest being nine years old, and my wife past childbearing.[6]

The eighteenth century's enlightened spirit brought the essay to the forefront as a means of criticizing society and religion. Its flexibility, brevity, and potential for ambiguity and allusions to contemporary situations made it an ideal tool for reformers throughout Europe and America. Among its adherents, Englishman Alexander Pope created in *An Essay on Man* (1733) a philosophical essay written in heroic couplets of iambic pentameter. The poem takes the form of four letters: (1) a survey of relations between humans and the universe; (2) a discussion of humans as individuals; (3) a discussion of the relationships between individuals and society; and (4) an exploration of questions involving the potential for happiness in individuals. In *An Essay on Man*, Pope describes the universe as a hierarchy of being that has humans, because of their ability to reason, at the top, above animals and plants. The brief excerpt that follows illustrates Pope's form and style in the piece.

An Essay on Man
Epistle I: Of the Nature and State of Man, With Respect to the Universe
Alexander Pope
1688–1744

ARGUMENT
Of Man in the abstract. I. That we can judge only with regard to our own system, being ignorant of the relations of

systems and things. <u>II.</u> That Man is not to be deemed imperfect, but a being suited to his place and rank in the creation, agreeable to the general order of things, and conformable to ends and relations to him unknown. <u>III.</u> That it is partly upon his ignorance of future events, and partly upon the hope of a future state, that all his happiness in the present depends. <u>IV.</u> The pride of aiming at more knowledge, and pretending to more perfection, the cause of Man's error and misery. The impiety of putting himself in the place of God, and judging of the fitness or unfitness, perfection or imperfection, justice or injustice, of his dispensations. <u>V.</u> The absurdity of conceiving himself the final cause of creation, or expecting that perfection in the moral world which is not in the natural. <u>VI.</u> The unreasonableness of his complaints against Providence, while, on the one hand, he demands the perfections of the angels, and, on the other, the bodily qualifications of the brutes; though to possess any of the sensitive faculties in a higher degree would render him miserable. <u>VII.</u> That throughout the whole visible world a universal order and gradation in the sensual and mental faculties is observed, which causes a subordination of creature to creature, and of all creatures to man. The gradations of Sense, Instinct, Thought, Reflection, Reason: that Reason alone countervails all the other faculties. <u>VIII.</u> How much further this order and subordination of living creatures may extend above and below us; were any part of which broken, not that part only, but the whole connected creation must be destroyed. <u>IX.</u> The extravagance, madness, and pride of such a desire. <u>X.</u> The consequence of all, the absolute submission due to Providence, both as to our present and future state.

Awake, my St. John! leave all meaner things
To low ambition and the pride of Kings.
Let us, since life can little more supply
Than just to look about us and to die,
Expatiate free o'er all this scene of man;
A mighty maze! but not without a plan;
A wild, where weeds and flowers promiscuous shoot,
Or garden, tempting with forbidden fruit.
Together let us beat this ample field,
Try what the open, what the covert yield;
The latent tracts, the giddy heights, explore
Of all who blindly creep or sightless soar;
Eye Nature's walks, shoot folly as it flies,
And catch the manners living as they rise;
Laugh where we must, be candid where we can,
But vindicate the ways of God to man.

I
Say first, of God above or Man below
What can we reason but from what we know?
Of man what see we but his station here,
From which to reason, or to which refer?
Thro' worlds unnumber'd tho' the God be known,
'Tis ours to trace him only in our own.

He who thro' vast immensity can pierce,
See worlds on worlds compose one universe,
Observe how system into system runs,
What other planets circle other suns,
What varied being peoples every star,
May tell why Heav'n has made us as we are:
But of this frame, the bearings and the ties,
The strong connexions, nice dependencies,
Gradations just, has thy pervading soul
Look'd thro'; or can a part contains the whole?
Is the great chain that draws all to agree,
And drawn supports, upheld by God or thee?[7]

Alexander Pope served as a model for an American poet, Phillis Wheatley. Perhaps of Fulani origin, in or near the current nation of Senegal, she came to America, captive, on the slaver "Phillis." At the age of seven, she was sold to John Wheatley, a Boston merchant. Recognizing her talent, the Wheatleys taught her to read and write not only in English but also in Latin. She read poetry, and at the age of fourteen, began to write. Her elegy on the death of George Whitefield (1770) brought her acclaim. With the 1773 publication of her *Poems on Various Subjects* in England, Phillis Wheatley's fame spread in Europe as well as America. She was freed in 1773 but remained with the Wheatley family as a servant and died in poverty. Her poetry follows Neoclassical style, has African influences, and reflects Christian concerns for morality and piety. In the short poem "On Virtue" the poet's language invokes imagery, figures, and allegory to make the moral quality of virtue a "bright jewel" and imbue it with personal characteristics. The unrhymed lines flow freely in iambic meter.

On Virtue
Phillis Wheatley
c. 1753–84

O Thou bright jewel in my aim I strive
To comprehend thee. Thine own words declare
Wisdom is higher than a fool can reach.
I cease to wonder, and no more attempt
Thine height t' explore, or fathom thy profound.
But, O my soul, sink not into despair,
Virtue is near thee, and with gentle hand
Would now embrace thee, hovers o'er thine head.
Fain would the heav'n-born soul with her converse,
Then seek, then court her for her promis'd bliss.
Auspicious queen, thine heav'nly pinions spread,
And lead celestial Chastity along;
Lo! now her sacred retinue descends,
Array'd in glory from the orbs above.
Attend me, Virtue, thro' my youthful years!

O leave me not to the false joys of time!
But guide my steps to endless life and bliss.
Greatness, or Goodness, say what I shall call thee,
To give me an higher appellation still,
Teach me a better strain, a nobler lay,
O thou, enthron'd with Cherubs in the realms of day.[8]

ASIA

Chinese Art

MING SCULPTURE AND CERAMICS Throughout the period of the Renaissance in Europe, the long-ruling Ming Dynasty (1368–1644) brought about a centralization of power and money in the court of the emperor of China. As a result, the demand for decorative arts caused a tremendous increase in the number and quality of ceramic works.

The celebrated Ming vases have become a symbol for the wide variety of ceramic ware produced during this period. Strong traditions in ceramic style and technique had been established much earlier. The Ming Dynasty capitalized on them and took ceramic art to even higher levels, especially in porcelains. By the fifteenth century an underglaze decoration of cobalt blue had been developed, and artisans achieved remarkable skill in color control. Familiar blue-and-white porcelains had their classic period between 1426 and 1435. They were marked by clarity of detail and variety of shapes. Over the next 100 years the palette was enriched by adding multicolored enamels to the basic blue. The result can be seen in a five-color covered jar from the reign of Wan Li (wahn-lee; 1573–1620; Fig. **11.32**). The complex process of adding layers of color called for refined designs and repeated firings. First, blue designs were applied to the white ground and were glazed and fired. Over this glaze, the decoration was completed in red, green, yellow, and brown; the work was then refired. The process resulted in a rich and delicate ceramic with freely painted narrative scenes and floral compositions of charm, grace, and appeal. Their content gives them a human quality of warmth.

Indian Art

Although Islam made incursions into India as early as the eighth century, with another push in the eleventh century, during the period of the European Renaissance India witnessed a significant clash of cultures as Muslims (the Mughals) strove again to conquer this Hindu subcontinent. Meanwhile, both cultures contributed significantly to the arts of India, in some cases with remarkable symbiosis.

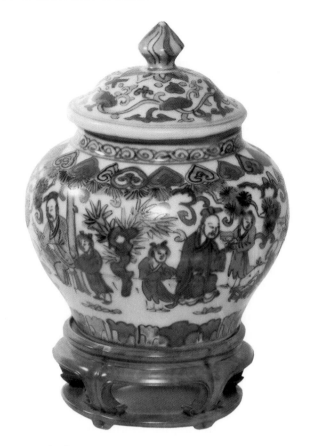

11.32 Mark of Wan Li, covered jar, c. 1600. Porcelain, height 4 ins (10.2 cm). Cleveland Museum of Art (John L. Severance Fund).

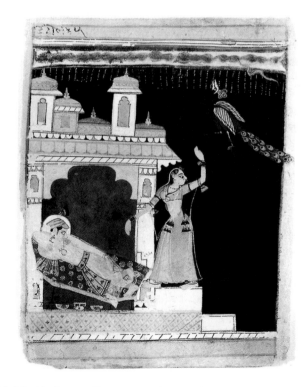

11.33 *Madhu Madhavi Ragini*, from Malwa, India, c. 1630–40. Color on paper, 7⁹⁄₁₆ × 5¹³⁄₁₆ ins (19.2 × 14.8 cm). Cleveland Museum of Art (Gift of J. H. Wade).

RAJPUT STYLE One style of Indian painting is called the Rajput style, after a group of clans in northern and central India who fought vigorously against the Muslim invaders. Their art has a folk quality and takes much of its subject matter from Hindu literature. Its treatment ranges widely, from abstract to intellectual to concrete and emotional. Figure 11.33, *Madhu Madhavi Ragini*, serves as a typical example. Its primary characteristic is its distinctive dark blue background. The title of the painting refers both to a musical mode and to a representation of a heroine who goes into the night to meet her lover with peacocks flying around her and lightning flashing. However, there seems little in this work that is ominous. Space is limited to the surface plane. Crossing diagonals give the work a sense of movement, and strong colors and contrasts make the painting forceful and appealing. The conventions of figure portrayal strike us as similar to those of Egypt (see p. 209).

PUNJAB STYLE Another major school of Indian painting, the Punjab hills style, comes from the northwest of the Indian subcontinent. It features linear drawings, in a gentle, lyrical mode.

Consider the example of *Gajahamurti*, which means "after the death of the elephant-demon" (Fig. **11.34**). This work presents deities posed formally in a perfectly balanced composition of gently curved forms and careful coloring. The gods Siva and Devi exhibit rigid formality, with Siva, the slayer of the demon, as the main focus. The two figures float in the sky on the elephant's hide. Swirling clouds seem to suggest a storm, especially in their strong contrast to the dark blue background. The sky takes predominance over a rather conventionally and sparsely illustrated earth. Nonetheless, the flowers show fine detailing and individuality. The ducks are also delicate and graceful, both in the water and in flight. Overall, the work has a subdued rather than a violent tone.

MUSLIM AND HINDU ARCHITECTURE The Mughal emperors of the seventeenth century proved to be great patrons of architecture, and the most famous of all Indian architectural accomplishments—the Taj Mahal at Agra, near Delhi (Fig. **11.35**)—is Islamic. It does, however, blend Persian and indigenous Indian styles. The Taj Mahal was built by Shah Jahan (1592–1666) as a mausoleum for his favorite wife Mumtaz Mahal (1593–1631). Such a tomb for a wife had no precedent in Islam, and possibly the building was also intended as an allegory of the day of resurrection: the building symbolically replicates the throne of God. Four intersecting waterways in the garden symbolize the four flowing rivers of Paradise, as described in the Koran. The building has immense

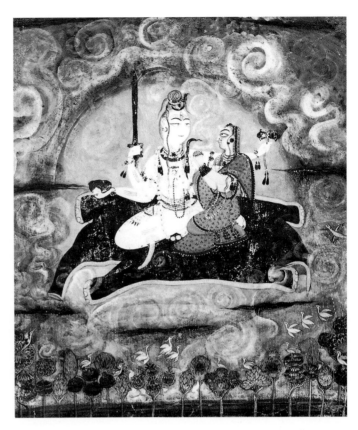

11.34 *Gajahamurti* (*Shiva and Devi on Gajasura Hide*), from Basohli, India, c. 1657–80. Color on paper, 9¼ × 6¼ ins (23.5 × 15.8 cm). Cleveland Museum of Art (Edward L. Whittemore Fund).

scale, and yet exquisitely refined details—entirely geometric and nonfigurative. Proportions are well-balanced and symmetrical. This huge, white, octagonal structure, with its impressive dome and flanking minarets, has a breathtaking effect.

By contrast, the Hindu architectural tradition is almost defiantly anti-Islamic, with an abundance of figurative sculpture celebrating a plurality of deities. Examples occur throughout India, but especially in the south, in the 10-square-mile city of Vijayanagar (vee-jay-YAH-nah-ghar), formerly the center of a Hindu empire established in the fourteenth century. Here, huge and exquisite temples come alive with brilliantly colored sculpture depicting the Hindu pantheon (Fig. **11.36**). Upward-striving terraces with ornate detail reach toward a vaulted pinnacle. In Vijayanagar the concept of the temple went beyond a single shrine and encompassed an entire complex of buildings within concentric enclosures. These were entered through tall gate towers called *gopuras*, packed with *friezes* of the Hindu gods, and increased in size as one moved from inner to outer walls.

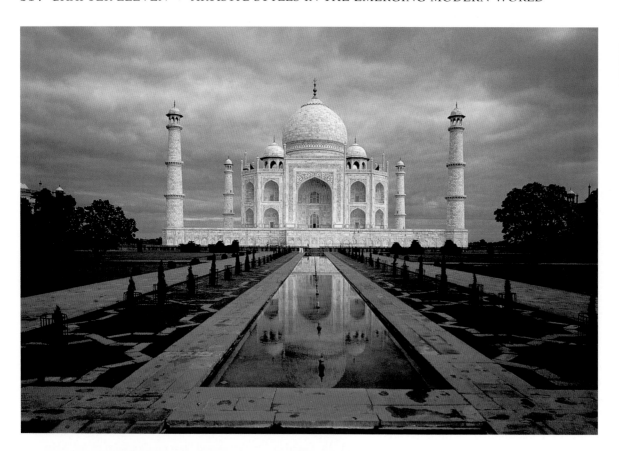

11.35 Ustad Ahmad Lahori (architect), Taj Mahal, Agra, India, 1632–48.

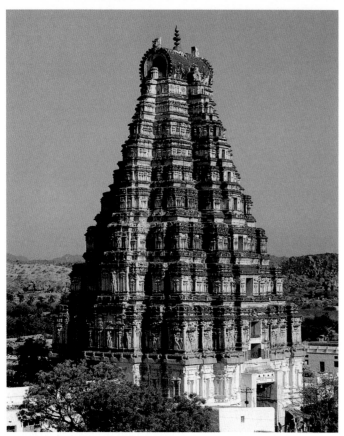

11.36 Pampapati Temple, Vijayanagar, India, *gopura* (gateway tower), 16th century (renovated in 17th century).

Japanese Art

PAINTING STYLE Tawayara Sotatsu (soh-that-soo; d. 1643) was a highly creative painter of the late sixteenth and early seventeenth centuries. In contrast with other Japanese painters, who tended to use Chinese motifs and patterns, Sotatsu painted in a style that emphasized boldness, severity, and asymmetry, with simplified silhouettes. He deftly broadened the color palette and use of ink, developing a notable skill in fading the edges of color areas and in creating blurred and pooled effects in wet colors by allowing ink and color to run together. He looked to sources in Japanese traditions for his subject matter. His hanging paper scroll *The Zen Priest Choka* (Fig. **11.37**) shows the priest sitting in a tree. The remarkable aspect of this painting is its use of space—the subject occupies only a small portion of the work. Choka sits in a tree, only faintly suggested at the left border: its trunk and limbs ebb and flow up the boundary and give us a glimpse here and there of their presence, but mostly leave a full configuration to our imagination. The priest himself is curiously de-emphasized. Sotatsu portrays him with pale color and soft lines of medium tonality. Although most of the painting stays void of images, it maintains balance. Sotatsu has cleverly split the universe of this work into halves divided on the lower left/upper right diagonals. This artwork is a fascinating example of how, both

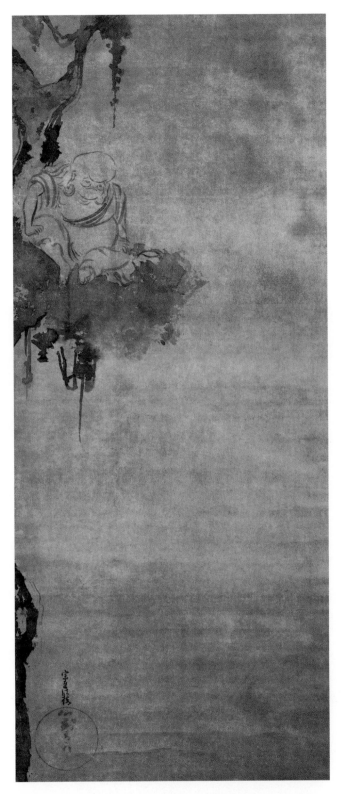

philosophically and visually, something can be balanced by nothing.

IMARI PORCELAIN The discovery of porcelain clay in Japan in the early seventeenth century, and the importation of Chinese techniques, led to some remarkable accomplishments in ceramic art. Typical of Japanese mastery of this medium, an Imari porcelain vase from the late seventeenth century (Fig. **11.38**) exhibits an exquisite curved silhouette with a relaxing flow. The proportions call attention to themselves as the design divides in half at the top of the lower bowl, balancing a gracefully slim neck that enlarges into an asymmetrical bulb, and ending in a delicate lip at the top. The ornate flowers have elegance and fine detail that give the vase delicacy and refinement. European figures often appear in this style of ceramics: Dutch and Portuguese men, and also Western ships. In the Imari vase, a sophisticated plan of proportional adjustment brings together three registers—or bands—of unequal proportion to make a smoothly unified whole. This compositional arrangement is reminiscent of the high chest of drawers illustrated in the Introduction (see Fig. **0.6**), and also reflects the complexities of the Baroque style.

11.37 Tawayara Sotatsu, *The Zen Priest Choka*, pre-1643. Ink on paper, 37¾ × 15¼ ins (95.9 × 38.7 cm). Cleveland Museum of Art (Norman O. Stone and Ella A. Stone Memorial Fund).

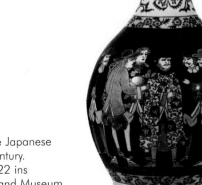

11.38 Imari ware Japanese vase, late 17th century. Porcelain, height 22 ins (55.9 cm). Cleveland Museum of Art (Gift of Ralph King).

KABUKI THEATRE Kabuki (kah-BOO-kee) drama began as "middle-class theatre" in the seventeenth century and, as such, was the object of contempt from the samurai and the court. The earliest Kabuki plays were simple sketches; two-act plays did not appear until the middle of the century.

The focus of a Kabuki play tends to be a climactic moment, as opposed to the plot. Connections between scenes tend to be vague, in contrast with much of Western theatre, whose plot development runs according to cause and effect. A narrator and chorus play predominant roles in Kabuki productions, because although there is a musical accompaniment, the actors themselves do not sing. The narrator describes the scene, comments on the action, and even speaks portions of the dialogue. The overall style of Kabuki drama tends to fall somewhere between convention and depiction. Every location is portrayed scenically, and scenery is changed in full view of the audience.

AFRICA

Benin Style

The spirit of discovery that took the Spanish to the Americas also took the Portuguese to Africa in the late fifteenth century, and that made an impact on artistry as well as culture. In Chapter 10 we experienced the artistic style of Ife (see p. 267). That culture probably gave birth to the artistry of the great city-state of Benin (beh-NEEN), approximately 150 miles (240 km) to the southeast. Local tradition suggests that the Benin style originated from either a master from Ife or the Portuguese, with whom the Benin came into contact in the late fifteenth century. We

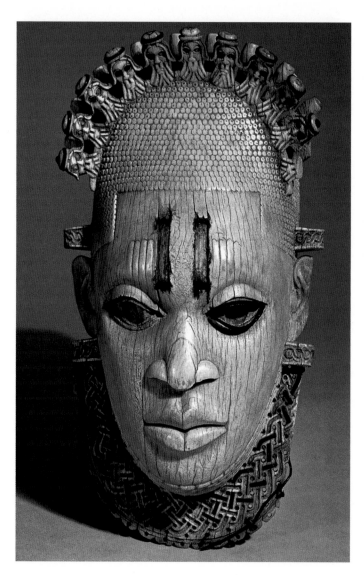

11.40 Pectoral or waist mask from Benin, early 16th century. Ivory, height 9¼ ins (25 cm). British Museum, London.

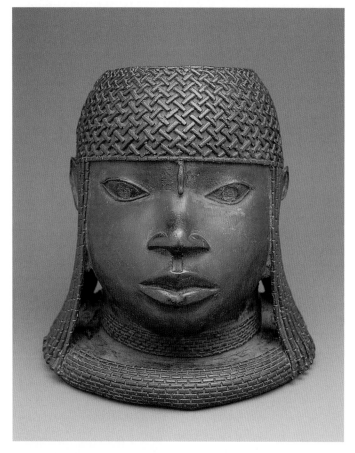

11.39 Memorial head from Benin, c. 1400–1550. Bronze, height 9¼ ins (23.4 cm), width 8⅝ ins (22 cm). Metropolitan Museum of Art, New York (The Michael C. Rockefeller Memorial Collection, Bequest of Nelson A. Rockefeller, 1979).

see the style of Ife, as in Figure **10.56**, represented some 200 years later in Benin in the memorial head pictured in Figure **11.39**. Here the work reflects mastery of the sculptural technique of casting—in this case, brass. Only the Oba, or King of Benin, could commission works in brass, and the tradition of casting memorial heads for the shrines of royalty continues today. Benin art developed into a widespread style of its own, marked by carefully executed lifelike features and a close attention to detail—as witnessed by the woven patterns of the headdress.

Another example of superb artistry in the Benin style occurs in the early sixteenth-century ivory mask pictured in Figure **11.40**. The carver has obvious mastery of the medium. The elongated head and stylized features create expressiveness, while the details of the mask are precise and delicate. Into the headdress the artist has skillfully woven heads of Portuguese men with beards. Their appearance holds some symbolic, yet unclear, meaning. The rendition strikes us in terms of its rich material, ivory—probably the exclusive property of the king (Oba)—and in terms of the artist's sophisticated artisanship in imparting such human character to the mask.

AMERICA

Aztec Art

The Aztecs did not have a written language, yet they did make written records. They chiefly used direct representation and varieties of hieroglyphic painting. Although the Spanish destroyed most Aztec books, several facsimiles of their drawings appear in Spanish documents. A page from *Codex Mendoza* (Fig. **11.41**) illustrates an idealized representation of Tenochtitlan and its sacred ceremonial precinct. Central to the drawing, an eagle perched on a prickly pear plant symbolizes the city. Waterways divide the city into fourths, with seated figures representing the wards of each of the quarters. The warriors at the bottom of the page symbolize Aztec conquests, while the house at the top center of the drawing probably symbolizes the Great Pyramid, a double, stepped pyramid with two temples on top, one of which served as the site for human sacrifice.

The statue of the mother of the principal Aztec god pictured in Figure **11.42** probably played a part in the ritual of an Aztec temple. Records indicate conquistadors seeing similar statues covered with blood inside a temple. The goddess has clawed hands and feet and a skirt of twisted snakes. Around her cling a pair of serpents and symbols of gushing blood. Her necklace contains sacrificial offerings of hands, hearts, and a skull. Originally, the statue would have been vividly painted to heighten its effect.

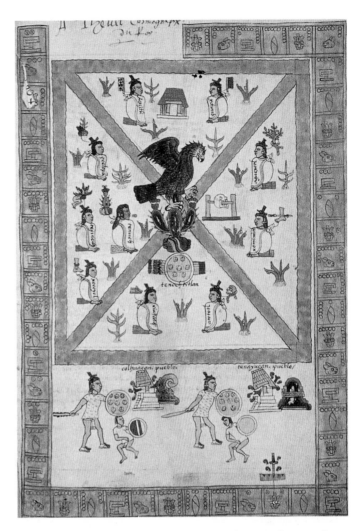

11.41 *The Founding of Tenochtitlan*, page from *Codex Mendoza*, 16th century. Ink and color on paper, 12⁹⁄₁₆ × 8⁷⁄₁₆ ins (31.5 × 21.5 cm). Bodleian Library, University of Oxford.

Incan Art

The Incas developed a functional style of architecture which exhibited strong engineering techniques and fine stone masonry (Fig. **11.43**). Their cities followed a plan based on broad avenues intersected by smaller streets converging on an open square lined by state buildings and temples. Structures were usually single-storied, displaying perfectly joined cut stones, although building materials differed from region to region. In mountainous areas—for example, at Machu Picchu (mah-choo PEE-choo; Fig. **11.44**)—their architecture often contained ingenious adaptation to the context. Machu Picchu straddles a ridge between two high peaks. It consists of stone buildings situated around central plazas. Narrow terraces devoted to agriculture step down the mountainside.

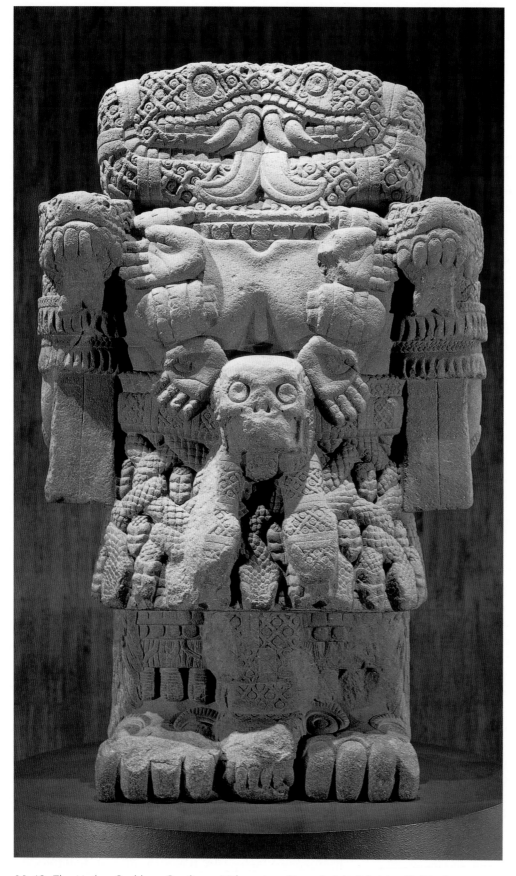

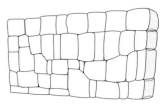

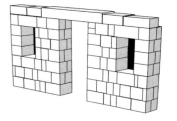

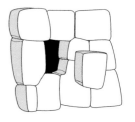

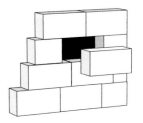

11.42 *The Mother Goddess, Coatlicue*, 15th century. Stone, height 8 ft 6 ins (2.65 m). Museo Nacional de Antropologia, Mexico City.

11.43 Inca building techniques.

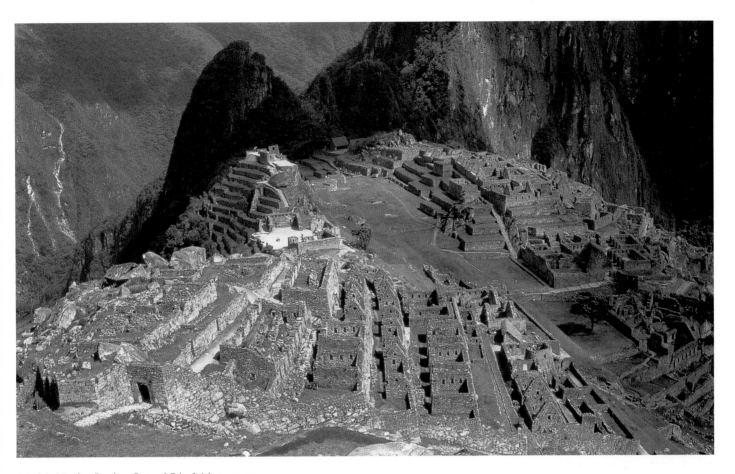

11.44 Machu Picchu, Peru, 15th–16th century.

The Incas developed excellent skills in metallurgy and, thus, in cast sculpture, as illustrated by the llama in Figure **11.45**. Unlike the Spanish, who sought gold and silver simply as materials of wealth, the Inca saw gold and silver as symbols of the sun and the moon respectively. This difference in philosophy accounts for the dearth of Inca statuary, which the conquistadors melted down for transport to Spain. For the Incas, gold was "the sweat of the sun" and silver the "tears of the moon." The llama, too, had significant religious meaning for the Incas, who connected it with the sun, rain, and fertility. Every morning and evening in the capital city of Cuzco, the Incas sacrificed a llama to the sun. A white llama kept in Cuzco symbolized the Incas themselves, and, bedecked with a red tunic and gold jewelry, it passed through the streets during religious celebrations. What we see here, in contrast, for example, to the qualities of Benin art just discussed, represents a lesser degree of lifelikeness and, perhaps—or arguably—a more symbolic investiture in their representations.

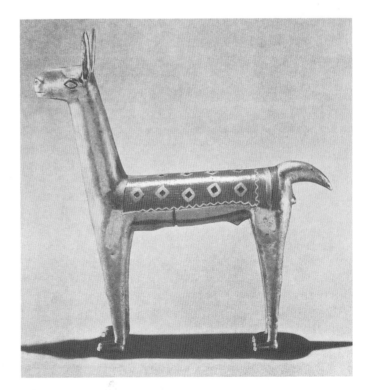

11.45 Llama, from Bolivia or Peru, found near Lake Titicaca, Bolivia, 15th century. Cast silver with gold and cinnabar, 9 × 8½ × 1¾ ins (22.9 × 21.6 × 4.4 cm). American Museum of Natural History, New York.

THINKING CRITICALLY

- Using the discussions of perspective and chiaroscuro set out in Chapter 1 (see pp. 62 and 63) as a guide, compare the ways in which Leonardo's *Last Supper* (Fig. **11.8**) and Rubens's *Henry IV Receiving the Portrait of Maria de' Medici* (Fig. **11.18**) achieve depth of space.

- Using the text on style in the Introduction (see pp. 30–36) and the discussions on Renaissance and Baroque art in this chapter as guides, explain why Masaccio's *Tribute Money* (Fig. **11.1**) and Rembrandt's *Night Watch* (Fig. **11.19**) are representative of each style.

- Listen to the first movement of Vivaldi's "Spring" (http://www.classicalarchives.com/main/) and the first movement of Mozart's *Symphony No. 40 in G Minor* (music CD track 13) then compare the use of motif, melody, and texture in each work. Explain how the pieces represent the Baroque and Classical styles, respectively.

- How are the Vivaldi and Mozart pieces, just mentioned, analogous to the visual representations of the same styles—for example, to Bernini's *David* (Fig. **11.20**; Baroque) and David's *Oath of the Horatii* (Fig. **11.26**; Neoclassical)?

CYBER STUDY

RENAISSANCE:
—Visual Art: Europe
http://www.artcyclopedia.com/history/early-renaissance.html
http://www.artcyclopedia.com/history/high-renaissance.html
http://www.artcyclopedia.com/history/northern-renaissance.html
—Visual Art: Asia
http://www.kamat.com/kalranga/art/timeline.htm
—Music
http://www.classicalarchives.com/early.html
—Theatre: Shakespeare; Marlowe
http://www.gutenberg.org/catalog/

BAROQUE:
—Visual Art
http://www.artcyclopedia.com/history/baroque.html
—Music: Vivaldi, Handel, Bach
http://www.classicalarchives.com/index_1.html

EIGHTEENTH CENTURY:
—Rococo
http://www.artcyclopedia.com/history/rococo.html
—Neoclassicism
http://www.artcyclopedia.com/history/neoclassicism.html
—Musical Classicism: Mozart, Haydn
http://www.classicalarchives.com/index_1.html
—Literature: Swift, Pope
http://www.gutenberg.org/catalog/

CHAPTER TWELVE

ARTISTRY IN AN AGE OF INDUSTRY

c. 1800 to c. 1900

— IMPORTANT TERMS —

Animism The belief that a spirit exists in every living thing.

Art Nouveau A style of architecture characterized by the lively, serpentine curve and a fascination with plant and animal life and organic growth.

Art song A solo musical composition for voice, usually with piano accompaniment.

Gesamtkunstwerk A comprehensive work of art in which music, poetry, and scenery are all subservient to the central generating idea.

Guardian figure An artistic manifestation believed to protect the remains of the dead.

Idée fixe A recurrent melodic motif representing a nonmusical idea.

Impressionism A style in painting emphasizing the presence of color and the interrelated mechanisms of the camera and the eye. A musical style exemplified by Debussy, using reduced melodic development and gliding chords.

Post-Impressionism A very diverse and personal style of visual art typically concerned with capturing sensory experience and insisting on "art for art's sake" and a return to form and structure.

Realism A style of painting and sculpture based on the theory that the method of presentation should be true to life.

Requiem A mass for the dead.

Romanticism A wide-ranging style and philosophy that emphasizes emotional appeal, personalization, and imagination.

THE CONTEXT

EUROPE

In Europe, the Industrial Revolution began in Britain and, at the conclusion of the Napoleonic wars in 1815, spread to France and then to the rest of Europe. It gained momentum as it spread, and irrevocably altered the fabric of civilization. By 1871, the first year of the unification of Germany, major industrial centers had developed all over Europe. Mechanization, especially in transportation and communications, made the nineteenth century and the international age while, at the same time, nations strove for individual power.

Drawn from pre-industrial home industries and farms, the new machine-worker class lived and worked in often deplorable conditions. No longer their own masters, they became virtual slaves. Unable to help themselves, they remained subject to severe organizing restrictions, hampered by lack of education, and threatened constantly by the prospect of unemployment. Slums, tenements, and horrifying living conditions awaited them. The middle classes, caught up in their own aspirations to wealth and political power, largely ignored their plight. Into this mix came the philosophy of Karl Marx (marks; 1818–83), a German economist and revolutionist, who developed the body of ideas known as Marxism. Together with Friedrich Engels (ENGH-ehls; 1820–95), he formed the basic tenets of modern socialism and communism. In 1859, Charles Darwin (1809–82) put forward the concept of natural selection as the explanation of species development in *The Origin of Species.* Evolution emerged as the framework that the science of biology would use for the foreseeable future.

Philosophy and psychology took fire and influenced the arts. One of the towering figures of modern times, the Austrian Sigmund Freud (froyd; 1856–1939) developed what he called "psychoanalysis"—the probing of the human "unconscious"—in the study of human behavior by exploring the world of dreams. At first his ideas met considerable skepticism because of their novel propositions regarding human sexuality. However, psychoanalysis gradually came to gain an important place in medicine and psychology.

The role of the artist changed significantly in the nineteenth century in Europe. For the first time in history, art could exist without the support of significant aristocratic and religious commissions and patronage. In fact, artists often deliberately resisted patronage, which imposed unwelcome limits on individual expression. In the late nineteenth century, a philosophical artistic thrust occurred called aestheticism, characterized by the slogan "art for art's sake." Those who championed this cause reacted against notions that a work of art must have uplifting, educational, or otherwise socially or morally beneficial characteristics.

ASIA

In Asia, the end of the eighteenth century saw Japan still under the rule of the Tokugawa Shogunate with increasing pressure to open up to the rest of the world. First, the Russians tried without success to establish trade relations. Other European nations followed, with equal lack of success. Eventually, the American Commodore Perry in 1853 and again in 1854 forced the Tokugawa government to open a limited number of ports for international trade. However, the trade remained very limited. Many Japanese people, however, recognized the advantages of the Western nations in science and military and favored opening up to the world. The stronger Western powers forced the Japanese to sign unequal treaties that gave the Westerners one-sided economical and legal advantages in Japan. In order to regain independence from the Europeans and Americans and establish itself as a respected nation in the world, Japan sought to close the economic and military gap by instituting reforms in practically every area of Japanese society. The new government tried to make Japan a democratic state with the resulting establishment of human rights such as religious freedom in 1873. In the end, an agrarian economy transformed into an industrial one. In 1889, Japan adopted a

European-style constitution and established a parliament (Diet), while leaving sovereignty with the emperor.

In 1894–95, conflicts with China over Korea led to the Sino–Japanese war, which Japan won and received Taiwan as a result. The intervention of Russia, France, and Germany forced Japan to return other territories. This "Triple Intervention" intensified Japan's activities to upgrade its military.

AFRICA

In Africa, the nineteenth century proved a century of European domination and partition. In the middle of the nineteenth century, Protestant missionaries proselytized on the Guinea coast, in South Africa, and in the Zanzibar dominions. Their work, largely beneficent, occurred in little-known regions and among unfamiliar peoples. In many instances missionaries turned explorers and pioneers of trade and empire.

While explorers solved the great mystery of Central Africa, explorers also unlocked the mysteries of other parts of the continent. They not only added considerably to geographical knowledge, but obtained invaluable information concerning the people, languages, and natural history of the countries in which they sojourned. In the last quarter of the nineteenth century, the map of Africa solidified and the continent became the theatre of European expansion. European nations drew lines of partition through trackless wildernesses and delineated their possessions. Railways penetrated the interior, and vast areas opened to Western occupation.

The prospect of Africa as an outlet for the energies of European powers in terms of markets for growing industries and a virgin soil for philanthropic and missionary activity proved too great to resist. European leaders saw the world as a finite place in which only the strong would predominate. Many saw in the newly discovered lands millions of "savages" to Christianize and "civilize." An international struggle began. Importantly, at the same time, in 1873, the great slave market in Zanzibar closed. Formal partition of the African continent by the European states came in 1876 with the establishment of "The International African Association," whose central idea was to put the exploration and development of Africa upon an international footing.

AMERICA

In America in the nineteenth century, the United States achieved its manifest destiny—a nation extending from the Atlantic to the Pacific Ocean—but at a tremendous cost to both American Indians and Black slaves. The country achieved its expansion through negotiation and purchases from European powers and by military conquest. The War of 1812 annexed the Great Lakes region and fixed the frontier with Canada. In 1823, President Monroe proclaimed the "Monroe Doctrine" of European noninterference—"America for Americans." White America hoped that the only remaining obstacle, "the savages," would disappear with the march of civilization. By the second half of the century, American Indian populations had been defeated by the army, decimated by epidemics, reduced to poverty, and confined to small reservations. Loss of traditional lands and conversions to Christianity threatened to remove even the remembrance of their cultures.

At the same time, slavery, an ethos counter to the ideology of independence, disappeared from the northern states in the early years of the century. The North–South conflict over slavery increased as the industrial age created a greater disparity between the two areas. By 1860, the North had industrialized, but the South, where 350,000 families (one-third of the white population) owned approximately three million slaves, maintained an agrarian, plantation economy. A series of unsatisfactory compromises attempted to settle the issue of slavery in the West, and in 1854, the Republican party emerged, standing for the abolition of all slavery. The Democratic Party championed the maintenance of slavery. When the country elected a Republican president, Abraham Lincoln, the South seceded and formed a new Confederacy. A minor military clash led to the outbreak of the Civil War. After the northern victory in the war, Blacks received their release from slavery, and it took ten years to reconstruct the union.

THE ARTS

EUROPE

Romanticism

In the late eighteenth century, Immanuel Kant proposed a philosophy that distinguished between a knowable world of sense perceptions and an unknowable world of essences. This reconciliation of philosophical extremes led to a nineteenth-century philosophy focused on the emotions. According to Kant, the real world, so far as humans could possibly rationalize it, is a mental reconstruction, an ideal world of the understanding. Thus, the nature of reality is of the nature of the mind—that is,

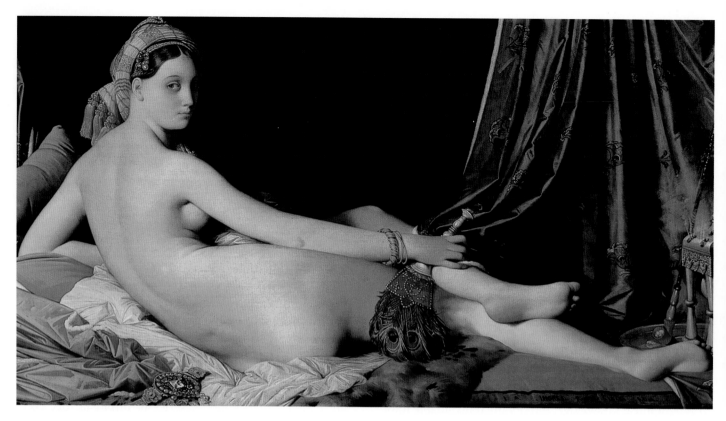

12.1 Jean-Auguste-Dominique Ingres, *Grande Odalisque (Harem Girl)*, 1814. Oil on canvas, 35¼ × 63¾ ins (89.5 × 161.9 cm). Louvre, Paris.

ideal. This doctrine was called *Kantian idealism* and also *Romanticism* and its reaction against eighteenth-century rationalism permeated both philosophy and the arts. The emphases of Romanticism were individualism, imagination, free expression, feeling, communion with nature, and the idea of the creative artist as visionary genius. Romanticism saw the artist as possessing ultimate insight into fundamental reality and revealing it, through impassioned self-expression, in a work of art that embodies, however imperfectly, a sublime ideal that transcends the ordinary world. Nature, wild and unspoiled, often became a metaphor for that idealism, and art was seen by some as the highest form of human endeavor.

PAINTING Romantic painting reflected a striving for freedom from social and artistic rules, coupled with an intense introversion. Formal content was subordinated to expressive intent. As the French novelist Emile Zola (1840–1902) said of Romantic naturalism, "A work of art is part of the universe as seen through a temperament." Romanticism explored the capacity of color and line to affect the viewer independently of subject matter.

Many Romantic painters are worthy of note, but a detailed look at Ingres, Goya, and Bonheur will suffice for our overview (see also Géricault, p. 65). The art of Jean-

Auguste-Dominique Ingres (AHNG-gruh; 1780–1867), and perhaps David as well, illustrates the confusing relationships and conflicts surrounding the Neoclassical and Romantic traditions in painting. Ingres's *Grande Odalisque*, or *Harem Girl* (Fig. **12.1**), has been called both Neoclassical and Romantic, and in many ways it represents both genres. Ingres professed to despise Romanticism, and yet his subject exudes Romantic individualism, exoticism, and escape. His sensuous textures appear emotional, not intellectual. At the same time, his line appears Neoclassically simple, his palette cool, and his spatial effects geometric. He uses precise and intellectually appealing linear rhythms.

The Spanish painter and printmaker Francisco de Goya (GOY-ah; 1746–1828) used his paintings to attack the abuses perpetrated by governments—both the Spanish and the French. His highly imaginative and nightmarish works capture the emotional character of humanity and nature, and often their malevolence.

Execution of the Citizens of Madrid, May 3, 1808 (Fig. **12.2**) depicts a true story. On that date, the citizens of Madrid rebelled against the invading army of Napoleon. People of the city were summarily executed. Using compositional devices to fragment the painting, Goya captures the climactic moment. The viewer cannot escape the focal point of the painting: the man in white who is about to be killed.

Goya leads us beyond the death of individuals here. These figures do not depict people realistically. Napoleon's soldiers are not even human types. Their faces are hidden, and their rigid, repeated forms become a line of subhuman automatons. Goya makes a powerful social and emotional statement. The murky quality of the background strengthens the value contrasts in the painting, and this charges the emotional drama of the scene. Color areas have hard edges, and a stark line of light running diagonally from the oversized lantern to the lower border irrevocably separates executioners and victims. Goya has no sympathy for French soldiers as human beings here; his subjectivity fills the painting.

Rosa Bonheur (buh-NUHR; 1822–99) is a painter who has been labeled both a Romantic and a Realist in style (we study Realism next; see p. 339). Her subjects are mostly animals, and she draws out their raw energy. "Wading in pools of blood," as she puts it, she studied animal anatomy, even in slaughter houses. She was particularly interested in animal psychology. *Plowing in the* *Nivernais* (Fig. **12.3**) expresses the tremendous power of the oxen on which European agriculture depended before the Industrial Revolution. The beasts appear almost monumental, and each detail is precisely executed. This painting reveals Bonheur's reverence for the dignity of labor and humankind's harmony with nature.

LITERATURE Literature in the 1770s witnessed the rise of a pre-Romantic movement called *Sturm und Drang* (shtoorm oont trahng), one of whose major exponents, Wolfgang von Goethe (GHUHR-tuh; 1749–1832), advocated freedom and a return to nature. The pre-Romantics took Shakespeare as one of their models and exalted the individual, personal experience, genius, and creative imagination. The movement's first novel, Goethe's *The Sorrows of Young Werther* portrayed Werther, a sensitive, ill-fated protagonist who proved the prototype of the Romantic hero. Goethe also chronicled the Faust legend, following Christopher Marlowe's story, which we discussed in Chapter 11. Part 1 of Goethe's sweeping two-part dramatic poem *Faust* (1808) details the magician Faust's despair, his pact with Mephistopheles, and his love

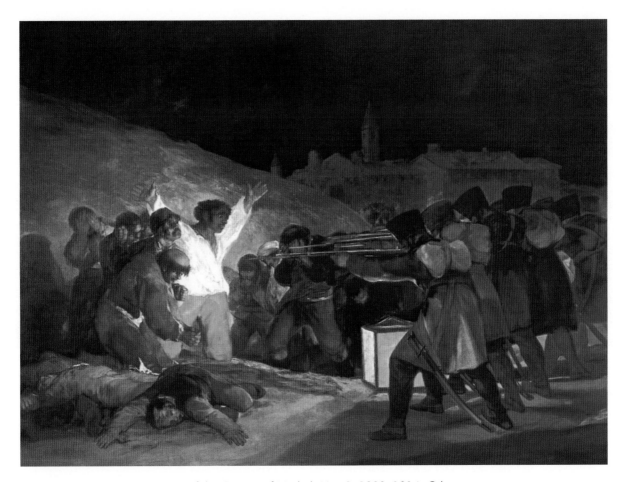

12.2 Francisco Goya, *Execution of the Citizens of Madrid, May 3, 1808*, 1814. Oil on canvas, 8 ft 6 ins × 11 ft 4 ins (2.59 × 3.45 m). Prado, Madrid.

Profile

Rosa Bonheur

One of the most significant and prominent women artists of the time, Rosa Bonheur (1822–99) focused her artistic attention almost solely on animals. Born in Bordeaux, France, she was the eldest of four children of an amateur painter. After early instruction from her father, she studied with Léon Cogniet (cuhn-YAY) at the École des Beaux-Arts (ay kohl day boh-ZAHR) in Paris, and soon began to specialize in animal subjects, studying them wherever she could. Her early paintings won awards in Paris, and in 1848 she won a first-class medal for *Plowing in the Nivernais* (Fig. **12.3**). By 1853 her work had reached full maturity, and she received high acclaim in Europe and the United States. Her paintings were much admired and she became widely known through engraved copies. She was also well known as a sculptor, and her animal subjects led to her success among her contemporary French sculptors.

Rosa Bonheur had an independent spirit, perhaps typical of the Romantic artist, and fought to gain acceptance on a level equal to that of male artists of the time. Her ability and popularity earned her the title of Chevalier of the Legion of Honor in 1865, and she was the first woman to receive the Grand Cross of the Legion. Befriended by Queen Victoria of Britain, who became her patron, Bonheur was also a favorite among the British aristocracy, although her last years were spent in France, and she died near Fontainebleau in 1899.

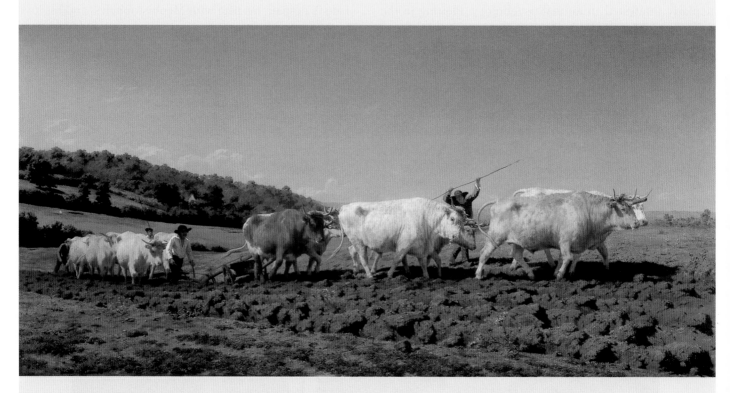

12.3 Rosa Bonheur, *Plowing in the Nivernais*, 1849. Oil on canvas, 5 ft 9 ins × 8 ft 8 ins (1.75 × 2.64 m). Musée Nationale du Château de Fontainebleau, France.

for Gretchen. Part II covers Faust's life at court, the wooing and winning of Helen of Troy, and his purification and salvation. Occasionally described as formless because of its array of lyric, epic, dramatic, operatic, and balletic elements, the work was probably conceived not as a play but as a dramatic poem.

In English literature, Romanticism proper began in the late 1790s with the publication of William Wordsworth and Samuel Taylor Coleridge's *Lyrical Ballads*. In Wordsworth's "Preface" to the second edition (1800), he described poetry as "the spontaneous overflow of powerful feelings." This sentiment underscored the English Romantic movement in poetry.

Wordsworth (1770–1850) charged the commonplace and everyday with transcendental and often indefinable significance. He created a new world of beauty through his closeness to nature and in the harmony he felt existed between humanity and nature. In 1795, he met the English poet Coleridge (1772–1834), and this friendship opened up his life and writing. Out of it came the *Lyrical Ballads*, which Wordsworth published anonymously along with four poems contributed by Coleridge. Among these ballads, "Tintern Abbey" reveals Wordsworth's love of nature. That love first appears as a sensuous animal passion, then as a moral influence, and finally as a mystical communion.

Lines Composed a Few Miles above Tintern Abbey, on Revisiting the Banks of the Wye during a Tour, July 13, 1798
William Wordsworth
1770–1850

Five years have past; five summers, with the length
Of five long winters! and again I hear
These waters, rolling from their mountain-springs
With a soft inland murmur.—Once again
Do I behold these steep and lofty cliffs,
That on a wild secluded scene impress
Thoughts of more deep seclusion; and connect
The landscape with the quiet of the sky.
The day is come when I again repose
Here, under this dark sycamore, and view
These plots of cottage-ground, these orchard-tufts,
Which at this season, with their unripe fruits,
Are clad in one green hue, and lose themselves
'Mid groves and copses. Once again I see
These hedge-rows, hardly hedge-rows, little lines
Of sportive wood run wild: these pastoral farms,
Green to the very door; and wreaths of smoke
Sent up, in silence, from among the trees!
With some uncertain notice, as might seem
Of vagrant dwellers in the houseless woods,

Or of some Hermit's cave, where by his fire
The Hermit sits alone.[1]

William Blake (1757–1827) was the third principal poet of Romanticism's early phase in England. Not only a poet, but also a painter, engraver, and visionary mystic, Blake hand-illustrated a series of lyrical and epic poems that comprise, arguably, one of the most original bodies of artistic work in the Western cultural tradition. Blake developed an etching technique called "illustrated printing," in which each page of the book appeared in monochrome from a plate containing both text and illustration.

English Romantic poetry achieved a high point in the works of Lord Byron, John Keats, and Percy Bysshe Shelley. George Gordon, Lord Byron (1788–1824) led a colorful and dramatic private life, supported the nationalist aspirations of the Greeks, and produced masterful, energetic verse. *Don Juan* (1819–24; dahn JOO-uhn), his greatest poem, rambles with rich irony through human frailties. The epic poem uses *ottava rima* (an Italian form composed of eight 11-syllable lines, rhyming *abababcc*) in sixteen cantos—a seventeenth remained unfinished. The poet uses the rhyme scheme to express different moods. The poem comprises a comic tale of the charming Don Juan, whom we follow through adventures with women, war, pirates, and politics in a timeless struggle between nature and civilization. Byron's hero, a "natural man," has instincts toward love and life constantly frustrated by brutality, hypocrisy, and conventionality.

Percy Bysshe Shelley (1792–1822) wrote in a more meditative and lyrical vein, with the passions of Romanticism never far below the surface. His poems reflect his passionate search for personal love and social justice. His works represent some of the greatest writing in the English language. Shelley married Mary Wollstonecraft Godwin, daughter of Mary Wollstonecraft. Mary Wollstonecraft Shelley earned her own fame as a Romantic writer with her novel *Frankenstein* (1818). Percy's works include "Ode to the West Wind," which invokes the spirit of the West Wind, "Destroyer and Preserver," through passionate language and symbolic imagery. The ode introduced a new form of stanza, consisting of five sonnets, each of which has four units of three lines each.

John Keats (1795–1821) devoted his life to perfecting poetry characterized by vivid imagery, sensuous appeal, and expression of philosophy through classical legend. We remember him for poems such as "Ode on a Grecian Urn" and "Ode to a Nightingale," which comprise essentially lyric meditations on an object or quality that prompts the poet to confront the conflicting impulses of his inner being and of the wider world around him.

Ode on a Grecian Urn
John Keats

Thou still unravish'd bride of quietness,
Thou foster-child of silence and slow time,
Sylvan historian, who canst thus express
A flowery tale more sweetly than our rhyme:
What leaf-fring'd legend haunts about thy shape
Of deities or mortals, or of both,
In Tempe or the dales of Arcady?
What men or gods are these? What maidens loth?
What mad pursuit? What struggle to escape?
What pipes and timbrels? What wild ecstasy?

Heard melodies are sweet, but those unheard
Are sweeter; therefore, ye soft pipes, play on;
Not to the sensual ear, but, more endear'd,
Pipe to the spirit ditties of no tone:
Fair youth, beneath the trees, thou canst not leave
Thy song, nor ever can those trees be bare;
Bold Lover, never, never canst thou kiss,
Though winning near the goal—yet, do not grieve;
She cannot fade, though thou hast not thy bliss,
For ever wilt thou love, and she be fair!

Ah, happy, happy boughs! that cannot shed
Your leaves, nor ever bid the Spring adieu;
And, happy melodist, unwearied,
For ever piping songs for ever new;
More happy love! more happy, happy love!
For ever warm and still to be enjoy'd,
For ever panting, and for ever young;
All breathing human passion far above,
That leaves a heart high-sorrowful and cloy'd,
A burning forehead, and a parching tongue.

Who are these coming to the sacrifice?
To what green altar, O mysterious priest,
Lead'st thou that heifer lowing at the skies,
And all her silken flanks with garlands drest?
What little town by river or sea shore,
Or mountain-built with peaceful citadel,
Is emptied of this folk, this pious morn?
And, little town, thy streets for evermore
Will silent be; and not a soul to tell
Why thou art desolate, can e'er return.

O Attic shape! Fair attitude! with brede
Of marble men and maidens overwrought,
With forest branches and the trodden weed;
Thou, silent form, dost tease us out of thought
As doth eternity: Cold Pastoral!
When old age shall this generation waste,
Thou shalt remain, in midst of other woe

Than ours, a friend to man, to whom thou say'st,
"Beauty is truth, truth beauty,"—that is all
Ye know on earth, and all ye need to know.

Jane Austen (1775–1817) lived and worked in the high years of the major English Romantics, but she shunned the Romantic cult of personality and remained largely indifferent to Romantic literature. She looked back to Neoclassicism and the comedy of manners as her sources, and her work portrays upper-class and middle-class people living in provincial towns and going about the daily routine of family life—a life of good breeding, wit, and a reasonable hope that difficulties can be resolved in a satisfactory manner. She occasionally portrayed disappointments in love and threatened or actual seduction, but, somehow, these seem less important than the ongoing and routine conversations and rituals of daily life. Merely because she portrayed a quiet form of life does not mean, however, that her characters lack depth or interest. She explored human experience deeply and with humor. She proved that one does not require spectacular events in order to provide engaging art.

Her early years produced a variety of works that parody the sentimental and romantic clichés of popular fiction. In her second period of writing, from 1810 on, she crowned her career with works such as *Mansfield Park* (1813), *Emma* (1815), and *Persuasion* (1818). *Emma* shows Jane Austen's ability to remain detached from her heroine, Emma Woodhouse, who represents self-deception, as she misreads evidence, misleads others, and discovers her own feelings only by accident. In her other works, Austen portrayed many gentle and self-effacing characters in the mode of her earlier masterpiece *Pride and Prejudice* (1813).

MUSIC In an era of Romantic subjectivity, music provided the medium in which many found an unrivaled opportunity to express emotion. In trying to express human emotion, Romantic music made stylistic changes to Classical music, and although Romanticism amounted to rebellion in many of the arts, in music it involved a more gradual and natural extension of Classical principles.

As in painting, spontaneity replaced control, but the primary emphasis of music in this era was on beautiful, lyrical, and expressive *melody*. Phrases became longer, more irregular, and more complex than they had been in Classical music. Much Romantic rhythm was traditional, but experiments produced new meters and patterns. Composers often suggested emotional conflict by juxtaposing different meters, and rhythmic irregularity became increasingly common as the century progressed. Romantic composers emphasized colorful harmonies and

Masterworks

Jane Austen, *Pride and Prejudice*

Pride and Prejudice (1813) contains little of the satire found in many works of the same period, but portrays an ironic and sympathetic view of human nature and its propensity for comic incongruity. The narrative, which Austen originally titled "First Impressions," describes the clash between Elizabeth Bennet, the daughter of a country gentleman, and Fitzwilliam Darcy, a rich and aristocratic landowner. Austen reverses the convention of first impressions: "pride" of rank and fortune, and "prejudice" against Elizabeth's inferiority of family, hold Darcy aloof; while Elizabeth is equally fired both by the pride of self-respect and by prejudice against Darcy's snobbery. Ultimately they come together in love and self-understanding.

The central comedy of *Pride and Prejudice* lies in the fully developed character that reveals a sense of human realities and values. For example, in the character of Mr. Bennet, Austen makes a symbolic comment on intelligence that exists without will or drive. In her two opposing protagonists, Darcy and Elizabeth, who reflect the title of the book, Austen depicts character overlaid with class superciliousness and character abounding in independence and sharpness of mind that acts with prejudgment, wrong-headedness, and self-satisfaction. In all situations, Jane Austen remains detached, witty, and good-humored. Her disturbances are minor intrusions in an unshakable moral universe in which one can point out an entire range of human frailties and yet not despair.

In the story, as summarized in *The Bloomsbury Guide to English Literature* (Prentice Hall, 1990), Mr. and Mrs. Bennet belong to the minor gentry and live at Longbourn, near London. Mr. Bennet is witty and intelligent, and bored with his foolish wife. They have five daughters, whose marriage prospects are Mrs. Bennet's chief interest in life, since the estate is "entailed"—that is, by the law of the period it will pass on Mr. Bennet's death to his nearest male relation, a sycophantic clergyman called Mr. Collins. The main part of the story is concerned with the relationship between the witty and attractive Elizabeth Bennet and the haughty and fastidious Fitzwilliam Darcy, who at first considers her beneath his notice and later, on coming to the point of asking her to marry him, finds that she is resolutely prejudiced against him.

Elizabeth is subjected to an insolent offer of marriage by Mr. Collins and the arrogant condescension of his patroness, Lady Catherine de Bourgh, Darcy's aunt. In the end, chastened by finding in one another a fastidiousness and pride that equal their own and despite a family scandal, they are united.

---

instrumentation. They utilized harmony as a means of expression, and therefore any previous "laws" regarding key relationships could be broken to achieve striking emotional effects. Harmonies became increasingly complex, and traditional distinctions between major and minor keys blurred in chromatic harmonies, complicated chords, and modulations to distant keys. In fact, some composers used key changes so frequently that their compositions turn into virtually nothing but whirls of continuous modulation.

As composers sought to disrupt the listener's expectations, more and more dissonance occurred, until it became an important focus of the music. They explored dissonance for its own sake, as a strong stimulant of emotional response rather than merely as a decorative way to get to the traditional tonic chord. By the end of the Romantic period, the exhaustion of chromatic usage and dissonance had led to a search for a completely different type of tonal system.

Exploring musical color to elicit feeling was as important to the Romantic musician as it was to the painter. Interest in tonal color, or timbre, led to great diversity in vocal and instrumental performance, and the music of this period abounds with solo works and exhibits a tremendous increase in the size and diversity of the orchestra. We have many options in how we might explore Romantic music, none of which we could pursue exhaustively. We will proceed by isolating some major genres and, within them, noting major composers as we pass. These choices remain arbitrary. More composers might be examined, but, again, this is a buffet: a sample provides a taste of the whole.

LIEDER In many ways, the "art song," or *Lied* (leed), characterized Romantic music. A composition for solo voice with piano accompaniment and poetic text, the art song allowed for a variety of lyrical and dramatic expressions and linked music directly with literature.

The burst of German lyric poetry in this period encouraged the growth of *Lieder*. Literary nuances affected music, and music added deeper emotional implications to the poem. This partnership had various results: some *Lieder* were complex, others simple; and some structured; others were freely composed. The pieces themselves depended on a close relationship between the piano and the voice. In many ways, the piano constituted an inseparable part of the experience, and certainly it served as more than accompaniment, for the piano explored mood and established rhythmic and thematic material, and sometimes had solo passages of its own. The interdependency of the song and its accompaniment stand basic to the art song.

The earliest, and perhaps the most important, composer of *Lieder*, Franz Schubert (1797–1828) led a troubled life and epitomized the Romantic view of the artist's desperate and isolated condition. Known only among a close circle of friends and musicians, Schubert composed almost one thousand works, from symphonies to sonatas and operas, to masses, choral compositions, and *Lieder*. None of his work was publicly performed, however, until the year of his death. He took his *Lieder* texts from a wide variety of poems, and in each case the melodic contours, harmonies, rhythms, and structures of the music were determined by the poem.

Schubert's song *Der Erlkönig* (*The Erlking*, 1815; music CD track 17; Fig. **12.4**) provides an excellent example both of Schubert's work and of Romantic music in general. The song consists of a musical setting of a poem about the supernatural by Goethe. Schubert uses a *through-composed setting*—he writes new music for each stanza—in order to capture the poem's mounting excitement. The piano plays the role of an important partner in transmitting the mood of the piece, creating tension with rapid octaves and menacing bass motif. Imaginative variety in the music allows Schubert's soloist to sound like several characters in the dramatic development.

Who rides so late through the night and the wind?
It is the father with his child;
He folds the boy close in his arms,
He clasps him securely, he holds him warmly.

"My son, why do you hide your face so anxiously?"
"Father, don't you see the Erlking?
The Erlking with his crown and his train?"
"My son, it's a streak of mist."

"Dear child, come, go with me!
I'll play the prettiest games with you.
Many-colored flowers grow along the shore;
My mother has many golden garments."

"My father, my father, and don't you hear
The Erlking whispering promises to me?"
"Be quiet, stay quiet, my child;
The wind is rustling in the dead leaves."

"My handsome boy, will you come with me?
My daughters shall wait upon you;
My daughters lead off in the dance every night,
And cradle and dance and sing you to sleep."

"My father, my father, and don't you see there
The Erlking's daughters in the shadows?"
"My son, my son, I see it clearly;
The old willows look so gray."

"I love you, your beautiful figure delights me!
And if you are not willing, then I shall use force!"
"My father, my father, now he is taking hold of me!
The Erlking has hurt me!"

The father shudders, he rides swiftly on;
He holds in his arms the groaning child,
He reaches the courtyard weary and anxious:
In his arms the child was dead.

Translated by Philip L. Miller

PIANO WORKS The development of the art song depended in no small way on nineteenth-century improvements in piano design. The instrument for which Schubert wrote had a much warmer, richer tone than earlier pianos, and improvements in pedal technique made sustained tones possible and gave the instrument greater lyrical potential.

Such flexibility made the piano an excellent instrument for accompaniment, and, more importantly, made it an almost ideal solo instrument. As a result, new works were composed solely for the piano, ranging from short, intimate pieces, similar to *Lieder*, to larger works designed to exhibit great virtuosity in performance. Franz Schubert wrote such pieces, as did Franz Liszt (1811–86). Liszt was one of the most celebrated pianists of the nineteenth

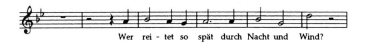

12.4 Franz Schubert, *The Erlking* (excerpt).

century and one of its most innovative composers. He enthralled audiences with his expressive, dramatic playing, and taught most of the major pianists of the next generation. He also influenced Richard Wagner (vahgh-nuhr) and Richard Strauss. His piano works include six *Paganini Études* (1851), concertos, and twenty *Hungarian Rhapsodies* based on Hungarian urban popular music rather than folk music. The technical demands of Liszt's compositions, and the rather florid way he performed them, gave rise to a theatricality, the primary purpose of which was to impress audiences with flashy presentation. This fitted well with the Romantic concept of the artist as hero.

The compositions of Frédéric Chopin (sho-pan; 1810–49) showed more restraint. Chopin wrote almost exclusively for the piano. Each of his *Études* (AY-tood; studies or pieces that were designed to help a performer master specific technical challenges) explored a single problem, usually set around a single motif. More than simple exercises, these works explored the possibilities of the instrument and became short tone poems in their own right. A second group of compositions included short intimate works such as preludes, nocturnes, and impromptus, and dances such as waltzes, polonaises, and mazurkas. (Chopin was Polish but lived in France, and Polish folk music had a particularly strong influence on him.) A final class of larger works included scherzos, ballades, and fantasies. Chopin's highly individual compositions, many without precedent, employ lyrical melodies and varying moods.

Chopin's "Revolutionary" *Etude in C Minor, Op. 10* (music CD track 16) has a blazing and furious quality perhaps inspired by the Russian takeover of Warsaw in Chopin's home country of Poland. As an *étude*, the "Revolutionary Etude" tackles the problem of developing speed and strength in the pianist's left hand: the piece requires the performer to play rapid passages throughout. The work begins with a dramatic explosion. High, dissonant chords couple with rushing downward passages culminating in the main melody played in octaves by the right hand. The melody's dotted rhythms and stormy accompaniment give the work a mounting tension. Near the end, after a climax, tension subsides briefly only to be followed by a fiery passage sweeping down the keyboard and coming to rest in strong closing chords.

PROGRAM MUSIC One of the new ways in which Romantic composers structured their longer works was to build them around a nonmusical story, a picture, or some other idea. Music of this sort is called "descriptive." When the idea is quite specific and closely followed throughout the piece, the music is called "programmatic" or "program music."

These techniques were not entirely new—we have already noted the descriptive elements in Beethoven's "Pastoral" Symphony—but the Romantics found them particularly attractive and employed them with great gusto. A nonmusical idea allowed composers to rid themselves of formal structure altogether. Of course, actual practice varied tremendously—some used programmatic material as their only structural device, while others subordinated a program idea to formal structure. Nevertheless, the Romantic period has become known as the "age of program music." Among the best-known composers of program music were Hector Berlioz (1803–69) and Richard Strauss (1864–1949).

Berlioz's *Symphonie Fantastique* (1830) employed a single motif, called an *idée fixe* (ee-DAY feex), to tie the five movements of the work together. The story on which the musical piece is based involves a hero who has poisoned himself because of unrequited love. However, the drug sends him only into semi-consciousness, in which he has visions. Throughout these visions the recurrent musical theme (the *idée fixe*) symbolizes his beloved. Movement 1 consists of "Reveries" and "Passions." Movement 2 represents "A Ball." "In the Country" is movement 3, in which he imagines a pastoral scene. In movement 4, "March to the Scaffold", he dreams he has killed his beloved and is about to be executed. The *idée fixe* returns at the end of the movement and is abruptly shattered by the fall of the axe. The final movement describes a "Dream of a Witches' Sabbath" in grotesque and orgiastic musical imagery (music CD track 15).

Not all program music depends for its interest upon an understanding of its text. Many people believe, however, that the tone poems, or symphonic poems, of Richard Strauss require an understanding of the story. His *Don Juan*, *Till Eulenspiegel*, and *Don Quixote* draw such detailed material from specific legends that program explanations and comments are integral to the works and help to give them coherence. In *Till Eulenspiegels lustige Streiche* (*Till Eulenspiegel's Merry Pranks*), Strauss tells the legendary German story of Till Eulenspiegel and his practical jokes. Till is traced through three escapades, all musically identifiable. He is then confronted by his critics and finally executed. Throughout, we find quite specific musical references.

SYMPHONIES Beethoven's powerful symphonies strongly influenced nineteenth-century composers. Schubert, whom we just discussed as a composer of *Lieder*, wrote eight symphonies, one of which, the so-called "Unfinished" (B Minor) has a darkly Romantic style. Hector Berlioz's *Symphonie Fantastique* (see above) illustrated that a symphony could be written in an entirely

Profile

Johannes Brahms

Although he was born into an impoverished family, Johannes Brahms (1833–97) appears to have had a relatively happy childhood. His father was an itinerant musician, who eked out a meager living playing the horn and double bass in taverns and nightclubs. The family lived in the slums of Hamburg, Germany, but, despite their economic hardships, they retained close and loving family relationships. Early in life, Johannes showed evidence of considerable musical talent, and the eminent piano teacher Eduard Marxsen agreed to give him tuition without pay.

By the time he was twenty, Brahms had gained acclaim as a pianist and accepted an invitation to participate in a concert tour with the Hungarian violinist Eduard Remenyi. The event was invaluable to the young Brahms, because it introduced him to Franz Liszt and Robert Schumann. Through Schumann's efforts, Brahms was able to publish several of his compositions, which opened the door to the wider artistic world and launched his prolific career. Brahms gained experience as musical director at the little court of Detmold and as founder and director of a women's chorus in Hamburg, for which he wrote several choral works. His musical creativity showed a deep love of folk music and a sensitivity of expression. He mastered German *Lieder* and remained devoted to the Romantic style throughout his career, notwithstanding his fondness for clarity of structure and form based in the Classical style of the previous century.

Although Brahms wanted to stay in Hamburg, he was passed over for a position, and, feeling betrayed and neglected by his native town, he moved to Vienna. That city's rich musical ambience enriched his talent and experience, and he gained tremendous success, serving as director of the Vienna Singakademie and as conductor of the Society of Friends of Music. In 1875, he resigned his positions and spent the rest of his days in creative endeavors. For the next twenty-two years, he sacrificed his personal life in pursuit of his career, and the results gained him—in his own lifetime—recognition as one of the world's greatest artists.

His work spanned several idioms, from solo piano compositions and chamber music to full orchestral works. He was never interested in music for the stage nor in program music, but he reveled in symphonic compositions ruled by purely musical ideas, favoring absolute music.

different manner from Beethoven's. Felix Mendelssohn (1809–47) followed Classical tradition in most of his symphonies, but we should note that although many Romantic symphonies followed Classical form, the form was employed more as a means to a Romantically expressive end and not for its own sake.

An outstanding example of the Romantic symphony, Brahms's *Symphony No. 3 in F Major* (1883), calls for pairs of flutes, oboes, clarinets, a bassoon, a contrabassoon, four horns, two trumpets, three trombones, two timpani, and strings—not an adventurous grouping of instruments for the period. Composed in sonata form, the first movement of the piece, allegro con brio (fast with spirit), begins in F major (Fig. 12.5).

The exposition section closes with a return to the opening motif and meter, employing rising scales and arpeggios. Then, following Classical tradition, the exposition is repeated.

The development section uses both the principal themes, with changes in tonal colors, dynamics, and modulation. The recapitulation opens with a forceful restatement of the opening motif, followed by a restatement and further development of materials from the exposition. Then comes a lengthy coda, again announced by the opening motif, and based on the first theme. A final, quiet, restatement of the opening motif and first phrase of the theme brings the first movement to an end.

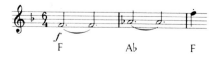

12.5 Johannes Brahms, *Symphony No. 3 in F major*, opening motif of first movement.

TRENDS The Romantic period also gave birth to new trends in music. The roots of such movements went deep into the past, but composers also wrote with the political circumstances of the century in mind. Folk tunes appear in these works as themes, as do local rhythms and harmonies. The exaltation of national identity stayed consistent with Romantic requirements, and it occurs in the music of nineteenth-century Russia, Bohemia, Spain, Britain, Scandinavia, Germany, and Austria.

Of all the composers of the Romantic period, the Russian Peter Ilyich Tchaikovsky (chy-KAWF-skee; 1840–93) has enjoyed the greatest popularity, with his *1812 Overture* perhaps topping the list, followed closely by his *Nutcracker* ballet. In his First Symphony, he imitates the lyricism of Russian folk song, and the traits of the nineteenth-century Russian salon song can be found in his Fifth and Sixth Symphonies.

The *symphonic poem*, an offshoot of the symphony proper, was a term invented by Franz Liszt to describe a series of orchestral works he wrote that take their musical form and rhetoric from nonabstract ideas, some of them poetic and others visual. Other composers followed Liszt's lead, and the model proved especially popular in topics stemming from nationalistic sources, among them Smetana (*My Country*), Dvořák (*The Noonday Witch*), Borodin (*In the Steppes of Central Asia*), Sibelius (*Tapiola*), and Elgar (*Falstaff*).

CHORAL MUSIC Vocal music ranged from solo to massive ensemble works. The emotional requirements of Romanticism were well served by the diverse timbres and lyricism of the human voice. Almost every major composer of the era wrote some form of vocal music. Franz Schubert is remembered for his masses, the most notable of which is the *Mass in A flat Major*. Felix Mendelssohn's *Elijah* stands beside Handel's *Messiah* and Haydn's *Creation* as a masterpiece of oratorio. Hector Berlioz marshaled full Romantic power for his *Requiem*, which called for 210 voices, a large orchestra, and four brass bands.

One of the most enduringly popular choral works of the Romantic period is Brahms's *Ein Deutsches Requiem* (*A German Requiem*). Based on selected texts from the Bible, in contrast with the Latin liturgy of traditional requiems, Brahms's work is not so much a mass for the dead as a consolation for the living. It is principally a choral work—the solos are minimal: two for baritone and one for soprano—but both vocal and instrumental writing are very expressive. Soaring melodic lines and rich harmonies weave thick textures. After the chorus sings "All mortal flesh is as the grass," the orchestra suggests fields of grass moving in the wind. The lyrical movement, "How lovely is thy dwelling place," soars with emotion. Brahms's *Requiem* begins and ends with moving passages aimed directly at the living: "Blest are they that mourn." Hope and consolation underlie the entire work.

An important factor in Brahms's music is its lyricism and its vocal beauty. Brahms explored the voice as a human voice, and not as another instrument or some other mechanism unaffected by any restrictions, as other composers have done. His parts are written and his words chosen so that no voice ever has to sing outside its natural range or technical capacity.

OPERA The spirit and style of Romanticism sum up in that perfect synthesis of all the arts, opera. Three countries, France (especially Paris), Italy, and Germany, dominated the development of opera.

Paris occupied an important position in Romantic opera during the first half of the nineteenth century. The spectacular quality of opera and the size of its auditoriums had made it an effective vehicle for propaganda during the Revolution, and as an art form, opera enjoyed great popular appeal among the rising and influential middle classes.

A new type of opera, called "grand opera," emerged early in the nineteenth century, principally through the efforts of Louis Veron, a businessman, the playwright Eugène Scribe, and Giacomo Meyerbeer, a composer. These three broke away from Classical themes and subject matter and staged spectacular productions with crowd scenes, ballets, choruses, and fantastic scenery, written around medieval and contemporary themes. Meyerbeer (1791–1864), a German, studied Italian opera in Venice and produced French opera in Paris. *Robert the Devil* and *The Huguenots* typify Meyerbeer's extravagant style; they achieved great popular success, although the composer Schumann called *The Huguenots* "a conglomeration of monstrosities." Berlioz's *The Trojans*, written in the late 1850s, had a more Classical base and more control musically. At the same time, Jacques Offenbach (1819–80) brought to the stage a lighter style (*opéra comique*; see p. 130) in which spoken dialogue mixed with the music. Offenbach used vaudeville humor to satirize other operas, popular events, and so forth. In between the styles of Meyerbeer and Offenbach a third form of Romantic opera occurred: lyric opera. Ambroise Thomas (1811–96) and Charles Gounod (1818–93) turned to Romantic drama and fantasy for their plots. Thomas's *Mignon* contains highly lyrical passages, and Gounod's *Faust*, based on Goethe's play, stresses melodic beauty.

Early Romantic opera in Italy featured the *bel canto* style, which emphasizes beauty of sound, and the works of Gioacchino Rossini (1792–1868) epitomize this feature. Rossini's *The Barber of Seville* takes melodic singing to new heights with light, ornamented, and highly appealing work, particularly for his soprano voices.

Great artists often stand apart from or astride general stylistic trends while they explore their own themes. Such is the case with the Italian composer Giuseppe Verdi (1813–1901). With Verdi, opera is truly a human drama, expressed through simple, beautiful melody.

In what might be described as typical of Romanticism, Verdi dared to make an operatic hero out of a hunchbacked court jester—Rigoletto—whose only redeeming quality seems to be his great love for his daughter, Gilda. Rigoletto's master is the licentious duke of Mantua, who, while posing as a poor student, wins Gilda's love. When the duke seduces the innocent girl, Rigoletto plots his death. Despite the seduction, Gilda loves the dissolute duke and ultimately gives her life to save his. Virtue does not triumph in this opera.

Act Three of *Rigoletto* contains one of the most popular of all operatic arias, "La donna è mobile" ("Woman is fickle"; Fig. **12.6**):

Woman is fickle
Like a feather in the wind,
She changes her words
And her thoughts.
Always a lovable
And lovely face,
Weeping or laughing,
Is lying.
Woman is fickle, etc.
The man's always wretched
Who believes in her,
Who recklessly entrusts
His heart to her!
And yet no one who never
Drinks love on that breast
Ever feels
Entirely happy!
Woman is fickle, etc.

Late in his career, Verdi wrote works such as *Aïda* (1871), grand operas of spectacular proportions built upon tightly woven dramatic structures. Finally, in a third

phase, he produced operas based on Shakespearean plays. *Otello* (1887) contrasts tragedy and *opera buffa*—comic opera, not *opéra comique*—and explores subtle balances among voices and orchestra, together with strong melodic development.

Richard Wagner (1813–83) was one of the masters of Romantic opera. At the heart of Wagner's artistry lay a philosophy that has affected the stage from the mid-nineteenth century to the present day. He laid out his ideas principally in two books, *Art and Revolution* (1849) and *Opera and Drama* (1851). Wagner's philosophy centered on the *Gesamtkunstwerk* (geh-ZAMT-koonst-VAIRK), a comprehensive work of art in which music, poetry, and scenery stay subservient to the central generating idea. For Wagner, the total unity of all elements had supremely importance. In line with German Romantic philosophy, which gives music supremacy over the other arts, music has the predominant role in Wagner's operas. Dramatic meaning unfolds through the *Leitmotif* (LYT-moh-TEEF), for which Wagner is famous, although he did not invent it. A *Leitmotif* is a musical theme that is tied to an idea, a person, or an object. Whenever that idea, person, or object appears on stage or comes to mind in the action, that theme appears. Juxtaposing *Leitmotifs* gives the audience an idea of relationships between their various subjects. *Leitmotifs* also give the composer building blocks to use for development, recapitulation, and unification.

We capture just a hint of the sweep and grandeur of Wagner's operatic music with the very well-known "Bridal Chorus" from *Lohengrin* (1850). To set the scene very briefly, in Act I, the German ruler tells his nobles of increased war with the Eastern hordes. The nobles agree to follow him. A local dispute, however, involves Telramund and Elsa, whom Telramund once intended to marry, over who should rule Brabant and Telramund's accusation that Elsa has murdered her own brother. But who will fight for Elsa? No one comes forward. Elsa prays fervently. Miraculously, an unknown knight (Lohengrin) appears. But before he will fight for Elsa, she must promise to marry him if he is victorious and never to ask his name or where he came from. He fights and defeats Telramund, but spares his life. Act II finds us in Antwerp where Elsa and Lohengrin will be married. Dawn begins to break. Knights and others gather in the courtyard of the cathedral. A herald announces Lohengrin as the new ruler of Brabant. Some turmoil over the still-simmering dispute arises again. But who is Lohengrin? The fatal question arises. Lohengrin will answer to no one but Elsa. Will she question him? She wavers but continues with the ceremony. Music associated with the fatal questions rise from the orchestra. Act III moves directly into the famous

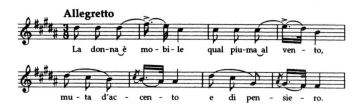

12.6 Giuseppe Verdi, "La donna è mobile," from *Rigoletto* (1851).

"Bridal Chorus" (music CD track 18). The attendants sing this to the happy couple on their wedding night and then leave them in the bridal chamber. Driven to madness by her curiosity, Elsa finally breaks and asks the fatal question: "Tell me thy name... Whence dost thou come? ... Where is thy home?" Before he can answer, Telramund and four knights burst into the chamber. Lohengrin dispatches them with one supernatural stroke of his sword. "Now all happiness is gone," he sighs. Before the king, Lohengrin reveals his secret: he belongs to a sacred band of knights who fight for the Holy Grail. Once every year a dove descends from heaven to renew its powers, and all the knights are protected by it in their fights for innocence and truth. His father is Percival, king of all the knights of the Grail. Now that his secret is known, he must return. There is a final twist as Elsa's brother, who had been turned into a swan by the sorceress Ortrud, returns miraculously. A dove descends with a chain and carries off Lohengrin in his boat. Elsa cries, "My husband, my husband" and falls lifeless into her brother's arms.

Theatre "The play-going world of the West End is at this moment occupied in rubbing its eyes, that it may recover completely from the dazzle of Thursday last, when, amid the acclamations of Queen Victoria's subjects, King Richard the Second was enthroned at the Princess's Theatre." Thus began the reviewer's comments in *The Spectator*, March 14, 1857. The dazzle of scenery, revivals, and a pot-pourri of uncertain accomplishments helped a stumbling theatre to keep up with the other arts that flourished through the early years of the nineteenth century.

Romanticism as a philosophy of art was its own worst enemy in the theatre. Artists sought new forms to express great truths, and they strove to free themselves from Neoclassical rules and restraints. They did, however, admire Shakespeare as an example of new ideals and as a symbol of freedom from structural confinement. Intuition reigned, and the artistic genius was set apart from everyday people and above normal constraints. As a result, Romantic writers had no use for any guide apart from their own imagination.

Unfortunately, the theatre operates within some rather specific limits. Many nineteenth-century playwrights penned unstageable and/or unplayable scripts, and great writers could not or would not abide by constraints of the stage, while the hacks, yielding to popular taste, could not resist overindulgence in phony emotionalism, melodrama (see chapter 5), and stage gimmickry. As a result, the best Romantic theatre performances came from the pen of William Shakespeare, whose work was revived in a great rush of nineteenth-century antiquarianism.

Poor as it may have been in original drama, the Romantic period did succeed in loosening the arbitrary rules of Neoclassical convention. Thus, it paved the way for a new theatrical era in the later years of the century.

The audiences of the nineteenth century played a significant part in determining what took the stage. Royal patronage was gone, and box office receipts were needed to pay the bills. A rising middle class had swelled the eighteenth-century audience and changed its character. Then, in the nineteenth century, the lower classes began attending the theatre. The Industrial Revolution had created larger urban populations and expanded public education to a degree. As feelings of egalitarianism spread throughout Europe and America, theatre audiences grew, and theatre building flourished. To appeal to this diverse audience, theatre managers had to put on plays for the popular as well as the sophisticated taste if they wanted to make money, so to offer something for everyone, an evening's theatre program might contain several types of fare and last over five hours. Fewer and fewer sophisticated patrons chose to attend, and the quality of the productions declined.

By 1850, theatres began to specialize, and sophisticated playgoers came back to certain theatres, although the multipart production remained typical until nearly the turn of the twentieth century. Audience demand was high, and theatre continued to expand.

Although theatre design was by now very diverse, some general similarities existed. Principally, the changes in nineteenth-century stages and staging were prompted by increased interest in historical accuracy and popular demand for depiction rather than convention. Before the eighteenth century, history had been considered irrelevant to art. Knowledge of antiquity that began with archeological excavations in Pompeii, however, aroused curiosity, and the Romantic dream of escape to the long ago and far away suggested that the stage picture of exotic places should be somehow believable. At first, such detail appeared inconsistently, but, by 1823, some productions claimed that they were entirely historical in every respect. Attempts at historical accuracy had begun as early as 1801, and in France, Victor Hugo and Alexandre Dumas *père* insisted on historically accurate settings and costumes during the early years of the century. However, actor-manager Charles Kean (1811–68) brought the spectacle of antiquarianism in the London theatre to fruition in the 1850s (Fig. **12.7**).

The onset of accuracy as a standard for production led to three-dimensionality in settings and away from drop and wing scenery to the box set. The stage floor was leveled—since the Renaissance it had been raked—and new methods of shifting and rigging were devised to meet

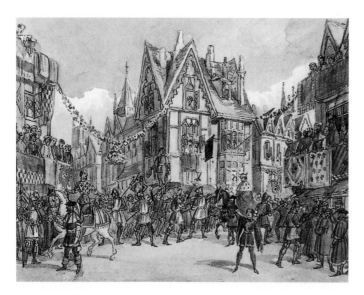

12.7 Charles Kean's production of Shakespeare's *Richard II*, London, 1857. Between Acts III and IV, the Entry of Bolingbroke into London. Contemporary watercolor by Thomas Grieve. Victoria & Albert Museum, London.

specific staging problems. Over a period of years, all elements of the production became integrated, much in the spirit of Wagner's totally unified artwork, the *Gesamtkunstwerk*. The distraction of numerous scene changes was eliminated by closing the curtain.

BALLET In a totally unrehearsed move, a ballerina leaped from the tomb on which she posed and narrowly escaped a piece of falling scenery. This and other disasters plagued the opening night performance of Meyerbeer's *Robert the Devil* in 1831. The novelty of tenors falling into trapdoors, and falling stagelights and scenery, however, was eclipsed by the startling novelty of the choreography for this opera. Romantic ballet poised at hand. To varying degrees, all the arts turned against the often cold formality of Classicism and Neoclassicism. The subjective (not the objective) viewpoint and feeling (rather than reason) sought release.

Two sources help in understanding the Romantic ballet, the writings of Théophile Gautier (goh-TYAY) and Carlo Blasis (blah-SEE). Gautier (1811–72), a poet and critic, held first of all that beauty was truth, a central Romantic conception. Gautier believed that dance comprised visual stimulation to show "beautiful forms in graceful attitudes." Dancing for Gautier was like a living painting or sculpture—"physical pleasure and feminine beauty." This exclusive focus on ballerinas placed sensual enjoyment and eroticism squarely at the center of his aesthetics. Gautier had significant influence, and accounted for the central role of the ballerina in Romantic ballet.

Male dancers were relegated to the background, strength being the only grace permissible to them.

The second general premise for Romantic ballet came from *Code of Terpsichore* (tuhrp-SIH-kuh-ree) by Carlo Blasis (1803–78). Blasis was much more systematic and specific than Gautier—he was a former dancer—and his principles covered training, structure, and positioning. Everything in the ballet required a beginning, a middle, and an ending. The basic "attitude" in dance, modeled on Giovanni Bologna's statue of *Mercury* (see Fig. 2.8), was to stand on one leg with the other brought up behind at a 90-degree angle with the knee bent. The dancer needed to display the human figure with taste and elegance. If the dancer trained each part of the body, the result would be grace without affectation. From Blasis comes the turned-out position, still considered fundamental to ballet today (Fig. 12.8; see also Fig. 7.2). These broad principles provided the framework, and, to a great extent, a summary, of objectives for Romantic ballet: delicate ballerinas, lightly poised, costumed in soft tulle, and moving *en pointe*, with elegant grace.

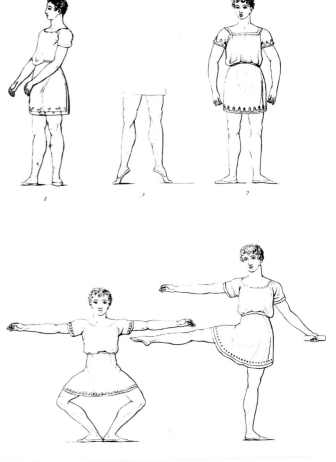

12.8 Illustrations from *The Art of Dancing*, 1820, by Carlo Blasis. The New York Public Library.

The first truly Romantic ballet, *Robert the Devil* told the story of Duke Robert of Normandy, his love for a princess, and an encounter with the devil. The ballet contains ghosts, bacchanalian dancing, and a spectral figure who was danced by the ballerina Marie Taglioni (tah-lee-OH-nee; Fig. **12.9**).

Taglioni went on to star in perhaps the most famous of all Romantic ballets, *La Sylphide* (sihl-FEED; 1832). Here the plot centered on the tragic impossibility of love between a mortal and a supernatural being. A spirit of the air, a sylph, falls in love with a young Scot on his wedding day. Torn between his real fiancée and his ideal, the sylph, he deserts his fiancée to run off with the spirit. A witch gives him a scarf, and, unaware that it is enchanted, he ties it around the spirit's waist. Immediately her wings fall off and she dies. She drifts away to sylphs' heaven. The young man, disconsolate and alone, sees his fiancée passing in the distance with a new lover on the way to her wedding. The Scottish setting was exotic, at least to

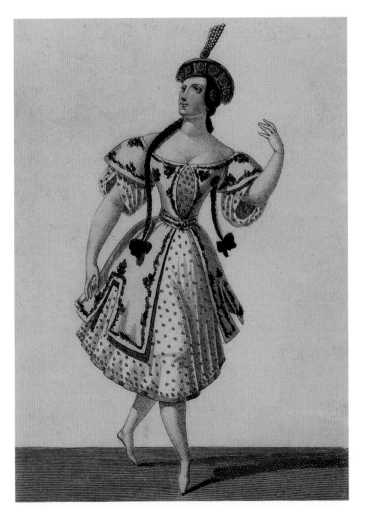

12.9 Marie Taglioni (1804–84). Engraving, 1834. The New York Public Library.

Parisians. Gaslight provided a ghostly, moonlit mood in the darkened auditorium. Taglioni danced the role of La Sylphide like "a creature of mist drifting over the stage" (assisted by flying machinery). Her lightness, delicacy, and modest grace established the standard for Romantic style in dancing. The story, exotic design, and mood-evoking lighting completed the production style, a style that prevailed for the next forty years— "moonbeams and gossamer," as some have described it.

Choreographers of Romantic ballet sought magic and escape in fantasies and legends. Ballets about elves and nymphs enjoyed great popularity, as did ballets about madness, sleepwalking, and opium dreams. Unusual subject matter came to the fore. For example, harem wives revolt against their oppressors with the help of the "Spirit of Womankind" in Filippo Taglioni's *The Revolt in the Harem*, possibly the first ballet about the emancipation of women. Women appeared not only as performers and as subjects of the dance, however. They also began to come to prominence as choreographers.

The ballet *Giselle* (zhee-ZEHL; 1841) marks the height of Romantic achievement. With its many fine dancing roles, both for women and for men, it has been a favorite of ballet companies since its first production.

The ballet has two acts; Act I is in sunlight, and Act II in moonlight. During a vine festival in a Rhineland village, Giselle, a frail peasant girl in love with a mysterious young man, discovers that the object of her affection is Albrecht, Count of Silesia. Albrecht is already engaged to a noblewoman. Giselle is shattered. She goes mad, turns from her deceitful lover, tries to commit suicide, swoons, and falls dead. In Act II, Giselle is summoned from her grave, deep in the forest, by Myrthe (MUHR-tuh), Queen of the Wilis, spirits of women who, having died unhappy in love, are condemned to lead men to destruction. (The word *wili* comes from a Slavic word for "vampire.") When a repentant Albrecht comes to bring flowers to Giselle's grave, Myrthe orders her to dance him to his death. Instead, Giselle protects Albrecht until the first rays of dawn break Myrthe's power.

In St. Petersburg, Russia, in 1862, an English ballet called *The Daughter of Pharaoh*, choreographed by Marius Petipa (peh-tee-PAH), sent Russian audiences into rapture. Petipa had come to Russia from France in 1842, and he remained a central figure in Russian ballet for almost sixty years. By the middle of the nineteenth century, ballet companies flourished in Moscow and St Petersburg. Dancers enjoyed positions of high esteem in Russia, as they did not in the rest of Europe.

In Russia, the influence of Petipa carried Russian ballet forward in a quasi-Romantic style. He shared the sentimental taste of his time, but his works often contained

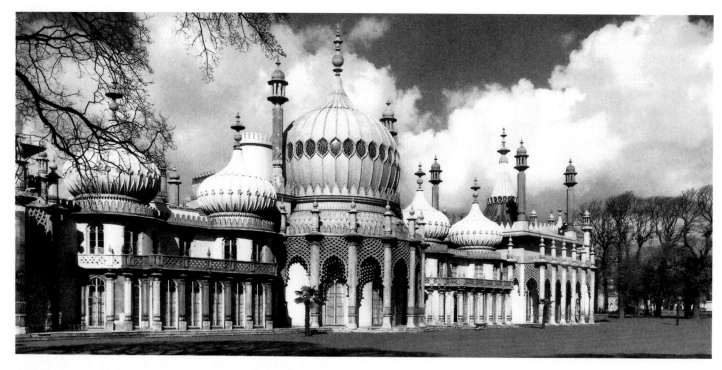

12.10 John Nash, Royal Pavilion, Brighton, England, remodeled 1815–23.

very strange elements and numerous anachronisms. Minor characters might wear costumes suggesting period or locale, but the stars wore conventional garb, often of Classical derivation. Prima ballerinas often appeared in stylish contemporary coiffures and jewels, even when playing the role of a slave. *Divertissements* (dee-vair-TEES-mawn)—light entertainments—were often inserted into a ballet. Petipa included many different kinds of dance in his ballets—Classical, character, and folk dance. His creative approach more than compensated for his anachronisms. As some have said in his defense, "No one criticized Shakespeare for having Antony and Cleopatra speak in blank verse."

From this Russian school came the ever-popular *Nutcracker* and *Swan Lake*, scores for both composed by Tchaikovsky. *Swan Lake* was first produced in 1877 by the Moscow Bolshoi and *Nutcracker* in 1892. *Swan Lake* popularized the *fouetté* (foo-eh-TAY), or whipping turn, introduced by the ballerina Pierina Legnani in Petipa's *Cinderella* and incorporated for her in *Swan Lake*. In one scene, Legnani danced thirty-two consecutive *fouettés*, and to this day that number is mandatory.

ARCHITECTURE One of the characteristics of Romantic architecture is its borrowing of styles from other eras. A vast array of buildings revived Gothic motifs, adding a major element of fantasy to create the Picturesque style. Eastern influence and whimsy abound in the Royal Pavilion at Brighton, England (Fig. **12.10**), designed

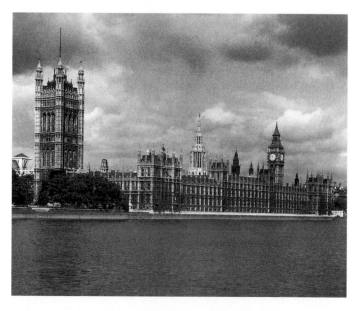

12.11 Sir Charles Barry and Augustus Welby Northmore Pugin, Houses of Parliament, London, 1839–52.

by John Nash (1752– 1835). Picturesque also describes the most famous example of Romantic architecture, the Houses of Parliament in London (Fig. **12.11**). Significantly, its exterior walls function as a screen, and suggest nothing of structure, interior design, or usage—a modern tendency in architectural design. Conversely, the inside of the building has absolutely no spatial

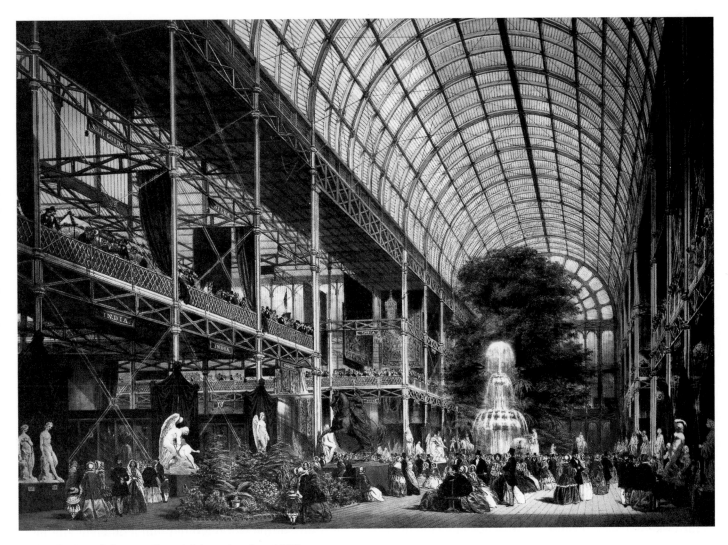

12.12 Sir Joseph Paxton, Crystal Palace, London, 1851.

relationship to the outside. Note, too, the strong contrast of forms and asymmetrical balance.

The nineteenth century was an age of industry, of experimentation and new materials. In architecture, iron, steel, and glass came to the fore. At first it took courage for an architect actually to display structural honesty by allowing support materials to be seen as part of the design. England's Crystal Palace (Fig. **12.12**) exemplifies the nineteenth-century fascination with new materials and concepts. Built for the Great Exhibition of 1851, this mammoth structure, completed in the space of just nine months, defined space by a three-dimensional grid of iron bars and girders, designed specifically for mass production and rapid assembly (in this case, disassembly as well—the entire structure was dismantled and rebuilt in 1852–4 at Sydenham). Like the Houses of Parliament, the Crystal Palace highlights the growing divergence of function (as reflected in the arrangement of interior spaces), surface decoration, and structure.

Realism

PAINTING A new painting style called *Realism* arose in the mid-nineteenth century. The term "reality" came to have special significance in the nineteenth century because the camera—a machine to record events, people, and locations—thrust itself into what had previously been considered the painter's realm.

The central figure of Realism, Gustave Courbet (coor-BAY; 1819–77), sought to make an objective and unprejudiced record of the customs, ideas, and appearances of contemporary French society. He depicted everyday life in terms of the play of light on surfaces, as seen in *The Stone Breakers* (Fig. **12.13**). This painting was the first to display his philosophy to the full. Courbet painted two men as he had seen them, working beside a road. The life-sized painting treats its subjects objectively, and yet it makes a sharp comment on the tedium and laborious nature

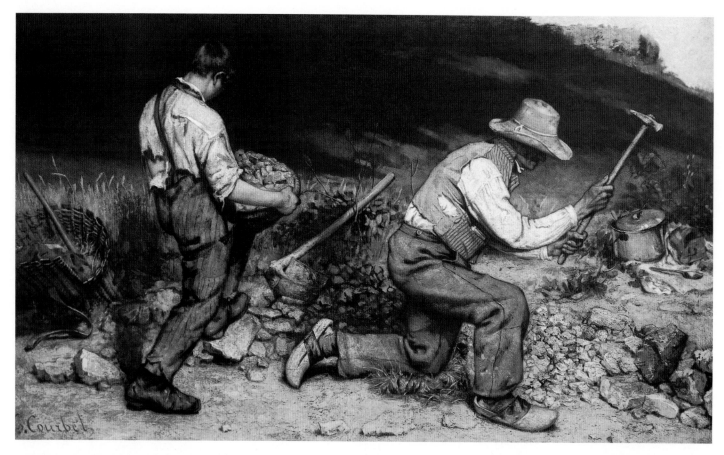

12.13 Gustave Courbet, *The Stone Breakers*, 1849. Oil on canvas, 5 ft 3 ins × 8 ft 6 ins (1.6 × 2.59 m). Formerly in the Gemäldegalerie, Dresden (destroyed 1945).

of the task. As a Social Realist, Courbet was more intent on conveying a political message than on producing a meditative reaction.

Edouard Manet (mah-NAY; 1832–83) strove to paint "only what the eye can see." Yet his works go beyond a mere reflection of reality to encompass an artistic reality: painting has an internal logic different from that of familiar reality. Manet thus liberated the canvas from competition with the camera. As indicated in the catalogue for an exhibition he produced when he was excluded from the International Exhibition in Paris in 1867, Manet believed that he presented in his art sincere—rather than faultless—perception.

His sincerity carried a form of protest—his impressions. To a certain extent Manet was both a conformist and a protester. He came from a comfortable bourgeois background and yet maintained a conviction about socialism. His work leans heavily on the masters of the past— for example, Raphael and Watteau—and at the same time explores completely new ground. He sought acceptance in salon circles while aiming to shock those same individuals. Striving to be a man of his own time, he rejected the superficiality he found in Romantic themes. He gave

the reality of the world around him a different and more straightforward interpretation. As a result, he is often hailed as the first modern painter.

Déjeuner sur l'herbe (day zhuh-NAY syoor-lairb; Fig. 12.14) shocked the public when it first appeared in 1863. Manet sought specifically to "speak in a new voice." The setting is pastoral, as in Watteau (see Fig. 11.23), for example, but the people in the foreground are real and identifiable: Manet's model, his brother, and the sculptor Leenhof. The apparent immorality of a naked frolic in a Paris park outraged the public and the critics. Had his figures been nymphs and satyrs, all would have been well; but Manet wanted both to be accepted by the official Salon, and to shock its organizers and visitors. The painting is contemporary while commenting upon similar themes of the past. But the intrusion of reality into the sacred confines of the mythical proved more than the public could handle.

Manet's search for harmonious colors, subjects from everyday life, and faithfulness to observed lighting and atmospheric effects led to the development of an artistic style that was described in 1874 by a hostile critic as Impressionist.

THEATRE AND LITERATURE The acknowledged master of realist drama, Norway's Henrik Ibsen (1828–1906), built powerful problem-dramas around carefully selected detail and plausible character-to-action motivations. His plays usually bring to conclusion events that began well in the past, with meticulous exposition. Ibsen's concern for detail carries to the scenery and costumes, and his plays contain detailed descriptions of settings and properties, all of which are essential to the action. The content of many of Ibsen's plays was controversial, and most deal with questions about moral and social issues that remain difficult today. In his late plays, however, Ibsen abandoned realism in favor of symbolist experiment.

Realism spread widely, finding expression in the work of the Russian writer Anton Chekhov (CHEHK-hawf, 1860–1904), although, like Ibsen, Chekhov incorporates symbolism into his works. Many people regard him as the founder of modern realism. He drew his themes and subject matter from Russian daily life, and they provide accurate portrayals of frustration and the depressing nature of existence. His structures flow in the same apparently aimless manner as the lives of his characters. While short on theatricality and compact structure, his skillfully constructed plots give the appearance of actuality.

Chekhov's masterpiece, *Uncle Vanya* (1897), provides deep insights into aimlessness and hopelessness. Uncle Vanya (Ivan Voynitsky) endures bitter disappointment when he realizes he has wasted his life tending to the business affairs of his former brother-in-law (Serebryakov), who is a second-rate academic. Meanwhile, Sonia, Serebryakov's daughter and Vanya's assistant, carries the torch of unrequited love for a local doctor. Vanya tries to shoot Serebryakov but misses. The play moves on, and nothing changes. Vanya cannot give up the work to which he has devoted his life, regardless of that work's meaninglessness.

The prolific Irish writer George Bernard Shaw (1856–1950) embodied the spirit of nineteenth-century realism, although his career overlapped the nineteenth and twentieth centuries. This witty, brilliant artist stood above all a humanitarian and although many Victorians considered him a heretic and a subversive (because of his devotion to socialism), his faith lay in humanity and its infinite potential.

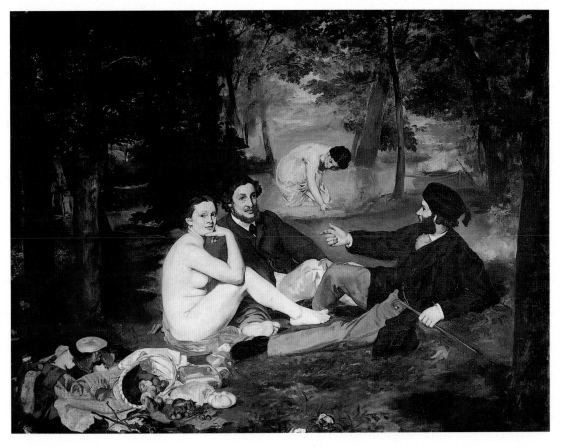

12.14 Edouard Manet, *Déjeuner sur l'herbe* (*The Picnic*), 1863. Oil on canvas, 7 ft × 8 ft 10 ins (2.13 × 2.69 m). Musée d'Orsay, Paris.

Shaw's plays deal with the unexpected, and they often appear contradictory and inconsistent in characterization and structure. In his favorite device he built up a pompous notion and then destroyed it. For example, in *Man and Superman*, when a respectable Victorian family learns that their daughter is pregnant, they react with predictable indignation. A character who appears to speak for the playwright comes to the girl's defense, attacking the family's hypocrisy and defending the girl. She, however, explodes in anger, not against her family, but against her defender. She had been secretly married all the time, and, as the most respectable of the lot, she condemns her defender's (and possibly the audience's) freethinking.

Shaw opposed the doctrine of "art for art's sake," and he insisted that art should have a purpose. He believed that plays made better vehicles for social messages than speeches or pamphlets. Although each play usually has a character who acts as the playwright's mouthpiece, Shaw does more than sermonize. His characters probe the depths of the human condition, often discovering themselves through some lifelike crisis.

Naturalism, a style closely related to realism, also flourished in the same period. Émile Zola (1840–1902), a leading proponent, proved more a theoretician and novelist than a playwright. Both realism and naturalism insisted on a truthful depiction of life, but naturalism went on to insist on the basic principle that heredity and environment determine behavior. Absolute objectivity, not personal opinion, formed naturalism's goal.

We have seen how realism took hold as a style in painting. Realism as a literary style held that art should depict life with absolute honesty—show things "as they really are." In pursuit of that goal, realists looked for specific, verifiable details rather than for sweeping generalities, and they valued impersonal, photographic accuracy more than the individual interpretation of experience. The triumph of realism, which began in the eighteenth century, came to full flower in the nineteenth and early twentieth centuries, influenced by the growth of science and by a revolt against the sweeping emotionalism of Romanticism. Because realists sought to avoid idealism and Romantic "prettifying," they tended to stress the commonplace and, often, sordid and brutal aspects of life. They also attempted to impose or convey their morals, value systems, and judgments—a characteristic that, among others, separated them from the naturalists.

Considered the father of the modern novel, Russian novelist Feodor Dostoyevski (dohs-tuh-YEF-skee; 1821–81) was born and raised in Moscow. He lost both his parents as a teenager—his father was murdered by his own serfs—and although interested in literature early on, he did not begin writing until he had finished military school and a two-year stint in the army. In 1846 he published a short story, "Poor Folk," which made him an instant success. He then associated with a group of political revolutionaries and Utopian reformers, and with the group's arrest, Dostoyevski received the death sentence, but was pardoned by the Czar at the last moment. Apparently, the Czar had planned to pardon the prisoners all along, but he let the matter proceed, right to the point where they stood before the firing squad, more as a whimsical joke than anything else. Dostoyevski was sent to Siberia for five years and then forced back into the army. In 1859 he was finally pardoned, but these experiences, plus the fact that he suffered from epilepsy, left him bitter. He believed that his imprisonment gave him an opportunity to expiate his sins, and his beliefs that humans required penitence and that salvation comes through suffering reached the point of obsession and recur constantly in his novels. Like Nietzsche, he believed that European materialism had led to decadence and decline.

We know Dostoyevski best for two works from among his many: *The Brothers Karamazov* and *Crime and Punishment*. *Crime and Punishment* (1866), a psychological novel, explores multiple personality—the hidden and confused motivations of human behavior—and explores a constant theme—moral redemption through suffering. Perhaps the most outstanding characteristic of the novel emerges as its capacity to force the reader to think seriously about the many problems it presents. Dostoyevski accomplishes this by refusing to allow us to confuse oversimplification with deep thought. For example, in tackling the issue of distinguishing between morality and respectability, Dostoyevski gives us one truly good character, the prostitute Sonia, who at the same time represents the most openly disreputable, and contrasts her with a truly evil character, Raskolnikov's sister, the most respectable of the characters. Thus, he forces us to see that morality consists of what a person is, while respectability represents the front that we put up in public, and that there need not be any connection between the two. He also shows that morality and respectability are not opposites, because, that, too, would be an oversimplification. The work forces us, through the objectively detailed manner of the realist, to think seriously about money, social position, sanity and insanity, and, above all, about crime and punishment. Dostoyevski presents these issues with such compelling insight that we cannot escape them or explain them away with superficial responses.

Impressionism

In France, Impressionism created a new way of expressing reality, in painting, sculpture, music and writing.

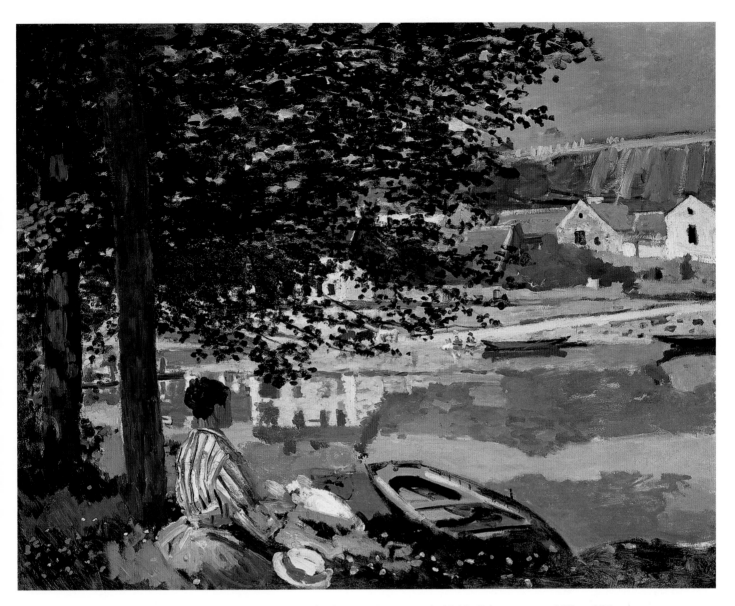

12.15 Claude Monet, *Au Bord de l'eau, Bennecourt* (*On the Seine at Bennecourt*), 1868. Oil on canvas, 31⅞ × 39½ ins (81.5 × 100.7 cm). Art Institute of Chicago (Potter Palmer Collection).

PAINTING Impressionist painting sought to capture "the psychological perception of reality in color and motion." It also emerged in competition with the newly invented technology of the camera, for the Impressionists tried to beat photography at its own game by portraying the essentials of perception that the camera cannot capture. The style lasted fifteen years in its purest form but deeply influenced all art that followed.

Working out of doors, the Impressionists concentrated on the effects of natural light on objects and atmosphere. They emphasized the presence of color within shadows and based their style on an understanding of the interrelated mechanisms of the camera and the eye: vision consists of the result of light and color making an "impression" on the retina. Their experiments resulted in a pro-foundly different vision of the world around them and a new way of rendering that vision. For them, the painted canvas was first of all a material surface covered with pigments and filled with small patches of color, which together create lively and vibrant images.

Despite the individualistic nature of the nineteenth century, Impressionism emerges as collective a style as any we have seen thus far. It reflects the common concerns of a relatively small group of artists who met frequently and held joint exhibitions. As a result, the style has marked characteristics that apply to all its exponents. The paintings are relatively small and use clear, bright colors. Composition appears casual and natural. Typical subjects include everyday scenes such as landscapes, rivers, streets, and cafés.

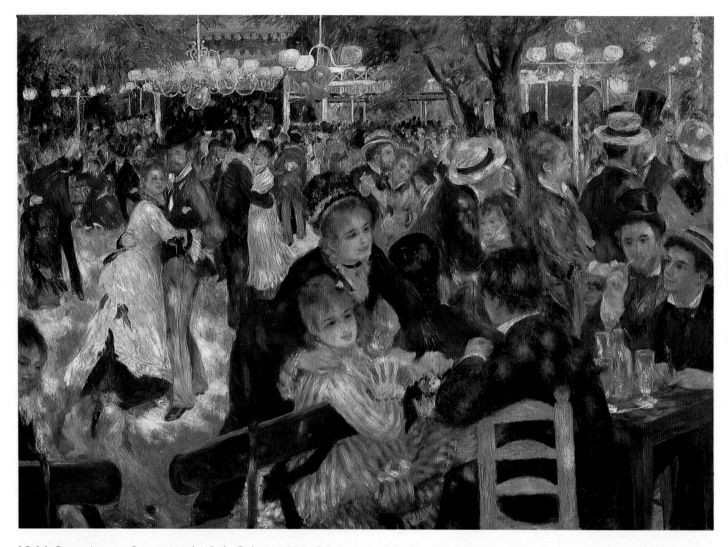

12.16 Pierre-Auguste Renoir, *Moulin de la Galette*, 1876. Oil on canvas, 51½ × 69 ins (131 × 175 cm). Musée d'Orsay, Paris.

Au Bord de l'eau, Bennecourt (*On the Seine at Bennecourt*) (Fig. **12.15**) by Claude Monet (muh-NAY; 1840–1926) illustrates several of the concerns of the Impressionists. It portrays a pleasant, objective picture of the times, in contrast with the often subjective viewpoint of the Romantics. It suggests a fleeting moment—a new tone in an era when the pace of life had increased. Monet, along with Renoir and Berthe Morisot (bairt muh-ree-SOH), among others, was a central figure in the development of Impressionism.

Pierre Auguste Renoir (rehn-WAH; 1841–1919) specialized in portraying the human figure, seeking out what was beautiful in the body. His paintings sparkle with the joy of life. In *Moulin de la Galette* (Fig. **12.16**) he depicts the bright gaiety of a Sunday crowd in a popular Parisian dance hall. He celebrates the liveliness and charm of these everyday folk as they talk, crowd the tables, flirt, and dance. Sunlight and shade dapple the scene and create a

floating sensation in light. A casualness pervades here, a sense of life captured in a fleeting and spontaneous moment. A much wider scene seems to extend beyond the canvas—the composition is an open one, not formally composed like David's *Oath of the Horatii* (see Fig. **11.26**). Rather, Renoir invites us to become part of the action. People go about their everyday routine with no reaction to the painter's presence. As opposed to the Classicist, who focuses on the universal and the typical, the Impressionist seeks realism in "the incidental, the momentary and the passing."

The original group of Impressionists included a woman, Berthe Morisot (1841–95), on equal terms. Gently introspective, her works often focus on family members. She edges her view of contemporary life with pathos and sentimentality. In *In the Dining Room* (Fig. **12.17**) she uses Impressionist techniques to give a penetrating glimpse of psychological reality. The servant

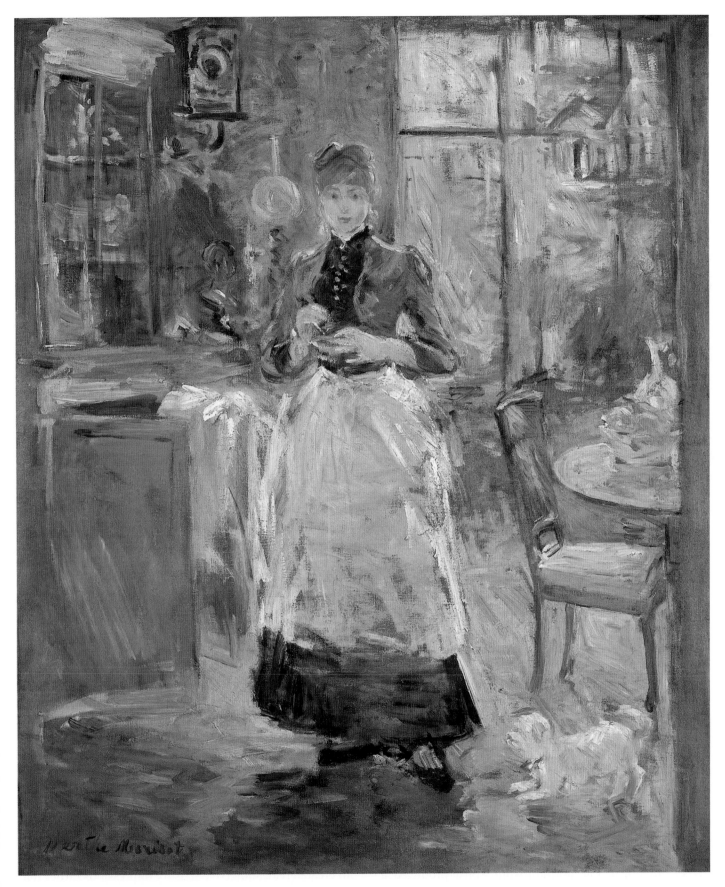

12.17 Berthe Morisot, *In the Dining Room*, 1886. Oil on canvas, 24⅛ × 19¾ ins (61.3 × 50 cm). National Gallery of Art, Washington, D.C. (Chester Dale Collection).

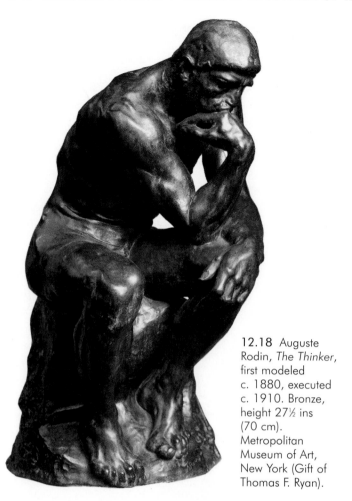

12.18 Auguste Rodin, *The Thinker*, first modeled c. 1880, executed c. 1910. Bronze, height 27½ ins (70 cm). Metropolitan Museum of Art, New York (Gift of Thomas F. Ryan).

girl has a personality, and she stares back at the viewer with complete self-assurance. The painting captures a moment of disorder: the cabinet door stands ajar with what appears to be a used tablecloth merely flung over it. The little dog playfully demands attention. Morisot's brushstroke is delicate, and her scenes are full of insight.

SCULPTURE The most remarkable sculptor of the era was Auguste Rodin (ruh-DAN; 1840–1917). Rodin uses textures that more than anything else, reflect Impressionism—his surfaces appear to shimmer as light plays on their irregular features. These textures affect more than reflective surfaces—they give his works dynamic and dramatic qualities. *The Thinker* (Fig. 12.18) shows the difficulty inherent in attempting to put into sculptural form what painters like Monet tried to do with color and texture (see Fig. 12.15). Although Rodin used a fair degree of lifelikeness, he nevertheless presented a reality beneath the surface.

MUSIC In music, the anti-Romantic spirit produced a style analogous to that of the Impressionist painters. There was some direct influence from the Impressionist painters, but mostly Impressionism in music turned to the *Symbolist* poets for inspiration.

Ironically, Impressionist music's primary champion, Claude Debussy (deh-boo-SEE; 1862–1918), did not like to be called an Impressionist. In fact, this is not surprising, for the label had been coined by a severe critic of the painters and was intended to be derogatory. Debussy maintained that he was "an old romantic who has thrown the worries of success out of the window," and he sought no association with the painters. However, similar motifs can be seen. His use of tone color has been described as "wedges of color" applied in a similar way to painters' individual brushstrokes. He delighted in natural scenes and sought to capture the effects of shimmering light. Debussy wished above all to return French music to fundamental sources in nature and move it away from the heaviness of the German tradition.

In contrast to his predecessors, Debussy abandoned chordal harmony's traditional progressions—perhaps his greatest break with tradition. Oriental influence appears in his use of the Asian five-tone scale and dissonance is common. He considered each chord strictly on the merits of its expressive capabilities and apart from any context of tonal progression. As a result, gliding chords (repetition of a chord up and down the scale) became a hallmark of musical Impressionism as we hear in *Clair de Lune* (music CD track 19).

Debussy reduced melodic development to short motifs—an analogy can again be drawn with the individual brushstrokes of the painters. Irregular rhythm and meter further distinguish his works. So, once more, form and content subordinate to expressive intent. His music tends to suggest, rather than to state, and to leave the listener with ambiguity—with an impression. Key elements of his style are freedom, flexibility, and non-traditional timbres. His most famous composition, the *Prélude à l'après-midi d'un faune* (*Prelude to the Afternoon of a Faun*; see also p. 128), is based on a sensual poem by the Symbolist Stéphane Mallarmé (mah-lahr-MAY; 1842–98). The piece uses a large orchestra, with emphasis on the harps and woodwinds, most notably in the haunting, chromatically sliding theme running throughout. Although freely ranging in an irregular 9/8 meter and virtually without tonal centers, the *Prélude* has a basically traditional ABA structure.

LITERATURE The Impressionists in literature, like those in painting and music that we have already studied, tried to depict scenes, emotions, and character details in order to create vivid, subjective sensory impressions rather than objective reality. One of the techniques to arise in the Impressionists' works, that of "stream of consciousness," takes the flow of numerous impressions—visual, auditory, physical, psychological, and so on—to create the sense of consciousness of the characters. Writers sought to capture the fullness, speed, and subtlety of the human mind by incorporating bits and pieces of incoherent thought, truncated language, and free association of ideas and images. Two writers stand out in this regard: James Joyce (*Ulysses;* 1922) and Virginia Woolf (*The Waves;* 1931).

James Joyce (1882–1941) was born in Dublin, Ireland, and had tried several occupations, including teaching, when he began writing a lengthy naturalistic novel about his own life. He interrupted that project to publish the stories that made up *Dubliners* (1914). Beset with financial difficulties, he continued to write. Living in Italy when that country entered World War I, Joyce took his family to Zurich, Switzerland, where he began work on *Ulysses.* Living off a series of grants, he published episodes from the book in *The Little Review* in 1918. The episodes continued until the work was banned in December 1920. In 1922, Sylvia Beach, who owned the Paris bookshop Shakespeare and Co., published the entire novel, which, because of its constant troubles with the censors, became famous immediately. Joyce constructed the novel as a modern parallel to Homer's *Odyssey,* with the action set in Dublin on a single day (June 16, 1904). The three main characters—Stephen Dedalus, Leopold Bloom, and Molly Bloom—stand as modern counterparts to Homer's Telemachus, Ulysses, and Penelope, and the novel's events reflect the major events in Odysseus' journey home from the Trojan War. Joyce renders deeply three-dimensional characters and imbues the work with humor. Above all, as we noted earlier, stands Joyce's use of the impressionistic device of stream of consciousness.

Virginia Woolf (1882–1941), who committed suicide during World War II, stood as one of the most gifted and innovative of the stream-of-consciousness writers. She wrote intensely subjective explorations, and worked toward high condensation and glimpses of moments of experience rather than attempting the illusion of a total picture. She advocated freedom for the novelist to capture the "shower of atoms" and the discontinuity of experience, and she pictured men and women as enclosed in their "envelope" of consciousness from birth to death. In *A Room of One's Own* (1929) she spoke out for women's liberation. The experimental, impressionistic novel *The Waves* (1931) presents her at her complex and innovative best. She strives for capturing the poetic rhythm of life, turning away from traditional focus on character and plot. The book consists of dramatic and occasionally narrative monologues that trace six friends through seven stages of their lives—from childhood to old age. Each position corresponds to a position of the sun and the tides.

Post-Impressionism

In the last two decades of the nineteenth century, Impressionism evolved into rather disparate styles called, simply, Post-Impressionism. In subject matter Post-Impressionist paintings are often similar to Impressionist ones—landscapes, familiar portraits, groups, and café and nightclub scenes. The Post-Impressionists, however, gave their subject matter a profoundly personal significance.

The Post-Impressionists were deeply concerned about the formal language of art and its ability to capture sensory experience. They maintained the contemporary philosophy of art for art's sake and moved beyond the Romantic and Impressionist world of pure sensation. They were more interested in the painting as a flat surface carefully composed of shapes, lines, and colors; an idea that became the foundation for most of the art movements that followed. The Post-Impressionists called for a return to form and structure in painting, characteristics they believed were lacking in the works of the Impressionists. Taking the evanescent light qualities of the Impressionists, they typically but not uniformly brought formal patterning to their canvases. They used clean color areas, and applied color in a systematic and almost scientific manner. The Post-Impressionists sought to return painting to traditional goals while retaining the clean palette of the Impressionists.

SEURAT Georges Seurat (suh-RAH; 1859–91) is often described as a Neo-Impressionist rather than a Post-Impressionist (he called his approach *divisionism*). He took the Impressionist technique a step further. He applied specks of paint with the point of the brush, one dot at a time. He used paint in accordance with his theories of optics and of color perception: *Sunday Afternoon on the Island of La Grande Jatte* (Fig. **12.19**) illustrates his concern for the accurate depiction of light and color. Its composition and depiction of shadow show attention to perspective, and yet Seurat willfully avoids three-dimensionality. Throughout the work we find conscious systematizing. The painting breaks into proportions of three-eighths and halves, which Seurat believed represented true harmony. He also selected his colors by formula. Physical reality for Seurat was just a pretext for the artist's search for a superior harmony, for an abstract perfection.

CÉZANNE Paul Cézanne (say-ZAHN; 1839–1906) is considered by many to be the father of modern art. In *Mont Sainte-Victoire* (Fig. **12.20**), he illustrates his concern for formal design with a nearly geometric configuration and balance. Foreground and background tie together systematically so that both join in the foreground to create pat-

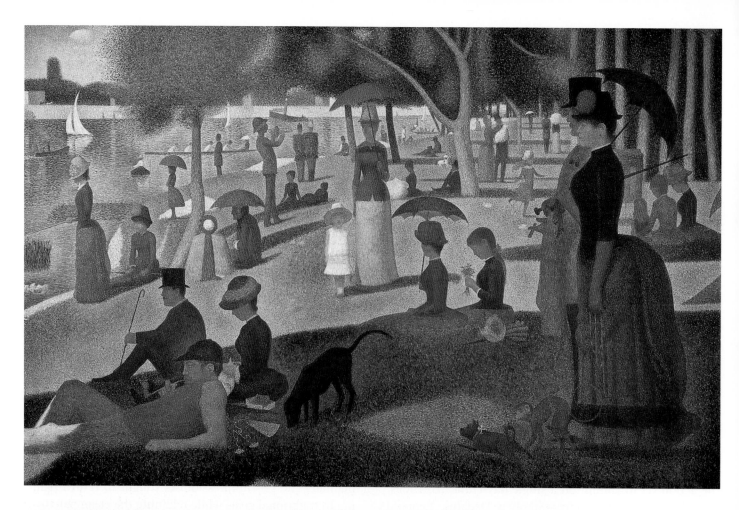

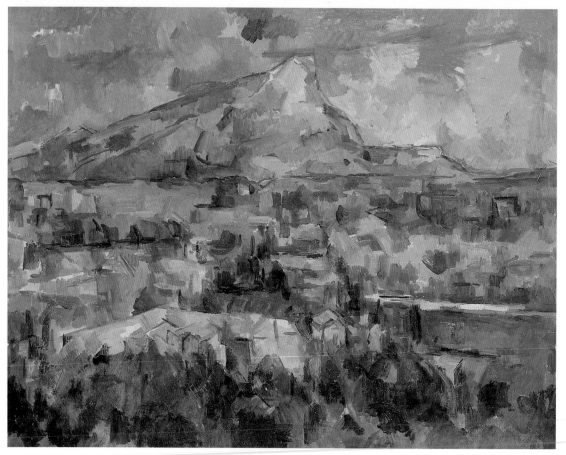

12.19 (above) Georges
Seurat, *Sunday
Afternoon on the Island
of La Grande Jatte*,
1884–6. Oil on canvas,
6 ft 9½ ins × 10 ft ⅜ ins
(2.07 × 3.06 m). Art
Institute of Chicago
(Helen Birch Bartlett
Memorial Collection).

12.20 (left) Paul
Cézanne, *Mont Sainte-
Victoire seen from Les
Lauves*, 1902–4. Oil on
canvas, 27½ × 35¼ ins
(70 × 90 cm).
Philadelphia Museum of
Art (George W. Elkins
Collection).

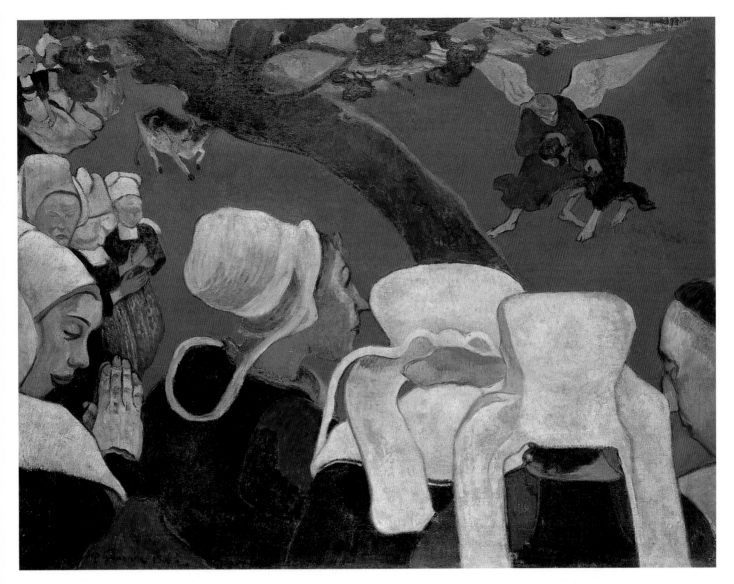

12.21 Paul Gauguin, *The Vision after the Sermon*, 1888. Oil on canvas, 28¾ × 36¼ ins (73 × 92 cm). National Gallery of Scotland, Edinburgh.

terns. Simplified shapes and outlining occur throughout. Cézanne employed geometric shapes—the cone, the sphere, and the cylinder—as metaphors of the permanent reality that lay beneath surface appearance.

Cézanne tried to invest his paintings with a strong sense of three-dimensionality. He took great liberty with color and also changed traditional ways of rendering objects, utilizing the cones and other geometric shapes just mentioned.

GAUGUIN A highly imaginative approach to Post-Impressionist goals came from Paul Gauguin (goh-GAN; 1848–1903). He and his followers were known as Symbolists or Nabis (the Hebrew word for prophet). His work shows an insistence on form and a resistance to realistic effects. *The Vision after the Sermon* (Fig. **12.21**) fea-

tures flat, outlined figures, simple forms, and symbolism. In the background Jacob wrestles with the angel, as described in Genesis, the first book of the Bible. Meanwhile, in the foreground, a priest, nuns, and women in Breton costume pray. The intense reds of this painting show symbolic and unnatural use of color, used here to portray the powerful sensations of a Breton folk festival.

VAN GOGH We move now to look at the work of the Dutch Post-Impressionist Vincent van Gogh (1853–90). His emotionalism in the pursuit of form is unique. Van Gogh's turbulent life included numerous short-lived careers, impossible love affairs, a tempestuous friendship with Gauguin, and, finally, serious mental illness. Works such as *The Starry Night* (see Fig. **1.7**) explode with frenetic energy manifested in the brushwork. Flattened

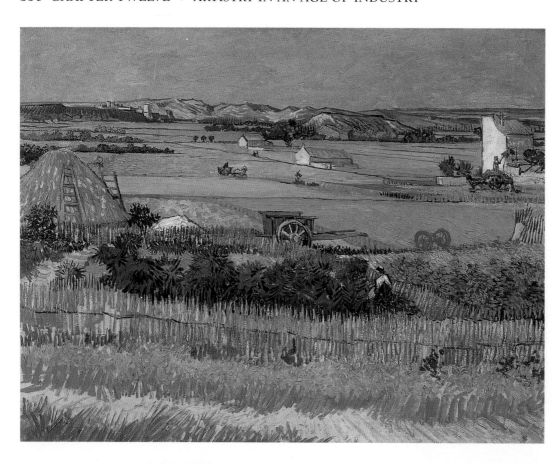

12.22 Vincent van Gogh. *Harvest at La Crau (The Blue Cart)*. 1888. Oil on canvas, 28½ × 36¼ ins (72.5 × 92 cm). Rijksmuseum, Vincent van Gogh, Amsterdam.

forms and outlining reflect Japanese influence (see Fig. **10.54**). *The Starry Night* exhibits tremendous power and controlled focus; dynamic, personal energy and mental turmoil. This work represents one of the earliest and most famous examples of Expressionism in painting. We will examine this in the next chapter.

Works such as *Harvest at La Crau* (*The Blue Cart*; Fig. **12.22**), reflect an interest in *complementary colors* (colors on opposite sides of the color wheel—see Chapter 1). Unlike Seurat, for example, who applied such colors in small dots, van Gogh placed large color areas side by side. Doing so, he believed, expressed the quiet, harmonious life of the rural community. Notice the active brushwork in the foreground while the fields in the background remain smooth. Subtle diagonals break up the predominantly horizontal line of the work. The painting suggests a return to a simple agrarian life.

Art Nouveau

In the 1890s and early 1900s a "new" art phenomenon occurred in Europe. Called "New Art" or Art Nouveau (ahrt noo-VOH), it grew out of the English Arts and Crafts Movement, emerging initially in response to a world's fair, the Paris Universal Exposition of 1889. Encompassing art, architecture, and design, Art Nouveau comprised a variety of examples, but typically it reflected the lively, serpentine curve known as the "whiplash." Overall, the style pursues a fascination with plant and animal life and organic growth. The influence of Japanese art is evident in Art Nouveau's undulating curves. In addition, the style incorporates organic and often symbolic motifs, treating them in a linear, relieflike manner.

Turning to the Paris Universal Exposition, the story of Art Nouveau emerges: the best known creation of the fair was and is the Eiffel Tower, designed by a civil engineer, Gustave Eiffel (1832–1923). The design for the tower was the winning entry in a contest for a monument to symbolize French industrial progress. At 984 feet (300 m), the tower stood as the tallest structure in the world at that time, its iron latticework resting on four huge legs reinforced by trussed arches similar to those Eiffel had used on his railroad bridges. The Eiffel Tower raised great concern in many quarters as regards its influence on the future of art in conjunction with the industrial age. Art Nouveau constituted one response. It sought to reflect modernism but to do so without losing a pre-industrial sense of beauty. As a consequence, the use of organic forms and traditional materials such as wood and stone emerged.

The issues addressed by Art Nouveau ranged beyond French borders. In fact, it was a Belgian, Victor Horta

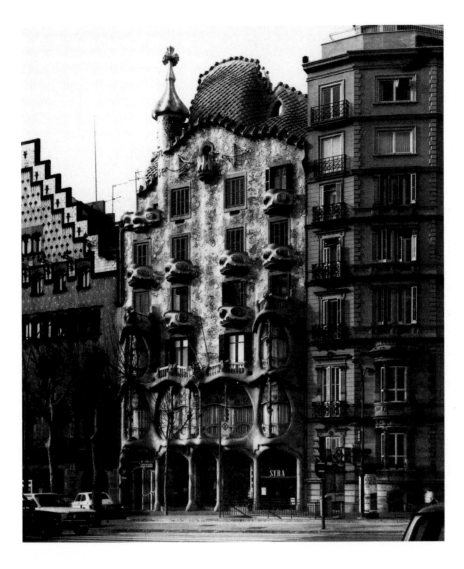

12.23 Antoni Gaudí,
Casa Batlló,
Barcelona, 1905–7.

(1867–1947), who launched the style. It spread throughout Europe, recognized by a variety of names in various countries: in Italy, *Stile floreale* ("floral style") and *Stile Liberty* (after the Liberty Department Store in London); in Germany, *Jugendstil* ("Youth Style"); in Spain, *Modernismo* (Modernism); in Vienna, *Secessionsstil* (after the secession from the Academy led by Klimt); in Belgium, *Paling Style* ("Eel Style"), and in France, a number of names including *moderne*. Eventually the name Art Nouveau settled on the movement after a shop in Paris (La Maison de l'Art Nouveau) that opened in 1895.

In France, where in Paris and Nancy the style proliferated, it was often called *style Guimard* after its leading practitioner, Hector Guimard (ghee-MAHR; 1867–1942), whose many works include the famous entrance portals for the Paris Métro (subway). In Spain, the man perhaps best remembered as a champion of the style, Antoni Gaudí (ghow–DEE, 1852–1926), transformed its characteristics into remarkable constructions; for example, Casa Batlló (baht-LOH; Fig. **12.23**) in Barcelona. Gaudí's approach took architecture in an astonishing direction: that of hand-crafted buildings made without plans other than what was in the head of the architect, and this effect clearly resonates from the example shown here.

ASIA

Our foray in Asia limits us to one country and one visual art genre: Japan and printmaking.

In the nineteenth century, as Japan began to look westward, the style of the country's two-dimensional art began to evolve. Some of the changes appear in the works of two printmakers, Katsushika Hokusai (hoh-KOO-sigh; 1760–1849) and Ando Hiroshige (hee-roh-SHEE-ghay; 1797–1858).

Hokusai broadened subject matter to include all aspects of Japanese life. In particular, his prints document in detail the streetlife in and around Edo. His works, entitled *Manga*, fill fifteen volumes, which he began to publish in 1814. Full of vibrancy, virility, and humor, his

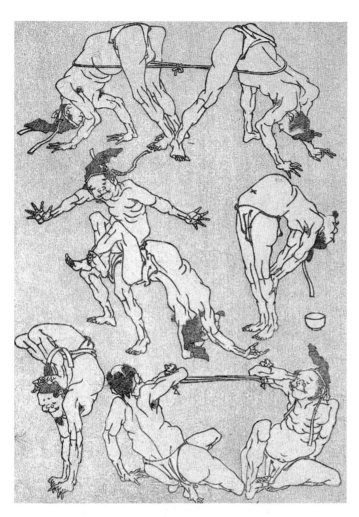

12.24 Katsushika Hokusai, page from *Manga*, vol. 8, 1817. Woodcut, 9 × 5¾ ins (22.8 × 14.6 cm). British Museum, London.

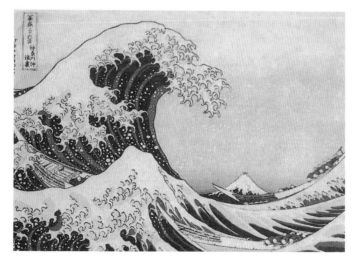

12.25 Katsushika Hokusai, *The Great Wave off Kanazawa*, 1823–9. Polychrome woodblock print, 10 × 14¾ ins (25.5 × 37.5 cm). Victoria & Albert Museum, London.

works show humankind in all its contrasting nobility and gracelessness. In a woodcut from *Manga* he portrays acrobats in various attitudes (Fig. **12.24**). They seem oblivious of any observer, and their antics reveal an earthy forthrightness that seems totally at odds with the graceful power one would normally associate with them. They seem cartoonish caricatures, and yet there is vitality, energy, and suppleness within the unflattering representation.

In his landscapes, Hokusai forged new directions in Japanese art. *The Great Wave off Kanazawa*, for example (Fig. **12.25**), is a boldly colored rendering that shows neither realism nor idealism. While Mount Fuji reposes calmly in the background, the great wave breaks over the boats with raging fury, and the foam reaches out like grasping fingers to crash down on the fragile craft. A new sense of directness occurs here, and yet Hokusai's response to natural forms and his decorative patterning lie firmly within the traditions of Japanese art.

A similar freshness emerges in the strongly colored landscape *Maple Leaves at the Tekona Shrine, Mamma* by Hiroshige (Fig. **12.26**). It shows deep space, using the foreground to "frame" the distance, and allowing the perspective to shift as described on page 62. The distance seems logical even though the colors and details are the same in foreground and background. Only the trees exhibit any degree of foreshortening. This pulls our vision back and forth in space as the red maple leaves—placed directly in our line of sight to the distance—constantly compete with middle ground and background for our attention. Thus, we are invited to focus on the series of huts staggered across a line, which divides the print into fourths. Downward-deflecting leaves and a strong, dark border redirect us into the painting at the top, while the framing diagonals of the tree trunks carry us back into the lower fourth of the work. Hiroshige cleverly manipulates hue, value, and contrast to keep interest and control. The red leaves and complementary gray-green limbs and mountains strike a harmonious visual chord, and the ocher grass, thatched roofs, and lightened sky stand in contrast—both in tone and value—to create a counterpoint and to hold our vision stable in the center of the work.

AFRICA

The nineteenth century, the focus of this chapter, brought significant changes to the entire world. Most certainly it changed Africa, as noted in the Context section. In tribal Africa at that time, animism and ancestor worship prevailed (the term "animism" is the belief that a spirit exists in every living thing). Ancestor worship takes a variety of forms, depending on the tribe, and its artistic manifestations also vary widely. One form is the *guardian figure*,

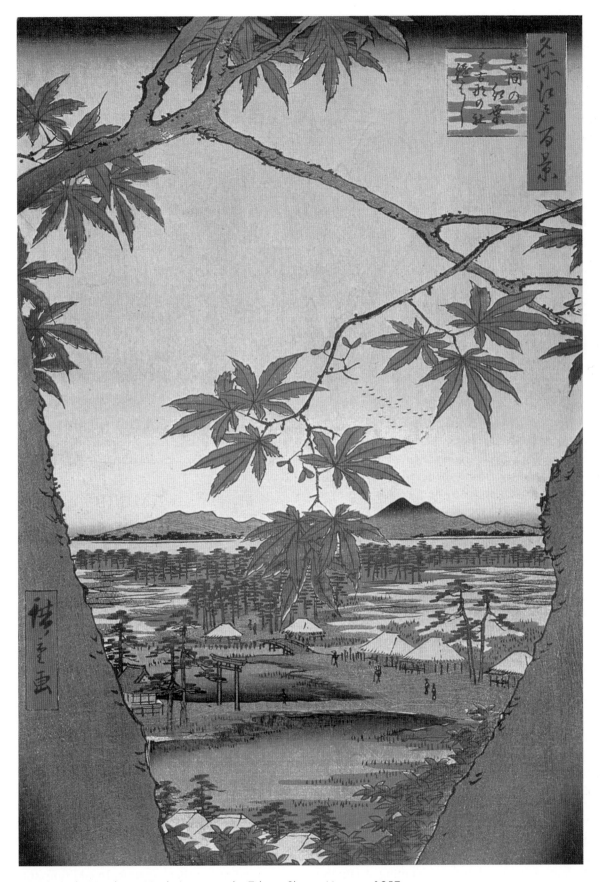

12.26 Ando Hiroshige, *Maple Leaves at the Tekona Shrine, Mamma*, 1857.
Polychrome woodblock print, 13¾ × 9¾ ins (35 × 24 cm). British Museum, London.

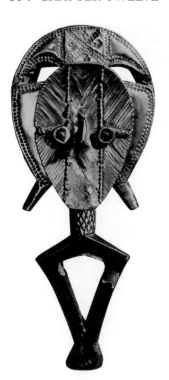

12.27 Guardian figure of the Kota tribe, from Gabon, late 19th century. Wood, brass, ivory eyes, height 16⅝ ins (42.2 cm). Metropolitan Museum of Art, New York (Michael C. Rockefeller Memorial Collection, Bequest of Nelson A. Rockefeller).

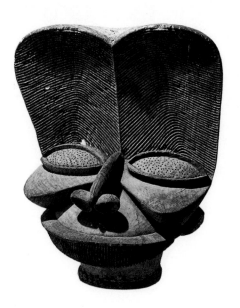

12.28 Mask, from the Bamenda area, Cameroon, late 19th century. Wood, height 26½ ins (67.3 cm). Rietberg Museum, Zürich (Heydt Collection).

used to protect the remains of the dead. In Gabon in Equatorial Africa, the Kota tribe of the nineteenth century produced polished metal figures that guarded large containers of skulls of ancestors—believed to be communal dwellings of ancestor spirits. The guardian figure in Figure **12.27** reflects an abstract geometric style typical of the art of tribal societies. Despite its abstraction, the anatomical parts of the body remain clearly defined. The entire design has been flattened into a single plane, perfectly symmetrical in balance. It has a calming effect: this guardian was clearly not intended to frighten the viewer. Compare it with the ancestor figure shown earlier in the book, Figure **2.7**.

The animism of the Kota people is all-embracing—for example, trees have spirits that must be appeased before the tree can be cut down; the individual tree spirit merges with a general "tree spirit"; this in turn merges with a larger "life spirit." Spirits are believed to dwell in rivers, lakes, forests, the sun, the moon, wind, and rain. In dealing with the spirit world, tribal peoples act out relationships with the spirits in dances and other dramatic ceremonies. Sometimes they disguise themselves so as to assume the role of the spirit temporarily. In the Bamenda area of Cameroon, the traditional costume for these ceremonies features a prominent mask. The one shown in Figure **12.28** is typical. Like the guardian figure, it has a symmetrical composition and distinct detailing. Again the abstract design leaves anatomical details recognizable. The elevated eyebrows with their delicate arching lines

give the mask a sophisticated and striking appearance. Its dignity and strength stem from its straightforwardness and the solidity of its detailing.

AMERICA

American Indian Art

In the nineteenth century, American Indian artists pursued many of the same goals as artists from any culture—they tried to evoke emotional responses in the viewer. But in the case of American Indian artists, the viewer might be a supernatural being. Much of their art deals with religious matters, and its purpose is like that of prayer—to entreat a benign god or placate a hostile one. Tradition dictates the manner or form. In fact, in American Indian culture a major criterion for "art" is how well the artist recognizes the force of tradition. Little room for artistic experimentation exists within the established tribal organization. However, exceptions do exist.

Naturally, many different factors have influenced American Indian works of art. Function is one factor. Environment is another: the accessibility of materials has played an important role in determining the nature of American Indian art. For example, availability of soapstone and lack of access to clay have meant that Inuit art is carved rather than ceramic. In addition, traditions have sometimes mixed as one people conquers another or as intertribal marriage occurs, thereby creating new traditions. Often, tribal groups such as the Hopi and Navajo share a common environment and lifestyle, and the function of their art is similar. Tradition and tribal integrity, however, keep their styles separate, and the works of both cultures remain distinguishable.

The meaning of works of art from American Indian cultures can prove baffling to someone raised in a Euro-centered culture. American Indian artists do not draw merely to recreate a picture of something, for they understand that they could not draw a tree as perfectly as it could be made by the Creator. This spiritual consciousness finds its way into the works of art. "Therefore, it can be said that Indian art is not so much drawings, carvings or reproductions *of* an object, but more the representation of the spirit *within* it. In short, it embodies the essence of the subject as well as its appearance."[2] American Indian art has a magical quality rather than a "meaning" in the sense that Western minds expect.

In a wide band of the Arctic, stretching right across North America, hundreds of tribes comprise the Inuit (IH-noo-iht) culture. All of them are related to each other culturally and/or linguistically. Out of the bleak and inhospitable environment of the North—where the quest for survival would seemingly leave little room for artistry—comes a tremendously imaginative artistic tradition. The long Arctic winter nights have given individuals ample time to carve ivory obtained from walrus and killer whales and, more recently, stone. Because of the difficulty of obtaining materials, Inuit art tends to be small in scale. In the case of tusk ivory, it is of necessity larger at one end than at the other. Characteristic of Inuit art is humor: caricatures found in the form of driftwood masks are common (Fig. **12.29**). This mask was originally decorated with snow goose feathers and typifies the elaborate or grotesque dance masks widely crafted among the Inuit people. They depict a variety of subjects—sacred and secular, human and animal.

The Pacific Northwest of North America produced stable American Indian cultures. This in great measure results from the abundance of resources and temperate climate, which figure prominently in the social and cultural fabric of the tribes. Fishing, hunting, and foraging produce ample means of sustenance, and therefore, the people of this region had no reason to cultivate crops or domesticate animals. Their cultures have tended to share certain features, probably because they traded and warred with one another. Artistic motifs are alike and they share a common religion, shamanism—an ancient form of magic, centered on wise, all-seeing men (shamans). (It is also shared with the hunting tribes of Siberia and various African cultures.) Although their pantheons and myths may differ, the Northwest tribes all acknowledge the

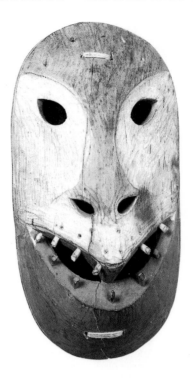

12.29 Carved dance mask of the Inuit tribe, from Mamtrek, Alaska, late 19th century. Wood (originally decorated with snow goose feathers), 8½ × 4½ ins (21.6 × 11.4 cm). National Museum of the American Indian, Smithsonian Institution, Washington, D.C.

power of shamans to contact the spirits of the forest and waters, to heal the sick, and to predict the future.

The rich forests of the area have provided artists with a wealth of materials for sculpting. Huge spruce and cedar trees abounded for many centuries, and when steel knives were obtained from fur traders and used as tools, Northwest-coast artists excelled in producing magnificent totem poles, carved posts for wooden dwellings, masks, rattles, and other objects. Figure **12.30** shows a carved housepost used inside a wooden dwelling to support the roof and to give additional decoration to the interior. It depicts the sea bear and has a frog carved in each ear. It was presented as a token of respect to Chief Frog Ears of Sukkwan by the people of a neighboring village. Proximity to the sea also provided abalone shells that were used as inlays to give luster to sculpted works.

Although many art objects from the area, such as masks, concern themselves with shamanistic religious rituals, a fair amount of art is secular. Like some African art, it serves to maintain the social fabric and bolster a ruler's power. In the Tlingit tribe, for example, communities comprise a number of families, each of which has its own chief who inherits his rank from his mother. Carefully devised social customs oblige both men and women to marry outside their own clan. In this way a balance is established in which no one family achieves dominance. Nonetheless, chiefs compete fiercely with each other in displays of riches. Totem poles form a part of this ostentation, proclaiming prestige and family pride through genealogy—much like the coats of arms of the

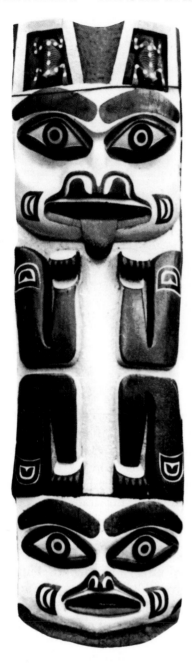

12.30 Housepost, from Haida, Alaska, 19th century. Wood, height 11 ft 6½ ins (3.52 m). National Museum of the American Indian, Smithsonian Institution, Washington, D.C.

European aristocracy. Totem poles are carved from single tree trunks and often reach a height of 90 feet (27.4 m). Probably originating as funerary monuments, by the nineteenth century they had become fixtures adorning the exteriors of chiefs' houses.

Eagles, beavers, and whales appear on the totem poles (Fig. 12.31), in essence as crests that a chief inherited from his ancestors. The Tlingit do not worship these figures or have any supernatural relationship with them. They are governed by traditional artistic principles. One of these, bilateral symmetry, places identical designs on

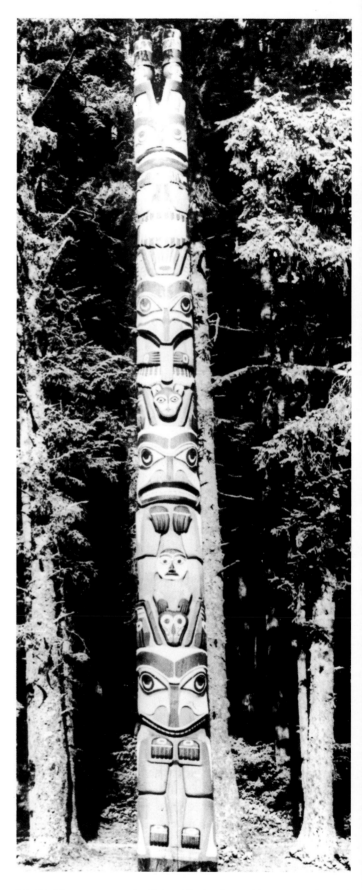

12.31 Tlingit totem pole, Sitka, Alaska, late 19th century. Carved and painted wood.

either side of the central axis. Another specifies the transition from one motif to another: each design must appear to grow from the one below. Thus, not only the overall vertical form of the totem pole, but also the design of its interior parts, leads the eye upward along its central axis. In our example, the patchwork of contrasting colors and upward striving line carry us with rhythmic precision from one motif to another until, finally, we reach the top. At the top, a darkly colored, triangular form and a strong horizontal capping band redirect the eye downward.

As historical documents that record the wealth, social position, and relative importance of the person who paid for them, totem poles function similarly to sculptural records from other cultures. The ultimate function of such art was probably to act as a gift: "The life goal of many of these tribes involved the belief that the greatest value was to give away all of one's possessions."[3] The actual working out of such a philosophy created some interesting scenarios. The more one gave away, the greater was one's prestige. In turn, one's rival was more or less obliged to give back the same or more material wealth in order to prove greater disdain for possessions. As a result, totems and other goods were often burned, thrown into the sea, or otherwise destroyed. It even went so far that slaves were occasionally killed and entire families sold into slavery.

African American Music

The European colonization of Africa had a negative impact on African art. The slave trade that serviced the plantations of the American South blended Euro- and African-centered cultures to create a significant African American artistic heritage. It emerged publicly during and immediately after the American Civil War (1861–5), and has been felt most strongly in music.

African American music consists of three basic types: folk music, art music, and popular music. Each has its own idiom, function, and place in the sociology of African American culture. Folk music—for example, the spiritual—has an anonymous origin, and oral transmission, and shows the "expressive melodic and racial feeling, character, and expression of the people."[4] This was a profoundly social musical form that defined a coherent experience for a dislocated people, supported people in distress, occasionally contained coded language of rebellion and escape, and provided a subtle language for exploring emotional extremities. Art music has a technical tradition in the hands of a group of highly trained specialists involved in both creation and performance. Popular music—for example, blues, ragtime, jazz, and soul—combines the art and folk traditions. It concerns itself with the contempo-

rary world, seeks novelty, and tends to be faddish. We will briefly examine some of the folk music of the African American tradition appropriate to the timeframe covered in this chapter.

As Northern soldiers, journalists, and missionaries arrived in the South toward the end of the Civil War, their reports created a new interest in and documentation of the culture of African Americans—especially their music. Numerous chronicles of this music can be found in newspaper and journal articles, letters, and other documents dating from the mid-1860s. In these lies the record of a musical heritage that expresses the joys and sorrows, thoughts and reactions of a people immersed in a struggle for freedom.

African Americans played numerous roles in the American Civil War: they were, for example, body servants for Southern officers, soldiers, cooks, hospital attendants, and railroad workers. Out of one unsuccessful attempt to organize freed men for military service came a plaintive song of regret:

Oh Lord, I want some valiant soldier,
I want some valiant soldier,
I want some valiant soldier,
To help me bear de cross.
For I weep, I weep,
For I weep, I weep,
I can't hold out;
If any mercy, Lord,
O pity poor me.[5]

On the eve of the expected Emancipation Proclamation, December 31, 1862, a prayer meeting and song service vigil held in the District of Columbia produced a spontaneous musical outpouring.

By the end of the Civil War, nearly 200,000 African Americans had served as soldiers in 166 regiments. Nearly 20,000 had served as sailors—almost one quarter of the entire United States Navy. Casualties numbered around 70,000, with approximately 30,000 killed. African Americans fought well and sang well. They linked their military struggle with their belief in a kind and liberating God.

The songs of slavery and the American South fill volumes. Clearly, music formed the core of the African American's life and culture during the two centuries of bondage. There were slave songs, religious folk songs, camp meeting songs, and spirituals. Most had strong religious themes—for example, the slave song "The Old Ship of Zion" (Fig. **12.32**).

The spiritual remains the most popular of the African American genres. A common misconception is that most

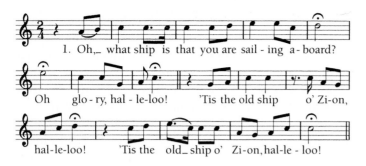

12.32 "The Old Ship of Zion," slave song.

of this music is in the minor key—it is not. It forms a commentary on the awful state of the African American's daily life, yet it shows patience for that life coupled with triumph in the life to come. Some songs focus on the present and some on the future, but the two were inexorably tied together, at least by implication. For example, in the spiritual "This World Almost Done" we hear the patient reminder,

Brudder, keep your lamp trimmin' and a-burnin',
Keep your lamp trimmin' and a-burnin',
Keep your lamp trimmin' and a-burnin',
    For dis world most done.
So keep your lamp trimmin' [etc.]
    For dis world most done.[6]

In "I Want to Go Home" the patience remains, but the final reward is proclaimed:

Dere's no rain to wet you,
    O, yes, I want to go home.
Dere's no sun to burn you,

O, yes, I want to go home.
O, push along, believers,
    O, yes, I want to go home.
Dere's no hard trials,
    O, yes, I want to go home.
Dere's no whips a crackin',
    O, yes, I want to go home.
My brudder on de wayside,
    O, yes, I want to go home.
O, push along, my brudder,
    O, yes, I want to go home.
Where dere's no stormy weather,
    O, yes, I want to go home.
Dere's no tribulation,
    O, yes, I want to go home.[7]

The first 250 years of African American cultural history reflect a diversity of reactions: sometimes the people howled out in alarm; sometimes they fought back and learned the advantages of resistance. They certainly did not "accept" slavery and oppression. The music of the time reflected the mind of the people and the circumstances they lived in.

The influence of this outpouring of musical expression in the folk idiom has been pervasive, and it has become a significant part not only of African American culture, but of American culture as a whole. In 1914 Henry Edward Krehbiel asserted:

Is it not the merest quibble to say that these songs are not American? They were created in America under American influences and by people who are Americans in the same sense that any other element of our population is American—every element except the aboriginal [American Indian].[8]

THINKING CRITICALLY

- Enumerate the basic characteristics of Romanticism and then, touching upon the elements of each art form (discussed in Chapters 1–8), compare Goya's *Execution of the Citizens of Madrid, May 3, 1808* (Fig. **12.2**), Wordsworth's "Tintern Abbey" (p. 327), Chopin's *Nocturne in E flat Major* (http://www.nifty.ne.jp/forum/fmidicla/mid/chonoc02.mid), and John Nash's Royal Pavilion (Fig. **12.10**) as representatives of the style.

- Explain how the styles of Realism, Impressionism, and Post-Impressionism are alike and/or different in the manner in which they utilize line, color, form, and personal emotion. Use examples from the text to illustrate your analysis.

- Compare Gaudí's Casa Batlló (Fig. **12.23**) and John Nash's Royal Pavilion (Fig. **12.10**) in terms of their basic stylistic approaches to architecture. In doing so, comment on line, scale, proportion, fenestration, structure, and expression of personal emotion. In addition, give your own personal reaction to each of these buildings and explain why you respond to them as you do.

CYBER STUDY

JAPAN:
—Printmaking: Hokusai, Hiroshige
http://www.ibiblio.org/wm/paint/auth/hiroshige/

AMERICAN INDIAN:
http://www.artcyclopedia.com/nationalities/
    Native_American.html

WESTERN ROMANTICISM:
—Visual Art
http://www.artcyclopedia.com/history/romanticism.html
—Music: Strauss, Schubert, Chopin, Liszt, Wagner, Brahms,
    Berlioz, Tchaikovsky
http://www.classicalarchives.com/index_1.html
—Literature: Austen, Goethe, Wordsworth, Coleridge,
    Byron, Shelley, Keats, Blake
http://www.infomotions.com/alex2/

NEW STYLES IN EUROPE AND AMERICA:
—Realism
http://www.artcyclopedia.com/history/realism.html
—Impressionism in Visual Art
http://www.artcyclopedia.com/history/impressionism.html
— Impressionism in Music: Debussy
http://www.classicalarchives.com/debussy.html
—Post-Impressionism
http://www.artcyclopedia.com/history/post-impressionism.html
—Art Nouveau
http://www.artcyclopedia.com/history/art-nouveau.html

CHAPTER THIRTEEN

THE ARTS IN A MODERN, POSTMODERN, AND PLURALISTIC WORLD

1900 to the Present

OUTLINE

——————————— IMPORTANT TERMS ———————————

Abstract Expressionism A painting style of the late 1940s and early 1950s, predominantly American, characterized by its rendering of expressive content by abstract or nonobjective means.

Cubism A style of art noted for the geometry of its forms, its fragmentation of the object, and its increasing abstraction.

Expressionism An art that stresses the psychological and emotional content of the work.

Fauvism An art movement characterized by its use of bold arbitrary color.

Futurism An art movement characterized by the desire to celebrate the movement and speed of modern industrial life.

Modernism Generally speaking, the various strategies and directions employed in twentieth-century arts to explore the particular formal properties of a given medium.

Musique actuelle Cutting-edge music drawing on jazz and rock to create vibrant, lively, personalized expressions.

Pop Art A style arising in the 1960s characterized by its emphasis on the forms and imagery of mass culture.

Postmodernism A term used to describe the willfully plural, eclectic, and typically anti-modern forms of art of the late twentieth century.

Serialism A system of musical composition emphasizing the tone row or twelve-tone technique.

Surrealism A style of art that emphasized dream imagery, chance operations, and rapid, thoughtless forms of notation that expressed the unconscious mind.

THE CONTEXT

More art has been produced since 1900 than in all the centuries that preceded it, and a glance at the styles of the last century suggest there have been more of them as well. In addition, since 1900 the world has become for the most part a single unit. Therefore, in this chapter we change our organization to reflect that global singularity. Rather than proceeding by continent, we will proceed by theme—pulling the world's arts together into three general topics: modern directions, postmodern directions, and pluralism. These three concepts represent three significant trends in the last century.

MODERNISM

Modernism in Western culture constitutes a general tendency to reject traditional conventions and forms in favor of innovation and experimentation, particularly as those innovations and experiments relate to societal change and technology. It encompasses a broad range of meanings, including the arts. In the arts, modernism developed in reaction to Romanticism and realism. Modernism in the arts rejected conventional narrative content and modes of expression to depict a world seen as altogether new and constantly in flux. As a movement, however, modernism has no coherence. Rather, it constitutes an approach to creation that broke old rules to express new thoughts and certain assumptions, often pessimistic, about the state of the world. We tend to view modernism as having begun around the end of the nineteenth century and lasting as a dominant expression until slightly after World War II.

We could also view modernism in a broader context as associated with a Renaissance concept of modernity that came into existence in the scientific revolution of the seventeenth century and carried forward to the Enlightenment. In those terms, modernism comprised a concept that denied the authority of the past—specifically the notion that Western culture reached its peak in ancient Greece and Rome—and gave credence to the idea of progress, rationalism, and technology.

POSTMODERNISM

Postmodernism grew out of modernism in the second half of the twentieth century, varying its onset among the arts. It continued some of the trends of modernism—for example, stylistic experimentation—but it disdained others, such as concern with purity of form. Perhaps most significantly, postmodernism questions the idea of metanarrative, or grand narrative: the attempt to explain all of human endeavor in terms of a single theory or principle such as Marxism and Freudian psychology. Such attempts to comprehensively account for human history and behavior are, according to postmodernism, posited in some respects in mutually incompatible terms. Postmodernism proposes to solve this contradiction by asserting that no final narrative exists to which one can reduce everything. Rather, a variety of perspectives on the world occur, none of which occupies a privileged position. This represents, arguably, a skeptical viewpoint stemming from the conviction that contemporary society is so hopelessly fractured—for example by the commercialization and trivialization of culture—that no coherent comprehension of it is possible. Within certain fields such as feminism and multiculturalism, postmodernism has created arguments between those who see it as supportive of their position (giving equal status with the prevailing Western narrative) and those who see postmodernism as so indiscriminate that it precludes any ground for political action.

The term "postmodernism" ("pomo" for short, and as opposed to "postmodern" or "post-modernity," which represent historical references) refers to aesthetic and artistic styles, ideas, and themes. Some of its indicators include eclecticism, anachronism (in which works may reflect and comment on a wide range of stylistic expressions and cultural-historical viewpoints), mixed genres or voices in a single work, fragmentation, open forms that recognize the presence of the audience, and irony. Often postmodernism results in an embrace of normlessness and cultural chaos, as well as a conscious attempt to break down distinctions between "high art" and popular culture—for example, performance art, which often involves a provocative mingling of musical, literary, and visual sources. The artist's self-conscious display of technique and artifice puts self-reference at the center of creation and presentation.

PLURALISM

The term pluralism has fallen easily into the vocabulary of the postmodern world because it has about it an implied inclusiveness and cultural and artistic egalitarianism previously unknown. Nonetheless, pluralism remains a vague concept that, in reality, encompasses or reacts against several adjacent concepts including ethnocentrism and cultural relativism. Pluralism often implies ethnically related activity—the acceptance and inclusion of works from various ethnicities outside the standard, previously accepted traditions of European or "Western" culture. In fact, the pluralism of the postmodern age has brought new emphasis on the arts of "ethnic minorities." Of course, such arts date to earliest recorded history and often represent sophisticated techniques and profound

visions. In the late twentieth and early twenty-first centuries, artists of minority ethnic and racial backgrounds gained inclusion in mainstream art circles, bringing to their works questions of identity and context. We will see this often in the chapter ahead. The emergence of emphasis on works of art from previously marginalized groups reflects an important conceptual shift within the various arts disciplines.

We need to note at this point that ethnic-centered emphasis and inclusion constitutes an opposite position from a concept that sounds almost the same: ethnocentrism. Ethnocentrism refers to the judging of other cultures by the standards and with the assumptions of one's own, and a belief in the superiority of one's own group to others. Although the current vogue applies ethnocentrism to Western or Eurocentrism, in fact, ethnocentrism occurs throughout the world and throughout history. Nonetheless, through the nineteenth century, most of Western history and social science proceeded from ethnocentric assumptions, viewing smaller-scale non-Western cultures as "primitive," less complex, and less morally developed.

In reaction to ethnocentrism, cultural relativism arose, asserting that beliefs, values, customs, and other expressions of cultures must be understood and judged within their own context rather than from outside viewpoints. The term "relativism" plays an important role in this point of view, because it maintains that no absolutes exist relative to truths or values. Rather, all truth and value lies relative to one's own personal, cultural, or historical perspective. Further, the approach of cultural relativism plays a vital role in the concept of multiculturalism, which seeks to overcome the dominance of Western cultural perspective, based on European civilization and Judeo-Christian religion, replacing it with expressions from a diversity of cultural and ethnic backgrounds. Some people argue that cultural relativism represents nonjudgmentality and, more importantly, a lack of critical insight that provides no basis for meaningful evaluation or cross-cultural analysis.

In the material ahead in this chapter, we will use the term "pluralism" as an organizing device that will allow us to examine artists and works of art by ethnic and racial topics in addition to discussion about styles.

HISTORY

In terms of historical context, in the early twentieth century, Europe found itself split into two camps: Germany, Austria-Hungary, and Italy versus Great Britain, France, and Russia. On August 3, 1914, Germany declared war on France and invaded Belgium. On August 4, Britain declared war on Germany. By 1918, after four of the bloodiest years in history, the Germans realized that they could no longer hope to turn things in their own favor. The first armistices were signed at the end of October and in November 1918 the Treaty of Versailles formally ended World War I.

In eastern Europe, a combination of military defeats, shortages, and hatred of the aristocracy made an explosive combination for Russia. In an uprising that lasted for five days in Petrograd, the revolution triumphed and Czar Nicholas II abdicated. Once the revolution had succeeded, however, Lenin and Stalin put the clamps on the nationalist movements.

Ten years later, a crisis beginning in the United States, and called the Great Depression, reflected not only the deep strains and stresses in world capitalism, but also a continuation of problems occurring in Europe since the second half of the nineteenth century. A wave of speculation on Wall Street caused the stock market to crash on October 24, 1929, and stocks and shares plummeted until 1932. The crisis spread throughout the world.

On January 30, 1933, Adolf Hitler (1889–1945) became chancellor of Germany. On September 1, 1939, Hitler invaded Poland, and war again engulfed Europe. Three years later, Japan attacked Pearl Harbor, and World War II reached around the globe. On May 8, 1945, Germany lay in ruin, and an unconditional surrender occurred. In the Pacific, resolution came when President Truman decided to drop two atomic bombs: one on Hiroshima on August 6, 1945, and one on Nagasaki on August 9, 1945.

After World War II, the United States and the Soviet Union dominated the world. The two former allies quickly grew apart as each sought to protect its sphere of influence from the other, and a period of tense conflict, the "Cold War," sometimes called "peaceful coexistence," lasted for the next forty-five years.

Before the end of World War II, much of the globe, especially in what we call the Third World, existed under the colonial rule of outside nations. After World War II that order began to change. During the late 1940s, decolonialization sprang from nationalist wars of independence. In the 1950s, as the Cold War polarized the world, violent popular revolutions challenged the remnants of colonialism in North Africa and southeast Asia. By the 1960s several African countries had achieved independence with the more-or-less freely given consent of their previous overlords.

As the Soviet Union under Mikhail Gorbachev (gahr-bah-chawf) and world communism in general disintegrated in the early 1990s, the large conflicts turned upon economics. The nations of Western Europe moved slowly but systematically toward an economically unified European community called the European Union (begun in the 1950s), with a common currency, the Euro. The draft political constitution of the EU failed to gain approval by all countries in 2005.

THE ARTS

MODERN DIRECTIONS

Expressionism

Expressionism traditionally refers to a movement in Germany between 1905 and 1930. Broadly speaking, however, it includes a variety of approaches, mostly in Europe, that aimed at eliciting in the viewer the same feelings the artist felt in creating the work—a sort of joint artist/viewer response to elements in the work of art. Any element—line, form, color—might be emphasized to elicit this response. The subject matter itself did not matter. What mattered was that the artist consciously tried to stimulate in the viewer a specific response similar to his or her own. The term "expressionism" as a description of this approach to visual art and architecture first appeared in 1911. It emerged following six years of work by an organized group of German artists who called themselves *Die Brücke* (dee brook-uh; "The Bridge"). Trying to define the group's purposes, the painter Ernst Ludwig Kirchner (KIRSH-nur; 1880–1938) wrote: "He who renders his inner convictions as he knows he must, and does so with spontaneity and sincerity, is one of us." They intended to protest against academic naturalism. The artists used simple media such as woodcuts and created often brutal, but nonetheless powerful, effects that expressed inner emotions.

The early expressionists maintained *representationalism* to a degree, but later expressionist artists, for example those of the Blue Rider group between 1912 and 1916, created some of the first completely abstract or nonobjective works of art. Color and form emerged as stimuli extrinsic to subject matter, and without any natural spatial relationships of recognizable objects, paintings took a new direction in internal organization.

In Max Beckmann's *Christ and the Woman Taken in Adultery* (Fig. **13.1**), the artist's revulsion against physical cruelty and suffering transmits through distorted figures crushed into shallow space. Linear distortion, changes of scale and perspective, and a nearly Gothic spirituality communicate Beckmann's reactions to the horrors of

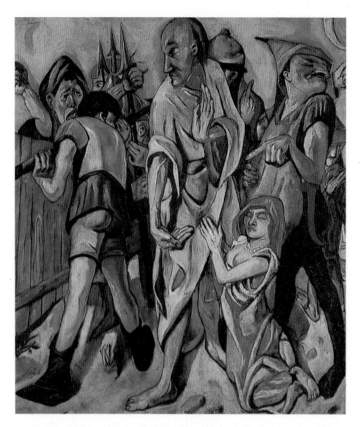

13.1 Max Beckmann, *Christ and the Woman Taken in Adultery*, 1917. Oil on canvas, 4 ft 10¾ ins × 4 ft 1⅞ ins (1.49 × 1.27 m). St. Louis Art Museum (Bequest of Curt Valentin).

World War I. In this approach, the meaning of the painting—the painter's meaning—transmits by very specific visual communication.

Expressionism found its way into the theatre in scenic design, as the painters' revolt against realism was adopted. But here we must tread carefully, because the theatre is both visual and oral. As regards concepts and plots, expressionism was merely an extension of realism, and disillusionment often came to the fore. Yet it allowed playwrights a more adequate means to express their own reactions to specific items in the universe around them. The Swedish dramatist August Strindberg (1849–1912), for example, turns inward to the subconscious in expressionistic plays such as the *Ghost Sonata*. In so doing, he creates a presentational rather than a representational style.

Expressionism also found its way to America. Elmer Rice's play *Adding Machine* depicts Mr. Zero, a cog in the great industrial machinery of twentieth-century life, who stumbles through a pointless existence. Finding himself replaced by an adding machine he goes berserk, kills his employer, and is executed. Then, adrift in the hereafter,

he is too narrow-minded to understand the happiness offered to him there. He becomes an adding machine operator in Heaven and finally returns to earth to begin his tortured existence all over again.

German expressionism made its mark in film as well as in the visual and other performing arts. The visual composition, strongly influenced by expressionist stagecraft, tried to convey through décor the subjective mental state of the protagonist. German expressionism emphasized visual design, and, as we have seen in painting and theatre, the style focuses on anxiety and tenor. In film, the sets reflect a deliberate artificiality: flat and obviously painted with no attempt at lifelikeness through perspective or scale. Expressionist film directors intended settings to represent a state of mind rather than a place, with an emphasis on diagonal lines in order to suggest instability and anguish. In 1919, expressionist cinema's most masterful example, Robert Wiene's (veen; 1881–1938) *The Cabinet of Dr Caligari*, astounded the film-going public. Macabre sets, surrealistic lighting effects, and distorted properties all combined to portray a menacing post-World War I German world. In the film—a morbid depiction of honor, menace, and anxiety—a madman relates to a madwoman his understanding of how he came to be in the asylum. The shadowy lighting and distorted streets and buildings on the set represent projections of his insane universe. The film's other characters also form visual symbols created through makeup and dress.

Whether in visual art, theatre, cinema, or literature, the expressionists turned to non-naturalistic techniques in order to express the subconscious thoughts and emotions of the artist and the inner realities of life. Primarily an outcry against materialism, urbanization, and industrialization of pre-World War I Europe, it forged a number of social protests. Expressionist writers pursued general truths rather than specific situations, and, thus, their characters exhibit the characteristics of symbols—of types—rather than the characteristics of fully developed individuals. We have also seen this in the theatre. Expressionist poets used nonreferential themes in seeking an "ecstatic, hymnlike lyricism" that had great associative power. Their approach stripped poetry down to strings of nouns with only a few adjectives or infinitive verbs. They eliminated narrative and description in order to get to the nub of feeling. Again, they sought to express their horror of urban life, and they frequently turned to apocalyptic scenes of civilization's destruction. This intensely personal approach tended toward vagueness, which made expressionist works seem inapproachable. As might be expected, that led to its demise, although in Germany, expressionism died at the hands of the Nazis, who labeled it as decadent and outlawed its publication or exhibition.

Fauvism

Closely associated with the expressionist movement was the style of the *fauves* (the French word for "wild beasts"). The label appeared in 1905 from an art critic in response to a sculpture that seemed to him "a Donatello in a cage of wild beasts."

Violent distortion and outrageous coloring mark the work of the fauves, whose two-dimensional surfaces and flat color areas were new to European painting.

The best-known artist of this short-lived movement was the Frenchman Henri Matisse (mah-TEES; 1869–1954). He tried to paint pictures that would "unravel the tensions of modern existence." In his old age, Matisse made a series of very joyful designs for the Chapel of the Rosary at Venice, not just as exercises in religious art but as expressions of joy and the nearly religious feeling that he had for living.

The *Blue Nude* (Fig. **13.2**) illustrates the wild coloring and distortions in the paintings of Matisse and the other fauves. The painting takes its name from the energetically applied blues, which occur throughout the figure as dark accents. For Matisse, color and line comprised indivisible devices, and the bold strokes of color in his work both reveal forms and stimulate a purely aesthetic response. Matisse literally "drew with color." He did not intend, of course, to draw a nude as he saw it in life. Rather, he tried to express his feelings about the nude as an object of aesthetic interest. Thus Matisse, along with the other fauve painters, represents one brand of expressionism.

Cubism

Between 1901 and 1912 a new approach to pictorial space emerged: *Cubism*. Cubist space violates all concepts of two- or three-dimensional perspective. In the past the space within a composition had been thought of as separate from the main object of the work. That is, if the subject were removed, the space would remain unaffected. Pablo Picasso (1881–1973) and Georges Braque (brahk; 1882–1963) changed that relationship to one in which the artist tried to paint "not objects, but the space they engender." The area around an object became an extension of the object itself. If the object were removed, the space around it would collapse. Cubist space is typically quite shallow and gives the impression of reaching forward toward the viewer, thereby intruding into space outside of the frame. Essentially the style developed as the result of independent experiments by Braque and Picasso with ways of describing form. Perhaps newly evolving notions of the time–space continuum proposed by German physicist Albert Einstein (1879–1955) at this time helped to make their works more acceptable.

Picasso influenced the visual arts of the twentieth century more than any other individual. Born in Spain, he moved in 1900 to France, where he resided for most of his life. In Paris he was influenced by Toulouse-Lautrec and the late works of Cézanne (see p. 347), particularly in terms of their organization, analysis of forms, and assumption of different viewpoints. He focused on form kept within the frame. Mass was "built up within [the frame] like a box within a box"[1] (see Figs. **1.24** and **1.26**).

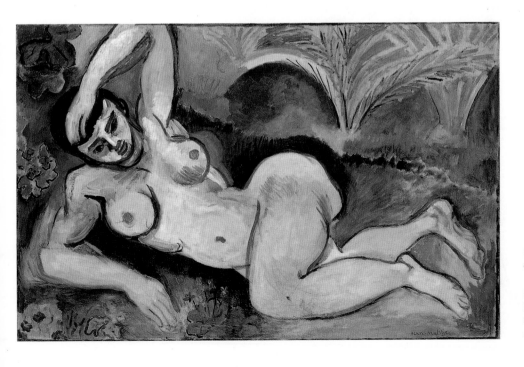

13.2 Henri Matisse, *Blue Nude* (*"Souvenir de Biskra"*), 1907. Oil on canvas, 36¼ × 55¼ ins (91 × 104 cm). Baltimore Museum of Art (Cone Collection, formed by Dr. Claribel Cone and Miss Etta Cone of Baltimore, Maryland). © Succession H. Matisse/Dacs 2001.

Very early on in his life, Picasso began to identify deeply with society's misfits and cast-offs. He was able to express this strongly in his art. Depression characterized his works from 1901 until around 1904 or 1905. This is known as his Blue Period and was followed by his Rose Period (1904–6) "in which he was less concerned with the tragic aspects of poverty than with the nostalgic charm of itinerant circus performers and the school of make-believe."

Les Demoiselles d'Avignon (lay duh-mwah-ZEHL dah-veen-YAWN; Fig. **13.3**) has become the single most discussed image in modern art. Its simplified forms and restricted color were adopted by many Cubists, as they reduced their palettes in order to concentrate on spatial exploration. A result of personal conflicts on the part of the artist, combined with his ambition to be recognized as the leader of the avant garde, the painting deliberately breaks with the traditions of Western illusionistic art. The painter denies both Classical proportions and the organic integrity and continuity of the human body.

Les Demoiselles d'Avignon (Avignon in the title refers to a street in Barcelona's red-light district) is aggressive and harsh, like the world of the prostitutes who inhabit it. Forms are simplified and angular, and colors are restricted to blues, pinks, and terracottas. Picasso breaks his subjects into angular wedges that convey a sense of three-dimensionality. We do not know whether the forms protrude out or recess in. In rejecting a single viewpoint, Picasso presents "reality" not as a mirror image of what we see in the world, but as images that have been reinterpreted within the terms of new principles. Understanding thus depends on knowing rather than seeing in the literal sense. Cubism uniformly reduced its palette range, thereby emphasizing the exploration of space.

The spatial structures of Cubism in painting found their way to literature as well. In the case of literature, abstraction of structure expressed itself in the narrative, and written attempts to reproduce the visual effects of Picasso and Braque resulted in bizarre associations and dissociations in imagery. Particularly, Cubist writers

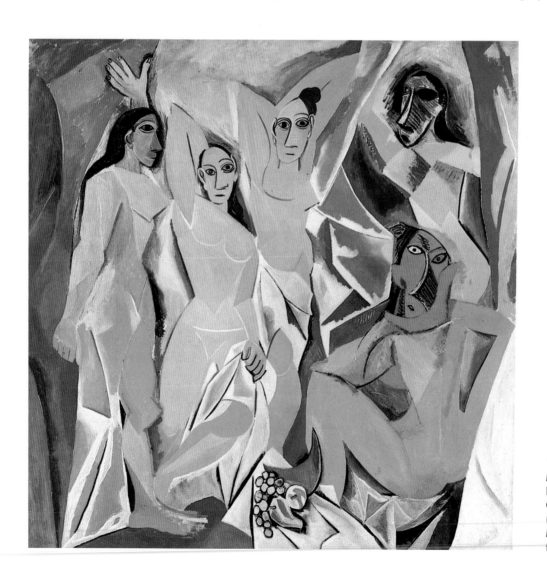

13.3 Pablo Picasso,
Les Demoiselles d'Avignon,
Paris, June to July 1907.
Oil on canvas, 8 ft × 7 ft 8 ins
(2.44 × 2.34 m). The Museum of
Modern Art, New York (Acquired
through the Lillie P. Bliss Bequest).

sought to present simultaneous occurrences of points of view toward the material. Perhaps the best-known of the writers attempting Cubist techniques was Gertrude Stein (stine; 1874–1946), who was a good friend of Picasso. She experimented in the style, creating in, for example, *Tender Buttons* (1914), obscure and unfathomable passages with an occasional, memorable turn of phrase:

Tender Buttons
Gertrude Stein

OBJECTS

A CARAFE, THAT IS A BLIND GLASS.

A kind in glass and a cousin, a spectacle and nothing strange a single hurt color and an arrangement in a system to pointing. All this and not ordinary, not unordered in not resembling. The difference is spreading.

GLAZED GLITTER.

Nickel, what is nickel, it is originally rid of a cover.

The change in that is that red weakens an hour. The change has come. There is no search. But there is, there is that hope and that interpretation and sometime, study any is unwelcome, sometime there is breath and there will be a sinecure and charming very charming is that clean and cleansing. Certainly glittering is handsome and convincing.

There is no gratitude in mercy and in medicine. There can be breakages in Japanese. That is no programme. That is no color chosen. It was chosen yesterday, that showed spitting and perhaps washing and polishing. It certainly showed no obligation and perhaps if borrowing is not natural there is some use in giving.

Futurism and Mechanism

Sculptors turned to further explorations of three-dimensional space and what they could do with it. Technological developments and new materials also encouraged the search for new forms to characterize the age. This search resulted in a style called "futurism," which constituted really more of an ideology than a style. Futurism encompassed more than just the arts, and it sought to destroy the past—especially the Italian past—in order to institute a totally new society, a new art, and new poetry. Its basis lay in "new dynamic sensations." In other words, the objects of modern life, such as "screaming automobiles" that run like machine guns, have a new beauty—speed—more beautiful than even the most dynamic objects of previous generations. Futurists found

in the noise, speed, and mechanical energy of the modern city a unique exhilaration that made everything of the past drab and unnecessary. The movement was particularly strong in Italy and among Italian sculptors. In searching for new dynamic qualities, the Italian futurists in the visual arts found that many new machines had sculptural form. Their own sculptures followed mechanistic lines and included representations of motion—described by some as Cubism with movement.

Unique Forms of Continuity in Space by Umberto Boccioni (boh-CHOH-nee; Fig. **13.4**) takes the mythological subject of Mercury, messenger of the gods (see Fig. **2.8**), and turns him into a futuristic machine. The overall form is recognizable and the connotations of the myth suggest subject matter. Nonetheless, this is primarily an exercise in composition of forms. The intense sense of energy and movement is created by the variety of surfaces and curves that flow into one another in a seemingly random yet highly controlled pattern. The overall impression is of a figure in motion, rather than of the figure itself.

Futurism in literature closely allied itself with the futurism of the visual arts. It violently rejected tradition and sought to give a formal expression to the energy and dynamism of mechanism. The movement rose in Italy with a manifesto by Filippo Marinetti (1876–1944), who coined the term. It spread to England and Russia. In the latter case, futurism took a radical turn in social and political outlook. Russian futurists attacked writers such as Dostoyevski, calling for new techniques in the writing of poetry. Rejection of logical sentence construction and traditional grammar and syntax typified futurism in Italy, England, France, and Russia. Futurists regularly used strings of incoherent words, stripped of their meaning, for the effects of their sounds alone. The Russian futurists actively and early supported the Bolshevik Revolution of 1917 and gained, as a result, a number of important cultural posts. Their approach, however, proved too unstable to support a long-lasting movement, and by 1930 their influence had ebbed close to extinction.

Themes dealing with mechanism proved popular in the early twentieth century, as life became more and more dominated by machines. Another brief movement in Italy, mechanism, sought to express the spirit of the age by capturing speed and power through representation of vehicles and machines in motion. Mechanistic themes appear clearly in the works of Marcel Duchamp (doo-SHAHWM; 1887–1968), often associated with the dada movement and whose famous *Nude Descending a Staircase, No. 2* (Fig. **13.5**) some call "protodadaist." To Duchamp, apparently, men and women were machines that ran on passion as fuel. Like those of the dadaists, many of Duchamp's works also exploit chance and accident.

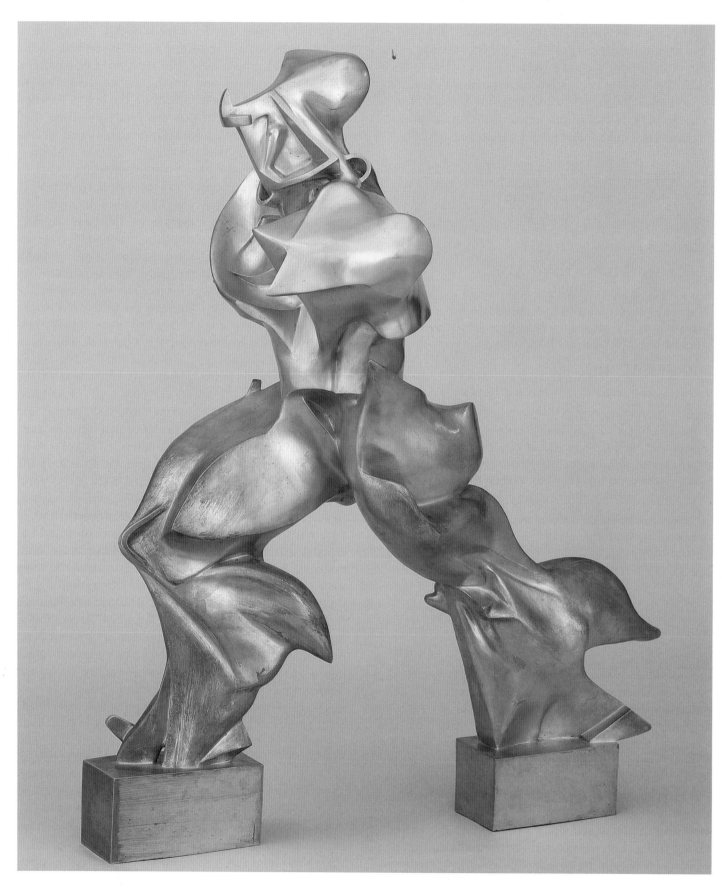

13.4 Umberto Boccioni, *Unique Forms of Continuity in Space*, 1913. Bronze (cast 1931), 43⅞ × 34⅞ × 15¾ ins (111.2 × 88.5 × 40 cm). The Museum of Modern Art, New York (Acquired through the Lillie P. Bliss Bequest).

By 1916, a few works of art by the Dadaists began to appear; many of them found objects and experiments in which chance played an important role. For example, Jean Arp (1888–1966) produced collages that he made by dropping haphazardly cut pieces of paper onto a surface and pasting them down the way they fell. Max Ernst (1891–1976) juxtaposed strange, unrelated items to produce unexplainable phenomena.

This use of conventional items placed in circumstances that alter their traditional meanings characterizes Dadaist art. Irrationality, meaninglessness, and harsh, mechanical images occur as typical effects. This nonsensical world shows pseudo-human forms with their bizarre features and proportions to suggest a malevolent unreality. Dada emphasizes protest and leads to the idea that the arts must shock (as with Duchamp's *Nude Descending a Staircase, No. 2*, Fig. **13.5**).

Abstraction

Abstraction in art takes two general forms: (1) the reduction of images from the natural world into shapes suggested by, but not conventionally representational of, actual objects; and (2) the "pure" use of color, line, shadow, mass, and other traditional, formal elements of painting and sculpture to create an image referring only to itself. In other words, abstract art seeks to explore the expressive qualities of formal design elements and materials for their own right. These elements stand apart from subject matter. The aesthetic theory underlying abstract art maintains that beauty can exist in form alone with no other quality needed.

Piet Mondrian (1872–1944) believed that the fundamental principles of life consisted of straight lines and right angles. A vertical line signified active vitality and life; a horizontal line signified tranquillity, rest, and death. The crossing of the two in a right angle expressed the highest possible tension between these forces, positive and negative.

Composition in White, Black, and Red (see Fig. **1.48**) explores Mondrian's philosophy in a manner characteristic of all his linear compositions. The painting's planes are close to the surface of the canvas, creating, in essence, no space, in contrast to the deep space of other styles. The palette is restricted to three hues. Even the edges of the canvas take on expressive possibilities as they provide additional points of interaction between lines. Mondrian believed that he could create "the equivalence of reality" and make the "absolute appear in the relativity of time and space" by keeping visual elements in a state of constant tension.

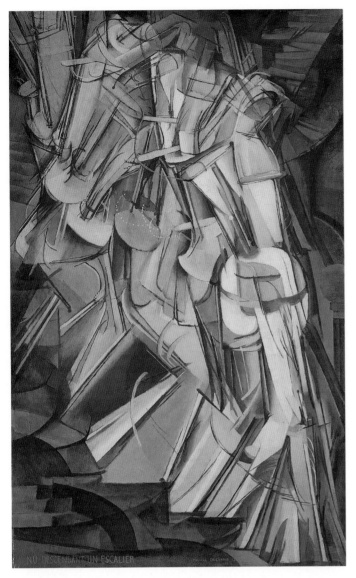

13.5 Marcel Duchamp, *Nude Descending a Staircase, No. 2*, 1912. Oil on canvas, 4 ft 10 ins × 2 ft 11 ins (1.25 × 0.6 m). Philadelphia Museum of Art (The Louise and Walter Arensberg Collection).

Dada

The horrors of World War I caused tremendous disillusionment. One expression of this emerged in the birth of "Dada." (Considerable debate exists about when and how the word "dada"—French for "hobby-horse"—came to be chosen. The Dadaists themselves accepted it as two nonsense syllables, like one of a baby's first words.) During the years 1915 and 1916, many artists gathered in neutral capitals in Europe to express their disgust at the direction Western societies were taking. Dada thus served as a political protest, and in many places the Dadaists produced more left-wing propaganda than art.

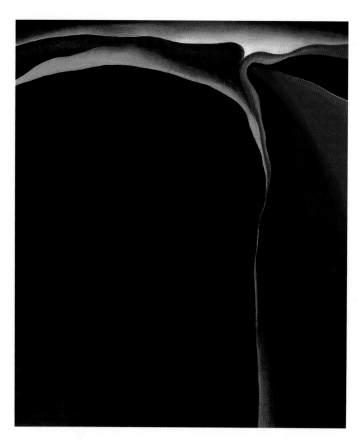

13.6 Georgia O'Keeffe, *Dark Abstraction*, 1924. Oil on canvas, 24⅞ × 20⅞ ins (63.3 × 53 cm). St. Louis Art Museum (Gift of Charles E. and Mary Merrill).

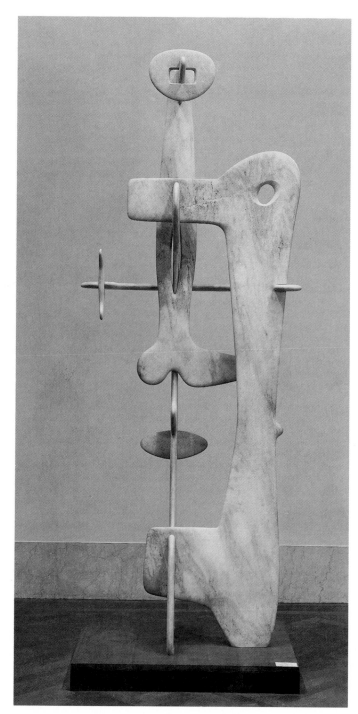

13.7 Isamu Noguchi, *Kouros (in nine parts)*, 1944–5. Pink Georgia marble, slate base, height approx. 9 ft 9 ins (2.97 m). Metropolitan Museum of Art, New York (Fletcher Fund).

The American Georgia O'Keeffe (1887–1986) was one of the most original artists of the twentieth century. Her imagery draws on a diverse repertoire of objects abstracted in a uniquely personal way. She takes, for example, an animal skull and transforms it into a form of absolute simplicity and beauty. In *Dark Abstraction* (Fig. **13.6**) an organic form becomes an exquisite landscape that, despite its modest size, appears monumental. Her lines flow gracefully upward and outward with skillful blending of colors and rhythmic grace. Whatever the subject of the painting, it expresses a mystical reverence for nature. O'Keeffe creates a sense of reality that takes us beyond our surface perceptions.

Isamu Noguchi (noh-GHOO-chee; 1904–88), seemingly less concerned with expressive content than others, experimented with abstract sculptural design from the 1930s onward. His creations go beyond sculpture to provide highly dynamic designs that inspired the choreography of Martha Graham, with whom he was associated for a number of years. Noguchi's *Kouros* figures (Fig. **13.7**) are an abstract response to archaic Greek sculpture, with exquisitely finished surfaces and exemplary technique. The highly original mobiles of Alexander Calder (1898–1976; see Fig. 2.6) put abstract sculpture into motion. Deceptively simple, these colorful shapes turn at the whim of subtle breezes or are powered by motors.

Surrealism

Surrealism, despite its Dada roots, in literature as in visual art, expressed more positive sentiments, particularly between World War I and World War II. It nonetheless built upon a reaction against the horrors of World War I. The spokesman of the group was Andre Breton (breh-TAHW; 1896–1966), himself a former Dadaist. In "The Surrealist Manifesto" (1924), he wrote that surrealism sought to reunite the conscious and unconscious realms of experience so fully that the world of dream and fantasy would join the everyday rational world in "an absolute reality, a surreality." Breton's poetry utilized a juxtaposition of words determined by psychological (unconscious) thought processes. Surrealist writers favored automatic writing because it relied on the powers of the subconscious. Automatic writing constitutes writing produced without conscious intention, often even without awareness, as in telepathic or spiritualistic occurrences. The phenomenon can appear during alert or hypnotic states and results in unrelated words, fragments of poems, puns, obscenities, or, even, rational fantasies. Surrealism had widespread influence including on absurdism.

As the work of Sigmund Freud became popular, artists became fascinated by the subconscious mind. By 1924, a Surrealist manifesto stated some specific connections between the subconscious mind and painting. Surrealist works were thought to be created by "pure psychic automatism," whose goal was to merge reason and unreason, consciousness and the unconscious into an "absolute reality—a super-reality." Its advocates saw Surrealism as a way to discover the basic realities of psychic life by automatic associations. Supposedly, a dream could be transferred directly from the unconscious mind of the painter to canvas without control or conscious interruption.

Two directions of Surrealist art emerged. The metaphysical fantasies of Giorgio de Chirico (KEE-ree-koh; 1888–1978), for example, present fantastic, hallucinatory scenes in a hard-edged, realistic manner. In works such as *The Nostalgia of the Infinite* (see Fig. **1.50**), strange objects are irrationally juxtaposed: they come together as in a dream. These bizarre works reflect a world that human beings do not control. In them, "there is only what I see with my eyes open, and even better, closed."

Another Surrealist of this same direction was Mexican painter Frida Kahlo (KAH-loh; 1907–54). Her works (more than one third of which are self-portraits) are studies in great pain and suffering, both mental and physical. Works such as *The Broken Column* (Fig. **13.8**) portray a nightmarish quality typical of Surrealism—here a myriad of emotions, as the subject appears both as a sufferer and a savior. The broken column displayed in the open chasm

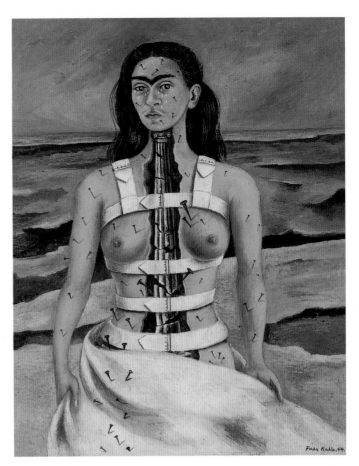

13.8 Frida Kahlo, *The Broken Column*, 1944. Oil on masonite, 15¾ × 12¼ ins (40 × 31 cm). Museo Dolores Olmedo, Mexico.

of the torso juxtaposes a graphic architectural form, perhaps suggesting her own spine and brokenness, with her body itself, punctured by numerous nails and held together by a cloth harness. The self-portrait stands before a barren monochromatic landscape and darkened sky.

The second direction of Surrealism—the abstract—can be seen in works by Joan Miró (see Fig. **1.25**). These are based on spontaneity and chance, using abstract images.

Absurdism

Many artists of this period had lost faith in religion, science, and humanity itself. In their search for meaning, they found only chaos, complexity, grotesque laughter, and perhaps insanity.

The plays of Luigi Pirandello (peer-an-DEHL-lo; 1867–1936) obsessively ask the question "'What is real?" with brilliant variations. In the psychological play, *Six Characters in Search of an Author* (1921), Pirandello sought to fragment reality by destroying conventional dramatic structures and adopting new ones. *Six Characters* features a play within a play. Pirandello sought to achieve perfect unity between ideas and dramatic structure by transferring the dissociation of reality from the plane of content to that of form. *Right You Are If You Think You Are* (1917) presents a wife, living with her husband in a top-floor apartment and not permitted to see her mother. She converses with her daily, the mother in the street and the daughter at a garret window. Soon a neighbor demands an explanation from the husband. He answers, but so does the mother, who has an equally plausible but different answer. Finally, someone approaches the wife, the only one who can clear up the mystery. Her response, as the curtain falls: loud laughter! Pirandello expressed his dismay at an incomprehensible world in mocking laughter directed at those people who thought they knew the answers.

Pirandello's work factored in the emergence of a movement called *"absurdism."* A philosophy that posited the essential meaninglessness—or unknowable meaning—of existence, and thus questioned the meaning of any action, was also emerging; "existentialism." It also contributed to absurdist style, especially in the literary arts.

From such antecedents came numerous dramas, the best-known of which were written by the French existentialist philosopher, writer, and playwright Jean-Paul Sartre (1905–80). Sartre held that no absolute or universal moral values existed and that humankind formed part of a world without purpose. Therefore, men and women had responsibility only to themselves. His plays attempted to draw logical conclusions from "a consistent atheism." Plays such as *No Exit* (1944) translate Sartre's existential views into dramatic form.

Albert Camus (kah-MOO; 1913–60) first applied the term "absurd" to the human condition. This he took to be a state somewhere between humanity's aspirations and the meaninglessness of the universe that is the condition of life. Determining which way to take a chaotic universe is the theme of Camus's plays, such as *Cross-Purposes* (1944). Absurdism continued as a theatrical genre after World War II.

Realism

In the twentieth century, pictorial objectivity continued in the realist tradition in the works of Grant Wood (1892–1942)—for example, *American Gothic* (see Fig. 0.4), a celebration of America's heartland and its simple, hardworking people. There is a lyric spirituality behind the façade of this down-home illustration. The upward movement of the elongated forms pull together at the top into a pointed arch that encapsulates the Gothic window of the farmhouse and escapes the frame of the painting through the lightning rod, in the same sense that the Gothic spire released the spirituality of the earth into heaven at its tip. Rural American reverence for home and labor is fêted here with gentle humor. There is a capricious two-dimensionality. All objects, and the people, line up horizontally. With no linear perspective in the middle ground, the buildings appear pressed against the backs of the farmer and his wife.

On April 23, 1896, at Roster and Bial's Music Hall in New York, the Leigh Sisters performed their umbrella dance. Then the astonished audience saw waves breaking upon the shore. Thus launched a new process for screen projection of movies—the Vitascope. Invented by Thomas Armat (although Thomas Edison has received much of the credit), the Vitascope was the latest in centuries of experiments on how to make pictures move. Relying on the "persistence of vision"—the continuance of a visual image on the retina for a brief time after the removal of the object—and basic photographic techniques, the Vitascope captured real objects in motion and presented those images on a screen.

Technological experiments in rapid-frame photography were common in the last half of the nineteenth century, but it remained for Thomas Armat and others to perfect a stop-motion device essential to screen projection. Two Frenchmen, the Lumière (loo-mee-AIR) brothers, usually receive credit for the first public projection of movies on a large screen in 1895. By 1897, the Lumières had successfully exhibited their *cinématographie* all over Europe, and their catalogue listed 358 films. Essentially, the Lumière brothers originated documentary film. They called their brief pieces *actualités* (ahk-tyoo-ah-lee-TAY), and shot them in angle takes. Fundamentally early newsreels, they often contained several different sequences without any cutting within a sequence. Thus, they represent the technique called the "sequence shot" (a complex action photographed in a continuous take, without cuts). The Lumières opened in America three months after the première of the Vitascope. Later that year, the American Biograph made its début using larger film and projecting twice as many pictures per minute, creating the largest, brightest, and steadiest picture of all.

At that point, movies did nothing more than record everyday life. It took Georges Méliès (may-lee-ES; 1861–1938) in France and Edwin S. Porter (1870–1941) in the United States to demonstrate the narrative and manipulative potential of the cinema. Between 1896 and 1914, Méliès turned out more than a thousand films. Méliès's crude narratives required using more than one shot. To accomplish tying together several shots into a sequence, Méliès, along with others, pioneered the style of "cutting to continuity." His narrative segments connect via a fade-out of one segment and a fade-in of the next, usually showing the same characters in a different location and different time. Edwin S. Porter, in charge of the Edison Company Studios, studied the narrative attempts of Méliès. Then, acting as his own scriptwriter, cameraman, and director, he spliced together old and freshly shot film into *The Life of an American Firefighter*. In 1903 Porter made *The Great Train Robbery*, the most popular film of the decade. It ran a total of twelve minutes and entranced the popular audience. People were flocking to electric theatres to see movies that could excite and thrill them with stories of romance and adventure. The movies helped to open a window to a wider world for the poor of America.

World War II and its aftermath brought radical change to the form and content of the cinema. A film came out in 1940 that stunned even Hollywood. Darryl Zanuck and John Ford's version of John Steinbeck's *Grapes of Wrath* took the social criticism of Steinbeck's portrayal of the Depression and presented it visually, creating art through superb cinematography and compelling performances. Social commentary burst forth again in 1941 with two outstanding works, *How Green was my Valley*, which dealt with exploited coal miners in Wales, and *Citizen Kane*, about wealth and power, and thought by some to be the best film ever produced. The cinematic techniques of *Citizen Kane* forged a new trail. Orson Welles, director and star, and Greg Toland, cinematographer, brilliantly combined deep-focus photography, new lighting effects, rapid cutting, and moving camera sequences.

But as the war ended and Italy overthrew the yoke of Fascism, a new concept set the stage for the years ahead. In 1945 Roberto Rossellini's (rah-seh-LEE-nee) *Rome, Open City* graphically depicted the misery of Rome during the German occupation. It was shot on the streets of the capital using hidden cameras and mostly nonprofessional actors and actresses. Technically, the quality of the work was deficient, but the effectiveness of its objective viewpoint and documentary realism changed the course of cinema and inaugurated a style called *Neorealism*.

Realism continued its strong tradition in the theatre throughout the postwar era, owing much of its strength to the works of the American playwrights Tennessee Williams (1912–83) and Arthur Miller (1915–2005). It has now expanded since its nineteenth-century conception in the works of Henrik Ibsen (*Ghosts*; *A Doll's House*) and George Bernard Shaw (*Pygmalion*; *Major Barbara*) to include more theatrical approaches, such as fragmented settings. Including many nonrealistic devices, such as symbolism, it has become broader and more eclectic, concluding that stage realism and life's realism are two separate issues.

Tennessee Williams skillfully blends the qualities of realism with whatever scenic, structural, or symbolic devices are necessary to meet his goals. His plays, such as *The Glass Menagerie*, deal sensitively and poignantly with the problems and psychology of everyday people. Character development is thorough and occupies the principal focus as he explores the mental and emotional ills of our society. Arthur Miller, too, probes the social and psychological forces that destroy contemporary men and women in plays such as *Death of a Salesman*.

Abstract Expressionism

The first fifteen years following the end of World War II were dominated by a style called Abstract Expressionism. Beginning essentially in New York, it spread rapidly throughout the world. Like most modern styles, it saw variation among individual artists. Two characteristics can be identified. One is freedom from traditional use of brushwork, and the other is the exclusion of representational subject matter. Individual expression used to reflect inner life gave artists rein to create works of high emotional and dynamic intensity. The freedom of this style appears to relate to the optimistic postwar sense of conquest over totalitarianism. By the early 1960s, when life was less certain and the implications of the nuclear age had sunk in, Abstract Expressionism as a force in art had reduced to a trickle.

The most heralded artist of this style was Jackson Pollock (1912–56). A rebellious spirit, he evolved a method of dripping and spilling paint onto huge canvases placed on the floor (Fig. **13.9**; see also Fig. **1.28**). Often called *action painting*, the controlled dripping gives a sense of tremendous energy, and a revolutionary concept of space, line, and form. Pollock rejected much of the European tradition in favor of cruder, rougher formal values identified with the American frontier. The term "action painting" (coined by an art critic) refers to active paint handling by the artist. Pollock indicated that he was more at ease with painting on the floor, believing that in that way he could literally be in the painting, and when in the painting, not aware of what he was doing. The result produced pure harmony. Thus, Pollock found deep pleasure in the technique, which provided him with a sense of being fully absorbed in action and freed from any estrangement from the world.

The Abstract Expressionist tradition continues in the work of Helen Frankenthaler (frahn-kehn-TAH-luhr; b. 1928). Her staining technique, as seen in *Buddha* (Fig. **13.10**), consists of pouring color across an unprimed canvas, creating amorphous shapes that seem to float in space. The image has infinite potential mean-

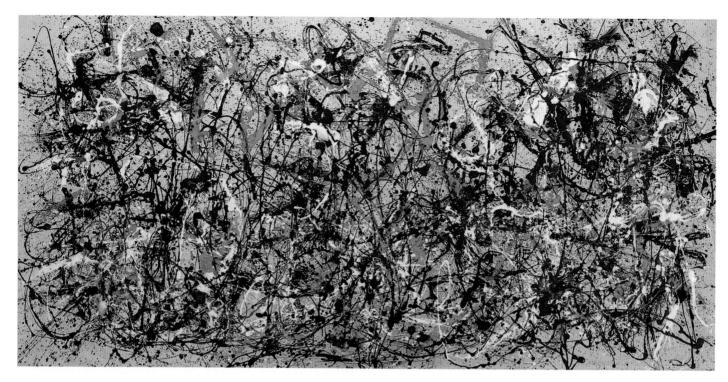

13.9 Jackson Pollock, *Autumn Rhythm*, 1950. Oil on canvas, 8 ft 9 ins × 17 ft 3 ins
(2.67 × 5.26 m). Metropolitan Museum of Art, New York (George A. Hearn Fund).

13.10 Helen Frankenthaler, *Buddha*, 1988. Acrylic on canvas, 6 ft 2 ins × 6 ft 9 ins
(1.88 × 2.06 m). Private collection.

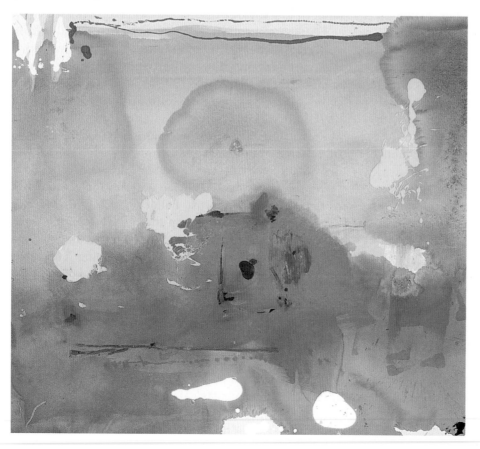

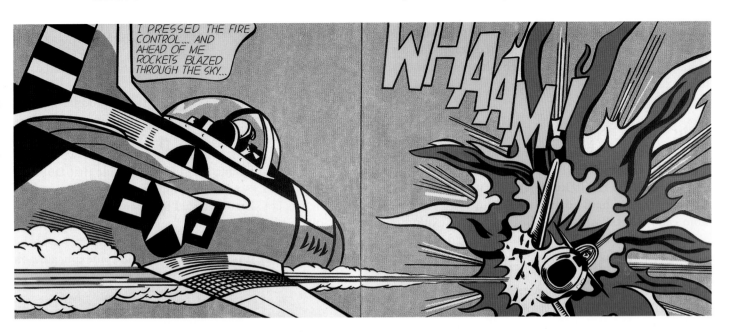

13.11 Roy Lichtenstein, *Whaam!*, 1963. Acrylic on canvas, 5 ft 8 ins × 13 ft 4 ins (1.73 × 4.05 m). Tate, London.

ing, apart from that suggested by the title. The very free-dom of the form symbolizes our freedom to choose its associations. However, the sensual quality of the work engages us. Its fluidity and the nonlinear use of color give it softness and grace.

Abstract Expressionism proved ultimately an American movement. Nowhere else did anything even remotely comparable emerge during this time. However, by the early 1960s the style reached its zenith. An entirely new perception of reality—one of consumerism and afflu-ence—began to sweep the world.

Following Abstract Expressionism, and in some instances as a reaction against that type of painting, there came a veritable explosion of styles and movements: Pop Art, Op Art, Hard Edge, Primary Structures, Minimal Art, Post-Minimal Art, Environmental Art, Body Art, Earth Art, Video Art, Kinetic Art, Photo Realism, and Concept-ualism. We have space to discuss only three of these.

Pop Art

Pop Art evolved in the 1950s, and concerns itself above all with image in a representational sense. Subjects and treatments in this style come from mass culture and com-mercial design. These sources provide Pop artists with what they consider to be essential aspects of their visual environment. Pop Art is essentially an ironic reflection of the contemporary scene. The term "Pop" was coined by the English critic Lawrence Alloway.

Probably the compelling depictions of Roy Lichten-stein (1923–97) are the most familiar (Fig. **13.11**). These

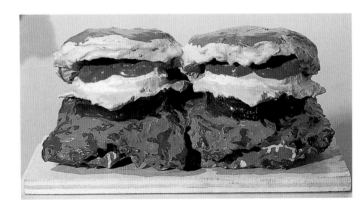

13.12 Claes Oldenburg, *Two Cheeseburgers, with Everything (Dual Hamburgers)*, 1962. Burlap soaked in plaster, painted with enamel, 7 × 14¾ × 8⅝ ins (17.8 × 37.5 × 21.8 cm). The Museum of Modern Art, New York (Philip Johnson Fund).

magnified cartoon-strip details use the Ben Day screen of dots by which colored ink is applied to cheap newsprint. Using a stencil about the size of a coin, the artist builds the image up into a stark and dynamic, if sometimes vio-lent, portrayal.

Pop objects serve as source materials for Claes Oldenburg (b. 1929). *Dual Hamburgers* (Fig. **13.12**) pres-ents an enigma to the viewer. For Oldenburg, art seems just another commercial product, but his intention really took the opposite turn, as Marilyn Stokstad (*Art History*, p. 1130) indicates, "to render more 'human' what he called the 'hostile objects' of commerce. He meant to fight the clean, antiseptic dehumanization of the American marketplace with objects that seemed to fairly ooze with life's juices. In 1961 he wrote: 'I am for an art that takes its lines from life itself, that twists and extends and accumulates' ... Oldenburg was confident that, in the end, 'the reality of art will replace reality.'"

Hard Edge

Hard Edge or Hard Edged Abstraction came to its height during the 1950s. The work of Ellsworth Kelly (b. 1923) and Frank Stella (b. 1936) best illustrates this style: flat color areas have hard edges that carefully separate them from each other. Essentially, Hard Edge is an exploration of design for its own sake. Stella often abandons the rectangular format in favor of irregular compositions to be sure that his paintings bear no relationship to windows. The shape of the canvas is part of the design itself, as opposed to being a frame or a formal border within which the design is executed. Some of Stella's paintings have iridescent metal powder mixed into the paint, and the metallic shine further enhances the precision of the composition. *Tahkt-i-Sulayman I* (Fig. **13.13**) stretches 20 ft (6 m) across and intersperses wonderfully surging circles and half-circles of yellow and green, reds and blues. The intensity of the surface counters the grace of its form with jarring fluorescence. The simplicity of these forms deceptively counters the variety of their repetitions. Stella's work exhibits pure bilateral symmetry, and yet the use of color changes all that through its seemingly infinite variations among the identically described semicircles. The work appeals through the complexity of its simplicity.

Environmental Art

Environmental Art creates an inclusive experience. In *Jardin d'Email* (zhahr-DAN deh-MEHL; Fig. **13.14**) by Jean Dubuffet (doo-boo-FAY; 1901–85), an area is made of concrete covered with white paint and black lines. It is capricious in form and surrounded by high walls. Inside the sculptural environment are a tree and two bushes made of polyurethane. We might conclude that Dubuffet has pushed the essence and boundaries of art to their limits. He has consistently opted for chaos, for *art brut*—the art of children, psychotics, and amateurs. The *Jardin d'Email* is one of a small series of projects in which he depicts the chaotic, disorienting, and inexplicable in three-dimensional form.

Architectural Modernism

The new age of experimentation took late-nineteenth-century architects in a new direction—upward. Late in the period—not until a man named Elisha Graves Otis (1811–61) had invented a safe elevator—the skyscraper was designed in response to the need to create commercial space on limited property in burgeoning urban areas.

An influential figure in the development of the skyscraper and in the whole philosophy of modern architecture was Louis Sullivan (1856–1924). The first truly modern architect, he worked in the last decade of the nineteenth century in Chicago, then the most rapidly developing metropolis in the world. Sullivan designed build-

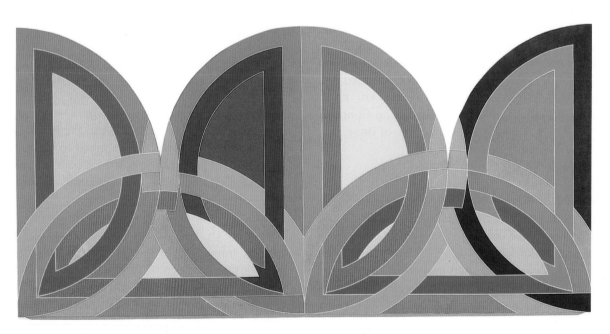

13.13 Frank Stella, *Tahkt-i-Sulayman I*, 1967. Polymer and fluorescent paint on canvas, 10 ft ¼ in × 20 ft 2¼ ins (3.04 × 6.15 m). Pasadena Art Museum, California (Gift of Mr. and Mrs. Robert A. Rowan).

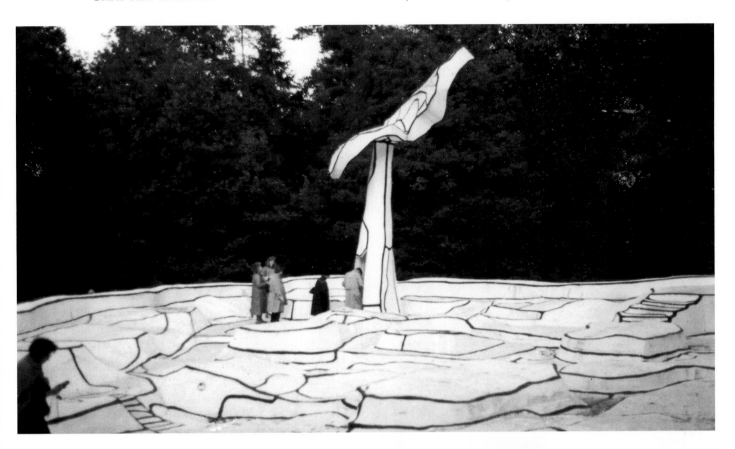

13.14 *(above)* Jean Dubuffet, *Jardin d'Email*, 1973–4. Concrete, epoxy paint, and polyurethane, 66 ft 8 ins × 100 ft (20 × 30 m). State Museum Kröller-Müller, Otterlo, The Netherlands.

ings characterized by dignity, simplicity, and strength. Most importantly, he created a rubric for modern architecture by combining form and function: in his theory, the former flows from the latter. As Sullivan said to an observer of the Carson, Pirie, & Scott building (Fig. **13.15**), "It is evident that we are looking at a department store. Its purpose is clearly set forth in its general aspect, and the form follows the function in a simple, straightforward way."[2]

Structural expression and preoccupation with building materials dominated the early twentieth century, as it had the nineteenth. Of vital importance in architecture was reinforced concrete, or ferroconcrete. It had been in use since around 1850, but nearly fifty years elapsed before it emerged fully as an important architectural material. Auguste Perret (peh-reh; 1874–1954) single-mindedly set about developing formulas for building with ferroconcrete, and his efforts were influential in the works of those who followed. Some of the implications are evident in Perret's Garage Ponthieu in Paris (Fig. **13.16**). The reinforced concrete structure protrudes from the façade, and glass or ceramic panels fill the open spaces. The result is a certain elegance and a logical expression of strength and lightness.

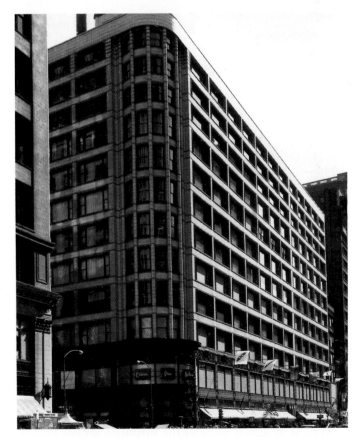

13.15 Louis Sullivan, Carson, Pirie, & Scott Department Store, Chicago, 1899–1904.

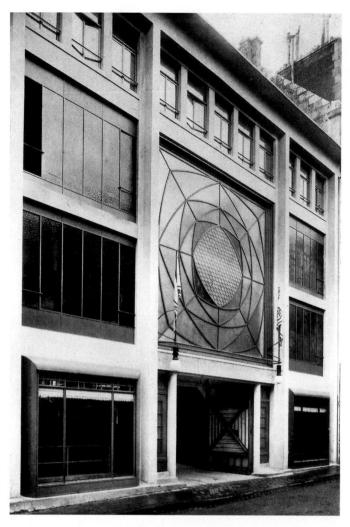

13.16 Auguste Perret, Garage Ponthieu, Paris, 1905–6.

Perret's contemporary, Frank Lloyd Wright (1867–1959; see Profile, p. 106), was one of the most innovative and influential of twentieth-century architects. While Perret encapsulated and continued earlier traditions, Wright initiated new ones. One of Wright's creations, the Prairie Style, which was developed around 1900 and drew upon the flat landscape of the Midwest for its tone. Wright's Prairie houses reflected Japanese influence in their simple horizontal and vertical accents.

As assistant to Louis Sullivan, Wright was influenced in his pursuit of form and functional relationships. Wright attempted to devise practical arrangements for his interiors and to reflect the interior spaces in the exterior appearance of the building (see Fig. 3.39). He also tried to relate the exterior of the building to its context or natural environment.

Wright designed some of the furniture for his houses; comfort, function, and design integration were his chief criteria. Textures and colors in the environment were duplicated in the materials, including large expanses of wood in both the house and its furniture. He made a point of producing multifunctional furniture—for example, tables also served as cabinets. He precisely designed all spaces and objects to present a complete environment. Wright was convinced that houses profoundly influence the people who live in them, and he saw the architect as a "molder of humanity." His works range from the simple to the complex, from the serene to the dramatic, and from interpenetration to enclosure of space. He always pursued experimentation: exploration of the interrelationships of spaces and geometric forms marks his designs (see Fig. 3.22).

A new concept in design emerges in the works of Le Corbusier in the 1920s and 1930s. He espoused a "domino" system of house construction, using a series of poured concrete slabs supported on slender columns. The resulting building was boxlike, with a flat roof that could be used as a terrace (see Fig. 3.31). Much machine-related art in the first half of the century sought depersonalization, but not Le Corbusier's design. Rather, it implied efficient construction from standard, mass-produced parts, logically planned for use in an efficient "house-machine."

World War II caused a ten-year break in architectural construction and, to a certain extent, separated what came after from what went before. However, the gap is bridged by the continuing careers of architects who achieved significant accomplishments before the war. Geographical focus shifted from Europe to the United States, Japan, and even South America. But the overall approach remained modern or international in flavor, which helps us to select a few examples to illustrate general tendencies.

As a type, the skyscraper saw a resurgence in the 1950s, in a glass-and-steel box form. The rectangle, which has so uniformly—and, in many cases, thoughtlessly—become the mark of contemporary architecture, leads us to one of its pre-war advocates.

The German architect Ludwig Mies van der Rohe (roh-uh; 1886–1969) insisted that form should not be an end in itself. Rather, he believed, the architect should discover and state the function of the building. His pursuit of those goals and his honesty in outwardly expressing the shapes of mass-produced materials, including bricks, glass, and manufactured metals, was the basis for the rectangularization that is the common ground of twentieth-century architecture. His search for proportional perfection can be traced, perhaps, to the German Pavilion of the Barcelona Exposition in 1929 and was expressed in projects such as New York's Seagram Building (Fig. 13.18).

Masterworks

Frank Lloyd Wright, Kaufmann House

Frank Lloyd Wright is one of the greatest American artists in any medium. His primary message is the relationship of architecture to its setting, a lesson that some modern architects seem to have forgotten. Wright's buildings seem to grow out of, and never violate, their environment.

One of his most inventive designs is the Kaufmann House, Fallingwater, at Bear Run, Pennsylvania (Fig. **13.17**). Cantilevered over a waterfall, its dramatic imagery is exciting. The inspiration for this house was probably the French Renaissance château of Chenonceaux, built on a bridge across the River Cher. However, Fallingwater is no house built on a bridge. It seems to erupt out of its natural rock site, and its beige concrete terraces blend harmoniously with the colors of the surrounding stone. Wright has successfully married two seemingly dissimilar styles: the house is a part of its context, yet it has the rectilinear lines of the International Style, to which Wright was usually opposed. He has taken those spare, sterile boxes and made them harmonize with their natural surroundings.

Wright's great asset, and at the same time his greatest liability, was his myopic insistence on his own vision. He could work only with clients who could bend to his wishes. So, unlike many architects, whose designs are tempered by the vision of the client, what Wright built was Wright's, and Wright's only. See the Companion Website: Architecture, Frank Lloyd Wright.

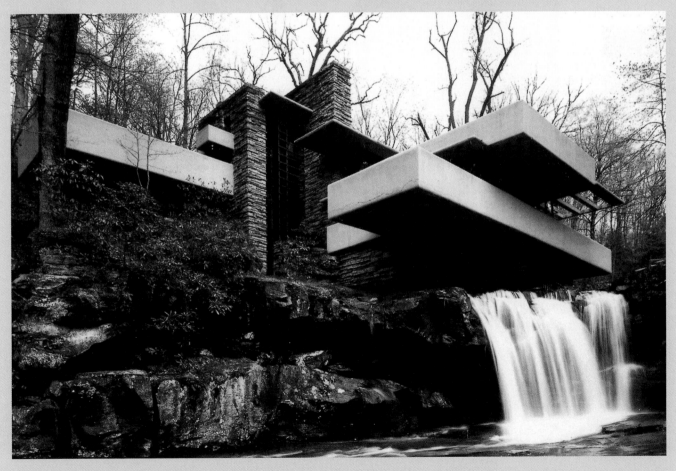

13.17 Frank Lloyd Wright, Fallingwater (Kaufmann House), Bear Run, Pennsylvania, 1936–7.

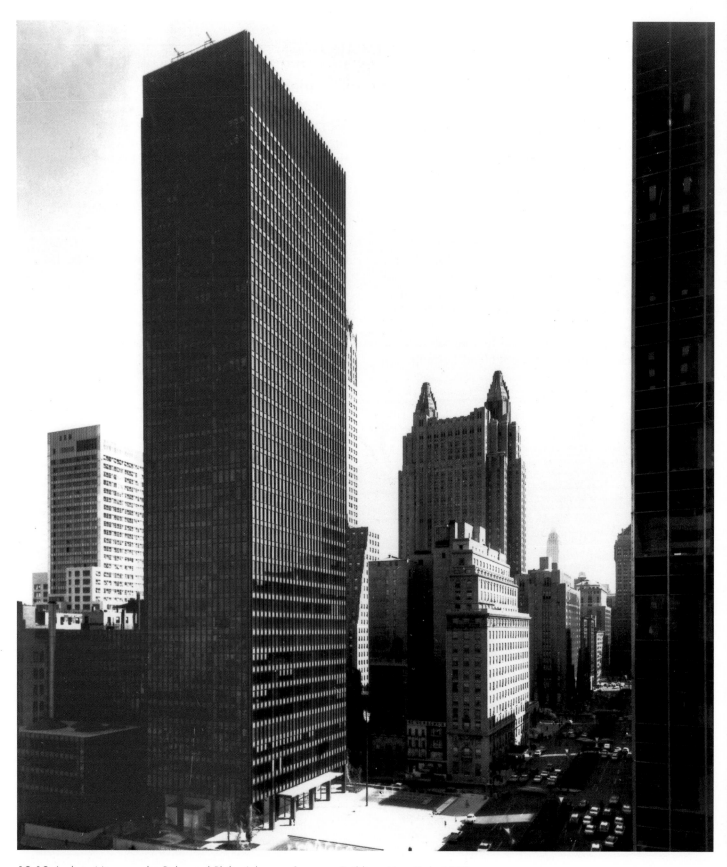

13.18 Ludwig Mies van der Rohe and Philip Johnson, Seagram Building, New York, 1958.

Contemporary design has ultimately pursued the question formulated by the American architect Louis I. Kahn (1901–74), "What form does the space want to become?" In the case of Frank Lloyd Wright's Guggenheim Museum (see Fig. 3.39), space has become a relaxing spiral that reflects the leisurely progress one should make through an art museum.

Modernism in Music

Modernism in music took no less radical a path from its nineteenth-century heritage than it did in painting and sculpture. Nevertheless, contemporary concert programs illustrate that response to works of art remains always in the present tense. Our own responses to the meanings in works of art are those of today, whether the artwork was created this morning or 20,000 years ago. So we have the luxury of sharing experiences directly with Michelangelo, Shakespeare, Leonardo da Vinci, J.S. Bach, and the architects of Athens, as well as with artists of our own era who illuminate and comment upon the events and circumstances that surround us. Our contemporaries may, and do, choose to follow the traditions of the past and invent new ones.

Twentieth-century music took both paths. The radical one diverges from the past essentially in three ways. The first is rhythmic complexity. Prevailing tradition since the Middle Ages has emphasized grouping beats together in measures. The accents of duple and triple meters have helped to characterize and unify compositions. But Modernist composers have done away with these regular accents, choosing instead to employ complex, changing rhythms in which it is virtually impossible to determine meter, or even the actual beat.

The second change from the past concerns dissonant harmonies. Prior to the late nineteenth century, musical convention in the West centered upon consonance as the norm to which all harmonic progressions returned. Dissonance was used to disturb the norm. The late nineteenth century witnessed significant tampering with that concept. By the twentieth century, composers were using more and more dissonance, focusing on it, and refraining from consonant resolution.

The third major change from the past was a rejection of traditional tonality and sense of key altogether. Traditional thinking held that one note, the *do* or tonic of a scale, was the most important. All music was composed with a specific key in mind. Modulations into distant or related keys occurred, but even then the tonic of the original key was the touchstone to which all progression related. In the twentieth century, many composers rejected that manner of systematizing musical sound and chose,

instead, to reject any sense of tonal center. All twelve tones of the chromatic scale thus become equal, and the system is known as *twelve-tone composition*, which was later refined into *serialism*.

The more conservative path saw a transition from the nineteenth to the twentieth century in France that rode primarily on the works of one major composer, the Impressionist Claude Debussy (see p. 346). Debussy's style linked him closely with the French composer Maurice Ravel (1875–1937), who began as an Impressionist but became more and more Classical in orientation as years went by. However, even in his earlier works, Ravel did not adopt Debussy's complex sonorities. Ravel's *Bolero* exhibits strong primitive influences and the unceasing rhythm of Spanish dance music. More typical works of Ravel—for example, his *Piano Concerto in G*— use Mozart and traditional Classicism as their models. As a result of Ravel's tendencies and the similar concerns of other composers—a Classically oriented style was adopted by Camille Saint-Saëns (san-SAHN; 1835–1921), for example—music in the early twentieth century took a Neoclassical direction, maintaining the established conventions of Western music but rejecting both Impressionist and serialist developments.

The American composer William Schuman also took the more traditional path in the 1930s and 1940s. His symphonies have bright timbres and energetic rhythms and focus on eighteenth- and nineteenth-century American folklore. The eighteenth-century American composer William Billings figures prominently in the works of Schuman in the *William Billings Overture* and the *New England Triptych*, based on three pieces by Billings. *American Festival Overture* is perhaps Schuman's most famous composition.

Traditional tonality can also be found in the works of Russia's Sergei Prokofiev. Notwithstanding this, his *Steel Step* reflects the encroachment of mechanization during the 1920s. The machine as a symbol for tremendous energy and motion found its way into music; in the *Steel Step* Prokofiev intentionally dehumanizes the subject in order to reflect contemporary life.

HINDEMITH Experimentation and departure from traditional tonality mark the compositions of the German composer Paul Hindemith (hin-duh-muhth or hin-duh-miht; 1895–1963). Concerned with problems of musical organization, he formulated a systematic solution in the *Craft of Musical Composition*. His music is extremely chromatic—almost atonal. He used "tonal centers," but abandoned the concepts of major and minor keys. He hoped that his new system would become a universal music language, but it did not. He was, however, extremely influential in twentieth-century music composition, both as a composer and a teacher. His works encompass many genres, including ten operas, art songs, cantatas, requiems, chamber music, sonatas, concertos, and symphonies.

BARTÓK The Hungarian composer Béla Bartók (bar-TAWK; 1881–1945) took another nontraditional approach to tonality. He was interested in folk music. His research into Eastern European folk music is significant, because much of it does not use Western major/minor modality. Bartók invented his own types of harmonic structure, which could accommodate traditional folk melodies. He also used tonal centers, and his music is often harshly dissonant.

As nontraditional as some of his work is, however, Bartók also employed traditional devices and forms. His style was precise and tightly structured. He often developed whole movements from one or two very short motifs. His larger works are unified by repetition of thematic material throughout. Occasionally he even used the Classical sonata form. Textures in Bartók's works are largely contrapuntal, which gives them a melodic emphasis on the motifs that are being developed.

Rhythm is important in Bartók's music—it has great rhythmic energy, employing many different devices, such as repeated chords and irregular meters (always to generate impetus). His use of polyrhythms—that is, various juxtaposed rhythms—creates a nonmelodic counterpoint of unique quality. In part, this reflects the influence of folk song and dance. Bartók's compositions—many piano pieces (including three concertos), six string quartets, the *Concerto for Orchestra*, an opera entitled *Duke Bluebeard's Castle*, and others—all possess a wonderfully spontaneous freshness.

STRAVINSKY Nontraditionalism was followed in other quarters, and with *The Firebird* the Russian composer Igor Stravinsky (1882–1971) came to prominence in 1910. *The Rite of Spring* (music CD track 21) created an even greater impact a couple of years later. Both works were scores for ballets. *The Firebird* was a commission for the Russian impresario Sergei Diaghilev, and premièred successfully at the Paris Opéra, while *The Rite of Spring* caused a near riot and a great scandal as a result of its revolutionary orchestrations, dissonance, and driving primitive rhythms. The piece had a great impact on twentieth-century music.

In later works, Stravinsky adopted a Neoclassical style as he attempted to revive Baroque and Classical elements and forms, for example in the oratorio *Oedipus Rex* and the opera *The Rake's Progress*. Toward the end of his life Stravinsky also experimented with serialism.

SCHOENBERG The movement that drew the most attention in the first half of the twentieth century grew out of German Romanticism and took a radical turn into atonality, and the composer at its root was Arnold Schoenberg (SHUHRN-bairk or SHUHRN-buhrg; 1874–1951). Between 1905 and 1912 Schoenberg turned away from the gigantic Post-Romantic works he had been composing to a more contained style. He broke down the musical texture, alternating timbres swiftly and fragmenting rhythm and melody. In 1911 Schoenberg wrote *Six Little Piano Pieces, op. 19*. In these he made some advances in his new style and eliminated some of the traditional procedures, for example, repetition or recall of earlier musical statements. These short pieces contain only nine to eighteen measures. Nonetheless, each constitutes a tiny but freestanding presentation of expression. Listen to number 5, "Etwas rasch" (rather quick) on the music CD track 20.

Although the word "atonality" (without tonality) is used to describe Schoenberg's works, he preferred the term "pantonality"—that is, inclusive of all tonalities. His compositions use any combination of tones without the necessity of having to resolve chordal progressions. He called that concept "the emancipation of dissonance."

By 1923 Schoenberg was composing in twelve-tone technique, in which a row or series of the twelve tones in an octave is used in order before any note can be repeated. The tone row can then be used upside down, backward, or upside down and backward. This serial arrangement can also be applied to rhythm and dynamics. The logical structure of the technique is mathematical and somewhat formalized, but it does maintain a complete absence of key sense, and a balance between emotion and mechanization. The important thing for a listener to understand about these works that stand outside conventional tonal organization is the fact that they contain their own internal logical order.

IVES AND COPLAND Ives and Copland were both Americans with experimental styles. Charles Ives (1874–1954) was so experimental and ahead of his time that many of his compositions were considered unplayable and did not receive public performances until after World War II. Content to remain anonymous, and financially able to do so, as he had a separate career working in insurance, Ives went unrecognized for many years. His melodies spring from folk and popular songs, hymns, and other, often familiar, material, which he treated in most unfamiliar ways. He experimented with quarter tones, polytonality, and polyrhythms. His rhythms are often irregular and without measure delineation except for an occasional bar line to indicate an accent beat. Some of the tone clusters in his piano music are unplayable without using a block of wood to depress all the necessary keys at once. Ives's experimentations, such as the *Unanswered Question*, employ ensembles placed in various locations to create stereophonic effects. For Ives, all music related to life's experiences and ideas, some of which were consonant and some dissonant, and his music reflected that philosophy accordingly.

Aaron Copland (1900–90) integrated national American idioms into his compositions. Jazz, dissonance, Mexican folk songs, and Shaker hymns all feature in his work. The latter figure prominently in Copland's most significant work, *Appalachian Spring*. First written as a ballet, it was later reworked as a suite for symphony orchestra. Some of Copland's music is reserved and harmonically complex, and some simple. He often used all the tones in the diatonic scale simultaneously, particularly in the opening chord of a work. Despite a diversity of influences, he achieved a distinctive personal style that is traditionally tonal. His manipulation of rhythms and chords was highly influential in twentieth-century American musical composition.

Modern Dance

DUNCAN Romantic ballet had become conventional and static by the late nineteenth century. The remarkable Isadora Duncan (1878–1927) introduced a revolutionary new style. By 1905 she had gained notoriety for her barefoot and deeply emotional dancing. She was considered to be controversial among balletomanes and dance reformers alike.

Although an American, Isadora Duncan achieved her fame in Europe. Her dances interpreted moods suggested to her by music or nature. Her costume was loose and flowing, inspired by Greek tunics and draperies, and the fact that she did not wear dancing shoes was deeply significant—this unconventional approach stuck, and it continues to this day in the modern dance tradition she helped to form.

DENISHAWN Isadora Duncan's contemporary Ruth St. Denis and her husband, Ted Shawn, were to lay more substantial cornerstones for modern dance. St. Denis's dancing began as a strange combination of exotic, Oriental interpretations and Delsartian poses. (Delsarte is a nineteenth-century system originated by François Delsarte as a scientific examination of the manner in which emotions and ideas are transmitted. His overzealous disciples formed his findings into a series of graceful gestures and poses, which supposedly denoted specific things.) St. Denis's impact on dance was solidified by the formation with her husband of the Denishawn company and school to carry on her philosophies and choreography. Their headquarters were in Los Angeles. A totally eclectic approach to dance was followed—any and all traditions were included, from formal ballet to Oriental and American Indian dances.

GRAHAM First to leave Denishawn was Martha Graham (1894–1991), probably the most influential figure in modern dance. Although the term modern dance defies accurate definition and satisfies few, it remains the most appropriate label for the nonballetic tradition Martha Graham has come to symbolize. She maintains that artistic individualism is fundamental. "There are no general rules. Each work of art creates its own code." Even modern dance has come to include its own conventions, however, principally because it tries so hard to be different from formal ballet. Ballet movements are largely rounded and symmetrical. Therefore, modern dancers emphasize angularity and asymmetry. Ballet stresses leaps and bases its line on toework, while modern dance hugs the floor and dancers go barefoot. As a result, the early works of Graham and others tended to be rather fierce and earthy, as opposed to graceful. But beneath it all was the desire to express emotion first and foremost, disregarding the execution of conventional positions and movements on which ballet is based. Martha Graham has described her choreography as "a graph of the heart."

Her ballets, often concerned with the psychological exploration of mythological themes, include *Primitive Mysteries* and *Circe*. After the Depression, when social criticism formed a large part of artistic expression, Graham pursued topical themes concerning the shaping of America, including her renowned work to the music of Aaron Copland, *Appalachian Spring*. It dealt with the effects of Puritanism and depicted the overcoming of its fire and brimstone by love and common sense (see box on p. 177).

CUNNINGHAM Martha Graham's troupe produced a radical and controversial choreographer who broke with many of the traditions of modern dance (as flexible as those traditions have been). He incorporated chance elements into his choreography and has often been associated with the composer John Cage. Merce Cunningham (b. 1919) uses everyday activity as well as dance movements in his works. His concern is for the audience to see dance in a new light; his choreography is radically different from anyone else's. His works show elegance and coolness, as well as a severely abstract quality. Dances such as *Summerspace* and *Winterbranch* illustrate Cunningham's use of chance, or indeterminacy. He thoroughly prepares numerous options and orders for sets, which can then be varied and intermixed in different orders from performance to performance (sometimes the choices are made by flipping a coin). The same piece may thus appear different from one night to the next. Cunningham also treats space as an integral part of the performance and allows focus to be spread across various areas of the stage, unlike classical ballet, which tends to concentrate its focus on center stage or downstage center alone. So Cunningham allows audience members to choose where to focus, as opposed to forcing that focus. Finally, he tends to allow each element of the dance to go its own way. As a result, the direct, beat-for-beat relationship that audiences have come to expect between music and footfalls in ballet and much modern dance simply does not exist.

LATER DEVELOPMENTS Since 1954, another graduate of Martha Graham's troupe (and also of Merce Cunningham's) has provided strong direction in modern dance. The work of Paul Taylor (b. 1930) has a vibrant, energetic, and abstract quality that often suggests primordial actions. Taylor, like Cunningham, often uses strange combinations of music and movement in highly ebullient and unrestrained dances such as *Book of Beasts*. Taylor's music often turns to Classical composers, such as Beethoven, and to specialized works like string quartets. The combination of such formal music with his wild movements creates challenge for the audience.

In a tradition that encourages individual exploration and independence, there have been many accomplished dancer/choreographers, among them Alvin Ailey (see p. 395) and Alwin Nikolais. Nikolais designs scenery, costumes, and lights and composes the music, as well as the choreography—his works tend to be mixed-media extravaganzas celebrating the electronic age. Often the display is so dazzling that the audience loses the dancers in the lighting effects and scenic environment. Twyla Tharp and Yvonne Ranier are other choreographers who have experimented with space and movement.

Literary Modernism

Modernism in literature, as in the other arts, represented a self-conscious break from traditional forms and subject matter in favor of a distinctly contemporary manner of expression. Early on, it had a radical and Utopian emergence from new ideas in the sciences and social sciences, particularly Freudian psychoanalysis. We can find modernism in both fiction and poetry. In fiction, characters involve themselves in some kind of quest. They seek to pull themselves together, find meaning in a confusing world, and live all they can. Modernist fiction writers

sought to illustrate the disorder of their environment, raising their characters to a level of honor and dignity in a largely dishonorable and undignified world. In so doing, the modernists strove for "newness," originality, and boldness.

Modernism, a widely diverse catch-all of approaches, included fiction writers such as D. H. Lawrence (1885–1930), Ernest Hemingway (1898–1961), and William Faulkner (1897–1962), to name but a few. These writers enriched subject matter and technique, challenging traditional forms of the novel, and traditional concepts of time and space.

Modernist poetry, as exemplified by the works of Ezra Pound (1885–1972) and T. S. Eliot (1888–1965), reflected a movement called imagism. Imagism, utilized concrete language and figures of speech, modern subject matter, and metrical freedom. It avoided romantic or mystical themes. Formulated by Pound around 1912, the imagists' verse had succinctness and clarity with exact visual images comprising a total poetic statement. T. S. Eliot reflects also the sobering effects of World War I, and *The Waste Land* (1922) presents a prevailing sense of disillusionment and fragmentation that represents the full emergence of modernism in poetry.

POSTMODERN DIRECTIONS

As suggested in the Context section of this chapter, postmodernism represents an amalgam of disparate, individual approaches dating variously to the post-World War II years. One artist who represents this melange of styles, sculptor Joel Shapiro (b. 1941), gradually evolved his art into the production of miniature clay, glass, copper, and lead pieces shaped objectively. One particular aspect of his works illustrates the use of a variety of media, some of which are new and require new techniques. The mixing of media in previously untried ways provides new avenues of experimentation and mastery as well as providing works of art that look different from those of the past. Shapiro's works graduated from clusters of small geometric pieces—spread out on the floors of galleries where the actual space in which they were assembled became an important element—to large-scale stick figures exhibiting precarious balance, such as *Untitled* (Fig. **13.19**). Cast in metal, it retains the texture and apparent construction methods of the wood from which Shapiro made it.

Neoabstraction

By the mid-1980s young artists sought to make their mark by reacting against the Postmodernist trends. Many of them returned to abstraction and near-abstraction,

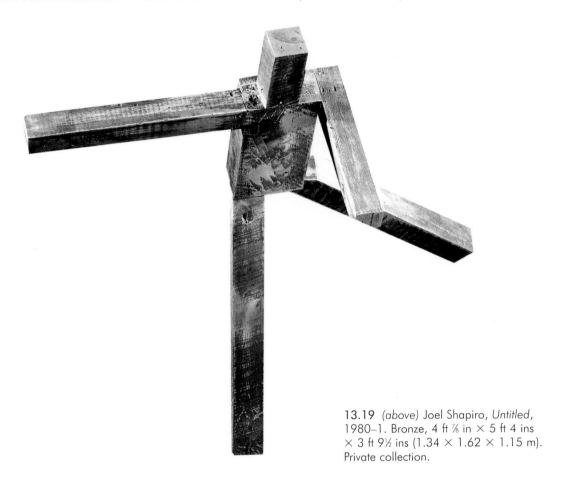

13.19 *(above)* Joel Shapiro, *Untitled*, 1980–1. Bronze, 4 ft ⅞ in × 5 ft 4 ins × 3 ft 9½ ins (1.34 × 1.62 × 1.15 m). Private collection.

including Hard Edge (see p. 376). These Neoabstractionists make up a loose confederation of mostly individualistic approaches. An example is the work of Lynda Benglis (b. 1941), a painter who has turned to sculpture. Her work also represents Process Art—that is, taking molten materials, letting them flow freely on the floor, and then adding color and/or shape to them. *Passat* (Fig. **13.20**) illustrates how she shapes knots, bows, and pleats into insectlike sculptures in shiny metal. Like the Postmodernists, Neoabstractionists borrow freely from others by modifying or changing the scale, media, or color of older works to give them a new framework and, hence, new meaning. Occasionally, the new meanings include sarcasm and satire and often comment on the decadence of contemporary American society.

"New" Realism

The realistic style of the nineteenth century (see p. 339) returns from time to time, and in the new century we find its evidence in the work of a number of young postmodern painters. Some of these approaches employ conventional techniques and traditional approaches to figure depiction in order to illuminate personal and ethnic narratives, including political statements. In other

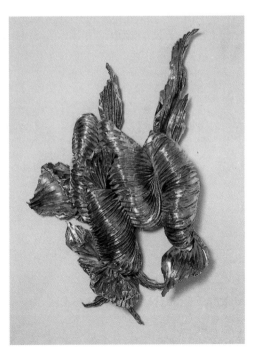

13.20 Lynda Benglis, *Passat*, 1990. Aluminum, 78 × 52 × 27 ins (198 × 132 × 68.5 cm). Paula Cooper Gallery, New York.

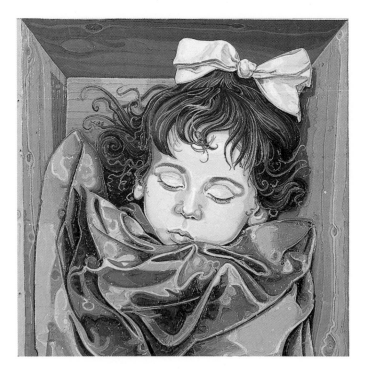

13.21 Julie Roberts, *The Little Girl Rosalia Lombardo, Embalmed*, 2000. Oil on canvas, 19¹¹⁄₁₆ × 19¹¹⁄₁₆ ins (50 × 50 cm). Courtesy Sean Kelly Gallery, New York.

cases, the "New" Realism searches for metaphorical connections between subject matter and ideas. What ties together this variety of individual approaches is the appearance of observable "reality" in the works. Illustrative of the "New" Realist tendency is Julie Roberts

(b. 1963), a Welsh painter based in London. In works such as *The Little Girl Rosalia Lombardo, Embalmed* (Fig. **13.21**), she takes a close look at the realism and drama of human life and death. With detailed clarity and smooth brushstroke, she brings a powerful statement to the viewer, leaving much to the imagination while at the same time creating an effective tension between the paint surface and the disturbing suggestion of the images.

Feminist Art

During the 1970s the feminist artists of the Women's Art Movement attempted to break down old barriers. Substantially as a result of this movement, women began to achieve increased recognition in the art world in America and beyond. Marches, protests, the organization of women's cooperative galleries, active promotion of women artists, critical exploration by women art historians, and the development of a Feminist Art Program at the California Institute of the Arts, in 1971, brought about significant results. One of the founders of the CalArts program, Judy Chicago, provides a good example of the feminist perspective. At the end of the 1960s she began to use feminine sexual imagery to reveal the sexism of the male-dominated art world. *The Dinner Party* (Fig. **13.22**) records the names of 999 notable women, and pays homage to thirty-nine legendary women, including an Egyptian queen and Georgia O'Keeffe (see p. 370). At each side of the triangular table are thirteen settings (the number of witches in a coven and the number of men

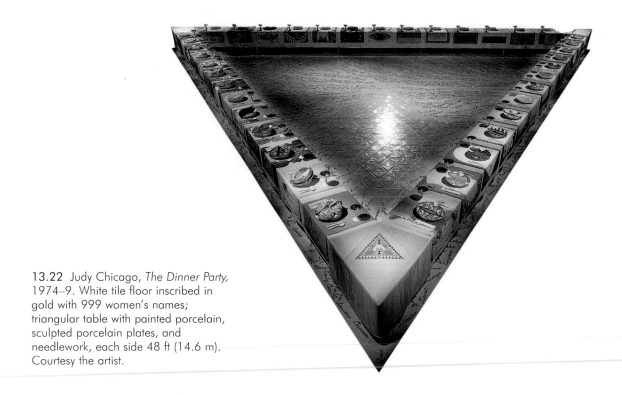

13.22 Judy Chicago, *The Dinner Party*, 1974–9. White tile floor inscribed in gold with 999 women's names; triangular table with painted porcelain, sculpted porcelain plates, and needlework, each side 48 ft (14.6 m). Courtesy the artist.

at the Last Supper). The triangular shape symbolizes woman. During the French Revolution it stood for equality. Each of the place settings at the table features a runner in a style appropriate to the woman it represents, in addition to a large ceramic plate. Included are traditional women's art forms such as stitching, needlepoint, and china painting, which Chicago wished to raise to the status given to painting and sculpture. Suggestions of female genitalia throughout the painting are the artist's comment that that was all the women at the table had in common.

Susan Lacy, whose analysis of the roles played by artists we examined on page 19, collaborated with Leslie Labowitz in a performance piece (see Performance Art, p. 137) called *In Mourning and Rage* (1977) outside the Los Angeles City Hall to protest violence against women in American cities. This example of political art, which we discussed as a function of art on page 21, utilized the image of mourning in a stark and elaborate event designed to promote action. The artists secured media coverage and followed the event with a number of talk-show appearances, a rape hotline, and other related activities.

Postmodern Architecture

Past styles find new manifestations in Postmodern or Revisionist architecture. The Spanish architect Ricardo Bofill (boh-FEEL; b. 1939) and the Italian Aldo Rossi (1931–97) have both derived much of their architectural language from the past. As Bofill remarked, his architecture takes "without copying, different themes from the past, but in an eclectic manner, seizing certain moments in history and juxtaposing them, thereby pre-figuring a new epoch." We see this in his public housing development called, with typical grandiosity, the Palace of Abraxas (Fig. **13.23**). Here columnar verticality is suggested by glass and by cornice/capitals, which dynamically present characteristics of Classicism. Postmodern architecture focuses on meaning and symbolism: the past and ornamentation are acceptable; functionalism no longer controls. The Postmodernist seeks to create buildings "in the fuller context of society and the environment." Social identity, cultural continuity, and sense of place become foundations for art.

In a clear repudiation of the glass and steel box of the International Style and other popular forms in mainstream architecture, the design for the Pompidou (pahm-pee-doo) Center in Paris (Fig. **13.24**) turns the building inside out, externalizing its network of ducts, pipes, and elevators while hiding the internal structure, which has no fixed walls—temporary dividers can be arranged in any desired configuration. The bright primary colors of the exterior combine with serpentine, plexiglass-covered

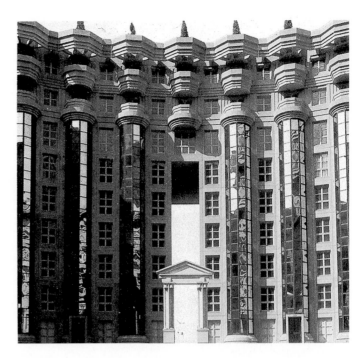

13.23 Ricardo Bofill, Palace of Abraxas, Marne-la-Vallée, near Paris, 1978–93.

escalators to give a whimsical, lively appearance to a functional building. The Pompidou Center (also known by Parisians as the Beaubourg) has become a tourist attraction rivaling the Eiffel Tower and, although controversial, has wide popular acceptance.

Frank Gehry (GHAIR-ee; b. 1929) has, since the 1970s, focused on projects that center on artistry. His approach creates functional works of sculpture rather than buildings in the traditional sense. The Walt Disney Concert Hall in Los Angeles, California (see Fig. **3.40**), suggests to some the sails of a ship. It can also suggest the turmoil of our times in its "visual chaos." This building, along with Gehry's Guggenheim Museum in Bilbao, Spain (1997), attempts to change the language of architecture. Both works stand like immense sculptures against the background of the city and continue a curvaceous, free-form style that has become the architect's signature. He utilized similar abstract components in other buildings such as the Gehry House in Santa Monica, California (1979) and the Fishdance Restaurant in Kobe, Japan (1986–9), which employs a similarly sleek curvaceous cladding. The forms of the building take on sculptured dimensions so complex that they required an advanced aerospace computer program to allow the contractor to build the building in a reasonable way. The sculptural design of Disney Hall may be so futuristic that it hearkens back to the style of futurism itself and Boccioni's *Unique Forms of Continuity in Space* (see fig. **13.4**).

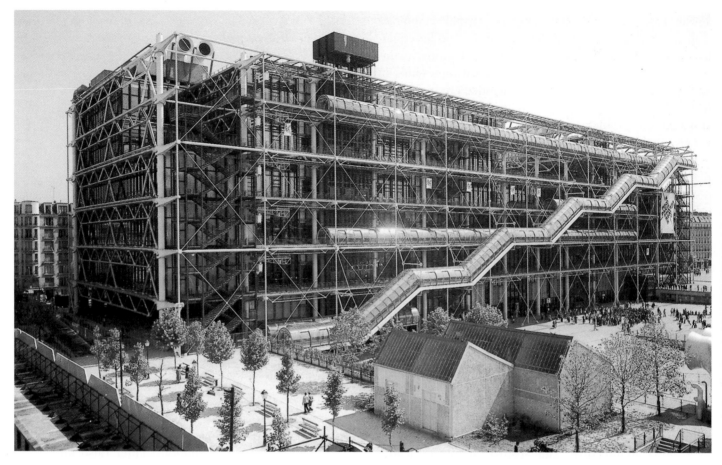

13.24 Renzo Piano and Richard Rogers, Pompidou Center, Paris, 1971–8.

Postmodern Music

Postmodern music challenges the very concept of "high art" or traditional Western concert music. Postmodernists would view "art music" as reflective of bourgeois (upper middle class) values. Finally, the aesthetic of postmodern music encompasses music from approximately 1960 to the present and employs an obvious use of mixed media, irony, humor, and self-parody. Our examination will pause briefly on four topics: minimalism, experimentation, improvisation and *musique actuelle*, and sound liberation.

MINIMALISM In the mid-1960s a musical development called minimalism occurred. Although sharing some roots with the modernist visual art style by the same name, minimalist music reacted against the complexity of serialism and the randomness of aleatory or chance music. The characteristics of minimalism in music include clear tonality, a steady beat, and repetition of short melodic patterns. It maintains a constancy of dynamic levels, texture, and harmony that tends to create almost a trancelike effect. Many of the minimalist composers showed strong influences of non-Western cultures. Another characteristic of minimalist music rests in the desire of its composers to bring their music to the widest possible audience. After the 1970s, minimalist music witnessed an increase in richness in its harmonies, tone colors, and textures. We glimpse a bit of this style in a short excerpt from Philip Glass's (b. 1937) opera *Akhnaten* (1984). The third of Glass's operas, it makes use of minimalist techniques in creating the aforementioned hypnotic repetitions of musical cells. The text uses various languages, including English, Egyptian, and Hebrew, with Akhnaten's "hymn to the sun," Aton (see p. 215), in the language of the audience, although our excerpt is instrumental (music CD track 24).

EXPERIMENTATION Experimentation with *microtones* has been of interest to composers and music theorists throughout history, and many non-Western cultures employ them routinely. Microtones comprise intervals smaller than a half step. The traditional Western system divides the octave into twelve equal half steps. But why

Profile

Richard Danielpour (b. 1956)

Richard Danielpour can be characterized as a "traditionalist" composer. He studied at the New England Conservatory and the Juilliard School, and also trained as a pianist. Speaking of his rise in the ranks of recognized composers, Danielpour reflected, "From the beginning, it was agonizing. It was like waiting for a Polaroid to develop, but the Polaroid took 10 years instead of 30 seconds." Indicative of his standing in the music world is his collaboration with Nobel Prize-winning writer Toni Morrison on a piece titled "Sweet Talk," premiered by Jessye Norman at Carnegie Hall.

In the early 1980s Danielpour moved away from the complexities of Modernism toward a more accessible style. As a result, his music's large and romantic gestures, brilliant orchestrations, and vibrant rhythms appeal to a wide cross-section of the public. In this regard, some critics have compared him to Leonard Bernstein, Aaron Copland, Igor Stravinsky, Dmitri Shostakovich, and other twentieth-century masters. "As I got older, I was aware of a number of different strands coming together in my music, rather than seeing myself on a mission with one particular ax to grind," he said. He calls himself an assimilator rather than an innovator. By utilizing familiar and unthreatening styles as a basis for his compositions, he has been able to win over even conservative audiences.

In the process of finding the means to express his message, Danielpour draws from many resources. "For me style is not the issue," he said. "It's how well a piece is written on a purely technical level. If other composers see themselves as superior just because their music may be more 'original,' that's O.K. That's not what I'm about." His "American-sounding rhythmic swagger," easy lyricism, and keen understanding of instrumental color create an appealing formula.

Although reluctant to discuss his music's spiritual component, he tends to label supposedly abstract instrumental works with intriguing, metaphysical titles. The movements of his Piano Quintet, for example, are "Annunciation," "Atonement," and "Apotheosis." Such titles, he admits, can be distracting. "Maybe it would be better not to have any at all," he said. When he does discuss spirituality in music, he doesn't hesitate to place himself in good company. "Some of my favorite composers," he said, "are also philosopher-composers who find themselves addressing questions about life and death in the very music they write: Mahler, Shostakovich, Bernstein."

He speaks of the creative process in spiritual and perhaps eccentric terms. "Where is the music received from?" he asked. "Where do your dreams come from? Composing is like being in a waking dream. To me the where is not important. It's intuition that has to lead the way and thinking that has to follow it. To speak of the mind first is worthless."

Perhaps typical of all professionals in today's music world, he has a sense of the business side of music. He knows about contracts and commissions and how to be in the right place at the right time. Nonetheless, Danielpour insists that he is no more active in self-promotion than his colleagues.[3] Learn more at www.schirmer.com/composers/danielpour_bio.html.

---

might the octave not be divided into twenty-four, fifty-three, ninety-five, or any number of parts? The possibilities are limited only by our ability to hear such intervals and a performer's ability to produce them. Alois Haba experimented in the early part of the century with quarter tones (twenty-four per octave) and sixth tones (thirty-six per octave) and Charles Ives did much the same thing. Musicians designed a number of instruments to produce microtones and experimented with them widely.

Composers also questioned the limitations of the traditional concert hall. Early work by Cage and others led to theatre pieces, multimedia or mixed-media pieces, so-called danger music, biomusic, soundscapes, happenings, and total environments that might include stimulation of all the senses in some way. Thus they often obscured the distinctions between the composer and the playwright, the filmmaker, the visual artist, and so on.

Theatre music, which is sometimes called "experimental music," may be relatively subtle, with performers playing or singing notated music and moving to various points on the stage, as in Luciano Berio's (b. 1925) *Circles* (1960). Or it may be more extreme, as in the works of La

Monte Young, where the performer is instructed to "draw a straight line and follow it," or to exchange places with the audience. In Nam June Paik's *Homage to John Cage*, the composer ran down into the audience, cut off Cage's tie, dumped liquid over his head, and ran out of the theatre. Later he phoned with the message that the composition had ended. Needless to say, such compositions contain a considerable degree of indeterminacy.

Some works were never intended to be performed, but only conceptualized, such as Nam June Paik's *Danger Music for Dick Higgins*, which instructs the performer to "creep into the vagina of a living whale" or Robert Moran's *Composition for Piano with Pianist*, which instructs the pianist to climb into the grand piano.

IMPROVISATION AND *MUSIQUE ACTUELLE* Composers such as Lukas Foss, who wrote a suite for soprano and orchestra that includes jazz improvisation, pursued an open, improvisatory tradition. Foss founded the Improvisation Chamber Ensemble, and a number of other improvisation groups sprang up in the United States during the 1960s. During this period, intense exploration of new sound possibilities using both conventional and electronic instruments also occurred. Electronically produced music, specifically the electronic altering of acoustically produced sounds, came to be called *musique concrète*.

In the late 1990s, improvised music, viewed as the cutting edge of musical style, took the name *musique actuelle* (mue-ZEEK akt-yoo-EL). It freely draws on jazz and rock and exudes vibrancy, liveliness, and personal expression. Its literal translation means "current," and it represents a number of subfactions. Illustrative of this approach, Gianni Gebbia's (JAHN-ee GEHB-ee-ah) trio reflects one of the heroes of musique actuelle, Evan Parker. Gebbia's music integrates three strains, American jazz, free improvising, and traditional Sicilian music. Always in musique actuelle there appears a strain of humor—for instance, the vocalist in Gebbia's trio might alternate between phrases reminiscent of opera and phrases utilizing nasal whines and fearsome guttural groans in two simultaneous pitches.

SOUND LIBERATION The Polish composer Krzysztof Penderecki (KRIHS-tov pen-der-EHT-skee; b. 1933) is widely known for his instrumental and choral works, including a major composition, the *Requiem Mass* (1985). Most notably, Penderecki has experimented with techniques to produce new sounds from conventional stringed instruments.

His *Polymorphia* (1961) uses twenty-four violins, eight violas, eight cellos, and eight double basses. He has invented a whole new series of musical markings listed at the beginning of the score. In performance, his timings are measured by a stop watch and have no clear meter. *Polymorphia* uses a free form, achieving its structure from textures, harmonies, and string techniques. The piece is dissonant and atonal.

It begins with a low, sustained chord. The mass of sound grows purposefully, with the entry of the upper strings, and then the middle register. Then comes a section of glissandos (slides), which can be played at any speed between two given pitches, or with what amounts to improvisation. A climax occurs, after which the sound tapers off. Then a number of pizzicato (plucked) effects are explored. Fingertips tap the instruments, and the palms of the hands hit the strings, leading up to a second climax. After another section exploring bowed, sustained, and sliding sounds, a third climax occurs. After an almost total dearth of melody and defined pitch, the work ends with a somewhat surprising C major chord.

Elliott Carter (b. 1908) developed a highly organized approach toward rhythm often called "metric modulation," in which the mathematical principles of meter, standard rhythmic notation, and other elements are carried to complex ends. Carter's use of pitch is highly chromatic and exact, and his music requires virtuoso playing both from the individual and the ensemble.

Eileen Taaffe Zwilich (b. 1939), who studied with Elliott Carter, earned her own place as an important composer. Her Symphony No. 1 (1983) won a Pulitzer Prize. The third movement of the symphony explodes with percussive effects, driving rhythms, juxtaposed timbres, dramatic dynamic changes, and a pyramidal climactic cadence. She has emerged as a national role model for women composers.

Postmodern Literature

Modernism in literature regarded language as a tool for dealing with philosophical origins—revealing truths about the world. Postmodernism, on the other hand, does not believe that language can reveal truths about the world, but rather, that systems like history and religion, which try to explain things, have only persuasive powers—not truth. In literature, postmodernism encompasses a variety of movements challenging the ideas and practices of modernism. Fundamentally, it has involved reacting against fixed ideas about the form and meaning of texts, especially in the use of *pastiche* and *parody*, the *absurd*, the *antihero*, and the *antinovel*. To illustrate postmodernism, we will comment on the writers Pynchon, Nabokov, and Sontag, and then examine three postmodern styles: concrete poetry, magic realism, and the confessionalists.

Thomas Pynchon (PIHN-chuhn; b. 1937), an American novelist and short-story writer, combines black humor and fantasy to portray human alienation in the chaos of modern society. His masterpiece, *Gravity's Rainbow* (1973) focuses on the idea of conspiracy, and Pynchon fills it with descriptions of paranoid fantasies, grotesque imagery, and esoteric mathematical language. The complex narrative relates the secret development and deployment of a rocket by the Nazis at the end of World War II. The hero, American intelligence officer Lieutenant Tyronne Slothrop, travels a nightmarish journey of "either historic discovery or profound paranoia," depending on the reader's—and the central character's—interpretation.

Vladimir Nabokov's (nuh-BAHW-kuhf or NAHB-uh-kahwf, 1899–1977) best-known novel, *Lolita* (1955), utilizes an antihero, the intellectual pedophile Humbert Humbert, to explore the topic of love in the light of lechery with stylish and intricate language and effects. *Pale Fire* (1962), however, extends Nabokov's mastery of unorthodox structure. It breaks down the boundaries between reality and fantasy. Written in both poetry and prose, it parodies literary scholarship, taking the form of a scholarly edition of a poem that tells the story through the foreword and notes. The plot centers on John Shade, whose last work, *Pale Fire*, has been edited by his next-door neighbor, Charles Kinbote. Both Shade and Kinbote teach at the Ivy League school, Wordsmith College. Kinbote, a refugee from the Eastern European country of Zembla, where a Russian-backed revolution has overthrown the monarchy, turns out to be the deposed king himself. He tries to persuade Shade to write a poetic lament for the Zemblian monarchy, describing his downfall. Zemblian extremists, looking to assassinate the former king, instead accidentally kill Shade. Things get complicated as Kinbote sets about editing the poem and reacting to its content. As illusion intrudes upon reality, we become less sure whether Shade constitutes a madman who thought himself a poet or Kinbote a madman who thought himself a king. The whole thing rings with an air of unreality. Nabokov uses a highly experimental structure with language loaded with external references.

Susan Sontag (1933–2004) gained her reputation through essays on modern culture. Her novel, the historical romance *The Volcano Lover* (1992), portrays the unstable nature of her subject through an examination of a "collection of fates" set primarily in Naples in the eighteenth century (the title refers to the central character's explorations of Mount Vesuvius). Sontag follows the life of Sir William Hamilton, British Ambassador to the King in Naples, through his various collections, and notes how he treated people, particularly his passionate and notorious love, and her infatuation with Lord Nelson. Purportedly factual, the book utilizes a constant narrative in which Sontag eschews the use of quotation marks.

CONCRETE POETRY Drawing on the influences of Dada, surrealism, and other early twentieth-century movements in art, concrete poetry has a strong visual element in which the poet's intent is conveyed through graphic patterns of letters, words, and symbols rather than through the conventional use of language to create expressive and evocative pictures. This differs from an earlier form of poetry, called "pattern poetry," in which words carry the major meaning (as in traditional poetry) but the poet shapes the poem's lines in such a way as to enhance the words' meaning. Concrete poetry relies so heavily on visual imagery that it cannot be read aloud with any sense of meaning. Its effects remain almost solely visual. Concrete poetry has much in common with *musique concrète* in terms of its origins and experimental objectives. Typical of poets using this form are the Brazilians Haroldo and Augusto de Campos (KAHM-poosh; b. 1929 and 1931, respectively) who produced the first exposition of concrete poetry in 1956.

MAGIC REALISM Magic realism, a Latin-American literary movement, incorporates fantastic or mythic elements into otherwise realistic fiction. Perhaps the master of this form is Gabriel García Márquez (ghahr-SEE-ah MAHR-kays; b. 1928), a Columbian-born author and journalist who won the 1982 Nobel Prize for Literature. His best-known work, *One Hundred Years of Solitude* (1967), tells the story of Macondo and its founders, the Buendía family. An epic tale of seven generations, it spans the years of Latin-American history from the 1820s to the 1920s during which patriarch Arcadio Buendía built the Utopian city of Macondo in the middle of a swamp. As time elapses, the city and the family slip into depravity. Finally, a hurricane totally obliterates the city. Complex fantasy combined with realism mark this book, making it a superb example of the magic realist genre.

CONFESSIONALISTS An important contribution to the postmodern movement comes from the confessional poets and writers who center upon autobiographical material (real or fictitious) which reveals intimate and hidden details of the subject's life. The revelation of such personal and often painful elements emerges particularly in the works of Sylvia Plath and Robert Lowell. Sylvia Plath (1932–63) wrote carefully crafted poems of deep personal imagery and intense focus. Many deal with themes such as alienation, death, and self-destruction. Little known at the time of her death by suicide, she had gained the status of a major contemporary poet by the 1970s. Robert Lowell (1917–77) won a 1947 Pulitzer Prize for his first major work, *Lord Weary's Castle*, which contained two of his most praised poems, "The Quaker

Graveyard in Nantucket" and "Colloquy in Black Rock." Active in the civil rights and anti-war campaigns of the 1960s, Lowell won a second Pulitzer Prize for literature in 1977.

PLURALISM

African American Art

HARLEM RENAISSANCE From 1919 to 1925 Harlem, a small enclave in New York City, became the international capital of African culture. "Harlem was in vogue" wrote the poet Langston Hughes (see p. 394). African American painters, sculptors, musicians, poets, and novelists joined in a remarkable artistic outpouring. The period became intensely controversial, its artistic merits attacked by some critics of the time as isolationist and conventional; the qualities of the Harlem Renaissance still provoke debate. Nonetheless, this period of intense creative activity by African Americans "gave the artists an identifiable artistic context for their work, propelled them to the forefront of the New Negro Movement, and inspired their art for the remainder of their careers."[4]

The artistic works of this period reached a national audience through exhibitions sponsored by the Harlem Foundation. The movement explored several themes: African American heritage; the traditions of African folklore; and the daily life of African American people. In every case the Harlem Renaissance artists broke with previous African artistic traditions. They celebrated their history and culture and "defined a visual vocabulary for Black Americans."[5]

Intellectuals such as W. E. B. Du Bois, Alain Locke, and Charles Spurgeon spearheaded the movement. Among the notable artists were social documenter and photographer James van der Zee (1886–1983), painter Palmer Hayden (1890–1973), the painter Aaron Douglas (1899–1979), painter William Henry Johnson (1901–70), the painter Jacob Lawrence (1917–2000), the sculptor Meta Vaux Warrick Fuller (1877–1968), and the poet Langston Hughes (1902–67).

Painter Palmer Hayden (Peyton Cole Hedgeman) trained at the Cooper Union in New York in 1919 and later at the Boothbay Art Colony. In 1927 he traveled to Europe and studied at the Ecole des Beaux Arts. His work was exhibited widely in New York and despite its symbols of ethnic heroism it drew heavy criticism from those who believed that his depictions mocked African American people and sustained negative stereotypes. Later in life he created the John Henry series, twelve oil paintings portraying the life and death of a folk hero. This was part of his focus on African American legends, which visually expressed the wealth of material from the African American oral culture of the rural South and from Africa itself. His main approach was to use folk themes to illustrate industrial America's dependence on the African American labor force.

Aaron Douglas, perhaps the foremost painter of the Harlem Renaissance, earned a bachelor of fine arts degree from the University of Nebraska and a master's degree from Columbia University. His training encouraged him to explore the rich vocabulary of African American myth and culture. His highly stylized work explores a palette of muted tones, and gained fame through its appearance as illustrations and cover designs for many books by African American writers. His mural *Aspects of Negro Life*, at the New York Public Library's Cullen Branch, documents in four panels the emergence of an African American identity. The first panel portrays the cultural background in images of music, dance, and sculpture. The next two bring to life slavery and emancipation in the American South and flight to the cities of the North. The fourth panel returns to the theme of music. Among Douglas's wide variety of stylistic approaches, his realistic portrait of Aalta (Fig. 13.25) provides a warm and relaxed composition. Its palette and expression show dignity, elegance, and stability.

William Henry Johnson trained at the National Academy of Design in New York, followed by a three-year fellowship in 1926 to study in Europe. Under the influence of the European Impressionists and Realists, his style grew in personal expressiveness. His many works focus on African American experience. Harlem, where he spent his childhood, is the central theme. Just prior to World War II his style changed again, moving from fully rounded to flat figures.

In Jacob Lawrence's works, such Modernist effects—for example, the flattening of space and the use of undifferentiated planes of color—are secondary to the need to convey an intelligible narrative to the viewer (Fig. 13.26). Having trained at the Harlem Art Workshop and the American Artists' School in New York, he is a fine example of an artist acutely aware of his privileged position and, at the same time, his membership of a dispossessed and disadvantaged section of society.

Sculptor Meta Vaux Warrick Fuller "was the first Black American artist to draw heavily on African themes and folklore for her subjects."[6] Years before the Harlem Renaissance, she began to express the pan-African ideals that later permeated the movement. After finishing graduate work at the Pennsylvania Museum and School for Industrial Arts, she studied in Paris at the Ecole des Beaux Arts and the Académie Colarossi. One of her mentors was the sculptor Auguste Rodin (see p. 346), and his

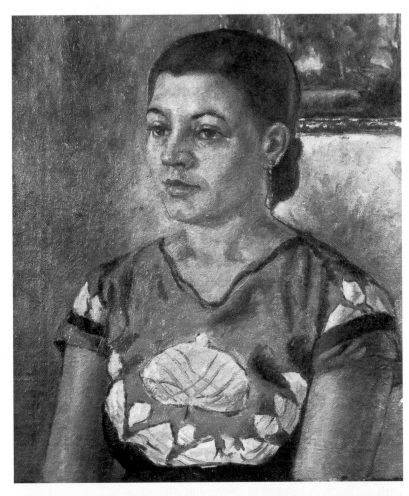

13.25 (*left*) Aaron Douglas, *Aalta*, 1936. Oil on canvas, 18 × 23 ins (45.7 × 58.4 cm). Carl Van Vechten Gallery of Fine Arts, Fisk University (Afro-American Collection of Art).

13.26 (*below*) Jacob Lawrence, "One of the most violent race riots occurred in East St. Louis," Panel 52 from *The Migration Series*, 1940–1; text and title revised by the artist, 1993. Tempera on gesso on composition board, 12 × 18 ins (30.5 × 45.7 cm). The Museum of Modern Art, New York (Gift of Mrs. David M. Levy).

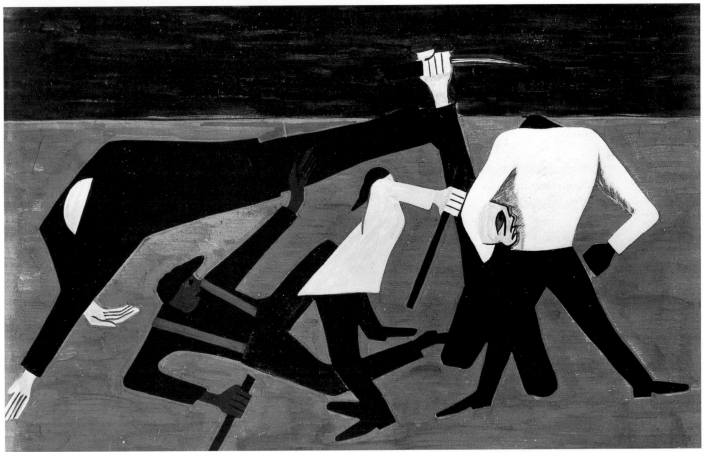

influence appears in her impressionistic surface treatment of Romantic Realist subjects. Fuller built her own studio in Framingham, Massachusetts, and focused on themes dealing with antislavery and protests against injustice to African Americans. In one of the earliest works by an American focusing on the African heritage, her sculpture *Ethiopia Awakening* shows an Egyptian woman emerging from her embalming wrappings. "The work symbolically represents the emergence of Black cultural awareness from the 'wrappings' of ignorance and oppression, and the beginnings of the end of colonial rule in Africa."[7] Works such as *The Talking Skull* are based on African models and illustrate the confrontation of humans with death, a prevalent theme in her career.

Poet Langston Hughes is often called the "poet laureate of Harlem." He portrays the life of the ordinary African American in the United States, catching with sharp immediacy and intensity the humor, pathos, irony, and humiliation of being black in America. His poetry particularly appeals to young people. He speaks of the basic qualities of life: love, hate, aspirations, and despair. Yet he writes with a faith in humanity in general. He interprets all life as it is experienced in the real world, as well as touching on the ideal. Hughes struggled within himself between what he wanted to express and what his audience expected him to write. Thus some of his work is militant, with broad sociopolitical implications.

Hughes received considerable attention as a poet as early as 1921 with his poem "The Negro Speaks of Rivers." In his novel *Not Without Laughter*, he creates a brilliant portrayal of an African American youth's passage into manhood. In the selections that follow, readers can sense something of the African American experience and perception of the universe.

Theme for English B

Langston Hughes
1902–67

The instructor said,
    Go home and write
    a page tonight.
    And let that page come out of you—
    Then, it will be true.
I wonder if it's that simple?

I am twenty-two, colored, born in Winston-Salem.
I went to school there, then Durham, then here
to this college on the hill above Harlem.
I am the only colored student in my class.
The steps from the hill lead down into Harlem
through a park, then I cross St. Nicholas.

Eighth Avenue. Seventh, and I come to the Y,
the Harlem Branch Y, where I take the elevator
up to my room, sit down, and write this page:
It's not easy to know what is true for you or me
at twenty-two, my age. But I guess I'm what
I feel and see and hear, Harlem, I hear you:
hear you, here me—we two—you, me, talk on this page.
(I hear New York, too) Me—who?
Well, I like to eat, sleep, drink, and be in love.
I like to work, read, learn, and understand life.
I like a pipe for a Christmas present,
or records—Bessie, bop, or Bach.
I guess being colored doesn't make me not like
the same things other folks like who are other races.
So will my page be colored that I write?
Being me, it will not be white.
But it will be
a part of you, instructor.
You are white—
yet a part of me, as I am a part of you,
that's American.
Sometimes perhaps you don't want to be a part of me.
Nor do I often want to be a part of you.
But we are, that's true!

As I learn from you
I guess you learn from me—
although you're older—and white—
and somewhat more free.

This is my page for English B.

Harlem

Langston Hughes

What happens to a dream deferred:

Does it dry up
like a raisin in the sun?
Or fester like a sore—
and then run?
Does it stink like rotten meat?
Or crust and sugar over—
like a syrupy sweet?

Maybe it just sags
like a heavy load.

Or does it explode?[8]

JAZZ Jazz developed out of a variety of venues—streets, bars, brothels, and dance halls—in New Orleans. Played mostly by African American musicians, it employed improvisation, syncopation, a steady beat, unique tone colors, and specialized performance techniques such as "blues," which became a national craze among African Americans in the 1920s. Probably the most popular blues song ever written in W. C. Handy's (1873–1958) "St. Louis Blues" (music CD track 25). The melody contains the Afro-Spanish habanera rhythms that Handy heard when he toured Cuba with his minstrel show at the turn of the twentieth century. He borrowed the final strain in the song from "Jogo Blues," an instrumental piece he had written the year before, whose melody came from Handy's preacher. Another type of blues, vocal blues, is intensely personal and often has references to sexuality, the pain of desertion, and unrequited love, with a very specific metrical and poetic form consisting of two rhythmic lines and a repeat of the first line. At the end of the nineteenth century, performers like Bessie Smith gave the blues an emotional quality, which the accompanying instruments tried to imitate.

We do not known exactly when jazz developed because for many years it existed solely in performance rather than being written down. Almost no jazz pieces found their way to recordings before 1923, and none at all before 1917 when the Original Dixieland Jazz Band made a recording. Jazz blended elements from diverse musical cultures, including West Africa, America, and Europe. Several important characteristics developed from the West African traditions. These included emphasis on improvisation, percussion, rhythmic complexity, and a characteristic called "call and response." Call and response forms the core of West African tribal music and consists of a soloist who sings a phrase to which a chorus responds. Jazz uses this when a voice or instrument is answered by an instrument or group of instruments.

Jazz found its materials in the rich fabric of black music such as spirituals, work songs, and gospel hymns. Out of this deep well came jazz as we know it in its wide variety of substyles, including New Orleans style (Dixieland), swing, bebop, cool jazz, and free jazz. In the New Orleans style, the front line, or melodic instruments improvise several contrasting melodic lines at once, supported by a rhythm section clearly marking the beat and providing a background of chords. New Orleans style typically has a march or church melody, ragtime piece, or popular song as its base.

Swing developed in the 1920s and flourished from 1935 to 1945. This is a "big band" style, ideal for dancing, and it worked its way into the forefront of American popular music. Bebop is a complex jazz style, typically for small groups. It developed in the 1940s and made its appeal to active listening rather than dancing. The term

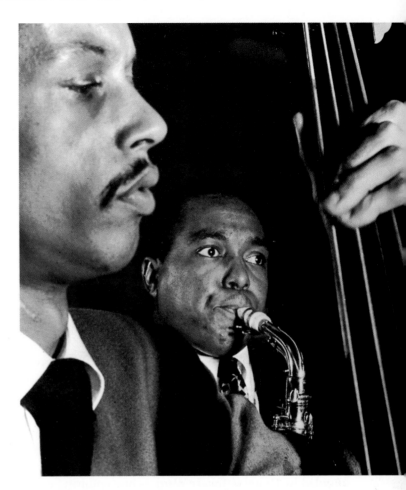

13.27 Saxophonist Charlie Parker in performance with Tommy Potter. Parker died prematurely in 1955, aged 35, but by that time he was already a legendary figure.

was coined as a result of the characteristic long-short triplet rhythm that ended many of its phrases. Its prime developers were alto saxophonist Charlie "Bird" Parker (Fig. 13.27) and trumpeter Dizzie Gillespie. Cool jazz developed in the 1950s and relates to bebop, but it has a more relaxed character that relies on arrangements. During the 1960s, free jazz developed and departed from traditional jazz in that it does not base on regular forms and established chord patterns.

The American dance scene has benefited from a number of exceptional choreographers of African American heritage who draw upon their culture. Among these was Alvin Ailey (1931–89), a versatile dancer whose company is known for its unusual repertoire and energetically free movements. Another form of dance that has its roots in Africa, but which draws upon the broad experiments of modern dance, is *jazz dance* (see Chapter 7). Like modern dance in general, its form and direction are still in flux. Nevertheless, stemming from sources as diverse and yet as allied as tribal Africa and the urban ghetto, it has seen significant activity and experimentation throughout the United States (see Figs. 7.8 and 7.9). Pioneered by choreographers such as Asadata Dafora Horton in the 1930s and Katherine Dunham and Pearl Primus in the 1940s, jazz dance flourished at the end of the century under choreographers such as Talley Beatty and Derglas MacKayle.

Theatrical liberation of the African American began in the 1960s. One manifestation of the civil rights movement of the 1950s and 1960s was the angry, militant African Americans who espoused "Black consciousness." Many converted to the African Muslim version of Islam, and many longed for a completely separate "Black nation." Radical groups talked about destroying Western society. A number of African Americans turned toward Africa and sought a new identity in the Third World. In the 1980s, there was a change in self-description from Black to African American. Many of these ideas were expressed in the works of playwrights such as LeRoi Jones (who became Imamu Amiri Baraka). His plays dramatize the dangers of Blacks allowing Whites into their private lives and call for racial separation. Charles Gordonne's *No Place to Be Somebody* renews Baraka's cause, and espouses violence as legitimate action in the penetrating story of a fair-skinned Black searching for his own racial identity.

Many new African American theatre companies emerged in the 1960s. The Negro Ensemble Company, founded by Douglas Turner Ward, is one enduring example. It staged a moving production of *Home* by Samm-Art Williams. *Home* traces the ups and downs in the life of an African American Southerner named Cephus. Raised on a farm, he leaves for the big city. Convicted of draft evasion and sent to jail, he progresses to joblessness and welfare, disease and despair. Finally, he returns to the honest labor and creative values on the farm. The poetic language and the conventions of its production format give *Home* a unique and endearing quality. Cephus is played by a single actor, but all the other roles—old, young, male, female, Black, White—are played by two women who take on whatever role they wish by changing costumes. Sometimes they are characters in Cephus's journey and other times they act as a chorus, helping the audience to follow leaps in time and space. The chorus format helps the audience to see Cephus from the point of view of African American history and culture. Although Cephus is constantly on the move, the stage setting never changes, and although the actresses play several different roles, they never change. Through these devices, the playwright suggests that "home" is at hand all the time, waiting to be grasped. The force that stands in the way is unwillingness: to acknowledge one's inner yearnings, to accept help from others, and to extend oneself by choosing a path of peace instead of confrontation.

The son of a White father and a Black mother, August Wilson (1945–2005) writes with an ear tuned to the rhythms and patterns of the blues and the speech of African American neighborhoods. He founded the Playwrights Center in Minneapolis. His plays range from *Jitney* and *Ma Rainey's Black Bottom* in the 1980s to *Two Trains Running* and *Seven Guitars* in the 1990s. Wilson believes that the African American has the most dramatic story of all humankind to tell. His concern lies with the stripping away of important African traditions and religious rituals from Blacks by Whites. In plays such as *The Piano Lesson*, he portrays the complexity of African American attitudes toward themselves and their past. Both the blatant and the more subtle conflicts between Black and White cultures and approaches form the core of Wilson's work and can be seen in plays such as *Fences*.

Fences treats the lives of African American tenement-dwellers in Pittsburgh in the 1950s. Troy Maxson, a garbage collector, takes great pride in his ability to hold his family together and to take care of them. As the play opens, Troy discusses his challenge to the union concerning Blacks' access to doing the same "easy" work as Whites. He is frustrated and believes that he has been deprived of the opportunities to get what he deserves—and this becomes a central motif. He describes his wrestling match with death in 1941 when he had pneumonia. He also tells of his days in the African American baseball leagues, barred from playing in the majors because of his race.

American Indian Art

Since World War II, American Indians struggled to avoid succumbing to a sense of despair about their culture's demise as it assimilated into the general American "melting pot." Writers in particular made the assault on such feelings a major focus of their works. In 1969, Scott Momaday's (b. 1934) novel *House Made of Dawn* won a Pulitzer Prize and made a new generation of American Indian writers aware of a powerful message: people caught between cultures can, despite a variety of problems, find ways to survive.

A House Made of Dawn explores the story of a young Tano Indian named Abel who returns to his village in New Mexico's Cañon de San Diego in 1945 after army service in World War II only to discover that he has entered a hell between two cultures. His grandfather Francisco's world—and the world of Francisco's fathers before him—remains a world of seasonal rhythms, a harsh and beautiful place defined by unremitting poverty; a land with creatures, traditions, and ceremonies reaching back thousands of years. However, the urban world of postwar white America, with its material abundance and promises of plenty, draws Abel away from his people. The choice causes Abel great pain. He winds up in prison, wanders to Los Angeles, and catapults into a life of dissipation, disgust, and despair. Torn between pueblo and city, between ancient ritual and modern materialism, between starlight and streetlight, Abel drops further and further into a state of anguish. He must find a way to reaffirm the ancient ways and truths of his people while discovering a place for himself in a world greatly at odds with those truths. "May it be beautiful all around me," prays the Night Chanter. Abel persists in seeking a path to that beauty.

Paula Gunn Allen (b. 1939) is a representative of many American Indian writers. She believes that Momaday's book created a new future for her: it "brought my land back to me." She says that she and many American Indians suffer from "land sickness"—a deep sense of exile caused by the loss of her land and birthright. In passages from *House Made of Dawn*, Gunn Allen found that she shared a familiarity with the places Momaday described: "I knew every inch of what he was saying." It gave her the strength and inspiration—the will—to continue. In her poem "Recuerdo," she creates images of movement, loss, and of searching. She looks for a sense of "being securely planted."

Recuerdo
Paula Gunn Allen

I have climbed into silence trying for clear air
and seen the peaks rise above me like the gods.
That is where they live, the old people say.
I used to hear them speak when I was a child
and we went to the mountain on a picnic
or to get wood. Shivering in the cold air then
I listened and I heard.

Lately I write, trying to combine sound and memory,
searching for that significance once heard and nearly lost.
It was within the tall pines, speaking.
There was one voice under the wind—something in it
that brought me to terror and to tears. I wanted
to cling to my mother so she could comfort me,
explain the sound and my fear, but I simply sat,
frozen, trying to feel as warm as the campfire,
the family voices around me suggested I should.

Now I climb the mesas in my dreams.
The mountain gods are still, and still I seek.
I finger peyote buttons and count the stalks of sweetsage
given me by a friend—obsessed with a memory
that will not die.
I stir wild honey into my carefully prepared cedar tea

and wait for meaning to arise,
to greet and comfort me.

Maybe this time I will not away.
Maybe I will ask instead what that sounding means.
Maybe I will find that exact hollow
where terror and comfort meet.
Tomorrow I will go back and climb the endless mesas
of my home. I will seek thistles drying in the wind,
pocket bright bits of obsidian and fragments
old potters left behind.[9]

CERAMICS AND PAINTING Pottery was the greatest of the prehistoric arts, and it continues almost completely as an aesthetic activity. Early pottery vessels, however, were designed for everyday use, and finishing techniques took second place to practical concerns—most important was to get the object into use. By the late twentieth century, time-honored traditions of Southwestern pottery rose in quality of finish and design to the status of high art. Thus, the culture has been sustained. American Indian potters today, however, face the challenge of deciding on the degree to which younger artists should master—that is, replicate—traditional forms, as opposed to expressing individual creativity while still maintaining cultural traditions. Lucy Lewis's ceramic bowl (Fig. **13.28**) reflects this challenge. It follows the traditions of Acoma pottery but does not reflect traditional design.

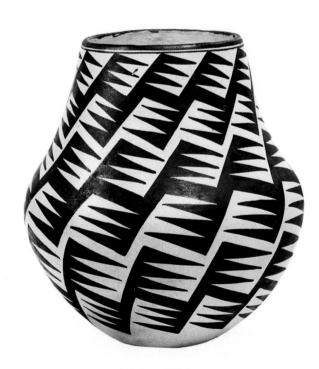

13.28 Lucy Lewis, ceramic bowl, from the Pueblo area, Acoma, New Mexico, 1969. National Museum of the American Indian, Smithsonian Institution, Washington, D.C.

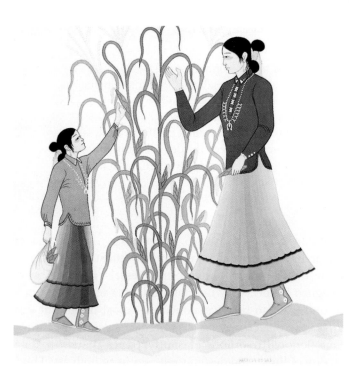

Other Southwestern artistic forms include silver-smithing—the popular silver and turquoise jewelry is still made—and sand painting. Sand paintings incorporate important religious meanings, and many rituals cannot be performed without them. The traditional materials of American Indian art—indigenous and easily accessible—were supplemented in the twentieth century by standard Western media—for example, watercolor. In Figure **13.29** one of the foremost Navajo painters documents typical American Indian life. One characteristic aspect of American Indian watercolor painting from the middle of the last century is this use of space: the painting stays on the surface plane and no background or spatial environ-

13.29 (*left*) Harrison Begay, *Women Picking Corn*, mid-20th century. Watercolor, 15 × 11½ ins (38.1 × 29.2 cm). National Museum of the American Indian, Smithsonian Institution, Washington, D.C.

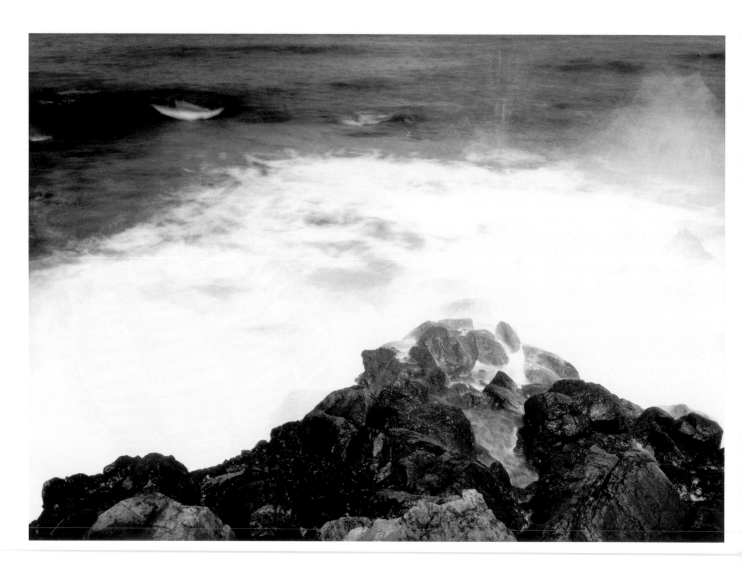

ment appears. The women and the corn are the only concerns. They are rendered in two dimensions with only the diminutive size of the woman on the left to hint at three-dimensional space or perspective. The horizon line, or viewer's eye level, is at the bottom of the painting.

Using an 1898 field camera and shooting only one image of each location, Thomas Joshua Cooper, a member of the Cherokee nation, composes his images, such as *The Mid North-Atlantic Ocean* (Fig. **13.30**), so that the scale of the composition is not always immediately apparent. The printing of the pieces further enhances the intensely emotive nature of his work. Renowned for his technical mastery of the photographic medium, Cooper uses subtly "under-painted" images with selenium and gold, resulting in blue and maroon tones in the photographic printing process. His painterly process ensures the uniqueness of each individual print. Cooper presents an image that comforts the viewer, in this case composing the picture with a stable (almost High Renaissance) triangle at the base of the image that counters the roiling sea. Despite the obvious "reality" of the photograph (we see precisely the details of rocks, waves, and sea), the work possesses an abstract quality in the manner in which Cooper divides the composition, tonally, into three distinct areas.

American Indian music continues as an important part of cultural reality. For example, Inuit music has developed into an artform with complex rhythms using contrasting accents and meters. Its melodies are fairly conjunct, creating a gentle and undulating quality, but the style can be declamatory—similar to the recitatives that are found in Western operas.

In Northwest-coast music, only the owner of a song is permitted to perform it. However, it is possible to buy a song, to inherit it, or even to obtain it by murdering the owner. Additionally, songs are owned by secret societies within the tribes. In musical terms, Northwest music uses parallel harmonies sung by separate voices and *drone* notes (single notes sustained while the remaining parts sing on). Rhythms tend toward strongly percussive and intricate patterns.

Songs among the Southwestern American Indians, especially the Pueblos, have a complex tonal system. They are based on six- or seven-note scales and stay at the low end of the register. This is in contrast to the music of the Plains Indians, who tend to use high pitches. Nearly every social occasion, holy day, and ceremony has its own special music.

13.30 *(left)* Thomas Joshua Cooper, *West—Mid North-Atlantic Ocean. Punta de la Calera, The Isle of La Gomera, The Canary Islands,* 2002. Silver gelatin print, 28 × 35.8 ins (71 × 91 cm).

Latino Art

Diego Rivera (ree-BAY-rah; 1886–1957) revived the fresco mural as an art form in Mexico in the 1920s. Working with the support of a new revolutionary government, he produced large-scale public murals that picture contemporary subjects in a style that blends European and native traditions. The fresco painting *Slavery in the Sugar Plantation* (Fig. **13.31**) creates a dramatic comment on that chapter in Mexican history. The composition is not unlike Goya's *Execution of the Citizens of Madrid, May 3, 1808* (see Fig. **12.2**). A strong diagonal sweeps across the work, separating the oppressed from the oppressor, and provides a dynamic movement stabilized by the Classically derived arcade framing the top of the composition. Rivera's wife, Frida Kahlo, whose work we discussed as an example of Surrealism (see p. 371), was one of the most celebrated painters of the early twentieth century. Her style reflects Mexican folk culture and her deep feeling for the power and beauty of folk art.

Rafael Ferrer (b. 1933), born in Puerto Rico, creates an exotic, mysterious world of the tropics in *El Sol Asombra* (Fig. **13.32**). A lively palette dominates the painting, and the relationship of the central structure to those surrounding it gives the work a slightly unsettling sense of space. The painting has a surface flatness, given its simplified and flattened shapes and tonally even colors. Ferrer's use of light energizes the composition and creates an inviting series of patterns. The title of the painting means "the sun with shade or shadow," and we suspect a play on words because, although the title describes the work accurately, there is mystery in the lightness juxtaposed against the dark.

Jose Bedia (BAY-dee-ah; b. 1959), a Cuban painter and installation artist, draws the viewer into *Si se quiere, se puede* (*If you want to, you can*; Fig. **13.33**). The painting raises ideas about leaving Cuba, and the image of a man on a boat shaped like an anvil, coupled with the title and the restricted palette, raises questions to which the viewer wants to respond. The flat starkness and black and blue palette of Bedia's rendering create a confrontational and engaging image. We are left to ponder the larger issues.

Theatre of the Spanish-speaking communities of America reflects and serves a diverse population. It dates to the conquistadors and grew significantly during the civil rights struggles of the 1960s. In the summer of 1965, Luis Valdez joined Cesar Chavez to use improvisational theatre to underscore the plight of the migrant worker and give political impetus to the farm workers' strike in Delano, California. This led Valdez to form El Teatro Campesino (Farm Workers' Theatre). Using Valdez as a model, a number of other Chicano theatre groups

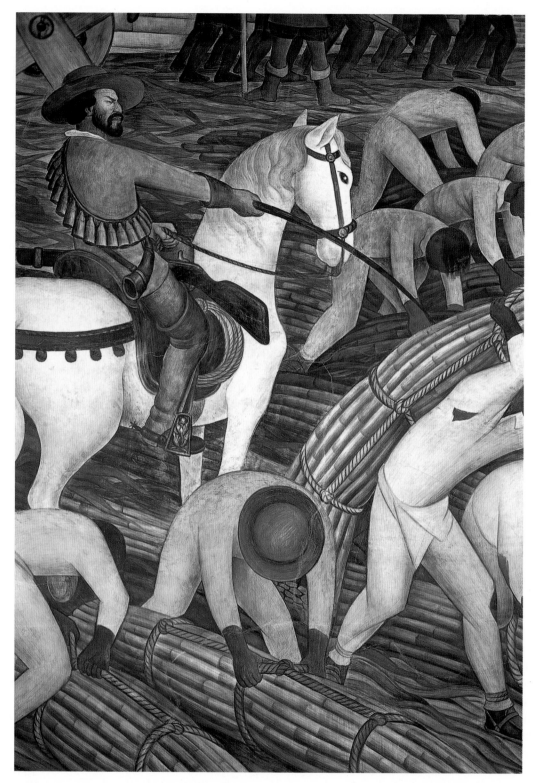

13.31 Diego Rivera, *Slavery in the Sugar Plantation, Tealtenago, Morelos* (detail), 1930–1. Fresco, 14 ft 3 ins × 9 ft 3 ins (4.35 × 2.82 m). Palace of Cortez, Cuernavaca, Mexico.

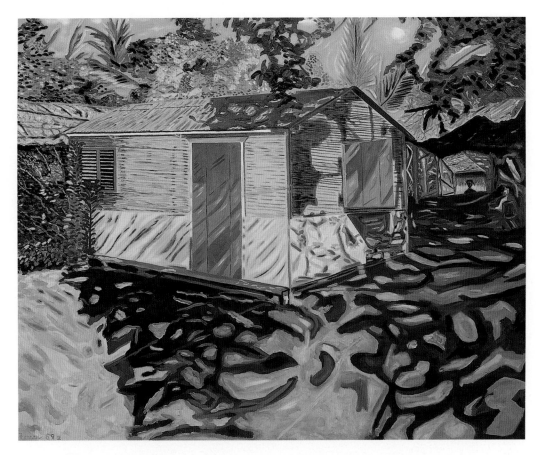

13.32 Rafael Ferrer, *El Sol Asombra*, 1989. Oil on canvas, 5 × 6 ft (1.52 × 1.83 m). Courtesy Nancy Hoffman Gallery, New York.

appeared during the 1960s and 1970s, including Jorge Huerta's (WAR-tah) Teatro de la Esperanza ("Theatre of Hope"). A number of Latino playwrights have emerged as well, including Estela Portillo Trambley.

The curious label *Nuyorican theatre* applies to Puerto Rican culture in New York, which typically deals with bilingual and working-class situations. This ethnic consciousness produces a diversity of street theatre, prison productions, and small non-profit Hispanic theatres such as Teatro Repertorio Español and the Puerto Rican Traveling Theatre. The term Nuyorican began to arouse negative responses when themes of crime, drugs, abnormal sexuality, and generally aberrant behavior became associated with the movement.

Nuyorican poetry came into being in the 1960s and 1970s and now enjoys a nationwide standing. Anthony Morales (b. 1981) represents the latest generation. He dedicated a poem read at the Nuyorican Poets Café, in New York City, to the founders of the stage where he stood—among them poet and playwright Miguel Piñero, subject of the film *Piñero* (2001), starring Benjamin Bratt:

to those stoned crazy prophets of revolution,
giving poetic solutions to political pollution,
organizing rhythmic confusion of assimilation
to this untied states nation of eggs, cheese and bacon
upon wakin'.

Morales, a native of the Bronx, majored in English and Latino studies at Columbia University and speaks of the heroin-infested, crime-ridden, self-destructive world of Piñero. His literary tradition, like that of Piñero, comes from the Puerto Rican experience in the United States. "My poetry is about trying to make sense of the world, of being a young Puerto Rican male. ... We have incredible stories we got to tell." Piñero's play *Short Eyes* (1974)—a prison drama presented by Joseph Papp's Public Theater and at Lincoln Center—won the New York Drama Critics Circle Award for best American play. It was developed in a workshop at the Ossining Correctional Facility (Sing Sing), where Piñero was serving time for armed robbery. That year Piñero, known as Miky, helped found the Nuyorican Poets Café. Piñero died of cirrhosis of the liver in 1988, at age 41 (*New York Times*, January 2, 2002).

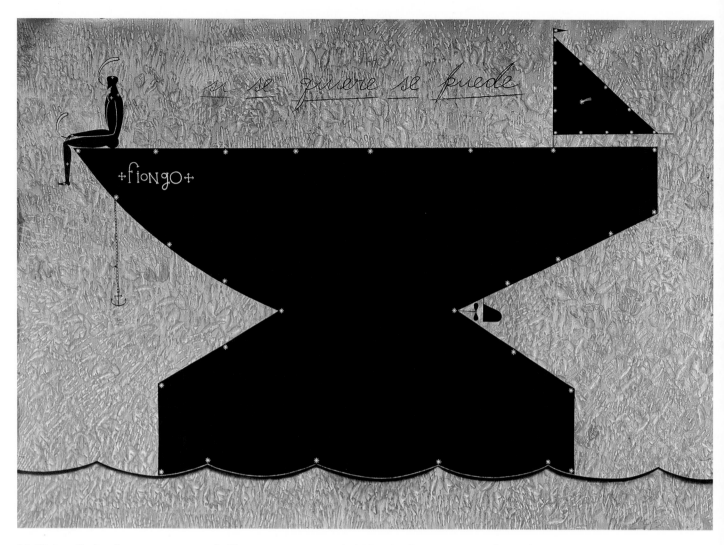

13.33 Jose Bedia, *Si se quiere, se puede (If you want to, you can)*, 1993. Acrylic on canvas, 5 ft × 7 ft 6 ins (1.52 × 2.29 m). Collection of Robertson, Stephens, Inc., San Francisco. Courtesy George Adams Gallery, New York.

Cuban-American theatre emerged as early as the nineteenth century in the Cuban-American communities of New York City and Ybor City-Tampa. The Cuban Revolution of 1959, which brought Fidel Castro to power in Cuba, resulted in large-scale theatrical activity in Cuban-American communities throughout the United States, but principally in Miami and New York. This was primarily political theatre of exile, and themes often include acculturation, bilingualism, culture conflict, and the generation gap between immigrants and their US-raised children.

Nilo Cruz (b. 1960), a Cuban-American playwright, came to America just before his tenth birthday on a Freedom Flight to Miami. He received a master's degree in playwriting at Brown University, and his work has been produced widely around the United States. Winner of a Pulitzer Prize in 2003, his *Anna in the Tropics* opens in 1929 with a mother and her daughters waiting expectantly for the arrival of a ship from Cuba that has on board a lector, someone who will read to them and their co-workers at a cigar-rolling factory in Tampa, Florida. Lectors comprise a long Cuban tradition as a way of enhancing manual labor with culture. Cruz focuses on his own community, using strongly developed female characters to depict the varieties of Latino experience. The central character, Anna, is taken from Tolstoy's novel *Anna Karenina*, which Cruz weaves into the fabric of the play by use of the figure of the lector.

THINKING CRITICALLY

- Using the elements and characteristics of poetry (see Chapter 8), analyze Paula Gunn Allen's poem, "Recuerdo" (see p. 397). What is your personal reaction to the poem and why do you respond to the work in that way?

- Using examples from the text to illustrate your point, compare a sculptural work from twentieth-century Africa with a painting from the Harlem Renaissance to develop an understanding of how the Black experience on two different continents may be alike or different, as seen through a work of art. What is your reaction to these works, and why?

- Using the elements of line and color as well as the characteristics of the styles discussed in the text, compare Picasso's *Demoiselles d'Avignon* (Fig. **13.3**) with Roy Lichtenstein's *Whaam!* (Fig. **13.11**). What is your reaction to these works, and what elements of the works cause it?

- Using the elements and principles of composition as well as the characteristics of the styles discussed in the text, compare Matisse's *Blue Nude* (Fig. **13.2**) with Georgia O'Keeffe's *Dark Abstraction* (Fig. **13.6**). What is your reaction to these works, and what elements of the works cause it?

CYBER STUDY

EXPRESSIONISM:
http://www.artcyclopedia.com/history/expressionism.html

CUBISM:
http://www.artcyclopedia.com/history/cubism.html

FAUVISM:
http://www.artcyclopedia.com/history/fauvism.html

FUTURISM:
http://www.artcyclopedia.com/history/futurism.html

ABSTRACTION:
http://www.artcyclopedia.com/history/neo-plasticism.html

SURREALISM:
http://www.artcyclopedia.com/history/surrealism.html

ABSTRACT EXPRESSIONISM:
http://www.artcyclopedia.com/history/abstract-expressionism.html

POP ART:
http://www.artcyclopedia.com/history/pop.html

NOTES

INTRODUCTION

1 Edwin J. Delattre, "The Humanities Can Irrigate Deserts," *The Chronicle of Higher Education*, October 11, 1977, p. 32.

CHAPTER FIVE

1 August Wilson, *Fences*, in Lee A. Jacobus, *The Bedford Introduction to Drama* (New York: St. Martin's Press, 1989), p. 1055.

2 Pierre Corneille, *Le Cid*, trans. and ed. John C. Lapp (New York: Appleton Century Crofts, 1955), pp. 36–7.

3 *American Theatre Magazine*, January 1991.

CHAPTER SEVEN

1 John Martin, *The Dance* (New York: Tudor Publishing Company, 1946), p. 26.

2 Agnes DeMille, *Martha, the Life and Work of Martha Graham* (New York: Random House, 1991), p. 261.

CHAPTER EIGHT

1 Alice Walker, "Roselilly," from *In Love & Trouble: Stories of Black Women* (Orlando: Harcourt Brace & Company, 1972), copyright © 1972 by Alice Walker, reprinted by permission of Harcourt, Inc.

2 Saki (H. H. Munro), *The Blood-Feud of Toad-Water: A West Country Epic*, from *Reginald in Russia and Other Sketches* (1910). Available online at http://www.ibiblio.org/gutenberg/etext99/rgrus10.txt.

3 Geoffrey Chaucer, *The Canterbury Tales*, trans. J. Nicolson (New York: Crown Publishing Group, 1934), pp. 120–3.

4 William Shakespeare, Sonnet XIX (*Sonnets* published by Thomas Thorpe in 1609). Available online at http://www.ibiblio.org/gutenberg/etext97/wssnt10.txt.

5 John Wesley, *God Brought Me Safe*.

6 Oliver Goldsmith, "The Benefits of Luxury, in Making a People more Wise and Happy."

7 William Shakespeare, "The Seven Ages of Man," from *As You Like It*, Act II, scene vii, 139–66.

8 Robert Frost, "Stopping by Woods on a Snowy Evening," from *The Poetry of Robert Frost*, ed. Edward Connery Lathem (New York: Holt, Rinehart & Winston, 1969). Copyright 1923, © 1969 by Holt, Rinehart, & Winston. Copyright 1951 by Robert Frost. Reprinted by permission of Henry Holt & Company.

9 K. L. Knickerbocker and W. Willard Reninger, *Interpreting Literature* (New York: Holt, Rinehart, & Winston, 1969), p. 218.

CHAPTER NINE

1 Common usage today has changed the references B.C. (Before Christ) and A.D. (*Anno Domini*, "the year of our Lord," i.e. after Christ) to B.C.E. (Before Common Era) and C.E. (Common Era).

2 Revised Standard Version Bible.

3 Homer, *The Iliad*, prose version by Andrew Lang, W. Leaf, and E. Myers (1883). Available online at http://www.ibiblio.org/gutenberg/etext02/iliab10.txt.

CHAPTER TEN

1 In each Greek tragic contest a playwright was required to present four plays in succession—three tragedies and a satyr play.

2 Aeschylus, *Agamemnon*, trans. Peter D. Arnott, in *An Introduction to the Greek Theatre* (Bloomington: Indiana University Press, 1963), pp. 76–7.

3 The chorus was a distinctive feature of Greek drama, portraying the dual function (in the same play) of narrator and collective character responding to the actors.

4 Virgil, *Aeneid*, trans. Theodore C. Williams (New York: Houghton Mifflin, 1938), p. 1.

5 Revised Standard Version Bible (Oxford: Oxford University Press, 1977).

6 "Rings around the Pantheon," *Discover*, March 1985, p. 12.

7 AOI: These three mysterious letters appear throughout the text. No one has ever adequately explained them, though every reader feels their effect.

8 *The Song of Roland*, trans. Frederick Goldin (New York: W. W. Norton, 1978).

9 Dante, *The Divine Comedy*, quoted in Cunningham and Reich, *Culture and Values*, vol. 1. (Harcourt Brace Jovanich College Publishers, 1994), p. 366.

10 Hugh Honour and John Fleming, *The Visual Arts: A History*, 4th edn. (Englewood Cliffs, NJ, and New York: Prentice Hall and Abrams, 1995), p. 94.

CHAPTER ELEVEN

1 Baldassare Castiglione, *The Book of the Courtier*, trans. George Bull (London: Penguin Classics, 1967). Copyright © 1967 George Bull.

2 Frederick Hartt, *Italian Renaissance Art*, 3rd ed, Englewood Cliffs, NJ and New York; Prentice Hall and Abrams, 1987, p. 592.

3 William Shakespeare, "To be, or not to be," from *Hamlet*, Act III, scene i.

4 Lilian Hornstein et al., *World Literature*, 2nd edn. (New York: Mentor, 1973), p. 155.

5 Germain Bazin, *The Baroque* (Greenwich, CT: New York Graphic Society, 1968), p. 30.

6 Jonathan Swift, "A Modest Proposal," in *The Norton Anthology of English Literature*, vol. 1, 3rd edn. (New York: W. W. Norton, 1974), p. 2094.

7 Alexander Pope, *An Essay on Man*, 1733–4. Available online at

http://www.ibiblio.org/
gutenberg/etext00/esymn10.txt.

8 Phillis Wheatley, "On Virtue," from
Poems on Various Subjects (1773).
Available online at
http://www.ibiblio.org/gutenberg/etext96
/whtly10.txt.

CHAPTER TWELVE

1 William Wordsworth, "Tintern Abbey,"
in *The Poetical Works of William
Wordsworth* (New York: Houghton
Mifflin, 1982), pp. 91–3.

2 Frederick J. Dockstader, *Indian Art of the
Americas* (New York: Museum of the
American Indian Heye Foundation,
1973), p. 14.

3 Ibid.

4 Dominique-Rene de Lerma, *Reflections
on Afro-American Music* (Kent, OH: Kent
State University Press, 1973), p. 162.

5 William Allen, Charles Ware, and Lucy
Garrison, *Slave Songs of the United States*
(New York: A. Simpson, 1867), p. 50; in
George R. Keck and Sherrill V. Martin,
Feel the Spirit (New York: Greenwood
Press, 1988), p. 3.

6 Bernard Katz, *The Social Implications of
Early Negro Music in the United States*
(New York: Arno Press and *The New
York Times*, 1969), p. 26.

7 Katz, op. cit., p. 14.

8 Henry Edward Krehbiel, *Afro-American*

Folksongs (New York: G. Schirmer, n.d.
[c. 1914]), p. 26.

CHAPTER THIRTEEN

1 H. W. Janson, *A Basic History of Art*,
5th edn. (Englewood Cliffs, NJ, and
New York: Prentice Hall and Harry N.
Abrams, 1995), p. 682.

2 Helen Gardner, *Art Through the Ages*
(New York: Harcourt Brace Jovanovich,
1980), p. 760.

3 *New York Times*, January 18, 1998,
Section 2, p. 41.

4 "Harlem Renaissance, Art of Black
America." Exhibition book for the
traveling exhibition under the auspices
of the American Federation of Arts, 1989.

5 Ibid.

6 Ibid.

7 Ibid.

8 Langston Hughes, "Theme for English
B" and "Harlem," from *The Collected
Poems of Langston Hughes* (New York:
Alfred A. Knopf, 1994). Copyright ©
1994 by the Estate of Langston Hughes.

9 Paula Gunn Allen, "Recuerdo," from
Shadow Country (Los Angeles:
University of California, American
Indian Studies Center, 1982). Copyright
© 1982 Regents of the University of
California. Reprinted from Joseph
Bruchac, *Survival This Way* (Tuscon, AZ:
University of Arizona Press, 1987), p. 3.

GLOSSARY
with Pronunciations

Cross-references are indicated by **bold** type.

abacus (A-buh-kuhs). The uppermost member of the capital of an architectural column; the slab on which the **architrave** rests.

absolute film (ab-suh-LOOT fihlm). A film that exists for its own sake: for its record of movement or form.

absolute music (ab-suh-LOOT myoo-zihk). Instrumental music free of any verbal reference or program.

absolute symmetry (ab-suh-LOOT SEHM-uh-tree). In visual art and architecture, when each half of a **composition** is exactly the same. See **symmetry.**

abstract (ab-STRAKT). Any art that does not depict objects from observable nature or transforms objects from nature into forms that resemble something other than the original model.

abstraction (ab-STRAK-shuhn). A thing apart, that is, removed from real life. Also, an early to mid-twentieth century art movement that stressed non**representation.**

Abstract Expressionism (ab-STRAKT-ehk-SPREH-shuhn-ihz-uhm). A mid-twentieth century visual art movement characterized by nontraditional brushwork, non**representational** subject matter, and **expressionist** emotional values.

absurdism (uhb-SUHRD-iz-uhm; uhb-ZUHRD-ihzm). In theatre and prose fiction, a philosophy arising after World War II in conflict with traditional beliefs and values and based on the contention that the universe is irrational and meaningless and that the search for order causes conflict with the universe. See **Theatre of the Absurd.**

academy (ah-KAD-uh-mee). From the grove (The Academeia) where Plato taught; the term has come to mean the cultural and artistic establishment that exercises responsibility for teaching and the maintenance of standards.

accent (AK-sehnt). In literature and music, a significant stress on the syllables of a **verse** or **tones** of a line, usually at regular intervals. In visual art and architecture, areas of strongest visual attraction.

accentual-syllabic (ak-SEHN-choo-uhl sih-LAH-bihk). A form of poetry in which the rhythm depends on there being a fixed number of syllables in each line.

acrylic (uh-KRIHL-lihk). An artist's **medium** made by dispersing pigment in a synthetic medium.

action painting (AK-shuhn PAYNT-ihng). A form of **Abstract Expressionism**, in which paint is applied with rapid, vigorous strokes or even splashed or thrown on the canvas.

additive (AD-ih-tihv). In sculpture, those works that are built (see **sculpture**). In **color**, the term refers to the mixing of **hues** of light.

aerial perspective (AIR-ee-yuhl-puhr-SPEHK-tihv). Also known as atmospheric perspective. In visual art, the indication of distance in painting through the use of light and atmosphere.

aesthetic (or esthetic) (ehs-THEHT-ihk). Relating to the appreciation of beauty or good taste or having a heightened sensitivity to beauty: a philosophy of what is artistically valid or beautiful.

aestheticism (ehs-THEH-tih-sihs-uhm). A late-nineteenth century arts movement that centered on the contention that art existed for its own sake, without need for social usefulness.

affective (uh-FEHK-tihv). Influenced by or resulting from the emotions.

aleatory (AY-lee-uh-tawr-ee). Dependent on chance. In music, using sounds chosen by the performer or left to chance. In film, composition on the spot by the camera operator.

allegory (AL-uh-gawr-ee). In literature and drama, a symbolic representation. The representation of abstract ideas or principles by characters, figures, or events in narrative, dramatic, or pictorial form. A fictional narrative that conveys a secondary meaning or meanings not explicitly set forth in the literal narrative.

allegro (uh-LAY-groh). A musical term meaning brisk.

alliteration (uh-lih-tuh-RAY-shuhn). In literature, the repetition of consonant sounds in two or more neighboring words or syllables.

altarpiece (AHL-tuhr-pees). A painted or sculpted panel placed above or behind an altar to inspire religious devotion.

ambulatory (AM-byoo-luh-tawr-ee). A covered passage for walking, found around the apse or choir of a church.

amphitheatre (AM-fih-thee-uh-tuhr). A building, typically Roman, that is oval or circular in form and encloses a central performance area.

anapestic (an-nah-PEHS-tihk). One of the four standard feet in poetry. Two light syllables are followed by a stressed syllable. See also **foot** and **meter.**

andante (ahn-DAHN-tay). In music, a moderately slow tempo.

antiphonal (an-TIH-fuh-nuhl). A responsive style of singing or playing, in which two groups alternate.

apse (aps). A large niche or nichelike space projecting from and expanding the interior space of an architectural form such as a basilica.

aquatint (AHK-wah-tihnt). An **intaglio** printmaking process in which the plate is treated with a resin substance to create textured tonal areas.

arcade (ahr-KAYD). In architecture, a series of arches placed side by side and supported by **columns**, **piers**, or pillars.

arch (ahrch). In architecture, a structural form taking a curved shape.

archaic (ahr-KAY-ihk). A style of art and architecture dating to ancient, pre-classical Greece (mid-fifth century B.C.E.), typified by the **Doric order**, **post-and-lintel** structure, geometric designs (especially in pottery), free-standing statues (**kouros** and **kore**) with stiff, frontal poses.

architrave (AHR-kih-trayv). In **post-and-lintel** architecture, the lintel or lowermost part of an **entablature**, resting directly on the **capitals** of the **columns**.

arena theatre (uh-REE-nuh-THEE-uh-tuhr). In theatre, a stage/audience arrangement in which the stage is surrounded on all sides by seats for the audience.

aria (AH-ree-uh). In music, a highly dramatic **solo** vocal piece with musical accompaniment, as in an **opera**, **oratorio**, and **cantata**.

Art Deco (ahrt-deh-KOH). In visual art and architecture, a style prevalent between 1925 and 1940 characterized by geometric designs, bold colors, and the use of plastic and glass materials.

art for art's sake. A phrase coined in the early nineteenth century that expresses the belief that art needs no justification—that is, it needs to serve no political, didactic or other end. See **aestheticism**.

articulation (ahr-tihk-yuh-LAY-shuhn). In the arts, the manner by which the various components of a work are joined together.

art nouveau (ahrt-noo-VOH). In architecture and design, a style prevalent in the late nineteenth and early twentieth centuries characterized by the depiction of leaves and flowers in flowing, sinuous lines (whiplash) treated in a flat, linear, and relieflike manner.

arts and crafts movement. In architecture and the decorative arts, a movement particularly in England and the United States from about 1870–1920 characterized by simplicity of design and the handcrafting of objects from local materials.

asymmetry (ay-SIHM-uh-tree). In visual art, a sense of balance achieved by placing dissimilar objects or forms on either side of a central axis. Also called "psychological balance." Cf. **symmetry**.

atmospheric perspective (at-muhs-FEER-ihk-puhr-SPEHK-tihv). See **aerial perspective**.

atonality (ay-toh-NAL-ih-tee). In music, the absence of a tonal center and of **harmonies** derived from a **diatonic scale** corresponding to such a center. Typical of much twentieth-century music.

avant-garde (ah-vahnt-GAHRD). The vanguard or intelligentsia that develops new or experimental concepts, especially in the arts. These concepts and works are usually unconventional, daring, obscure, controversial, or highly personal ideas.

balance (bal-uhns). In visual art, the placement of physically or psychologically equal items on either side of a central axis. Or the compositional equilibrium of opposing forces. In literature, the

syntactically parallel placement of similar, contrasting, or opposing ideas—for example, "To err is human; to forgive, divine."

ballet (ba-LAY). In dance, a **classical** or formal tradition resting heavily on a set of prescribed movements, actions, and positions. See **first position**; **second position**; **third position**; **fourth position**, and **fifth position**.

balloon construction (buh-LOON-cuhn-STRUHK-shuhn). In architecture, construction of wood using a skeletal framework. See **skeleton frame**.

baroque (buh-ROHK). A diverse artistic style taking place from the late sixteenth to early eighteenth century marked typically by complexity, elaborate form, and appeal to the emotions. In literature it witnessed bizarre, calculatedly ingenious, and sometimes intentionally ambiguous imagery.

barrel vault (tunnel vault) (BAR-uhl-vawlt). In architecture, a series of arches placed back to back to enclose space.

bearing wall (BAIR-ihng wahl). In architecture, construction in which the wall supports itself, the roof, and floors. See **monolithic construction**.

beat (beet). In music, the equal parts into which a measure is divided.

bel canto (behl-KAN-toh). In music, a style of operatic singing utilizing full, even tones and virtuoso vocal technique. Italian for "beautiful singing."

bilateral symmetry (by-LAT-uhr-uhl-SIHM-uh-tree). In visual art and architecture, when the overall effect of a composition is one of **absolute symmetry** even though clear discrepancies exist side to side. See **symmetry**.

binary (BY-nuh-ree). In music, having two sections or subjects.

biography (by-AHG-ruh-fee). In literature, a type of **nonfiction**, the subject of which is the life of an individual. *See also* **hagiography**.

biomorphic (by-oh-MAWR-fihk). In visual art, representing lifeforms, as opposed to geometric forms.

bridge (brihj). In music, a section or passage, or in literature and drama a section, passage, or scene that serves as a transition between two other sections, passages, or scenes. In music, it occurs in the **exposition** of the **sonata form** between the first and second **themes**.

buttress (BUHT-rihs). In architecture, a structure typically brick or stone built against a wall, vault, or arch for reinforcing support.

cadence (CAY-duhns). In music, a particular arrangement of chords to indicate the ending of a musical passage. In literature, a rhythmic sequence or flow of sounds in language; a particular rhythmic sequence of a particular author or literary composition. Or, the rising or falling order of strong, long, or stressed syllables and weak, short, or unstressed syllables. Or, an unmetrical or irregular arrangement of stressed and unstressed syllables in prose of free verse that is based on natural stress groups.

calotype (KAL-uh-typ). In photography, the first process invented to utilize negatives and proper positives. Invented by William Henry Fox Talbot in the late 1830s.

camera obscura (KAM-uh-ruh ahb-SKYUHR-uh). In visual art, a dark room or box with a small hole in one side, through which an inverted image of the view outside is projected on the opposite wall, screen, or mirror. The image can then be traced. A prototype for the modern camera.

cantata (kuhn-TAH-tuh). In music, a composition in several movements for orchestra and chorus often with a **sacred** text, and utilizing **recitatives**, **arias**, and choruses.

cantilever (KAN-tih-lee-vuhr). In architecture, a structural system in which an overhanging beam is supported only at one end.

capital (Kap-ih-tuhl). In architecture, the top part of a pillar or column. The transition between the top of a **column** and the **lintel**.

cella (CHEH-luh or CHAY-lah). The principal enclosed room of a temple; the entire body of a temple as opposed to its external parts.

chiaroscuro (kee-ah-ruh-SKOOR-oh). In visual art, the technique of using light and shade to develop three-dimensional form. In theatre, the use of light to enhance the three-dimensionality of the human body or the elements of scenery.

chord (kohrd). In music, three or more pitches sounded simultaneously.

choreography (kohr-ee-AHGH-ruh-fee). In dance, the art of creation of a dance work. Also, the arrangement of patterns of movement in a dance.

chroma (KROHM-uh). In visual art, the degree of **saturation** or purity of a color or **hue**.

chromatic scale (kroh-MAT-ihk-scayl). In music, a **scale** consisting of 12 **semitones** or half steps.

cinéma vérité (see-nay-MAH-vay-ree-TAY). In film, a style of presentation based on complete **realism** that uses **aleatory** methods, a minimum of equipment, and a **documentary** approach.

cire-perdue (lost wax) (sihr-pair-DOO). In sculpture, a method of casting metal in a mold, the cavity of which is formed of wax, which is then melted and poured away.

classic (KLAS-ihk). A work of art from ancient Greece and/or Rome. A work of art or artist of enduring excellence.

classical (KLAS-ih-kuhl). Adhering to traditional standards. May refer to a style in art and architecture dating to the mid-fifth century B.C.E. in Athens, Greece or ancient Rome, or any art that emphasizes simplicity, harmony, restraint, proportion, and reason. In Greek classical architecture, **Doric** and **Ionic orders** appear in **peripteral** temples. In vase painting, geometry remains from the **archaic style**, but figures have a sense of **idealism** and lifelikeness. In music, classical refers to a style of the eighteenth century that adhered to classical standards but had no known classical antecedents. See **neoclassicism**.

classicism (KLAS-uh-sihz-uhm). The principles, historical traditions, aesthetic attitudes, or style of the arts of ancient Greece and Rome, including works created in those times or later inspired by those times. Or, **classical** scholarship. Or, adherence to or practice of the virtues thought to be characteristic of classicism or to be universally and enduringly valid—that is, formal elegance and correctness, simplicity, dignity, restraint, order, and proportion.

clerestory (or clearstory) (KLIHR-stawr-ee). The upper portion of a wall containing windows, when it extends above any abutting aisles or secondary roofs: especially in the **nave**, **transept**, and **choir** of a church. Provides direct light into the central interior space.

coda (KOH-duh). In music, drama, and literature, the concluding portion of a work that typically integrates or rounds off previous themes or ideas.

cognitive (KAHG-nuh-tihv). Facts and objectivity as opposed to emotions and subjectivity. Cf. **affective**.

collage (koh-LAZH). In visual art, a composition of materials and objects pasted on a surface. In literature, a work composed of borrowed and original materials.

colonnade (KAHL-uh-nayd). In architecture, a series of **columns** placed at regular intervals usually connected by **lintels**.

color (KUH-luhr). In visual art, the appearance of surfaces in terms of **hue**, **value**, and **intensity**. In music, the quality of a tone—also called **timbre**. In literature, the vividness or variety of emotional effects of language—for example, sound and image. See also **complementary color**; **primary color**; **secondary color**; **tertiary color**.

column (KAHL-uhm). In architecture, a supporting pillar consisting of a base, cylindrical shaft, and **capital**.

composition (kahm-poh-ZIH-shuhn). In visual art and architecture, the arrangement of line, form, mass, and color. Also, the arrangement of the technical qualities of any artform.

compressive strength (kuhm-PREHS-ihv-strehngth). In architecture, the ability of a material to withstand crushing. See **tensile strength**.

concerto (kuhn-CHAIR-toh). In music, an extended composition for orchestra and one or more soloists, typically in three movements: fast, slow, and fast.

concerto grosso (kuhn-CHAIR-toh-GHROH-soh). In music, a composition for orchestra and a small group of instrumental soloists, typically late **baroque**.

conjunct melody (KAHN-juhngkt; kuhn-JUHNGKT MEHL-oh-dee). In music, a melody comprising notes close together in the scale.

consonance (KAHN-soh-nuhns). In music, tones that sound agreeable or harmonious together, as opposed to **dissonance**. In literature, repetition of identical or similar consonants. In all arts, a feeling of comfortable relationship. Consonance may be both physical and cultural in its ramifications.

contrapposto, counterpoise (kahn-truh-POHS-toh; COWN-tuhr-poyz). In sculpture, the arrangement of body parts so that the weight-bearing leg is apart from the free leg, thereby shifting the hip–shoulder axis.

convention (kuhn-VEHN-shuhn). In all the arts, a generally accepted practice, technique, or device.

Corinthian order (kaw-RIHN-thee-uhn-AWR-duhr). One of three ancient Greek architectural orders (along with **Doric** and **Ionic**). Corinthian is the most ornate and is characterized by slender **fluted columns** with an ornate, bell-shaped **capital** decorated with **acanthus** leaves.

counterpoint (KOWN-tuhr-point). In any art, the use of contrast in major elements. In music, the use of **polyphony** as a texture. In literature the term refers to metrical variation in poetry.

cover shot (KUHV-uhr shaht). In film, extra shots of a scene that can be used to bridge transitions in case the planned footage fails to edit as planned.

crescendo (kreh-SHEHN-do). In music, a gradual increase in volume or intensity.

crosscut (KRAWS-cuht). In film, the technique of alternating between two independent actions that are related thematically or by **plot** to give the impression of simultaneous occurrence.

Cubism (KYOOB-ihz-uhm). An art style originated by **Picasso** and **Braque** around 1907 that emphasizes **abstract** structure rather than **representationalism**. Objects are depicted as assemblages of geometric shapes. The early mature phase (1909–11) is called Analytical Cubism. A more decorative phase called synthetic or **collage** Cubism appeared around 1912. In literature, Cubist writing uses abstract structure to replace the narrative.

cut (kuht). In film, the joining of shots together during the editing process. Examples are: **jump cut, form cut, montage, crosscut,** and **cutting within the frame.**

cutting within the frame. In film, a **cut** that changes the viewpoint of the camera within a shot by moving from a long or medium shot to a close-up, without cutting the film.

Dada or Dadaism (DAH-dah; DAH-dah-ihz-uhm). A nihilistic movement in the arts from around 1916 to 1920.

daguerreotype (duh-GHAIR-uh-typ). In photography, a process (or photograph made from it) using a light-sensitive, silver-coated metallic plate.

decrescendo (day-kruh-SHEHN-doh). In music, gradually diminishing loudness or force.

dénouement (day-noo-MAHN). In theatre, film, and literature, the final resolution of a dramatic or narrative plot—that is, the events following the climax.

depth of focus (dehpth uhv FOHK-uhs). In film, when both near and distance objects are clearly seen.

development (dih-VEHL-uhp-muhnt). In music, in **sonata form**, the second section in which the **themes** of the **exposition** are freely developed. See also **recapitulation.**

diatonic (dy-uh-TAHN-ihk). In music, relating to the seven tones of a standard scale without chromatic alterations.

diatonic minor (dy-uh-THAN-ihk-MY-nuhr). In music, the standard minor **scale** achieved by lowering by one half step the third and sixth of the diatonic or standard major scale.

diptych (DIHP-tihk). A painting on two hinged panels.

direct address (dih-REHKT-uh-DREHS). In theatre and film, when a character addresses the audience directly.

disjunct melody (dihs-JUHNKT MEHL-uh-dee). In music, **melody** characterized by skips or jumps in the scale. The opposite of **conjunct melody.**

dissolve (dih-ZAHLV). In film, a transition from one **shot** to another by fading out and fading in.

dissonance (DIHS-uh-nuhns). In music or visual art, any harsh disagreement between elements of the composition—that is, discord. In music, a combination of sounds used to suggest unrelieved tension. Cf. **consonance.**

divertissement (duh-VUHR-tihs-munt; dee-vair-tees-MAHN). In dance, a short balletic performance presented as an interlude in a play or opera or any short dance or musical work designed strictly as an amusement.

documentary film (dahk-yuh-MEHN-tuh-ree-fihlm). In film, a work that presents its subject factually, often with interviews and narration.

dome (dohm). In architecture, a circular, vaulted roof.

Doric order (DAWR-ihk-AWR-duhr). In architecture, the oldest and simplest of the three Greek architectural orders (along with **Ionic** and **Corinthian**). It is characterized by heavy columns with plain, saucer-shaped capitals and no base.

drypoint (DRY-poynt). In visual art, an **intaglio** printmaking process in which a metal plate is scratched with a sharp needlelike tool called a **stylus.**

dynamics (dy-NAM-ihks). The various levels of loudness and softness of sounds; the increase and decrease of **intensities.**

editing (EHD-iht-ihng). In film, the composition of a finished work from various **shots** and sound tracks.

empathy (EHM-puh-thee). Identification with another's situation. In theatre and film, a physical reaction to events witnessed on the stage or screen.

engaged column (ehn-GHAYJ-d KAHL-uhm). A **column**, often decorative, which is part of, and projects from, a wall surface.

engraving (ehn-GRAYV-ihng). In printmaking, an **intaglio** process in which sharp, definitive lines are cut into a metal plate.

en pointe (ahn-pwant). See **on point.**

entablature (ehn-TAB-luh-chuhr).The upper portion of a **classical** architectural order above the **column capital.**

ephemeral (ih-FEHM-uhr-uhl). In visual art, a work designed to last only a short time.

epic (EHP-ihk). In literature, a long narrative poem in elevated style celebrating heroic achievement. In film, a **genre** characterized by bold and sweeping themes and a **protagonist** who is an ideal representative of a culture.

essay (EHS-ay). In literature, a short composition treating a single subject usually from the personal point of view of the author.

establishing shot (eh-STAB-lihsh-ihng shaht). In film, a long shot at the beginning of a scene to establish the time, place, and so forth. See **master shot.**

etching (EHCH-ihng). In visual art, a type of **intaglio** printmaking in which the design comprises lines cut into a metal plate by acid.

exposition (ehk-spoh-ZIH-shuhn). In theatre, film, and literature, the aspect of **plot** in which necessary background information, introduction of **characters**, and current situation are detailed. In music, the first section of **sonata form**, in which the first **subject** (in the **tonic** key) and second subject (in the **dominant** key), also sometimes further subjects, are played and often repeated. See development and **recapitulation.** Also, the first thematic statement of a **fugue** by all players in turn.

expressionism (ek-SPREHSH-uh-nihz-uhm). An artistic movement of the late nineteenth and early twentieth centuries that stresses the subjective and subconscious thoughts of the artist and seeks to evoke subjective emotions on the part of the respondent. The struggle of life's inner realities are presented by techniques that include abstraction, distortion, exaggeration, **primitivism**, fantasy, and **symbolism**.

farce (fahrs). In theatre, a light, comic work using improbable situations, stereotyped characters, horseplay, and exaggeration.

fenestration (fehn-ih-STRAY-shuhn). In architecture, an opening such as a window in a structure.

ferroconcrete (FAIR-oh-kahn-kreet). See **reinforced concrete**.

fiction (FIHK-shuhn). In literature a work created from the imagination of the writer.

fluting (FLOO-tihng). In architecture, vertical grooves cut in the shaft of a **column**.

flying buttress (fly-ihng-BUH-truhs). A semidetached **buttress**.

focus (focal point; focal area) (FOH-kuhs). In visual art and architecture, an area of attention. In photography and film, the degree of acceptable sharpness in an image.

foil (foyl). In theatre, film, and literature, a character presented as a contrast to another character so as to point out or show to advantage some aspect of the second character.

folk dance (fohk dans). In dance, a body or group of dances performed to traditional music that is stylistically identifiable with a specific culture, for which it serves as a necessary or informative part.

foot (fuhwt). In literature, the basic poetic unit of verse meter consisting of any of various fixed combinations or groups of stressed and unstressed or long and short syllables.

foreground (FAWR-grownd). In two-dimensional art, an area of a picture, usually at the bottom, that appears closest to the viewer.

foreshortening (fahwr-SHOHWR-tuhn-ihng). Something that is compact, abridged, or shortened. In visual art, the compacting of three dimensions by **linear perspective** in order to show depth of space.

form (fahwrm). In any art, a type or genre. Or, the shape, structure, configuration, or essence of something. Or, the organization of ideas in time or space.

form cut (fawrm-kuht). In film, a **cut** that jumps from one image to another, both of which have a similar shape or contour.

forte (FAWR-tay). In music: loud and forceful.

found sculpture or object (fownd). In visual art, an object taken from life that is presented as an artwork.

frame tale (FRAYM tayl). Overall unifying story within which one or more tales are related.

fresco (FREHS-koh). In painting, a work done on wet plaster with water-soluble paints. The image becomes part of the wall surface as opposed to being painted on it. Also known as *buon fresco*, or "true fresco." Cf. **fresco secco**.

fresco secco (FREHS-koh SEHK-oh). In painting, a work done on dry plaster.

frieze (freez). In architecture, a plain or decorated horizontal part of an **entablature** between the **architrave** and **cornice**. Also, a decorative horizontal band along the upper part of a wall.

fugue (fyoog). In music, a **polyphonic** composition in which a **theme** or themes are stated successively in all voices.

full-round (fuhl-rownd). In sculpture, works that explore full three-dimensionality and are meant to be viewed from any angle. See **sculpture**.

genre (ZHAHN-ruh). A distinctive type or category or art, drama, literature, music, etc, characterized by a particular style, form, or content. Also, a style of painting representing an aspect of everyday life, such as a domestic interior, a still life, or a rural scene.

geodesic dome (jee-uh-DEHS-ihk). In architecture, a domed or vaulted structure of lightweight straight elements made up of interlocking polygons.

gesamtkunstwerk (guh-ZAHMT-kuhnst-vuhrk). A complete, totally integrated artwork; associated with the music dramas of **Richard Wagner** in nineteenth-century Germany.

glyptic (GHLIHP-tihk). In sculpture, works emphasizing the qualities of the material from which they are made.

Gothic (gothic) (GHAHTH-ihk). In architecture, painting, and sculpture, a medieval style based on a pointed-arch structure and characterized by simplicity, verticality, elegance, and lightness. In literature, a style of fiction of the late eighteenth and early nineteenth centuries characterized by medieval settings, mysterious, and violent actions. In the mid-twentieth century, the term Southern Gothic was used to describe literary works characterized by grotesque, macabre, or fantastic incidents in an atmosphere of violence and decadence.

gouache (gwahsh). In visual art, a watercolor medium in which gum is added to ground opaque colors and mixed with water.

Greek cross (greek krahws). A cross in which all arms are the same length.

Greek revival (ghreek ree-VYV-uhl). In architecture, a style that imitates the elements of ancient Greek temple design. Popular in the United States and Europe during the first half of the nineteenth century.

Gregorian chant (ghrih-GHAWR-ee-uhn-chant). In music, an unaccompanied, vocal, monophonic, and **consonant** liturgical chant named for Pope Gregory I (540–604 C.E.) and comprising a body of sacred—that is, religious—music. Chants were sung in a flexible **tempo** with unmeasured **rhythms** following the natural **accents** of normal Latin speech. Also called chant, plainchant, or plainsong.

groin vault (ghroyn vawlt). In architecture, a ceiling formation created by the intersection of two **tunnel** or **barrel** vaults.

hagiography (ha-jee-AHGH-ruh-fee; hay-). In literature, writings about or study of the lives of the Saints. A sacred form of **biography**.

harmony (HAHR-muh-nee). In music, the arrangement and progression of chords. In visual art, the relationship of like elements such as colors and repeated patterns. In literature, an arrangement of parallel passages for the purpose of showing agreement. Cf. **consonance** and **dissonance**.

Hellenistic (hehl-uh-NIHS-tihk). In visual art, architecture, and theatre, a style dating to the fourth century to the second century B.C.E. that encompassed a diversity of approaches reflecting an increasing interest in the differences between individual humans and characterized by emotion, drama, and interaction of sculptural forms with the surrounding space. In architecture, it reflected a change in proportions from the **classical** and introduced the **Corinthian order**.

hierarchy (HY-uhr-ahrk-ee). Any system of persons or things that has higher and lower ranks.

hieratic (hy-yuhr-AT-ihk). A style of depicting sacred persons or office, particularly in Byzantine art.

hieroglyph, hieroglyphic (HY-roh-ghlihf; hy-roh-GHLIH-fihk). A picture or symbol of an object standing for a word, idea, or sound; developed by the ancient Egyptians into a system of writing.

high relief or haut-relief (HY ruh-leef; OH reh-LEEF). In sculpture, **relief** works in which the figures protrude from the background by at least half their depth.

High Renaissance (hy REHN-eh-sahns). A movement dating to the late fifteenth to early sixteenth centuries that followed **classical** ideals and sought a universal ideal through impressive themes and styles. In visual art, figures became types rather than individuals.

homophony (huh-MAH-fuh-nee). In music, a **texture** characterized by chordal development supporting one melody. Cf. **monophony** and **polyphony**.

horizon line (huh-RYZ-uhn-lyn). In visual art, a real or implied line across the picture plane, which, like the horizon in nature, tends to fix the viewer's vantage point.

hypostyle (HY-puh-styl). A building with a roof or ceiling supported by rows of **columns**, as in ancient Egyptian architecture.

iambic (y-AM-bihk). In literature, one of the four standard feet in poetry. A light syllable is followed by a stressed syllable. See **foot** and **meter**.

icon (Y-kahn). Greek for "image." An artwork whose subject matter includes idolatry, veneration, or some other religious content. Specifically, in visual art, an image or representation of a sacred personage.

idée fixe (ee-day-FEEX). In music and literature, a recurring **motif** or **theme**.

Impressionism (ihm-PREHSH-uh-nihz-uhm). A mid- to late-nineteenth century style originating in France. In painting it sought spontaneity, harmonious colors, subjects from everyday life, and faithfulness to observed lighting and atmospheric effects by seeking to capture the psychological perception of reality in color and motion. It emphasized the presence of color within shadows and the result of color and light making an "impression" on the retina. In music it freely challenged traditional tonality with new tone colors, Oriental influence, and harmonies away from the traditional. Gliding chords—that is, repetition of a chord up and down the scale—was a hallmark.

inciting incident (ihn-SYT-ing Dm-suh-duhnt). In theatre, an event or decision that creates a complication leading to the resolution of the drama.

intaglio (ihn-TAHL-yo; -TAL-). A printmaking process in which ink is transferred from the grooves of a metal plate to paper by extreme pressure. It includes **engraving**, **etching**, and **drypoint**.

interval (IHN-tuhr-vuhl). In music, the difference (usually expressed in number of steps) between two pitches.

Ionic (Ionic order) (y-AHN-ihk). Relating to Ionia in ancient Greece. In architecture, one of three orders of Greek architecture (along with **Doric** and **Corinthian**), characterized by two opposed **volutes** in the **capital**. In literature, a foot of verse that comprises either two long and two short syllables or two short and two long syllables.

iris (Y-ruhs). In film, a masking device that blacks out portions of the screen, allowing only part of an image to be seen. The device is usually circular or oval in shape and can be expanded or contracted.

irony (Y-ruh-nee). In literature, words used to express something other than, and particularly the opposite of, the literal meaning.

jazz (jaz). In music, a form of music native to America and calling on the African American heritage characterized by strong, flexible **rhythms**, **syncopation**, and improvisation.

jazz dance (jaz). In dance, a form arising partly from African dance customs, and with a strong improvisational nature, that developed into American social and entertainment dances.

jump cut (juhmp-cuht). In film, the instantaneous **cut** from one scene to another or from one **shot** to another; often used for shock effect.

key (kee). In visual art, the relative lightness or darkness of a picture or the colors employed in it. See **value**. In architecture, the **keystone** in an **arch**. In music, a tonal system consisting of seven **tones** in fixed relationship to a **tonic**.

kouros (KOO-rohs). In sculpture, an archaic Greek statue of a standing nude male youth. See **kore**.

labanotation (lab-uh-noh-TAY-shuhn). In dance, a system for writing down movements.

lap dissolve (lap-dih-ZAHLV). In film, the simultaneous fade in and fade out of two scenes so that they briefly overlap. See **dissolve**.

largo (LAHR-goh). In music, a very slow tempo, with great dignity.

Latin cross (la-tihn). A cross in which the vertical arm is longer than the horizontal arm, through whose midpoint it passes.

legato (lih-GAH-toh). In music, a smooth, even style without breaks between the notes.

leitmotiv or leitmotif (lyt-moh-TEEF). In music and literature, a dominant recurring theme, phrase, or sentence often associated with a character, situation, or element, as in Wagnerian opera.

lento (LEHN-toh). In music, in a slow tempo.

libretto (lih-BREHT-oh). In music and theatre, the text of an opera or any other kind of musical theatre.

linear perspective (LIHN-ee-uhr-puhr-SPEHK-tihv). In two-dimensional art, the creation of the illusion of distance through the convention of **line** and **foreshortening**.

linear sculpture (LIHN-ee-uhr-SKUHLP-chuhr). In sculpture, works that emphasize two-dimensional materials such as wire.

lintel (LIHN-tl). In architecture, a horizontal structural member typically of stone that spans the space between uprights such as **columns**.

lithography (lih-THAHGH-ruh-fee). In printmaking, a **planographic** process using an image rendered on a flat surface, such as a stone, and treated to retain ink while nonimage areas are treated to repel ink. See also **chromolithography**.

lost-wax (lawst-wax). See **cire-perdue**.

low relief (loh-ruh-LEEF). Also called bas-relief. In sculpture, a **relief** work in which figures and forms project only slightly from the background. Cf. **high relief**.

madrigal (MAD-rih-ghuhl). In music, a secular part song, originating in Italy, for two or three unaccompanied voices. In literature, a medieval short lyrical poem specifically about love. Common in the **Renaissance**.

magnitude (MAG-nuh-tood). In theatre and film, the scope of universality of the theme.

manipulation (muh-nihp-yoo-LAY-shuhn). In sculpture, a technique in which materials such as clay are shaped by skilled use of the hands.

mass (mas). In visual art and architecture, three-dimensional form having physical bulk. Also the illusion of such a form on a two-dimensional surface.

master shot (MAST-uhr shaht). In film, a single shot of an entire piece of action. See **establishing shot**.

measure (MAY-zhuhr). In music, a basic rhythmic division of a composition marked in the score by vertical lines (bar lines) and containing a fixed number of **beats**.

melismatic (meh-lihz-MA-tihk). Music where a single syllable or text is sung on many notes.

melodrama (MEHL-oh-drahm-uh). In theatre, a genre characterized by stereotyped characters, implausible plots, and emphasis on spectacle.

melody (MEHL-uh-dee). In music, a succession of individual tones that create a recognizable whole.

metaphor (MEHT-uh-fawr). In literature, a **figure of speech** that substitutes one word or phrase for another, suggesting a likeness between them. Or an implied comparison between two otherwise unlike elements, meaningful in a figurative rather than literal sense.

meter (MEE-tuhr). In music, the regular succession of rhythmical impulses or beats. In literature, a systematically arranged and measured rhythm in verse. Also in literature, a fixed metrical pattern or a verse form.

microtone (my-kroh-tohn). A musical interval smaller than a half step.

mime (mym). In theatre, a type of Greek and Roman **farce**; or a performance using only body movement and gestures, without the use of words. In dance or theatre, actions that imitate human or animal movements.

mise-en-scène (meez-ahn-sehn). In theatre, film, and dance, the complete visual environment of the production, including scenery, lighting, properties, costumes, and physical structure of the theatre.

mobile (MOH-beel). A constructed structure whose components have been connected by joints to move by force of wind or motor.

modern dance (MAHD-uhrn-dans). A form of concert dance relying on emotional use of the body, as opposed to formalized or conventional movement such as **ballet**, and stressing human emotion and the human condition.

modulate (MAHJ-uh-layt). In music, to change **pitch**, intensity, or tone, or to move from one **key** to another.

monolithic construction (mahn-oh-LIH-thihk-kuhn-STRUHK-shuhn). In architecture, a variation of **bearing-wall** construction in which the wall material is not jointed or pieced together.

monophony (muh-NAHF-uh-nee). In music, a texture comprising a single melodic line. Cf. **homophony**; **polyphony**.

monoprint (MAHN-oh-prihnt). In visual art, a single print pulled from a hard surface prepared with a painted design. Each print comprises an individual artwork.

montage (mahn-TAHZH). In the visual arts, the process of making a single composition by combining parts of other pictures so the parts form a whole, and yet remain distinct. In film, montage is a type of **cut** handled either as an indication of compression of elongation of time, or as a rapid succession of images to illustrate an association of ideas.

monumental (mohn-yoo-MENT-uhl). In visual art and architecture, works actually or appearing larger than life-size.

mosaic (moh-ZAY-ihk). A decorative work for walls, vaults, floors, or ceilings, composed of pieces of colored material set in plaster or cement.

motet (moh-TEHT). In music, a **polyphonic** composition for choir based on a sacred Latin text (other than the Mass) and typically sung without accompaniment.

motif (or motive) (moh-TEEF; MOH-tihv) In visual art, music, theatre, film, dance, or literature, a short, recurring theme, idea, melody, or other element.

movement (MOOV-muhnt). In music, a self-contained section of an extended composition such as a **symphony**.

musique actuelle (myoo-ZEEK-ak-CHWEHL). In music, an approach from the 1990s that comprises **improvised** music freely drawing on **jazz** and rock and eliciting vibrancy, liveliness, and personal expression. Its literal translation means "current," and it represents a number of subfactions from various localities, always seeming to involve a strain of humor.

musique concrète (moo-ZEEK-kahn-KREHT). In music, a twentieth-century approach in which conventional and recorded sounds are altered electronically or otherwise and recorded on tape to produce new sounds.

nave (nayv). The great central space in a church, usually running from west to east, where the congregation sits.

neoclassicism (nee-oh-CLAS-uh-sihz-uhm). Adherence to or practice of the ideals and characteristics of classical art, literature, and music. In painting it emerged in the eighteenth century; in theatre, the sixteenth; and in music, the eighteenth century as **classicism** and in the early twentieth century as Neoclassicism. In architecture it was eclectic; in painting, it reflected a perception of grandeur in antiquity with classical details, starkness of outline, and strong geometric composition. Likewise in sculpture. In theatre, the "**unities**" of time, place, and action were reinterpreted from the writings of Aristotle. In music, eighteenth-century **classicism** rejected the excessive ornamentation of the **baroque** seeking instead to achieve order, simplicity, and careful attention to **form** through variety and contrast in mood, flexibility of **rhythm**, **homophonic** texture, memorable **melody**, and gradual changes in dynamics. Twentieth-century Neoclassicism in music is marked by emotional restraint, balance, and clarity.

nonobjective (nahn-uhb-JEHK-tihv). Without reference to reality; may be differentiated from **abstract**.

nonrepresentational (nahn-rehp-ree-zehn-TAY-shuhn-uhl). Without reference to reality; including **abstract** and **nonobjective**.

novel (NAH-vuhl). In literature, a lengthy and complex **fictional** prose **narrative** dealing imaginatively with the human condition using a connected series of events and a group of **characters** in a specific setting.

objective camera (ahb-JEHK-tihv KAM-uh-ruh). In film, a camera position based on a third-person viewpoint.

octave (AHK-tihv; -tayv). In music, eight **tones** comprising a **scale**. The **interval** between two **pitches**, one of which is double the frequency of the other. In literature, a stanza of eight lines.

on point (ahn poynt). In dance, a ballet technique utilizing special shoes in which the dancer dances on the points of the toes.

opera buffa (AHP-uh-ruh BOO-fuh; AHP-ruh-; OH-pair-uh-BOOF-fah). Comic opera that usually does not have spoken dialogue and typically uses satire to treat a serious topic with humor.

opéra comique (AHP-uh-ruh-kah-MEEK; AHP-ruh; oh-pay-rah-kah-MEEK). Any opera, regardless of subject matter, that has spoken dialogue.

opera seria (AHP-uh-ruh-SIHR-ee-uh; OHP-air-uh-SAIR-). Serious opera, usually grand in scale and tragic in tone. Highly stylized and treating heroic subjects such as gods and heroes of ancient times.

operetta (ahp-uh-REHT-uh). A type of opera that has spoken dialogue but usually refers to a style of opera characterized by popular themes, a romantic mood, and often a humorous tone. Frequently considered more theatrical than musical, its story line is usually frivolous and sentimental.

opus (OH-puhs). A single work of art.

oratorio (awr-uh-TAWR-ee-oh; -TOH-). In music, a semidramatic work, without acting, scenery, or costumes, often on a religious theme, for **orchestra**, choir, and soloists.

orchestra (AWRK-ih-struh). In music, a large instrumental ensemble divided into sections such as strings, woodwinds, brass, and percussion. In theatre, the section of seats on the ground floor of the auditorium directly in front of the stage. Also, the circular playing area of an ancient Greek theatre.

order (AWR-duhr). In architecture, one of the systems used by the Greeks and Romans to decorate and define their buildings. See **Corinthian order, Doric order,** and **Ionic order.**

palette (PAL-eht). In visual art, the composite use of color by an artist in an artwork. Or, a flat piece of board or other material that a painter holds and on which pigments can be mixed. In music and literature, the range of qualities employed by a composer or writer in a particular work.

pan (pan). In film, to follow a moving object with the camera.

pantheon (PAN-thee-ahn). A Greek word meaning "all the gods."

pas de deux (pah-duh-DUH). In dance, a dance for two individuals, especially in **ballet.**

pathos (PA-thaws or PAY-thaws). The "suffering" aspect of drama usually associated with the evocation of pity.

pediment (PEHD-uh-muhnt). In architecture, a wide, low-pitched **gable** atop the façade of a Greek-style building. Also a similar triangular element used above window or door openings.

pendentive (pehn-DEHN-tihv). In architecture, a triangular section of vaulting used to anchor a dome to the rectilinear structure below it.

persistence of vision (puhr-SIHST-uhns uhv VIHZH-uhn). In film, the continuance of a visual image on the retina for a brief time after the removal of the object.

perspective (puhr-SPEHK-tihv). In two-dimensional art, the representation of distance and three-dimensionality on a two-dimensional surface. See **aerial perspective** and **linear perspective.**

piano (pee-AN-oh). In music: softly or quietly.

picaresque novel (pihk-uh-REHSK). In literature, a type of **novel** dealing with the episodic adventures of a rogue.

pitch (pihch). In music, the quality of a sound—its highness or lowness—which is governed by a specific number of vibrations per second. In architecture, the angle of a roof.

plainchant (PLAYN-chant). See **Gregorian chant.**

planography (pluh-NAHG-ruh-fee). In printmaking, a process that prints from a smooth surface—for example, **lithography.**

plastic (PLAS-tihk). In visual art and film: capable of being shaped or molded; or, three-dimensional.

platemark (PLAYT-mahrk). In printmaking, a ridged or embossed effect created by the pressure used in transferring ink to paper from a metal plate in the **intaglio** process.

poetry (POH-uh-tree). One of the major divisions or **genres** of literature. A work designed to convey a vivid and imaginative sense experience through the use of condensed language selected for its sound and suggestive power and meaning, and employing specific technical devices, such as **meter, rhyme,** and **metaphor.** There are three major types of poetry: **narrative,** dramatic, and **lyric.**

pointe (pwahnt). See **on point.**

pointillism (POYNT-ihl-lihz-uhm). A style of painting in which the paint is applied to the surface by dabbing the brush so as to create small dots of color.

polyphony (puh-LIHF-uh-nee). In music, a texture comprising two or more independent melodic lines sounded together. Cf. **monophony** and **homophony.**

polyrhythm (pah-lee-RIH-thuhm). The use of contrasting rhythms at the same time in music, post and beam (pohst-and-beem). See **post-and-lintel.**

post-and-lintel (pohst-and-LIHNT-uhl). In architecture, a structural system in which horizontal pieces (**lintels**) are held up by vertical columns (**posts**); similar to post and beam structure, which usually utilizes wooden posts and beams held together by nails or pegs.

Postimpressionism (pohst-ihm-PREHSH-uh-nihz-uhm). In visual art, a diverse style dating to the late nineteenth century that rejected the objective **naturalism** of **Impressionism** and used form and color in more personal ways. It reflects an "**art for art's sake**" philosophy.

post-tensioned concrete (pohst-TEHN-shuhnd-KAHN-kreet). In architecture, concrete using metal rods and wires under stress or tension to cause structural forces to flow in predetermined directions.

precast concrete (pree-kast-KAHN-kreet). In architecture, concrete cast in place using wooden forms around a steel framework.

pre-Columbian (pree-kuh-LUHM-bee-uhn). Originating in the Americas prior to the arrival of Columbus in 1492.

prestressed concrete (pree-strehst-KAHN-kreet). See **post-tensioned** concrete.

program music (PROH-gram-MYOOZ-ihk). Music intended to depict or suggest nonmusical ideas or images through a descriptive title or text. Cf. **absolute music**.

proportion (pruh-PAWR-shuhn). In visual art and architecture, the relation, or ratio, of one part to another and of each part to the whole with regard to size, height, width, length, or depth.

proscenium (proh-SEE-nee-uhm). In theatre, a form of theatre architecture in which a frame (arch) separates the audience from the stage (picture frame stage); also, the frame or arch itself; also, in the Greek **classical** theatre, the area between the background (**skene**) and the **orchestra**.

protagonist (proh-TAG-uh-nihst). In theatre, film, and literature, the leading actor or personage in a play or narrative work—that is, the major **character** around whose decisions and actions the **plot** revolves.

putti (POO-tee). Nude male children—usually winged—especially shown in **Renaissance** and later art.

rack focus (rak FOH-kuhs). Also called differential focus (dihf-uh-REHN-shuhl). In film, when an object is clearly shown while the remainder of the scene is out of focus.

radial symmetry (RAY-dee-uhl-SIHM-uh-tree). In visual art, the **symmetrical** arrangement of elements around a central point.

realism (REE-uhl-ihz-uhm). In visual art and theatre, a mid-nineteenth-century style seeking to present an objective and unprejudiced record of the customs, ideas, and appearances of contemporary society through spontaneity, harmonious colors, and subjects from everyday life with a focus on human motive and experience.

recapitulation (rih-cuh-pihch-uh-LAY-shuhn; ree-). In **sonata form**, the third section in which the **exposition** is repeated, often with variations. See **development**.

recitative (rehs-ih-tuh-TEEV; rehch-). In music (in **opera**, **cantata**, and **oratorio**), a vocal line that imitates the **rhythms** and **pitch** fluctuations of speech and often serving to lead into an **aria**.

reinforced concrete (ree-ihn-FAWRST; -FOHRST; -KAHN-kreet). In architecture, poured concrete containing steel reinforcing bars or mesh to increase its **tensile strength**.

relief (rih-LEEF). See **sculpture**.

relief printing (ruh-LEEF-PRIHNT-ihng). In printmaking, a process by which the ink is transferred to the paper from raised areas on a printing block.

representational (rehp-rih-zehn-TAY-shuhn-uhl). In visual art and theatre, having the appearance of observable reality. Cf. **abstract** and **nonrepresentational**.

requiem (REHK-wee-uhm). In music, a composition for a **mass** for the dead.

rhyme (or rime) (rym). In literature, an echoing by two or more words with similar-sounding final syllables.

rhythm (RIHTH-uhm). The relationship, either of time or space, between recurring elements of a **composition**. The regular or ordered

repetition of dominant and subordinate elements or units within a design or composition.

ribbed vault (rihbd-vawlt). In architecture, a structure in which arches are connected by diagonal as well as horizontal members.

ritardando (rih-tahr-DAHN-doh). In music, a decrease in tempo.

ritornello form (rih-tohr-NEHL-oh fawrm). In music, a type of composition usually in a **baroque concerto grosso**, in which the **tutti** plays a **ritornello**, alternating with one or more soloists playing new material.

ritual dance (RIH-choo-uhl dans). In dance, a group of dances that perform some religious, moral, or ethical purpose in a society.

Rococo (ruh-KOH-koh; roh-koh-KOH). An eighteenth-century style in architecture and visual art, developed in France from the **baroque** and characterized by elaborate and profuse ornamentation, often in the form of shells, scrolls, and the like. In architecture it manifested itself in interior design and furniture. In painting and sculpture, a decorous style exhibiting intimate grace, charm, and delicate superficiality.

satire (SA-tyr). In literature and drama, the use of ridicule, **irony**, or sarcasm to hold up to ridicule and contempt vices, follies, abuses, and so forth. Also, a work of literature that uses satire.

saturation (sach-uh-RAY-shuhn). In visual art, the degree of white present in a hue. The more white, the less saturated is the hue.

scale (skayl). In visual art and architecture, a building's size and the relationship of the building and its decorative elements to the human form. In music, an ascending or descending arrangement of pitches.

sculpture (SKUHLP-chuhr). A form of visual art or a three-dimensional artwork. Among the major types of sculpture are *full-round*, which is free-standing and fully three-dimensional; *relief*, which is attached to a larger background (see **low-relief** and **high-relief**; and linear, which emphasizes linear materials such as wire. Among the methods of execution are *cast*, which is created from molten material in a mold (see **substitution**); *built* or assembled (see *additive*), which is created by the addition of, often, prefabricated elements; *carved* (see **subtraction**); and *manipulated*—that is, constructed by manipulating soft materials such as clay.

serialism (SIHR-ee-uh-lihz-uhm). In music, a mid-twentieth century type of composition based on the **twelve tone system**. In serialism the techniques of the twelve-tone system are used to organize musical dimensions other than pitch, for example, rhythm, dynamics, and tone color.

serigraphy (suh-RIHGH-ruh-fee). In printmaking, a process in which ink is forced through a piece of stretched fabric, part of which has been blocked out—for example, **silk-screening** and stenciling.

sfumato (sfoo-MAH-toh). A smoky or hazy quality in a painting, with particular reference to Leonardo da Vinci's work.

short story. In literature, a brief **fictional prose narrative** usually concerning a single effect portrayed in a single episode or scene and with a limited number of **characters** focusing on unity of characterization, **theme**, and effect.

silk-screen (also silkscreen) (SIHLK-skreen). In printmaking, a type of stenciling using a screen of silk or other mesh on which a design is imposed and through which ink is forced with a squeegee onto the printing surface.

skeleton frame (SKEHL-uh-tuhn-fraym). In architecture, construction in which a skeletal framework supports the building. See **balloon construction** and **steel cage construction**.

sonata (suh-NAH-tuh). In music, an instrumental piece, usually in three or four movements and usually for one or two players.

sonata form (suh-NAH-tuh-fawrm). In music, a type of structure usually used in the first movement of a **sonata**. The three parts are the **exposition**, **development**, and **recapitulation**.

song cycle (sawng-SY-kuhl). In music, a group of **art songs** combined around a similar text or theme.

sonnet (SAHN-uht). In literature, a fixed **verse** form of Italian origin comprising fourteen lines usually of five-foot iambics rhyming according to a prescribed scheme. See also **Petrarchan sonnet**; **Shakespearean sonnet**.

spine (or super objective) (spyn). In the theatre, the motivating aspect of a character's persona that an actor seeks to reveal by physical means.

steel cage construction (steel-kayj-kuhn-STRUHK-shuhn). In architecture, construction using a metal framework. See **skeleton frame**.

stream of consciousness. In literature, a **narrative form** in **fiction** that attempts to capture the whole range and flow of a **character's** mental processes.

strophic form (STRAH-fikh fawrm). Form of vocal music in which all stanzas of the text are sung to the same music.

style (styl). The individual characteristics of a work of art that identify it with a particular artist, nationality, historical period, or school of artists.

stylized (STY-uh-lyzd). A type of depiction in which true-to-lifeness has been altered for artistic effect.

stylobate (STY-loh-bayt). The foundation immediately below a row of **columns**.

substitution (suhb-stih-TOO-shuhn). In sculpture, a technique utilizing materials transformed from a plastic, molten, or fluid into a solid state.

subtraction (suhb-TRAK-shuhn). In sculpture, works that are carved. In color, the mixing of pigments as opposed to the mixing of light.

superobjective (soo-puhr-ahb-JEHK-tihv). See **spine**.

surrealism (suhr-REE-uh-lihz-uhm). A movement in art developed in the 1920s in which artists and writers gave free rein to the imagination, expressing the subconscious through the irrational **juxtapositions** of objects and themes. The movement took two directions: **representational** and **abstract**.

symbol (SIHM-buhl). A form, image, or subject standing for something else.

symbolism (SIHM-buhl-ihz-uhm). The suggestion through imagery of something that is invisible or intangible.

symmetry (SIHM-ih-tree). In visual art, balancing of elements in design by placing physically equal objects on either side of a central axis. Cf. **asymmetry**.

symphony (SIHM-fuh-nee). In music, an extended musical composition for **orchestra** usually consisting of three or four **movements**. Also, see **orchestra**.

syncopation (sihng-kuh-PAY-shuhn). In music, the displacement of **accent** from the normally accented **beat** to the offbeat.

tempera (TEHMP-uh-ruh). In painting, an opaque watercolor medium, referring to ground pigments, and their color binders such as gum, glue, or egg.

tempo (TEHMP-oh). In music, the rate of speed at which a composition is performed. In theatre, film, and dance, the rate of speed of the overall performance.

tensile strength (TEHN-suhl-strehngth). In architecture and sculpture, the ability of a material to withstand twisting and bending.

tertiary color (TUHR-shee-air-ee). In visual art, colors that result from mixing **secondary hues** in equal proportions.

text painting (tehkst paynt-ihng). See **word painting**.

texture (TEHKS-chuhr). In painting and sculpture, the two-dimensional or three-dimensional quality of the surface of a work. In music, the melodic and harmonic characteristics of a composition. In literature, the elements—for example, metaphors, imagery, meter, and rhyme—that are separate from the structure or argument of the work.

theatricality (thee-ya-trih-KAL-uh-tee). Exaggeration and artificiality. The opposite of lifelikeness.

theme (theem). The dominant idea of a work of art, music, film, dance, and literature. In music, a principal melodic phrase in a composition.

thrust stage (thruhst-stayj). In theatre, a production arrangement in which the audience sits on three sides of the **stage**.

timbre (TAM-bur). In music, the quality of a tone that distinguishes it from other tones of the same pitch. Also called color or tone color.

tint (tihnt). A color or **hue** that has been modified by the addition of a small amount of another color.

toccata (tuh-KAH-tah). A baroque keyboard composition intended to display technique.

tonality (toh-NAL-ih-tee). In music, the specific key in which a composition is written. See **key**. In the visual arts, the characteristics of **value**.

tone (tohn). In visual art, the overall degree of brightness or darkness of a work. In music, sound that has a definite pitch, or frequency.

tone color, (tohn KUHL-uhr). In music, the **timbre** of a voice or instrument, tonic (TAHN-ihk). In music, the root tone (do) of a key.

tragedy (TRAJ-uh-dee). A serious drama or other literary work in which conflict between a **protagonist** and a superior force (often fate) concludes in disaster for the protagonist.

tragic flaw (traj-ihk flaw) A flaw that beings about a hero's downfall.

tragicomedy (traj-ih-KAHM-uh-dee). A drama combining the qualities of **tragedy** and **comedy**.

transept (TRAN-sehpt). The crossing arm of a cruciform church, at right angles to the nave.

triptych (TRIHP-tihk). An altar piece or devotional picture composed of a central panel and two wings.

trompe l'oeil (trawmp-LOY). French for "trick the eye" or "fool the eye." A two-dimensional artwork, executed in such a way as to make the viewer believe that a three-dimensional object is being perceived.

trope (trohp). A medieval dramatic elaboration of the Roman Catholic mass or other offices, tunnel vault (TUHN-uhl vawlt). See **barrel vault**.

twelve-tone (twehlv-tohn). In music, relating to or based on an arrangement of the twelve chromatic tones. Also an atonal system of composition based on use of the twelve tones, invented in the 1920s by Arnold **Schoenberg**, who preferred the term "pantonal."

tympanum (TIHM-puh-nuhm). The space above the door beam and within the arch of a medieval doorway.

unity (YOO-nuh-tee). The combination of the parts of a work of art, literature, or building that creates a sense of completeness or undivided total effect.

value (VAL-yoo). Also value scale or key. In the visual arts, the range of tonalities from white to black or dark to light.

vanishing point (VAN-ihsh-ihng poynt). In **linear perspective**, the point on the horizon toward which parallel lines appear to converge and at which they seem to vanish.

variation (veh-ree-YAY-shuhn). Repetition of a theme with minor or major changes, vault (vawlt). See **barrel vault**.

verisimilitude (vair-ih-sih-MIHL-ih-tood). In the arts and literature, the semblance of reality—that is, nearness to truth.

verismo (vay-REEZ-moh). In literature, **realism** as it developed in Italy in the late nineteenth and early twentieth century. Also a style of opera utilizing realistic librettos and production style.

wash and brush (wahsh and bruhsh). In visual art, a wet drawing medium similar to **watercolor** in painting.

watercolor (WAH-tuhr-kuhl-uhr). In visual art, a paint made up of pigment in a water-soluble binder.

wet-plate collodion process (weht playt cuh-LOHD-ee-uhn PRAH-sehs). In photography, a process, developed around 1850, that permitted short exposure times and quick development of the print.

wipe (wyp). In film, a line that passes across the screen eliminating one scene as it reveals the next.

woodcut (WUD-kuht). In printmaking, a **relief** printing technique in which the work is printed from a design cut into the plank (side) of the grain of a piece of wood.

wood engraving (wud ehn-GRAYV-ihng). In printmaking, a **relief** printing technique in which the work is printed from a design cut into the butt (end) of the grain of a piece of wood.

word painting (wuhrd payn-tihng). The use of language by a poet or playwright to suggest images and emotions; in music, the use of expressive melody to suggest a specific text.

zoom shot (zoom shaht). In film, a change, in one continuous movement, from wide-angle to telephoto, and vice versa.

BIBLIOGRAPHY

Abcarian, Richard, and Marvin Klotz (eds.). *Literature, the Human Experience*. New York: St. Martin's Press, 1998.

Acton, Mary. *Learning to Look at Paintings*. London: Routledge, 1997.

Ambrosio, Nora. *Learning About Dance* (2nd edn.). Dubuque, IA: Kendall Hunt, 1999.

Anderson, Jack. *Dance*. New York: Newsweek Books, 1974.

Andreae, Bernard. *The Art of Rome*, New York: Abrams, 1977.

Arnheim, Rudolph. *Art and Visual Perception: A Psychology of the Creative Eye*. Berkeley: University of California Press, 1997.

Arnheim, Rudolph. *Film as Art*. Berkeley: University of California Press, 1992.

Arnott, Peter D. *An Introduction to the Greek Theatre*. Bloomington: Indiana University Press, 1963.

Artz, Frederick. *From the Renaissance to Romanticism*. Chicago: University of Chicago Press, 1962.

Bacon, Edmund N. *Design of Cities*. New York: Viking Press, 1976.

Bazin, Germain. *The Baroque*. Greenwich, CT: New York Graphic Society, 1968.

Benbow-Pfalzgraf, Taryn. *International Dictionary of Modern Dance*. New York: St James Press, 1998.

Bobker Lee R. *Elements of Film*. New York: Harcourt Brace Jovanovich, 1979.

Booth, Michael. *Victorian Spectacular Theatre 1850–1910*. Boston: Routledge & Kegan Paul, 1981.

Bordwell, David, and Kristin Thompson. *Film Art: An Introduction*. Reading, MA: Addison-Wesley, 1996.

Braider, Christopher. *Refiguring the Real: Picture and Modernity in Word and Image: 1400–1700*. Princeton, NJ: Princeton University Press, 1993.

Brindle, Reginald Smith. *The New Music: The Avant-Garde Since 1945*. London: Oxford University Press, 1975.

Brockett, Oscar G. *History of the Theatre*. Boston: Allyn & Bacon, 1968.

Brockett, Oscar G.. *The Essential Theatre* (5th edn.). New York: Holt, Rinehart, & Winston, 1992.

Cameron, Kenneth M., and Patti Gillespie. *The Enjoyment of the Theatre* (4th edn.). Boston, MA: Allyn & Bacon, 1996.

Campos, D. Redig de (ed.). *Art Treasures of the Vatican*. Englewood Cliffs, NJ: Prentice Hall, 1974.

Canaday, John. *What Is Art?* New York: Alfred A. Knopf, 1990.

Cass, Joan. *Dancing Through History*. Englewood Cliffs, NJ: Prentice Hall, 1993.

Chadwick, Whitney. *Women, Art, and Society*. New York: Norton, 1991.

Ching, Frank D. K., and Francis D. Ching. *Architecture: Form, Space, & Order* (2nd edn.). New York: John Wiley & Sons, 1996.

Cook, David A. *A History of Narrative Film*. New York: Norton, 1996.

Le Corbusier. *Towards a New Architecture*. New York: Dover, 1986.

Corner, James S. *Taking Measures Across the American Landscape*. New Haven, CT: Yale University Press, 1996.

Davis, Phil. *Photography*. Dubuque, IA: William C. Brown, 1996.

Dean, Alexander, and Lawrence Carra. *Fundamentals of Play Directing*. New York: Holt, Rinehart, & Winston, 1990.

De la Croix, Horst, Richard G. Tansey, and Diane Kirkpatric. *Gardner's Art Through the Ages* (9th edn.). San Diego, CA: Harcourt, 1991.

De Lerma, Dominique-Rene. *Reflections of Afro-American Music*. Kent, OH: Kent State University Press, 1973.

Diehl, Charles. *Byzantium*. New Brunswick, NJ: Rutgers University Press, 1957.

Dockstader, Frederick J. *Indian Art of the Americas*. New York: Museum of the American Indian; Heye Foundation, 1973.

Ernst, David. *The Evolution of Electronic Music*. New York: Schirmer, 1977.

Finn, David. *How to Look at Sculpture*. New York: Harry N. Abrams, 1989.

Frampton, Kenneth. *Modern Architecture: A Critical History* (3rd edn.). London: Thames and Hudson, 1992.

Gardner, Helen. *Art Through the Ages* (9th edn.). New York: Harcourt Brace Jovanovich, 1991.

Garraty, John, and Peter Gay. *A History of the World* (2 vols.). New York: Harper & Row, 1972.

Giannetti, Louis. *Understanding Movies* (2nd edn.). Englewood Cliffs, NJ: Prentice Hall, 1996.

Giedion, Sigfried. *Space, Time and Architecture: the Growth of a New Tradition* (5th edn.). Cambridge, MA: Harvard University Press, 1967.

Gilbert, Cecil. *International Folk Dance at a Glance*. Minneapolis, MN: Burgess Publishing, 1969.

Gilbert, Creighton. *History of Renaissance Art Throughout Europe: Painting, Sculpture, Architecture*. New York: Abrams, 1973.

Glasstone, Victor. *Victorian and Edwardian Theatres*. Cambridge, MA: Harvard University Press, 1975.

Golding, John. *Visions of the Modern*. Berkeley, CA: University of California Press, 1994.

Grabar, André. *The Art of the Byzantine Empire*. New York: Crown Publishers, 1966.

Graziosi, Paolo. *Paleolithic Art*. New York: McGraw-Hill, 1960.

Griffiths, Paul. *A Concise History of Avant-Garde Music*. New York: Oxford University Press, 1978.

Grimm, Harold. *The Reformation Era*. New York: Macmillan, 1954.

Groenewegen-Frankfort and Bernard Ashmole. *Art of the Ancient World*. Englewood Cliffs, NJ: and New York: Prentice Hall and Abrams, n.d.

Grout, Donald Jay. *A History of Western Music* (rev. edn.). New York: W. W. Norton, 1973.

Hamilton, George Heard. *Nineteenth and Twentieth Century Art: Painting, Sculpture, Architecture*. New York: Abrams, 1970.

Hartnoll, Phyllis, and Peter Found (eds.). *The Concise Oxford Companion to the Theatre* (2nd edn.). New York: Oxford University Press, 1992.

Hartt, Frederick. *Art* (4th edn.). Englewood Cliffs, NJ, and New York: Prentice Hall and Abrams, 1993.

Hartt, Frederick. *Italian Renaissance Art* (3rd edn.). Englewood Cliffs, NJ, and New York: Prentice Hall and Abrams, 1987.

Hawkes, Jacquetta, and Sir Leonard Wooley. *History of Mankind: Prehistory and the Beginnings of Civilization*. New York: Harper & Row, 1963.

Held, Julius, and D. Posner. *17th and 18th Century Art*. New York: Abrams, n.d.

Helm, Ernest. *Music at the Court of Frederick the Great*. Norman, OK: University of Oklahoma Press, 1960.

Henig, Martin (ed.). *A Handbook of Roman Art*. Ithaca, NY: Cornell University Press, 1983.

Heyer, Paul. *Architects on Architecture: New Directions in America*. New York: Walker and Company, 1978.

Highwater, Jamake. *Dance: Rituals of Experience* (3rd edn.). New York: Oxford University Press, 1996.

Hitchcock, Henry-Russell. *Architecture; Nineteenth and Twentieth Centuries*. Baltimore: Penguin, 1971.

Honour, Hugh, and John Fleming. *The Visual Arts: A History* (4th edn.). Englewood Cliffs, NJ, and New York: Prentice Hall and Abrams, 1995.

Hornstein, Lilian, G. D. Percy, and Sterling A. Brown. *World Literature* (2nd edn.). New York: Mentor, 1973.

Hubert, J., J. Porcher and W. F. Volbach. *The Carolingian Renaissance*. New York: George Braziller, 1970.

Hyman, Isabelle, and Marvin Trachtenberg. *Architecture: From Prehistory to Post-Modernism/The Western Tradition*. New York: Harry N. Abrams, 1986.

Janson, H. W. *History of Art* (5th edn.). Englewood Cliffs, NJ, and New York: Prentice Hall and Abrams, 1995.

Jones, LeRoi. *Black Music*. New York: William Morrow, 1967.

Kamien, Roger. *Music: An Appreciation* (5th edn.). New York: McGraw-Hill, 1995.

Katz, Bernard. *The Social Implications of Early Negro Music in the United States*. New York: Arno Press and *The New York Times*, 1969.

Keck, George R., and Sherrill Martin. *Feel the Spirit*. Westport, CT: Greenwood Press, 1988.

Keutner, Hubert. *Sculpture: Renaissance to Rococo*. Greenwich, CT: New York Graphic Society, 1969.

Kjellberg, Ernst, and Gosta Saflund. *Greek and Roman Art*. New York: Thomas Y. Crowell, 1968.

Kramer, Jonathan D. *Listen to the Music: A Self-Guided Tour Through the Orchestral Repertoire*. New York: Schirmer Books, 1992.

Krehbiel, Henry Edward. *Afro-American Folksongs*. New York: G. Schirmer, n.d. (c. 1914).

Lacy, Susan, *Mapping the Terrain: New Genre Public Art*. Seattle: Bay Press, 1995.

Lee, Sherman. *A History of Far Eastern Art* (4th edn.). Englewood Cliffs, NJ, and New York: Prentice Hall and Abrams, 1982.

Lippard, Lucy R. *Pop Art*. New York: Oxford University Press, 1966.

Lloyd, Seton. *The Archaeology of Mesopotamia*. London: Thames & Hudson, 1978.

Mango, Cyril. *Byzantium*. New York: Charles Scribner's Sons, 1980.

Marshack, Alexander. *The Roots of Civilization*. New York: McGraw-Hill, 1972.

Martin, John. *The Modern Dance*. Brooklyn: Dance Horizons, 1965.

McDonagy, Don. *The Rise and Fall of Modern Dance*. New York: E. P. Dutton, 1971.

McLeish, Kenneth. *The Theatre of Aristophanes*. New York: Taplinger Publishing, 1980.

Muthesius, Stefan. *The High Victorian Movement in Architecture 1850–1870*. London: Routledge & Kegan Paul, 1972.

Nesbitt, Kate (ed.). *Theorizing a New Agenda for Architecture: An Anthology of Architectural Theory 1965–1995*. New Haven, CT: Princeton Architectural Press, 1996.

Newton, Norman T. *Design on the Land: the Development of Landscape Architecture*. Cambridge, MA: Harvard University Press, 1971.

Nyman, Michael. *Experimental Music: Cage and Beyond*. New York: Schirmer Books, 1974.

Ocvirk, Otto G. et al. *Art Fundamentals* (7th edn.). Madison, WI, and Dubuque, IA: Brown & Benchmark, 1994.

Ostransky, Leroy. *Understanding Jazz*. Englewood Cliffs, NJ: Prentice Hall, 1977.

Pfeiffer, John E. *The Creative Explosion*. New York: Harper & Row, 1982.

Pignatti, Terisio. *The Age of Rococo*. London: Paul Hamlyn, 1969.

Politoske, Daniel T. *Music* (5th edn.). Englewood Cliffs, NJ: Prentice Hall, 1992.

Powell, T. G. E. *Prehistoric Art*. New York: Frederick Praeger Publishers, 1966.

Preble, Duane. *We Create, Art Creates Us*. New York: Harper & Row, 1976.

Rasmussen, Steen Eiler. *Experiencing Architecture*. Cambridge, MA: MIT Press, 1984.

Read, Benedict. *Victorian Sculpture*. New Haven, CT: Yale University Press, 1982.

Rice, David Talbot. *The Art of Byzantium*. New York: Abrams, n.d.

Richter, Gisela. *Greek Art*. Greenwich, CT: Phaidon, 1960.

Robertson, Martin. *A Shorter History of Greek Art*. Cambridge, MA: Cambridge University Press, 1981.

Roters, Eberhard. *Painters of the Bauhaus*. New York: Praeger Publishers, 1965.

Ryman, Rhonda. *Dictionary of Classical Ballet Terminology*. Princeton, NJ: Princeton Book Company, 1998.

Sachs, Curt. *World History of the Dance*. New York: W. W. Norton, 1937.

Savill, Agnes. *Alexander the Great and His Times*. New York: Barnes and Noble, 1993.

Schonberger, Arno, and Halldor Soehner. *The Rococo Age*. New York: McGraw-Hill, 1960.

Sherrard, Philip. *Byzantium*. New York: Time, 1966.

Sitwell, Sacheverell. *Great Houses of Europe*. London: Spring Books, 1970.

Snell, Bruno, *Discovery of the Mind: The Greek Origins of European Thought*. New York: Harper, 1960.

Sorell, Walter. *Dance in its Time*. Garden City, NY: Doubleday Anchor Press, 1981.

Sporre, Dennis J. *The Art of Theatre*. Englewood Cliffs, NJ: Prentice Hall, 1993.

Sporre, Dennis J. *The Creative Impulse* (5th edn.). Upper Saddle River, NJ: Prentice Hall, 2000.

Sporre, Dennis J., and Robert C. Burroughs. *Scene Design in the Theatre*. Englewood Cliffs, NJ: Prentice Hall, 1990.

Stanley, John. *An Introduction to Classical Music Through the Great Composers & Their Masterworks*. New York: Reader's Digest, 1997.

Stearns, Marshall, and Jean Marshall. *Jazz Dance*. New York: Macmillan, 1968.

Steinberg, Cobbett. *The Dancing Anthology*. New York: Times Mirror, 1980.

Steinberg, Michael. *The Symphony: A Listener's Guide*. New York: Oxford University Press, 1995.

Stockstad, Marilyn. *Art History*. Upper Saddle River, NJ: Prentice Hall, 1995.

Summerson, John Newenham. *Classical Language of Architecture*. Cambridge, MA: MIT Press, 1984.

Thompson, Kristin, and David Bordwell. *Film History: An Introduction*. New York: McGraw-Hill, 1994

Tirro, Frank. *Jazz: A History*. New York: W. W. Norton, 1977.

Trythall, Gilbert. *Principles and Practice of Electronic Music*. New York: Grosset & Dunlap, 1973.

Vacche, Angela Dalle. *Cinema and Painting: How Art Is Used in Film*. Austin, TX: University of Texas Press, 1996.

Van Der Kemp, Gerald. *Versailles*. New York: Vendome Press, 1977.

Wheeler, Robert Eric Mortimer. *Roman Art and Architecture*. New York: Praeger Publishers, 1964.

Yenawine, Philip. *How to Look at Modern Art*. New York: Harry N. Abrams, 1991.

Zarnecki, George. *Art of the Medieval World*. Englewood Cliffs, NJ: Prentice Hall, 1975.

Zorn. Jay D. *Listen to Music*. Englewood Cliffs, NJ: Prentice Hall, 1994.

INDEX

CREDITS

Front cover Philadelphia Museum of Art,
The Louise and Walter Arensberg Collection
© Succession Marcel Duchamp/ADAGP, Paris
and DACS, London 2005
Page 1 Ansel Adams Publishing Rights Trust
Page 2 Photo Vatican Museums
Page 12 The Art Archive © The Estate of Diego
Rivera. Banco de Mexico

INTRODUCTION
Page 15 Photograph by Schecter Lee © 1986
The Metropolitan Museum of Art
0.1   AKG Images
0.2   A/B © Christo 1997. Photo: Wolfgang Volz
0.4   Photography © The Art Institute of Chicago
0.6   Alinari
0.7   VAG (UK) Ltd.
0.10 Photograph © The Board of Trustees, The
      National Gallery of Art, Washington.
      Chester Dale Collection 1963.10.111
0.11 © Succession Picasso/DACS 2005
0.12 © 2005 The Museum of Modern Art, New
      York/Photo Scala, Florence
0.13 © 2005 The Museum of Modern Art, New
      York/Photo Scala, Florence. © ARS, New
      York and DACS, London 2005
0.14 Novosti, London
0.16 Novosti, London

Page 37 National Galleries of Scotland

CHAPTER 1
1.1   Photograph © The Board of Trustees,
      The National Gallery of Art, Washington.
      1991.150.1.a. Photo by: Dean Beasom
1.2   Photograph © The Board of Trustees,
      The National Gallery of Art, Washington.
      1986.82.1. Photo by: Dean Beasom
1.3   Courtesy Bernice Steinbaum Gallery,
      Miami, FL. Photo: Adam Reich

1.4   Photograph © The Board of Trustees,
      The National Gallery of Art, Washington.
      1979.41.1. Photo by: Dean Beasom
1.5   Photograph © The Board of Trustees,
      The National Gallery of Art, Washington.
      1942.9.670. Photo by: Dean Beasom
1.7   Digital Image © 2005 The Museum of
      Modern Art, New York/Photo Scala,
      Florence
1.14 © Thomas Hart Benton Trust/VAGA New
      York/DACS London 2005
1.19 © ARS, New York and DACS, London
      2005
1.20 Ansel Adams Publishing Rights Trust
1.21 © 2005 Museum of Modern Art (MOMA),
      New York/Scala, Florence. Gift of James
      Thrall Soby. 112.1941
1.22 © Bettman/Corbis
1.23 © Bettman/Corbis
1.24 © Succession Picasso/DACS 2005
1.26 © 2005 The Museum of Modern Art,
      New York/Photo Scala, Florence. © ARS,
      New York and DACS, London 2005
1.28 © 2005 The Museum of Modern Art,
      New York/Photo Scala, Florence. © ARS,
      New York and DACS, London 2005
1.39 Photograph © The Board of Trustees,
      The National Gallery of Art, Washington.
      Andrew W. Mellon Collection 1937.1.53
1.40 © Photo RMN
1.41 © 2005 The Museum of Modern Art, New
      York/Photo Scala, Florence. © Salvador
      Dali, Gala-Salvador Dali Foundation,
      DACS, London 2005
1.48 © 2005 The Museum of Modern Art, New
      York/Photo Scala, Florence/©
      Mondrian/Holzman Trust, c/o Beeldrecht,
      Amsterdam, Holland
1.50 © 2005 The Museum of Modern Art, New
      York/Photo Scala, Florence. © DACS 2005
1.51 Photograph © The Board of Trustees, The
      National Gallery of Art, Washington.
      Chester Dale Collection 1943.7.2

CHAPTER 2
2.1   National Galleries of Scotland
2.2   Photo: Lee Stalsworth
2.4   Giraudon, Paris
2.6   © ARS, NY and DACS, London 2005
2.7   © The British Museum, London
2.10 Hirmer Fotoarchiv, Munich
2.11 © 2005 The Museum of Modern Art, New
      York/Photo Scala, Florence. © ADAGP,
      Paris and DACS, London 2005

2.12 © 2005 The Museum of Modern Art, New
      York/Photo Scala, Florence. © DACS 2005
2.16 © Christo 1997. Photo: Wolfgang Volz

CHAPTER 3
3.1   Britain on View (B.T.A.), London
3.2   A.C. & R. John Donat, London
3.5   Hirmer Fotoarchiv, Munich
3.6   © Patrick Ward/Corbis
3.13 Photograph © The Board of Trustees,
      The National Gallery of Art,
      Washington.Samuel H. Kress Collection
      1939.1.24
3.14 A.F. Kersting, London
3.20 Library of Congress
3.21 Wayne Andrews/ESTO, Mamaroneck
3.22 Ezra Stoller/Esto, Mamaroneck
3.26 Ralph Liebermann, North Adams, MA
3.27 Wayne Andrews, Chicago
3.28 TWA - Trans World Airlines, Inc.
3.29 © FLC/ADAGP Paris/DACS London 2005
3.31 © FLC/ADAGP Paris/DACS London 2005
3.32 Norman McGrath, New York
3.33 Giraudon/Bridgeman Art Library
3.35 Photo Scala, Florence
3.37 Photo Scala, Florence
3.38 Washington Area Convention and Visitors
      Association
3.39 Solomon R. Guggenheim Museum/Robert
      E. Mates © ARS, NY and DACS, London
      2005
3.40 John Edward Linden/Arcaid
3.41 Stefano Cellai/Superstock

CHAPTER 4
4.10, 4.12 Trudy Lee Cohen, Philadelphia

CHAPTER 5
5.6, 9, 11, 13 University of Arizona Theatre
5.7, 8 Old Globe Theatre, San Diego
5.10 State University, New York
5.12 University of Iowa Theatre
5.14 University of Illinois
5.15 Black Star, New York. Photo: Steve Schapiro

CHAPTER 6
6.1   Getty Images, Inc./Hulton Archive Photos
6.2, 4 B.F.I., London
6.3   © Universal Pictures, a Division of
      Universal Studios Inc. All Rights Reserved

CHAPTER 7
7.1, 6, 10 Dee Conway Ballet and Dance Picture
      Library